RAC

HISTORIC BRITAIN
AND IRELAND
1989

Published by
RAC Motoring Services Limited, Croydon
in association with
British Leisure Publications, East Grinstead

Contents

Cover picture: Blickling Hall, Norfolk. *National Trust*
Title page: Filching Manor and Motor Museum, East Sussex. *Photo* Roy Day

ISBN 0-86211-073-4
CIP catalogue record for this book is available from the British Library.
Cartography: Engineering Surveys Ltd
© 1989 The Royal Automobile Club (pages 1–16)
© 1989 Reed Information Services Ltd (pages 17–238)

Printed and bound in Great Britain by William Clowes Limited, Beccles and London

"If you come into the yard slightly nervous they sense it straight away"

"It came to me on a Wednesday, that that's what I wanted to do for a living and by Friday I was out looking for an apprenticeship." That's how Mike Sinstadt, mobile farrier around Nantwich, Cheshire, describes his decision to become a blacksmith.

In contrast, the training takes 4 long years apprenticed to a master from the Worshipful Company of Farriers, learning how to deal with several hundred pounds of apprehensive horseflesh. Mike reckons his "patients" have long memories, so it pays to "introduce yourself to the horse quietly", as he puts it.

First of all, the worn out shoes have to come off and the horse's feet are carefully trimmed. The shoe is made on the spot, individually, to fit the particular horse, then nailed onto the hoof, which, like a human fingernail, has no sensitivity. The shoeing nails are rasped off to a certain length and any excess hoof filed away.

In the old days, farriers' tools, fashioned from different materials, lasted much longer than today. Mike's rasps last just about a week, shoeing hammers wear out after a couple of years and knives are used for perhaps a year. Unlike the farriers of the last century, Mike cannot hand down the tools of the trade, but at least he can pass on something more important – his craftsmanship.

No. 13 in a series on 'BRITAIN'S CRAFT HERITAGE'.

The Royal Bank of Scotland plc

Registered Office: 36 St. Andrew Square, Edinburgh EH2 2YB.
Registered in Scotland No.90312.

850 BRANCHES THROUGHOUT THE UK

Introduction

A glance through the pages of this Guide illustrates clearly the scope and variety of places open to visitors throughout Britain and Ireland, some world famous, others hardly known outside their immediate neighbourhood. We hope readers will be tempted to visit some of these lesser known houses and museums which have much to offer.

The very roads you travel along may be as much a part of our history as the buildings you visit. Stone Age man made our first roads for trade and flint for tools and weapons was a prime commodity, only found in some locations. One such source was **Grimes Graves**, near Thetford in Norfolk, an extensive network of 500 Stone Age flint mines, two of which are maintained open, making it possible to descend 30 to 40 feet to subterranean caves and experience an essential part of life 5,000 years ago.

Trading in flint from Norfolk led to the marking out of the Icknield Way. Commencing close to Grimes Graves it leads to the high open Salisbury Plain in Wiltshire — a veritable spaghetti junction of ancient trackways. Hence the importance of Stonehenge, Woodhenge and the proliferation of barrows and burial mounds in this area. An initial trip to the tiny **Alexander Keiller Museum** by the church in Avebury before visiting prehistoric sites in Wiltshire, will prove rewarding for it explains the significance and construction of all the surrounding examples like Silbury Hill, Stonehenge and Avebury itself — a village which is actually built within a great Stone Age circle.

A contemporary village exists at Skara Brae in the Orkney Islands and at **Chysauster**, near Lands End in Cornwall, there are remains of an Iron Age Village of approximately 500 BC, each house being built round a courtyard with its own terrace.

It was a long time before the people of this Cornish settlement had more than tracks to walk on for even the Romans got no further than Exeter with their road building. Seven thousand miles of Roman road can still be traced in Britain, laid mainly to the east of their 180-mile Fosse Way. This runs between Lincoln and Axminster traversing en route the scenic beauty of the Cotswold Hills where it may be identified as the A429. Here, two miles east of Guiting Power on the River Windrush and beside another Roman road, Buckle Street, **Cotswold Farm Park** is a rare breeds survival centre created in 1970 in an area of outstanding natural beauty.

At one time the land here was used to quarry slate. It has been left in an uneven state to provide natural shelter for a thriving collection of rare animals. The small brown Soay sheep is a good example. This was the last survivor of the early domestic sheep of Europe, which continued to exist wild on the Hebridean island of Soay, one of the St. Kilda group. Jacob sheep are so called because of the account in Genesis of how Jacob was paid for his work with all those of the flock having spotted fleece. Other rare breeds include Highland cattle, Longhorns, Shire horses and a team of working oxen who also do TV assignments. Of the wide variety of pigs, some are similar to those which roamed our forests in pre-historic times. Other smaller hairy examples run free to greet visitors and are very much like dogs.

There is superb scenic driving in every direction from this central Cotswold location. The Tudor Manor, **Snowshill,** for instance is only four miles to the north. Its eccentric owner, Charles Wade, lived here in the utmost frugality, spending his considerable fortune, magpie fashion, on an extraordinary haphazard collection of unusual and rare items. Rooms have exotic names like, "Zenith", "Seraphim", "Top Royal" and "Dragon", chosen by Mr. Wade to relate to their contents. "Admiral", for instance, contains a large collection of navigation and marine instruments. "Seventh Heaven", toys — wind toys, model trains, a theatre of 1825 with several sets of scenery, 19th century doll's houses plus a series of occupants and their furniture. In the "Green Room", a company of Samurai warriors in full armour are presented standing, sitting and apparently holding council.

Samurai warriors at Snowshill Manor

Mr. Wade put the panelling and coffered waggon vault into the "Music Room" which displays an astonishing variety of instruments. The house is stuffed; each room filled to bursting point just as Charles Wade left it when he presented Snowshill and its contents to the National Trust in 1951.

The garden here is an additional attraction. Mr. Wade persuaded Major Lawrence Johnston, his neighbour at nearby **Hidcote Manor,** to advise him on a layout to take the form of a series of cottage gardens. Keen gardeners will no doubt be aware of the charms of **Hidcote Manor Garden**, a series of enclosed gardens, similar in concept to those created by Vita Sackville-West at **Sissinghurst**.

At one time, Snowshill Manor was owned by Queen Catherine Parr, given to her by Henry VIII as part of her dowry. Her home, **Sudeley Castle** is quite near at Winchcombe. It also contains a toy collection – the largest in private ownership in all Europe – in a castle which still has some of its 12th century remains and many royal connections.

Another Queen's house is **St. Paul's Walden Bury** where Queen Elizabeth, the Queen Mother, spent much of her childhood. The house is not open to the public but the garden is – perhaps only two or three days in the year but it is certainly worth looking for those days in these pages.

The house is deep in a part of Hertfordshire which is as yet undeveloped, making it a pleasant excursion from central London. The front with its octagonal wings is thought to be by Robert Adam. The garden was laid out mainly in the early 18th century and epitomizes English landscape gardening of that period, which aimed to harmonize with and blend into the surrounding countryside. This has been achieved by a series of grass allées or avenues which, enclosed by hedges of beech, radiate from the house presenting various vistas whilst leading to a flower garden or a terraced theatre or perhaps to the pond. One avenue terminates in a view of the distant church.

The Queen Mother's childhood Scottish home, **Glamis Castle**, is also open to the public.

Sudeley Castle

Shelton toll house, Blists Hill Museum

Scotland produced both Telford and Macadam who in the 18th and 19th centuries made major improvements in road building. Finance for this was raised in the form of tolls levied from travellers at tollgates and administered by turnpike trusts throughout the country. Telford was of the opinion that tollkeepers should have good houses complete with privy and pig-sty. The tollhouse at Shelton has been rebuilt to his specification as part of a small industrial Victorian town reproduced over 42 acres at **Blists Hill Open Air Museum**. What already existed here has been preserved and restored. Other examples of machines, shops, workshops, workers' cottages and similar buildings of significance to the early industrial life of the Ironbridge Gorge have been transported here and rebuilt under the auspices of the Gorge Museum Trust formed in 1968 to preserve for posterity one of the most important periods in British history.

Exploring these frequently misty streets busy with costumed workers pursuing their trades with the help of carts drawn by Shire horses, will more than fill a day. The northern boundary is marked by part of the Shropshire Canal which passes close to the Blists Hill Mine. At the pit head one may enter the winding house to watch the cage being lowered 600 feet. Mined coal was transported via the canal to the Hay Inclined Plane. This is a fascinating device by means of which the five or six ton tub boats were floated onto wheeled cradles which carried the boats on iron rails up and down a steep incline.

David and Samson are a pair of beam engines built in 1851 and reconstructed here in 1971. They are magnificent and impressive as are the three original blast furnaces used to produce pig iron.

On the lighter side, workers' cottages are fully furnished and their tiny yards well stocked with pigs, goats and fowl. The Shire horses keep the blacksmith busy and the candle maker too puts in a hard day. His produce is for sale as are beer, sandwiches and hot snacks in a Victorian pub under the watchful eye of the Mission Church.

Blists Hill in all its variety of interest is only one part of **the Ironbridge Gorge Museum** complex to be found in the town of Telford near the famous Iron Bridge.

This and the 1,000 foot long Menai Bridge, opened in 1826 to connect Wales to the island of Anglesey, are the two bridges for which Thomas Telford is best remembered.

It was from Anglesey that architect Thomas Hopper chose his stone when in 1827 he was commissioned to construct a massive castle for the wealthy owner of Penrhyn slate quarries. Thus **Penrhyn Castle** came to be built close to the Menai Bridge near Bangor in a style which on first sight looks like a typical Norman fortification. Inside, it is far from plain as the architect imposes extravagant 19th century Gothic embellishments on a neo-Norman frame.

Naturally slate abounds throughout. The great hall is floored with it. The extravagant plaster work and carvings are also Hopper's creation as is most of the remaining furniture giving a homogenous atmosphere to this almost unique example of a short-lived period of neo-Norman revival which took place in the 19th century.

Penrhyn Castle

It is well worth crossing the Menai Bridge. At 100 feet above high water the views up and down the Strait are impressive. On the far side, the ruins of **Beaumaris Castle** — a genuine medieval fortification begun in 1295 — make an interesting contrast to Penrhyn. The tiny town of Beaumaris has about 2,000 inhabitants and many ancient buildings of interest including a visitable goal of 1829, complete with tread-wheel and condemned cell. **(Beaumaris Goal)**

So many people visit the Lake District that the roads can hardly cope! One way of avoiding traffic delays is to choose a house to visit which is off the beaten track but has enough entertainment to keep a family happy for a whole day. **Holker Hall** in the southern part of the Lake District fills the bill admirably. It is rare for a house of this size to offer such a range of events throughout the season. There are horse riding and carriage driving trials, model aircraft and model car rallies, hot air balloon and archery events and because this is the home of the Lakeland Motor Museum, historic vehicle rallies are organised here too.

The house is very much the home of the young Cavendish family, descendants of the Dukes of Devonshire. In 400 years it has never been bought or sold. There can be no doubt that Holker is much loved by its family They occupy the 'old' wing which survived a disastrous fire of 1871 in which many treasures were destroyed including a fine collection of paintings by Sir Joshua Reynolds. One most unusual of these, a caricature, survives in the Billiards Room.

Fireplace in 'Wedgewood' dressing room, Holker Hall

The post-fire west wing is in Elizabethan style but is clearly Victorian. It contains a magnificent library of some 3,500 books which survived the fire. Here, as elsewhere, the electric lighting installed in 1911, is concealed in order to preserve the symmetry of ornately moulded ceilings. Even the switches are hidden behind dummy books near the doorway! There is much fine wood carving to admire, from four different forms of linen-fold panelling to one hundred balusters, each a different design, in a magnificent cantilevered staircase. Those who love classical china will find examples of Minton washstands, delicate miniature Crown Derby, exuberent floral Wemyss ware and a Wedgwood bedroom.

A mild climate encourages tender and unusual shrubs in 23 acres of formal and woodland gardens containing also an Adventure Playground, a Baby Animal House and a Craft & Countryside Exhibition — something for everyone at Holker Hall.

Drawing room at Hill House

It is one of Telford's roads which links the Lake District at Carlisle with Glasgow where the School of Art buildings is the major masterpiece of a native born architect, Charles Rennie Mackintosh. Second in importance to this is his **Hill House** in Helensburgh, built in 1902 for publisher Walter Blackie who gave Mackintosh a free hand in respect of the architecture, decorative design and some of the furniture. The result is a house one could visualise living in today; an individual house, a delight of asymmetrical composition based on Mackintosh's reliance on nature for inspiration so that this building seems to grow out of the hill on which it is placed to overlook the River Clyde. The slightly severe and essentially Scottish pebble dash walls and turret beneath steeply sloping roofs contrast sharply with a soft interior.

In the drawing room, white walls are decorated with a stylised briar rose motif supported by trellis work under a dark 'plum' ceiling. The bay window here is a delight of light and space. Delicate pierced pillars separate a long white window seat from book shelves at either end. Small leaded lights carry out the rose theme as does the fireplace with its five ovals of coloured and mirrored glass. High ladder-backed chairs, for which Mackintosh is famous, are dramatic against their white background. The white bedroom has a pair of these. Much of the furniture has remained here since it was designed for the house. Other pieces by Mackintosh have been acquired to further enhance this time capsule of its period.

On the top floor, an attic school room for the Blackie children has been taken over by the Landmark Trust and converted into a holiday flat so that you too may experience the delight of staying in an historic house overlooking the Clyde.

The National Museum of Science & Industry

Science Museum

Science Museum
Exhibition Road
London SW7 2DD

Opening times: Weekdays 10.00 – 18.00
Sundays   11.00 – 18.00

Nearest Underground: South Kensington

Admission charged

Major Cathedrals

The Cathedrals of Britain are amongst our greatest architectural treasures. Some, like Salisbury and St Paul's, London, are built all in one style to one design, but most are amalgams of many different architectural styles as succeeding generations rebuilt, altered and extended these great buildings.

As well as a brief description of the main architectural features of each Cathedral, we give for most the opening times, the times of services, any charges made and details of any special events taking place in 1989-90.

Please note that visitors must not walk around a Cathedral during a service, though all are welcome to participate in it.

BIRMINGHAM – St Philip
An early 18th-century classical-style building with a concave-sided Baroque tower surmounted by a dome and cupola. Burne-Jones stained glass.
Open: 7.15am–5.30pm; *Services:* Sun 9.15am, 11am, 4pm; Mon 7.30am, 3.30pm; Tues, Wed, Fri 7.30am, 6.15pm; Thur 10.30am, 3.30pm; Sat 9.30am, 3.30pm.

BRISTOL – Holy Trinity
A rare example of a 'hall church' with the aisles, nave and choir all the same height. Superb Norman Chapter House, exquisite Early English Lady Chapel. Note the choir vault and the star-shaped tomb niches.
Open: 8am–6pm. *Services:* Sun 7.40am, 8am, 10am, 3.30pm; Mon, Tues, Wed, Fri 8.40am, 12.30pm, 5.15pm; Thur 8.15am, 5.15pm; Sat 8.40am, 12.30pm, 3.30pm.

BURY ST EDMUNDS – St James
Originally a 16th-century parish church, it is dwarfed by the ruins of the great abbey. Note the Victorian hammerbeam roof and the Elizabeth Frink statue of St Edmund.
Open: 8.30am–10pm (Jun–Aug), 8.30am–6pm summertime, 8.30am–5.30pm winter. *Services:* Sun 8am, 10am, 11.30am, 3.30pm; Mon 9am, 5pm; Tues 7.30am, 9am, 5pm; Wed 9am, 11am, 5pm; Thur 7.30am, 9am, 5pm; Fri 7.30am, 9am, 7pm; Sat 9am.

CANTERBURY – Christ Church
For many people, the greatest of England's Cathedrals, as befits the senior See, with a magnificent Norman crypt, the first English Gothic choir, a lovely Perpendicular nave leading to the 15th-century choir screen and topped by the superb Bell Harry tower. Look particularly for the 12th-century wall painting, the glorious 12th- and 13th-century glass, the tomb of the Black Prince, St Augustine's chair and the site of the shrine of St Thomas à Becket.
Open: 8.45am–7pm, 8.45am–5pm (Oct–Easter), Crypt 10am–4.30pm; Sun 12.30pm–2.30pm, 4.30pm–5.30pm. *Services:* 8am, 9.30am, 11am, 3.15pm, 6.30pm; weekdays 7.30am (not Sat), 8am, 11am (Wed), 3.15pm, (Sat), 5.30pm, 6.15pm (Thur). Mystery Plays 28 Jul–18 Aug.

CARLISLE – Holy Trinity
The short Norman nave (the rest was destroyed in the Civil War) is narrower than the Early English East end. The nine-light East window has superb tracery and original glass.

CHESTER – Christ & St Mary
A mainly Gothic Cathedral (Early English Lady Chapel, Decorated choir, Perpendicular tower) in red sandstone but the north transept and part of the nave are Norman. Wonderful canopied choir stalls (c. 1390).
Open: 7am–6.30pm. *Services:* Sun 8am, 10.15am, 11.30am, 3.30pm, 6.30pm; weekdays 7.45am, 9.30am, 5.15pm (4.15pm on Sat). Chester Music Festival 23–30 July.

CHICHESTER – Holy Trinity
A basically Norman building with some Gothic remodelling. The 13th-century central tower and its 14th-century spire collapsed in 1861 but were restored. Note the John Piper tapestry and 12th-century carved stone panels.
Open: 7.40am–7pm, 7.40am–5pm (Oct–Apr). *Services:* Sun 8am, 10am, 11am, 3.30pm; weekdays 7.40am, 8am, 5.30pm. *Charges:* treasury 10p. Southern Cathedrals Festival 20–23 July.

COVENTRY – St Michael
The 15th-century Cathedral was almost destroyed in a bomb attack in 1940. The new Cathedral, designed by Sir Basil Spence, was built next to the ruins. Notable are Epstein and Moore sculptures, the Sutherland tapestry and stained glass by Piper and Reyntiens.
Open: 7.30am–7.30pm, 9.30am–5.30pm winter. *Services:* Sun 7.40am, 8am, 10.30am, 5.30pm; Mon 7am, 5pm; Tues 9am, noon, 1.05pm, 5pm; Wed 5pm; Thur 7.30am, 9am, 5pm; Fri 9am, noon, 5pm; Sat 8.30am, 9am, 3.30pm. *Charges:* £1 donation (voluntary); tower £1, children 50p.

DURHAM – Christ & St Mary
A magnificent building dominating the town from a rock high above the River Wear. Sophisticated late Norman with Europe's first rib vaulting, though the Nine Altars chapel is Early English. Note the sanctuary knocker, the Neville screen, the elaborate Renaissance font cover, the shrine of St Cuthbert and tomb of the Venerable Bede.
Open: 7.15am–8pm, 7.15am–6pm (Sept–Apr). *Services:* Sun 8am, 10.15am, 11.30am, 3.30pm; weekdays 7.30am, 9am, 5.15pm. *Charges:* £1 donation (voluntary).

ELY – Holy Trinity
Standing on a small hill, yet visible for miles in the flat fen country, Ely has a great Norman nave, an Early English retrochoir and an exquisite, light and airy Decorated Lady Chapel, but its masterpiece is the Octagon over the crossing whose wooden vault supports the timber lantern tower.
Open: 7am–7pm, 7.30am–6pm in winter (till 5pm on Sun). *Services:* Sun 8.15am, 10.30am, 3.45pm; weekdays 7.40am, 8am, 5.30pm. *Charges:* £2 (students/OAPs £1.20); tower £1.50 (students/children 90p); stained glass museum adults 80p, children 40p. Special Harvest Festival Exhibition 6–8 October.

EXETER – St Peter
The flanking towers remain of the Norman Cathedral but beginning with the fine Lady Chapel, it was rebuilt, mostly in the Decorated style. The nave and choir have the longest unbroken stretch of vaulted roofing (over 300ft) in the world.
Open: 7.30am–6.30pm. *Services:* Sun 8am, 9.45am, 11.15am, 3pm, 6.30pm; weekdays 7.30am, 7.45am, 3pm (Sat), 5.30pm (Mon–Fri). *Charges:* £1 donation (adults, voluntary).

GLOUCESTER – Holy Trinity
A Norman Cathedral transformed in the 14th century by the addition of a new clerestorey, elaborate vaulting and a huge East window. Magnificent late Perpendicular Lady Chapel and outstanding cloisters with superb fan vaulting.
Open: 7.30am–7pm, 7.30am–6pm (winter). *Services:* Sun 7.40am, 8am, 10.15am, noon, 3pm; weekdays 8am, 4pm (Sat only), 5.30pm (not Sat); *Charges* £2 donation invited. Exhibition on history of the Cathedral: Single 75p, families £1.50. **1089–1989** — 900th anniversary of present building. 19-26 August – Three Choirs Festival.

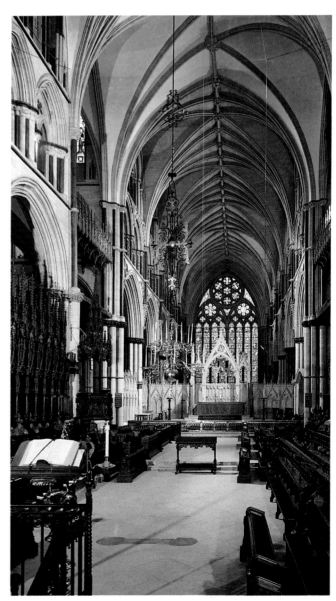

Lincoln Cathedral: choir

Photo: *Woodmansterne*

GUILDFORD – Holy Spirit
Built in red brick and strikingly set on top of Stag Hill, the Cathedral was completed in 1964. The plain interior is enlivened by the specially designed sanctuary carpet, the famous and colourful hassocks and the tall gold brocade reredos.
Open: 8.30am–5.30pm. *Services:* Sun 8am, 9.45am, 11.15am, 6.30pm; weekdays 8.45am, 9am, 4pm (Sat), 5.30pm (not Wed).

HEREFORD – St Mary & St Ethelbert
A Norman Cathedral progressively altered, beginning with an Early English upper stage to the choir, through Wyatt's gothicisation of the nave in the 18th century to a new West Front in 1904–8. Treasures include the chained library, some superb brasses and the 'Mappa Mundi' (replica now on view).
Open: 7.15am–6.15pm. *Services:* Sun 8am, 10am, 11.30am, 3.30pm; weekdays 7.30am, 8am, 5.30pm. *Charges:* tower £1, children 50p; treasury 25p; chained library 25p.

LEICESTER – St Martin of Tours
Hemmed in by city centre development, this 13th-century parish church was made a Cathedral in 1927. Most of the present building dates from 1844 when the church was remodelled by Raphael Brandon and the tower and spire added.
Open: 7.30am–6.30pm (Sun till 5pm). *Services:* Sun 8am, 10.30am, 4pm; weekdays 7.45am, 8am, 6.15pm.

LICHFIELD – St Mary & St Chad
A Gothic Cathedral famous for its three-spired silhouette and a splendid West Front whose three tiers of canopied recesses now contain Victorian statues.
Open: 7.30am–6.30pm (Sun 8pm, 5pm in winter). *Services:* Sun 8am, 10.30am, 3.30pm; weekdays 9.30am, 5.30pm. *Charges:* £1 donation (voluntary), Chapter House 25p. Lichfield Festival 7–16 July.

LINCOLN – St Mary
The great Cathedral stands high on a hill above the town. Parts of the West Front and the twin towers are Norman, but the nave is superb Early English with two lovely rose windows in the transepts, while the 'Angel' choir with the great East window is one of the finest examples of 'Geometric' Gothic. Notable carvings.
Open: 7.15am–10pm (Sun till 6pm), 7.15am–6pm (Sun till 5pm) in winter. *Services:* Sun 7.45am, 8am, 9.30am, 11am, 12.15pm, 3.45pm; weekdays 8am, 9.15am, 10.30am (Tues & Thur), 5.15pm (except Wed and in hols). *Charges:* £1 earning adults, 20p others (voluntary); tower 60p adults, 40p children (summer holidays only); roof tours (on advance application only) £2.50 per person. Lincoln Mystery Plays 13–15, 17–22 July.

LIVERPOOL – Cathedral Church of Christ
Completed in 1978, having taken 75 years, this huge and dignified building was designed by Sir Giles Gilbert Scott and built out of locally quarried sandstone. It is the largest church in England. Towering above, in a central position is the Vestey Tower (331ft) which holds 13 bells.
Open: 9am–6pm. *Services:* Sun 10.30am, 3pm, 4pm; weekdays 9am, 3pm. *Charges:* £1.50, students/OAPs £1, children 50p (all voluntary).

LIVERPOOL – Christ the King (Roman Catholic).
In complete contrast, this Cathedral took only five years to complete (1962–7). A circular building with a metal and glass lantern tower, it stands on top of a crypt built for a Lutyens-designed Baroque Cathedral which was never completed.
Open: 8am–6pm (Sun 5pm in winter). *Masses:* 8.30am, 10am, 11am, 3pm, 4pm, 7pm; weekdays 8am, 12.15pm, 5.45pm (not Sat), 6.30pm (Sat).

LONDON – St Paul's
Wren's unique contribution to British Cathedrals arose out of the ashes of the Great Fire of London (1666). The Renaissance building, with its impressive dome, dominated the City skyline until the 1960s. The climb up inside the Dome to the Whispering Gallery, above the crossing, and on to the top, with a wonderful view of the City, is worth the effort.
Open: 10am–4.15pm. *Services:* Sun 10.30am, 11.30am, 3.15pm (4pm in July); weekdays 8am, 12.30pm, 5pm. *Charges:* Dome £1, children 50p; crypt 80p, children 40p; ambulatory 60p, children free.

LONDON – Westminster Abbey
A Gothic masterpiece of the 13th–15th centuries, the Abbey is the crowning place of almost all and the burial place of many of our monarchs. Do not miss the Royal Tombs, the Coronation Chair with the Stone of Scone or Poets Corner.
Open: 8am–6pm (Wed 8am–7.45pm); Royal Chapels, choir etc 9am–4.45pm, Sat 9am–2.45pm and 3.45–5.45pm. *Services:* Sun 8am, 10am, 11.15am, 3pm, 6.30pm; Mon–Fri 7.30am, 8am, 12.30pm, 5pm; Sat 8am, 9.20am, 3pm. *Charges:* Royal Chapels £2, students/OAPs £1, children 50p.

LONDON – Westminster Cathedral (Roman Catholic)
This large Byzantine-style building with its red and white bell tower, which commands a good view over London, is best approached from the piazza off Victoria Street. Designed by J. F. Bentley, it is constructed entirely of brick and was built between 1895 and 1903.
Open: 6.45am–8pm. *Masses:* Sun 7am, 8am, 9am, 10.30am, noon, 5.30pm, 7pm; weekdays 7am, 8am, 8.30am, 9am, 10.30am, 12.30pm, 1.05pm, 5.30pm. *Charges:* tower 70p, children/OAPs 35p. Flower Festival 11–14 May.

LONDON – Southwark Cathedral
A simpler Gothic building with an Early English eastern end; the nave was rebuilt in Victorian Gothic. The pinnacled central tower is 15th century but like most of the exterior has been much restored. The original cloisters have long disappeared leaving the Cathedral hemmed in between Borough Market and the railway lines.

MANCHESTER – St Mary, St Denis & St George
An oddly truncated building with a short, very wide nave in the Perpendicular style, built between 1422 and 1513 and much restored in the 19th century. Note the superb carved choir stalls of the 15th and 16th centuries.
Open: 7.30am–6.30pm. *Services:* Sun 8.45am, 9am, 10.30am, 3.30pm, 7pm; weekdays 7.45am, 8am, 1.10pm (Wed, Fri), 3.30pm (Sat), 5.30pm (Mon–Fri).

NEWCASTLE – St Nicholas
Originally one of the largest parish churches in England, most of the building

dates from the 14th and 15th centuries. On top of the West tower is a fine example of a 'crown' spire.
Open: 7am–6pm. *Services:* Sun 7.30am, 8am, 9.30am, 6pm; weekdays: 7.30am, (Fri 7am), 8am, (Sat 8.40am), 10.30am (Wed), 12.30pm, (Tues, Thur), 5.30pm (not Sat).

NORWICH – Holy Trinity
An impressive 15th-century spire, 312ft high, tops the tower of one of the most notable Norman Cathedrals. The Eastern apse with its flying buttresses has a splendidly bossed vault. Note the early Tudor stalls, the episcopal chair and the beautifully vaulted cloisters.
Open: 7am–7pm, 7am–6pm in winter. *Services:* Sun 7.35am, 8am, 11am, 3.30pm, 7pm; weekdays 7.35am, 8am, 11am (Tues & Thur), 12.30pm (Wed & Fri), 5.15pm.

OXFORD – Christ
The smallest Cathedral in England is also the chapel of Christ Church College. The Norman nave and choir have an intricate late Perpendicular vault, while the early 13th-century tower and spire are the oldest of any Cathedral.

PETERBOROUGH – St Peter, St Paul & St Andrew
The solid Norman Cathedral is overshadowed by a flamboyant 13th-century West Front. Note the lovely fan vaulting in the Perpendicular-style New Building at the East end and a unique 13th-century painted ceiling in the nave.
Open: 7.30am–8pm, 7.30am–6pm (winter). *Services:* Sun 7.30am, 8am, 9.45am, 11am, 3.15pm, 6.30pm; weekdays 7.30am, 8am, noon (Wed), 5.30pm. *Charges:* £1 donation (voluntary).

RIPON – St Peter & St Wilfred
Though the simple crypt may be Saxon, Ripon is a mixture of Gothic styles. Its glories include a seven-light East window and choir in the 'Geometric' style and the intricately carved 16th-century choir stalls.
Open: 7am–7pm, 7am–6pm in winter. *Services:* Sun 8am, 9.30am, 11.30am, 12.30pm, 6.30pm (4pm in winter); weekdays 9am, 5.30pm plus 9.20am (Mon & Thur), 7.30am (Tues & Fri), 7.30am & 11am (Wed), 8.30am (Sat). *Charges:* £1 (optional); treasury 25p.

ROCHESTER – Christ & St Mary
Built on the site of a Saxon church by Bishop Gandulf, who also built the Tower of London, Rochester is still predominantly Norman though the East end is an Early English addition. Memorial to Charles Dickens.
Open: 8.30am–6pm, 8.30am–5pm (winter). *Services:* Sun 8am, 9.45am, 10.30am, 3.15pm, 6.30pm (except mid July–mid Sept); weekdays 8am, 12.45pm (Thur), 3.15pm (Sat), 5.30pm. *Charges:* £1 donation (voluntary).

ST ALBANS – St Alban
The Norman nave, at 275ft the longest in England, and the arcade built from old Roman bricks and tiles, make up for some rather heavy handed Victorian work.
Open: First service–6 45pm, 5.45pm in winter. *Services:* Sun 8am, 9.15am, 11am, 12.15pm, 6.30pm; Mon–Fri 7am, 7.30am, 5pm; Sat 8.30am, 9am, 4pm. *Charges:* £1 donation (voluntary). International Organ Festival 8–15 July; Benedictine week 16–24 Sept; Flower Festival 5–8 Oct.

SALISBURY – St Mary
With the tallest spire in England (404ft), Salisbury is unique amongst English Cathedrals in being solely of Early English design, keeping very definitely to the pyrimidal ideal.
Open: 7.30am–6pm. *Services:* Sun 8am, 9.15am, 11am, noon, 3.15pm, 6.30pm; weekdays 7.30am, 8am, 5.30pm. *Charges:* adults £2, children £1.

SHEFFIELD – St Peter & St Paul
Originally a 15th-century parish church, it has been altered and added to in both the 19th and 20th centuries. The West entrance now is under a modern narthex tower, lit by a striking stained glass 'crown of thorns' lantern.
Open: 7.30am–6pm. *Services:* 8am, 9.30am, 11am; weekdays 8am (Sat 8.30am), 5.30pm (Fri 6.30pm).

SOUTHWELL – St Mary
Norman, Early English and Decorated styles are all represented here. Note the impressive triple Norman arcading in the nave and the exquisite Decorated Chapter House with some marvellous naturalistic stone carving.
Open: 8am–7pm, 8am–dusk (winter). *Services:* Sun 8am, 9.30am, 11am, 3.15pm; weekdays 7.30am (Tues, Wed, Thur, Fri), 9am (Mon, Sat), 5.30pm.

WELLS – St Andrew
A Gothic Cathedral set in a lovely precinct with a moated Bishop's Palace. The elaborate West Front still has its 13th-century statues while the choir is a superb example of the Decorated style. The central tower and the delicate octagonal Chapter House are other glories.
Open: 7.15am–dusk, 7.15am–6pm (winter). *Services:* 8am, 10am, 11.30am, 3pm; weekdays 7.40am, 8am, 10am (Wed), 5pm. *Charges:* adults £1, children/OAPs 50p. 7–14 Aug Embroidery Exhibition.

WINCHESTER – Holy Trinity
The original Norman Cathedral, still visible in tower and transepts, was gothicised in the 13th and 14th centuries with a new West Front, clerestorey and vault, a magnificent sight in this, England's longest Cathedral. Note the elaborate choir stalls, reredos and chantry chapels.
Open: 7.30am–6.30pm. *Services:* Sun 8am, 10.30am, 11.30am, 3.30pm; weekdays 7.40am, 8am, 5.30pm. *Charges:* £1 donation (voluntary).

WORCESTER – Christ & St Mary
Above a Norman crypt, the Cathedral was rebuilt mostly in Decorated style though the attractive tower is Perpendicular as is the intricate chantry to Prince Arthur, Henry VIII's elder brother.
Open: 7.45am–7pm, 7.45am–5.30pm. *Services:* 7.45am, 8am, 9.30am, 11am, 4pm, 6.30pm; weekdays 7.45am, 8am, 11.30am (Fri), 1.05pm (Wed), 4pm (Thur), 5.30pm (not Thur). *Charges:* £1 donation (voluntary); tower £1, children 50p.

YORK – St Peter
Surrounded by the cobbled streets of the old town, the massive Gothic Minster has great interior height, a suitable setting for its greatest glory, superb stained

glass from the 13th–16th centuries. The South Transept and its rose window, badly damaged by fire in 1984 have been restored to former glory with some modern touches such as the face of the astronaut Neil Armstrong carved on a boss. Museum in the Norman undercroft.
Open: 7.30am–8pm, 7.30am–6pm (winter). *Services:* Sun 8am, 9.45am, 10.30am, noon, 3.15pm, 6.30pm; weekdays 7.30am, 8am, 1.05pm (Wed, Fri), 5.30pm. *Charges:* £1 donation (voluntary); tower £1.50, children 50p; Museum 80p, children 40p.

SCOTLAND

ABERDEEN – St Machar
Founded in 1136, the present Cathedral is a mainly 15th-century granite building containing two 14th century sandstone pillars. Interesting West Front with castellated towers. Note the painted Heraldic ceiling in the nave dating from 1520.
Open: 9am–5pm. *Services:* Sun 11am, 6pm.

EDINBURGH – St Giles
John Knox preached from the pulpit of St Giles. Considerable restoration in the Gothic style in the 19th century fortunately left the 15th-century crown steeple, the finest example in Scotland, unscathed.
Open: 9am–7pm, 9am–5pm (Oct–Mar). *Services:* Sun 8am, 10am, 11.30am, 8pm; weekdays noon. *Charges:* Chapel of the Order of the Thistle 30p.

GLASGOW – St Mungo
The saint himself lies in a splendid tomb surrounded by magnificent pillars and vaulting. It is the only complete medieval cathedral on the Scottish mainland. Note the 13th century work on the choir and tower and the splendidly carved door leading to the Chapter House.
Open: 9.30am–1pm & 2pm–7pm (winter until 4pm); Sun 2pm–5pm (winter until 4pm). *Services:* Sun 11am, 6.30pm; weekdays noon.

KIRKWALL, Orkney – St Magnus
Founded in 1137 by the nephew of St Magnus, himself later canonised, the remains of both saints are sealed in pillars in the Cathedral. Desecration by the Roundheads was later completed by a bolt of lightning hitting the spire and destroying it. The 20th century has seen the restoration of the Cathedral to its former glory.
Open: 9am–1pm & 2pm–5pm. *Services:* Sun 11.15am.

WALES

LLANDAFF – St Peter and St Paul
Impressively restored, Llandaff is unique in that it has no transepts. Neglected over 300 years until the 18th century when a church in the style of an Indian temple was built within its walls, it was restored in the 19th century then all but destroyed by a land mine in 1941. Post-war restoration was completed in the 1960s. Note the pre-Raphaelite decoration and the remains of the Indian temple.

ST ASAPH
The smallest Cathedral in Britain, it contains interesting roof paintings and gilding commemorating the investiture of the Prince of Wales in 1969.
Open: 7.30am–8pm, 7.30am–6.30pm in winter. *Services:* 8am, 11am, 3.30pm; Mon, Tues, Wed, Sat 7.40am, 6pm; Thurs 8am, 6.30pm; Fri 10am, 6pm. September: Gerard Manley Hopkins Centenary Exhibition; 24–30 September: North Wales Music Festival.

ST DAVID'S
Built on the reputed site of St David's own monastry, the Gothic Cathedral is flanked by the ruins of the old Bishop's Palace. Of particular interest is the tomb of Edmund Tudor, father of Henry VII.
Open: 9am–6.30pm. *Services:* Sun 8am, 9.30am, 11am, 6pm; weekdays 7.30am, 8am, 6pm. May: Bach Festival.

Stay in an historic hotel

After the church and the great house, whether castle or mansion, the local inn was often the most significant building in a village or town in pre-industrial Britain. A surprising number of them have survived through the centuries and now, modernised and often discreetly added to, make fascinating places to stay. Stately homes, too, have sometimes found new roles as country-house hotels.

The following RAC hotels are in historic buildings of architectural interest ranging from 14th century inns, with beams and huge open fireplaces, to elegant Lutyens-designed Edwardian country houses.

The star ratings indicate the level of comfort, service and amenities.

♨ shows a country house hotel.

H C R are the RAC Hotel Awards for outstanding Hospitality, Comfort and Restaurant quality.

〜 is the Blue Ribbon Award for the RAC hotels which are, overall, the best in their classification.

Acc and H/Acc are Acclaimed and Highly Acclaimed awards to listed RAC hotels.

♙ Tankard Awards for Inns.

ENGLAND

ALDERMINSTER ♨ ★★★★ **C** **Ettington Park** CV37 8BS Tel. (0789) 740740 *Beautifully restored 19th-century Château-style mansion.*

ALFRISTON ★★★ **Star Inn**, High St, BN26 5TA Tel. (0323) 870495 *Picturesque 14th-century timber-framed inn.*

ALFRISTON ★★ **George Inn**, High St, BN26 5SY Tel. (0323) 870319 *Half-timbered 14th-15th-century inn in centre of village.*

ASHFORD ♨ ★★★★ **Eastwell Manor**, Boughton Aluph, TN25 4HR Tel. (0233) 35751 *Superbly furnished Tudor house.*

BAINBRIDGE ★★ **Rose & Crown**, Nr Leyburn, DL8 3EE Tel. (0969) 50225 *Ancient coaching inn overlooking village green.*

BARNSLEY ★ **Royal**, 11 Church St, S70 2AD Tel. (0226) 203658 *Handsome 18th-century building.*

BARROW-IN-FURNESS ★★★★ **Abbey House**, Abbey Rd, LA13 0PA Tel. (0229) 38282 *Mansion designed by Sir Edwin Lutyens.*

BATH ★★★★ **Royal Crescent**, Royal Cres, BA1 2LS Tel. (0225) 319090 *Luxury hotel in the centre of famous Georgian crescent.*

BATH ★★★ **Dukes**, Great Pulteney St, BA2 4DN Tel. (0225) 63512 *Gracious Georgian house in a wide street of literary renown.*

BATH ★★★ **Pratt's**, South Parade, BA2 4DN Tel. (0225) 60441 *Georgian terrace hotel in quiet area. Once home of Sir Walter Scott.*

BATH ★★★ **Royal York**, York Buildings, George St, BA1 2DY Tel. (0225) 61541 *Bath-stone terrace hotel near city centre.*

BATH **Chesterfield** (Acc), 11 Great Pulteney St, BA2 4BR Tel. (0225) 460953 *Georgian terrace hotel in famous street.*

BATH **Millers**, 69 Great Pulteney St, BA2 4DL Tel. (0225) 65798 *Hotel in Georgian terrace.*

BELLINGHAM ★★ **Riverdale Hall**, Hexham, NE48 2JT Tel. (0660) 20254 *Spacious 19th-century mansion.*

BIBURY ♨ ★★ **R** **Bibury Court**, Nr Cirencester, GL7 5NT Tel. (028 574) 337 *Jacobean country house of Cotswold stone.*

Feathers Hotel, Ludlow

BILLESLEY ⚑ ★★★ **R** **Billesley Manor**, Alcester, B49 6NF Tel. (0789) 400888 *Elizabethan country house.*

BRAINTREE ★★★ **White Hart**, Bocking End, CM7 6AB Tel. (0376) 21401 *Charming 15th-century, half timbered coaching inn.*

BRENTWOOD ★★★★ **Brentwood Moat House**, London Rd, CM14 4NR Tel. (0277) 225252 *Well-preserved hunting lodge of Henry VIII.*

BRIGHTON ★★★ **Old Ship**, Kings Rd, BN1 1NR Tel. (0273) 29001 *Regency building on the seafront.*

BRISTOL ★★ **Parkside**, 470 Bath Rd, Avon, BS4 3FQ Tel. (0272) 711461 *Stone-built, part Georgian hotel.*

BURNHAM-ON-CROUCH ★ **Ye Olde White Harte**, The Quay, CM0 8AS Tel. (0621) 782106 *Attractive waterside inn.*

BUXTON ★★ **Grove**, Grove Parade, SK17 6AJ Tel. (0298) 3804 *An 18th-century building in a spa town.*

CANTERBURY ★ **Three Tuns**, Watling St, Kent Tel. (0227) 67371 *A 16th-century inn on a Roman road in the city centre.*

CHARLBURY ★★ **Bell**, Church St, OX7 3AP Tel. (0608) 810278 *Lovely Cotswold stone 17th-century hotel.*

CHIPPING CAMPDEN ★★★ **C R** **Cotswold House**, The Square, GL55 6AN Tel. (0386) 840330 *Regency stone building in town centre.*

CHIPPING CAMPDEN ★★ **Noel Arms**, High St, GL55 6AT Tel. (0386) 840317 *A 14th-century inn with an open courtyard.*

COCKERMOUTH ★★ **Globe**, Main St, CA13 9LE Tel. (0900) 822126 *Handsome red-brick Georgian hotel in town centre.*

COLEFORD ★★ **Speech House**, GL16 7EL Tel. (0594) 22607 *A 17th-century court house in the Forest of Dean.*

CONGLETON ★★ **Lion & Swan**, Swan Bank, CW12 1JR Tel. (0260) 273115 *Timber-framed 16th-century coaching inn with an impressive porchway.*

CORNHILL ON TWEED ⚑ ★★★ **Tillmouth Park**, TD12 4UU Tel. (0890) 2255 *Imposing, stone-built Victorian mansion.*

COTTINGHAM ★★ **Hunting Lodge**, High St, Nr Market Harborough, LE16 8XN Tel. (0536) 771370 *Attractive 16th-century house.*

CRANBORNE ★★ **Fleur de Lys**, 5 Wimborne St, BH21 5PP Tel. (072 54) 282 *Charming olde-worlde inn.*

CUCKFIELD ★★★ **H C R** **Ockenden Manor**, Ockenden Lane, RH17 5LD Tel. (0444) 416111 *A 16th-century manor house with beamed and panelled rooms.*

DARLINGTON ★★★★ **M Blackwell Grange Moat House**, DL3 8QH Tel. (0325) 380888 *Brick-built 17th-century mansion.*

DARTMOUTH ★★★ **Royal Castle**, 11 The Quay, TQ6 9PS Tel. (08043) 4004 *Quayside 16th-century inn with later facade.*

DERBY ⚑ ★★★ **Breadsall Priory**, Moor Rd, Morley, DE7 6DL Tel. (0332) 832235 *Stone-built mansion in parkland.*

DORCHESTER ★★★ **Kings Arms**, High St, DT1 1HF Tel. (0305) 65353 *Bow-windowed 18th-century coaching inn with Hardy associations.*

DUNSTER ★★★ **C** **Luttrell Arms**, High St, TA24 6SG Tel. (0643) 821555 *Stone-built hotel, originally the guest house of Cleeve Abbey.*

DURHAM ★★★ **Ramside Hall**, DH1 1TD Tel. (091 386) 5282 *Part-Tudor, part-Victorian castle.*

EGHAM ★★★★ **Great Fosters**, Stroude Rd, TW20 9UR Tel. (0784) 33822 *Elizabethan manor house with antique furniture.*

FLITWICK ⚑ ★★★ 🎀 **Flitwick Manor**, Church Rd, MK45 1AE Tel. (0525) 712242 *Substantial 18th-century house.*

FOREST ROW ★★★ **Roebuck**, Wych Cross, RH18 5LF Tel. (034 282) 3811 *Red-brick Georgian building.*

GISBURN ★★★ **Stirk House**, Clitheroe, BB7 4LJ Tel. (020 05) 581 *Creeper-clad 16th-century manor house.*

GLASTONBURY ★★★ **George & Pilgrims**, High St, BA6 9DP Tel. (0458) 31146 *Lovely stone-built 15th-century building.*

GOUDHURST ★★ **H C R** **Star & Eagle**, High St, TN17 1AL Tel. (0580) 211512 *Charming 16th-century beamed and half-timbered inn.*

GRANTHAM ★★★ **Angel & Royal**, High St, NG31 6PN Tel. (0476) 65816 *A 13th-century stone building said to be England's oldest inn.*

HAREWOOD ★★ **C** **Harewood Arms**, Nr Leeds, LS17 9LH Tel. (0532) 886566 *Traditional stone-built inn.*

HARROGATE ★★★★ **Old Swan**, Swan Rd, HG1 2SR Tel. (0423) 500055 *Elegant stone-built hotel dating from 1770.*

HARROGATE ★★★ **Hotel St. George**, Ripon Rd, HG1 2SY Tel. (0423) 61431 *Fine 19th-century hotel with spacious rooms.*

HASSOP ⚑ ★★★ **H C R** **Hassop Hall**, Nr Bakewell, DE4 1NS Tel. (062 987) 488 *Mostly 17th-century country house in parkland.*

HEXHAM ⚑ ★★★ **Langley Castle**, Langley-on-Tyne, NE47 5LU Tel. (0434 84) 8888 *A 14th-century castle with walls 7 feet thick.*

HORLEY **Langshott Manor** (H/Acc), RH6 9LN Tel. (0293) 786680 *Beautifully restored 16th-century manor house.*

Sir Christopher Wren's House, Windsor

HORNCASTLE ★ **Bull**, Bull Ring, LN9 5HU Tel. (065 82) 3331 *A 400-year-old inn situated in a market town.*

HORTON CUM STUDLEY ⚑ ★★★ **Studley Priory**, OX9 1AZ Tel. (086 735) 203 *Elizabethan manor built on to 12th-century nunnery.*

HUNGERFORD ★★★ **R** **Bear**, Charnham St, RG17 0EL Tel. (0488) 82512 *A 13th-century former coaching inn with Civil War connections.*

HUNTINGDON ★★★ **George**, George St, PE18 6AB Tel. (0480) 432444 *Historic old posting inn with galleried courtyard.*

HURLEY ★★★ **R** **Bell**, Nr Maidenhead, SL6 5LX Tel. (062 882) 5881 *Gabled hotel dating back to 12th century.*

IPSWICH ⚑ ★★★★ **H C R** **Hintlesham Hall**, Hintlesham, IP8 3NS Tel. (047 387) 334 *Fine Elizabethan manor with Georgian facade.*

KENILWORTH ★★ **Clarendon House**, Old High St, CV8 1LZ Tel. (0926) 57668 *Beamed 15th-century inn.*

KESWICK ★★ **George**, St. John St, CA12 5AZ Tel. (076 87) 72076 *A 16th-century inn situated in heart of town.*

KILDWICK ⚑ ★★★ **Kildwick Hall**, Nr Keighley, BD20 9AW Tel. (0535) 32244 *Handsome Jacobean stone building.*

KINGSBRIDGE ⚑ ★★★ 🎀 **Buckland Tout Saints**, Goveton, TQ7 2DS Tel. (0548) 3055 *Elegant 17th-century country house.*

LAVENHAM ★★★★ **Swan**, High St, CO10 9QA Tel. (0787) 247477 *Splendidly preserved Elizabethan house, inn and woolhall, now combined into a luxury hotel.*

LEWES ★★ **Shelleys**, High St, BN7 1XS Tel. (0273) 472361 *Georgian building in town centre.*

LICHFIELD ★★★ **George**, Bird St, WS13 6PR Tel. (0543) 414822 *Coaching inn close to the Cathedral.*

LONG MELFORD ★★★ **Bull**, CO10 9JG Tel. (0787) 78494 *Fine timbered 15th century inn.*

LOUTH **Priory** (Acc), Eastgate, LN11 9AG Tel. (0507) 602930 *Small private hotel in ancient priory building.*

LOWER SLAUGHTER ⚑ ★★★ **C R** **Manor**, GL54 2HP Tel. (0451) 20456 *Imposing 17th-century stone-built manor house.*

LUDLOW ★★★ **Feathers**, Bull Ring, SY8 1AA Tel. (0584) 5261 *Magnificent 17th-century half-timbered inn with richly decorated interior.*

LYME REGIS ★★ 🎀 **Kersbrook**, Pound Rd, DT7 3HX Tel. (029 74) 2596 *Thatched 18th-century hotel.*

MAIDSTONE **Tanyard** (H/Acc), Wierton Hill, Boughton Monchelsea, ME17 4JT Tel. (0622) 44705 *Small hotel in heavily beamed medieval farmhouse.*

MALMESBURY ★★★ **Old Bell**, Abbey Row, SN16 0BW Tel. (0666) 822344 *Stone building of 12th-century origins next to the Abbey.*

MATLOCK ⚑ ★★★ **Riber Hall**, DE4 5JU Tel. (0629) 582795 *Luxurious Elizabethan country house.*

MAYFIELD ★★ **Middle House**, High St, TN20 6AB Tel. (0435) 872146 *Heavily beamed Tudor building furnished in appropriate style.*

MIDHURST ★★★ **Spread Eagle**, South St, GU29 9NH Tel. (073 081) 6911 *Fine timber-framed 15th-century inn.*

NORTON ⚑ ⚑ ⚑ **C** **Hundred House**, Shifnal, TF11 9EE Tel. (095 271) 353 *Stylish 18th-century inn with Tudor courtyard buildings.*

OUNDLE ★★★ **Talbot**, New St, PE8 4EA Tel. (0832) 73621 *A 17th-century stone-built hotel.*

PADSTOW ★★ **Old Customs House Inn**, South Quay, PL28 8BY Tel. (0841) 532359 *Delightful old inn with harbour views.*

RIPON ★★ **Unicorn**, Market Place, HG4 1BP Tel. (0765) 2202 *An 18th-century posting house.*

ROCHESTER (Northumberland) ★ **Redesdale Arms**, NE19 1TA Tel. (0830) 20668 *Stone-built coaching inn.*

ROWSLEY ★★★ **H C R** **Peacock**, Nr Matlock, DE4 2EB Tel. (0629) 733518 *A 17th-century building with antique furniture.*

RYDE **Georgian**, 22 George St, I.O.W., PO33 2EW Tel. (0983) 63989 *An 18th-century hotel in centre of Ryde.*

RYE ★★★ **The Mermaid**, Mermaid St, TN31 7EY Tel. (0797) 223065 *Rebuilt in 1420 – the wine cellar is dated 1106 – this lovely timbered inn is one of the oldest in England.*

SAFFRON WALDEN ★★ 🄷🄁 **Saffron Hotel**, 10/18 High St, Essex, CB10 1AY Tel. (0799) 22676 *Old coaching inn situated in town centre.*

SALISBURY ★★★ **Rose & Crown**, Harnham Rd, SP2 8JQ Tel. (0722) 27908 *Charming half-timbered 14th-century inn.*

SANDBACH ★★ **Old Hall**, Newcastle Rd, CW11 0AL Tel. (0270) 761221 *Half timbered Jacobean building.*

SCARBOROUGH ★★★★ **Royal**, St Nicholas St, YO11 2HE Tel. (0723) 364333 *Delightful Regency seaside hotel.*

SOUTHWELL ★★★ **Saracen's Head**, Market Place, NG25 0HE Tel. (0636) 812701 *A 16th-century inn opposite the Minster.*

STAMFORD ★★★ 🄷🄒🄁 **George of Stamford**, St Martins PE9 2LB Tel. (0780) 55171 *Famous 16th-century coaching inn.*

STAMFORD ★★ **Crown**, All Saints Place, PE9 2AG Tel. (0780) 63136 *Lovely stone-built hotel in town centre.*

STORRINGTON 🏌 ★★★ **Little Thakeham**, Merrywood Lane, RH20 3HE Tel. (090 66) 4416 *Designed by Sir Edwin Lutyens in a garden planned by Gertrude Jekyll.*

STRATFORD UPON AVON ★★★★ **Shakespeare**, Chapel St, CV37 6ER Tel. (0789) 294771 *Classic Elizabethan black and white architecture.*

STRATFORD UPON AVON ★★★ **Falcon**, Chapel St, CV37 6HA Tel. (0789) 205777 *A 16th-century black and white inn, close to the Royal Shakespeare Theatre.*

SUTTON COLDFIELD 🏌 ★★★★ **New Hall**, Walmley Rd, B75 7UU Tel. 021-378 2442 *Crenellated medieval manor house, reputed to be the oldest inhabited moated house in England.*

TEDBURN ST MARY ★★ **King's Arms**, EX6 6EG Tel. (064 76) 224 *A typical old coaching inn.*

TEWKESBURY ★★★ **Bell**, 52 Church St, GL20 5SA Tel. (0684) 293293 *Black and white timbered 15th-century inn opposite the Abbey.*

TEWKESBURY ★★ **Tudor House**, High St, GL20 5BH Tel. (0684) 297755 *Attractive Tudor house in town centre.*

THORNBURY 🏌 ★★★ 🎗 **Thornbury Castle**, Nr Bristol, BS12 1HH Tel. (0454) 418511 *Beautifully furnished Tudor castle.*

UPPER SLAUGHTER 🏌 ★★★ 🄷🄒🄁 **Lords of the Manor**, GL54 2JD Tel. (0451) 20243 *Attractive 17th-century Cotswold stone manor house.*

WAKEFIELD ★★★ **Waterton Park**, The Balk, Walton WF2 6PW Tel. (0924) 257911 *Georgian mansion on an island in a lake.*

WALLINGFORD ★★★ **George**, High St, OX10 0BS Tel. (0491) 36665 *Tudor hotel with charming courtyard.*

WANSFORD ★★★ **Haycock**, Great North Road, PE8 6JA Tel. (0780) 782223 *Famous old stone-built coaching inn on the London – York road.*

WARWICK ★★ **Lord Leycester**, Jury St, CV34 4EJ Tel. (0926) 491481 *Georgian coaching inn close to town centre.*

WESTON-UNDER-REDCASTLE 🏌 ★★★ **Hawkstone Park**, Nr Shrewsbury, SY4 5UY Tel. (093 924) 611 *Elegant Georgian country house.*

WINDSOR ★★★ **Sir Christopher Wren's House**, Thames St, SL4 1PX Tel. (0753) 861354 *Elegant residence built by Wren for himself.*

WITHAM ★★ **White Hart**, Newland St, CM8 2AF Tel. (0376) 512245 *Heavily beamed 15th-century inn.*

WOBURN ★★★★ **Bedford Arms**, George St, MK17 9PX Tel. (0525) 290441 *Georgian coaching inn with old-world charm.*

WOODSTOCK ★★ **Marlborough Arms**, Oxford St, OX7 1TS Tel. (0993) 811227 *A 15th-century inn with a Georgian front.*

YORK 🏌 ★★★★ 🎗 **Middlethorpe Hall**, Bishopthorpe Rd, YO2 1QP Tel. (0904) 641241 *Handsome Queen Anne Mansion.*

SCOTLAND

BALLACHULISH ★★★ **Ballachulish Hotel**, PA34 4JY Tel. (085 52) 606 *Large, stone-built hotel, originally a drovers inn.*

BANCHORY 🏌 ★★★ 🄷🄒🄁 **Banchory Lodge**, Dee St AB3 3HS Tel. (033 02) 2625 *Lovely riverside hotel, part dating from 16th century.*

BANCHORY 🏌 ★★★ 🄒 **Raemoir**, AB3 4ED Tel. (033 02) 4884 *Elegant Georgian stone-built mansion with historic 'Ha Hoose' in grounds.*

BRORA ★★ **Royal Marine**, KW9 6QS Tel. (0408) 21252 *A mansion designed by Sir Robert Lorimer.*

DOLPHINTON 🏌 ★★★ **Dolphinton House**, West Linton, EH46 7AB Tel. (0968) 82286 *Early 19th-century red sandstone country house.*

EDINBURGH ★★★★ **Carlton Highland**, North Bridge, EH1 1SD Tel. 031-556 7277 *Impressive hotel by Waverley station.*

EDINBURGH ★★★ 🄒 **Roxburghe**, 38 Charlotte Sq, EH2 4HG Tel. 031-225 3921 *Handsome stone-built hotel in an Adam Square.*

GIFFORD ★★ **Tweeddale Arms**, High St, EH41 4QU Tel. (062 081) 240 *A traditional stone-built Victorian inn.*

GLENBORRODALE 🏌 ★★ **Glenborrodale Castle**, Ardnamurchan, Acharacle, PH36 4 JP Tel. (097 24) 266 *'Scottish baronial' Victorian Castle on shores of Loch Sunart.*

GULLANE 🏌 ★★★ 🄷🄒🄁 **Greywalls**, Duncur Rd, Muirfield, EH31 2EG Tel. (0620) 842144 *Edwardian country house designed by Lutyens set in a Jekyll garden.*

KELSO ★★★ **Cross Keys**, 36-37 The Square, TD5 7HI Tel. (0573) 23303 *Georgian hotel dominating the town square.*

LETHAM 🏌 ★★★ **Fernie Castle**, Ladybank, Nr Cupar, KY7 7RU Tel. (033 781) 381 *Lovely stone-built 14th-century castle.*

MOFFAT ★★★ **Moffat House**, High St, DG10 9HI Tel. (0683) 20039 *Stone-built Georgian manor house.*

NEWTON STEWART 🏌 ★★ **Creebridge House**, DG8 6NP Tel. (0671) 2121 *Elegant 18th-century building.*

ONICH ★★★ 🄷 **Lodge on the Loch**, PH33 6RY Tel. (085 53) 606 *Traditional Highland hotel with spectacular views.*

PORT ASKAIG ★★ **Port Askaig Hotel**, Isle of Islay, PA46 7RD Tel. (049 684) 245 *An 18th-century Highland hotel, incorporating a 16th-century inn.*

STIRLING ★★★ **Golden Lion**, 8 King St, FK8 1BD Tel. (0786) 75351 *Stone-built hotel part dating back to 16th-century.*

UPHALL 🏌 ★★★ 🄁 **Houstoun House**, EH52 6JS Tel. (0506) 853831 *A 16th-century laird's fortified house.*

WALES

BALA ★★ **White Lion Royal**, High St, LL23 7AE Tel. (0678) 520314 *Famous old coaching inn.*

BEAUMARIS ★★★ **Bulkeley Arms**, Castle St, LL58 8AW Tel. (0248) 810415 *Traditional Welsh hotel.*

BRECON ★★ 🄒 **Wellington**, The Bulwark, LD3 7AD Tel. (0874) 5225 *Georgian hotel in town centre.*

CAERSWS 🏌 ★★ **Maesmawr Hall**, SY17 5SF Tel. (068 684) 255 *Half-timbered 16th-century house.*

CHEPSTOW ★★★★ M **St Pierre Park**, NP6 6YA Tel. (029 12) 5261 *A 14th-century manor house with adjacent country club.*

CHEPSTOW ★★ **Beaufort**, Beaufort Sq, NP6 5EP Tel. (029 12) 2497 *A 16th-century inn with elegant Georgian windows.*

LLANDUDNO 🏌 ★★★ 🎗 **Bodysgallen Hall**, LL30 0DS Tel. (0492) 84466 *A beautifully restored 17th-century mansion in lovely gardens.*

PEMBROKE ★★★ **Court**, SA71 5NY Tel. (0646) 672273 *Elegant Georgian mansion with imposing portico.*

RUTHIN ★★★ **Castle**, St Peters Sq, LL15 1AA Tel. (082 42) 2479 *Elizabethan and 18th century building.*

CHANNEL ISLANDS

ST PETER PORT ★★★ **Moore's**, Pollet, Guernsey Tel. (0481) 24452 *Georgian terrace building in town centre.*

ST PETERS ★★★ M **Mermaid**, Jersey Tel. (0534) 41255 *Modern hotel built round an historic tavern.*

NORTHERN IRELAND

BALLYGALLY ★★★ **Ballygally Castle**, 274 Coast Rd, Nr Larne, BT40 2QZ Tel. (0574) 83212 *A 17th-century castle facing a sandy beach.*

BUSHMILLS ★★★ **Bushmills Inn**, 25 Main St, BT57 8QA Tel. (026 57) 32339 *A 19th-century coaching inn situated in an historic village.*

Fernie Castle, Letham

NAVAL HERITAGE

AT PORTSMOUTH

MARY ROSE

HMS VICTORY

HMS WARRIOR 1860

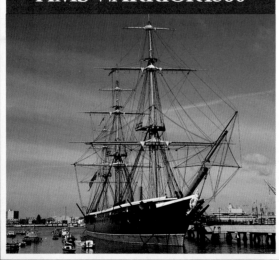

ROYAL NAVAL MUSEUM

The World's greatest Maritime Spectacle!

OPEN DAILY IN PORTSMOUTH NAVAL BASE

For further details of opening times and admission prices telephone: 0705-839766

  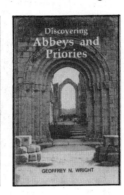  
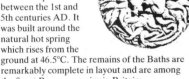

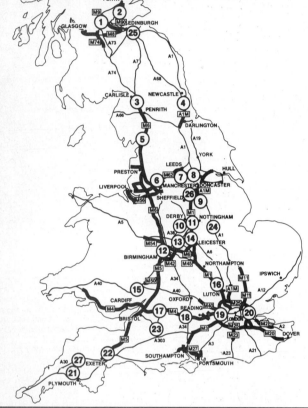

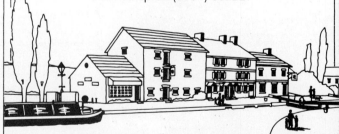

ENGLAND

Properties are listed in alphabetical order of counties and towns within counties.

Avon

BATH

BATH INDUSTRIAL HERITAGE CENTRE *(Camden Works)*
Julian Road. Tel: (0225) 318348.
The entire stock-in-trade of J.B. Bowler, Victorian brass founder, engineer and mineral water manufacturer, displayed in authentic settings – some working machinery. Also 'The Story of Bath Stone' including a mock-up of a hand worked mine face. 2–5 daily Feb 1 to Nov 30. 2–5 weekends only in winter. Parties all year by appointment. *Closed* Dec 24 and 25. Adm £1.00, Chld and OAPs 50p; Family ticket £2.00.

BATH POSTAL MUSEUM
8 Broad Street.

BECKFORD'S TOWER
Telephone: Bath (0225) 336228
(The Beckford Tower Trust)

Built 1827 by William Beckford of Fonthill. A Beckford Museum (first floor); fine views from Belvedere (156 steps).
Location: 2 m from Bath Spa Station via Lansdown Road.
Station: Bath Spa (2 m).
Opening Times: Apr 2 to Oct 30—Sats, Suns & Bank Hol Mons 2–5. Adm £1p, Chd & OAPs 50p. *Parties other days by arrangement.*

COSTUME AND FASHION RESEARCH CENTRE
(Bath City Council)
4 Circus. Tel: (0225) 461111, Ext. 2752.
Facilities for study and research, including extensive reference library and study collection of costume. Mon to Fri 10–1, 2–5, by appointment.

GEOLOGY MUSEUM *(Avon County Council)*
18 Queen Square. Tel: (0225) 28144.
On display are a wealth of, mainly local, minerals, rocks and fossils. They were collected and donated by an eminent geologist of the last century – Charles Moore (1814–1881). Mon to Fri 9.30–6. Sat 9.30–5. *Closed* Sun and Bank Hol weekends. Adm Free. Parties welcome, worksheets available on request. The Curator is available to assist with identifications and answer general enquiries: Miss Diana Smith.

GUILDHALL *(Bath City Council)*
High Street. Tel: (0225) 461111, Ext. 2785.
18th century Banqueting Room. Mon to Thurs 8.30–5; Fri 8.30–4.30. Subject to Bookings.

HERSCHEL HOUSE AND MUSEUM
19 New King Street BA1 2BL. Tel: (0225) 27160.
Displays on William Herschel, discoverer of Uranus, for the William Herschel Society by the National Maritime Museum. Mar to Oct: open daily 2–5. Adm. charge.

HOLBURNE MUSEUM AND CRAFTS STUDY CENTRE
Great Pulteney Street. Tel: (0225) 66669.
The Holburne Museum, Bath, is a successful combination of ancient and modern. Set in an elegant 18th century building the collection of decorative and fine art which it contains was made by Sir Thomas William Holburne (1793–1874) and includes superb English and continental silver and porcelain, Italian maiolica and bronzes, together with glass, furniture, miniatures and old master paintings. Fine examples of work by British 20th century artist-craftsmen are also on view in the Crafts Study Centre. This collection and archive embraces printed and woven textiles, pottery, furniture, and calligraphy. Study facilities by appointment. Temporary exhibitions and events throughout the year. Licensed Teahouse. Free Parking. Coaches welcome by prior appointment. Mon to Sat 11–5, Sun 2.30–6. Open Bank Holidays except Christmas. *Closed* mid Dec to mid Feb and Mons Nov to Easter. Adm £1; Chld, Students and OAPs 50p.

THE HUNTINGDON CENTRE
The Countess of Huntingdon's Chapel, The Vineyards. The Paragon. Tel: (0225) 333895.
A restored Georgian Gothic Chapel used as a centre for the appreciation of the history and architecture of Bath. Scale model of the city, tape-slide programmes, talk, and walks. Exhibition about the work of Selina, Countess of Huntingdon for her Connexion in England and America. Tues to Sat 10.30–4. Groups at other times by prior arrangement. *Closed* last week in Dec. Adm 75p; Chld and concessions 40p.

MUSEUM OF BOOKBINDING *(Hylton Bayntun-Coward)*
Manvers Street. Tel: (0225) 66000.
Showing the historical and contemporary practice of the craft, a reconstruction of a 19th century bindery and examples of the art. Open office hours – Mon to Fri. Adm £1. National Car Park nearby.

MUSEUM OF COSTUME *(Bath City Council)*
Assembly Rooms, Bennett Street. Tel: (0225) 461111, Ext. 2785.
400 years of personal style are to be seen at one of Britain's greatest costume collections. Flapper, Gigolo, Courtier, Society Hostess, Fop, Masher, Beau and Dandy all parade their distinctive dress. From ancient bodices to Body Map, this unique display informs and entertains with the added gloss of jewellery, underwear and all other accessories. Special sections on Royal apparel, children's toys, dolls and games of the past, make a visit here an experience not to be missed. There are guided tours throughout the day, and a museum souvenir shop. Winter: Weekdays 10–5; Sun 11–5. Summer: Weekdays 9.30–6; Sun 10–6. Adm £1.50; Chld 95p. Reduction for parties.

NUMBER ONE, ROYAL CRESCENT
Telephone: Bath (0225) 28126
(Bath Preservation Trust)

A Georgian Town House at the eastern end of Bath's most magnificent crescent; redecorated and furnished to show the visitor how it might have appeared in the late 18th century.
Location: Bath.
Opening Times: Mar to end Oct: Tues to Sat 11–5; Sun 2–5. Bank Hol Mon (last adm 4.30). Nov & Dec: Sat, Sun 11–3 (last adm 2.30). Adm £1.50, Chd, OAPs & Students 80p. Museum shop.

ROMAN BATHS MUSEUM *(Bath City Council)*
Abbey Church Yard, near Bath Abbey. Tel: (0225) 461111, Ext. 2785.
Adjoins the extensive remains of the Roman Baths and includes material from that and other Roman sites, including architectural fragments, inscriptions, metalware and offerings from the sacred spring. Winter: Mon to Sat 9–5; Sun 10–5. Summer: Daily 9–6 (July and Aug 9–7). Adm (including entrance to Pump Room, Roman Baths and Temple Precinct) £2, Chld £1.15. Reductions for parties.

THE R.P.S. NATIONAL CENTRE OF PHOTOGRAPHY
(The Royal Photographic Society)
The Octagon, Milsom Street. Tel: (0225) 62841.
Five Galleries with changing exhibitions.

VICTORIA ART GALLERY *(Bath City Council)*
Bridge Street. Tel: (0225) 461111, Ext. 2772.
Exhibitions from permanent collections and temporary exhibitions frequently changed. Paintings, prints and drawings, glass, ceramics, watches, coins and tokens. Local topography. Mon to Fri 10–6; Sat 10–5. *Closed* Sun and Bank Holidays. Admission free.

BRISTOL

ARNOLFINI GALLERY
16 Narrow Quay.

BARSTAPLE HOUSE (TRINITY ALMSHOUSES)
Telephone: Bristol (0272) 265777 (Warden)
(Bristol Municipal Charities)

Victorian almshouse with garden courtyard.
Location: Old Market Street, Bristol; ½ m from City centre on A420.
Station: Bristol Temple Meads (¾ m).

Opening Times: GARDEN & EXTERIOR OF BUILDINGS ONLY. All the year—Weekdays 10–4. Adm free. *The Almshouse is occupied mainly by elderly residents & their rights for privacy should be respected.*

BRISTOL INDUSTRIAL MUSEUM *(City of Bristol)*
Princes Wharf, Bristol. Tel: (0272) 299771.

BRISTOL MUSEUM AND ART GALLERY *(City of Bristol)*
Queen's Road, Bristol BS8 1RL. Tel: (0272) 299771.

CHATTERTON HOUSE *(City of Bristol)*
Redcliffe Way.

THE EXPLORATORY HANDS-ON SCIENCE CENTRE
The Victoria Rooms, Queen's Road, Clifton, Bristol. Wed–Sat 10–5; Sun and Bank Holidays 11–5. (*Closed* Christmas Day). Adm £2, Chld £1.50, concessions £1. School and coach parties by appointment only please. All correspondence to: The Exploratory Workshop, 131 Duckmoor Road, Bristol BS3 2BH. For further information tel. 0272 634321.

GEORGIAN HOUSE
Telephone: Bristol (0272) 299771 ext 237
(City of Bristol)

A merchant's town house, completed in 1791. Furnished in the style of the period, both 'above' and 'below' stairs.
Location: 7 Great George St., Bristol 1.
Station: Bristol Temple Meads (¾ m).
Opening Times: All the year—Mon to Sat 10–1, 2–5. *Closed Christmas Day, Boxing Day, New Year's Day, Good Friday. May 1 & Spring Bank Hol Mon.* Adm free.

HARVEYS WINE MUSEUM
12 Denmark Street. Tel: (0272) 277661.
Please telephone to arrange or join a guided tour Mon to Fri, price guide £2–£4.50, or call in on Fri mornings (Bank Hols excepted) between 10–12, to view at your leisure. Adm £1.50. Visitors must be aged 18 or over.

KINGSWESTON ROMAN VILLA *(City of Bristol)*
Long Cross, Lawrence Weston.

MARITIME HERITAGE CENTRE *(City of Bristol)*
Wapping Wharf, Gas Ferry Road. Tel: (0272) 260680.

RED LODGE
Telephone: Bristol (0272) 299771 ext 236
(City of Bristol)

Late 16th century house with period panelling and plasterwork; some rooms altered c.1730. Furnished in the style of both periods.
Location: Park Row, Bristol 1.
Station: Bristol Temple Meads (¾ m).
Opening Times: All the year—Mon to Sat 10–1, 2–5. *Closed Christmas Day, Boxing Day, New Year's Day, Good Friday, May 1 & Spring Bank Hol Mon.* Adm free.

ST. NICHOLAS CHURCH MUSEUM *(City of Bristol)*
St. Nicholas Street Tel: (0272) 299771.

CHIPPING SODBURY

LITTLE SODBURY MANOR
Telephone: Chipping Sodbury 312232
(Mr & Mrs Gerald Harford)

Medieval House with fine Great Hall. There are Tudor, Jacobean and Queen Anne additions.
Location: 2½ m from Chipping Sodbury off A46.
Opening Times: Apr to Sept—By appointment only. Adm £2.
Refreshments: Teas on request.

CLAVERTON

CLAVERTON MANOR
Telephone: Bath (0225) 60503
(The American Museum in Britain)

A Greek Revival house high above the valley of the Avon. Completely furnished rooms, 17th, 18th and 19th century brought from the U.S.A.
Location: 2½ m from Bath Station via Bathwick Hill; 3¾ m SE of Bath via Warminster Road (A36) & Claverton village.
Station: Bath Spa (2½ m).
Opening Times: Mar 24–Oct 29—Daily (except Mons) 2–5; Bank Hols Sun and Mon 12–5. *Mornings and winter months on application only.* School parties by previous arrangement, except Jan. Educational Tel 63538. Adm (1988) House & Grounds £3, Chd £2, and Senior Citizens £2.50. Grounds only £1. Parties of children not admitted during normal opening hours. *Pre-arranged parties over 30 at reduced rate.* Gardens open throughout the season (*except Mon*) 12–6.
Refreshments: Tea with American cookies (*Gingerbread cooked in 18th century oven*).

ORCHARD HOUSE
(Rear Adm & Mrs Hugh Tracy)

Plantsman's garden of 2½ acres in which owners have tried to combine botanical interest with attractive and informal layout. Collections of foliage plants, herbs, alpines, ground-cover and silver plants; rock gardens, herbaceous borders, lawns, shrubs, views.
Location: 3½ m from centre of Bath via A36 (Warminster) road; turn off at signpost for American museum: or ½ m down hill from American Museum, Claverton.
Station: Bath Spa (2½ m).
Opening Times: GARDEN ONLY. Weds Apr 26, May 3, 10, 17, 24, 31; June 7, 14. Adm 80p, Chd 30p. *In aid of National Gardens Scheme & King George's Fund for Sailors.* No dogs. Plants for sale. Small (wholesale) nursery.

CLEVEDON

CLEVEDON COURT, The National Trust
A 14th century manor house incorporating a 12th century tower and a 13th century hall with terraced 18th century garden; rare shrubs and plants. The home of the Elton family. Important collections of Nailsea glass and Eltonware.
Location: 1½ m E of Clevedon on the Bristol Road B3130.
Station: Yatton (3 m).
Opening Times: Mar 26 to Sept 28—Weds, Thurs & Suns, also Bank Hol Mons 2.30–5.30 (last adm 5).
Adm £2, Chd £1 (children under 17 must be accompanied by an adult). No dogs. Unsuitable for wheelchairs & coaches.
Refreshments: Teas at the house.

DYRHAM

DYRHAM PARK, The National Trust
Telephone: Abson 2501 &
Late 17th century house in a splendid deer park. The Blathwayt furniture and Dutch paintings in a fine series of panelled rooms.
Location: 12 m E of Bristol approach from Bath/Stroud Road (A46), 2 m S of Tormarton interchange with M4, 8 m N of Bath.
Opening Times: Park—Daily 12–6 (or dusk if earlier).
House & Garden: Mar 25 to Oct 29—Daily (except Thurs & Fris) 2–6. Last adm 5.30.
Adm House, Gardens & Park £3, Chd £1.50. *Pre-booked parties of 15 or more £2.* Park only 80p, Chd 40p. Dogs in park on leads, please. Wheelchairs provided.
Refreshments: Teas in the Orangery.

HENBURY

BLAISE CASTLE HOUSE MUSEUM
Telephone: Bristol (0272) 506789
(City of Bristol)

18th century house set in landscaped park; containing collections illustrating everyday life of the last 300 years.
Location: 4 m NW of central Bristol.
Station: Sea Mills (2 m).
Opening Times: All the year—Sats to Weds 10–1, 2–5. *Closed Thurs & Fris; Christmas Day, Boxing Day, New Year's Day & Good Friday.* Adm free.
Refreshments: Tea bar (in park).

VINE HOUSE
Telephone: Bristol (0272) 503573
(Professor & Mrs T. F. Hewer)

Two acres. Trees, shrubs, small water garden; bulbs; naturalised garden landscape.
Location: 4 m NW of Bristol centre next to 'Salutation' Public House.
Stations: Bristol Parkway; Bristol Temple Meads each about 4 m from Henbury.
Opening Times: GARDENS ONLY. Suns & Mons Mar 26 & 27, May 28 & 29, 2–7. Also open by appointment throughout the year. Adm 60p, Chd & OAPs 30p. Dogs on leads. *In aid of National Gardens Scheme & 'Friends of Blaise'.*

HORTON

HORTON COURT, The National Trust &
A Cotswold manor house restored and altered in the 19th century. 12th century hall and late Perpendicular ambulatory in garden only shown.
Location: 3 m NE of Chipping Sodbury, ¼ m N of Horton, 1 m W of Bath/Stroud Road (A46).
Opening Times: Hall & Ambulatory only: Mar 25 to Oct 28—Weds & Sats 2–6 (or sunset if earlier).
Other times by written appointment with the tenant. Adm 80p. *No reduction for parties or children.* No dogs. Unsuitable for coaches. Wheelchairs—ambulatory only.

Avon — *continued*

WALTON-IN-GORDANO

THE MANOR HOUSE
Telephone: Clevedon (0272) 872067
(Mr & Mrs Simon Wills)

Four acres—mainly shrubs and fine trees, bulbs, alpines and herbaceous plants, mostly labelled.

Location: W of Bristol; via B3124 from Clevedon to Portishead; driveway on left before 1st houses in Walton-in-Gordano.
Station: Yatton (6 m).
Opening Times: GARDEN ONLY: Apr 12 to Sept 14 every Wed & Thurs 10–4. Suns Apr 30, May 28, Aug 27, 2–6; Mons May 1 & 29, Aug 28, 2–6. Open by appointment all year. Adm 75p, accompanied Chd free. Plants for sale. No dogs. Coaches by appointment only. In aid of National Gardens Scheme and St. Peter's Hospice.

WESTON SUPER MARE

WOODSPRING MUSEUM
Burlington Street. Tel: (0934) 21028.
A friendly local museum for all the family. Set around a palm-lined courtyard, in the old Gaslight Co's workshops are displays of the Seaside Holiday, local industries, Mendip mining, local archaeology, costume rooms, camera collection and indoor nature trail. Also the Peggy Nisbet collection of costume dolls and frequent temporary exhibitions. Clara's Cottage adjoining, is displayed as seaside lodgings of the 1900 period. Souvenir shop and refreshments in central courtyard. Mon to Sat 10–5; Open Bank Hol. Mon. Adm free.

The AMERICAN MUSEUM
CLAVERTON MANOR, BATH

The American Museum stands high above the Avon Valley. Eighteen furnished period rooms combine with galleries of textiles, pewter, glass and silver to illustrate the background of American domestic life between the 17th and 19th centuries. Special sections are devoted to the American Indians, Pennsylvania Germans and the Shakers. American gardens, American Arboretum and teas with American cookies.

HARVEYS WINE MUSEUM

Please telephone to arrange or join a guided group tour Monday to Friday. (Bank Hols excepted) or call in on Fridays between 10.00 and 12.00 to view at your leisure.

Admission £1.50.

We look forward to seeing you.

Visitors must be aged 18 or over

12 Denmark St. Bristol   *Tel: 277661*

s.s. GREAT BRITAIN

The s.s. "Great Britain" was built and launched in Bristol on July 19th, 1843. She was the first ocean-going, propeller-driven, iron ship in history. Designed by I. K. Brunel, she had a varied active life for 43 years, both as a liner and a cargo vessel. Her first voyages were to America then for some 25 years she carried thousands of emigrants to Australia; the voyages to Australia were interrupted twice when she became a troopship for the Crimean War and the Indian Mutiny. Abandoned in the Falkland Islands in 1886, the ship provided storage facilities in Port Stanley for 50 years. In 1970 she was towed back to Bristol and is now being restored to her original 1843 appearance.

Tel: (0272) 260680 for party bookings and further information.
BORN AGAIN IN BRISTOL at
Great Western Dock, Gas Ferry Road, (off Cumberland Road), Bristol
OPEN EVERY DAY
10 a.m. – 6 p.m. Summer 10 a.m. – 5 p.m. Winter
Car and Coach Park, Souvenir Shop, Museum

HOLBURNE MUSEUM & CRAFTS STUDY CENTRE

Great Pulteney Street, Bath BA2 4DB
Tel: 0225-66669

Elegant 18th century building housing an excellent collection of 17th–18th century fine and decorative art. Work by British 20th century artist-craftsmen on view in the Crafts study centre including pots by Bernard Leach. Temporary exhibitions throughout year.

Open weekdays 11–5, Sundays 2.30–6. Closed mid-December - mid-February and Mondays November to Easter.

Licensed Teahouse. Open Easter to October.

Free Parking.

Gainsborough's Portrait of Dr. Rice Charleton.

Bedfordshire

BEDFORD

BEDFORD MUSEUM *(North Bedfordshire Borough Council)*
Castle Lane. Tel: (0234) 53323.
The Museum for North Bedfordshire with displays of local material including archaeology, local and social history, natural history and geology. Two large new galleries recently opened. Temporary exhibition programme. Tues to Sat 11–5; Sun and Bank Hol Mons 2–5.

BROMHAM MILL *(Bedfordshire County Council Leisure Services)*
Bromham. Tel: (0234) 228330.
Restored water mill and machinery. Natural history room, special exhibitions, art gallery and craft cabinets. Adjoining picnic site. Apr to Oct: Wed to Fri 10.30–4.30. Sat, Sun and Bank Hol 11.30–6. Adm (1988 rates) 35p, Chld and OAPs 20p. Party rates on application. Car parking for 30 cars. Some parts of this property are not suitable for disabled.

THE BUNYAN MEETING LIBRARY AND MUSEUM
(Trustees of Bunyan Meeting)
Mill Street.
Contains all the surviving personal relics of John Bunyan. World Famous collection of 'The Pilgrim's Progress' in 169 languages. Apr to Sept: Tues to Sat 2–4. Adm 30p, Chld 20p.

CECIL HIGGINS ART GALLERY & MUSEUM
Telephone: Bedford (0234) 211222 &
(Gallery jointly owned and administered by the North Bedfordshire Borough Council and the Trustees of the Cecil Higgins Art Gallery)

Award-winning re-created Victorian Mansion, original home of Cecil Higgins. Rooms displayed to give 'lived-in' atmosphere, including bedroom with furniture designed by William Burges (1827–1881). Adjoining gallery with outstanding collections of ceramics, glass and watercolours. Situated in gardens leading down to the river embankment.
Location: Centre of Bedford, just off The Embankment.
Station: Bedford Midland (1 m).
Bus Station: (½ m).
Opening Times: Tues–Frid 12.30–5, Sat 11–5, Sun 2–5. *Closed Mons (except Bank Hol Mons), Christmas Day, Boxing Day, Good Fri.*
Adm free. Group bookings and refreshments by prior arrangement. Facilities for the disabled. Trains from London (St. Pancras), and King's Cross Thameslink – fast trains 36 mins. National Express. United Counties 131/132 Bedford/Milton Keynes – Buckingham – Bicester – Oxford, 128/129 Northampton – Bedford – Cambridge and Express Service from London.

ELSTOW MOOT HALL
(Bedfordshire County Council Leisure Services)
Elstow. Tel: (0234) 228330.
Medieval market hall containing 17th century collection associated with John Bunyan. Apr to Oct: Tue to Sat 2–5, Bank Hol Mon 2–5; Sun 2–5.30. Adm (1988 rates) 35p, Chld 20p; party rates on application.

BIGGLESWADE

THE SWISS GARDEN
Telephone: Bedford (0234) 228330 &
(Bedfordshire County Council)

An unusual Romantic landscaped garden dating from the early 19th century, containing original buildings, ironwork and other features together with many interesting plants and trees, some of great rarity. Attractive lakeside picnic area in adjoining woodlands.
Location: 2½ m W of Biggleswade, adjoining Biggleswade/Old Warden Road; approximately 2 m W of A1.
Station: Biggleswade (3 m).
Opening Times: Apr to Oct—Weds, Thurs, Sats, Suns (but closed the last Sun in each month), & Bank Holidays. Mons 2–6 (last admission 5.15). Adm (1988 rates) 60p, Chd (5–16) and OAPS 30p. Special rates for School parties & group visits by prior arrangement. Wheelchair access by special arrangement. Lakeside picnic area open at all times. Public lavatory (facilities for disabled).
Refreshments: Cafeteria at adjoining Shuttleworth Aeroplane Collection.

LUTON

LUTON HOO
Telephone: Luton (0582) 22955
(The Wernher Family)

Exterior commenced by Robert Adam, 1767. Interior remodelled in the French style early in this century. Magnificent art collection includes Fabergé jewels and unique porcelain collection. Park landscaped by 'Capability' Brown.
Location: Entrance at Park Street Gates Luton 30 m N of London via M1 (exit 10, junction A1081 – formerly A6). Railway & Bus Stations 3 m.
Station: Luton (2½ m).
Opening Times: House & Gardens. Easter then Apr 15 to Oct 15, 1988. Open daily 2–5.45; closed Mons *except Bank Hols;* last adm 5; £3, Chd £1.50. Reduced rates for parties by prior arrangement (minimum 30 adults). No dogs admitted to House or Gardens.

LUTON MUSEUM AND ART GALLERY *(Luton Museum Service)*
Wardown Park, Luton LU2 7HA. Tel: (0582) 36941–2.
Collections/Displays Archaeology, Costume, Dolls and Toys. Fine and Decorative Art, Local History, Social History, Military (Beds and Herts Regiment), Natural History/Geology, Lace, Straw Plait. Changing Exhibitions. Study access to reserve collections by appointment only. Educational group visits welcome by prior booking. (0582) 36941 × 221. Open: Weekdays and Sat 10–5, Sun 1–5. *Closed* Dec. 25, 26, Jan 1. For further details Telephone above number.

STOCKWOOD CRAFT MUSEUM AND GARDENS
(Luton Museum Service)
Stockwood Park, Farley Hill, LU1 4BH (near M1 exit 10). Tel: (0582) 38714.
Collections/Displays Rural crafts and trades including Thatching, Saddlery, Shoemaking, Rushwork, Blacksmithing, Wood Crafts, Wheelwrighting and Agriculture, Wheeled Vehicles. Also to be seen: craft workshops, regular weekend craft demonstrations, period gardens and sculptures by Ian Hamilton Finlay. Educational group visits welcome by prior booking (0582) 36941 × 221. Open Mar–Apr to Oct: Weekdays and Sat 10–5; Sun 10–6. *Closed* Mon and Tues (except Bank holiday Mondays). For further details Telephone above number or 36941.

OLD WARDEN

THE SHUTTLEWORTH COLLECTION
Nr Biggleswade. Tel: (076 727) 288.
At The Shuttleworth Collection you will find the whole history of aviation laid before you in the form of real *flyable* veteran aeroplanes. Housed in a small grass aerodrome that is the timeless magic of Old Warden, it is the only collection of its kind in Europe. There are some 34 aircraft in all, ranging from the 1909 Bleriot type IX to a Spitfire Mark VC and fully half of them are sole surviving examples of their type. But there are many exhibits of general transport interest including early motor cars, cycles, fire engines and horse drawn vehicles. Open daily throughout the year but closed for one week during Christmas period. Opening hours: 10–5. (4 during winter time), last admission one hour before closing. A wide variety of events including flying days from Apr to Oct. Details on request.

SHEFFORD

CHICKSANDS PRIORY
Telephone: Biggleswade 315674
(Ministry of Defence Property Administered by RAF Commander. Friends of Priory licensed to open Priory to public and redecorate interior)

Chicksands Priory was founded by Payne De Beauchamp and his wife Countess Rohese for Nuns and Canons of the English Order of Gilbertines c 1150. Dissolved and surrendered 1538, it was sold by Henry VIII for £810 11s 8d to the Snowe family 1540. Acquired by the Osborne family in 1576, it so remained their family home until sold to The Crown, 1936. 13th and 15th century monastic remains survive with architectural work by Isaac Ware (1740) and James Wyatt (1813). Stained glass, Chinese wallpaper, Coade statuary have been uncovered since the Anglo-American Group of Friends opened the building to the public, 1975. The 18th century Venetian Prayer Book purchased by Sir Danvers Osborn, 3rd Baronet, is shown in the refurbished Private Chapel. Ghosts of former inhabitants are said to haunt the building; a plaque boasts of a walled up Nun within the cloisters and remains of monastic residents are buried in the still landscaped gardens. Game larder, Orangery and grapevines are on show exclusive of guided tour of the interior, which takes approximately 45 minutes. Past visitors to Chicksands include St Thomas Becket, King James I, HRH Princess Alice, Duchess of Gloucester, the Duke of Bedford, Terence, Cardinal Cooke. Following intensive external restoration by the Ministry of Defence, The Friends are decorating and restoring the interior.
Location: 1¼ miles from Shefford. Entrances on A507 Shefford to Ampthill Road and on A600 Shefford to Bedford Road.
Opening Times: 1st & 3rd Suns of Month Apr to Oct 2–5; last tour 4.30. Guided tours only. No adm charge—donations for interior decoration requested. Parties by appointment only. Car Parking. Unsuitable for wheelchairs.
Refreshments: Light refreshments at Priory. Nearest hotels at Biggleswade, Bedford & Hitchin, all being 7 miles from Chicksands.

SILSOE

WREST PARK HOUSE AND GARDENS
Telephone: (0525) 60718
(English Heritage)

Here is a history of English gardening in the grand manner from 1700–1850, which would not, of course, be complete without some designs by 'Capability' Brown. Every whim of fashion is represented, whether it be for a Chinese bridge, artificial lake, classical temple or rustic ruin. The present house was built about 1839 by the Earl de Grey, whose family had lorded it over the Manor of Wrest for 600 years. The State Rooms and gardens are open to the public.
Location: ¾ m (1 km) east of Silcoe.
Opening Times: Good Friday to Sept 30, weekends and Bank Hols only 10–6. Adm £1.10, OAPs 80p, Chd 55p.

STAGSDEN

STAGSDEN BIRD GARDENS
Telephone: Oakley (023 02) 2745

A large Bird Zoo and breeding establishment for birds with over 1300 specimens in approximately 150 species. Also a collection of shrub roses.

Location: 5 m W of Bedford, 7 m N of A422. Turn N at Stagsden Church.
Opening Times: Every day of the year 11–6 (or dusk if earlier). Adm £1.50, Chd (4–15 inc.) 70p, OAPs £1.30.

WOBURN

WOBURN ABBEY
Telephone: Woburn (0525) 290666; Catering (0525) 290662; Antiques Centre (0525) 290350
(The Marquess of Tavistock and Trustees of the Bedford Estates)

Home of the Dukes of Bedford for over 300 years. Rebuilt by Henry Flitcroft mid-18th century, and added to by Henry Holland in early 19th century. 3000 acre deer park landscaped by Humphry Repton. Very important and extensive art collection.

Location: In Woburn 8½ m NW of Dunstable on A418. 42 m from London off M1 at junction with A5120, exit 12 or 13.
Station: Ridgmont (3 m).
Opening Times: House and Gardens. Dec 31 to Mar 19 — Sats & Suns only. House 11–4.45; Park 10.30–3.45. Mar 20 to Oct 29 — Daily. House: Weekdays 11–5.45; Suns 11–6.15. Park: Weekdays 10–4.45; Suns 10–5.45. *Last adm to House 45 mins before closing time every day.* House Adm £4, Chd (7–16) £1.50, OAPs £3.
Party rates are available.
Free car park.
Refreshments: Flying Duchess Pavilion Coffee Shop, Restaurants for pre-booked parties.

WOBURN ABBEY
BEDFORDSHIRE

The Deer Park has lots of wild life, including nine species of deer, roaming freely. One of these, the Pere David, descended from the Imperial Herd of China, was saved from extinction at Woburn and is now the largest breeding herd of this specie in the world. In 1985 twenty-two Pere David were given by the Family to the People's Republic of China with the hope that the specie may become re-established in its natural habitat. The Marquess of Tavistock visited Beijing (Peking) to release the herd at Nan Haizi, the former Imperial hunting ground outside Beijing (Peking). Happily the deer have already bred, and as further consolidation, the Family gave another 15 Pere David to the Republic in 1987.

The Abbey contains one of the most important private art collections in the world, including paintings by Canaletto, Van Dyck, Cuyp, Teniers, Rembrandt, Gainsborough, Reynolds, Velazques and many other famous artists. French and English 18th century furniture, silver and the fabulous Sèvres dinner service presented to the 4th Duke by Louis XV of France.

The tour of the Abbey covers three floors, including the Crypt and it is regretted that wheelchairs can only be accommodated in the House by prior arrangement.

The 40 shop Antiques Centre is probably the most unusual such centre outside London – the shop fronts having been rescued from demolition sites in various parts of Britain. Shipping can be arranged on a world-wide basis.

All catering is operated by ourselves with banqueting, conferences and receptions our speciality, in the beautiful setting of the Sculpture Gallery, overlooking the private gardens. There is a Pottery and Garden Centre, and summer weekend events are arranged.

Extensive picnic areas with ample coach and car parking. Gift shops. Pottery and a Garden & Camping Equipment Centre.

CECIL HIGGINS ART GALLERY AND MUSEUM, BEDFORD

Venetian-style glass, possibly German, late 17th century. Latticino decoration with painted butterflies and insects.

Pablo Picasso. "Après le Pique", 1956. Linocut.

The Gallery's outstanding collections have been re-displayed in a major extension and in room settings, the latter evoking a late Victorian family home. It has won 4 national awards: 1978 Museum of the Year runner-up, 1981 Sotheby's Best Fine Art Museum and twice highly commended by the British Tourist Authority in the 'Come to Britain Trophy'.

Tallboy, mahogany, English, about 1760. Serpentine front with brass rococo handles and key escutcheons.

Berkshire

BURGHFIELD

THE OLD RECTORY
(Mr & Mrs R. R. Merton)

Garden of horticultural interest; roses, hellebores, lilies, many rare and unusual plants from China and Japan; old-fashioned cottage plants; autumn colour.
Location: 5½ m SW of Reading, between M4 junctions 11 & 12.
Stations: Reading and Mortimer (3½ m).
Opening Times: GARDEN ONLY. Weds: Feb 22, March 29, April 26, May 31, June 28, July 26, Aug 30, Sept 27, Oct 25, 11–4. Adm 50p, Chd 10p. *In aid of National Gardens Scheme.* (Share to Save the Children & BB & O NCCPG). Plants & produce for sale. No dogs.

COOKHAM ON THAMES

STANLEY SPENCER GALLERY
King's Hall. Tel: Bourne End (062 85) 24580/20043.

Major Spencer collection (*The Last Supper* 1920, *Christ Preaching at Cookham Regatta* 1959, etc) in village immortalized by the artist. Gallery shop. Easter–Oct: daily, 10.30–5.30. Nov–Easter: Sat, Sun and Bank Holidays, 11–1, 2–5. Adm 50p, students & OAPs 25p, chld 10p. Enquiries (including group visits), Tel: on the above number.

HUNGERFORD

LITTLECOTE
Telephone: (0488) 84000

An impressive Tudor Manor House, built between 1490 and 1520. Colonel Alexander Popham garrisoned his private army here during the Civil War. The magnificent Great Hall contains a 30ft Shovel Board table (possibly the longest in the world), and the unique collection of Cromwellian armour belonging to the Royal Armouries. The grounds include a working rare breeds farm, Tudor style rose gardens, and a 'period village' with craftsmen and shopkeepers in Tudor costume. Visitors can also enjoy daily falconry displays and jousting tournaments. Important Roman excavations and Orpheus mosaic.
Location: 4 m S of M4 (junction 14) nr. Hungerford. B4193 W to Chilton Foliat and Swindon, into village of Chilton Foliat, then 1 m out of village and follow signposting.
Opening Times: Mar 19 to Oct 1: Daily from 10 am.
Refreshments: Tavern, licensed restaurant, picnic area.

MAIDENHEAD

COURAGE SHIRE HORSE CENTRE
Maidenhead Thicket. Tel: Littlewick Green (062 882) 4848.

No animal on earth can match the Shire Horse's unique combination of size, strength, grace and beauty and nowhere will you get a better chance to see Shires in their home environment than at the Courage Shire Horse Centre. Knowledgeable trained guides offer free tours and a rare insight into the world of the 'Gentle Giants' or you can wander around the Centre at your own pace. Every horse has its own stable, looking out across a communal courtyard, where the horse's names and characteristics are displayed to help visitors to get to know each horse individually. The Courage Shire Horse Centre is a working stable and the care and preparation that prize-winning Shires demand is evident wherever you look. Daily grooming and harnessing and polishing the harnesses and brasses calls for hard work and devotion, but the reward is displayed for visitors to see in the shape of hundreds of prize rosettes. The farrier's workshop is normally in use on three days a week when the farrier can be seen silhouetted against his furnace making horseshoes or attending to the horses' feet. Additional attractions at the Centre include a free audio visual presentation featuring popular TV 'Animal Man' Johnny Morris, a well-stocked souvenir shop, children's playground and a small animal and bird area. The Centre's newly-refurbished Tea Rooms sell a range of hot and cold food and drinks. If you prefer to take your own food, there are several picnic areas inside the Centre. The Centre is situated on the A4, 2 miles west of Maidenhead and within a few miles of junction 8/9 of the M4. Open daily from 11am with last admission at 4pm from Mar 1 to Oct 31. £1.75 for adults, £1.25 for children and OAPs. Suitable for disabled visitors. Car parking is free.

HENRY REITLINGER BEQUEST
Oldfield, Guards Club Road, SL6 8DN. Tel: (0628) 21818.

NEWBURY

NEWBURY DISTRICT MUSEUM
The Wharf. Tel: (0635) 30511.
In picturesque 17th and 18th century buildings. Displays: Ballooning; Kennet & Avon Canal; Traditional Crafts; Costume; Civil War battles of Newbury (with audio-visual). Local collections: archaeology, history, geology and birds. Also cameras, pewter and pottery. Apr to Sept: Mon to Sat 10–6; Sun and Bank Hol 2–6. Oct to Mar: Mon to Sat 10–4. *Closed* Wed all year.

PANGBOURNE

BASILDON PARK, The National Trust
Telephone: Pangbourne (07357) 3040

Classical house built 1776. Unusual Octagon room; fine plasterwork; important paintings and furniture. Garden and Woodland walks.
Location: 7 m NW of Reading between Pangbourne and Streatley on A329.
Stations: Pangbourne (2½ m); Goring and Streatley (3 m).
Opening Times: Mar 25 to end Oct—Weds to Sats 2–6; Suns & Bank Hol Mons 12–6. *Last adm to house half-hour before closing.* Adm House & Grounds £2. Grounds only £1, Chd half price. Reductions (except Suns and Bank Hol Mons) to House & Grounds for parties of 15 or more (Booking essential). *Closed Mons (except Bank Hols), Tues & Weds following Bank Hols and Good Friday.* Shop. Dogs in grounds only on leads. House unsuitable for wheelchairs.
Refreshments: Tea room in house accessible to wheelchairs.

READING

BLAKE'S LOCK MUSEUM *(Reading Corporation)*
Gasworks Road, off Kenavon Drive. Tel: (0734) 590630.
Displays the history of the industrial and commercial life of Reading and the development of its waterways. Mon to Fri 10–5, Sat and Sun 2–5.

THE COLE MUSEUM OF ZOOLOGY *(The University of Reading)*
Whiteknights. Tel: (0734) 875123.
A specialist collection for teaching purposes consisting of dissections, skeletons and models. By appointment.

MUSEUM AND ART GALLERY *(Reading Corporation)*
Blagrave Street Tel: (0734) 575911 Ext. 3409.
Displays of natural history and local archaeology. Roman collection from Silchester. Changing art exhibitions each month. Thames Conservancy collection of prehistoric and Medieval metalwork. Historical collections. Mon to Fri 10–5.30; Sat 10–5; Sun 2–5.

MAPLEDURHAM HOUSE
Telephone: Reading (0734) 723350 or 723277
(J J Eyston and Lady Anne Eyston)

Late 16th century Elizabethan home of the Blount Family. Original moulded ceilings, great oak staircase, fine collection of paintings and private chapel. Unique setting in grounds running down to the Thames. 15th century Water-mill nearby is now restored and operating.
Location: 4 m NW of Reading on North Bank of Thames. Signposted off Caversham/Woodcote Road on A4074. Boats from Caversham Bridge 2pm on open days. (Caversham Bridge is ½ m from Reading Station).
Opening Times: House. Easter Sun to end of Sept—Sats, Suns & Bank Hols 2.30–5.30. Last admission 5. Midweek party visits, see advertisement for details. Watermill and Country Park/Picnic area—see advertisement for details.
Refreshments: Tea room serving home made afternoon/cream teas.

MUSEUM OF ENGLISH RURAL LIFE *(The University of Reading)*
Whiteknights. Tel: (0734) 318660.
A national collection of material relating to the history of the English country-side, including agriculture, crafts, domestic utensils and village life. There is a permanent exhibition open to the general public and, in addition, study collections of objects and documentary material which may be consulted on application to the Secretary. Tues to Sat 10–1, 2–4.30. *Closed* Sun, Mon and Public Hols.

NATIONAL DAIRY MUSEUM
Wellington Country Park, Riseley. Tel: Reading (0734) 326444.
Exhibits and displays showing the growth of dairying from a small rural activity to a large countrywide industry. Mar 1 to Oct 31: Daily 10–5.30; also weekends in winter. Adm (includes entry to Country Park) £1.70, Chld 90p (1988 charges). Party reduction.

THE URE MUSEUM OF GREEK ARCHAEOLOGY
(The University of Reading)
Whiteknights.
Greek pottery. Mon to Fri 9–5. Open for individual visits. Parties by appointment.

SWALLOWFIELD

SWALLOWFIELD PARK
(Country Houses Association Ltd)

Built by the Second Earl of Clarendon in 1678.
Location: In the village of Swallowfield 6 m SE of Reading.
Opening Times: May to September—Weds & Thurs 2–5. Adm £1, Chd 50p. Free car park. No dogs admitted.

WINDSOR

FROGMORE GARDENS
(Her Majesty The Queen)

Beautifully landscaped gardens with trees, shrubs and lake.
Location: Entrance to garden through Long Walk Gate. *(Visitors are requested kindly to refrain from entering grounds of the Home Park).*
Stations: Windsor & Eton Central; Windsor & Eton Riverside (both 20 mins walk).

Opening Times: GARDEN ONLY. Open on Wed May 3 & Thurs May 4: 10.30–7 (last adm 6.30). Adm £1, accompanied Chd free. No dogs. Free car park. Coaches by appointment only (apply to National Gardens Scheme, 57 Lower Belgrave Street, London SW1W 0LR. Tel: 01-730 0359, stating whether am or pm pass is required). The Royal Mausoleum also open on above 2 days, adm free. (In addition Mausoleum open Wed May 24: 11–4, but *not* the gardens).
Refreshments: Tent at car park—May 4 & 5.

SAVILL GARDEN
(Crown Property)

Mainly a woodland garden of 35 acres together with a formal area of roses and herbaceous plants, all of which offer great interest and beauty at every season of the year.

Location: To be approached from A30 via Wick Road & Wick Lane, Englefield Green.
Station: Egham (3 m).
Opening Times: Open daily 10–6. *Closed for a short period at Christmas.* Adm £1.80, OAPs £1.60. Parties of 20 and over £1.60, accompanied Chd (under 16) free.

VALLEY GARDENS
(Crown Property)

Extensive woodland gardens of 400 acres which include a large heather garden offering beauty and charm at all seasons of the year.

Location: To be approached from Wick Road off A30 (1 m walk).
Station: Egham (3 m).
Opening Times: Open daily from sunrise to sunset. Adm free to pedestrians. Car park adjoining gardens. £1.50 per car (£2 in Apr & May).

WINDSOR CASTLE
Telephone: Windsor (0753) 868286
(Official residence of H.M. The Queen)

Perhaps the largest fortress of its kind in the world, Windsor Castle has belonged to the Sovereigns of England for over 900 years, and is by far, the oldest residence still in regular use. The Castle has the following areas open to the public:–
State Apartments (except when HM The Queen in official residence).
Queen Mary's Dolls' House.
Exhibition of Drawings.
Exhibition of The Queen's Presents and Royal Carriages.

Location: 3m off J6 of M4.
Opening Times: The Curfew Tower: Tues to Sat 11–1, 2–4. *Closed Sun and Mon.* Adm 20p, Chd (accompanied) 10p. **St. George's Chapel:** Summer: weekdays 10.45–4, Sun 2–4. Winter: 10.45–3.45, Sun 2–3.45. *Closed in Jan (except for services) and occasionally at other times for special services.* Adm £1.50, Chd (5–16) and retirement pensioners 60p. **Albert Memorial Chapel:** Weekdays: 10–1, 2–3.45. *Closed Sun.* **Castle precincts:** open daily from 10–4.15, or 10–7.15 (depending on time of year. Adm free. **State Apartments:** Jan 4 to Mar 12 and Oct 23 to Dec 10: Mon to Sat 10.30–3, *Closed Sun.* May 1 to June 5, and June 26 to Oct 22: Mon to Sat 10.30–5, Sun 1.30–5. Adm £1.80, Chd 80p. **Queen Mary's Dolls' House and Exhibition of Old Master Drawings:** Jan 4 to Mar 27, Oct 23 to Dec 31: Mon to Sat 10.30–3: Mar 28 to Oct 22: Mon to Sat 10.30–5, Sun 1.30–5. *Closed Apr 3, 10, 17, 24, June 13, Dec 24–27.* Adm 80p, Chd 40p. **Exhibition of the Queen's Presents and Royal Carriages:** Jan 24 to Mar 27, and Oct 23 to Dec 31: Mon to Sat 10.30–3. *Closed Sun;* Mar 28 to Oct 22: Mon to Sat 10.30–5, Sun 10.30–3. Adm 80p, Chd 40p. *Closed Good Friday, Apr 3, 10, 17, 24 and Dec 24–27.* **Group Discounts:** during Nov 1 to Mar 31 a discount of 20% is available for parties of 15 or more who have pre-booked and pre- paid. This applies to the following: The State Apartments, Exhibition of Old Master Drawings, Exhibition of the Queen's Presents and Royal Carriages, Queen Mary's Dolls' House.
Whilst there is every intention to adhere to the above schedule this cannot be guaranteed as Windsor Castle is always subject to closure, sometimes at short notice. All enquiries (about Chapel only): Tel: Windsor 65538.
Refreshments: Castle Hotel (opposite).

MAPLEDURHAM
4 miles west of Reading on the north bank of the River Thames

MAPLEDURHAM HOUSE

Elizabethan Mansion built by Sir Michael Blount in 1588, now the home of his descendants Mr John and Lady Anne Eyston and their family. It stands on the bank of the Thames and is set in an unspoilt village of great charm, with its church, almshouses and watermill. This romantic house was frequently visited by Alexander Pope, and among the portraits are those of the beautiful sisters, Martha and Teresa Blount, to whom he dedicated much of his poetry. Great oak staircases, moulded ceilings of late Tudor plasterwork, fine collection of pictures and family portraits of 16th, 17th and 18th centuries. The family chapel built in 1797 by special licence is decorated in Strawberry Hill Gothick.

OPEN: Easter Sunday to the end of September on Saturdays, Sundays and Public Holidays.

HOUSE: 2.30 to 5.30 pm.

WATERMILL & COUNTRY PARK PICNIC AREA: Watermill open 1.00 to 5 pm Saturday, Sunday and Bank Holidays Easter to September. Also open 2 to 4 pm Sundays from October to April.

COUNTRY PARK: 12 to 7 pm, as above, also weekdays in July and August.
N.B. Weekday opening in July and August is provisional at this stage.

GUIDED PARTY VISITS of House and Watermill: Tuesday, Wednesday and Thursday afternoons by appointment only. Reduced Rates for Parties.

Shop for gifts, flour and other Watermill produce.

Home made cream/afternoon teas available.

Visit Mapledurham by river. A passenger boat leaves Reading from Caversham Promenade at 2 pm each day the House is open. This boat can also be hired for party visits.

For all enquiries and details of prices please contact: The Estate Office, Mapledurham House, Reading RG4 7TR. Telephone (0734) 723350/ 723277

MAPLEDURHAM WATERMILL

The picturesque Corn and Grist Mill in the grounds of Mapledurham House, dates from the 15th century. Visitors will often be able to see flour being ground by the old millstones in the traditional Oxfordshire manner. The wooden machinery powered by an undershot water-wheel also built of wood, is a unique working example of a Thames watermill. Its two pairs of millstones are set up to produce wholewheat flour which may be purchased in the shop.

Buckinghamshire

AYLESBURY

BUCKINGHAMSHIRE COUNTY MUSEUM

(Buckinghamshire County Council)
Church Street. Tel: (0296) 82158 and 88849.
Displays illustrating county geology, natural history, archaeology and history; costume; small collection of paintings. Temporary exhibitions. Mon to Fri 10–5; Sat 10–12.30, 1.30–5. *Closed* Christmas Day, Boxing Day, New Year's Day and Good Friday.

NETHER WINCHENDON HOUSE

Telephone: Haddenham 290101   &
(Mrs John Spencer Bernard)
Correspondence to Administrator, R.V. Spencer Bernard Esq.

Tudor manor house with 18th century additions. Home of Sir Francis Bernard, Governor of New Jersey and Massachusetts, 1760.
Location: 1 m N of A418 Aylesbury/Thame Road, nr village of Lower Winchendon, 6 m SW Aylesbury.
Station: Aylesbury (7½ m).
Opening Times: May to Aug: Thurs 2.30–5.30. Bank Hol weekends (i.e. Sat, Sun, Mon) 2.30–5.30; first weekend in June (Sat & Sun) 2.30–5.30; Second weekend in Aug (Sat & Sun) 2.30–5.30. Parties at any time of year by written appointment. Adm £1.50, Chd (under 12) £1; OAPs £1 (Thurs only).

BUCKINGHAM

BUCKINGHAM MOVIE MUSEUM

Printers Mews, Market Hill.

STOWE (Stowe School)

Famous 18th century house formerly the home of the Duke of Buckingham. Garden and garden buildings by Bridgeman, Kent, Gibbs, Vanburgh and 'Capability' Brown.
Location: 4 m N of Buckingham town.
Opening Times: Grounds, Garden Buildings & Main State Rooms: Mar 24 to Apr 16 and July 9 to Aug 28. Daily from 12. Adm £1.40, Chd & OAPs £1.
Refreshments: Light refreshments.

CHALFONT ST GILES

CHILTERN OPEN AIR MUSEUM

Telephone: Chalfont St Giles (024 07) 71117
(Chiltern Open Air Museum Ltd)

A museum of historic buildings, rescued from demolition and re-erected in Newland Park. Barns, Granaries, Stables, Forge, Toll House plus an Iron Age House. Woodland Nature Trail.
Location: Between Chalfont St Peter and Chalfont St Giles; 4½ m Amersham, 8 m Watford, 6 m Beaconsfield; 2 m A413 at Chalfont St Peter, 4 m from junction 17 on the M25 via Maple Cross and the Chalfonts.
Station: Chorleywood (2 m via footpath).
Opening Times: Mar 26 to end Oct—Weds, Suns & Bank Hols 2–6, Wed to Sun incl July 1 to Sept 10. Parties & School parties by arrangement weekdays all year round. Adm £1.50, OAPs £1, Chd under 16yrs £1, under 5 free.
Refreshments: Home-made teas.

MILTON COTTAGE

Telephone: Chalfont St Giles 2313   &
(Milton's Cottage Trust)

The Cottage where John Milton completed 'Paradise Lost' and began 'Paradise Regained', contains many Milton relics and a library including first and early editions. Preserved as it was in 1665. Charming Cottage Garden.
Location: ½ m W of A413; on B4442 to Beaconsfield.
Station: Seer Green (2½ m).
Opening Times: Mar to Oct—Tues to Sats 10–1, 2–6; Suns 2–6. Spring & Summer Bank Hol Mons 10–1, 2–6. *Closed Mons (except Bank Hols) & Jan, Feb, Nov & Dec.* Adm £1, Chd (under 15) 40p, Parties of 20 or more 80p.

CHENIES

CHENIES MANOR HOUSE

Telephone: Little Chalfont 2888
(Lt Col & Mrs MacLeod Matthews)

Charming 15th/16th century Manor House and garden in picturesque village.
Location: Off A404 between Amersham & Rickmansworth (M25 – junction 18).
Station: Chorleywood (1½ m).
Opening Times: First week in April to end of Oct Weds and Thurs 2–5. Also open Bank Hol Mons May 29 & Aug 28, 2–6. Adm £2.10, Chd (under 14) half-price. Gardens only £1. Parties throughout the year by prior arrangement—min charge £40. Free parking. No dogs.
Refreshments: Home-made teas.

DORNEY

DORNEY COURT

Telephone: Burnham (062 86) 4638 (please note from early 1989 tel. no. will be (0628) 604638)
(Mr & Mrs Peregrine Palmer)

Beautiful Tudor pink brick and timber Manor House which has been in the family for over 450 years. Superb collection of furniture and paintings.
Location: 2 m W of Eton & Windsor in village of Dorney on B3026.
Stations: Burnham (2 m).
Opening Times: Easter weekend Fri to Mon then Suns & Bank Hol Mons to second Sun in June; also Mons & Tues in June, July, Aug & Sept; 2–5.30. Adm £2.30, Chd over 9 £1. 10% discount for National Trust members and OAPs on Mons & Tues *(excluding Bank Holidays).* Parties at other times by arrangement.
Refreshments: Home-made cream teas.

HIGH WYCOMBE

THE DISRAELI MUSEUM   *(National Trust)*

Hughenden Manor. Tel: (0494) 32580.
Home of Benjamin Disraeli, Earl of Beaconsfield (1847–81). Disraeli relics, furniture, pictures and books.

HUGHENDEN MANOR, The National Trust

Telephone: High Wycombe (0494) 32580   &

Home of Benjamin Disraeli, Earl of Beaconsfield (1847-1881). Small formal garden.
Location: 1½ m N of High Wycombe on W side Gt Missenden Road (A4128).
Station: High Wycombe (2 m).
Opening Times: House & Garden. Mar 4–Mar 19—Sats & Suns only 2–6 (or sunset if earlier), Easter Sat to end of Oct—Weds to Sats 2–6; Suns & Bank Hol Mons 12–6. *Closed Good Friday.* Adm £2, Chd half price. Shop open mid-March to end Oct as House and pre-Christmas. *Parties must book in advance.* Dogs in Park & car park only. Wheelchair provided. Parties Weds to Fris only if booked in advance.

WYCOMBE CHAIR MUSEUM   *(Wycombe District Council)*

Castle Hill, Priory Avenue, High Wycombe. Tel: (0494) 23879.
The making of Windsor Chairs and the story of the woodland Bodgers of the Chilterns is the subject of this fascinating craft museum. Exhibitions on linked crafts of chair caning, rushing and lace making are also on show. Open all year Mon-Sat 10–5 (*closed* Sun and Bank Hols) admission free.

MILTON KEYNES

STACEY HILL MUSEUM OF INDUSTRY & RURAL LIFE

Southern Way, Wolverton. Tel: Milton Keynes (0908) 319148 or 316222.
Extensive exhibition of agricultural, industrial and domestic items. Refreshments available. May to Oct: Mon to Frid 2–4, first & third Sun 2–5. Working displays events weekends 20–21 May, 17–18 June, 15–16 July, 16–17 Sept, 11–5.30. Suitable for the disabled. Admission charge. Special parties by arrangement. Telephone for further details.

NEWPORT PAGNELL

CHICHELEY HALL

Telephone: North Crawley (023 065) 252
(Trustees of the Hon Nicholas Beatty)

Beautiful Baroque house and gardens built 1719–1723. Fine panelling. Naval pictures and mementoes of Admiral Lord Beatty. Sir John Chester's unique Hidden Library.
Location: 2 m E of Newport Pagnell; 11 m W of Bedford on A422.
Opening Times: Mar 24 to May 30, and Aug 6 to Sept 24. Suns and Bank Holiday Mons 2.30–6. Last tour 5. Day or evening parties, with or without meals, by appointment at any time throughout the summer. Adm £2.20, Chd £1, parties (over 20) £1.60.

OLNEY

COWPER & NEWTON MUSEUM

Telephone: Bedford (0234) 711516

Personal belongings of William Cowper and Rev. John Newton. Bobbin lace and items of local interest.
Location: Market Place, Olney; N of Newport Pagnell via A509.
Opening Times: Easter—Oct 31: Tues to Sats 10–12, 2–5. Open Bank Hol Mons. Limited winter opening. Adm £1.

PRINCES RISBOROUGH

PRINCES RISBOROUGH MANOR HOUSE, The National Trust   &

17th century red-brick house with Jacobean oak staircase.
Location: Opposite church off market square in town centre.
Station: Princes Risborough (1 m).
Opening Times: Open by written appointment only—Weds 2.30–4.30. Last adm 4. Two rooms only shown. Adm £1, Chd 50p. No reductions for parties. No dogs. Wheelchair access.

Buckinghamshire – *continued*

CLIVEDEN, The National Trust
Telephone: Burnham (06286) 5069

Gardens contain temples by Giacomo Leoni. Box parterre, fountain, formal walks; amphitheatre, water garden, rose garden, herbaceous borders. Views of Thames.
Location: 3 m upstream from Maidenhead; 2 m N of Taplow on Hedsor Road (B476). Main entrance opposite Feathers Inn.
Stations: Taplow (3 m) (not Suns); Maidenhead (4¼ m).
Opening Times: Grounds: Mar to Dec—Daily 11–6 or sunset if earlier. *Closed Jan & Feb.* House: Apr 2 to Oct 29, Thurs & Suns 3–6 (last adm 5.30). Adm Grounds £2.40. House 80p extra (timed ticket), Chd half price. *Parties must give advance notice. No dogs in House or in gardens, elsewhere only on lead.* Wheelchairs (available) in parts of garden & house. Shop: Good Friday to end Oct, Weds to Suns (incl Good Friday) & Bank Hol Mons 1–5.30.
Refreshments: Light lunches, coffee, teas in Orangery Restaurant Good Friday to end Oct (Weds to Suns).

WADDESDON

WADDESDON MANOR, The National Trust
Telephone: Aylesbury (0296) 651211 or 651282

Built 1874–89 for Baron Ferdinand de Rothschild in the style of a French Renaissance château and bequeathed to the National Trust by Mr James A. de Rothschild in 1957. Rooms with 18th century French panelling furnished with French royal furniture, Sèvres and Meissen porcelain, and Savonnerie carpets. Dutch, Flemish and Italian paintings, and portraits by Gainsborough, Reynolds and Romney. Other rooms contain French 17th and 18th century drawings, also lace, buttons and fans, and an exhibition of ladies' clothes of c.1865, together with personal mementoes and pastimes of the family. In the Bachelors' Wing, open on Fridays only (except Good Friday), are 15th, 16th and 17th century works of art and European small arms. Extensive grounds with 18th century style aviary and small herd of Japanese Sika deer. Fine trees and views. Play area for young children.
Location: At W end of Waddesdon village; 6 m NW of Aylesbury on Bicester Road (A41).
Station: Aylesbury (6 m).
Buses: Red Rover 1, 15, 16, from Aylesbury. (Tel: Aylesbury 28686).
Opening Times: Mar 15 to Oct 22. House: Weds to Suns 1–5 (open until 6 on Sat & Sun in May to Sept). Bachelors' Wing open Fris (except Good Friday). Grounds & aviary: Weds to Sats from 1, Suns from 11.30. Good Friday and Bank Hol Mons House and Grounds 11–6. *Completely closed Weds following Bank Hol Mons.* Adm House, grounds & aviary £3. Bachelors' Wing £1 extra. Chd 10–17 years, half price; Chd under 10 not admitted to house. Grounds & aviary only, £1.50; Chd from 5–17 half price; Chd under 5 free. Parties by arrangement (no reduction except pre-booked parties of OAPs Weds, Thurs Sats). Private morning guided tours by arrangement, £7.50. Free car park. Shops with books, gifts, plants and flowers. Dogs in grounds only, excluding aviary and children's play area. Wheelchairs provided on request. *No photography indoors.*
Shops: Two shops during the summer season, special Christmas shop Oct 27 to Dec 23, Fri, Sat & Sun 12–5. Free entry and free parking.
Refreshments: Light lunches and afternoon teas available.

WEST WYCOMBE

WEST WYCOMBE MOTOR MUSEUM
Chorley Road.

WEST WYCOMBE PARK (1750), The National Trust
Telephone: High Wycombe (0494) 24411

Palladian house with frescoes and painted ceilings. 18th century landscape garden with lake and various classical temples, including the newly reconstructed Temple of Venus.
Location: At W end of West Wycombe, S of Oxford Road (A40), 2½ m W High Wycombe.
Station: High Wycombe (2½ m).

Opening Times: Grounds only: Apr & May Mons to Thurs 2-6, and Easter, May Day and Spring Bank Hols. Sun & Mon 2–6. *Closed* Good Friday. **House & Grounds:** June, July & Aug, Suns to Thurs inc Summer Bank Hol Mon 2–6 (last adm 5.15). Adm House & Grounds £2.60; Grounds only £1.60, Chd half price. *No reduction for parties.* Dogs in car park only. House unsuitable for wheelchairs.

WING

ASCOTT, The National Trust
Telephone: Aylesbury (0296) 688242

Anthony de Rothschild collection of fine pictures. French and Chippendale furniture, exceptional Oriental porcelain containing examples of the Ming, K'ang Hsi and Chun ware of the Sung dynasty. Gardens contain unusual trees, flower borders, topiary sundial, naturalised bulbs and water lilies.
Location: ½ m E of Wing; 2 m SW of Leighton Buzzard, on the S side of Aylesbury/Leighton Buzzard Road (A418).
Station: Leighton Buzzard (2 m).
Opening Times: House & Gardens. July 18–Sept 17, Tues to Suns 2–6. Bank Hol Mon Aug 28, closed Tues Aug 29. Garden only: Apr to July 13 and Sept 21, 24, 28; every Thurs and last Sun in each month 2–6. Last adm 5.30. Adm House & Gardens £2.60, Chd £1.80; Gardens only £1.60, Chd 80p. *No reduction for parties.* Dogs on leads, in car park only. Wheelchair access to ground floor and part of garden only. Enquiries: Estate Manager.
NB Owing to large number of visitors, entry is by timed ticket. Occasionally there will be considerable delays in gaining admission to the House.

WINSLOW

CLAYDON HOUSE, The National Trust
Telephone: Steeple Claydon (029673) 349

Built mid 18th century as an addition to an earlier house. The stone-faced West front contains a series of magnificent and unique rococo state-rooms including Florence Nightingale Museum, her bedroom and sitting room.
Location: Nr the village of Middle Claydon, 13m NW of Aylesbury, 3½ m SW of Winslow.
Opening Times: Mar 25 to end of Oct—Sat to Wed 2–6, Bank Hol Mons 1–6. Last adm 5.30. *Closed Thurs & Fris (inc Good Friday).* Adm £2, Chd £1. Parties write to Custodian. Dogs in car park only. Wheelchairs provided.
Refreshments: Available at house.

WINSLOW HALL
Telephone: (029 671) 2323
(Sir Edward & Lady Tomkins)

Built 1698–1702. Almost certainly designed by Sir Christopher Wren. Has survived without major structural alteration and retains most of its original features. Modernized and redecorated by the present owners. Good eighteenth century furniture, mostly English. Some fine pictures, clocks and carpets. Several examples of Chinese art, notably of the Tang period. Beautiful gardens with many unusual trees and shrubs.
Location: At entrance to Winslow on the Aylesbury road (A413).
Opening Times: Visits by appointment.
Refreshments: Catering by arrangement.

WOTTON UNDERWOOD

WOTTON HOUSE
(Administrator Mrs Patrick Brunner)

Built 1704, on the same plan as Buckingham House, which later became Buckingham Palace Interior remodelled by Sir John Soane 1820. Wrought iron by Tijou and Thomas Robinson. 'Capability' Brown landscape 1757-1760.
Location: In Wotton Underwood 2 m S of A41 midway between Aylesbury and Bicester.
Opening Times: Aug to end of Sept—Weds. Tours 2 and 3 (last tour). Small parties by arrangement.

Cambridgeshire

CAMBRIDGE

CAMBRIDGE AND COUNTY FOLK MUSEUM
2 and 3 Castle Street. Tel: (0223) 355159.
Museum occupying the former White Horse Inn, contains domestic and agricultural bygones, toys, pictures, trades exhibits illustrating the life of the people of the County covering three centuries. Mon to Sat 10.30–5; Sun 2.30–4.30. Adm 80p, Chld and OAPs 40p.

DENNY ABBEY
Telephone: (022 024) 489

After a brief life as a Benedictine priory, the abbey passed to the Knights Templar who used it as a hospital for their sick and aged members. In 1308 the Order was suppressed and the inmates arrested. The abbey remained empty until 1339 when the widowed Countess of Pembroke acquired it and moved the Franciscan nuns from her Abbey at Waterbeach to Denny. Most of the monastic buildings were demolished in the 16th century, but there are remnants of the 12th century church and 14th century additions.

Location: 6 m (9.7 km) north of Cambridge on A10. OS map ref TL495684.
Opening Times: Good Friday to Sept 30, daily 10–6; Oct 1 to Maundy Thursday, Sun only 10–4. *Closed Christmas and New Year.* Adm 80p, OAPs 60p, Chd 40p.

FITZWILLIAM MUSEUM
Trumpington Street. Tel: (0223) 332900–3.
Picture gallery of old and modern masters. Collections of antiquities, ceramics and applied arts, coins, drawings and prints, historical and Medieval manuscripts, special exhibitions. Tues to Sat: Lower Galleries 10–2, Upper Galleries 2–5; Sun: all Galleries 2.15–5. *Closed* Mon (except Easter, Spring and Summer Bank Hols). *Closed* Good Friday and Dec 24 to Jan 1 inclusive.

KETTLES YARD *(University of Cambridge)*
Castle Street, Cambridge CB3 0AQ. Tel: (0223) 352124
Permanent collection of early 20th century art, including Gaudier-Brzeska, David Jones, Alfred Wallis, Christopher Wood etc, maintained in a domestic setting. Gallery showing continuous series of temporary exhibitions of modern and contemporary art. House open 2–4 Tues to Sun, Gallery 12.30–5.30 Tues–Sat *(until 7 Thurs)*, 2–5.30 (Sun). Adm free. Parties for house please book if over 10 only. Suitable for disabled only with help.

THE SCOTT POLAR RESEARCH INSTITUTE
Lensfield Road. Tel: (0223) 336555.
Current scientific work in the Arctic and Antarctic. Expedition relics and equipment. Eskimo and general polar art collections. Mon to Sat 2.30–4.

SEDGWICK MUSEUM OF GEOLOGY
Downing Street. Tel: (0223) 333456.
Fossils and subordinate collections of rocks, building stones and ornamental marbles. Mon to Fri 9–1, 2–5; Sat 10–1 throughout the year. *Closed* one week at Christmas also Good Friday and Easter Monday.

UNIVERSITY BOTANIC GARDEN
(Cambridge University)

Fine specimen trees and shrubs. Founded 1761.
Location: In Cambridge, 1 m S of City Centre.
Station: Cambridge (½ m).
Opening Times: All the year—Daily 8–6 (dusk in winter).
Adm free, weekdays (Suns, May to Sept only 2.30–6.30). *Open to ticketholders only, Suns at other times throughout year.* Picnic area.

UNIVERSITY COLLECTION OF AERIAL PHOTOGRAPHS
Mond Building, Free School Lane CB2 3RF. Tel: (0223) 334578.
A collection of aerial photographs illustrating different aspects of agriculture, archaeology, geography, geology, history, vegetation, and the social and economic past and present of the United Kingdom. By appointment only. Curator: D.R. Wilson M.A.

UNIVERSITY MUSEUM OF ARCHAEOLOGY AND ANTHROPOLOGY
Downing Street. Tel: (0223) 337733.
Archaeological collections illustrating world prehistory and Britain from the earliest period until post-Mediaeval times. Anthropological galleries temporarily closed for refurbishment. Mon to Fri 2–4; Sat 10–12.30.

UNIVERSITY MUSEUM OF CLASSICAL ARCHAEOLOGY
Sidgwick Avenue site. Tel: (0223) 335153.
Representative collection of casts of Greek and Roman sculpture. Mon to Fri 9–1, 2.15–5; Sat (in term) 9–1.

WHIPPLE MUSEUM OF THE HISTORY OF SCIENCE
Free School Lane. Tel: (0223) 334540.
Collection of historic scientific instruments from the 16th to 19th century. Special exhibitions. Mon to Fri 2–4. During vacations the museum may be closed.

DUXFORD

IMPERIAL WAR MUSEUM
Duxford Airfield, Cambridge CB2 4QR.
Tel: Cambridge (0223) 833963 or 835000 (answer-phone)
A505 Royston–Newmarket Road; by junction 10 on M11. The finest collection of military and civil aircraft in Britain, displayed in the historic surroundings of a preserved Battle of Britain fighter station. Over 100 aircraft, from the First World War to Concorde. Also tanks, military vehicles, naval exhibits, special exhibitions. Full programme of flying days and special events. Shops, restaurant. Open daily from 10.30 except Dec 24, 25, 26 and Jan 1. Adm charge. Limited viewing in winter months – please telephone for details.

ELY

ELY MUSEUM
High Street. Tel: (0353) 663135.
All new displays opening early 1989 covering the social and natural history of the Isle of Ely. Collections include local archaeology, Fenland farm and craft instruments, the bicycle which won the world's first bicycle race and much more besides. Something for everybody! Small admission charge.

PRIOR CRAUDEN'S CHAPEL
Telephone: (0353) 662837
(The Bursar, The King's School)

Built as a private chapel in 1324/1325 for Prior Crauden, the Prior of the Mediaeval Benedictine Monastery from 1321 to 1341. Recently restored to show glimpses of coloured walls, painted glass and wall paintings. In 1649 Cromwell's Commissioners planned to destroy the Chapel, but it was saved by being turned into a dwelling house for two hundred years, until a restoration in 1850. Now on view to the public and used for services by the King's School, Ely.

Location: In the precincts of Ely Cathedral.
Opening Times: Mon to Fri 9–5, excluding statutory and Bank Hols. Adm free. Parking in Cathedral Car Park. Not suitable for disabled visitors.
Refreshments: Lamb Hotel, and restaurants in City of Ely.

THE STAINED GLASS MUSEUM
North Triforium, Ely Cathedral. Tel: (0353) 665103 or (0223) 60148.
Stained glass from medieval to modern times, including important 19th century collection, mainly rescued from redundant churches and now displayed at eye level. Models of a modern workshop, origins and history of the craft. Mar to Oct. Mon to Fri 10.30–4, Sat and Bank Hols 10.30–4.30, Sun 12–3. Adm charges, party reductions.

GODMANCHESTER

ISLAND HALL
(Mr Christopher & The Hon Mrs Vane Percy)

A mid 18th century Mansion, of architectural importance with fine panelled rooms, in a tranquil riverside setting, with an ornamental island forming part of the gardens.

Location: In centre of Godmanchester next to the car park. 1 m S of Huntingdon (A1); 15 m NW of Cambridge (A604).
Station: Huntingdon (1 m).
Opening Times: June 11–Sept 17 Suns only 2.30–5.30. Parties particularly welcome May–Sept by appointment. Party rate £1.50 groups over 30. Adm House and Grounds £2, Chd £1 (grounds only). Grounds only £1.
Refreshments: Teas.

HADDENHAM

FARMLAND MUSEUM
50 High Street CB6 3XB. Tel: Ely (0353) 740381.
Agricultural implements, bygones, rural crafts. Open first Sun each month 2–dusk and Weds Easter to end Sept. Adm 50p, Chld 30p.

HUNTINGDON

THE CROMWELL MUSEUM *(Cambridgeshire County Council)*
Grammar School Walk. Tel: (0480) 425830.
Oliver Cromwell was born in Huntingdon in 1599, and spent his early life in the town. The Museum illustrates the life of Oliver Cromwell and the Parliamentary side of the Puritan Revolution 1642–1660. The Museum is in Cromwell's old school in the centre of the town. Open all year round. Apr–Oct: 11–1, 2–5 Tues to Fri; 11–1, 2–4 Sat & Sun. Nov–Mar: 2–5 Tues to Fri; 11–1, 2–4 Sat; 2–4 Sun. Admission is free. Party bookings are welcome. Coach parking and refreshments available nearby. For further details and leaflet write or telephone above number.

KIMBOLTON

KIMBOLTON CASTLE
(Governors of Kimbolton School)

Tudor manor house associated with Katherine of Aragon, completely remodelled by Vanbrugh (1708-20); courtyard c. 1694. Fine murals by Pellegrini in chapel, boudoir and on staircase. Gatehouse by Robert Adam.

Location: 8 m NW of St Neots on A45; 14 m N of Bedford.
Station: St Neots (9 m).
Opening Times: Easter Sun & Mon; Spring Bank Hol Sun & Mon; Summer Bank Hol Mon; also July 23 to Aug 27 – Suns only: 2–6. Adm 75p Chd & OAPs 30p.

Cambridgeshire – *continued*

LODE

ANGLESEY ABBEY, The National Trust
Telephone: Cambridge (0223) 811200 &

The Abbey, founded in the reign of Henry I, was later converted to an Elizabethan manor. Contains Fairhaven collection of art treasures. About 100 acres of grounds, including flower borders, trees, avenues, unique garden statuary and a working water mill that grinds corn.
Location: In village of Lode 6 m NE of Cambridge on B1102.
Station: Cambridge (6 m).
Opening Times: HOUSE & GARDEN. Mar 25 to Oct 15 — Wed to Sun & Bank Hol Mons 1.30–5.30. *Closed Good Friday.* Adm £3.50. Pre-booked parties of 15 or more £2.50 (Weds, Thurs & Fris only).
GARDENS ONLY. Mar 25 to July 2, Wed to Sun & Bank Holiday Mons 12–5.30; July 3–Oct 15 daily 12 noon–5.30. Adm £1.50, Chd (with adult) half price. No dogs. Indoor photography by permission only. Wheelchair access (house difficult); chairs provided. Free car park & picnic area. Shop *(closed Mons & Tues).*
Lode Mill: Mar 25 to Oct 15 — Sat, Suns & Bank Hol Mons 1.30–5.30.
Refreshments: Restaurant open same days as House, 12–5, lunches and teas. Table licence.

PETERBOROUGH

ELTON HALL
(Mr & Mrs William Proby)

The Proby family have lived at Elton Hall for over 3 centuries. This romantic and gracious house with its mixture of medieval, gothic and classical styles contains excellent pictures and furniture and one of the finest collections of books in private hands. Rose garden restored and new herbaceous borders.
Location: On A605, 5 m W of Peterborough.
Opening Times: Every Wed June 1 to Sept 30; Every Sun July 1 to Sept 30. Guided tours. Bank Hols: Easter Sun & Mon, Mar 26, 27; May Sun & Mon, Apr 30, May 1; Whit Sun & Mon, May 28, 29; Aug Sun & Mon, Aug 27, 28. Open 2–5. Parties other days by appointment. Prices on application. Adults: £2.40, Chd £1.20. Free parking.
Refreshments: Home-made teas. Suppers and lunches by arrangement. Shop.

LONGTHORPE TOWER
Telephone: (0733) 268482

This three-storey tower, added to an existing fortified manor house about 1300, is remarkable for the richness and completeness of its early 14th century wall-paintings. These were discovered less than 40 years ago under layers of limewash and distemper, and depict scenes from the Bible and of life in the East Anglian countryside; the most complete set of such paintings of the period in England.
Location: 2 m (3.2 km) west of Peterborough on A47. OS map ref TL163983.
Opening Times: Good Friday to Sept 30, daily 10–6; Oct 1 to Maundy Thursday, daily 10–4. *Closed Mons, Christmas and New Year.* Adm 80p, OAPs 60p, Chd 40p.

PETERBOROUGH MUSEUM & ART GALLERY
(Peterborough City Council)
Priestgate. Tel: (0733) 43329.
Archaeology, local history, Geology and Wildlife, Costume gallery, Victorian rooms and Period Shop. Also large collection of Prisoner-of-War artefacts. Small collection of paintings, ceramics and glass (and varied programme of temporary exhibitions throughout the year). Military gallery and an 18th century watchmaker's shop. May to Sept: Tues to Sat 10–5. Oct to Apr: Tues to Frid 12–5; Sat 10–5. *Closed* Sun and Mon.

RAILWORLD *(Museum of World Railways)*
Oundle Road PE2 9NR. Tel: (0733) 44240.
A museum about trains, people and countries to depict railway travel world-wide, past and present. The project is scheduled to open to the public in 1990.

SACREWELL WATER MILL
Farming and Country Life Centre. Tel: Stamford (0780) 782222.
Large open air museum on attractive farm site. Easily accessible from A47, 8m W of Peterborough. Working 18th century watermill on Domesday site. Very large collection of hand implements, tools, and equipment relating to farming, and the Mill's history, housed in 18th century farm buildings; traditional building materials. Always open.

ST. IVES

NORRIS MUSEUM *(St. Ives Town Council)*
The Broadway
Local history of Huntingdonshire: fossils, archaeology, bygones, crafts, research library. Tues to Fri 10–1, 2–5 (winter closes at 4); Sat 10–12. May to Sept also open 2–5 Sat and Sun. *Closed* Mon and Bank Hol weekends.

SHEPRETH

DOCWRA'S MANOR
Telephone: (0763) 60235, 61473 or 61557
(Mrs John Raven)

Two acres of choice plants in a series of enclosed gardens.
Location: Opposite War Memorial in centre of Shepreth village; ½ m W of Cambridge –Royston Rd (A10) bus stops at gate.
Station: Shepreth.
Opening Times: GARDEN ONLY. Suns Apr 2, May 7, June 4, July 2, Aug 6, Sept 3, Oct 1, 2–6, also Bank Holiday Mons Mar 27, May 1, May 29, Aug 28 10–5; Mar 15–Oct 13: every Wed & Fri 10–5. Adm £1, accompanied Chd free. Proceeds for garden upkeep. Also Suns May 14, June 11, 2–7 *in aid of National Gardens Scheme.* Also open by appointment. Plants for sale. No dogs.
Refreshments: Teas Suns May 14, June 11.

WIMPOLE

WIMPOLE HALL, The National Trust
Telephone: Cambridge (0223) 207257

An architecturally refined house of aristocratic proportions, sumptuous 18th and 19th century staterooms, set in a beautifully undulating park devised by the best of the landscape architects. Exhibition at Stable Block.
Location: 8 m SW of Cambridge; signposted off A603 at New Wimpole.
Stations: Shepreth (5 m) (not Suns); Royston (7 m).
Opening Times: House, Garden & Park. Mar 25 to Oct 29 — Daily except Mons & Fris 1–5, Bank Hol Mon 11–5. Adm: £3.50 Chld £1.75. Pre-booked parties of 15 or more £2.50 (Tues to Thurs only). Joint ticket Hall & Farm £4.50. Picnic area. Shop. Dogs allowed in park only on leads. Wheelchair access, 3 chairs provided.
Refreshments: Lunches & teas in the Dining Room 12–5. Table licence. Light refreshments at stable block.

WIMPOLE HOME FARM, The National Trust

An historic farm, faithfully restored by the National Trust, set in 350 acres of beautiful parkland. Approved Rare Breeds Centre. Children's corner. Agricultural museum. Adventure playground. Shop. Film loft.
Location: 8 m S of Cambridge; signposted off A603 at New Wimpole.
Stations: Shepreth (5 m); Royston (7 m).
Opening Times: Mar 25 to Oct 29 — Daily (except Mons & Fris) (open Bank Hol Mon) 10.30–5. (Mar, Apr and Oct: 11–4). Adm £2.50, NT members £1, Chd £1 parties (pre-booked) £2. Joint ticket for Hall and Farm £4.50.
Refreshments: Lunches & teas at Wimpole Hall. Snacks at Home Farm.

WISBECH

PECKOVER HOUSE AND GARDEN, The National Trust
Telephone: Wisbech 583463 &

Important example of early 18th century domestic architecture. Fine rococo decoration. Interesting Victorian garden contains rare trees, flower borders, roses. Under glass are orange trees. Georgian stables.
Location: Centre of Wisbech town on N bank of River Nene (B1441).
Station: March (9½ m).
Opening Times: Principal Rooms & Gardens: Mar 25 to Oct 15; Sat, Sun & Mon. 2–5.30. Adm £1.50, Chld 75p. Party rate £1. No dogs. Wheelchairs garden only.
Refreshments: In the Old Kitchen.

WISBECH AND FENLAND MUSEUM
Museum Square Tel: (0945) 583817.
Local history, archaeology, natural history, geology, ceramics, bygones. Library (by appointment only). Tues to Sat 10–5 (closes at 4 in winter).

ISLAND HALL
GODMANCHESTER, CAMBRIDGESHIRE

On the banks of the Great Ouse, overlooking the Island from which it takes its name, this beautiful house, very much a family home, contains lovely rooms with fine period detail and interesting possessions relating to the owners ancestors since their first occupation of the house in 1800.

ADMISSION – SEE EDITORIAL REFERENCE

The National Trust in
CAMBRIDGESHIRE

ANGLESEY ABBEY

PECKOVER HOUSE

WIMPOLE HALL

ADMISSION – SEE EDITORIAL REFERENCE

Channel Islands

GUERNSEY

CANDIE GARDENS
St. Peter Port. Tel: (0481) 26518.
Guernsey's new museum tells the story of the island and its people. It also includes an art gallery, audiovisual theatre and tea room. Daily 10.30–5.30. Adm 80p, Chld 30p, OAPs 40p.

CASTLE CORNET
St. Peter Port. Tel: (0481) 21657.
Medieval castle with important Elizabethan, Georgian, Victorian and German Second World War additions. Museums with C.I. Militia, Occupation, R.A.F., armoury and maritime collections. Picture galleries. Apr to Oct: Daily 10.30–5.30. Conducted parties at 10.45 and 2.30. Adm £1.20, Chld 40p, OAPs 60p.

FORT GREY
Rocquaine Bay, St. Peter's. Tel: (0481) 65036.
Napoleonic fort restored as a maritime museum specialising in shipwrecks. May to Sept: Daily 10.30–12.30, 1.30–5.30. Adm 60p, Chld 25p, OAPs 30p.

Education service, Tel: (0481) 23688.
Joint ticket available to all three museums £1.75.

GERMAN OCCUPATION MUSEUM
Forest
Wartime street; occupation kitchen, bunker rooms. Tearoom and garden. Apr to Oct: Daily 10.30–5. Winter: Sun and Thurs afternoons 2–4.30. Adm £1, Chld 50p.

ST. PETER PORT

HAUTEVILLE HOUSE

JERSEY

ELIZABETH CASTLE *(Jersey Museums Service)*
St. Aubins Bay Tel: (0534) 23971.
Elizabethan fortress built on an islet about one mile from shore. Eighteenth century garrison buildings with interpretive displays and museum of Jersey militia, refortified by the German occupying forces in 1940–44. Apr to Oct: Daily 9.30–5.30 including Bank Hols. Adm £1, Chld, OAPs 50p. Parties by arrangement. Booked schools free. Refreshments. Director of Museums Michael Day B.A., A.M.A.

JERSEY MUSEUM *(Jersey Museums Service)*
9 Pier Road, St. Helier. Tel: (0534) 75940.
Granite built merchant's house, c.1815. Four floors of displays. Major extension planned for 1992. Social and political history. Silver, coins, medals, fine art. Mon to Sat 10–5 throughout the year. Adm £1p, Chld, OAPs 50p. Parties by arrangement. Special reductions for local schools. Car parking at nearby multi-storey in Pier Road. Director of Museums Michael Day B.A., A.M.A.

LA HOUGUE BIE MUSEUM *(Jersey Museums Service)*
Grouville Tel: (0534) 53823.
3,000 B.C. Neolithic tomb – open to the public, two Medieval chapels, museums of archaeology, geology, agriculture and the German occupation. Mar to Nov: Tues – Sun 10–5. Adm £1, Chld, OAPs 50p. Parties by arrangement. Car parking. Director of Museums Michael Day B.A., A.M.A.

MONT ORGUEIL CASTLE *(Jersey Museums Service)*
Gorey, St. Martins. Tel: (0534) 53292.
Medieval fortress. Small archaeological museum of local finds. Tableaux illustrating the Castle's history. Apr to Oct: Daily 9.30–5.30. Adm £1p, Chld, OAPs 50p. Booked schools free. Parties catered for. Refreshments. Director of Museums Michael Day B.A., A.M.A.

SIR FRANCIS COOK GALLERY *(Jersey Museums Service)*
Route de la Trinité, Augrès. Tel: (0534) 63333.
Converted methodist chapel – permanent collection of work of Sir Francis Cook and special exhibitions. Open as advertised locally. Adm free. Car parking. Director of Museums Michael Day B.A., A.M.A.

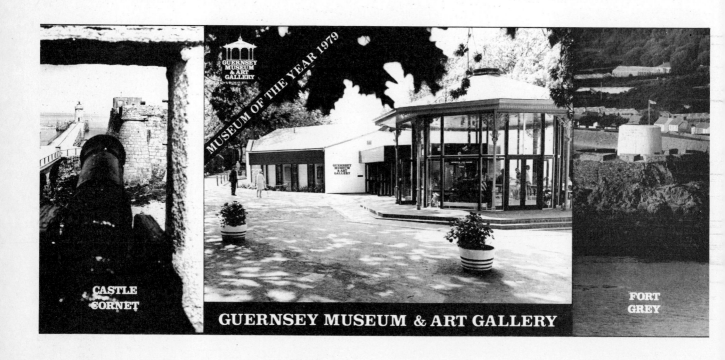

GUERNSEY MUSEUM & ART GALLERY

Cheshire

ADLINGTON

ADLINGTON HALL
Telephone: Prestbury 829206
(Charles Legh, Esq.)

Great Hall dates from about 1450, Elizabethan half-timbered 'black and white' portion 1581.
Location: 5 m N of Macclesfield on the Stockport/Macclesfield Road (A523).
Station: Adlington (½ m).
Opening Times: Good Friday to Oct 1—Suns & Bank Hols; also Aug—Weds & Sats 2–5.30. Adm £1.75, Chd 85p. *Special parties by arrangement other days (over 25 people £1.25).*
Refreshments: At the Hall.

ALDERLEY EDGE

HARE HILL GARDEN, The National Trust

Walled garden with pergola, rhododendrons and azaleas; parkland.
Location: Between Alderley Edge and Prestbury off B5087 at Greyhound Road. Link path to Alderley Edge.
Stations: Alderley Edge (3½ m); Prestbury (2½ m).
Opening Times: GARDEN ONLY. Easter Sun to end of Oct—Weds, Thurs, Sats, Suns and Bank Hol Mons 10–5.30. Special opening for rhododendrons and azaleas May 22 to June 9, daily 10–5.30. Adm £1. Parties by appointment in writing to the Head Gardener, Garden Lodge. Unsuitable for school parties. Wheelchair access – some assistance needed.

NETHER ALDERLEY MILL, The National Trust
Telephone: Wilmslow (0625) 523012

15th century corn-mill in use until 1939 and now restored; tandem overshot water wheels. Flour ground occasionally for demonstration.
Location: 1½ m S of Alderley Edge on E side of A34.
Station: Alderley Edge (2 m).
Opening Times: Easter Sunday to June 30 & Oct—Weds, Suns & Bank Hol Mons 2–5.30. *Closed* Good Friday. July, Aug & Sept—Daily (except Mons but open Bank Hol Mons) 2–5.30. Adm £1.10, Chd 50p. No dogs. Unsuitable for disabled or visually handicapped. Parties by prior arrangement with Mrs Pamela Ferguson, 7 Oak Cottages, Styal, Wilmslow.

Nr. ALTRINCHAM

DUNHAM MASSEY, The National Trust
Telephone: 061-941 1025

Fine 18th century house with Georgian and Edwardian interiors. Huguenot silver collection, fine furniture and family portraits. Extensive gardens recently restored, woodlands, deer park and water mill.
Location: 3 m SW of Altrincham off A56; junction 19 off M6; junction 7 off M56.
Opening Times: Mar 25 to Oct 29—Daily (except Fris). Garden, restaurant & shop 12–5.30 (Suns & Bank Hol Mons 11–5.30). House 1–5 (Suns & Bank Hol Mons 12–5). Last adm 4.30. Guided evening tours by arrangement at an extra charge. Coaches free. Adm: House and Garden £3, Chd £1.50. Family ticket £8. Reduced rates for pre-booked parties. Dogs in park only on lead. Wheelchairs provided—access to shop, garden and park. Limited access to house. Information from the Administrator, Dunham Massey Hall, Altrincham, Cheshire. WA14 4SJ.
Refreshments: Lunches & teas available. Also open for booked parties, functions etc – by arrangement. Tel: 061-941 2815. Restaurant and shop also open Nov to Dec 17, Thur to Sun 12–4, and Jan 6 to Mar 25 1990, Sat and Sun 12–4.

BUNBURY

BEESTON CASTLE
Telephone: (0829) 260464
(English Heritage)

Built on an isolated crag, Beeston Castle is visible for miles around. The view across the Cheshire plain extends to the Pennines in the east and westwards to Wales. Begun about 1220 by Ranulf de Blundeville, the castle was further fortified by Edward I. The ditch alone can have been no small task, as it is hewn from the solid rock. There is an exhibition on the history of the castle in the museum.
Location: 2 m (3.2 km) west of Bunbury. 11m (18 km) south east of Chester. OS map ref SJ537593.
Opening Times: Good Friday to Sept 30, 10–6; Oct 1 to Maundy Thurs, daily 10–4. *Closed* Mon, Dec 24–26 and Jan 1. Adm £1.30, OAPs £1, Chd 65p.

CHESTER

THE CASTLE STREET GEORGIAN HOUSE
Tel: (0244) 21616.

Part of the Grosvenor Museum dating from c.1680, the former Town House of the Swettenham and Comberbach families. Contains particularly fine late 17th century staircase and 17th and 18th century panelled rooms, Stuart, Mid-Georgian and Victorian Period rooms with many examples of local furniture and reconstructions of a Victorian kitchen and laundry. Also a small gallery of 19th and 20th century costumes. Adm to Museum and Georgian House free. Mon to Sat 10.30–5; Sun 2–5.

CHESTER HERITAGE CENTRE
St. Michael's Church, Bridge Street Row. Tel: (0244) 317948

Britain's first Heritage Centre, housed in the former St. Michael's Church in the heart of the ancient city. The building has been sensitively converted to provide exhibitions illustrating Chester's history, architecture and conservation programme. A colourful three-screen audio-visual show tells the story of Chester from Roman times to the present day. Adm: Adults 60p, Chld 30p. Open: Apr–Sept weekdays 10–5. Suns 2–5. *Closed* Weds. Oct to Mar: Daily (except Weds) 1.30–4.30.

GROSVENOR MUSEUM
Grosvenor Street. Tel: (0244) 21616.

Founded in 1886, the museum contains internationally renowned displays illustrating the organisation of the Roman Army and an extensive collection of Roman tombstones and inscriptions. Other collections cover the natural history, local history and archaeology of Chester and Cheshire. The museum is noted for its local paintings and watercolours by artists such as Louise Rayner, and for its silver, much of which was made and assayed in Chester. One of the most intriguing displays is the Mayor's Parlour from the King's Arms Kitchen, the reconstruction of an early 19th century pub interior, where the 'Honourable Incorporation', a debating and wagering club, staged a satire on the City Council, electing its own Mayor, Sheriffs and other officials. Adm to Museum and Georgian House free. Mon to Sat 10.30–5; Sun 2–5.

KING CHARLES TOWER
City Walls. Tel: (0244) 318780

Built c.13th or 14th centuries; heavily damaged during the Civil War and subsequently rebuilt in its present form. From the roof King Charles I watched the defeat of his army at the Battle of Rowton Moor in 1645. Displays on the Civil War and the Siege of Chester. Apr to Oct: Mon to Fri 1–5; Sat 10–5; Sun 2–5.30. Nov to Mar: Sat 1–4.30 (or dusk); Sun 2–4.30 (or dusk). Adm charge.

ST. MARY'S CENTRE
St. Mary's Hill (off Castle Street). Tel: (0244) 603321.

The beautiful redundant 15th century church of St. Mary-on-the-Hill incorporating a fine Tudor roof, two 17th century monumental effigies, medieval glass, traces of wall painting. A centre for educational and cultural activities in the city of Chester. Open to visitors as part of the local heritage 2–4.30 each weekday and by arrangement. *Closed* Aug and public holidays. '500 years of history at work today.'

CONGLETON

LITTLE MORETON HALL, The National Trust
Telephone: Congleton (0260) 272018 &

Begun in the 15th century, one of the most perfect examples of a timber-framed moated manor house in the country. Remarkable carved gables. The recently discovered and restored 16th century wall paintings are on view. Attractive knot garden.
Location: 4 m SW of Congleton off Newcastle-under-Lyme/Congleton Road (A34).
Opening Times: Mar & Oct—Sats & Suns 1.30-5.30. Easter Mon 11.30–5.30. *Closed* Good Friday. Apr to end Sept; 1.30–5.30 every day except Tues. Bank Holiday 11.30–5.30, last adm 5. School parties: Apr to end Sept mornings only not Tues by prior arrangement with Administrator (sae please). Guided tours usually each afternoon. Adm weekends & Bank Hols £2.50; weekdays £2; Family ticket £6, reduced rate for pre-booked parties. Dogs in car park and grass area in front of Hall only. Wheelchairs provided. Shop.
Refreshments: Light lunches and home made teas from 1.30.

DISLEY

LYME PARK, The National Trust
(Cared for by Stockport Metropolitan Borough Council)
Telephone: Disley (0663) 62023

An Elizabethan House with 18th and 19th century alterations, particularly by Giacomo Leoni in the 1730's. A lively visitor centre evokes the atmosphere of Edwardian Lyme.
Formal gardens, including a spectacular Dutch Garden. Over 1,300 acres of Parkland and Moorland, set on edge of the Peak District and populated with herds of Red and Fallow Deer.
Opening Times: HALL: Mar 24–Apr 9, daily free flow 2–5 (last entry 4.15). Apr 9–Apr 30, Sun only free flow 2–5 (last entry 4.15). May 1–June 29 Tues, Weds, Thurs, Sat, Sun plus Bank Holiday, weekdays guided tours hourly 2–4. Sat guided tours half hourly 2–4.30. Sun free flow 2–5 (last entry 4.15). May 27–June 11, free flow 2–5 (last entry 4.15). July 1–Aug 31, Tues, Weds, Thurs, Sat, Sun plus Bank Holiday, free flow 2–5 (last entry 4.15). Sept 2–Oct 1, Tues, Weds, Thurs, Sat, Sun, weekdays guided tours hourly 2–4. Sat guided tours half hourly 2–4.30. Sun free flow 2–5 (last entry 4.15). Oct 8–Dec 10, Sun only guided tours half hourly 2–4.30. SHOP: open as Hall, 1 hour before to ½ hour after Hall times. Special bookings when Hall is closed by arrangement with the Manager. Adm for car, including occupants: Park and Gardens incl. N.T. £2.50. Park, Gardens and Hall £6.00 (N.T. £2.50). GARDENS: Mar 24–Sept 30, daily 11–6. Oct 1–Apr 1 1990, 11–4. *Closed* Christmas Day & Boxing Day. INFORMATION CENTRE: Open Sat Mar 18–Oct 1 and Oct School Holiday, daily 10–6. Oct–Mar 1990 (inclusive) 11–4.
Refreshments: Kiosk – weekends and school holidays and June, July, Aug, daily from 11. Servants Hall Tea Room: dates as Hall, from midday.
Other Activities: Pitch and putt course, fishing and horse riding permits, children's adventure playground, orienteering course (open all year), nature trail. Function facilities. 1989 Events – See events leaflet. Guided walks and Chapel services throughout the year. For further information contact The Manager, address above, or Tel: Disley (0663) 62023.

ELLESMERE PORT

THE BOAT MUSEUM, Britains Premier Canal Museum
The National Waterways Museum, Dockyard Road, L65 4EF.
Access from junction 9 of M53. Tel: (051 355) 5017.

A working museum in the old docks at the junction of the Shropshire Union and Manchester Ship Canals. Over 50 historic canal boats, steam driven pumping engines; exhibitions, including worker's cottages, and blacksmith's forge; craft workshops; The Tom Rolt education conference centre. Daily 10–5 (10–4 in winter). Regular boat trips. Tel for bookings and information. **Winner Sandford Award.**

FADDILEY

WOODHEY CHAPEL
Telephone: Faddiley (027 074) 215
(The Trustees of Woodhey Chapel)

'The Chapel in the Fields.' A small private chapel, recently restored, dating from 1699.
Location: 1 m SW of Faddiley off A534 Nantwich/Wrexham Road.
Opening Times: Apr to Oct—Sats & Bank Hol Mons 2–5. Adm 50p, Chd 25p. At other times by appointment.

HANDFORTH

HANDFORTH HALL
(Dr J. C. Douglas)

Small 16th century half-timbered manor house. Fine Jacobean staircase. Collection of oak furniture.
Location: ½ m E of Handforth on B5358.
Station: Handforth (few mins walk).
Opening Times: June to Sept by written appointment only.

KNUTSFORD

PEOVER HALL
Telephone: Lower Peover 2135
(Randle Brooks)

House dates from 1585. Fine Caroline stables. Mainwaring Chapel. 18th century landscaped park. Large garden with Topiary work, also Walled and Herb gardens.
Location: 4 m S of Knutsford off A50 at Whipping Stocks Inn.
Opening Times: Beginning of May to end of Sept (except Bank Holidays). House, Stables & Gardens—Mons 2.30–5. Adm £1.80, Chd 90p. Thurs Stables & Gardens Only 2–5. Adm £1. Enquiries: N. Brooks, Peover Hall Farm.
Refreshments: Teas in the Stables on Mons.

TATTON PARK, The National Trust
(financed and managed by Cheshire County Council)
Telephone: Knutsford (0565) 54822   &

Seat of the late Lord Egerton of Tatton. Fine Georgian mansion by Samuel and Lewis Wyatt, beautifully furnished and decorated. Family museum. Restored 15th century Old Hall. 1930s working Farm. Magnificently varied 50 acre garden, showhouse, fernery, waterfowl, 1,000 acre deer park, two large meres, swimming, sailing, fishing, riding. Medieval village trail. Historical nature trail. Gift shop and Garden sales.
Location: 2 m N of Knutsford; 3½ m off M6 (exit 19); 4 m S of M56 (exit 7) fully signposted. A556 Chester Rd, or A50 from Stoke on Trent.
Station: Knutsford (2 m).
Opening Times: PARK AND GARDENS open all year (except Christmas Day). MANSION open daily—Easter to Oct 31. House (Suns & Public hols in brackets): Easter to mid-May & Sept/Oct: Park 11–6 (10–6); Garden 11.30–5 (10.30–5.30); Mansion 1–4 (1–5); Old Hall 12–4 (12–5); Farm 12–4 (12–4). Mid-May to Aug: Park 10.30–7 (10–7); Garden 11–5.30 (10.30–6); Mansion 1–4 (1–5); July/Aug 1–5 (12–5); Old Hall 12–4 (12–5); July/Aug 12–5 (12–5); Farm 11–4 (11–4). Nov to Apr 1: Park 11–dusk (11–dusk); Garden 1–4 (12–4). *Everything closed June 20 & 21.* Farm closed but open Suns in Nov & Mar 1–4 (Old Hall closed). Exits remain open for 1 hour after adm times. Adm Mansion £1.35; Garden £1; Old Hall £1; Farm 95p. Reduction for parties of 12 or more weekdays on application only. Park: cars £1.20 (incl NT members), coaches free. Knutsford Gate car park: cars 60p (incl NT members). Information from: Secretary, Tatton Park, Knutsford. Send sae for full calendar of events.
Refreshments: Restaurant.

MACCLESFIELD

CAPESTHORNE
Telephone: Chelford 861221 or 861439
(Lt Col Sir Walter Bromley-Davenport)

Recent research has revealed that Francis and William Smith of Warwick were almost certainly the original architects of this Jacobean style house built in 1722. Later alterations were made by Blore and Salvin. Pictures, furniture, Capesthorne collection of vases, family muniments and Americana.
Location: 7 m S of Wilmslow, on Manchester/London Road (A34); 6½ m N of Congleton, Junction 18 (M6).
Station: Chelford (3 m).
Opening Times: Park, Gardens and Chapel 12–6, Hall 2–5. April—Suns; May & Sept—Sats, Suns & Weds; June, July & Aug—Tues, Weds, Thurs, Sats & Suns.

Open Good Fri and all Bank Hols. Adm Park, Gardens & Chapel £1.20, Chd (5–16 years) 50p, Park, Gardens, Chapel & Hall £2.40, Chd £1. Budget Family ticket £6. Visitors to Gardens, Caravanners etc, may visit the Hall by paying the excess of £1.20, Chd 50p, at the desk in the Hall entrance. Chd under 5 years accompanied by an adult free. Coach and Car Park free. Dogs are allowed in the Park area only. Organised parties are welcome daily (except Mons and Fris) by appointment (please send for booking form and coloured brochure). Special reductions for parties of 20 or more at £1.70 per person to Hall, Park, Gardens & Chapel. Evening parties are also welcome from May to July (by appointment). Evening party rate £2 per person, minimum number 20.
Refreshments: Garden Restaurant & Bromley room.

GAWSWORTH HALL
Telephone: North Rode (0260) 223456
(Mr & Mrs Timothy Richards)

Tudor half-timbered manor house with tilting ground. Former home of Mary Fitton, Maid of Honour at the Court of Queen Elizabeth I, and the supposed 'dark lady' of Shakespeare's sonnets. Pictures, sculpture and furniture. Open air theatre with covered grand stand—June/July/August.
Location: 3 m S of Macclesfield on the Congleton/Macclesfield Road (A536).
Opening Times: Mar 26 to Oct 9–Daily 2–6. Adm £2.20, Chd £1.10. *Evening parties by arrangement.* Free car park.
Refreshments: In the Pavilion.

MACCLESFIELD SILK MUSEUM AND HERITAGE CENTRE
(Trustees of Macclesfield Museums Trust)
Roe Street. Tel: (0625) 613210.
Silk Museum (Britain's first) – The story of silk in Macclesfield, audio visual, models and costume displays, silk shop. Admission Fee Charged. *Heritage Centre* – Free exhibitions on the history of Macclesfield and the history of the Sunday School building. Tea Room. Tues to Sat 11–5; Sun 2–5. *Closed* Mon (except Bank Hols), Christmas Day, Boxing Day, New Year's Day and Good Friday. Parties at other times by arrangement. *Victorian Schoolroom* – Educational parties by appointment only. Director: Moira Stevenson.

PARADISE MILL SILK MUSEUM
(Trustees of Macclesfield Museums Trust)
Old Park Lane. Tel: (0625) 618228.
26 silk hand looms with Jacquards, demonstrations of hand weaving, room settings of 1930's, design and card cutting rooms, Manager's office. Silk shop. Tues–Sun 2–5. *Closed* Mon (except Bank Hols), Christmas Day, Boxing Day, New Year's Day, Good Friday. Adm charge. Parties by arrangement, mornings and evenings. Tea room in Heritage Centre, 5 minutes walk. 1985 Museum of the Year Award for achievement with limited resources. Director: Moira Stevenson.

WEST PARK MUSEUM & ART GALLERY
(Trustees of Macclesfield Museum Trust)
Prestbury Road. Tel: (0625) 24067.
Fine and decorative art, Egyptology. Work by C.F. Tunnicliffe, A.R.A. Tues to Sun 2–5. Adm free. *Closed* Mon (except Bank Holiday) Christmas Day, Boxing Day, New Year's Day and Good Friday. Director: Moira Stevenson.

MALPAS

CHOLMONDELEY CASTLE GARDENS
Telephone: Cholmondeley (082 922) 383 or 203
(The Marquess of Cholmondeley)

Lakeside picnic area, rare breeds of farm animals, and romantically landscaped gardens full of variety. Ancient private chapel in Park. Evening service 6.30 every third sun in month.
Location: Off A41 Chester/Whitchurch Road and A49 Whitchurch/Tarporley Road.
Opening Times: GARDEN & FARM ONLY. Easter Sun to Sept 24—Suns & Bank Hols only 12–5.30. Adm £1.50, OAPs £1, Chd 50p. Enquiries to: The Secretary, Cholmondeley Castle, Malpas, Cheshire. Gift Shop, Plants for sale. (House not open to public.)
Refreshments: Tea room.

NANTWICH

DORFOLD HALL
Telephone: Nantwich (0270) 625245
(R. C. Roundell, Esq.)

Jacobean country house built 1616. Beautiful plaster ceilings and panelling. Attractive gardens. Guided tours.
Location: 1 m W of Nantwich on A534 Nantwich/Wrexham Road.
Station: Nantwich (1½ m).
Opening Times: Apr to Oct—Tues & Bank Hol Mons 2–5. Adm £2, Chd £1. *At other times by appointment only.*

NANTWICH MUSEUM *(Nantwich Museum Trust Ltd.)*
Pillory Street, CW5 5BQ. Tel: (0270) 627104.
Local history, cheese-making and temporary exhibitions.

NESTON

NESS GARDENS
Telephone: 051-336 2135   &
(Liverpool University Botanic Gardens)

Finest collection of rhododendrons and azaleas in the NW. Superb specimen

trees and shrubs. Large rock, water, heather and terrace gardens. Visitor centre with slide shows, indoor exhibitions and shop.
Location: Between Neston and Burton; NW of Chester off A540.
Station: Neston (1½ m).
Opening Times: All the year—Daily 9 to sunset. *Closed Christmas Day.* Adm £1.80, Chd & OAPs £1, Family ticket £4. Picnic area.
Refreshments: Tea room facilities Mar—Sept (party catering by prior arrangement).

NORTHWICH

ARLEY HALL AND GARDENS
Telephone: Arley (056 585) 353
(The Hon M L W Flower)

Victorian country house and private Chapel (c 1840). Gardens of great variety and charm—topiary, rhododendrons, azaleas, herbaceous border, shrub roses, walled gardens, herb garden, woodland garden and woodland walk.
Location: 5 m N of Northwich; 6 m W of Knutsford; 7 m S of Warrington; 5 m off M6 at junction 19 & 20; 5 m off M56 at junction 9 & 10.
Opening Times: Mar 24 to Oct 8 — Tues to Suns & Bank Hol Mons Gardens 2–6 (June, July & Aug 12–6). Hall 2–5.30 throughout. Last adm Hall 5, Gardens 5.30. 1988 charges not available at time of going to press. Special rates, opening hours and catering for organised parties by appointment.
Refreshments: In converted Tudor Barn.

SALT MUSEUM *(Cheshire County Council)*
London Road. Tel: (0606) 41331.
Museum of the salt industry in Cheshire from the Roman period to the present day. Slide and tape programme. Displays include models and reconstructions as well as old salt-working tools and equipment. Temporary exhibitions. Daily (except Mon) 2–5. Open Bank Hol Mons. Adm charge. Car park, shop.

RUNCORN

NORTON PRIORY MUSEUM
Telephone: Runcorn (092 85) 69895
(Norton Priory Museum Trust)

The beautiful woodland gardens covering 16 acres contain the 12th century undercroft and excavated remains of the Priory. Displays of mediaeval tiles, stonework, ceramics etc. Shop, picnic area, refreshments.
Location: From M56 (junction 11) turn towards Warrington and follow Norton Priory Road signs.
Opening Times: Mar to Oct—Sats, Suns & Bank Hols 12–6; Mons to Fris 12–5. Nov to Feb—Daily 12–4. *Closed Dec 24, 25 & 26.* Special arrangements for groups. Adm £1.20, Chd, Students & OAPs 60p.

SCHOLAR GREEN

RODE HALL
Telephone: Alsager 3237
(Sir Richard Baker Wilbraham Bt.)

18th century country house with Georgian stable block. Later alterations by L. Wyatt and Darcy Braddell.
Location: 5 m SW of Congleton between A34 & A50.
Station: Alsager (2¼ m).
Opening Times: Closed in 1989 for repairs.
Refreshments: Bleeding Wolf Restaurant, Scholar Green.

STRETTON

STRETTON MILL *(Cheshire County Council)*
Stretton, near Farndon (signposted off A534 at Barton). Tel: (0606) 41331.
Water-powered corn mill dating from the 17th century restored to working order. Demonstrations daily Mar 1 to Oct 31. Daily (except Mon) 2–6. Open Bank Hols. Adm charge. Car park. Picnic area. Shop.

STYAL

QUARRY BANK MILL,
The National Trust & Quarry Bank Mill Trust Ltd
Telephone: Wilmslow (0625) 527468

Award-winning working museum of the cotton industry housed in a 200-year-old spinning mill. Skilled demonstrators operate vintage machinery showing cotton processes from carding and spinning to weaving on Lancashire looms. Displays on water power, the lifestyle of the mill-owning Greg family plus the millworkers' world at home and at work in the 19th century. Giant 1850 waterwheel restored to working order. Renovated Apprentice House. The millworkers' village of Styal and the mill are set in the 250 acre Styal County Park. Museum of the Year 1984. A winner of the Sandford Award for Heritage Education 1987.
Location: 1½ m N of Wilmslow off B5166.
Stations: Styal (½ m) (not Suns); Wilmslow (1½ m).
Opening Times: Oct–Mar 11–4 Tues–Sun, April/May 11–5 Tues–Sun, June–Sept 11–5 daily. Open Bank Holidays. Mill and Apprentice House: £3.75, Chd £2.75. Mill only: £2.75, Chd £2. Apprentice House only £1.50, Chd £1.25. Family tickets: Mill & Apprentice House £12; Mill only £8. Apprentice House only £5. NT members free. Car park £1 per vehicle. (NT members may park free of charge). Parties should apply for details of special rates and booking form at least 4 weeks in advance. Disabled visitors asked to telephone before visit. No coach parties Suns or Bank Holidays. **Sandford Award for Heritage Education.**
Refreshments: Licensed restaurant. Mill shop.

WARRINGTON

MUSEUM AND ART GALLERY *(Warrington Borough Council)*
Bold Street WA1 1JG. Tel: (0925) 35961 or 30550.
General collections of natural history, geology, ethnology, Egyptology and weapons. Local history is well represented in the Prehistory, Roman and Medieval periods. Good collections of pottery, porcelain, local glass and clocks. Frequent temporary exhibitions are arranged in the Art Galleries including periods when the permanent collections of fine Victorian oils and important 19th century English watercolours are shown. Museum Education service operates. Mon to Fri 10–5.30; Sat 10–5. *Closed* Sun and Bank Hols.

WALTON HALL *(Warrington Borough Council)*
Walton Lea Road, Higher Walton, WA4 6SN. Tel: (0925) 601617.
Victorian Hall, formerly home of Greenall Family (well known local brewers). Situated in attractive parkland. Permanent displays and A.V. show illustrate family history. Two rooms furnished with fine antiques from L.J. Gibson bequest. Imposing staircase with oils by Luke Fildes R.A., Henry Woods R.A. and James Charles. Small temporary exhibition space. Easter–Sept. Thurs, Fri, Sat, Sun and Bank Hols 1–5. Winter: Sun only 12.30–4.30. 40p, Chld/OAPs 20p.

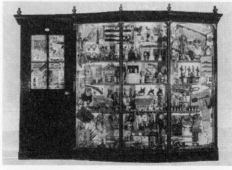

Cleveland

GUISBOROUGH

GISBOROUGH PRIORY
Telephone: (0287) 38301

Founded in the 12th century for Augustinian canons by Robert de Brus, the priory was among the richest and most magnificent in the north. The remains include an impressive gatehouse, and the wonderful east wall, an important example of early Gothic architecture.

Location: Guisborough, next to the parish church. OS map ref NZ618163.
Opening Times: Good Friday to Sept 30, daily 10–6; Oct 1 to Maundy Thursday, daily 10–4. *Closed Mons, Christmas and New Year.* Adm 55p, OAPs 40p, Chd 25p.

HARTLEPOOL

GRAY ART GALLERY AND MUSEUM
(Hartlepool Borough Council)
Clarence Road. Tel: (0429) 268916.
Nineteenth and 20th century paintings, oriental antiquities. Museum displays illustrate the archaeology, social history and natural history of the district. Ground displays include Hart Smithy, Brine Pump and reconstructed Tram office. Mon to Sat 10–5.30; Sun 2–5. *Closed* Christmas Day, Boxing Day, New Year's Day and Good Friday.

MARITIME MUSEUM *(Hartlepool Borough Council)*
Northgate. Tel: (0429) 272814.
Maritime history of the town including fishing, ship-building, marine engineering etc. Displays include simulated fisherman's cottage and ship's bridge and an early gas-lit lighthouse lantern, net store and boat builder. Mon to Sat 10–5. *Closed* Sun, Christmas Day, Boxing Day, New Year's Day and Good Friday.

KIRKLEATHAM

KIRKLEATHAM 'OLD HALL' MUSEUM AND PAVILION
(Langbaurgh on Tees Borough Council)
Tel: Redcar (0642) 479500.
A newly restored Queen Anne building dating from 1710, once a free school endowed by Sir William Turner, now housing displays reflecting the life and industry of the area and recalling the history of the Turner family. Apr to Sep: Daily (except Mon) 9–5. Oct to Mar: Daily (except Mon) 10–4. Administrator: Mr. M. D. H. Warren.

MIDDLESBROUGH

CAPTAIN COOK BIRTHPLACE MUSEUM
(Middlesbrough Borough Council)
Stewart Park. Tel: (0642) 311211 or 813781.
Illustrating Captain Cook's early life and voyages of exploration; Cook personalia; natural history and ethnography of Australia, New Zealand, North America and Pacific Islands. Cafeteria. Daily 10–6 (summer), 9–4 (winter). (Last tickets 45 mins before closing.) Adm 30p, Chld, OAPs 10p. Changing exhibitions. Souvenir Shop. Full access for the disabled.

CLEVELAND CRAFTS CENTRE
57 Gilkes Street, TS1 5EL. Tel: (0642) 226351
The Cleveland Crafts Centre houses a major collection of contemporary ceramics with fine examples representing the entire period, from work by the pioneer potters to the masters of the 1970s and 1980s. The ceramics are on open display. There is also a national and international collection of contemporary jewellery. Both collections are part of the Cleveland County Museums collection. The exhibition area of 1000 sq.ft. is a venue for in-house and touring exhibitions of high quality craft and design. There are also 9 self-contained workshops occupied by craftspeople and designers, one of whom is a Crafts-person in Residence, funded by Northern Arts. Tue to Sat 10–5. *Closed* Bank Holidays. Adm free. Car park adjacent. Suitable for disabled persons. Administrator: Susan Hoyal (Crafts Officer).

CLEVELAND GALLERY *(Cleveland County Museum Service)*
Victoria Road, TS1 3QS. Tel: (0642) 225408.
Exciting range of temporary exhibitions which change every four to six weeks. The Gallery houses the County Museum Service's permanent collection of modern drawings and paintings, decorative art from the seventeenth century to the present day, and collections of antique maps and lace, all of which are exhibited from time to time. Open: Tues–Sat 12–7. *Closed* bank holidays. Free car park. Disabled Access.

DORMAN MUSEUM *(Middlesbrough Borough Council)*
Linthorpe Road. Tel: (0642) 813781.
Local, social, industrial and natural history. Permanent display of regional and Linthorpe pottery. Exhibition on History of Middlesbrough. Temporary exhibition programme. Mon to Fri 10–6; Sat 10–5. Admission free.

MIDDLESBROUGH ART GALLERY
(Middlesbrough Borough Council)
Linthorpe Road. Tel: (0642) 247445.
Exhibitions of regional and national importance. Permanent collection of British 20th Century art and 17th to 19th Century collection. Both shown through temporary exhibitions. Outdoor Sculpture Court, Mar to Oct: Mon–Sat 10–6. Admission free.

NEWHAM GRANGE LEISURE FARM
(Middlesbrough Borough Council)
Coulby Newham. Tel: (0642) 300261 or 245432, Ext. 3831
Agricultural museum with displays of farming in Cleveland including saddlers, vet's surgery and farmhouse kitchen. Farm stocked with rare breeds of farm animals. Apr to Oct: Daily 10–6. (last ticket 3.15). Adm 50p, Chld 25p.

ORMESBY HALL, The National Trust
Mid-18th century house. Contemporary plasterwork. Small garden.
Location: 3 m SE of Middlesbrough.
Station: Marton (1½ m) (not Suns April, Sept & Oct).
Opening Times: Easter to end Oct, Mar 24–27: 2–5.30. Apr and Oct, Wed and Sun: 2–5.30. May–Sept, Weds, Thurs and Sun: 2–5.30. Adm £1, Chd (accompanied) 50p. *Pre-booked parties of 15 or over 80p each adult, 30p Chd.* No dogs (except guide dogs). Wheelchair access to ground floor only. Small shop.

STOCKTON ON TEES

BILLINGHAM ART GALLERY *(Stockton Borough Council)*
Queensway, Billingham.
A purpose built modern art gallery with a constantly changing programme of exhibitions. Mon to Sat 9.30–5. *Closed* Sun and Bank Holidays.

GREEN DRAGON MUSEUM *(Stockton Borough Council)*
Finkle Street, Stockton.
Local history museum showing the development of Stockton including a large permanent display from local potteries. Mon to Sat 9.30–5. *Closed* Sun and Bank Holidays.

PRESTON HALL MUSEUM *(Stockton Borough Council)*
Yarm Road, Stockton.
Social history depicted through the use of an open air period street with working craftsmen and reconstructed period rooms. Galleries showing pewter, toys, costume and carriage transport. Also a fine collection of weapons and George de La Tour's 'The Diceplayers'. Large park with zoo, play and picnic areas, café, riverside walks. Mon to Sat 9.30–5.30; Sun 2–5.30. Last admission 5.

HARTLEPOOL MUSEUMS & ART GALLERY

Trawler Deck, Maritime Museum

GRAY ART GALLERY & MUSEUM
Permanent collections of 19th & 20th century pictures, local history, archaeology and natural history, and a variety of temporary exhibitions. The museum grounds contain a reconstructed blacksmith's shop, the Hartlepool Electric Tram offices and a 'nodding donkey' brine pump.

MARITIME MUSEUM
Housed in a building overlooking the docks. The museum contains ship models and displays relating to all aspects of Hartlepool's maritime history, including one of the World's first gas-lit lighthouse lanterns.

GISBOROUGH PRIORY

Cornwall

BODMIN

BODMIN TOWN MUSEUM
Tel: (0208) 4159.
Local history collection. Enquiries to Bodmin Town Council, Shire House, Mount Folly Square, Bodmin.

LANHYDROCK, The National Trust
Telephone: Bodmin 73320. Restaurant 74331. &

The great house of Cornwall, with 36 rooms open to the public. 17th century long gallery. Fine plaster ceilings. Family portraits 17th to 20th centuries. The extensive kitchen and servants' quarters (1883) are also shown. Formal garden with clipped yews, and parterre, laid out in 1857. Rhododendrons, magnolias, rare trees and shrubs. Woodland garden and parkland setting.
Location: 2½ m SE of Bodmin on Bodmin/Lostwithiel Road (B3268).
Station: Bodmin Parkway (1¾ m by signposted carriage-drive to house; 3 m by road).
Opening Times: House, Garden and Grounds – Mar 24 to end of Oct—Daily except Mon (*open Bank Holiday Mons*) 11–6 (last adm 5.30) 11–5 in Oct. Nov to end of Mar—Garden and Grounds – open daily during daylight hours. Adm £3.50, Chd £1.75; Garden only £1.60, Chd 80p. Pre-booked parties £2.80, Chd £1.40. *Organisers should book visits & arrange for meals beforehand with The Administrator.* Dogs in park only on leads. Wheelchairs provided. Shop (also open Nov & Dec).
Refreshments: Teas in restaurant at House; snacks in stable block (last adm 5.30).

BOLVENTOR

POTTERS MUSEUM OF CURIOSITY
Jamaica Inn, Nr. Launceston. Tel: (0566) 86838.
Life work of Victorian naturalist and taxidermist, plus numerous curiosities from all over the world.

CALSTOCK

COTEHELE HOUSE, The National Trust
Telephone: Liskeard 50434. Restaurant 50652. &

Fine mediaeval house former home of Earls of Mount Edgcumbe. Armour, furniture, tapestries. Terrace garden falling to the sheltered valley, ponds, stream, unusual shrubs. Memorial Watermill and Cotehele Quay museum.
Location: On W bank of the Tamar, 1 m W of Calstock by footpath, (6 m by road). 8 m SW of Tavistock; 14 m from Plymouth via Tamar Bridge.
Station: Calstock (1½ m) (not Suns).
Opening Times: Mar 24 to end of Oct—Garden, Mill and Quay every day, House every day *except Friday,* but open Good Friday 11–6 (last adm 5.30) 11–5 in Oct. Closes dusk if earlier. Nov to Mar—Garden open daily during daylight. Adm House, Gardens, Cotehele Mill and Quay £3.50, Chd £1.75. Gardens, Cotehele Mill and Quay £1.60 Chd 80p. *Reduced fee of £2.80, Chd £1.40 for pre-booked coach parties. Organisers should book visits & arrange for meals beforehand with the Administrator.* DOGS IN WOOD ONLY – on lead. Wheelchairs provided; house only accessible. Shop.
Refreshments: Available.

CAMBORNE

CAMBORNE SCHOOL OF MINES GEOLOGICAL MUSEUM
Pool, Redruth. Tel: (0209) 714866.
Collection of minerals and ores. Mon to Fri 9–4.30. *Closed* Bank Hols. Adm free.

CORNISH ENGINES *(National Trust)*
East Pool Mine, Pool.
The 30-in. rotative beam winding engine (1887) and the 90-in. beam pumping engine (1892) both stand complete in their houses. Apr 1 to Oct 31: Daily 11–6 (last tour at 5.30). Adm £1.00, Chld 50p. *No reduction for parties.*

CAMELFORD

NORTH CORNWALL MUSEUM AND GALLERY
The Clease. Tel: (0840) 212954.
A privately owned museum of rural life in North Cornwall from 50 to 100 years ago. Two wagons and a dog cart; sections on agriculture, cidermaking, slate and granite quarrying, blacksmith's and wheelwright's tools, cobbling, the dairy and domestic scene. Pilgrim Trust award 1978. Apr to Sep: Mon to Sat 10.30–5. *Closed* Sun.

FALMOUTH

FALMOUTH ART GALLERY *(Falmouth Town Council)*
The Moor. Tel: (0326) 313863.
Programme of regularly changed exhibitions throughout the year, comprising one-man shows by contemporary artists, travelling exhibitions, and subjects of local interest, in addition to one exhibition of major artistic importance each year. Permanent collection on display periodically includes works by Waterhouse, Munnings and Tuke and fine 18th and 19th century maritime paintings and prints. Mon to Fri 10–1, 2–4.30. *Closed* between Christmas and New Year. Adm free. All enquiries to the Curator.

FALMOUTH MARITIME MUSEUM
C/o Hon Secretary, Higher Penpol House, Mawnan Smith, Nr. Falmouth.
Tel: (0326) 250507.
Cornwall's Maritime History. Historic steam tug with unique engine and exhibition on board. Open Easter–Oct. Building with theme displays and ship models, normally open throughout the year.

PENDENNIS CASTLE
Telephone: (0326) 316594
(Cornwall English Heritage)

Henry VIII's reply to the Pope's crusade against him was to fortify his coastline. Two castles guarded the Fal Estuary, Pendennis and St Mawes. Built high on a promontory, Pendennis saw action in the Civil War when 'Jack-for-the-King' Arundell held the castle for five terrible months. It continued in military use until 1946. Also see Museum exhibition, 1588 gundeck tableau.
Location: Pendennis Head 1 m (1.6 km) south east of Falmouth.
Opening Times: Good Friday to Sept 30, daily 10–6; Oct 1 to Maundy Thurs, daily 10–4. *Closed* Mons, Dec 24–26, Jan 1. Adm £1.30, OAPs £1, Chd 65p.

HELSTON

FLAMBARDS TRIPLE THEME PARK
Culdrose Manor. Tel: (0326) 573404/574549.
Three major award winning all-weather attractions for just one admission fee all set in beautiful landscaped prize winning gardens.
1. Flambards Victorian Village – Much extended this year, an authentically reconstructed life-size village with cobbled streets, shops, carriages and fashions. New this year the famous Chemist Shop Time Capsule.
2. Britain in the Blitz – A recreation of a life-size wartime street offering a unique Blitz experience. Opened by Dame Vera Lynn D.B.E., LL.D.
3. Cornwall Aero Park – Many new vibrant displays that encourage participation.
Also included: Special Exhibitions – Kodak's Planet Protection – celebrating the World Wildlife Fund's 25th Anniversary ☆ Historic Motor Vehicles ☆ Battle of Britain War Gallery. Live Entertainment and Huge **FREE** Adventure Playground.
Discounted tickets and wristbands available for those amusements **not included in the admission fee**. Including the New Attraction for 1988, from Mid-May to Mid-Sept the Fabulous Circus Perrier.
Open every day 10 to last admissions 5, Mar 30 to Oct 31. Tel: Helston (0326) 574549 & 573404.

GODOLPHIN HOUSE
(Mrs. Schofield)
Tudor house. Colonnaded front added 1635. A former house of the Earls of Godolphin.
Location: 5 m NW of Helston; between villages of Townshend and Godolphin Cross.
Opening Times: Bank Hol Mons; May & June—Thurs 2–5. July & Sept—Tues 2–5, Thurs 2–5, Aug—Tues 2–5, Thurs 10–1, 2–5. Adm £1.50, Chd 50p (1988 rates, 1989 charges not known at time of going to press). Open at other times for pre-booked parties & all year round for arranged parties.

HELSTON FOLK MUSEUM
Old Butter Market.
Folk Museum dealing with all aspects of local life in the Lizard Peninsula. Daily 10.30–1, 2–4.30 (Wed 10.30–12 noon).

POLDARK MINE
Wendron, 3 miles N. of Helston on B3297 (Redruth to Helston Road).
Underground tour with museums of Cornish mining. Restaurant, gardens, shops. Apr to Oct: Daily 10–6, last tour 5; Aug 10–10, last tour 8. Total visit will exceed 3 hours. Adm charge.

ISLES OF SCILLY

THE VALHALLA FIGUREHEAD COLLECTION
Abbey Gardens, Tresco. Tel: (0720) 22849.
Figureheads and ships' carvings from wrecks around the Isles of Scilly. A National Maritime Museum Outstation. Daily Apr to Oct, 10–4.

LAUNCESTON

LAUNCESTON CASTLE
Telephone: (0566) 2365

The impressive round keep stands high on its grassy mound within a circular wall. Inside, a tall cylindrical tower soars from the centre. The space between tower and keep was roofed. Like Launceston itself, the castle was important in the Middle Ages. Small site museum.
Location: Launceston. OS map ref SX330846.
Opening Times: Good Friday to Sept 30, daily 10–6; Oct 1 to Maundy Thursday, daily 10–4. *Closed Mons, Christmas and New Year.* Adm 80p, OAPs 60p, Chd 40p.

LISKEARD

THORBURN MUSEUM AND GALLERY
Tel: (0579) 20325/21129.

LOSTWITHIEL

RESTORMEL CASTLE
Telephone: (0208) 872687

Crowning a hill overlooking the River Fowey, the castle rises steeply above a dry but deep, wide moat. The outer 12th century wall is a perfect circle. Domestic buildings were later added inside and a rectangular chapel outside.
Location: 1½ m (2.4 km) north of Lostwithiel. OS map ref SX104614.
Opening Times: Good Friday to Sept 30, daily 10–6; Oct 1 to Maundy Thursday, daily 10–4. *Closed Mons, Christmas and New Year.* Adm 80p, OAPs 60p, Chd 40p.

MAWNAN SMITH

GLENDURGAN GARDEN, The National Trust
A valley garden of great beauty with fine trees and shrubs, overlooking estuary. Giant's Stride and maze much enjoyed by children.
Location: 4 m SW of Falmouth ½ m SW of Mawnan Smith on road to Helford Passage.
Opening Times: Mar 1 to end of Oct—Mons, Weds & Fris (except Good Friday) 10.30–5.30 (last adm 4.30). Adm £1.60, Chd 80p. *No reduction for parties.* No dogs. Unsuitable for wheelchairs.

MEVAGISSEY

MEVAGISSEY FOLK MUSEUM
East Quay.

MOUNT EDGCUMBE

MOUNT EDGCUMBE HOUSE & COUNTRY PARK
Telephone: Plymouth (0752) 822236
(City of Plymouth & Cornwall County Council)

Stretching along 10 miles of spectacular coastline from Plymouth to Whitsand Bay, the Park contains one of only three Grade I Historic Gardens in Cornwall. The first landscape park in Cornwall, it was designed 240 years ago with wonderful woodland walks and views and includes a deer park and Formal Gardens in the Italian, French and English styles. It is the site for the collection of International Camellia Society. Mount Edgcumbe House, a restored Tudor mansion with the Earls Garden surrounding it was the home of the Edgcumbe family for 400 years and has recently been refurbished and redecorated to reflect the late 18th century.
Location: On Rame Peninsula, 12 m from Torpoint or from Trerulefoot (A38) via A374 to Antony or Crafthole, and B3247 to Mount Edgcumbe, or by Cremyll (pedestrian) Ferry from Plymouth (Stonehouse) to Park entrance.
Opening Times: Country Park, including Landscaped Park and Formal Gardens open every day, all year round, Free. House and Earls Garden open Mar 24 to Oct 31 11–5.30 Wed to Sun and Bank Hol Mons. Adm £2 adult, Chd £1, concessions £1.50 including pre-booked parties of 10 or more. Visitor Centre and Shop selling guides and souvenirs open Mar 24 to Oct 31 every day.
Refreshments: Lunches, teas and light refreshments available in the Orangery Restaurant/Cafe, Mar 24 to Oct 31, Reservations and enquiries telephone Plymouth (0752) 822586.

NEWLYN

NEWLYN ART GALLERY
Tel: (0736) 63715.
Exhibitions of contemporary works by leading West Country artists. Supported by South West Arts. Mon to Sat 10–5.

PADSTOW

PRIDEAUX PLACE
Telephone: (0841) 532945
(The Prideaux-Brune family)

An Elizabethan Mansion House set in extensive grounds including 20 acres of deer park. Guided tours through this family home include a visit to the Great Chamber with its interesting embossed plaster ceiling dating from 1585.
Location: 7 m from Wadebridge.
Opening Times: House, shop, tearoom – Good Fri for two weeks then Spring Bank Hol to end of Sept, Sun to Thurs inclusive, 1.30–5.30. Adm House & grounds £2. Grounds only 50p. Chd half price. Special party rates. Open all the year round by written appointment. Large public car park on A389 nearby. Enquiries to the Administrator, Prideaux Place, Padstow PL28 8RP. Tel: (0841) 532945.

PENZANCE

CHYSAUSTER ANCIENT VILLAGE
Telephone: (0736) 61889

Halfway up a hillside, through a stone passage, lie the stone houses erected by our prehistoric ancestors. By the time the Romans came the village had already existed for two centuries. Each house, built around a courtyard, had its own terrace. Were these the earliest gardens?
Location: 2½ m (3.5 km) north west of Gulval, near Penzance. OS map ref SW473350.
Opening Times: Good Friday to Sept 30, daily 10–6; Oct 1 to Maundy Thursday, daily 10–4. *Closed Mons, Christmas and New Year.* Adm 80p, OAPs 60p, Chd 40p.

PENLEE HOUSE MUSEUM AND ART GALLERY
(Penzance Town Council)
Penlee Park.   Tel: (0736) 63625 or 63405.
Local antiquities and Natural History. Exhibition of paintings, including some fine examples of the Newlyn school.

ST MICHAEL'S MOUNT, The National Trust
Telephone: Penzance 710507

Home of Lord St Levan. Mediaeval and early 17th century with considerable alterations and additions in 18th and 19th century.
Location: ½ m from the shore at Marazion (A394), connected by causeway. 3 m E Penzance.
Opening Times: Mar 24 to end of Oct: Mons to Fri 10.30–5.45. Nov to end of Mar: Guided tours as tide, weather and circumstances permit. *NB: ferry boats do not operate a regular service during this period).* Adm £2.50, Chd £1.25, Family ticket £7. Shop and restaurant—Mar 24 to end of Oct, daily. No dogs. Unsuitable for wheelchairs.

TRENGWAINTON GARDEN, The National Trust   ♿

Large shrub and woodland garden. Fine views. A series of walled gardens contain rare sub-tropical plants.
Location: 2 m NW of Penzance ½ m W of Heamoor on Morvah Road (B3312). *Station: Penzance (2 m).*
Opening Times: Mar 1 to Oct—Weds, Thurs, Fris, Sats & Bank Hol Mons 11–6, 11–5 in Mar and Oct. Adm £1.50, Chd 75p. *No reduction for parties.* No dogs. Wheelchair access.

PORT ISAAC

LONG CROSS VICTORIAN GARDENS
Telephone: Port Isaac (0208) 880243

Late Victorian gardens set amidst majestic pines with panoramic sea views.
Location: Just off B3314 between Port Isaac & Port Quin, Trelights & St Endellion: 7 m NE of Wadebridge.
Opening Times: Easter to Oct—Daily 11 to dusk. Children's playground; family room. Adm free. *Collection box in aid of MacMillan Nurses.*
Refreshments: Beer Garden, coffee & refreshments, cream teas.

PROBUS

TREWITHEN HOUSE AND GARDENS
Telephone: St Austell (0726) 882418/882764

The name means 'House of the trees' which truly describes this fine early Georgian house in its splendid setting of wood and parkland. The house has been described by Christopher Hussey in *Country Life* magazine as **'one of the outstanding West Country houses of the 18th century'**. The origins of the house go back to the 17th century, but it was the architect Thomas Edwards of Greenwich who was responsible for the fine building we see today. Bought by Philip Hawkins in 1715, who commissioned the substantial rebuilding, it was completed only some 40 years later. The house has been lived in and cared for by the same family for over 250 years. Some of the magnolias and rhododendron species in the Garden are well known throughout the world. Plants and shrubs, of which many are exported, are for sale. These Gardens are particularly spectacular between March and the end of June, and again the Autumn, although there is much to see throughout the year. There is a 25 minute video of the House and Gardens.
Location: On A390 between Probus and Grampound, adjoining County Demonstration Gardens.
Opening Times: Gardens: Open Mar 1 to Sept 30, Mon to Sat 10–4.30. *Closed* Sun. Free car parking. Plants for sale. Dogs on leads. Adm Gardens: Mar–June £1.50, Chd (under 15) 75p; July to Sept £1.20, Chd (under 15) 60p. House: £2 per person. There are guided tours around this charming house on Mons & Tues (2–4.30) Apr to July & August Bank Holiday Monday. Parties by arrangement please.

ST. AUSTELL

MID CORNWALL GALLERIES
St. Austell PL24 2EG on A390 at St Blazey. Tel: (0726) 81 2131.
3 m E of St. Austell on A390, the gallery is a Victorian School converted to well lit modern gallery showing a very comprehensive range of contemporary arts and crafts. Approximately 8 Exhibitions/Group Shows a year featuring work by both National and South West artists and craftsmen. Work on show includes paintings, etchings, ceramics, jewellery, sculpture, woodwork, metalwork, glass, silks . . . all work for sale. Open: Mon to Sat 10–5 all year round. Adm free. Ample car parking. Suitable for disabled persons. Coffee, cakes available.

ST. AUSTELL CHINA CLAY MUSEUM
Carthew.

ST. IVES

THE BARBARA HEPWORTH MUSEUM *(The Tate Gallery)*
Barnoon Hill. Tel: (0736) 796226.
The house, studio, sculpture garden and workshops of the famous sculptor. Mon to Sat: Spring/Summer 10–5.30; Autumn/Winter 10–4.30. *Closed* Sun, Good Friday, Christmas and Boxing Days. Adm 50p, Chld, Students and OAPs 25p.

OLD MARINERS CHURCH *(St. Ives Society of Artists)*
Norway Square. Tel: Penzance (0736) 795582.
Exhibitions of the St. Ives Society of Artists.

ST. MAWES

ST MAWES CASTLE
Telephone: (0326) 270526

Shaped like a clover leaf, this small 16th century castle, still intact, nestles among rock plants and tropical shrubs. During the Civil War the Governor capitulated without gunfire or bloodshed, unlike Pendennis on the opposite shore.
Location: St Mawes. OS map ref SW842328.
Opening Times: Good Friday to Sept 30, daily 10–6; Oct 1 to Maundy Thursday, daily 10–4. *Closed Mons, Christmas and New Year.* Adm 80p, OAPs 60p, Chd 40p.

ST. NEWLYN EAST

TRERICE, The National Trust
Telephone: Newquay 875404   ♿

A small Elizabethan house, fine furniture, plaster ceilings and fireplaces, in a recently planted garden. A small museum in the Barn traces the development of the lawn mower.
Location: 3 m SE of Newquay A392 & A3058 (turn right at Kestle Mill).
Station: Quintrel Downs (1½ m).
Opening Times: Mar 24 to end of Oct—Daily 11–6 (last adm 5.30), 11–5 in Oct. Adm £2.60, Chd £1.30. *Reduced rate of £2, Chd £1 for pre-booked parties.* No dogs. Wheelchairs available; access to house only. Shop.
Refreshments: In the barn 11–6 (last adm 5.30). *Parties must book.*

SALTASH

COTEHELE QUAY – NATIONAL MARITIME MUSEUM OUTSTATION *(with The National Trust)*
Tel: (0579) 50830.
Display on shipping and trade of the River Tamar. Home of the NMM/NT restored Tamar sailing barge *Shamrock*. Daily Apr to Oct, 11–4. Resident NMM staff.

TINTAGEL

TINTAGEL CASTLE
Telephone: (0840) 770328
(English Heritage)

Amazing that anything has survived on this wild, windswept coast. Yet fragments of Earl Reginald's great hall, built about 1145, and Earl Richard's 13th century wall and iron gate still stand in this incomparable landscape. No wonder that King Arthur and his Knights were thought to have dwelt here. Site exhibition.
Location: ½ m (0.8 km) north west of Tintagel. OS map ref SX048891.
Opening Times: Good Friday to Sept 30, daily 10–6; Oct 1 to Maundy Thurs, daily 10–4, *closed Mons, Dec 24–26, Jan 1.* Adm 1.30, OAPs £1, Chd 65p.

TINTAGEL – THE OLD POST OFFICE, The National Trust   ♿

A miniature 14th century manor house with large hall.
Location: Nos 3 & 4 in the centre of Tintagel.
Opening Times: Mar 24 to end of Oct—Daily 11–6 (or sunset if earlier), (Oct closed 5). Adm £1, Chd 50p. *No reduction for parties.* No dogs. Wheelchair access. Shop.

TORPOINT

ANTONY HOUSE, The National Trust
Telephone: Plymouth (0752) 812191

The home of Mr. Richard Carew Pole. Built for Sir William Carew 1711-1721. Unaltered Queen Anne house, panelled rooms. Fine furniture. Extensive garden.
Location: 5 m W of Plymouth via Torpoint car ferry. 2 m NW of Torpoint, N of A374.
Opening Times: Mar 27 to end of Oct—Tues, Weds & Thurs; also Bank Hol Mons and Suns in June, July and Aug 2–6 (last adm 5.30). Adm £2.40, Chd £1.20. Pre-arranged parties £1.80, Chd 90p. No dogs. Unsuitable for wheelchairs. Shop.

ANTONY WOODLAND GARDEN
(Carew Pole Garden Trust)

A woodland garden extending to over 50 acres bordering the Lynher Estuary, an area designated as one of Outstanding Natural Beauty and a Site of Special Scientific Interest. Established in the late 18th century with the assistance of Humphrey Repton, the gardens feature extensive woodland and riverside walks with over 300 types of Camellias and a wide variety of Magnolias, Rhododendrons, Hydrangeas, Azaleas and other flowering shrubs together with many fine specimen indigenous and exotic hardwood and softwood trees.

Location: 5 m W of Plymouth via Torpoint Car Ferry. 2 m NW of Torpoint off A374.
Opening Times: Mar 15–May 31 and Sept 15–Oct 31, Mon–Fri 11.30–5.30. Suns 2.30–5.30. *Closed* Sats. Special openings in aid of Charities by arrangement. Adm £1, Chd 50p. Car parking available. No dogs allowed.

TRURO

COUNTY MUSEUM AND ART GALLERY
(Royal Institution of Cornwall)
River Street. Tel: (0872) 72205.
Local antiquities and history. Ceramics and art. World-famous collections of Cornish minerals. Mon to Sat 9–5. *Closed* Sun and Bank Hols.

TRELISSICK GARDEN, The National Trust
Telephone: Truro 862090

Large shrub garden. Beautiful wooded park overlooking the river Fal. Woodland walks. Particularly rich in rhododendrons, camellias and hydrangeas.
Location: 4 m S of Truro on both sides of B3289 overlooking King Harry Ferry.
Opening Times: Gardens only: Mar 1 to end of Oct—Mons to Sats 11–6 (or sunset if earlier), Suns 1–6 (or sunset if earlier), 11–5 in Mar and Oct. Entrance on road to King Harry Passage. Adm £1.90, Chd 95p. *No reduction for parties.* Shop, with special plants section. New Art and Craft gallery. Dogs in woodland walk and park only, on leads. Wheelchairs provided.
Refreshments: In the barn.

Cumbria

AMBLESIDE

RYDAL MOUNT
Telephone: Ambleside (05394) 33002
(Mrs Mary Henderson—nee Wordsworth)

Wordsworth home from 1813–1850. Family portraits and furniture, many of the poet's personal possessions, and first editions of his works. The garden which was designed by Wordsworth has been described as one of the most interesting small gardens to be found anywhere in England. Two long terraces, many rare trees and shrubs. Extends to 4½ acres.
Location: Off A591, 1½ m from Ambleside, 2½ m from Grasmere.
Opening Times: Mar 1 to Oct 31—Daily 9.30–5. Nov 1 to Mar 1—10–4. *(Closed Tues in winter).* Adm House & Gardens £1.50, Chd 50p. Parties, £1. See Lake District National Park Visitor Centre for out of season package.

BARROW IN FURNESS

FURNESS ABBEY
Telephone: (0229) 23420

At the time of its suppression in 1537, the abbey was one of the wealthiest monasteries in the land. Founded in 1124 by King Stephen, the abbey belonged at first to the Order of Savigny, then to the Cistercians. Ruined buildings of red sandstone evoke a vision of past splendour. Magnificent still are the canopied seats in the presbytery and the Chapter House. Exhibition in the museum at the entrance.
Location: 1½ m (2.4 km) north of Barrow-in-Furness. OS map ref SD218717.
Opening Times: Good Friday to Sept 30, daily 10–6; Oct 1 to Maundy Thursday, daily 10–4. *Closed Mons, Christmas and New Year.* Adm £1.10, OAPs 80p, Chd 55p.

FURNESS MUSEUM *(District Council)*
Ramsden Square LA14 1LL. Tel: (0229) 20650
Illustrates all aspects of the Furness area. Vickers collection of ship models. Finds from prehistoric sites, chiefly Stone Age. Furness bygones. Mon, Tues, Wed and Fri 10–5; Thur 10–4; Sat 10–4. *Closed* Sun and Bank Hols.

BRAMPTON

LANERCOST PRIORY
Telephone: (069 77) 3030

Just south of Hadrian's Wall, in the wooded valley of the River Irthing, stands this noble Augustinian priory founded by Robert de Vaux in the 12th century. Centre-piece is the priory church, 800 years old, and the nave is still a parish church. English Heritage has the cloistral area and the ruined East End of the church.
Location: 2 m (3.2 km) north east of Brampton. OS map ref NY556637.
Opening Times: Good Friday to Sept 30, daily 10–6. Adm 55p, OAPs 40p, Chd 25p.

NAWORTH CASTLE
Telephone: Brampton (069 77) 2692 (Curator)
(The Earl of Carlisle MC)

Set amid rugged Hadrian's Wall country this historic Border fortress (referred to several times in Sir Walter Scott's novels) is neither ruin nor museum, but a lived-in family home. Its Great Hall is breathtaking with huge heraldic beasts and eight Gobelin tapestries, which are one of the most important collections in the country. Also woodland walk, dungeon, garde robes and original fish, White Knight, griffin, etc. from 'Alice Through the Looking Glass' as well as work by Salvin, Burne Jones and Philip Webb.
Location: 12 m from Carlisle, 2 m from Brampton, just off the A69 to Newcastle.
Opening Times: Easter Sun & Mon, thereafter Weds and Suns to Sept 30; also Sats in July and Aug and Bank Hols. Adm £1.50, Chd/OAPs 75p. Parties by arrangement on other days. Free car park. Not suitable for disabled.

BROUGH

BROUGH CASTLE
Telephone: (093 04) 219

The importance of Brough-under-Stainmore, lying between Carlisle and York, did not escape the Romans. So it is hardly surprising that the Normans built a stronghold on the site of that derelict Roman fort. The Scots destroyed it in 1174 and the present castle is a product of the rebuilding that followed. Until 1204 Brough was a royal castle; then King John granted it to Robert de Vipont, ancestor of the Lords Clifford. Part of the 11th century wall remains and much of the 17th century repair work carried out by that energetic restorer of castles, Lady Anne Clifford.
Location: 8 m (13 km) south east of Appleby. OS map ref NY791141.
Opening Times: Good Friday to Sept 30, daily 10–6; Oct 1 to Maundy Thursday, daily 10–4. *Closed Mons, Christmas and New Year.* Adm 55p, OAPs 40p, Chd 25p.

CARK-IN-CARTMEL

HOLKER HALL
Telephone: Flookburgh (044 853) 328
(Mr & Mrs Hugh Cavendish)

Former home of the Dukes of Devonshire and still lived in by members of the family. 120 acre Deer Park, formal and woodland gardens. Exhibitions including **The Lakeland Motor Museum,** a fine collection of over 80 historic vehicles, tel (044 853) 509. Victorian, Edwardian and Wartime Kitchens Exhibition from the Zanussi Collection.
Location: ½ m N of Cark-in-Cartmel on B5278 from Haverthwaite; 4 m W Grangeover-Sands.
Opening Times: House, Gardens & Motor Museum. Easter Sun to last Sun in Oct—Daily (ex Sat) 10.30–4.30. Park open until 6. *Thurs evenings until 9 for booked groups of 20 or more.* Group rates for parties of 20 or more. Free Coach and Car Park. Gift Shop.
Refreshments: Clock Tower Cafe serving salads, sandwiches, home made cakes and pastries, beverages including wine and beer. *Group catering by prior arrangement.*

CARLISLE

CARLISLE CASTLE
Telephone: (0228) 31777
(English Heritage)

Twenty-six years after the Battle of Hastings, Carlisle remained unconquered. In 1092 William II marched north, took the city and ordered the building of a stronghold above the River Eden. Since William's time the castle has survived 800 years of fierce and bloody attacks, extensive rebuilding and continuous military occupation. A massive Norman keep contains an exhibition on the history of the castle. D'Ireby Tower now open to the public, containing furnishings to authentic medieval design, an exhibition and shop.
Location: North of town centre. O.S. map NY 397563.
Open: Good Friday to Sept 30, daily 10–6; Oct 1 to Maundy Thurs, daily 10–4. *Closed* Mons, Dec 24–26, Jan 1. Adm £1.30, OAPs £1, Chd 65p.

CARLISLE MUSEUM AND ART GALLERY
(Carlisle City Council)
Tullie House, Castle Street. Tel: (0228) 34781.
Jacobean house (1689) with Victorian extensions and attractive grounds; 19/20th century British paintings; 18/19th century English porcelain; costume, toys and dolls; Prehistoric and Roman archaeology of Cumbria; British birds; Geology including minerals. Temporary exhibitions. Mon to Sat 9–5, Sun 10–4 (June to Aug). Spring and Summer Bank Hols 10–4. Hours subject to alteration.

THE GUILDHALL MUSEUM *(Carlisle City Council)*
Greenmarket. Tel: (0228) 34781.
Early 15th century half-timbered house. Displays of Guild, Civic and local history, including medieval items. Open May 18 to Sept 4: Wed to Sun 12–4. By appointment at other times. Adm free.

COCKERMOUTH

ETHNIC DOLL & TOY MUSEUM
(Mr and Mrs A.L. Pickering, Mr R. Moore)
Bank's Court, Market Place. Tel: (0900) 85259/823254
Ethnic costume dolls, Kent & Sussex Wealden scale model houses, miniature rooms, mainly British toys from 1900, working Hornby 0 and 00 railway layouts. Mar to Oct: Daily 10–5; winter by appointment. Adm charge. Parties welcome. Reduction for group of over 20. Unsuitable for disabled.

WORDSWORTH HOUSE, The National Trust
Telephone: Cockermouth (0900) 824805

North country Georgian House built in 1745, birthplace of the poet Wordsworth, furnished in the style of his time, with some of his belongings. The pleasant garden is referred to in his 'Prelude'. Static and audio-visual displays.
Location: In Main Street.
Opening Times: Mar 24–Nov 5—Mons to Sats (except Thurs) 11–5; Suns 2–5 (last admission 4.30). Adm £1.50, Chd 75p. Reductions for pre-booked parties except on Suns. No dogs. Shop open daily in summer & Nov to Dec 24 (except Thurs & Suns) 10–4.30. Unsuitable for wheelchairs.
Refreshments: Light refreshments & lunches in the old kitchen (licensed).

CONISTON

BRANTWOOD
Telephone: (0966) 41396
(Brantwood Educational Trust)

The home of John Ruskin from 1872–1900. Large collection of pictures by Ruskin and his associates. Ruskin's coach, boat, furniture and other associated items. Ruskin's woodland gardens are currently being restored. There is a delightful nature walk around the 250 acre estate.
Location: 2½ m from Coniston. Historic House signs at Coniston, Head of Coniston Water & Hawkshead.
Opening Times: Open all year. Mid-Mar to mid-Nov—Daily 11–5.30. Winter season—Weds to Suns 11–4. Adm House, Wainwright Exhibition & Nature Walks £2, Chd 90p; Family Ticket (2 adults and children) £5.25, Nature trails only 50p, Chd 25p. Steam Yacht Gondola sails regularly from Coniston Pier. Free car park. Parking for disabled near house. Toilets (incl for disabled). Lakeland Guild Craft Gallery and shop.
Refreshments: Tea room/coffee; light meals available.

THE RUSKIN MUSEUM
Tel: (053 94) 41387.
Works by John Ruskin and his circle. Sections for Ruskin lace, local history and Campbell water speed records. Easter to Oct 31: Daily 10 to 5.30. Adm charge.

GRASMERE

DOVE COTTAGE AND WORDSWORTH MUSEUM
Tel: (09665) 544/547
Combined ticket gives access to Dove Cottage (home of Wordsworth during his most creative years, 1799–1808) and the museum which has an extensive display of verse manuscripts, paintings and special exhibitions providing a context for the poet's life and work. 9.30–5.30 *(last admission 5)*. Reductions for parties. Restaurant, book and gift shop.

THE HEATON COOPER STUDIO *(John Heaton Cooper)*
The Studio LA22 9SX. Tel: (09665) 280
In the centre of the village is an exhibition of original watercolour paintings and a unique collection of colour reproductions by W. Heaton Cooper R.I. and A. Heaton Cooper (1863–1929) who through their paintings of mountains and lakes are recognised as the foremost artists of the area. There are also many examples of sculpture by Ophelia Gordon Bell. Reproductions and originals may be purchased from The Studio at Grasmere or Bowness together with books and greetings cards. Open: Easter to end Oct: Daily 9–6 (Sun 12–6); Nov to Easter: Mon to Sat 9–5. Open Bank Hols *(except Christmas)*. Parties welcome; car park; suitable for disabled.

KENDAL

ABBOT HALL ART GALLERY
& MUSEUM OF LAKELAND LIFE & INDUSTRY
Telephone: Kendal (0539) 22464   &
(Lake District Art Gallery & Museum Trust)

Impressive Georgian House; comprehensive collections of portraits by George Romney and Daniel Gardner, Lake District landscapes and furniture by Gillows of Lancaster displayed in elegant 18th C. rooms; lively temporary exhibition programme; craft shop selling work by leading artist-craftsmen. Adjacent Museum of Lakeland Life & Industry recaptures unique flavour of everyday life in Lake District: everything from hip baths to sheep dips; Arthur Ransome room; first Museum of the Year. Also visit award winning Kendal Museum of Natural History & Archaeology, Station Road.
Location: Off Kirkland nr Kendal Parish Church. From M6 exit 36.
Station: Oxenholme (1½ m); Kendal (¾ m).
Opening Times: All the year – daily except Dec 25, 26, Jan 1 and Good Friday. Mon–Fri 10.30–5, Sat & Sun 2–5, (Spring Bank Holiday – Oct 31; Sat 10.30–5). Adm charge; concessions for OAPs, Chd, Students and families. Lift for disabled (Mon–Fri only).
Refreshments: Coffee shop (in season).

LEVENS HALL
Telephone: Sedgwick (053 95) 60321   &
(C. H. Bagot, Esq.)

Elizabethan family home with fine plaster-work, panelling, paintings and Jacobean furniture. World famous topiary garden laid out in 1692.
Location: 5 m S of Kendal on the Milnthorpe Road (A6); Exit 36 from M6.
Opening Times: Easter Sunday to Sept 30. House, Garden, Gift Shop, Tea-rooms, Plants for sale, Play Area and Picnic Area. Suns, Mons, Tues, Weds & Thurs 11–5. Steam Collection 2–5. Closed Fris & Sats. Adm House & Garden £2.60, Garden £1.40. Groups and OAPs: House and Garden £2.10; Garden £1.25. Chd half price. Regret House not suitable for wheelchairs.
Refreshments: Home-made light Lunches and teas.

SIZERGH CASTLE AND GARDEN, The National Trust
Telephone: Sedgwick (05295) 60070

The 14th century Pele tower (the oldest part of the castle) rises to 60 feet, contains some original windows, floors and fireplaces; 15th century Great Hall, extended in later centuries; 16th century panelling and ceilings; contents include French and English furniture, china, family portraits, Stuart portraits and relics; extensive garden includes ⅔ acre limestone rock garden, the largest owned by the Trust with large collection of Japanese maples, dwarf conifers, hardy ferns and many perennials and bulbs; water garden; herbaceous borders; wild flower banks; fine autumn colour.
Location: 3½ m S of Kendal NW of A6/A591 interchange; 2 m from Levens Hall.
Opening Times: Castle & Garden; Mar 26 to Oct 30—Suns, Mons, Weds & Thurs; 2–6 (last admission 5.30). Garden & Shop open from 12.30 same days. Adm £2.00 (House and Garden), Chd half-price. Garden only: £1, Chld 50p. Parties by arrangement with The Administrator, Sizergh Castle, Tel: Sedgwick 60070. Please send sae. Shop. No dogs. Wheelchairs (one provided) in garden only.

KESWICK

FITZ PARK MUSEUM AND ART GALLERY
Station Road.
Contains original Southey, Wordsworth and Walpole manuscripts. Local geology and natural history. Apr to Oct: Mon to Sat 10–12.30, 2–5.30. *Closed Sun.* Adm 50p, Chld, OAPs 25p. Schoolchld in parties 10p per chld.

MIREHOUSE
Telephone: Keswick (076 87) 72287   &
(Mr & Mrs Spedding)

Seventeenth century Manor House with 19th century additions. Portraits and manuscripts of Francis Bacon and many literary friends of the Spedding family including Tennyson, Wordsworth, Southey. Walk through grounds to Bassenthwaite Lake. Adventure Playgrounds. Norman Lakeside Church of St. Bega.
Location: 4½ m N of Keswick on A591 (Keswick to Carlisle Road).
Opening Times: Apr to Oct – Lakeside Walk, Adventure Playgrounds—Daily 10.30–5.30. House—Suns, Weds & Bank Hol Mons 2–5. Parties welcome at other times by appointment.
Refreshments: Old Sawmill Tearoom open daily 10.30–5.30; specialises in salad & sandwiches made to order, home baking. Parties please book (Tel: Keswick (07687) 74317).

RAILWAY MUSEUM *(Derwent Railway Society)*
28 Main Street, Keswick.
Railwayana & relics mainly associated with railways of Cumbria.

MARYPORT

MARITIME MUSEUM *(Allerdale District Council)*
Senhouse Street. Tel: Maryport (0900) 813738
Maritime and local history. Steamship section in adjacent harbour.

MILLOM

MILLOM FOLK MUSEUM *(Millom Folk Museum Society)*
St. Georges Road.
Unique full-scale model of a Hodbarrow iron mine drift, miner's cottage, smithy and many other items.

NEWBY BRIDGE

STOTT PARK BOBBIN MILL
Telephone: (0448) 31087

The Victorian mill buildings forming Stott Park are virtually the same today as they were 150 years ago. The bobbin mill developed from man's ability to harness the power of the fast-flowing Lakeland streams to run machinery and also from the abundance of local coppice wood. Restored as a working industrial monument, much of the machinery still remains, including a turbine and steam engine.
Location: On unclassified road north of the village of Finsthwaite, 2 m (3.2 km) north of A590 Kendal/Barrow-in-Furness Road at Newby Bridge (near east bank of Lake Windermere). OS map ref SD373883.
Opening Times: Good Friday to Oct 31, daily 10–6 (or dusk if earlier). Adm £1.30, OAPs £1, Chd 65p.

PENRITH

BROUGHAM CASTLE
Telephone: (0768) 62488

The oldest part of the surviving building, the keep, was constructed in Henry II's reign after the Scots had relinquished their hold on the north west of England. The keep, later heightened, and its gatehouses formed an impregnable fortress, while also providing a lordly residence of spacious proportions.
Location: 1½ m (2.4 km) east of Penrith. OS map ref NY537290.
Opening Times: Good Friday to Sept 30, daily 10–6; Oct 1 to Maundy Thursday, daily 10–4. *Closed Mons, Christmas and New Year.* Adm 80p, OAPs 60p, Chd 40p.

DALEMAIN
Telephone: Pooley Bridge (085 36) 450
(Mr & Mrs Bryce McCosh)

Medieval, Tudor and early Georgian house and gardens lived in by the same family for over 300 years. Fine furniture and portraits. Countryside museum and picnic areas, Agricultural Museum, Westmorland and Cumberland Yeomanry Museum and Adventure Playground, Fell Pony Museum. Interesting garden as portrayed in various publications. Plant Centre.
Location: 3 m from Penrith on A592. Turn off M6 exit 40 onto A66 (A592) to Ullswater.
Opening Times: Easter Sun—Mid Oct daily except Fris and Sats, 11.15–5. Adm charged. Car park and picnic area free.
Refreshments: Coffee from 11.15. Bar lunches 12–2.30. Home made teas from 2.30 pm.

HUTTON-IN-THE-FOREST
Telephone: Skelton (085 34) 449
(Lord Inglewood)

One of the ancient manors in the Forest of Inglewood, and the home of Lord Inglewood's family since the beginning of the 17th century. The House stands in magnificent gardens and woodland.
Location: 6 m NW of Penrith on B5305 Wigton Road (from M6 exit 41).
Opening Times: Bank Hol Suns & Mons also Thurs, Fris and Suns from June 1–Oct 1. Grounds open every day 11–5. Private parties by arrangement any day from Apr 1. Adm: House & Grounds: £2, Chd (accompanied) free of charge. Grounds only: £1.00.
Refreshments: Fresh home-made teas available in the cloisters when house open.

PENRITH MUSEUM *(Eden District Council)*
  Robinson's School, Middlegate. Tel: (0768) 64671.
Local history, archaeology and geology. Exhibition of the history of the Eden Valley, from early man to present day. The museum building, dating from 1670, was a charity school. Shares premises with Tourist Information Centre. Jun 1 to Sept 30: Mon to Sat 10–7; Sun 1–6. Nov 1 to Mar 31: Mon, Tues, Thurs 10–5. Apr 1 to May 31 and Oct 1 to Oct 31: Mon to Sat 10–5 (including *all* Bank Hols). Adm free. Curator Mrs Judith Clarke AMA.

RAVENGLASS

MUNCASTER CASTLE
(Mrs P. Gordon-Duff-Pennington)

Seat of the Pennington family since 13th century. Famed rhododendron and azalea gardens. Superb views over Esk Valley (Ruskin's Gateway to Paradise).
Location: 1 m SE of Ravenglass village on A595 (entrance ½ m W of Church). *Station: Ravenglass (¼ m).*
Opening Times: Grounds and Bird Garden; Good Friday to Sept 30—Daily (except Mons but open Bank Hols) 12–5. Castle; Good Friday to Sept 30—Daily (except Mons but open Bank Hols) 1.30–4.30 (last adm). Adm Grounds only £1.25, Chd 90p; Inclusive Ticket £2.50, Chd £1.25. Special party rates.

ROCKCLIFFE

CASTLETOWN HOUSE
Telephone: Rockcliffe (0228 74) 205
(Giles Mounsey-Heysham, Esq.)

Georgian Country House set in attractive gardens and grounds. Fine ceilings. Naval pictures, furnishings and model engines.
Location: 5 m NW of Carlisle on Solway coast, 1 m W of Rockcliffe village and 2 m W of A74.
Opening Times: HOUSE ONLY. Apr to Sept—Weds & Bank Hol Mons 2–5. Other times & parties by prior arrangement. Adm £1.50, Chd (accompanied) & OAPs £1.
Refreshments: Hotels & refreshments in Carlisle.

TEMPLE SOWERBY

ACORN BANK GARDEN, The National Trust

This 2½ acre garden is protected by fine oaks under which grow a vast display of daffodils. Inside walls are two orchards with medlar, mulberry, cherries, quince and apples. Surrounding the orchards are mixed borders with herbaceous plants and many flowering shrubs and climbing roses. The adjacent herb garden has the largest collection of culinary, medicinal and narcotic herbs in the north. The red sandstone house is let to the Sue Ryder Foundation and is open on application.
Location: Just N of Temple Sowerby, 6 m E of Penrith on A66.
Opening Times: GARDEN ONLY. Easter to end October—Daily 10–6. Adm 80p, Chd 40p. No reduction for parties. No dogs. Wheelchair access to parts of garden only. Small shop. Plant sales.

TROUTBECK

TOWNEND, The National Trust
Telephone: Ambleside (05394) 32628

17th century Lakeland farmhouse with original furnishings including much woodcarving in traditional style. Home of the Browne family for 300 years, and last remaining glimpse into the old farming way of life.
Location: At S end of Troutbeck village, 3 m SE of Ambleside.
Opening Times: Mar 24–Nov 5. Daily (except Mons & Sats but open Bank Hol Mons) 2–6 or dusk if earlier). Last adm 5.30. Adm £1.50, Chd 75p. *No reductions for parties. No dogs. No coaches.* Unsuitable for wheelchairs.

WHITEHAVEN

19/20 IRISH STREET
Telephone: Whitehaven (0946) 3111, Ext 287 ♿
(Copeland Borough Council)

1840-50 Italianate design, possibly by S. Smirke. Stuccoed 3-storey building now occupied by the Council Offices.
Location: In town centre.
Station: Whitehaven.
Opening Times: All the year during office hours. For details & appointments telephone Mr J. A. Pomfret. Ground floor only suitable for disabled.
Refreshments: Hotels and restaurants in town centre.

WHITEHAVEN MUSEUM AND ART GALLERY
  (Copeland Borough Council)
  Civic Hall, Lowther St., Whitehaven CA28 7SH. Tel: (0946) 3111, Ext. 307.
Local History including coal and iron mining, maritime history, archaeology, pottery etc. Programme of temporary exhibitions throughout the year. Open Mon–Fri 9–5; Sat 10–4. *Closed* Sun and Bank Holidays.

WINDERMERE

WINDERMERE STEAMBOAT MUSEUM
  Rayrigg Road. Tel: (096 62) 5565
Unique and Historic collection of Steam and Motor boats including 'Dolly', one of the two oldest working mechanically powered boats in the world, plus displays and many other historic craft. Easter to Oct, inclusive, daily 10–5. Adm charge. Reduction for families and parties.

WORKINGTON

HELENA THOMPSON MUSEUM
  (Allerdale District Council)
  Park End Road. Tel: (0900) 62598
Costumes and applied art; local history collection. Mon to Sat Apr 1–Oct 31: 10.30–4; Nov 1–Mar 31: 11–3.

BRANTWOOD
CONISTON, CUMBRIA

The home of John Ruskin, from 1872-1900. Brantwood is the most beautifully situated house in the Lake District, with the best lake and mountain views in England. The house contains a fine collection of Ruskin drawings and watercolours. There is a delightful nature walk around the Brantwood Estate. Also the Lakeland Guild Craft Gallery, the Wainwright Exhibition (the famous walker and artist), and a well stocked bookshop. Excellent tea room with delicious cakes. Steam yacht 'Gondola' sails regularly to Brantwood from Coniston Pier.

ADMISSION – SEE EDITORIAL REFERENCE

Holker Hall
&
Lakeland Motor Museum

**Cark-in-Cartmel, Grange-over-Sands
Cumbria LA22 7PL**

Easter Sunday to last Sunday in October daily
(ex Saturday)
10.30 am to 6.00 pm. Last admission 4.30 pm.

Holker Hall
Tel. (044 853) 328

Lakeland Motor Museum
Tel. (044 853) 509

Enjoy the peace and tranquillity of Holker Hall. There are no ropes or barriers and visitors are welcome to take as much time as they wish looking at the fine furniture, paintings, and magnificent woodcarving.

The formal and woodland gardens cover 22 acres and contain many unusual species. A herd of Fallow Deer grace the 120 acre Deer Park.

Also
Victorian/Edwardian and Wartime Kitchens Exhibition from the Zanussi Collection
Craft and Countryside Museum – Baby Animal House
Adventure Playground – Gift Shop – Café – Picnic Areas
Equestrian Trials, Model Aircraft, Hot-Air Balloon and Historic Vehicles Rallies during the season in the Park. (Write or call for details.)

Hot-Air Ballooning many Sundays. (Weather permitting.)

NAWORTH CASTLE

Set serenely amid the rugged Border countryside Naworth Castle stands today as a token of permanence in a turbulent world. Within sight of the Scottish border and Hadrian's Wall, battles and skirmishes have taken place around it but Naworth has remained the family home of the Earls of Carlisle and their ancestors for seven centuries. Its supreme glory is the Great Hall, hung with tapestries, with its four heraldic beasts and superb roof and fireplace —still used by the Earl and Countess for present-day entertaining.

Derbyshire

BAKEWELL

CHATSWORTH
Telephone: Baslow (024 688) 2204
(Chatsworth House Trust)

Built by Talman for 1st Duke of Devonshire between 1687 and 1707. Splendid collection of pictures, drawings, books and furniture. Garden with elaborate waterworks surrounded by a great park. CHATSWORTH'S TEMPLE OF FLORA, a botanical exhibition in the Sculpture Gallery. **Regret House impossible for wheelchairs, but they are most welcome in the garden.**
Location: ½ m E of village of Edensor on A623, 4 m E of Bakewell, 16 m from junction 29, M1. Signposted via Chesterfield.
Opening Times: HOUSE & GARDEN. Mar 22 to Oct 29—Daily 11.30–4.30. FARMYARD & ADVENTURE PLAYGROUND. Mar 22 to Oct 1—Daily 10.30–4.30. Adm charges not available at time of going to press. Gift shops. Baby Room. All details subject to confirmation.
Refreshments: Home-made refreshments. Coach Drivers' Rest Room.

HADDON HALL
Telephone: Bakewell 2855
(His Grace the Duke of Rutland)

Fine example of medieval and manorial home containing priceless tapestries, wood carvings and wall paintings. Delightful terraced garden noted for wall and bed roses, and many old fashioned flowers.
Location: 2 m SE Bakewell & 6½ m N of Matlock on Buxton/Matlock Road (A6).
Opening Times: Mar 24 to Oct 1—Tues–Sun, 11–6. *Closed Mons except Bank Hols, also closed Suns in July and Aug except Bank Hol weekends.* Adm £2.60, Chd £1.50; Party rate £2, OAPs £2.
Refreshments: Morning coffee, lunches, afternoon teas at Stables Restaurant.

OLD HOUSE MUSEUM
(Bakewell & District Historical Society)

An early Tudor house with original wattle & daub screen and open chamber. Costumes and Victorian kitchen, children's toys, craftsmen's tools and lacework.
Location: Above the church in Bakewell. ¼ m from centre.
Opening Times: HOUSE ONLY. Mar 24 to Oct 31—Daily 2–5. Parties in morning or evening by appointment (Telephone Bakewell (062 981) 3647. Adm 75p, Chd 35p.

BOLSOVER

BOLSOVER CASTLE
Telephone: (0246) 823349
(English Heritage)

Castle in name only, the present mansion was built during the 17th century by Sir Charles Cavendish and his son William on the site of a 12th century castle. The Little Castle, separate and self-contained, is a delightful romantic folly decorated in Jacobean style.
Location: Bolsover 6 m east of Chesterfield on A632. OS map ref SK471707.
Opening Times: Good Friday to Sept 30, daily 10–6; Oct 1 to Maundy Thurs, daily 10–4. *Closed* Mons, Dec 24–26, Jan 1. Adm £1.30, OAPs £1, Chd 65p.

BUXTON

BUXTON MUSEUM AND ART GALLERY
(Derbyshire Museum Service)
Terrace Road SK17 6DJ. Tel: (0298) 4658.

Local history, archaeology and extensive collections connected with local caves; local fossils, minerals and ornaments of Blue John and Ashford Marble presented in new thematic displays. Exhibition galleries with programme of temporary exhibitions from a variety of local, regional and national sources.

CASTLETON

LOSEHILL HALL
Telephone: Hope Valley (0433) 20373
(Peak National Park Centre)

Victorian Hall with formal garden, parkland and Victorian woodlands. Organises holidays, talks, guided visits to local historic houses and gardens.
Location: ½ m E of Castleton Village on A625 towards Hope. Turn left after leaving Castleton before Losehill Caravan Site.
Station: Hope (2 m).
Opening Times: Holidays on the theme of Great Houses and Gardens for individuals and families, Mar 25–Mar 31, July 29–Aug 5, Aug 5–Aug 12. Visits to Chatsworth, Haddon, Hardwick, Kedleston, etc. Special residential holidays are organised for private parties. Booked parties only, guided day visits of Losehill Hall with talk about Peak National Park. Prices on application.
Refreshments: Teas for booked parties. Full accommodation for holidays.

PEVERIL CASTLE
Telephone: (0433) 20613

The castle was built to control Peak Forest, where lead had been mined since prehistoric times. William the Conqueror thought so highly of this metal—and of the silver that could be extracted from it—that he entrusted the forest to one of his most esteemed knights, William Peveril.
Location: In Castleton on A625, 15 m west of Sheffield. OS map ref SK150827.
Opening Times: Good Friday to Sept 30, daily 10–6; Oct 1 to Maundy Thursday, daily 10–4. *Closed Mons, Christmas and New Year.* Adm 80p, OAPs 60p, Chd 40p.

CHESTERFIELD

HARDWICK HALL, The National Trust
Telephone: Chesterfield (0246) 850430

Built 1591–1597 by "Bess of Hardwick". Notable furniture, needlework, tapestries. Gardens with yew hedges and borders of shrubs and flowers. Extensive collection of herbs. Information Centre in Country Park.
Location: 2 m S of Chesterfield/Mansfield Road (A617) 6½ m NW of Mansfield and 9½ m SE of Chesterfield. Approach from M1 exit 29.
Opening Times: House & Garden. Mar 25 to Sept 17. House—Weds, Thurs, Sats, Suns & Bank Hol Mons 1–5.30 (or sunset if earlier). Last adm to Hall 5 pm. Garden open daily to end Oct, 12–5.30. *Closed Good Friday,* Adm: House & Garden £4, Chd £2; Garden only £1.50, Chd 70p. *No reduction for parties (including schools). School parties must book.* Car park (gates close 6.30). Dogs in park only, on leads. Wheelchairs in garden only. *Enquiries to The National Trust, Hardwick Hall, Doe Lea, nr Chesterfield, Derbys. Access to Hall may be limited at peak periods.*
Refreshments: In the Great Kitchen of Hall 2.30–5. Lunches 12–2 (last orders 15 mins before closing) on days when hall is open.

PEACOCK HERITAGE CENTRE *(Chesterfield Borough Council)*
Low Pavement. Tel: (0246) 207777.
Sixteenth century timber-framed building with first floor room open to the timber frame; fully restored in 1981. Mon to Sat 12–5 for a continuous programme of changing exhibitions and a short sound slide show on 'Chesterfield and Its Setting'.

REVOLUTION HOUSE *(Chesterfield Borough Council)*
Old Whittington. Tel: (0246) 35928.
Originally an inn where three conspirators met to plot the Revolution of 1688. Temporary exhibition of local material, audio-visual presentation available of the events of 1688. Open Jan 4–Oct 29 (1989) daily 10–4; Nov 4–Dec 24 (1989) Sat & Sun only 10–4.

CRICH

THE NATIONAL TRAMWAY MUSEUM
(The Tramway Museum Society)
Crich, near Matlock. Tel: Ambergate 2565.
Unique collection of restored horse, steam and electric trams built 1873–1953. Tram services regularly operated over one mile scenic track. Open weekends and Bank Hols Apr to end of Oct: 10–6.30; also May to Sept: Mon to Thurs 10–5.30, plus Fris in summer holidays (dates subject to confirmation).

CROMFORD

ARKWRIGHT'S MILL
Cromford, near Matlock. Tel: Wirksworth (062 982) 4297.
The world's first successful water powered cotton spinning mill. The Arkwright Society are in the process of restoring the mills. Exhibitions, audio-visual slide display, mill shop. Guides available any time. Adm and times tel. above No.

CROMFORD AND HIGH PEAK RAILWAY (HIGH PEAK TRAIL)
Tel: Wirksworth (062 982) 3204/2831.
Railway Workshops at High Peak Junction, the junction of the railway with the Cromford Canal, approx. 1½ miles from Cromford village, signposted from the Cromford to Crich road. Contains many artefacts of the Cromford and High Peak Railway including a section of original 1825 cast iron fish-bellied rails still in situ, a working forge and hand bellows, tools etc.

DERBY

DERBY INDUSTRIAL MUSEUM
The Silk Mill, off Full Street. Tel: (0332) 293111 ext. 740.
Displays form an introduction to the industrial history of Derby and Derbyshire. They also include a major collection of Rolls-Royce aero engines ranging from an Eagle of 1915 to an RB211 from the first TriStar airliner. The first section of a new railway engineering gallery and the Power for Industry gallery, now open. Open Tues to Fri 10–5, Sat 10–4.45. *Closed* Sun, Mon and Bank Hols. Admission free.

DERBY MUSEUMS & ART GALLERY
The Strand. Tel: (0332) 293111, Ext. 782.
Museum. Archaeology, military and social history, coins and medals, natural history, geology, reconstruction of a Derby public house bar. Special exhibitions. Museum shop. **Art Gallery.** Major works by 18th century painter Joseph Wright of Derby, including examples of his unusual scientific and industrial subjects. The art collection also specialises in works by other local artists and topographical views of Derby and Derbyshire. The Derby porcelain gallery displays an unrivalled collection. Temporary exhibitions. School Service: term-time lessons and holiday activities for children. **Regimental Museum of the 9th/12th Royal Lancers (Prince of Wales's), Derbyshire Yeomanry,** and material of the **Sherwood Foresters.** Tues to Sat 10–5. *Closed* Sun, Mon and Bank Hols. Admission free.

KEDLESTON HALL
Telephone: Derby (0332) 842191

One of the best examples of neo-classical architecture in the country. Robert Adam designed the late 18th century house for Sir Nathaniel Curzon. Fine collection of furniture, tapestries and portraits. Landscaped park includes further examples of Adam's work.
Location: 4 m NW of Derby on Derby/Hulland Road via the Derby Ring Road Queensway.
Opening Times: House, park and garden: Mar 25 to end Oct, Sats to Wed including Bank Holiday Mons. Park: from 11. Gardens and tea room: 12–5. House and Shop: 1–5.30 (last adm 5). £3, Chld £1.50. Coach parties welcome on days when the property is open, but **must** book well in advance in writing to the Administrator. 1989 events – details from Administrator.

PICKFORD'S HOUSE MUSEUM
41 Friar Gate. Tel: (0332) 293111 ext. 402 or 782.
Part of this Georgian town house opens in late 1988 as a social history museum interpreting domestic life at various points over the past two centuries, both above and below stairs. Displays of Georgian and later period rooms, and special collections. Opening times: please telephone. Admission free.

ROYAL CROWN DERBY MUSEUM
Osmaston Road. Tel: (0332) 47051.
The only factory allowed to use the words 'Crown' and 'Royal', a double honour granted by George III and Queen Victoria. The museum, opened by the Duchess of Devonshire in 1969, traces the development of the company from 1748 to the present day. Weekdays 9–12.30, 1.30–4. Factory tours, factory shop.

ELVASTON

ELVASTON CASTLE MUSEUM *(Derbyshire Museum Service)*
The Working Estate, Elvaston Castle Country Park, Borrowash Lane DE7 3EP.
Tel: (0332) 71342.
This unusual museum re-creates the past through displays and demonstrations in and around the original workshops and cottage providing visitors with opportunities to experience and involve themselves in the life and work of the craftsmen, tradesmen, labourers and their families about 1910. The site includes gipsy caravans, agricultural machinery, livestock, corn mill, machines for the preparation of timber, estate craft workshops – wheelwright, blacksmith, farrier, plumber, joiner, saddler and cobbler and an estate cottage with gardens, laundry and a dairy. Apr 1 to Nov 1: Wed to Sat 1–5; Sun and Bank Hols 10–6. School and organised parties by prior arrangement. Adm charge.

ILKESTON

EREWASH MUSEUM *(Erewash Borough Council)*
High Street. Tel: (0602) 440440, Ext. 331.
Eighteenth century town house, set in pleasant gardens, housing local history collections in room settings and galleries. Thur, Fri and Sat 10–4. Adm free.

LEA

LEA GARDENS
(Mr & Mrs Tye)

A rare collection of rhododendrons, azaleas, alpines and conifers in a lovely woodland setting.
Location: 5 m SE of Matlock off A6.
Station: Whatstandwell (2¾ m).
Opening Times: GARDEN ONLY. Mar 20 to July 31—Daily 10–7. Adm: Season ticket £1.50, Chd 50p. *Donation to National Gardens Scheme.* Coaches by appointment only. Plants for sale.
Refreshments: Light lunches, teas, home baking.

MATLOCK

WINSTER MARKET HOUSE, The National Trust
Telephone: Thorpe Cloud (033 529) 245

A stone market house of the late 17th or early 18th century in main street of Winster.
Location: 4 m W of Matlock on S side of B5057.
Opening Times: Afternoons most summer weekends. Adm free. Shop and Information Centre. No dogs. Unsuitable for wheelchairs.

MIDDLETON-BY-WIRKSWORTH

MIDDLETON TOP ENGINE HOUSE *(Derbyshire County Council)*
Tel: Wirksworth (062 982) 3204/2831.
Signposted from the B5036 Cromford to Wirksworth road. Beautifully restored Beam Winding Engine dating from 1830 when the railway was built to link the Cromford Canal with the Peak Forest Canal.

REPTON

REPTON SCHOOL MUSEUM
Tel: (0283) 702249.
By appointment.

SUDBURY

SUDBURY HALL, The National Trust
Telephone: Sudbury (028 378) 305

A 17th century brick built house. Contains plasterwork ceilings. Laguerre murals staircase carved by Pierce and overmantel by Grinling Gibbons. Museum of childhood.
Location: At Sudbury, 6 m E of Uttoxeter off A50 Road.
Opening Times: Mar 25 to end of Oct—Weds to Suns and Bank Holiday Mons 1–5.30 (last adm 5). Adm £2.50, Chd £1.20. Pre-booked parties special rates. Museum small adm charge. Shop. Dogs in grounds only, on lead. Wheelchairs in garden only. 1989 events – details from the Administrator.
Refreshments: Light lunches & teas in Coach House, same open days as property, 12.30–5.30.

TICKNALL

CALKE ABBEY AND PARK, The National Trust
Telephone: Melbourne (033 16) 3822

Calke Abbey was built 1701-1703. Visitor route includes the Caricature room, Saloon, Drawing room and Butler's Pantry. Information Room, carriage and display in Stable Block. Calke Park is a fine landscaped setting (approx. 750 acres). Park accessible via Ticknall entrance only. (One-way system in operation).
Location: 9m S of Derby on A514 at Ticknall between Swadlincote and Melbourne.
Opening Times: Mar 25–end Oct: Sat–Wed including Bank Holiday Mon. *Closed* Good Friday. 1–5.30 (last adm 5). Admission by time of ticket only. Parties **must** book in advance with the Administrator. Adm £3.50, Chd £1.70.

DERBY MUSEUMS and ART GALLERY

A charcoal self-portrait by Joseph Wright of Derby, A.R.A., 1734-97.

Rolls-Royce RB2II aero engine display annexe at Derby Industrial Museum.

Rare experimental piece of Derby porcelain by Andrew Planché, c.1756, modelled as figures and a watchstand.

The Derby Museum and Art Gallery are housed in the city centre between the Strand and the Wardwick. The Art Gallery has the finest collection of paintings and drawings by Joseph Wright of Derby, an extensive topographical collection and an unrivalled collection of Derby Porcelain. The Museum has expanding collections of Derbyshire antiquities, natural history and geology. There is a full programme of special and temporary exhibitions throughout the year. Derby Industrial Museum shows the Rolls-Royce aero engine collection and the development of local industries. Pickford's House Museum is a Georgian town house with social history and period room displays.

Devon

ASHBURTON

ASHBURTON MUSEUM
1 West Street.
Local antiquities, implements, bronze age flints, geology, lace, American Indian antiques. Mid May to end Sept: Tues, Thur, Fri and Sat 2.30–5.

BARNSTAPLE

NORTH DEVON MUSEUMS SERVICE
(North Devon District Council)
Museum of North Devon, The Square, EX32 8LN. Tel: (0271) 46747.
All correspondence to Museums Officer at above address.

THE MUSEUM OF NORTH DEVON
(North Devon District Council)
The Square, EX32 8LN. Tel: (0271) 46747.
Headquarters of North Devon Museums Service. Collections closed to general public until summer 1989 when the former Athenaeum building will re-open as a major new museum displaying and interpreting the natural and human history of North Devon and its environs. The museum will include collections originating from the museum of the Barnstaple Literary and Scientific Institution founded in 1845, the North Devon Athenaeum Museum founded in 1888 and St. Anne's Chapel Museum founded in 1930. In addition the new museum will feature the collections of the Royal Devon Yeomanry formerly displayed in Exeter and a "Victorian Fernery" displaying growing British ferns and their varieties linked to displays on the Victorian fern craze as it affected North Devon. The new museum will be the regional museum for the Natural History, Archaeology, Militaria and Pottery Industry of northern Devon. "A NEW MUSEUM ON OLD FOUNDATIONS". All correspondence to Museums Officer, North Devon Museums Service (see above).

ST. ANNE'S CHAPEL AND OLD GRAMMAR SCHOOL MUSEUM
(North Devon District Council)
St. Peter's Churchyard, High Street.
Tel: (0271) 46747 or (when open) 78709.
St. Anne's Chapel itself is probably 13th century in origin but it was used as Barnstaple Grammar School from the 16th century until 1910 and was used by Huguenot refugees for their Sunday worship from the late seventeenth to mid eighteenth centuries. The museum has recently been completely changed to reflect the history of the building and features a recreation of the school room (with its original unique oak furniture) as it would have been at the end of the seventeenth century when the poet John Gay was a pupil there. The newly cased museum in the crypt describes the history of schooling in North Devon and Britain as a whole. Admission free. Dates of opening under review. All correspondence to Museums Officer, North Devon Museums Service (see above).

WOODSIDE
Telephone: Barnstaple (0271) 43095
(Mr & Mrs Mervyn Feesey)

2 acre plantsman's garden, south sloping, raised beds. Collection of ornamental grasses, bamboos, sedges and other monocots; unusual and rare dwarf shrubs and plants; troughs; variegated and peat-loving shrubs and conifers; New Zealand collection.
Location: N outskirts of Barnstaple; off A39 to Lynton (400 yds. beyond Fire Station).
Station: Barnstaple Junction (1 m).
Opening Times: GARDEN ONLY. Sat May 20, Suns June 18, July 16; 2–6. Adm 75p, Chd 25p. *In aid of National Gardens Scheme.* Other days by appointment.

BICKLEIGH

BICKLEIGH CASTLE
Telephone: Bickleigh (088 45) 363
(Mr & Mrs O. N. Boxall)

Medieval romantic home of the heirs of the Earls of Devon. Great Hall. Armoury Guard Room, Stuart farmhouse, Elizabethan bedroom. 11th century Chapel. Tower Museum and spy & escape gadgets, Exhibition showing Bickleigh Castle's connection with Tudor maritime history and the Mary Rose, also a feature on the "Titanic". Moated Gardens.
Location: 4 m S of Tiverton A396. At Bickleigh Bridge take A3072 and follow signs.
Opening Times: Easter Week (Good Fri to Fri) then Weds, Suns & Bank Hol Mons to Spring Bank Hol; then to early Oct—Daily (except Sats) 2–5. *Parties of 20 or more by prior appointment only (preferably at times other than above) at reduced rates.* Adm £2, Chd half-price (1988 prices). Free coach & car park. Souvenir shops.
Refreshments: Tea in the thatched Barn.

BIDEFORD

BURTON ART GALLERY *(Torridge District Council)*
Victoria Park, Kingsley Road.
Contains the Hubert Coop Collection of paintings and other objects of art. Apr to Oct: Mon to Sat 10–1, 2–5; (also Summer Bank Hols) Sun 2–5; Nov to Mar: Mon–Sat 10–1, 2–4. Full programme of visiting exhibitions.

BRIXHAM

BRITISH FISHERIES MUSEUM
The Old Market House, The Quay. Tel: (080 45) 2861.
Five hundred years of British deep-sea fishing. A National Maritime Museum Outstation run with Torbay Borough Council. Daily Apr to Oct, 9–6; limited winter opening.

BRIXHAM MUSEUM *(The Brixham Museum and History Society)*
Bolton Cross TQ5 8LZ. Tel: (080 45) 6267.
Local and maritime history. Coastguards. Easter to end-Oct: Daily 10–5.30.
Adm 60p, Chld 20p, OAPs 30p. Family, 2 adults and children £1.50. Central car
park 100 yds.

BUDLEIGH SALTERTON

FAIRLYNCH ARTS CENTRE AND MUSEUM *(Trustees)*
27 Fore Street. Tel: Budleigh Salterton 2666.
Early 19th century cottage with thatched roof, adjacent to sea front, on two
floors. Reference library. Emphasis on local material, local history, archaeology
and geology, natural history. Period costume, especially Victorian. Lace. Lace
making demonstrations. Special exhibitions of general interest, summer and at
Christmas. Easter to mid Oct: 2.30–5; mid July to end Aug additionally 10.30–
12.30. *Closed* Sun mornings. 3 weeks from Boxing Day 2.30–4.30. No special
arrangements for Bank Hols. Adm 40p, Chld, OAP, Students 20p. Parties by
arrangement. Car parking on sea front. Suitable for disabled persons on ground
floor only. Curator Mrs P.M. Hull.

OTTERTON MILL CENTRE AND WORKING MUSEUM
Otterton (off the A376 between Newton Poppleford and Budleigh Salterton).
Water mill museum; wholemeal flour production using water power. Gallery
with fine art and craft exhibitions (Easter to Dec). Workshops, restaurant and
bakery, picnic area, shop. Christmas hol activities. Daily: summer 10.30–5.30;
winter 2–5. Adm charge.

CADBURY

FURSDON HOUSE
Telephone: Exeter (0392) 860860
(E D Fursdon, Esq)

Georgian fronted manor house, home of the Fursdon family who have lived
here for over 700 years in unbroken male succession. Regency Library, family
portraits, costumes and mementos. House set in farmland with superb views
across estate. Informal garden undergoing restoration. Primarily a family home.
Location: 9 m N of Exeter, 6 m SW of Tiverton; ¾ m off A3072 Tiverton/
Crediton Road.
Opening Times: Easter – Sat to Mon incl. May to Sept 30: Thurs, Bank Holidays
and the Suns immediately preceding Bank Hol Mon 2–5 each open day. Parties
by arrangement please. Adm House & Grounds £1.90, Chd under 16 £1; under
10, free.
Refreshments: Tea room (open days). Food available at Inns in Bickleigh (2 m)
& Thorverton (2 m).

CHAGFORD

CASTLE DROGO, The National Trust
Telephone: Chagford (064 73) 3306   &

Granite castle designed by Sir Edwin Lutyens, standing at over 900ft overlooking the wooded gorge of the River Teign. Terraced garden and miles of
splendid walks.
Location: 4 m NE of Chagford; 6 m S of A30.
Opening Times: Good Friday to end of Oct—Daily 11–6, 11–5 during Oct (last
adm ½ hour before closing). Adm £2.80; Grounds only £1.30. Chd half-price.
*Reduced rates for parties (£2) on application to the Administrator. Parties who
do not pre-book will be charged at full rate.* No dogs except guide dogs.
Wheelchairs provided. Shop. The restored croquet lawn is open. Equipment for
hire from the Administrator.
Refreshments: Coffee, light lunches (licensed) & teas at the castle 11–½ hour
before closing.

CHUDLEIGH

UGBROOKE HOUSE
Telephone: Chudleigh (0626) 852179

The original house and church were built about 1200 and redesigned by Robert
Adam. The Clifford family live in the house, and the rooms are in constant use.
Ugbrooke contains fine furniture and paintings, beautiful embroideries and
uniforms. The grounds by Capability Brown provide delightful walks and a
pleasant picnic area. Afternoon snacks and teas are served in the Wyvern Cafe
in the original 18th century stable block. Also on display is a fine collection of
maps dating back to the 18th century and a unique collection of Indian
weaponry captured during the Indian mutiny. Items of nostalgia include:
letters and photographs. Lakeside walks.
Location: Chudleigh
Opening Times: May 27 to Aug 28, Sat, Sun and Bank Hols only. GROUNDS –
1–5. Guided tours of House at 2.15 and 3.45. Adm £2.80, Chd (5–16) £1.30,
Groups (over 20) £2.30.
Refreshments: Snacks & afternoon teas at the Wyvern Café, 1.30–5.

COLETON

COLETON FISHACRE GARDEN, The National Trust
Telephone: Kingswear (080 425) 466   &

18 acre garden in a stream-fed valley. Garden created by Lady Dorothy D'Oyly
Carte between 1925 and 1940; planted with wide variety of uncommon trees
and exotic shrubs.

Location: 2 m from Kingswear; take Lower Ferry Road, turn off at tollhouse &
follow 'Garden Open' signs.
Opening Times: Good Friday to end Oct—Weds, Fris & Suns 11–6. Adm £1.50,
Chd half price. Pre-booked parties £1.10. Limited wheelchair access.

DARTMOUTH

DARTMOUTH CASTLE
Telephone: (08043) 3588
(English Heritage)

Boldly guarding the narrow entrance to the Dart Estuary, this castle was among
the first in England to be built for artillery. Construction began in 1481 on the
site of an earlier castle. 1861 Battery with fully equipped guns opening 1989.
Location: 1 m (1.6km) south east of Dartmouth.
Opening Times: Good Friday to Sept 30, daily 10–6; Oct 1 to Maundy Thurs,
daily 10–4. *Closed* Mons, Dec 24–26, Jan 1. Adm £1.10, OAPs 80p, Chd 55p.

DARTMOUTH TOWN MUSEUM *(Dartmouth Town Council)*
The Butterwalk.
Housed in former merchant's house built 1640. Original panelling and ceilings.
Historic and maritime exhibits.

NEWCOMEN ENGINE HOUSE *(Newcomen Society)*
adjacent to The Butterwalk. Tel: (080 43) 2923.
Contains one of Newcomen's original atmospheric pressure/steam engines
circa 1725. May be seen working. Open Easter–Oct 31.

DAWLISH

DAWLISH MUSEUM
Brunswick House, Brunswick Place.

EXETER

THE BRUNEL ATMOSPHERIC RAILWAY
(The Brunel Atmospheric Railway Trust)
Brunel Pumping House, Starcross, Nr. Exeter. Tel: (0626) 890000.
Historic listed building built by I.K. Brunel in 1844. Incorporates demonstration
atmospheric railway and Victorian scientific curiosities. Daily 10–5 Easter to
end Oct. Adm £1.50, Chld 80p. Car parking. Curator Mr R.A. Forrester.

EXETER MARITIME MUSEUM *(International Sailing Craft Assoc.)*
The Haven. Tel: (0392) 58075.
The world's largest collection of the world's boats with over 140 boats, most of
which are on display, afloat, ashore and under cover. Many can be boarded and
explored. Car parking, tea rooms, boat hire.

GUILDHALL *(Exeter City Council)*
High Street.
One of the oldest municipal buildings in the country. Main structure medieval,
tudor frontage and oak door added in 1593. City regalia, silver and historical
portraits. Mon to Sat 10–5.30 (subject to civic functions). Enquiries to Royal
Albert Memorial Museum.

KILLERTON, The National Trust
Telephone: Exeter (0392) 881345   &

Late 18th century house in a beautiful setting containing the Paulise de Bush
Collection of Costume. Lovely throughout the year, with flowers from early
spring, and splendid late autumn colours. 19th century Chapel and Ice House.
Estate exhibition in Stables. Paths lead up the hill to the Dolbury, an isolated
hill with an Iron Age hill fort site.
Location: 7 m NE of Exeter on W side of Exeter Cullompton (B3181—formerly
A38); from M5 s'bound exit 28/B3181; from M5 n'bound exit 29 via Broadclyst
& B3181.
Opening Times: House: Good Friday to end of Oct—Daily 11–6, 11–5 during
Oct (last adm ½ hour before closing). Park: All the year during daylight hours.
Adm. House and Garden £2.80 (tickets available at Stable Block), Chd half-
price; Garden only £1.50. *Reduced rates for parties (£2) on application to the
Administrator. Parties who do not pre-book will be charged at full rate.* The
Conference Room may be booked for meetings, etc. Applications (in writing) to:
The Administrator, Killerton House, Broadclyst, Exeter, Devon. Shop in Stables.
Dogs in Park only. Wheelchairs provided. Motorised buggy for disabled visitors
to tour the garden.
Refreshments: Licensed restaurant at House, entrance from garden—tickets
necessary, available in Stables. Light refreshments and ice cream in Coach
House, home baked bread and pastries for sale and to take away.

QUAY HOUSE INTERPRETATION CENTRE
(Exeter City Council)
The Quay. Tel: (0392) 265213
Exhibition and audio-visual presentation on the history of the quay and the
city. Admission free. Open daily all year.

ROUGEMONT HOUSE MUSEUM OF COSTUME AND LACE
(Exeter City Council)
Castle Street. Tel: (0392) 265858.
New museum of costume in period room settings in fine Georgian House.
Magnificent displays of lace. Admission charge but free on Fri. Open all year
round Mon–Sat 10–5.30; July and Aug: Sun 2–6 & Wed 10–7.30.

ROYAL ALBERT MEMORIAL MUSEUM AND ART GALLERY
(Exeter City Council)
Queen Street. Tel: (0392) 265858.
Important collections of natural history, archaeology, Exeter silver, ethnography, English paintings, ceramics and glass. An active programme of temporary exhibitions. Tues to Sat 10–5.30. Adm free.

ST. NICHOLAS PRIORY *(Exeter City Council)*
The Mint, Fore Street. Tel: (0392) 265858.
Fine Monastic guesthouse, including a Norman crypt, and a 15th century Guest Hall. Tues to Sat 10–1, 2–5.30.

EXMOUTH

A LA RONDE
Telephone: Exmouth (0395) 265514 &
(Mrs Ursula Tudor Perkins)

A unique sixteen sided house designed in 1795 by the Misses Jane and Mary Parminter. Almost unchanged and still owned by the same family, it combines contrived 18th century fashions with total practicability. Parkland. Panoramic views of sea and estuary; Shell Gallery, Gothic grottos.

Location: 2 m N of Exmouth on A376.
Station: Lympstone (1¼ m).
Opening Times: Good Friday–Oct 31: Daily 10–6, Sun 2–7. Coaches – day & evening visits by appointment.
Refreshments: Devon cream teas (in old kitchen). Summer & Winter meals, functions etc. on request.

GREAT TORRINGTON

ROSEMOOR GARDEN
(The Royal Horticultural Society)

Important plantsman's garden of eight acres which has recently been given by Lady Anne Palmer to the RHS and is being enlarged to 40 acres; rhododendrons (species and hybrid), ornamental trees and shrubs, dwarf conifer collection, species and old-fashioned roses, scree and alpine beds, arboretum. Nursery selling rare plants.

Location: 1 m SE of Great Torrington on B3220 to Exeter.
Opening Times: Daily 8–7 or dusk. Nursery open 8–5. Adm £1.50, Chd 50p. Parties of over 20 persons £1.35 each. In aid of National Gardens Scheme on Jun 17 & Jul 23.
Refreshments: Teas Suns, Weds and to order.

HARTLAND

HARTLAND ABBEY
Telephone: Hartland 559
(Sir Hugh Stucley, Bt.)

The Abbey was founded soon after 1157. Much of the house has been rebuilt through various periods. The original cloisters have been used in the basement. There is a Queen Anne wing built in 1705 and further alterations to the front of the house were completed in 1779. Since the dissolution of the monasteries the house has descended to the present day through a series of marriages and has never been sold. It contains a unique collection of documents dating from AD1160 and pictures, furniture and porcelain collected over many generations. Either side of the house are shrub gardens containing mostly rhododendrons, azaleas and camellias. The house is set in an area of outstanding natural beauty.

Location: NW Devon (Hartland Point); 15 m from Bideford; 5 m approx from A39.
Opening Times: May to Sept incl – Weds 2–5.30. Bank Hols (Easter to Summer) Suns & Mons 2–5.30. Adm £2, Chd £1. Parties welcomed £1.75. Ample car parking close to house.
Refreshments: Cream teas provided at house.

HARTLAND QUAY MUSEUM
near Bideford.
A museum devoted to the Hartland coastline displaying four centuries of shipwreck, natural history, geology, Hartland Quay and coastal trades and activities. Easter week then Whitsun to Sept 30: Daily 11–5. Adm 40p, Chld 15p.

HONITON

ALLHALLOWS MUSEUM
High Street (next to St. Paul's Church). Tel: Farway (040 487) 307.
Comprehensive exhibition of Honiton Lace with frequent demonstrations of lace making. Local history. Easter then mid May to end Oct: Weekdays 10–5 *(During Oct 10–4)*. Adm 50p, Chld 20p.

ILFRACOMBE

ILFRACOMBE MUSEUM
Wilder Road (opposite Runnymeade Gardens).
Collections: Natural History, Victoriana, Costume, China, Maritime, Railway, Engravings, Pictures and Brass Rubbing Centre. Open from 10, all year. Adm 40p, Chld 10p, OAPs 20p.

INSTOW

TAPELEY PARK
Telephone: Instow (0271) 860528 &
(H T C Christie Esq.)

A fine historic house, basically William and Mary but with later neo-classic façades by John Belcher. Standing in one of the most beautiful settings in North Devon, with magnificent views over the Taw and Torridge estuary. Italian gardens with many rare plants, lily ponds, woodland walks with lakes, walled kitchen garden, ice house, shell house, peacocks, rare breed sheep, picnic areas.

Location: Between Barnstaple & Bideford on A39; 1 m SW of Instow.
Opening Times: Easter to Oct (Gardens open all year, during daylight hours only) 10–6, daily except Sat. House tours regularly through day provided minimum of 10 adults. Adm Gardens: £1.50, Chd 50p; House: (extra) £1.50, Chd 50p. Reduced rates for coaches.
Refreshments: The Queen Anne Dairy is open all day for light lunch, cream tea & other refreshments.

IVYBRIDGE

FLETE
(Country Houses Association Ltd)

Built around an Elizabethan manor.
Location: 11 m E of Plymouth.
Opening Times: May to Sept – Weds & Thurs, 2–5. Adm £1, Chd 50p. Free car park. No dogs admitted.

KINGSBRIDGE

COOKWORTHY MUSEUM OF RURAL LIFE IN SOUTH DEVON
The Old Grammar School, 108 Fore Street.
Social and economic life in the area in the last 150 years. Includes restored Victorian kitchen, dairy and pharmacy. Costume, old photographs, tools and farm gallery. Programme of craft demonstrations. Easter to Sept 10–5 (except Sun). Oct 10–4.30 (not weekends). Adm charge.

MARLDON

COMPTON CASTLE, The National Trust
Telephone: Kingskerswell (080 47) 2112

Fortified manor house. Great Hall (restored), Solar, Kitchen, Chapel and rose garden.
Location: 1 m N of Marldon off A381.
Opening Times: Easter Mon to end of Oct – Mons, Weds & Thurs 10–12.15, 2–5 (last adm 30 mins before closing). Adm £1.50, Chd half-price. Parties £1.20 – *organisers should please notify the Secretary*. No dogs except guide dogs. Additional parking and refreshments at Castle Barton, opposite entrance.

MARWOOD

MARWOOD HILL
(Dr J A Smart)

Extensive collection of camellias under glass and in the open, daffodils, rhododendrons, rare flowering shrubs: rock and alpine garden, rose garden, waterside planting. Bog garden. 18 acre garden with 3 small lakes. Australian native plants. Many clematis.

Location: 4 m N of Barnstaple; opposite church in Marwood.
Opening Times: GARDENS ONLY. All the year – Daily (except Christmas Day) dawn to dusk. Adm £1, Chd 10p. *In aid of National Gardens Scheme*. Plants for sale. Dogs allowed, on leads only.
Refreshments: Teas. Apr to Sept, Suns & Bank Hols, or by prior arrangement for parties.

MORWELLHAM QUAY

MORWELLHAM QUAY OPEN AIR MUSEUM
(Morwellham Recreation Company)
off A390 between Tavistock and Gunnislake. Tel: Tavistock (0822) 832766.
Information only: 833808.
Once 'the greatest copper port in Queen Victoria's empire'. Meet the Blacksmith and Cooper, Assayer and Servant Girls, Quay workers and Coachmen dressed in period costume to re-create the bustling boom years in this picturesque old port. Ride underground into a copper mine and enjoy a heavy horsedrawn wagonette ride along the Duke of Bedford's carriageway. Unspoilt country, riverside and woodland trails, slide shows and other exhibits will help in discovering a thousand years of history. Open daily (except Christmas week) summer: 10–5.30 (last adm 4); winter: 10–4 (last adm 2.30) All inclusive adm charge.

NEWTON ABBOT

BRADLEY MANOR, The National Trust
Small, roughcast 15th century manor house with perpendicular chapel, set in woodland and meadows.

Location: W end of town, 7½ m NW of Torquay opp Old Totnes Road Junction. On W side of A381.
Station: Newton Abbot (1½ m).
Opening Times: Apr 1 to end of Sept—Weds 2–5; also Thurs, Apr 6 & 13, Sept 21 & 28. Adm £1.50, Chd half-price. *No reduction for parties.* Parties of 15 or more must book in writing. No indoor photography. No access for coaches—Lodge gates too narrow. No dogs. Unsuitable for disabled or visually handicapped.

OKEHAMPTON

OKEHAMPTON CASTLE
Telephone: (0837) 2844

Rebellion broke out in the south west after the Battle of Hastings and a stronghold was built here to subdue it. The castle passed from Baldwin FitzGilbert to Robert de Courtenay in 1172 and remained with this family, off and on, for 3½ centuries. The last Courtenay to own it, the Marquis of Exeter, was beheaded in 1538 and the castle dismantled.
Location: 1 m (1.6 km) south west of Okehampton. OS map ref SX584942.
Opening Times: Good Friday to Sept 30, daily 10–6; Oct 1 to Maundy Thursday, daily 10–4. *Closed Mons, Christmas and New Year.* Adm 80p, OAPs 60p, Chd 40p.

OKEHAMPTON & DISTRICT MUSEUM OF DARTMOOR LIFE
3 West Street. Tel: (0837) 3020.
Set in old mill with waterwheel. Displays cover geology, prehistory, later history, living conditions, industries, crafts, farming etc. Courtyard features craft and gift shops, tourist information centre and tea rooms. Open all year Mon–Sat, 0–5 (*closed* for Christmas). Adm 50p, OAPs 40p, Chld 30p. Reduction of 10p per person for group bookings. Free car park.

OTTERY ST. MARY

CADHAY
Telephone: Ottery St Mary 2432
(Lady William-Powlett)

Cadhay is approached by an avenue of lime-trees, and stands in a pleasant listed garden, with herbaceous borders and yew hedges, with excellent views over the original mediaeval fish ponds. Cadhay is first mentioned in the reign of Edward I, and was held by a de Cadehaye. The main part of the house was built about 1550 by John Haydon who had married the de Cadhay heiress. He retained the Great Hall of an earlier house, of which the fine timber roof (about 1420) can be seen. An Elizabethan Long Gallery was added by John's successor at the end of the 16th century, thereby forming a unique and lovely courtyard. Some Georgian alterations were made in the mid 18th century. The house is viewed by conducted tour. Photography is permitted outside.
Location: 1 m NW of Ottery St Mary on B3176.
Station: Feniton (2½ m) (not Suns).
Opening Times: Spring (May 28 & 29) & Summer (Aug 27 & 28) Bank Hol Suns & Mons; also Tues, Weds & Thurs in July & Aug: 2–6 (last adm 5.30). Adm £2, Chd 50p. *Parties by arrangement.*

FERNWOOD
(Mr & Mrs H Hollinrake)

2 acre woodland garden; wide selection of flowering shrubs, conifers and bulbs giving colour over a long period; species and hybrid rhododendrons and azaleas.
Location: 1½ m W of Ottery St Mary; ¼ m down Toadpit lane (off B3174).
Opening Times: GARDEN ONLY. Apr 1 to Sept 30—Daily, all day. *In aid of National Gardens Scheme.* No dogs. Adm 50p, accompanied chd free.

PAIGNTON

KIRKHAM HOUSE
Telephone: (0803) 522775
(English Heritage)

This well-preserved house near the church is an interesting example of 15th century architecture. It was probably the home of a prosperous merchant. Display of modern furniture.
Location: Kirkham Street, Paignton.
Opening Times: Good Friday to Sept 30, daily 10–6. Adm 80p, OAPs 60p, Chd 40p.

TORBAY AIRCRAFT MUSEUM
(Mr Keith Fordyce)
Higher Blagdon TQ3 3YG. Tel: (0803) 553540.
Four attractions all on one site.

PILTON

THE BULL HOUSE
(Mr M.L. Corney)

Text book example of small late mediaeval mansion almost unaltered. Former Prior's House and Guest Lodging of Pilton Priory. Great hall, solar, parlour, guest chambers etc. with moulded oak roofs, ceilings, panelling and stone arches.
Location: ½ m N of Barnstaple, off A39, beside Pilton churchyard.
Opening Times: Apr to Oct by appointment. Adm £1.25 adults only.

PLYMOUTH

CITY MUSEUM AND ART GALLERY
(Plymouth City Council)
Drake Circus. Tel: (0752) 264878.
Collections of paintings, silver, Plymouth and other porcelain. Cottonian collection of Old Master drawings, Reynolds' family portraits and early printed books. Local and natural history collections. Mon to Fri 10–5.30; Sat 10–5. Adm free.

ELIZABETHAN HOUSE *(Plymouth City Council)*
32 New Street.
A 16th century house in Plymouth's historic quarter furnished according to period. Mon to Fri 10–5.30; Sat 10–5. *Closed* 1–2.15. (*Closes* 4.30 in winter); Sun (summer only) 3–5. Details of adm charge from City Museum & Art Gallery.

HEMERDON HOUSE
Telephone: Plymouth (0752) 223816 (Office hours);
337350 (weekend & evenings)
(J H G Woollcombe, Esq)

Regency house containing West country paintings and prints, with appropriate furniture and a Library.
Location: 2 m from Plympton.
Opening Times: May – 22 days including Bank Holidays and Aug – 8 days including Bank Holiday 2–5.30. For opening dates please contact the Administrator. Adm £1.50.

MERCHANT'S HOUSE *(Plymouth City Council)*
33 St. Andrew's Street.
A town house with 16th and early 17th century features, containing a museum of Plymouth social history. Mon to Fri 10–5.30; Sat 10–5. *Closed* 1–2; Sun (Easter to 30 Sept) 3–5. Details of adm charges from City Museum and Art Gallery.

SALTRAM HOUSE, The National Trust
Telephone: Plymouth (0752) 336546

A George II house, built around and incorporating remnants of a late Tudor mansion, in a landscaped park. Two exceptional rooms by Robert Adam. Furniture, pictures, fine plasterwork and woodwork. Great Kitchen. Beautiful garden with Orangery. Octagonal summer-house, rare shrubs and trees. Shop in stables.
Location: 2 m W of Plympton 3½ m E of Plymouth city centre, between A38 & A379 main roads.
Opening Times: Nov to end of Mar. Garden open daily 11–6. Good Friday to end Oct. House: Suns–Thurs, Good Friday and Bank Hol, Sats 12.30–6, 12.30–5 during Oct; Kitchen, Shop & Art Gallery 11–6, 11–5 during Oct; Garden 11–6 (open daily). Last adm ½ hour before closing. Adm £3.20, Chd half-price; Garden only £1.20. *Reductions for parties (£2.40) at certain times of day by prior arrangement for visits/meals with the Administrator.* The Chapel may be booked for meetings, etc. Applications (in writing) to: The Administrator, Saltram House, Plympton, Plymouth. Dogs in grounds only. Wheelchairs provided.
Refreshments: Licensed restaurant in House (entrance from Garden); Suns–Thurs & Bank Hols 11–6, 11–5 during Oct (last adm ½ hour before closing). Light refreshments at Coach House near car park during peak periods.

ROBOROUGH

BICKHAM HOUSE
(The Lord Roborough)

Shrub garden; camellias, rhododendrons, azaleas, cherries, bulbs, trees. Lovely views.
Location: 8 m N of Plymouth on Roborough Down turn for Maristow.
Opening Times: GARDEN ONLY: Suns Mar 26–June 4 incl, and Sun June 18, Mons Mar 27, May 1, 29, 2–6. Adm 50p. *In aid of National Gardens Scheme. No dogs.*
Refreshments: Home-made teas, parties catered for by appointment up to the end of June.

SALCOMBE

OVERBECKS MUSEUM & GARDEN, The National Trust
Telephone: Salcombe (054 884) 2893

6 acres of garden with rare and tender plants and beautiful views eastwards over Salcombe Bay. Part of house forms museum of local interest and of particular interest to children.
Location: 1½ m SW of Salcombe signposted from Malborough & Salcombe.
Opening Times: Gardens. All the year—Daily 10–8, or sunset if earlier. Museum: Good Friday to Oct 31—Daily 11–5. Last adm ½ hour before closing. Adm Museum & Garden £1.70, Chd half-price. Garden only £1.30. *No reduction for parties.* Dogs allowed in gardens & conservatory only on leads, not in Museum. Shop. Picnicking allowed in gardens. Not suitable for coaches.

SHIRWELL

ARLINGTON COURT, The National Trust
Telephone: Shirwell (027 182) 296   &

Regency house furnished with the collections of the late Miss Rosalie Chichester; including shells, pewter and model ships. Display of horse-drawn vehicles in the stables. Good trees. Victorian formal garden.

Location: 8 m NE of Barnstaple on E side of A39.
Opening Times: Nov to Mar 24: Garden & park open daily during daylight hours. House, Carriage Collection, Stables, Shop: Good Friday to end of Oct— Daily (except Sats but open Sats of Bank Hol Weekends) 11–6, 11–5 during Oct. (Last adm ½ hour before closing.) Garden & Park: Good Friday to Oct—Daily 11–6. Open Good Friday. Adm: House & Carriage Collection £3, Chd £1.50. Gardens, Ground & Stables £1.60, Chd half-price. *Reduced fee of £2.30 for parties of 15 or more on application to the Administrator. Parties who do not pre-book will be charged full rate.* Shop. Dogs in grounds only, on leads. Wheelchairs provided. Carriage rides.
Refreshments: Licensed restaurant at the House: Mar 24 to end of Oct—days and times as for House.

SIDBURY

SAND
(Lt Col P V Huyshe)

Lived in Manor house owned by Huyshe family since 1560, rebuilt 1592–4, situated in unspoilt valley. Screens passage, panelling, family documents, heraldry. Also **Sand Lodge** roof structure of late 15th century Hall House.

Location: ¾ m NE of Sidbury; 400 yds from A375, Grid ref 146925.
Opening Times: Suns & Mons—Mar 26, 27; May 28, 29, July 30, 31, Aug 27, 28 2–5.30. Last tour 4.45. Adm £1.50, Chd & Students 20p. Sand Lodge and outside of Sand by written appointment, £1.
Refreshments: Light teas in house, cream teas in Sidbury (free car parking).

SIDMOUTH

THE VINTAGE TOY AND TRAIN MUSEUM
First Floor, Field's Dept. Store, Market Place. Tel: (039 55) 5124 Ext. 34.
Fifty years of tinplate and die-cast toys and trains 1925–1975. Museum shop. Easter to end Oct: Daily 10–5 (except Sun and Bank Hols). **Member AIM**.

SOUTH MOLTON

SOUTH MOLTON MUSEUM *(South Molton Town Council)*
Town Hall.
Local trades, agricultural implements, fire engines, pewter collection. Mar to Nov: Tues, Thurs, Fri 10.30–1, 2–4; Wed and Sat 10.30–12.30. *Closed* Sun, Public Hols and Mons. Adm free.

STARCROSS

POWDERHAM CASTLE
(The Earl and Countess of Devon)

Medieval castle built c 1390 by Sir Philip Courtenay, ancestor of the present Earl of Devon. Damaged in the Civil War and restored and altered in 18th and 19th centuries. Music Room by Wyatt. Park stocked with deer. A family home.

Location: 8 m SW of Exeter off A379 to Dawlish.
Station: Starcross 1½ m.
Opening Times: May 28–Sept 14—Suns–Thurs 2–5.30 (last adm 5). Closed Fris & Sats. Extended tour: Tues, Wed, Thurs. For information please contact: The Administrator Tel. Starcross (0626) 890 243. Teas, souvenirs. Good free parking. Dogs admitted to shaded car park only.

TIVERTON

KNIGHTSHAYES COURT, The National Trust
Telephone: Tiverton (0884) 254665   &

One of the finest gardens in Devon with specimen trees, rare shrubs, spring bulbs, summer flowering borders; of interest at all seasons. House by William Burges, begun in 1869, decorated by J D Crace.

Location: 2 m N of Tiverton; turn off A396 (Bampton/Tiverton Road) at Bolham.
Opening Times: Good Friday to end of Oct—Garden daily 11–6, 11–5 during Oct. House – daily except Fri (but open Good Friday) 1.30–6, 1.30–5 during Oct (last adm ½ hour before closing). *Nov and Dec: Sun 2–4; pre-arranged parties only.* Adm £2.90, Chd £1.45. Garden & Grounds only £1.70. *Reduced rates for parties (£2.20) on application to the Administrator. Parties who do not pre-book will be charged at full rate.* Shop. Plants available at garden shop. Dogs in park only on leads. Wheelchairs provided.
Refreshments: Licensed restaurant for coffee, lunches and teas 11–½ hour before closing, daily. Picnic area in car park.

TIVERTON CASTLE
Telephone: (0884) 253200 or 01-727 4854
(Mr and Mrs A.K. Gordon)

Originally a Royal Castle built in 1106, then a Tudor palace and Civil War fortress, now enclosing a private house. Important Civil War Armoury. Medieval gatehouse and towers. Entrances to secret passageways extending throughout the town. Romantic ruins of towers, walls and chapel. Famous Victorian murder mystery exhibit. New World Tapestry. Fine furniture and pictures.

Location: Next to St. Peter's Church. The Castle is well signposted in Tiverton.
Opening Times: Good Friday to last Sun in Sept—Suns to Thurs 2.30–5.30. Adm £1.80, Chd under 7 free, 7–16 £1. OAPs and students £1.25. Party bookings at special rates. Free parking inside. Coach parties by appointment only.
Refreshments: Devon cream teas during Summer. Light lunches, evening parties by appointment.

THE TIVERTON MUSEUM
St. Andrew Street. Tel: (0884) 256295.
Award-winning ('Museum of the Year 1977') large local museum. Railway Gallery and Lace Machine Gallery. Weekdays 10.30–4.30. *Closed* Sun and Dec 22 to Jan 29.

TOPSHAM

TOPSHAM MUSEUM
25 The Strand, Topsham.
History of the port and trade of Topsham including 19th century shipbuilding.

TORQUAY

TORQUAY MUSUEM
Babbacombe Road. Tel: (0803) 23975.
Impressive natural history gallery; important finds from Kents Cavern and elsewhere; archaeology of South Devon; overseas ethnography; Devon folk life; new gallery devoted to Victoriana. Weekdays 10–4.45 (Sat; Easter to Sept and Sun mid-July to mid-Sept). *Closed* Good Friday. Adm charge.

TORRE ABBEY
Telephone: Torquay (0803) 23593
(Torbay Borough Council)

12th century monastery converted into a private residence after the Dissolution in 1539. Extensively remodelled in the early 18th century and currently undergoing complete renovation and restoration. Contains furnished period rooms, family chapel, extensive collection of paintings and other works of art, and the Dame Agatha Christie memorial room, containing many mementos of the Torquay born authoress. Over 20 rooms now open to the public including those in the newly restored South-West wing. Ruins of medieval Abbey also on show, including the remains of the Abbey Church, excavated in 1987/8. Formal gardens containing tropical palm house, summer bedding, rockeries and spring bulbs.

Location: On Torquay Sea front.
Station: Torquay (¼ m).
Opening Times: HOUSE: Apr to Oct—Daily 10–5 (last adm 4.30). Other times by appointment. Adm (1988 rates) 75p, OAPs 40p, Chd Free (if accompanied). GARDENS: All the year—Daily. Adm free.

TOTNES

BOWDEN HOUSE
Telephone: Totnes (0803) 863664
(Mr & Mrs C V Petersen)

Dating back to the 9th century Bowden became the residence of the De Broase family, builders of 13th century Totnes Castle. Parts of the house date from this period. An Elizabethan mansion was created in 1510 with a Queen Anne facade added in 1704. The Grand Hall is decorated in Neo-classical Baroque style.

Location: 1 m from centre of Totnes, follow Historic House signs.
Station: Totnes (1 m).
Opening Times: Open from first Tues in Apr to last Thurs in Oct, Tues, Weds and Thurs, plus Suns and Mons during July and Aug, and Bank Holidays. Grounds, cafe, Photographic Museum open 12 noon. House: guided tours from 2 (1.30 in high season). Last tour 4.30. **Tours given in Georgian costume**. Adm £2, reduction for chd. Photographic Museum £1 extra. Reductions for chd.
Refreshments: Licensed café, cream teas, ploughmans lunches served by wenches (open 12–5). **Picnic and play area**.

DEVONSHIRE COLLECTION OF PERIOD COSTUME
Bogan House, 43 High Street.
Exhibitions from the Collection, changed annually, on show in historic house. Spring Bank Hol to Oct 1: Mon to Fri 11–5, Sun 2–5. Adm charge.

MOTOR MUSEUM
Steamer Quay TQ9 5AL. Tel: (0803) 862777.
Vintage, sports, racing cars, motorbikes, engines and model cars displayed on 2 floors. Easter to Oct, daily 10–5.

TOTNES CASTLE
Telephone: (0803) 864406

The Normans also built a stronghold here to overawe the townspeople. But they surrendered without a blow, as they did again in the Civil War. The remains date largely from the 14th century, although the huge earth mound on which the castle rests is Norman.

Location: Totnes. OS map ref SX800605.
Opening Times: Good Friday to Sept 30, daily 10–6; Oct 1 to Maundy Thursday, daily 10–4. *Closed Mons, Christmas and New Year.* Adm 80p, OAPs 60p, Chd 40p.

TOTNES (ELIZABETHAN) MUSEUM *(Joint Committee)*
  70 Fore Street. Tel: (0803) 863821.
Period furniture and costumes; local tools, toys, domestic articles and archaeological exhibits. C. Babbage room – memorabilia and exhibition. Victorian
grocers shop – local reference library.

**BUCKLAND ABBEY, Jointly managed by The National
Trust, and Plymouth City Council**
Telephone: Yelverton (082 285) 3607

13th century Cistercian monastery bought by Sir Richard Grenville in 1541,
altered by his grandson Sir Richard Grenville, of the 'Revenge', in 1576. Home
of Drake from 1581 and still contains many relics of the great seaman, including
Drake's drum. Exhibition to illustrate the Abbey's history. Restored buildings,
including the monk's guesthouse and 18th century farm buildings. Great Barn.

Location: 11 m N of Plymouth 6 m S of Tavistock between the Tavistock/
Plymouth Road (A386) & River Tavy.

Opening Times: Good Friday to end Oct: daily 11–6, 11–5 during Oct. Last
admissions ½ hour before closing time. Nov to Mar 1990: Weds, Sats and Suns
2–5. Adm £2.80. Chd half price. Reduced rate for parties (£2); school parties
£1.20 on application to the Administrator. Parties who do not pre-book will be
charged at full rate. Dogs in grounds only on leads. Shop.

Refreshments: Licensed Restaurant serving home-made lunches and teas as
well as warming coffee. Good Friday to end Oct; 11 to ½ hour before closing;
Nov–Mar 1990 11–5.

THE GARDEN HOUSE
Telephone: Yelverton 854769
(The Fortescue Charitable Trust)

8 acre garden of interest throughout the year and including a 2 acre walled
garden that is one of the finest in the country. Fine collections of herbaceous
and woody plants.

Location: 5 m S of Tavistock; from Yelverton on A386 turn W; 10 m S
Plymouth.

Opening Times: GARDENS ONLY. Apr 1 to Sept 30—Daily 12–5. Adm £1, Chd
50p. *In aid of National Gardens' Scheme.* No dogs. Coaches & parties by
appointment. Car park. Unusual plants for sale.

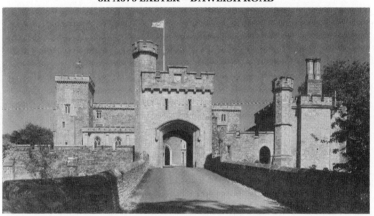

ROUGEMONT HOUSE

Museum of Costume and Lace

CASTLE STREET, EXETER.

for further details phone (0392) 265858

Dorset

ABBOTSBURY

**ABBOTSBURY–SWANNERY
& SUB-TROPICAL GARDENS**
Telephone: Abbotsbury (030 587) 387
(Strangways Estates)

Owned by the Strangways family since 1541 it received a Conservation award in 1975. The Swannery—unique colony of mute swans; 17th century duck decoy; reed bed walk. Sub-Tropical Gardens—20 acres of woodland and walled gardens containing tender and exotic plants growing outdoors. Peacocks.
Location: On B3157 Weymouth/Bridport Road; may be approached from A35 at Winterbourne Abbas.
Opening Times: The Swannery mid May to mid Sept 9.30–4.30. The Gardens mid Mar to mid Sept 10–6.
Refreshments: Tea garden at sub-tropical gardens.

BEAMINSTER

MAPPERTON
Telephone: (0308) 862645
(Mr J. Montagu)

Terraced and hillside gardens with daffodils, formal borders and specimen shrubs and trees. Modern orangery in classical style, 17th century stone fish ponds and summer house. Tudor manor house, enlarged under Charles II. Magnificent views.
Location: 1 m off B3163, 2 m off B3066.
Opening Times: Mar 15–Oct 31, Sun–Fri 2–6. Adm £1.20, under 18 and OAPs 60p, under 5 free. House also open to group tours by appointment, prices as for gardens.

PARNHAM
Telephone: Beaminster (0308) 862204
(Mr & Mrs John Makepeace)

An Elizabethan manor, restored by Nash and surrounded by gardens landscaped by Inigo Thomas, extensively replanted over recent years by Jennie Makepeace. In the workshop, furniture designed by John Makepeace is made for public and private collections.
Location: On A3066, 1 m S of Beaminster; 5 m N of Bridport.
Opening Times: Good Friday Mar 24 to Sun Oct 29—Weds, Suns & Bank Hols 10–5. Group visits on these and other days by prior arrangement only. Adm Principal rooms, gardens, workshops, car parks, picnic areas: £2.50, Chd (10–15) £1.20; under 10, free.
Refreshments: Light lunches, teas etc in licensed 17th century buttery.

BLANDFORD

BLANDFORD FORUM MUSEUM
Old Coach House, Bere's Yard, Market Place.

BOURNEMOUTH

BOURNEMOUTH NATURAL SCIENCE SOCIETY'S MUSEUM
39 Christchurch Road. Tel: (0202) 23525.
History, archaeology, botany, geology, physics, chemistry, zoology, geography and astronomy. Open by arrangement.

CASA MAGNI SHELLEY MUSEUM
(Bournemouth Borough Council)
Boscombe Manor, Shelley Park, Beechwood Avenue, Boscombe.
Tel: (0202) 21009.
The Museum, which includes a Reference Library on the Romantic Period, occupies two rooms on the ground floor. June to Sept: Mon to Sat 10.30–5. Thur, Fri and Sat rest of year. All enquiries to the Russell-Cotes Art Gallery and Museum.

MOBILE MUSEUM *(The Russell-Cotes Art Gallery and Museum)*
Tel: (0202) 21009.
An ex-Bournemouth Corporation Transport double-deck bus has been converted by the Transport Department into a mobile museum with the aid of a grant from the Area Museum Council for the South-West. It entered service on June 23, 1977. A second mobile museum has been converted from an ex-Bournemouth Corporation Transport single-deck bus. Tel. or write to the Curator, Russell-Cotes Art Gallery and Museum for details of current exhibition, location and opening times. Adm free.

RUSSELL-COTES ART GALLERY AND MUSEUM
(A Registered Charity governed by Bournemouth Borough Council)
East Cliff. Tel: (0202) 21009.
Designed in 1894 by Fogerty as a villa for Sir Merton Russell-Cotes, the interior is decorated in the Italian manner. Seventeenth to 20th century oil paintings, tempera, watercolours, sculpture, miniatures, ceramics, Japanese, Chinese, Burmese, theatrical (Irving). Lucas collection of early Italian paintings and pottery, English porcelain, 17th century furniture, Victorian bygones and pictures, ethnography, arms and armour, ship models, shells and pictures, local and exotic butterflies and moths. Collection of 'Pictures You May Borrow' available to resident and non-resident subscribers. Geological terrace. Mon to Sat 10–5. Adm 50p, Chld 10p (under 5 free).

TRANSPORT AND RURAL MUSEUM
(Bournemouth Borough Council and Bournemouth Passenger Transport Association)
Tel: (0202) 21009.
This new Museum will not be completely open for some time but on Wed during June, July, Aug and Sept tram-cars, trolley-buses and diesel buses will be on exhibition at Mallard Road Depot, 10.30–3.30. Visitors must first report to the Mobile Museum which will be parked at the entrance to the Depot. Adm 50p, Chld 10p (under 5 free). Tel. or write to the Curator, Russell-Cotes Art Gallery and Museum for details.

BRIDPORT

BRIDPORT MUSEUM & ART GALLERY
(West Dorset District Council)
South Street. Tel: (0308) 22116.
Items connected with the town's historic rope and net making trade and rural bygones. Extensive collection of dolls from all over the world. Open weekday mornings throughout the year and on Mon, Tues, Wed and Fri afternoons from June 1 to Sept 30.

CERNE ABBAS

MINTERNE
Telephone: Cerne Abbas (03003) 370
(The Lord Digby)

Important rhododendron and shrub garden, many fine and rare trees, landscaped in the 18th century with lakes, cascades and streams.
Location: On A352 2 m N of Cerne Abbas; 10 m N of Dorchester, 9 m S of Sherborne.
Opening Times: Apr 1 to Oct 31—Daily 10–7. Adm £1, accom chd free. Free car park.

CHETNOLE

MELBURY HOUSE
(The Lady Teresa Agnew)

Large garden; very fine arboretum; shrubs and lakeside walk; beautiful deer park.
Location: 13 m N of Dorchester.
Station: Chetnole (2 m).
Opening Times: GARDEN ONLY. Thurs June 15 & 22; July 6 & 20, Aug 31, Sept 7 (for St John's Ambulance). Adm will be charged. Teas and plants available. *In aid of the National Gardens Scheme and the MacMillan Trust.*

CHETTLE

CHETTLE HOUSE
Telephone: Chettle (0258 89) 209
(J. P. C. Bourke)

One of the finest examples of a Queen Anne House in the English Baroque style by Thomas Archer. Set in 5 acres of garden with many unusual herbaceous plants and shrubs. Fine Art Gallery and vineyard.
Location: 6 m NE of Blandford on A354 & 1 mile W.
Opening Times: Adm £1. Car and Coach park. Wheelchairs garden only. Apr–Oct daily (except Tues) 10.30–5.30. Plant Centre specialising in unusual herbaceous plants. No dogs.
Refreshments: Many pubs within 2 miles. Picnic area available, teas weekends.

CHRISTCHURCH

CHRISTCHURCH TRICYCLE MUSEUM
Quay Road. Tel: (04252) 3240.
World's first museum devoted to multi-wheeled cycles. Approx. 40 exhibits. Easter to Oct. Adm 75p, Chld 40p, Family, OAP and group reductions.

RED HOUSE MUSEUM, ART GALLERY AND GARDENS
(Hampshire County Museum Service)
Quay Road. Tel: (0202) 482860.
Regional museum for natural history and antiquities; also 19th century fashion plates, costume, dolls and objects of social and domestic life. Temporary exhibitions in the art gallery. New costume gallery. In fine Georgian house with herb and other gardens. Tues to Sat 10–5; Sun 2–5. *Closed* Mon. Adm 50p, Chld/OAPs 30p. Curator: Alison J. Carter, BA, MA, AMA.

CORFE CASTLE

CORFE CASTLE, The National Trust
Telephone: Corfe Castle 480921

Ruins of former royal castle, sieged and 'slighted' by Parliamentary forces in 1646.
Location: In the village of Corfe Castle: on A351 Wareham-Swanage road.
Opening Times: Feb 11 to Nov 5: every day 10–4.30 pm or sunset if earlier. Nov 5 to Feb 10; Sat and Sun (weather permitting) 12–4 pm (or sunset if earlier). Adm: Adults £1.60, Chd 80p, parties (15 or more) £1.20. Not suitable for wheelchairs. N.T. Shop and refreshments.

CRANBORNE

CRANBORNE MANOR GARDENS
Telephone: Cranborne 248
(The Viscount and Viscountess Cranborne)

Walled gardens, yew hedges and lawns; wild garden with spring bulbs, herb garden, Jacobean mount garden, flowering cherries and collection of old-fashioned and specie roses. Gardens originally laid out by John Tradescant.
Location: 18 m N of Bournemouth, B3078; 16 m S of Salisbury, A354, B3081.
Opening Times: GARDENS ONLY. Apr to Sept—Weds 9–5. Free car park. GARDEN CENTRE open Tues–Sats 9–5, Suns 2–5 (not Jan & Feb). *Closed* Mons except Bank Holidays. Something for every gardener, but specialising in old-fashioned and specie roses, herbs, ornamental pots and Italian statuary and garden furniture.

EDMONDSHAM HOUSE AND GARDENS
Telephone: Cranborne (072 54) 207
(Mrs J. E. Smith)

A family home since the 16th century, and a fine blend of Tudor and Georgian architecture, with a Victorian stable block and dairy, interesting furniture, lace and other exhibits. The Gardens include an old-fashioned walled garden, cultivated organically, with an excellent display of spring bulbs, shrubs, lawns and herbaceous border.
Location: Between Cranborne and Verwood, off the B3081.
Opening Times: HOUSE AND GARDENS: Easter Sun 2.30–5. Bank Holiday Mon and Wed in Apr 2.30–5. Parties and individuals by arrangement at other times. Adm £1.20, Chd 60p. GARDENS: Apr, May, June and Oct: Wed–Sat incl. 10–12, and at other times when the owner is at home. Adm 60p, Chd 30p.

DORCHESTER

THE DINOSAUR MUSEUM *(Archosaur Society)*
Icen Way.
The only dinosaur museum in Britain.

DORSET COUNTY MUSEUM
(Dorset Natural History and Archaeological Society)
Tel: (0305) 62735.
A Regional Museum whose collections cover Dorset geology, natural history, prehistory, bygones and history with Thomas Hardy Memorial room. Temporary exhibitions each month. Mon to Sat 10–5. *Closed* Christmas Day, Boxing Day and Good Friday. Adm £1, Chld (5–16 years) and OAP, 50p.

DORSET MILITARY MUSEUM
The Keep, Dorchester. Tel: (0305) 64066.
Exhibits of Dorset Regiment, Dorset Militia and Volunteers, Queen's Own Dorset Yeomanry and Devonshire and Dorset Regiment. Mon to Fri 9–1, 2–5; Sat 10–1 (July to Sep 9–1, 2–5). Adm 50p, Chld 25p. Parties by appointment. Free car park.

WOLFETON HOUSE
Telephone: (0305) 63500
(Capt. N. T. L. Thimbleby)

Outstanding medieval and Elizabethan manor house with magnificent wood and stone work, fireplaces and ceilings; Great Hall and stairs; parlour, dining room, Chapel and Cider House.
Location: 1½ m from Dorchester on Yeovil road (A37); indicated by Historic House signs.
Stations: Dorchester South and West 1¾ m.
Opening Times: May to Sept—Tues, Fris and Bank Hol Mons 2–6. At other times throughout the year, parties by arrangement. Adm charges not available at time of going to press.
Refreshments: Ploughman's lunches, teas and evening meals for parties, by prior arrangement. Cider for sale.

FORDE ABBEY

FORDE ABBEY AND GARDENS
Telephone: (0460) 20231
(Trustees of Forde Abbey)

Cromwellian Country House created out of a 12th century Cistercian Monastery. Famous Mortlake tapestries. 25 acres of outstanding gardens.
Location: 1 m E of Chard Junction, 4 m SE of Chard. 7 m W of Crewkerne.
Opening Times: GARDENS AND PLANT CENTRE: open daily throughout the year 10.30–4.30; HOUSE: Easter–Mid Oct. Suns, Weds & Bank Hol Mons, 2–5.30. Adm £2.50; Gardens only £1.50, Chld free.
Refreshments: Tea room open mid-day.

HIGHER BOCKHAMPTON

HARDY'S COTTAGE, The National Trust
Telephone: Dorchester 62366   ♿

Birthplace of Thomas Hardy 1840–1928. A thatched cottage, built by his grandfather; little altered.
Location: 3 m NE of Dorchester; ½ m S of Blandford Road (A35).
Opening Times: Interior: by prior appointment with the custodian. Adm to interior £1.50. Garden: between Easter–Oct 30 (except Tues am) from 11–6 or sunset if earlier. Exterior and garden free. Approached by 10 mins walk from car park via woods. Wheelchairs, garden only.

KIMMERIDGE

SMEDMORE
Telephone: Corfe Castle 480717   ♿
(Major and Mrs John Mansel)

17th/18th century manor house, still lived in by the family who built it. Plenty to see including 18th century marquetry furniture, Dresden china, antique dolls, Nelson letters. Walled gardens, interesting shrubs, fuchsias and hydrangeas.
Location: 7 m S of Wareham.
Opening Times: June 7 to Sept 13—Weds 2.15–5.30 (last adm 5). Also Sun, Aug 27, 2.15–5.30. Adm House & Gardens £1.50, Chd 75p. Gardens only 75p, Chd free. Organised parties Weds afternoons during same period by arrangement. Written guides in French, German & Dutch.
Refreshments: Tea at Kimmeridge (1 m).

LANGTON MATRAVERS

COACH HOUSE MUSEUM
Behind Parish Church.
Museum of the Purbeck Stone Industry. Open Apr 1 to Oct 31. Mon to Sat 10–12, 2–4, or by appointment.

LYME REGIS

THE LYME REGIS MUSEUM
Bridge Street. Tel: (029 74) 3370.
Old prints and documents, fossils and lace; an old Sun fire engine of 1710. Apr 1 to Oct 31: Daily 10.30–1, 2.30–5 (*closed* Sun mornings).

MILBORNE PORT

PURSE CAUNDLE MANOR
Telephone: Milborne Port 250400
(Michael de Pelet, Esq)

Interesting 15th/16th century Manor House. Lived in as a family home. Great Hall with minstrel gallery; Winter Parlour; Solar with oriel; bedchambers; garden.
Location: 4 m E of Sherborne; ¼ m S of A30.
Opening Times: Easter Mon to Sept 28, Thurs, Suns & Bank Hols, 2–5. Coaches welcomed by appointment. Adm £1.50, Chd 50p. Free car park.
Refreshments: Home-made cream teas by prior arrangement.

MILTON ABBAS

MILTON ABBEY
(The Council of Milton Abbey School Ltd)

A fine Abbey Church (Salisbury Diocese) partially completed 15th century on site of 10th century Abbey. Georgian Gothic Mansion (Milton Abbey School). Architect Sir William Chambers, with ceilings and decorations by James Wyatt. Incorporates Abbots Hall, completed 1498, with fine hammerbeam roof and carved screen.
Location: 7 m SW of Blandford, just N of A354 from Winterborne Whitechurch or Milborne St Andrew.
Opening Times: HOUSE & GROUNDS. Mar 24–Apr 2 and July 16–Sept 3 inc.— Daily 10–6.30. Adm 60p, Chd free. ABBEY CHURCH: Throughout the year. Free except for above dates.
Refreshments: Available when House is open in summer only.

POOLE

GUILDHALL MUSEUM *(Poole Borough Council)*
Market Street.
The development of the town of Poole is portrayed in the displays at this fine example of a two-storey Georgian Market House. See Scaplen's Court (below) for Opening times and Adm charges.

MARITIME MUSEUM *(Poole Borough Council)*
Paradise Street.
The displays which illustrate Poole's links with the sea from prehistoric times until the early 20th century are housed in a late 15th century woolhouse. See Scaplen's Court (below) for Opening times and Adm charges.

THE OLD LIFEBOAT HOUSE
East Quay.
Poole's 1938 lifeboat *Thomas Kirk Wright*, veteran of Dunkirk. Now on loan from the National Maritime Museum to, and for the support of, the RNLI, Poole branch. Easter to end Sept, daily 10.15–12.30, 2.30–5.30.

SCAPLEN'S COURT *(Poole Borough Council)*
High Street. Tel: Poole (0202) 675151.

One of the finest examples of a 15th century town house to be seen on the south coast. This medieval merchants house provides the setting for a range of displays which cover everyday life in Poole throughout the ages. Opening times and Adm charges for all three museums: Mon to Sat 10–5; Sun 2–5. *Closed* Christmas Day, Boxing Day, New Year's Day and Good Friday. Adm 50p, Chld 25p. Combined ticket for all museums £1, Chld 50p, prices subject to alteration.

WATERFRONT POOLE *(Poole Borough Council)*
An exciting new complex due to open in 1989. It will incorporate the Maritime Museum as well as the adjoining 6 floor warehouse. Displays range from the crafts & trades of the Port to Underwater Archaeology. Refreshments, toilet and shop facilities.
Opening times and admission – to be announced.

PORTLAND

PORTLAND CASTLE
Telephone: (0305) 820539

Built in the middle of the 16th century on the northern shore of the Isle of Portland, the castle was part of Henry VIII's coastal defences and is little altered. Unusually shaped, like a segment of a circle, it was seized by Royalists in the Civil War, changing hands twice before yielding to Parliament in 1646.

Location: Overlooking Portland Harbour, adjacent to RN helicopter base. OS map ref SY684743.
Opening Times: Good Friday to Sept 30, daily 10–6. Adm 80p, OAPs 60p, Chd 40p.

PORTLAND MUSEUM *(Weymouth and Portland Borough Council)*
217 Wakeham.

The exhibits consist of objects of local, historical and folk interest and natural history.

PUDDLETOWN

ATHELHAMPTON
Telephone: Puddletown (0305) 848363
(Lady Cooke)

One of the finest medieval houses in England. 10 acres of formal and landscape gardens.
Location: ½ m E of Puddletown on Dorchester/Bournemouth Road (A35); 5 m NE of Dorchester.
Opening Times: Easter to Oct 15, 2–6 on Weds, Thurs & Suns; Good Fri & Bank Hols; also Mons & Tues in Aug: 2–6. Entrance and Garden: £1.25, House £1.25 extra. (Chd free of charge in gardens). Special rate for pre-booked parties £2 incl. Dogs admitted only to shaded car park.
Refreshments: Tea at the House.

SANDFORD ORCAS

SANDFORD ORCAS MANOR HOUSE
Telephone: Corton Denham (096 322) 206
(Sir Mervyn Medlycott, Bt)

Tudor Manor House in remarkable original state of preservation, with gate-house, spiral staircases, and Tudor and Jacobean panelling. Fine collections of 14th–17th C. stained glass, Queen Anne and Chippendale furniture, Elizabethan and Georgian needlework, and 17th C. Dutch paintings. Mature terraced gardens, with topiary, and herb garden.
Location: 2½ m N of Sherborne, ent. next to Church.
Opening Times: Easter Mon 10–6 then May to Sept—Suns 2–6 & Mons 10–6. Adm £1.20, Chd 60p. Pre-booked parties (of 10 or more) at reduced rates on other days if preferred.

SHAFTESBURY

SHAFTESBURY ABBEY AND MUSEUM
(Shaftesbury Abbey and Museum Trust Company Limited)
Park Walk. Tel: (0747) 2910.

Excavated ruins of Alfred the Great's Benedictine Abbey Church. Museum houses excavated artifacts and related historical material. Open daily, Apr to Oct (including Sun and Bank Hols) 10.30–5.30. Adm 50p, Chld 25p. 10p per person for organised schools parties. Public car parks in town close by.

SHERBORNE

SHERBORNE CASTLE
Telephone: Sherborne (0935) 813182
(Simon Wingfield Digby, Esq)

16th century mansion in continuous occupation of the Digby family since 1617.
Location: 5 m E of Yeovil off A30 to S.
Station: Sherborne (few mins walk).
Opening Times: Easter Sat to end of Sept—Thurs, Sats, Suns & Bank Hol Mons 2–6. Grounds open 12 noon Sats, Suns and Bank Hol Mons and Thurs 1.30. Adm charges available on request by telephone. *Special terms & days for parties by arrangement.* Gift shop.
Refreshments: Tea at the house.

SHERBORNE OLD CASTLE
Telephone: (0935) 812730

The powerful and wealthy Bishop Roger de Caen built the castle in the early 12th century, but by 1135 it had been seized by the Crown. In 1592 the castle passed to Sir Walter Raleigh who built Sherborne Lodge in the grounds. The buildings were largely demolished after the Civil War, but a gatehouse, some graceful arcading and decorative windows survive.

Location: ½ m (0.8 km) east of Sherborne. OS map ref ST647167.
Opening Times: Good Friday to Sept 30, daily 10–6; Oct 1 to Maundy Thursday, daily 10–4. *Closed Mons, Christmas and New Year.* Adm 80p, OAPs 60p, Chd 40p.

STURMINSTER NEWTON

FIDDLEFORD MILL HOUSE

14th century house, altered in the early 16th century, comprising a hall and solar block, both with elaborate roofs.
Location: 1 m (1.6 km) east of Sturminster Newton off A357. OS map ref ST801136.
Opening Times: Good Friday to Sept 30, daily 10–6. Adm 80p, OAPs 60p, Chd 40p.

WAREHAM

WAREHAM TOWN MUSEUM *(Wareham Town Council)*
East Street. Tel: (09295) 3006 or 2771

Local history. Archaeology. Pictorial collection 'Lawrence of Arabia'. Adm free. Open Easter–mid Oct: daily except Sun 10–1, 2–5. Max 12 persons in parties. Car parking nearby. Suitable for disabled.

WEST MOORS

HIGHBURY
Telephone: Ferndown 874372
(Mr & Mrs Stanley Cherry)

Half acre garden in mature setting; many rare and unusual plants and shrubs. Specialist collections. Botanical and horticultural interest with everything labelled.
Location: 8 m N of Bournemouth. In Woodside Road off B3072, Bournemouth/Verwood (last Road N end of village).
Opening Times: GARDEN ONLY. Apr 2 to Sept 3—Suns & Bank Hol Mons 2–6. Parties other days by appointment. Adm 45p, Chd 25p. *In aid of National Gardens Scheme.* No dogs.
Refreshments: Teas in the orchard when fine.

WEYMOUTH

WEYMOUTH LOCAL HISTORY MUSEUM
(Weymouth and Portland Borough Council)
Westham Road.

Local illustrations and bygones, shipwrecks and transport.

WIMBORNE MINSTER

DEANS COURT
(Sir Michael & Lady Hanham)

Partly wild garden, specimen trees, interesting birds, organic kitchen garden.
Location: 2 m walk South from Wimborne Minster & Square; nr free car parks in town.
Opening Times: GARDEN. Bank Hols Mar 27, May 1 and 29, Aug 28, 10–6; Suns Mar 26, Apr 30, May 28, June 25, July 23, Aug 27, Sept 24. 2–6. Thurs in Apr, May, June, July & Sept, 2–6. Adm £1, Chd 50p. No dogs or unaccompanied children. *Special arrangements and car park for disabled on application at gate.* Parties by prior **written** appointment. Organically-grown produce for sale. Vegetable sanctuary. GARDEN HERITAGE WEEK APR 29 TO MAY 7. Telephone Tourist Information Office Wimborne (0202) 886116 for details of special daily events.
Refreshments: Wholefood teas on all Suns and Bank Hols, & Thurs in June & July. Coffee on Bank Hol morning.

KINGSTON LACY, The National Trust
Telephone: Wimborne 883402

17th century House designed by Sir Roger Pratt but with considerable alterations by Sir Charles Barry in the 19th century. Important Italian and English paintings collected by W.J. Bankes. Set in 250 acres of wooded park.
Location: on B3082—Wimborne–Blandford Road, 1½ m W of Wimborne.
Opening Times: Mar 25 to Oct 29—Sats to Weds incl. HOUSE: 1–5. PARKS AND GARDEN: 12–6 (last adm half-hour before closing). Guided Tours Sat 10–12 by written appointment only. Adm: HOUSE & GARDEN: £3.50, Chd £1.80, Guided Tours £5. PARK & GARDEN ONLY: £1, Chd 50p. House not suitable for wheelchairs. One wheelchair available for use in Garden. Guide dogs admitted to grounds. Parties by arrangement **only. Timed Tickets.**
Refreshments: Lunches and cream teas. National Trust Shop.

PRIEST'S HOUSE MUSEUM AND GARDEN
Telephone: Wimborne 882533
(Mrs K. Callow, Curator)

A partly Tudor house, with beautiful, large walled garden, in the town centre.

Location: Centre of Wimborne Minster.
Opening Times: Easter Mon to Sept 30: Daily 10.30–4.30, Sun 2–4.30, also open for short Christmas period 2–4.30, please telephone for details. Small charge includes admission to garden.

WOOL

CLOUDS HILL, The National Trust

The cottage home of T E Lawrence (Lawrence of Arabia) after the first World War; contains his furniture and other relics.

Location: 1 m N of Bovington Camp, 1½ m E of Waddock crossroads (B3390), 9 m E of Dorchester.
Opening Times: Apr to end Sept—Weds, Thurs, Fris (inc Good Friday) Suns & Bank Hol Mons 2–5. Oct to Mar—Suns only 1–4. Adm £1.50. *No reduction for children or parties.* No photography. Unsuitable for wheelchairs & coaches.

THE TANK MUSEUM
(Royal Armoured Corps and Royal Tank Regiment)
Near Wool. Tel: (0929) 462721, Ext. 329/463 or (0929) 463953.

Over 200 examples of AFVs from 1915. Daily (most of the year) 10–5. Adm charge. Chld and OAPs half price. Special rates for parties. Large car and coach parks, self-service restaurant, picnic area, video theatre, large shop. Major expansion & modernisation in progress.

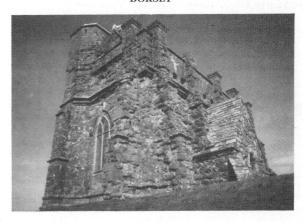

County Durham

BARNARD CASTLE

BARNARD CASTLE
Telephone: (0833) 38212

Named after its founder, Bernard de Baliol, the castle overlooks the River Tees from a craggy cliff-top. Its ownership was disputed by the Bishops of Durham, one of whom seized it in 1296. He added a magnificent hall and refortified the castle. Part of the castle has recently been excavated to discover more of its complex building history.

Location: In Barnard Castle. OS map ref NZ049165.
Opening Times: Good Friday to Sept 30, daily 10–6; Oct 1 to Maundy Thursday, daily 10–4. *Closed Mons, Christmas and New Year.* Adm 80p, OAPs 60p, Chd 40p.

THE BOWES MUSEUM *(Durham County Council)*
Tel: Teesdale (0833) 690606.
The main collections are representative of European art from the late Medieval period to the 19th century. They comprise paintings, tapestries, furniture, porcelain, glass, jewellery, sculpture and metalwork. Paintings by Italian, Spanish, Flemish, Dutch, French and English artists. Mon to Sat 10–5.30 (Oct, Mar, Apr 10–5; Nov to Feb 10–4); Sun 2–5 (winter 2–4). Adm (at time of going to press) £1.50, Chld and OAPs 50p. Tea Room in the building (Apr to Sep). Free parking. Good facilities for the disabled. Attractive gardens.

ROKEBY PARK
Palladian House built by Sir Thomas Robinson in 1735. Fine rooms, furniture and pictures (including exceptional collection of 18th century needlework pictures by Anne Morritt).

Opening Times: May 1, then each Mon from May 29 to Sept 11, each Tues from July 18 to Sept 12, and each Thur from Aug 3–Aug 31, 2–5 (last adm 4.30). Parties of 25 or more will also be admitted on other days if a written appointment is made with the Curator.

BEAMISH

NORTH OF ENGLAND OPEN AIR MUSEUM
Near Chester-le-Street. Tel: (0207) 231811.
Buildings from the North of England have been rebuilt, in 200 acres of beautiful countryside, to show Northern life around the turn of the century. The Town has Co-operative shops, a Victorian pub with stables, town houses, printers workshop and Tea Rooms. At the Colliery visitors can go down a 'drift' mine, see Colliery buildings and visit furnished pit cottages. Home Farm with traditional farm house also has animals, poultry and exhibitions. Locomotives can often be seen in steam at Rowley Station, the centrepiece of the railway area. Also electric tramway, transport collection and fairground. Apr to Oct: Daily 10–6. Nov to Mar: Daily (except Mon) 10–5. Last adm always 4pm.
Museum of the Year 1986. European Museum of the Year awarded in 1987.

BISHOP AUCKLAND

AUCKLAND CASTLE
Telephone: Bishop Auckland (0388) 609766
(The Church Commissioners)

Historic home of the Bishops of Durham with parts dating from 12th century. Very fine private Chapel remodelled by Bishop Cosin from 1660. 14th century Hall, gothicised by James Wyatt in 1795. Also large public park and unusual 18th century deerhouse.

Location: In Bishop Auckland, at the end of Market Place.
Station: Bishop Auckland.
Opening Times: Castle and Chapel: May 15 to Sept 29—Suns & Weds 2–5. Chapel only Thurs 10–12. Adm 75p, Chd 30p, OAPs 50p. Park: Daylight hours throughout the year.

DARLINGTON

DARLINGTON ART GALLERY *(Borough of Darlington)*
Crown Street. Tel: (0325) 462034
Loan exhibitions, local exhibitions and selections from the permanent collection. Mon to Fri 10–8; Sat 10–5.30.

DARLINGTON MUSEUM *(Borough of Darlington)*
Tubwell Row. Tel: (0325) 463795 (Curator).
Social history of Darlington. Natural history of Teesdale. Historic fishing tackle. Observation beehive during summer months. Mon to Fri 10–1, 2–6 (except Thur 10–1 only); Sat 10–1, 2–5.30.

DARLINGTON RAILWAY CENTRE AND MUSEUM
(Darlington Borough Council)
North Road Station. Tel: (0325) 460532.
Based on the restored 1842 station of the Stockton & Darlington Railway and associated buildings. Engines and rolling stock from 1825, including "Locomotion", the first locomotive to run on a public railway. Models, documents, pictures and other exhibits relating to the railways of north-east England. Daily 9.30–5 (except Christmas/New Year). Adm 80p, OAP 60p, chld 40p. Party rates available on application. Pre-booked school groups free. Suitable for the disabled. Hours and charges subject to revision.

DURHAM

BOTANIC GARDEN, UNIVERSITY OF DURHAM
Telephone: (091) 3742671
(University of Durham)

18 acres of trees and shrubs, set in mature woodland.
Location: Take the Durham turn off at A167 at Cock o' the North Roundabout. 1 m from Durham, along Hollingside Lane.
Opening Times: All year including Bank Holidays 10–4.30. Parties welcome, guided tours charged. Attractive Visitor Centre. Free parking. Not suitable for disabled.

THE CATHEDRAL TREASURY
Tel: (091) 3844854.
The relics of St. Cuthbert, Medieval seals, vestments, manuscripts, church plate, the Sanctuary knocker.

DURHAM CASTLE
(The University of Durham)

The Norman castle of the prince bishops has been used by Durham University since 1832.
Location: In the centre of the city (adjoining Cathedral).
Station: Durham (½ m).
Opening Times: All the year; first three weeks in Apr then July, Aug & Sept— Weekdays 10–12, 2–4.30. Other months—Mons, Weds & Sats 2–4. Adm 95p, Chd 45p.

DURHAM LIGHT INFANTRY MUSEUM AND ARTS CENTRE
Near County Hall. Tel: (091) 384 2214.
Lower Galleries: uniforms, medals, weapons and illustrations tell the story of the County Regiment's 200 years of history. Upper Galleries: changing exhibitions of arts and crafts. Coffee Bar. Car Park. Weekdays (except Mon) 10–5; Sun 2–5. Open Bank Hol Mons. *Closed* Christmas Day and Boxing Day. Adm (subject to alteration) 60p, Chld and OAPs 25p. Suitable for the disabled (including lift and toilet facilities).

DURHAM UNIVERSITY ORIENTAL MUSEUM
Elvet Hill, South Road. Tel: (091) 374 2911.
A wide range of artefacts from all periods and cultures of the Orient from Ancient Egypt to Japan. Mon to Sat 9.30–1 and 2–5, Sun 2–5. *Closed* Christmas and weekends Nov–Feb inclusive. Adm 50p, Students/ Chld/OAPs 30p. Organised school parties 15p.

FINCHALE PRIORY
Telephone: (0385) 63828

This 13th century priory was built around the tomb of St Godric, who founded a hermitage here in 1110. St Godric led an adventurous life as a travelling pedlar, then a sailor, until a vision summoned him to Finchale. His stone tomb can still be seen in the chapel, but the coffin is now empty.
Location: 5½ m (9 km) north of Durham. OS map ref NZ297471.
Opening Times: Good Friday to Sept 30, daily 10–6; Oct 1 to Maundy Thursday, daily 10–4. *Closed Mons, Christmas and New Year.* Adm 80p, OAPs 60p, Chd 40p.

OLD FULLING MILL, MUSEUM OF ARCHAEOLOGY
The Banks. Tel: (091) 374 3623.
Permanent archaeological collections of local and national importance and varied programme of temporary exhibitions. Daily Apr to Oct 11–4; Nov to Mar 1–3.30. 50p, Schoolchildren free, OAPs, Students and UB40s 25p.

STAINDROP

RABY CASTLE
Telephone: Staindrop (0833) 60202
(The Lord Barnard, T.D.)

Principally 14th century, alterations made 1765 and mid-19th century. Fine pictures and furniture. Collection of horse-drawn carriages and fire engines. Large walled Gardens.
Location: 1 m N of Staindrop village, on the Barnard Castle/Bishop Auckland Road (A688).
Opening Times: Easter weekend (Sat–Wed) then Apr 29 to June 30, Weds & Suns; July 1 to Sept 30, daily (except Sats); May, Spring and Aug Bank Hols, Sat–Tues; Castle 1–5; Park & Gardens 11–5.30. Adm Castle, Gardens & Carriage collection £2, Chd & Senior Citizens £1.20; Park, Gardens & Carriages only 80p, Chd & Senior Citizens 60p. Separate adm charge for Bulmer's Tower when open. Special terms for parties over 25 people on above and other days by arrangement (Tel Curator). Picnic area.
Refreshments: Tea at the Stables.

AUCKLAND CASTLE

BISHOP AUCKLAND, CO. DURHAM

THE CHURCH COMMISSIONERS

Steeped in the history of the ancient and important See of Durham, the Castle has been the home of successive bishops since 1183. The medieval Chapel, the size of a parish church, has recently been splendidly restored, and the State Rooms include a Gothick Throne Room lined with the portraits of past bishops. Gardens.

Bishop Auckland is 11 miles South-West of Durham via A167 & A688.

ADMISSION — SEE EDITORIAL REFERENCE

ROKEBY PARK

Nr BARNARD CASTLE

ADMISSION — SEE EDITORIAL REFERENCE

Essex

BELCHAMP WALTER

BELCHAMP HALL
Telephone: Sudbury (0787) 72744
(M. M. J. Raymond, Esq)

Queen Anne period house with period furniture and 17th and 18th century family portraits. Gardens.
Location: 5 m SW of Sudbury.
Opening Times: By appointment only. May to Sept—Tues & Thurs and Easter, Spring & Summer Bank Hol Mons 2.30–6. Adm £1.40, Chd 70p. Reduction for parties.

BILLERICAY

BARLEYLANDS FARM MUSEUM
(H.R. Philpot & Son (Barleylands) Ltd.)
Barleylands Farm, Barleylands Road. Tel: (0268) 282090.
Barleylands Farm museum covers nearly an acre of ground and includes a vintage collection of over 1,000 exhibits, some dating back to the 16th century, including a corn grinding mill, 65 tractors and 2 steam ploughing engines. The exhibits are housed mainly in renovated cow sheds and stables adjacent to a large arable farm and pick-your-own unit and farm shop. Oct 1 to Mar 31, Wed–Sat 11–4.30 and Sun 1–5. Apr 1 to Sept 30, Wed–Sat 11–5 and Sun 1–5.30. Open Bank Hols except Christmas Day & Boxing Day. Adm £1, OAPs, Chld over 5 & students 50p. People in wheelchairs half published price. Parties of all sizes catered for. Car parking for cars and coaches. Suitable for disabled persons.

BRENTWOOD

THE MAGNOLIAS
Telephone: Brentwood 220019
(Mr & Mrs R. A. Hammond)

It is hoped that the small front garden doesn't put the potential visitor off as the back garden seems to go on and on. Cleverly laid out paths lead the visitor up and down, maximising the half acre informal plantsman's garden. The ground is intensively planted with a wide variety of trees, shrubs, climbers, herbaceous groundcover and bulbs. Here can be seen good collections of Acer, Magnolia, Rhododendron, Camellia, Pieris, Hosta and ferns plus the N.C.C.P.G. National Collection of Arisaema. There are seven ponds including one in a green house, some with Koi Carp.
Location: 1 m from Brentwood High Street (A1023). At Wilsons Corner turn S down A128; after 300 yds turn right at traffic lights; over railway bridge: St. John's Ave 3rd on right.
Opening Times: Weds Apr, May and June 2–5; Suns Mar 26, Apr 2, 16, 30, May 14, 28, June 11, 25, 10–5. Adm 70p, Chd 30p. Parties by appointment. Not suitable for disabled.
Refreshments: Teas.

BURNHAM ON CROUCH

THE BURNHAM MUSEUM
Providence
Houses a fine collection of agricultural machinery and tools, interesting Maritime and pre-historic pieces from the Dengie Hundred area. Open Mar to Dec: Wed and Sat 11–4; Sun and Bank Hols 2–4.30. Adm 20p. Parties welcome at other times by arrangement.

CASTLE HEDINGHAM

COLNE VALLEY RAILWAY
Halstead. Tel: (0787) 61174.
Running through one of the prettiest parts of the Colne Valley this vintage steam Railway can offer: Wine & Dine Trains.

HEDINGHAM CASTLE
Telephone: Hedingham (0787) 60261 or 60804
(The Hon Thomas & Mrs Lindsay)

Home of the famous medieval family the de Veres, Earls of Oxford. Besieged by King John and visited by King Henry VII and Queen Elizabeth I. Visitors can see the Garrison Chamber, the Banqueting Hall with Minstrel's Gallery and the beautiful Tudor bridge built in 1496.
Location: On B1058 4 m N of Halstead, turn off A604; 9 m N of Braintree; 30 m SE of Cambridge.
Opening Times: Easter Weekend & May to end of Oct—Daily 10–5. Parties & schools welcome all year round by appointment with the Curator. Adm £2, Chd £1.
Refreshments: Light refreshments.

CHELMSFORD

CHELMSFORD AND ESSEX MUSEUM, ESSEX REGIMENT MUSEUM
(Chelmsford Borough Council)
Oaklands Park, Moulsham Street CM2 9AQ. Tel: (0245) 353066.
Chelmsford & Essex Museum – tel: 353066.
Long-term displays, from the permanent collection, of natural history, archaeology, social history, costume, glass, paintings and local industries: full temporary exhibition programme.
Essex Regiment Museum – tel: 260614
Displays tracing the history of the Essex Regiment.

COGGESHALL

PAYCOCKE'S, The National Trust

Richly ornamented merchant's house, dating from about 1500. Special display of local lace. Delightful garden leading down to small river.
Location: On A120; S side of West St. Coggeshall next to Fleece Inn; 5½ m E of Braintree.
Station: Kelvedon (2½ m).
Opening Times: Mar 25 to Oct 6—Tues, Thurs, Suns and Bank Hol Mons 2–5.30. Adm £1.10, Chd (accompanied) half-price. *Parties exceeding six should make prior arrangements with the tenant.* No reduction for parties. No dogs.
Refreshments: In Coggeshall.

COLCHESTER

BETH CHATTO GARDENS
(Mrs Beth Chatto)

5-acre garden, attractively landscaped with many unusual plants in wide range of conditions.

Location: 4 m E of Colchester on A133 Colchester/Clacton Road. *Station: Colchester.*
Opening Times: GARDEN ONLY. All the year—Mons to Sats 9–5 Mar to Oct. Mon–Fri 9–4 Nov to Feb. *Closed Suns & Bank Hols also Sats Nov 4 to end of Feb.* Adm £1, Chd free. *In aid of National Gardens Scheme.* Adjacent nursery also open. *Parties by arrangement.* No dogs please.

THE CASTLE *(Colchester Borough Council)*
Tel: (0206) 712490.

A Norman Keep which stands on the foundations of a Roman temple. It contains archaeological material of all kinds from Essex and the extensive finds from Roman Colchester. Mon to Sat 10–5 (Oct to Mar closes 4 on Sat); Sun (Apr to Sept) 2.30–5. Adm 85p, Chld 45p. Tours of vaults and prisons in summer 65p, Chld 35p.

COLCHESTER AND ESSEX MUSEUM
(Colchester Borough Council)
14 Ryegate Road. Tel: (0206) 712481/2.

All correspondence to Resource Centre at above address. Adm and tour prices subject to alteration.

HOLLYTREES MUSEUM *(Colchester Borough Council)*
Tel: (0206) 712493.

A house of 1718 used as a museum of later social history including costume. Mon to Sat 10–1, 2–5 (Oct to Mar closes 4 on Sat). Adm free all year.

THE MINORIES ART GALLERY *(Victor Batte-Lay Trust)*
74 High Street.

Exhibitions of historical and contemporary arts and crafts in a Georgian House. Own permanent collection. Incorporates the Colchester Film Makers workshop.

NATURAL HISTORY MUSEUM
(Colchester Borough Council)
All Saints Church, High Street. Tel: (0206) 712494.

The natural history of Essex. Mon to Sat 10–1, 2–5 (Oct to Mar closes 4 on Sat). Adm free all year.

OLIVERS
Telephone: (0206) 330575
(Mr & Mrs D. Edwards)

Twenty acres of landscaped gardens slope down from redbrick, mainly Georgian house (not open). Fine trees and shrubs including rhododendrons and azaleas, underplanted with Spring bulbs. Three lakes and stream with bluebells and primulas. Yew hedges back mixed shrub and herbaceous borders with a wide variety of planting. Shrub roses. Eighteenth century dovecote.

Location: 3 m SW of Colchester between B1022 and B1026. Olivers Lane is a turning off Gosbeck's Road.
Opening Times: Sat & Sun May 6 & 7. All Weds in May 2–6. Adm £1, Chd free. Parties by appointment any time of year. Ample car parking. Suitable for disabled, no wheelchairs available. Plants for sale.
Refreshments: Teas at house in May. From June–Oct, strawberry cream teas at adjoining pick-your-own orchard.

SOCIAL HISTORY MUSEUM
(Colchester Borough Council)
Holy Trinity Church, Trinity Street. Tel: (0206) 712491.

County life and crafts. Mon–Sat 10–1, 2–5 (Oct to Mar closes 4 on Sat). Adm free all year.

TYMPERLEYS CLOCK MUSEUM *(Colchester Borough Council)*
Trinity Street. Tel: (0206) 712492.

A selection of Colchester made clocks from the Mason Collection displayed in the 15th century house which Bernard Mason restored and presented to the town. Tues–Sat 10–1, 2–5. Apr to Oct (closes 4 on Sat in Oct). Adm 40p, Chld 25p. *Closed* Mons (except Bank Hols).

DEDHAM

CASTLE HOUSE
Telephone: (0206) 322127   &

Home of the late Sir Alfred Munnings. KCVO, President of the Royal Academy 1944-1949. The house and studios contain many paintings, drawings, sketches and other works.

Location: ¾ m Dedham village, 7 m NE Colchester 2 m E of Ipswich Road (A12).
Opening Times: Apr 30 to Oct 1—Weds, Suns & Bank Hol Mons, also Thurs & Sats in Aug, 2–5. Adm £1.50, Chd 25p, OAPs 75p.

EAST TILBURY

COALHOUSE FORT
Tel: (03752) 4203.

A splendid example of a Royal Commission Fort built from 1861–1874 for the defence of the Thames.

THURROCK LOCAL HISTORY MUSEUM
(Thurrock Borough Council)
Central Complex, Orsett Road. Tel: (0375) 383325.

Prehistoric, Romano-British and pagan Saxon archaeology, social, agricultural and industrial history of locality. Mon to Fri 10–8; Sat 10–5. *Closed* Bank Hols.

GREAT SALING

SALING HALL
(Mr & Mrs Hugh Johnson)

12 acre garden; wall garden dated 1698; small park with fine trees, extensive new collection of unusual plants with emphasis on trees; water gardens.

Location: 6 m NW of Braintree; mid-way between Braintree & Dunmow (A120); turn off N at Saling Oak Inn.
Opening Times: GARDEN ONLY. Weds in May, June & July 2–5. Suns May 28, and July 9, 2–6. *Parties other days by arrangement.* Adm £1, accompanied Chd free. No dogs please. *In aid of National Gardens Scheme & Village Church Fund.*

GREAT WALTHAM

PARK FARM (GARDEN)
Telephone: (0245) 360871
(Mrs Jill Cowley & Mr Derek Bracey)

Young garden still to be completed on farmyard site. Two acres of bulbs, herbaceous plants and especially roses planted in separate rooms formed by new hedges. There is also a newly-constructed pond garden.

Location: A131 to Braintree from Chelmsford: on Little Waltham Bypass turn W to Chatham Hall Lane: Park Farm ½ m on left hand side.
Opening Times: Every Sun in May, June and July 2–6; Mon evenings 6pm–dusk. Adm 60p, Chd 30p. Parties by arrangement. Not suitable for disabled.
Refreshments: Teas provided in Victorian Dairy.

HALSTEAD

GOSFIELD HALL
(Country Houses Association Ltd).

Very fine Tudor gallery.

Location: 2½ m SW of Halstead on Braintree/Haverhill Road (A131).
Opening Times: May to Sept—Weds & Thurs 2–5. Adm £1, Chd 50p. Free car park. No dogs admitted.

HARLOW

HARLOW MUSEUM *(Harlow District Council)*
Passmores House, Third Avenue. Tel: (0279) 446422.

A Tudor and Georgian farmhouse set in pleasant landscaped grounds. Local archaeology and history collections including Roman and Post-Medieval, Folk Life and Farming plus Geology and Natural History. Ground floor only suitable for the disabled. Adm free. Open daily 10–5, but closed 12.30–1.30 on Sat and Sun.

MARK HALL CYCLE MUSEUM AND GARDENS
(Harlow District Council)
Muskham Road, off First Avenue. Tel: (0279) 39680.

A converted 19th century stable block housing a fine collection of bicycles from the 1818 Hobby Horse to the 1982 Plastic Itera incorporating the Collins Collection. The large accessory collection includes lamps of all types, tools, saddles, pumps and a wide range of components. The grounds include three walled period gardens. Suitable for the disabled. Daily 10–5. Adm free.

HARWICH

HARWICH REDOUBT *(The Harwich Society)*
Main Road.

180ft diameter circular fort built 1808 to defend port against Napoleonic invasion. Now being restored by Harwich Society, and part is museum. Eleven guns on battlements. May to Sept: Daily 9–5; Oct to Apr: Suns only 10–12, 2–5. Adm 50p. Family accompanied chld free: no unaccompanied chld. Schools 25p per person. Parties by prior arrangement (with 11 Bay Road). Car parking in Harbour Crescent. Light drinks available. Curator: A. Rutter.

PORT OF HARWICH MARITIME MUSEUM *(The Harwich Society)*
Harwich Green.

Housed in a disused lighthouse on the edge of Harwich Green with specialised displays on RNLI, RN and commercial shipping. Sun 2–5, Easter to Oct. Adm 25p. Accompanied chld free: no unaccompanied chld. Parties by prior arrangement (to 11 Bay Road). Car parking in Harbour Crescent. Curator: P. Gates.

LAYER BRETON

SHALOM HALL
(Lady Phoebe Hillingdon)

19th century house containing a collection of 17th and 18th century French furniture and porcelain and portraits by famous English artists including Thomas Gainsborough, Sir Joshua Reynolds etc.

Location: 7 m SW of Colchester; 2 m from A12.
Opening Times: Aug—Mon to Fri 10–1, 2.30–5.30. Adm free.

MALDON

I.C.S. HISTORY OF JAGUAR MUSEUM
Mill Lane CM9 7LD. Tel: (0261) 53311.

The I.C.S. History of Jaguar Museum traces the history of Jaguar from the Swallow Sidecar, through the Swallow bodied and S.S. cars, to the full range of XK engined Jaguars, including competition cars.

NEWPORT

PRIOR'S HALL BARN, WIDDINGTON
Telephone: (0799) 41047

One of the finest surviving medieval barns in south-east England, this is typical of aisled barns and representative of a group of such structures centred on north-west Essex. It displays a number of unusual features and has been restored where necessary with seasoned English oak and new roof tiles made in Sussex.

Location: 2 m (3.2 km) south east of Newport, Essex. OS map ref TL538319.
Opening Times: Good Friday to Sept 30, 10–6 weekends and Bank Holidays only. Adm 55p, OAPs 40p, Chd 25p.

RETTENDON

HYDE HALL
(Hyde Hall Garden Trust)

Varied collection of trees and shrubs, spring bulbs, roses and ornamental greenhouse plants.

Location: 7 m SE of Chelmsford (off A130).
Opening Times: GARDEN ONLY. Suns, Weds and Bank Holidays 11–6 from Easter to Oct 29. Adm £1, Chd 25p. *In aid of National Gardens Scheme & other charities.* Plant stall. Dogs on leads allowed.
Refreshments: Light refreshments available.

ST. OSYTH

ST. OSYTH PRIORY
Telephone: (0255) 820492
(Somerset de Chair)

Great gatehouse c 1475, "unexcelled in any monastic remains in the country", *Country Life.* A unique group of buildings dating from the 13th, 15th 16th, 18th and 19th centuries, surrounding a wide quadrangle like an Oxford or Cambridge college. Gardens include Rose garden, Topiary garden, Water Garden etc. Art collection in Georgian wing includes world-famous paintings George Stubbs ARA.

Location: 65 miles from London via A12, A120; A133 12 miles from Colchester; 8 miles from Frinton.
Opening Times: Easter weekend. Then May 1–Sept 30. Gardens and Ancient Monuments open 10–5. Art Collection 10.30–12.30, 2.30–4.30. Adm £2, Chld 50p, OAPs £1. Parties by arrangement. Free car parking. Gardens suitable for disabled persons. Gardens overlook but do not include deer park on the estuary of the River Colne. Contact Mrs Colby tel (0255) 820242.
Refreshments: In village 100 yards from entrance.

SAFFRON WALDEN

AUDLEY END HOUSE AND PARK
Telephone: (0799) 22399

James I is said to have remarked that Audley End was too large for a king but not for his Lord Treasurer, Sir Thomas Howard, who built it. The house was so large in fact that early in the 18th century about half of it was demolished as being unmanageable, but this still leaves a very substantial mansion. The interior contains rooms decorated by Robert Adam, a magnificent Jacobean Great Hall, a picturesque 'Gothick' chapel and a suite of rooms decorated in the revived Jacobean style of the early 19th century.

Location: ¾ m (1 km) west of Saffron Walden off B1383. OS map ref TL525382.
Opening Times: Good Friday to Sept 30, daily 1–6. Park and Gardens open at 12 noon. Last admissions one hour before closing. Adm £3, OAPs £2, Chd £1.50.

SAFFRON WALDEN MUSEUM
Museum Street (near Church). Tel. (0799) 22494.

Collections of archaeology, natural history, geology, local history, ceramics, glass, costume, furniture, dolls and toys, ethnography. Also special exhibitions. Castle ruins in grounds. Mon to Sat 11–5 (Oct to Mar 11–4); Sun and Bank Hols 2.30–5. *Closed* Good Friday, Christmas Eve and Christmas Day. Adm free.

SOUTHEND ON SEA

BEECROFT ART GALLERY *(Borough of Southend-on-Sea)*
Station Road, Westcliff-on-Sea. Tel: (0702) 347418.

Contains the Municipal, Thorpe Smith and Beecroft Collections. Loan exhibitions changed monthly. Mon to Thur 9.30–5.30; Fri 9.30–5; Sat 9.30–5.30.

CENTRAL MUSEUM *(Borough of Southend-on-Sea)*
Victoria Avenue. Tel: (0702) 330214.

Administrative headquarters. The human and natural history of south-east Essex. Temporary exhibitions throughout the year. Mon 1–5; Tues to Sat 10–5. *Closed* Sun.

PRITTLEWELL PRIORY MUSEUM *(Borough of Southend-on-Sea)*
Priory Park. Tel: (0702) 342878.

Originally a Cluniac Monastery, now a museum of local history and natural history with a large collection of radios, televisions, gramophones and printing equipment. Tues to Sat 10–1, 2–5. *Closed* Sun and Mon. Parties in the mornings by arrangement.

SOUTHCHURCH HALL *(Borough of Southend-on-Sea)*
Southchurch Hall Close. Tel: (0702) 67671.

Moated timber-framed manor house, early 14th century, with small Tudor wing, the open hall furnished as a Medieval manor; with exhibition room. Tues to Sat 10–1, 2–5. *Closed* Sun and Mon. Parties in the mornings by arrangement.

TILBURY

THURROCK RIVERSIDE MUSEUM *(Thurrock Borough Council)*
Civic Square. Tel: (0375) 856886, Ext. 3.

History of the local River Thames, its landscape and fortifications. Normally Tues to Fri 10–1, 2–5.30; Sat 10–1, 2–5. *Closed* Sun, Mon and Bank Hols. Please telephone if coming from a distance.

TILBURY FORT
Telephone: (037 52) 78489

After an audacious raid up the Thames by the Dutch in 1667, Charles II commissioned plans for a defensive fort at Tilbury, on the site of Henry VIII's smaller fortification. It took 13 years to build but never saw the action for which it was designed. In the First World War a German Zeppelin was gunned down from the parade ground. Entry is now from the landward side across two restored bridges. In 1988 Tilbury Fort will celebrate Queen Elizabeth I's visit to rally her troops against the Armada threat. An Armada centre will be open Apr–Sept.

Location: ½ m (0.8 km) south east of Tilbury. OS map ref TQ651754.
Opening Times: Good Friday to Sept 30, daily 10–6; Oct 1 to Maundy Thursday, daily 10–4. *Closed Mons, Christmas and New Year.* Adm £1.10, OAPs 80p, Chd 55p.

TIPTREE

LAYER MARNEY TOWER
Telephone: Colchester 330202
(Major & Mrs Gerald Charrington)

1520 Tudor brick house with eight-storey gate tower. Terracotta dolphin cresting and windows. Formal yew hedges, rose bushes and lawns. Adjoining church contains three effigy tombs of the Marneys and original St Christopher wall painting.

Location: 3 m from Tiptree, 1 m S of B1022. Colchester/Maldon Road.
Opening Times: Apr 1 to Sept 30 — Suns & Thurs 2–6; Bank Hols 11–6; also Tues 2–6 during July & Aug. Adm £1.25, Chd 50p. *Parties other days by prior arrangement.*

UPMINSTER

UPMINSTER TITHE BARN AGRICULTURAL AND FOLK MUSEUM
(London Borough of Havering and Hornchurch & District Historical Society)
Hall Lane. Tel: Romford (0708) 44297.

Collections of agricultural implements, craft and farm tools, local bricks and domestic bygones, displayed in 15th century timber and thatched barn.

WALTHAM ABBEY

EPPING FOREST DISTRICT MUSEUM
39/41 Sun Street EN9 1EL. Tel: (0992) 716882.

Opened in 1981, the museum is situated in two timber-framed buildings dating from 16th and 18th centuries. Displays illustrate daily life in the Epping Forest District from the Stone Age to the 20th century. Key exhibits include some magnificent oak panelling carved for the Abbot of Waltham during the reign of Henry VIII and now on loan from the Victoria and Albert Museum. Social history relating to the Epping Forest District. Also growing collection of contemporary art by artists living or working in the historic County of Essex. Regularly changing programme of temporary exhibitions. Research and reference room available by prior appointment. Herb garden. Shop. Tea/Coffee. *Special Events:* 'Tudor Market Fayre' in May – a Tudor festival involving local schools, adult groups and traders. 'Artists in Essex' – annual exhibition of contemporary work by Essex artists. Please contact the museum for dates and further details. Fri, Sat, Sun, Mon 2–5. Tues 12–5. Wed, Thurs *Closed* (except for booked parties). Open all Bank Hols (except Christmas Day, Boxing Day, New Year's Day). Adm free.

EPPING FOREST DISTRICT MUSEUM

WALTHAM ABBEY

Local history Museum

Temporary exhibition programme.

Collection of contemporary work by Essex artists.

Shop – souvenirs, booklets, replicas etc.

Herb garden

Refreshments

SEE EDITORIAL ENTRIES FOR FURTHER DETAILS.

Epping Forest District Museum opened November, 1981.

SOUTHEND-ON-SEA MUSEUMS

PRITTLEWELL PRIORY MUSEUM
BEECROFT ART GALLERY, Westcliff-on-Sea
SOUTHCHURCH HALL MUSEUM
SOUTHEND CENTRAL MUSEUM
Telephone: 0702 330214

Gloucestershire

BARNSLEY

BARNSLEY HOUSE GARDEN
Telephone: Bibury 281
(Mrs D. C. W. Verey)

Garden laid out 1770, trees planted 1840. Re-planned 1960. Many spring bulbs. Laburnum avenue (early June). Lime walk, herbaceous and shrub borders. Ground cover. Knot garden. Autumn colour. Gothic summerhouse 1770. Classical temple 1780. House 1697 (not open). Vegetable garden laid out as decorative potager.
Location: 4 m NE of Cirencester on Cirencester to Burford Road (A433).
Opening Times: GARDEN ONLY. All the year—Mon–Sat 10–6 (or dusk if earlier); Adm (Mar to Nov inc) £1.50, OAPs £1. Season tickets £4. Guided Parties minimum charge £50 VAT. Dec to Feb free. Plants for sale.
Refreshments: Lunch and supper – The Village Pub, Barnsley. Tea – Bibury & Cirencester.

BERKELEY

BERKELEY CASTLE
Telephone: Dursley (0453) 810332
(Mr & Mrs R. J. Berkeley)

One of the most historic castles, over 800 years old, and still lived in by the Berkeleys. Scene of the murder of Edward II (1327).
Location: S of the town of Berkeley, midway between Bristol and Gloucester, just off A38.
Opening Times: Apr—Daily (exc Mons) 2–5, May to Aug—Tues to Sats 11–5, Suns 2–5; *closed Mons.* Sept—Daily (exc Mons) 2–5; Oct—Suns only 2–4.30, also Bank Hol Mons 11–5. Grounds open until 6 pm (5.30 in Oct) also Bank Hol Mons 11–5. Admission charges not available at time of going to press. *Reduced terms for prearranged parties of 25 or over—apply Custodian.*
Refreshments: Light lunches (May to Aug) and teas at Castle.

BIBURY

ARLINGTON MILL
Telephone: Bibury 368
(Mrs D. C. W. Verey)

Large 17th century Mill. Old Mill machinery. Country Museum. Very pretty village. Arts & Crafts furniture. Changing exhibitions contemporary art, craft displays at weekends. Old breeds of farm animals, and picnic area.
Location: 7 m NE of Cirencester on the Cirencester to Burford Road (A433).
Opening Times: Mar to Oct—Daily 10.30–7 or dusk if earlier. Also open weekends in winter. Adm £1.50, OAPs £1.20, Chd 60p. Family ticket (2 adults, 2–4 Chd) £3.60. Season ticket £5. Museum shop.
Refreshments: Swan Hotel, Bibury.

Nr. BROADWAY

SNOWSHILL MANOR, The National Trust
Telephone: Broadway 852410

A Tudor house with c1700 facade; 21 rooms containing interesting collection of craftsmanship, including musical instruments, clocks, toys, bicycles and Japanese armour, with small formal garden.
Location: 3 m SW of Broadway, 4 m W of junction A44 & A424.
Opening Times: Easter Sat to Mon 11–1, 2–6. Apr & Oct. Sat & Sun 11–1, 2–5. May to end Sept: Wed to Sun & Bank Hol Mon 11–1, 2–6. Last admissions to house ½ hour before closing. *Closed Good Friday.* Adm £2.80, Chd £1.40. Parties by prior written arrangement only. No dogs. Liable to serious overcrowding on Bank Holiday weekends. Disabled – limited access to house (ground floor) and part of garden.

STANWAY HOUSE
Telephone: Stanton 469
(Lord Neidpath)

Location: 1 m off A46 Cheltenham/Broadway road; on B4077 Toddington/Stow-on-the-Wold road; M5 junction 9.
Opening Times: June, July and Aug—Tues and Thurs 2–5. Adm £1.75, OAPs £1.50, Chd 75p.
Refreshments: Teas in Old Bakehouse in village (Stanton 204).

CHELTENHAM

CHELTENHAM ART GALLERY AND MUSEUM
(Cheltenham Borough Council)
Clarence Street. Tel: (0242) 237431.
Nationally important Arts and Crafts Movement collection; notable 17th century Dutch paintings; British painting 17th–20th century. Large collection of English and Oriental ceramics; pewter collection; social history and archaeological material relating to Cheltenham and the Cotswolds. Temporary exhibitions held throughout the year. Mon to Sat 10–5.30. *Closed* Sun and Bank Hols. Access for Disabled. Adm free.

GUSTAV HOLST BIRTHPLACE MUSEUM
(Trustees: administered by Cheltenham Borough Council)
4 Clarence Road, Pittville. Tel: (0242) 524846.
House where the composer was born in 1874, containing rooms with period furnishings and working Victorian kitchen. Gustav Holst personalia and reference collections. Parties welcome by arrangement. Tues to Fri 12–5.30; Sat 11–5.30. *Closed* Sun, Mon and Bank Hols. Adm free.

PITTVILLE PUMP ROOM MUSEUM
(Cheltenham Borough Council)
Pittville. Tel: (0242) 512740.
Cheltenham's Gallery of Fashion: a visual presentation of the life and history of the town from the 1760s up to the 1960s. Historic settings based on rich costume collections with displays of jewellery and accessories and temporary exhibitions. Apr to Oct: Tues to Sun 10.30–5. Nov to Mar: Tues to Sat 10.30–5. Open Easter, Spring and Summer Bank Hols. Last adm 4.40. Small adm charge. Free car park.

CHIPPING CAMPDEN

HIDCOTE MANOR GARDEN, The National Trust
Telephone: Mickleton 333   &

One of the most beautiful English gardens.
Location: 4 m NE of Chipping Campden, 1 m E of A46 off B4081.
Opening Times: Mar 25 to end of Oct—Daily (except Tues & Fris) 11–8 (last adm 7 or one hour before sunset) (*closed* Good Fri). Adm £2.90, (£3.20 on Sun and Bank Hol Mon) Chd £1.45. *Parties by prior written arrangement only.* No dogs. Liable to serious overcrowding on Bank Holiday Weekends and fine Sundays. Wheelchair access to part of garden only, wheelchairs provided.
Refreshments: Coffee, light lunches & cream teas 11–5.

KIFTSGATE COURT
(Mr & Mrs J. G. Chambers)

Garden with many unusual shrubs and plants including tree paeonies, abutilons etc, specie and old fashioned roses.
Location: 3 m NE of Chipping Campden 1 m E of A46 and B4081.
Opening Times: GARDENS ONLY. Apr 1 to Sept 30—Weds, Thurs & Suns 2–6; also Bank Hols 2–6. Adm £1.70, Chd 70p. Coaches by appointment only. *Unusual plants for sale on open days.*
Refreshments: Whit Sun to Sept 1.

CINDERFORD

DEAN HERITAGE MUSEUM TRUST
Camp Mill, Soudley GL14 7UG. Tel: (0594) 22170.

The Centre, set by a mill pond in a beautiful wooded valley, exists to interpret the unique heritage of the Forest of Dean by providing the visitor with various attractive displays and facilities within a peaceful environment. The attractions now include: A new display, "The Living Forest" depicting both the natural and man-made forest; A forest smallholding with animals; Nature trails; Charcoal burning; Adventure playground; Barbecue and picnic sites; Museum with A-V sequence; Reconstructed miners' cottage c1900 and mine; Archaeological display; 12′ overshot Waterwheel; Working craftspeople – including pottery, ornamental ironwork, glass engraving and poker work, hand-painted wood. Home-baking from the Heritage Kitchen; Hand-crafted gifts from the Craft Centre and Gallery; Car and coach parking. During 1988 a new Bradley Hill Display is being prepared to demonstrate man's interaction with his environment. Old farm carts, a cider press and the Lightmoor Colliery Beam Engine are being restored to working order. Guided tours of the Museum, and of the Countryside around the Centre are also available. Lecture Room – available for day and evening hire – for art exhibitions, craft displays, etc. Open daily (except Christmas Day and Boxing Day). Apr to Oct 10–6. Nov to Mar 10–5. Wheelchair facilities, with new level nature trail around nearby S.S.S.I. Soudley Ponds.

CIRENCESTER

CIRENCESTER LOCK-UP *(Cotswold District Council)*
Trinity Road. Tel: (0285) 5611.
Newly-restored two-cell town lock-up dating from early 19th century and incorporating interpretative displays on lock-up and workhouse history plus exhibition of architectural conservation in the Cotswolds. Details from Corinium Museum; open daily by arrangement. Adm free.

CORINIUM MUSEUM *(Cotswold District Council)*
Park Street. Tel: (0285) 5611.
A regional museum for Cirencester and the Cotswolds displaying one of the finest collections of antiquities from Roman Britain from the site of Corinium (modern Cirencester). Full-scale reconstructions of kitchen, dining room and mosaic craftsman's workshop bring Corinium to life. New gallery of Cotswold prehistory. Special exhibitions programme of local history and archaeology. Award winning displays; in the Good Museums Guide 'Top Twenty'. Open throughout the year: Apr to Sept: Daily 10–5.30, Sun 2–5.30; Oct to Mar: Tues to Sat 10–5, Sun 2–5. Open all Bank Hols, *closed* Christmas. Adm Adults 60p, Chld 30p, OAPs/Students/Party groups 40p.

RODMARTON MANOR GARDEN
Telephone: (028584) 219
(Mrs Anthony Biddulph)

Cotswold House (not open except chapel), designed by Earnest Barnsley. Featured in Country Life, RHS Journal, Stately Gardens of Britain, The English Garden in Over Time (Brown), and English Gardens (Peter Coats). English Topiary Gardens – Ethne Clarke. Vita Sackville West admired its long, cool facade looking over an enchanting garden. Terrace and leisure garden. Herbaceous borders – long vistas. Hornbeam avenue. Beech, Holly and Yew hedges. Topiary. Many 'rooms'. A series of gardens, many enclosed with hedges. A present day garden in keeping with the traditional house, and with many weed suppressing plantings such as hostas, potentillas, and lavender planted in paving.
Location: 6½ m Cirencester, 20 m M4 via Cricklade by-pass. 4 m Tetbury.
Opening Times: Open daily every Thurs from 2–5, Mar 1 to Aug 31. For further open days which have not yet been decided, please see the NGS 'Yellow Book'. Adm £1. No special reductions. Car park. Suitable for disabled persons (wheelchairs not available).
Refreshments: Teas can be provided if booked in advance.

GLOUCESTER

BLACKFRIARS, GLOUCESTER
Telephone: (0452) 27685

The Black Friars of St Dominic were welcomed enthusiastically as they spread across Europe at the beginning of the 13th century. In England houses were set up for them in Oxford, London and, in 1239, Gloucester. No less a notability than King Henry III donated oak for the roofs of the Gloucester Black Friary, some of which are still almost complete. The friary buildings were inevitably changed in the 16th century when they were bought by a local alderman.
Location: Ladybellegate Street. OS map ref SO830186.
Opening Times: Good Friday to Sept 30, daily 10–6. Adm 80p, OAPs 60p, Chd 40p.

CITY EAST GATE *(Gloucester City Council)*
Eastgate Street.
Roman and medieval gate towers and moat in an underground exhibition chamber. May to Sept: Wed and Fri 2–5; Sat 10–12, 2–5. Adm free.

CITY MUSEUM AND ART GALLERY
(Gloucester City Council)
Brunswick Road. Tel: (0452) 24131.
The Marling bequest of 18th century walnut furniture, barometers and domestic silver. Paintings by Richard Wilson, Gainsborough, Turner etc. supplemented by art exhibitions throughout the year. Local archaeology including mosaics and sculptures; natural history including a freshwater aquarium. Mon to Sat 10–5. Open some public hols. Adm free.

FOLK MUSEUM *(Gloucester City Council)*
99–103 Westgate Street. Tel: (0452) 26467.
A group of half-timbered houses, Tudor and Jacobean, furnished to illustrate local history, domestic life and rural crafts. Civil War armour, Victorian toys. Severn fishing traps, wooden ploughs etc. Reconstructed Double Gloucester dairy, ironmongers, carpenter's and wheelwright's shop. Pin factory with 18th century forge. Mon to Sat 10–5. Open some public hols. Adm free.

HARDWICKE COURT
Telephone: (0452) 720212
(C.G.M. Lloyd-Baker)

Late Georgian house designed by Robert Smirke, built 1816–1817. Entrance hall, drawing room, library and dining room open. Gardens under course of restoration.
Location: 5 m S of Gloucester on A38 (between M5 access 12 S only and 13).
Opening Times: Easter Mon to End Sept – Mons only 2–4. Other times by prior written appointment. Adm £1. Parking for cars only. Not suitable for disabled.

NATIONAL WATERWAYS MUSEUM
Llanthony Warehouse, The Docks. Tel: (Gloucester) (0452) 25524.
An enthralling collection portraying the history of Britain's canals and inland waterways in the beautiful setting of Gloucester's remarkable inland docks. The Museum itself is centred on the magnificent Victorian Llanthony Warehouse where three floors of innovative displays and fascinating exhibits bring to life the long history of our canals. A growing collection of historic boats is on display in the Barge Arm. From traditionally decorated narrowboats to the massive power of a steam dredger, the boats form a working background to the land-based displays. An outdoor exhibition area creates the environment of a canal maintenance yard and live displays demonstrate the range of jobs and skills which went into the vital business of running a canal. Afterwards visit the Museum's shops to choose from souvenirs, hand-crafted canal ware, traditional chandlery and a wide range of books and guides. For details of admission charges, party rates and for general information, please telephone the Museum. Opening times: British Summertime: 10–6 daily. Winter: 10–5; daily (*except* Mon).

THE ROBERT OPIE COLLECTION, MUSEUM OF ADVERTISING AND PACKAGING
Albert Warehouse, Gloucester Docks. Tel: (0452) 302309.
A nostalgic journey back through the memories of one's childhood, brought vividly to life by this unique collection of packaging and advertising material, dating from the mid-1800's to the present day.

TRANSPORT MUSEUM *(Gloucester City Council)*
Bearland.
Horse-drawn vehicles visible from the road at all times.

LITTLEDEAN

LITTLE DEAN HALL
(D. E. & D. M. Macer-Wright, Esq.)

Little Dean or correctly Dean Hall gets its name from the Dene family, Lords of Dene from 1080–1327. The oldest part of the Hall can be seen in the cellar where the remains of a sunken floored open hall of Saxon type has been identified, surviving to over mid wall height and dating from the 11th century. Present knowledge indicates Dean Hall is the oldest lived in house in England. The Jacobean front includes panelled rooms and carved chimney pieces. Civil War connections. Historical and museum displays covering over 2000 years of history. In the grounds are terraced lawns, remarkable trees some over 500 years old, water garden with ornamental fish, temple and outstanding views. The restored and reconstructed remains of the largest Roman water shrine known in Britain are unique. This is believed by Dr. Anne Ross to have been the cult shrine of Sabrina, goddess of the Severn. The panorama walk to the Old Castle of Dene provides the finest view in Gloucestershire over the famous Severn horseshoe bend.

Location: 12 W of Gloucester; 2 m E of Cinderford; 400 yds from A4151 on Littledean/ Newnham-on-Severn Road, turn at King's Head.
Opening Times: Gardens & House. Good Friday to Oct—Daily 10.30–6. Adm £2, Chd (5–16) £1. Dogs on lead. Picnic grounds.
Refreshments: Lunches at Littledean House Hotel.

LYDNEY

LYDNEY PARK
Telephone: (Office) Dean (0594 42844)
(Viscount Bledisloe)

Extensive Woodland Garden with lakes and a wide selection of fine shrubs and trees. Museums and Roman Temple Site. Deer Park (picnics). Country shop.

Location: ½ m W of Lydney on A48 (Gloucester to Chepstow).
Opening Times: Easter Sun and Mon; every Sun, Wed and Bank Hol from Apr 23 to June 11, but every day from Sun May 28 to Sun June 4, 11–6. Dogs on lead. **Coaches and parties** on Open Days and on other days by appointment (minimum 25). Easter to mid June; thereafter to end Sept for Temple Site and Museum only.
Refreshments: Teas in house (house not otherwise open).

MISERDEN

MISARDEN PARK GARDENS
Telephone: Miserden 303   &
(Major M T N H Wills)

The garden has a timeless quality of a typically English Garden. A particular feature is the extensive yew topiary. To the south of the house is a wide Terrace laid with York paving. Sir Edward Lutyens Wing contains a Loggia overhung with Wisteria and on a lower terrace against the wing is a magnificent Magnolia 'Soulangeana'. On the south lawn are two flights of finely detailed grass steps. West of the main lawn are a series of terraced lawns leading to the Nurseries. To the east of these lawns is a broad grass walk lined by two substantial and very colourful herbaceous borders and beyond this is a traditional rose garden. There are many fine specimen trees throughout the garden and the bulbs in variety and blossom in the Spring are other particular features. The garden stands high overlooking the wooded 'Golden Valley'.

Location: Miserden 7 m from Gloucester, Cheltenham, Stroud & Cirencester; 3 m off A417 (signed).
Opening Times: Every Wed & Thurs from Mar 29 to Sept 28, 10–4.30. Adm £1 (includes guide), Chd (accompanied) free. Reductions for parties by appointment. Car parking provided. Suitable for disabled. No wheelchairs available. Nurseries adjacent to garden open daily (except Mons) throughout the year.
Refreshments: Carpenters Arms in village serves good meals.

MORETON-IN-MARSH

BATSFORD ARBORETUM
Telephone: Blockley (0386) 700409 or Moreton (0608) 50722.
(The Batsford Foundation.)

Over 1000 species of different trees set in fifty acres of delightful Cotswold countryside overlooking the Vale of Evenlode, with a unique collection of exotic shrubs and bronze statues from the Orient.

Location: 1½ m NW of Moreton-in-Marsh on A44 to Evesham. Turn right into Park drive prior to Bourton-on-the-Hill.
Station: Moreton-in-Marsh (2½ m).
Opening Times: Garden only: Apr 1 to Oct 31—every day 10–5. Adm £1.50, Chd & OAPs 75p *(1987 rates)*. Parties by arrangement. Free parking. Garden Centre open all year round 9–5.30 (Suns 10–5).
Refreshments: Tea room for coffee, light lunches and teas (Apr to Oct except Mons). Picnic area.

SEZINCOTE
(Mr & Mrs D. Peake)

Oriental water garden by Repton and Daniell with trees of unusual size. House in 'Indian' style inspiration of Royal Pavilion, Brighton.

Location: 1½ m W of Moreton-in-Marsh on A44 to Evesham; turn left by lodge before Bourton-on-the-Hill.
Opening Times: GARDEN. Thurs, Fris & Bank Hol Mons 2–6 (or dusk if earlier) throughout year, except Dec. Adm £1.60, Chd 50p. No dogs. HOUSE May, June, July & Sept, Thurs & Fris 2.30–6. Parties by appointment. Adm House & Garden £2.75.
Refreshments: Hotels & restaurant in Moreton-in-Marsh.

NORTHLEACH

COTSWOLD COUNTRYSIDE COLLECTION
   (Cotswold District Council)
   Fosseway. Tel: (0451) 60715 or (0285) 5611.

Opened in 1981 this new museum of rural life displays the Lloyd-Baker Collection of agricultural history including wagons, horse-drawn implements and tools, exhibited in a 'seasons of the year' display. A Cotswold gallery records the social history of the area. New 'Below Stairs' exhibition of laundry,

dairy and kitchen. The museum's home is a House of Correction and its history is displayed in a restored cell-block and court-room. Audio and video sequences. Award-winning displays: Civic Trust 1982, Museum of the Year Award commendations 1983 and 1985, Come to Britain Trophy certificate of distinction 1984. Open daily Apr to Oct inc: 10–5.30 and Sun 2–5.30. Adm Adults 60p, Chld 30p, OAPs/Students/ Party rate 40p. No additional charge for events programme. Free car parking. Weekend refreshments. Easy access from A429 Fosse Way.

PAINSWICK

PAINSWICK ROCOCO GARDEN
Telephone: Painswick 813204
(Lord & Lady Dickinson)

This beautiful six acre garden, set in a hidden combe, is a rare and complete survivor of the brief eighteenth century taste for the Rococo in garden design.
Location: ½ m from Painswick on B4073.
Opening Times: GARDEN ONLY: **Snowdrops Feb 1 to Feb 28, Wed to Suns.** Easter Fri to Mon; May to Sept—Weds to Suns incl, Bank Hols 11–5. Groups: (minimum 15) by arrangement all the year. Dogs on leads. Adm £1.50, Chd 75p.
Refreshments: In licensed restaurant, morning coffees and home made light lunches and afternoon teas. Present Collection shop.

SANDHURST

NATURE IN ART *(The International Centre for Wildlife Art)*
   Wallsworth Hall. Tel: (0452) 731422.
A unique collection of fine wildlife art from all parts of the world, and all historical periods, including porcelain, mosaic, furniture, etc. Displayed in a Georgian building c. 1780, with interesting features. Tues–Sun 10–5, Bank holiday Mon 10–5. *Closed* Mon and Dec 24, 25, 26. £2.25, Chld/OAPs £1.25. Parties welcome by arrangement. Free parking. Suitable for disabled, but please telephone first. The Swan coffee shop, art shop, play area.

STROUD

STROUD DISTRICT (COWLE) MUSEUM *(Stroud District Council)*
   Lansdown. Tel: (045 36) 3394.
Also in Lansdown hall. Collections cover geology, archaeology, crafts and industries, farming and household equipment, ceramics, dolls etc. Records of local houses and mills. Weekdays 10.30–1, 2–5.

TAYNTON

RYELANDS HOUSE
(Captain & Mrs Eldred Wilson)

Fascinating sunken garden of 1½ acres with great variety of plants, many rare and unusual, in beautiful unspoilt country setting. Country walk to see abundance of wild flowers and spectacular views; landscaped lake in woodlands.

Location: 8 m NW of Gloucester; on B4216 halfway between Huntley (A40) & Newent (B4215).
Opening Times: Suns, Apr 2, 9, 16, 23, 30; Mon May 1; Suns June 11, 18, 25; July 16, 23, Sun Aug 27, Mon Aug 28. Adm £1.25. All dates 2–6. Parties by appointment. In aid of National Gardens Scheme. Dogs welcome on walk. Plants for sale.
Refreshments: Home made teas Suns and Bank Hol Mons.

TETBURY

CHAVENAGE
Telephone: Tetbury 52329
(David Lowsley-Williams, Esq)

Elizabethan House (1576) with Cromwellian associations. 16th and 17th century furniture and tapestries. Family Chapel and medieval barn. Personally conducted tours.

Location: 2 m N of Tetbury signposted off A46 B4014.
Opening Times: Easter Sun & Mon then May to Sept—Thurs, Suns & Bank Hols 2–5. Adm £2, Chd half-price. Parties by appointment as above and also on other dates and times.

TEWKESBURY

THE JOHN MOORE MUSEUM
   41 Church Street.
Countryside collections and natural history. Also The Little Museum, restored Medieval merchant's cottage. Easter to Oct: Tues to Sat and Bank Hols 10–1, 2–5.

THE MUSEUM
   Barton Street.
In an old half-timbered building, items concerning the history of the town. Small Heritage Centre display. Model of Battle of Tewkesbury. Apr to Oct: Daily 10–1, 2–5. Small admission charge.

WESTBURY ON SEVERN

WESTBURY COURT GARDEN, The National Trust
Telephone: Westbury-on-Severn 461   &

A formal Dutch water-garden with canals and yew hedges, laid out between 1696 and 1705; the earliest of its kind remaining in England.

Location: 9 m SW of Gloucester on A48.
Opening Times: Mar 25 to Oct (*closed* Good Fri) – Weds to Suns & Bank Hol Mons 11–6. Adm £1.20, Chd 60p. Parties by prior written arrangement only. Picnic area. No dogs. Wheelchairs provided.

WHITTINGTON

WHITTINGTON COURT
Telephone: (0242) 820218.
(Mrs R. J. Charleston)

Small Elizabethan stone-built manor house with family possessions.
Location: 4½ m E of Cheltenham on A40.
Opening Times: Mar 25 to Apr 9: Aug 14 to 28. Daily 2–5. Adm £1.50, OAPs £1, Chd 50p. Open to parties by arrangement.

WINCHCOMBE

HAILES ABBEY
Telephone: (0242) 602398

His life in danger at sea, Richard, Earl of Cornwall, vowed he would found a religious house if he lived. In 1245 his brother, King Henry III, gave him the manor of Hailes so that he could keep his pledge. After its establishment Richard's son, Edmund, presented the Cistercian monks of the abbey with a phial said to contain the Blood of Christ and from then until the Dissolution Hailes became a magnet for pilgrims. Extensive ruins survive and there is an excellent museum.
Location: 2 m (3.2 km) north east of Winchcombe. OS map ref SP050300.
Opening Times: Good Friday to Sept 30, daily 10–6; Oct 1 to Maundy Thursday, daily 10–4. *Closed Mons, Christmas and New Year.* Adm £1.10, OAPs 80p, Chd 55p.

SUDELEY CASTLE
Telephone: Cheltenham (0242) 602308
(The Lady Ashcombe)

Beautiful 12th century home of Queen Katherine Parr, rich in Tudor history. Art treasures include Constable, Rubens and Van Dyck. Lovely gardens with historic Elizabethan garden as main highlight. Falconry exhibition with Flying Displays each Tues, Wed and Thurs from May to Aug (see inside back cover). Traditional Craft Exhibition, incorporating craftsmen at work.
Location: 6 m NE of Cheltenham on A46. Access A40, A438, M5 (at Tewkesbury turn off).
Opening Times: Apr to Oct – Daily (inc Bank Hols) 12–5. Grounds open from 11. All inclusive adm £3.25, Chd £1.75. Special rates for OAPs and parties. Ample free car parking. (Guides in major rooms. Guided tours available in Apr, Sept & Oct by prior arrangement.) Educational material relating to Civil War and the Tudors, available for school parties on request. *Closed Nov–Mar inclusive.*
Refreshments: The Old Kitchen Restaurant is open daily from 11–5 for coffees, buffet lunches and afternoon teas.

WINCHCOMBE RAILWAY MUSEUM *(T.R. Petchey)*
23 Gloucester Street. Tel: (0242) 602257.
A collection of items of British Railway interest, from tickets and labels to horse-drawn railway road vehicles, lineside features and signals. Many exhibits can be operated by the visitor. Open daily 1–6 (dusk if earlier). *Closed* Christmas Day. Adm £1, Chld accompanied by adult free. Unaccompanied Chld 65p. OAPs 65p. Parties of 8 or more 20% reduction. Car parking available on street at entrance. Suitable for disabled persons.

WOTTON UNDER EDGE

NEWARK PARK, The National Trust
Telephone: Dursley 842644

Elizabethan Hunting Lodge built on cliff edge, modified in 1790's by James Wyatt and rehabilitated by present tenant. Woodland garden.
Location: 1½ m E of Wotton under Edge, 1½ m S of junction of A4135 and B4058.
Opening Times: Apr, May, Aug & Sept; Weds & Thurs 2–5. Adm £1, Chd 50p. Parties by prior written arrangement only. No reductions. Not suitable for coaches or wheelchairs. No dogs.

YANWORTH

CHEDWORTH ROMAN VILLA, The National Trust
Telephone: Withington 256   ♿

The best exposed Romano-British villa in Britain. It was built about AD120 and extended and occupied until about AD400. There are good fourth century mosaics in the bath suits and triclinium (dining room). The villa was excavated in 1864, and a museum has a good range of household objects.
Location: 3 m NW of Fossebridge on Cirencester–Northleach road (A429).
Opening Times: Mar to end Oct: Tues to Sun & Bank Hol Mon 10–5.30. Last admissions 5. *Closed* Good Friday. Nov to 10 Dec: Wed to Sun 11–4. Feb: pre-booked parties only, subject to weather conditions. Adm £1.80, Chd 90p. Parties by prior written arrangement only. Disabled – all parts accessible but some with difficulty. Disabled WC.

BERKELEY CASTLE GLOUCESTERSHIRE

The Castle and Gardens are open to the public: April—Daily (except Mondays) 2 to 5 pm. May to August—Weekdays (except Mondays) 11 am to 5 pm; Sundays 2 to 5 pm. September—Daily (except Mondays) 2 to 5 pm. October—Sundays only 2 to 4.30 pm. Also Bank Holiday Mondays 11am to 5 pm.

Refreshments, light lunches and afternoon teas available.
Luncheons, to order only, for parties of 20 or more persons in separate room. Free Coach and Car Park. Dogs not allowed.

Charge for admission: Not available at time of going to press.

For further information apply to the Custodian. Berkeley Castle, Glos. (stamped addressed envelope please). Telephone 0453 810332.

Built in 1153, the castle stands in a state of perfect preservation. This, the oldest inhabited castle in England, has everything one expects to find in such an historic building.

Here is the massive Norman Keep, Dungeon, Great Hall and Kitchen, and the cell which was the SCENE OF THE MURDER OF KING EDWARD II.

The State Apartments contain a magnificent collection of furniture, rare paintings and tapestries. Part of the world-famous Berkeley silver is also on display. The lovely Elizabethan Terraced Gardens, with an ancient bowling alley, overlook the watermeadows, the Kennels of the Berkeley Hounds and beyond, the Deer Park with its Red and Fallow Deer, Butterfly House. Picnic area adjacent to coach and car parks.

ENGLANDS MOST FAMOUS HISTORIC HOME

Cotswold District Council

Cotswold's Museums

 CORINIUM MUSEUM
Roman Britain comes alive
PARK STREET, CIRENCESTER
Telephone: (0285) 5611

 COTSWOLD COUNTRYSIDE COLLECTION
A Museum of Rural Life
FOSSE WAY, NORTHLEACH
Telephone: (0451) 60715

 AWARD WINNING MUSEUM!

 CIRENCESTER LOCK-UP
TRINITY ROAD, CIRENCESTER
Telephone: (0285) 5611

For further information, opening hours etc, please see editorial

GLOUCESTER MUSEUMS AND ART GALLERY

*Left:
puppets at the
City Museum*

*Right:
wheelwright's
shop at the
Folk Museum*

The City Museum collections cover the archaeology and natural history of the city and county of Gloucester. On the first floor is the art gallery (temporary exhibitions throughout the year) and collections of English furniture, pottery, silver, glass and costume.
The Branch Museum at the Folk Museum contains collections illustrating the post-medieval history of Gloucester and the trades, crafts and industries of the surrounding countryside.

Cheltenham Art Gallery & Museums

An extended Art Gallery & Museum with improved visitor facilities will be opening in 1989

Sudeley Castle and Gardens

Sudeley, the lovely Cotswold home of Lord and Lady Ashcombe, is rich in Tudor history, art treasures, antiques, arms and armour. The dungeon tower houses craft workshops. The tomb of Queen Katherine Parr lies in the 15th Century chapel. Falconry displays are held each Tuesday, Wednesday and Thursday May to August.
Open daily from Easter to October.
Sudeley Castle Holiday Cottages are available all year round.

 Winchcombe, Gloucestershire. Telephone: Cheltenham (0242) 602308

Greater Manchester

ASHTON-UNDER-LYNE

THE MUSEUM OF THE MANCHESTERS. A SOCIAL AND REGIMENTAL HISTORY
(Tameside Metropolitan Borough)
Ashton Town Hall, The Market Place. Tel: 061 344 3078.
The history of the Manchester Regiment, displayed with the social history of the community in which it was based. Mon–Sat 10–4. *Closed* Sun and Bank Hols. Adm free.

PORTLAND BASIN INDUSTRIAL HERITAGE CENTRE
(Tameside Metropolitan Borough)
Portland Place, Portland Street South. Tel: 061 308 3374.
200 years of Tameside's social and industrial history displayed in a former canal warehouse with a waterwheel on the wharf. Tues to Sat, 10–5; Sun 1–5. *Closed* Mon. Adm free.

BOLTON

BOLTON MUSEUM AND ART GALLERY
(Bolton Metropolitan Borough Council)
Le Mans Crescent. Tel: (0204) 22311, Ext. 2191.
Collections of archaeology, local and industrial history, natural history, geology and Egyptology. Art gallery containing collection of 18th century watercolours; sculpture, ceramics; temporary exhibitions gallery. Mon, Tues, Thurs and Fri 9.30–5.30; Sat 10–5. *Closed* Wed, Sun and Bank Hols.

BOLTON STEAM MUSEUM *(Northern Mill Engine Society)*
The Engine House, Atlas No 3 Mill, Chorley Old Road.
Display of the Society's collection of restored stationary steam engines, mainly from the north-west textile industry. Currently 8 rebuilt engines plus photos, models etc. Suns (static viewing); Steam days as advertised. Static viewing free; charge on Steam days. Parties welcome. Car parking off-road and free. Refreshments on Steam days only. Curator: J. Phillp (Hon Secretary).

HALL I' TH' WOOD
Telephone: Bolton (0204) 51159
(Bolton Metropolitan Borough)

Dating from latter half of the 15th century and furnished throughout in the appropriate period. The Hall, built in the post and plaster style, dates from 1483, a further extension was added in 1591, the last addition being made in 1648. Home of Samuel Crompton in 1779 when he invented the Spinning Mule. House contains Crompton relics.
Location: In Green Way, off Crompton Way; 2 m NE of town centre off A58 (Crompton Way); signposted. Hall i' th' Wood (½ m).
Station: Bolton (2½ m); Bromley Cross (1¼ m). Hall i' th' Wood (½ m).
Opening Times: Apr to Sept: Tues to Sat 11–5; Sun 2–5. *Closed* Mons except Bank Holidays. Oct to Mar: *Closed* to general public. Open to pre-booked parties and evening party tours.

MUSEUM OF LOCAL HISTORY
Little Bolton Town Hall, St. George's Street. Tel: (0204) 22311, Ext. 2192.
The museum displays various aspects of the social history of the region. Mon to Sat 10–12, 1–5. *Closed* Thurs, Sun and Bank Hols.

SMITHILLS HALL
Telephone: Bolton (0204) 41265
(Bolton Metropolitan Borough)

Dating from the 14th century with later additions. Great Hall with open roof. Fine linenfold panelling. 16th and 17th century furnishings. Grounds contain nature trail and trailside museum.
Location: Off Smithills Dean Road; 1½ m NW of town centre off A58 (Moss Bank Way); signposted.
Station: Bolton.
Opening Times: Apr to Sept: Tues to Sat 11–5, Sun 2–5. *Closed* Mons except Bank Holidays. Oct to Mar: *Closed* to general public. Open to pre-booked educational parties and to evening party tours.

TONGE MOOR TEXTILE MUSEUM
The Library, Tonge Moor Road. Tel: (0204) 21394/22311, Ext. 2195.
Houses a collection of important early textile machines including Crompton's Mule, Hargreaves' Jenny and Arkwright's Water Frame. Mon and Thurs 9.30–7.30; Tues and Fri 9.30–5.30; St 9.30–12.30. *Closed* Wed, Sun and Bank Hols.

BROMLEY CROSS

TURTON TOWER *(Lancashire County Council)*
Chapeltown Road, Bromley Cross, Bolton. Tel: (0204) 852203.
Medieval Pele Tower with Tudor Revival interiors and Elizabethan half timbered wing. Permanent collection of 17th century furniture, Civil War arms and armour; local history. Temporary exhibitions. Adm 70p, Chld 35p, OAPs 50p and £1.70 family tickets (2 adults/2 chld). Parties and guided tours by appointment. Car parking. Open Mar, Apr, Oct. Sat–Wed 2–5; May–Sept Mon to Fri 10–12 and 1–5, Sat and Sun 1–5. Nov and Feb, Sun only 2–5. Open Bank Holidays. *Closed* Dec and Jan. Tea room in Victorian Kitchen.

LEIGH

TURNPIKE GALLERY *(Wigan Metro. Borough)*
Leigh. Tel: (0942) 679407.
Some major touring exhibitions, local exhibitions. Small water-colour collection.

MANCHESTER

ATHENAEUM GALLERY *(Manchester City Art Galleries)*
Princess Street (next door to the City Art Gallery). Tel: 061-236 9422.
A newly restored and expanded exhibition Gallery for temporary shows both from Manchester City Arts Galleries' own collections and touring exhibitions. Please write or telephone for details of current programme. Adm free.

CITY ART GALLERY *(Manchester City Art Galleries)*
Mosley Street. Tel: 061-236 9422.
An imposing Greek Revival style Gallery designed by Charles Barry, houses one of the greatest collections of paintings, drawings, sculpture and decorative arts in the country. The interior has been recently restored with elaborate stencilling and gilding to a 19th century scheme to provide a background for works by (among others) Souch, Claude Lorrain, Bellotto, Batoni, Cuyp, de Hooch, Boucher, Stubbs, Gainsborough, Palmer, Turner and the famous collection of Pre-Raphaelite and Victorian paintings. Two rooms now house small temporary exhibitions. There is also a new display: Mr Lowry at Home, featuring a reconstruction of the artists living room and studio. There are also outstanding collections of sculpture, furniture, ceramics, silver and glass from 16th century to 19th century. Mon to Sat 10–6; Sun 2–6. Adm free.

FACULTY OF ART AND DESIGN, HOLDEN GALLERY
Manchester Polytechnic, Cavendish Street, All Saints M15 6BR.
Tel: 061-228 6171.
Temporary exhibitions, chiefly of contemporary art and design, arranged frequently during the academic year also permanent exhibition of historic craftwork on view Oct to May. During term: Mon to Fri 10–6.

FLETCHER MOSS MUSEUM AND ART GALLERY
Telephone: 061-236 9422 enquiries
(Manchester City Art Galleries)

A late Georgian and early Victorian parsonage set in pleasant gardens. A local heritage centre displaying works by artists related to the North West.
Location: 5 m S of City centre on main Wilmslow Road.
Opening Times: Open Apr to Sept. Please telephone to check times before visit. Adm free.

GALLERY OF ENGLISH COSTUME *(Manchester City Art Galleries)*
Platt Hall, Platt Fields, Rusholme. Tel: 061-224 5217.
One of the finest costume collections in the country outside London. Displays include clothes and fashions from 16th century embroidered garments to present day designs by Zandra Rhodes and Caroline Charles. Please write or telephone for details of current special displays. The costume library and study collection is open to students on request. Open every day (except Tues) 10–6; Sun 2–6 (Nov to Feb, the Gallery closes at 4).

THE GREATER MANCHESTER MUSEUM OF SCIENCE AND INDUSTRY
Liverpool Road. Tel: 061-832 2244.
A new museum developed at the world's first passenger railway station utilising the site's historic buildings. The Museum features the Power Exhibition Hall, which tells the story of power using working exhibits (water wheel, steam engines, locomotives etc.). National Electricity Gallery (discovery and uses of electricity, period room settings, restored Power Station generating set), Air and Space Gallery (Shackleton, Spitfire etc.), a Liverpool/Manchester Railway exhibition, the Warehouse Exhibition (printing, papermaking, textile manufacture, computers), special events, Museum shop and refreshments. Opening during 1988 "Greater Manchester Story" and "Underground Manchester" exhibitions. Daily 10–5. Last adm 4.30. *Closed* December 23 to 25.

GREATER MANCHESTER POLICE MUSEUM
(Greater Manchester Police)
Newton Street. Tel: 061-855 3290.
Set in a Victorian Police Station, the Police Museum features a reconstructed Charge Office of the 1920's, the station cells and in three other rooms collections of uniforms, equipment, forgery exhibits and photographic displays. Open only by appointment. Open throughout the year. *Closed* weekends, Public and Bank Hols. All visits free of charge. Parties – no minimum number, but a maximum size of 20 persons only per visit. Curator: Mr Duncan Broady.

HEATON HALL
Telephone: 061-236 9422 enquiries
(Manchester City Art Galleries)

Former home of the Earls of Wilton and designed by James Wyatt in 1772 the Hall has a unique decorated interior. Described by Pevsner as one of the finest country houses of its period in the country.
Location: 6 m N of City centre.
Station: Heaton Park (½ m).
Opening Times: Open Apr to Sept, including Bank Holidays. Please telephone to check times before visit. Adm free.

MANCHESTER JEWISH MUSEUM
(Trustees of Manchester Jewish Museum)
190 Cheetham Hill Road. M8 8LW. Tel: 061 834 9879 or 832 7353
The museum is in a former Spanish and Portuguese synagogue built in 1874. Downstairs the synagogue has been restored to its original condition but upstairs, in the former ladies gallery, there is an exhibition on the history of Manchester's Jewish community over the last two hundred years.
Temporary exhibition area and programme of trails, demonstrations, talks and concerts. Open Mon–Thurs 10.30–4; Sun 10.30–5. *Closed* Fri, Sat and Jewish holidays. Adm 60p, concessions 40p, family ticket £2. No charge for teachers with school parties or on preliminary visits. Car parking on street nearby. Suitable for disabled persons on ground floor only. All parties must be booked in advance.

MANCHESTER MUSEUM
The University, Oxford Road M13 9PL. Tel: 061-275 2634.
Important collections of geology, botany, zoology, entomology, archaeology, Egyptology, ethnology, numismatics, the Simon Archery Collection and the Cannon Aquarium and Vivarium; museum education service and frequent temporary exhibitions. Museum shop. Mon to Sat 10–5. *Closed* a few days at Christmas and on Good Friday and May Day Bank Hol. Buses from Albert Square and Piccadilly 41 to 49 inclusive. Car parking. **Museum of the Year 1987.**

THE PANKHURST CENTRE
60-62 Nelson Street, Chorlton-cum-Hardy.
Restored Georgian terraced house, grade 2 listed, No 62 with 2**. Former residence of Mrs Emmeline Pankhurst and her family between 1897–1907.

PLATT HALL
Telephone: 061-224 5217
(Manchester City Art Galleries)

A Georgian country house of the 1760's, designed by John Carr of York and Timothy Lightoler for the Worsleys, it is now the internationally famous Gallery of English Costume, showing the changing styles in clothes and accessories from the 17th century to the present day.
Location: In Platt Fields, Rusholme 2 m S of City on Wilmslow Road.
Station: Levenshulme.
Opening Times: Open all year. Please telephone to check times before visit. Adm free.
Refreshments: Teas in the park.

WHITWORTH ART GALLERY *(University of Manchester)*
Oxford Road. Tel: 061-273 4865.
Outstanding collections of British watercolours, Old Master drawings, Post-Impressionist and 20th century Continental drawings. Contemporary paintings and sculpture. Prints ranging from the Renaissance period to the present day, including Japanese colour woodcuts. Historic wallpapers. Important textiles collection notable for its Coptic and Peruvian cloths, Spanish and Italian vestments, Renaissance reliefs, ethnographical textiles, tribal rugs and contemporary fabrics. Major exhibitions. Gallery Shop and Gallery Bistro. Mon to Sat 10–5 (Thurs 10–9). *Closed* Sun and Christmas to New Year also Good Friday. Car Parking. Buses 40, 46, 48, 157, 158, 190, 191, W42, P11, B5, B6.

WYTHENSHAWE HALL
Telephone: 061-236 9422
(Manchester City Art Galleries)

A timber framed country house which was the home of the Tatton family for over 500 years. 17th century furniture, oil paintings and rare, recently discovered Tudor wall paintings.
Location: 7 m S of City centre in Wythenshawe Park, on the Altrincham/Stockport Road.
Opening Times: Open Apr to Sept. Please telephone to check times before visit. Adm free.
Refreshments: Teas at the Hall.

OLD TRAFFORD

MANCHESTER UNITED MUSEUM AND VISITOR CENTRE
Old Trafford. Tel: 061 872 1661.
The first, purpose built museum in British football. Covers the history of Manchester United in words, pictures, sound and vision. More than 300 exhibits on display, including historical shirts, trophies, tickets, programmes and international caps. Lunches and refreshments available in the Sir Matt Busby Suite daily from 12–2.30. Museum open 10–4 Sun to Fri. £1.50, Chld £1, under five free. Parking facilities. Generous reductions for organised parties. Ground tours for groups available by prior arrangement, and usually comprise a visit to the dressing rooms, players' lounge, trophy room, and a walk down the players' tunnel to view the pitch and stadium, as well as the entrance to the museum. Club's mural, painted by Walter Kershaw, can be seen in the Sir Matt Busby suite.

OLDHAM

ART GALLERY *(Oldham Leisure Services)*
Union Street. Tel: 061-678 4651.
Frequently changed exhibitions of contemporary art and photography. Also Oldham collections comprising early English watercolours, British 19th and 20th century paintings, modern prints, English ceramics and glass, plus small Oriental collection. Mon, Wed, Thurs and Fri 10–5; Tues 10–1; Sat 10–4. *Closed* Sun.

LOCAL INTEREST CENTRE *(Oldham Leisure Services)*
Greaves Street. Tel: 061-678 4655.
Two floors devoted to changing exhibitions of local interest. Local Studies Library and Tourist Information point in adjacent building. Mon, Wed, Thurs and Fri 10–5; Tues 10–1; Sat 10–4. *Closed* Sun.

SADDLEWORTH MUSEUM & ART GALLERY
High Street, Uppermill. Tel: (045 77) 4093.
Local heritage museum. Art exhibitions, events, shop, tourist information. Open daily, parties and educational visits welcome.

ROCHDALE

ROCHDALE ART GALLERY
Tel: (0706) 342154.
A lively and exciting gallery with a commitment to showing art in a social and public context. The gallery organises exhibitions which try to represent the art of the past to a wide audience, shows contemporary art in a more accessible and critical way and has a positive policy towards the work of Black artists and women. The Gallery wishes to involve local communities in art and organises community projects, workshops and discussions. Shows planned for 1989 include 'Artists for Animals', artists producing work on animal rights, Black women photographers, a video project based in the community, a historic investigation into Laura Knight and the role of women during the war years. Workshops and discussions during most exhibitions. Mon to Fri 10–5; Wed 10–1; Sat 10–4. Adm free.

ROCHDALE COLLEGE OF ARTS AND DESIGN
Leo Solomon Gallery, St. Mary's Gate, OL12 6RY. Tel: (0706) 345346.
Exhibitions (all media) and performance by students and invited artists. An active programme of temporary shows and events. Open during College terms Mon to Thurs 10–7.30, Fri 10–3, Sat 10–12. Adm free. Annual students' Exhibition and Open Days mid June.

ROCHDALE MUSEUM *(Rochdale Metro. Borough)*
Sparrow Hill. Tel: (0706) 47474, Ext. 4924.
Situated in 18th century vicarage next to the Parish Church. Displays of local history, rural industries, interiors, costume, geology, natural history, decorative arts, John Bright and Gracie Fields memorabilia. Collections also include Egyptology, furniture, folk life. Temporary exhibitions. Mon to Fri 12–5; Sat 10–1, 2–5. *Closed* Sun and Public Hols.

ROCHDALE PIONEERS CO-OPERATIVE MUSEUM
Toad Lane. Tel: 061-832 4300.
Houses the original store of the Rochdale Co-operative Pioneers containing documents, pictures and other material of British and international co-operative interest.

SALFORD

MONKS HALL MUSEUM *(City of Salford)*
42 Wellington Road, Eccles. Tel: 061-789 4372.
Closed for refurbishment.

MUSEUM AND ART GALLERY *(City of Salford)*
Peel Park, The Crescent. Tel: 061-736 2649.
The main museum exhibit is that of a period street typical of a northern industrial town at the time of the turn of the century. The Art Gallery permanently displays a comprehensive collection of the works of L.S. Lowry and holds frequent exhibitions by artists of this region. Mon to Fri 10–5; Sun 2–5.

MUSEUM OF MINING *(City of Salford)*
Buile Hill Park, Eccles Old Road. Tel: 061-736 1832.
The museum is devoted to the history and technology of coal-mining and reproductions of an underground mine and a drift mine illustrate this theme. Organised school parties on pre-arranged visits are welcome. Mon to Fri 10–12.30, 1–5.30; Sun 2–5.

ORDSALL HALL MUSEUM *(City of Salford)*
Taylorson Street. Tel: 061-872 0251.
This largely 15th to 17th century building has been restored for use as a museum and apart from its architectural interest it contains period rooms and local history displays. It is used as a regular concert venue. Mon to Fri 10–12.30, 1.30–5; Sun 2–5.

PHOTOGRAPHIC HERITAGE CENTRE *(City of Salford)*
Vulcan House, Crescent. (Opposite Museum & Art Gallery).
The Centre is devoted to Salfords History in photographs plus regular contemporary photographic exhibitions. Tues to Fri 10–5; Sun 2–5.

STALYBRIDGE

THE ASTLEY CHEETHAM ART GALLERY
(Tameside Metropolitan Borough)
Trinity Street. Tel: 061-338 2708.
The Cheetham Collection of paintings; 14th century Italian gold ground paintings to Burne-Jones. Monthly exhibition programme covering fine art, craft and photography. Mon, Tues, Wed and Fri 1–7.30; Sat 9–4. *Closed* Sun and Thur. Adm free.

STOCKPORT

BRAMALL HALL
Telephone: 061-485 3708
(Metropolitan Borough of Stockport)

Bramall Hall is one of the most splendid of Cheshire's black and white timber framed houses. The oldest parts date back to the fourteenth century, and there are many interesting features from later centuries. The magnificent 16th century wall paintings are some of the finest in the North West, and the Elizabethan withdrawing room has a fine plaster ceiling and overmantel. The Victorian additions are in the most romantic spirit and include attractive wrought iron fittings. Special events and concerts are arranged throughout the year. The Hall stands in a landscaped park with streams, lakes and woods. Shop.

Location: 4 m S of Stockport; off A5102.
Station: Cheadle Hulme (½ m).
Opening Times: Apr–Sept daily 1–5; Oct–Jan 1: Tues–Sun 1–4; Jan 2–Jan 31: *Closed* Feb–Mar: Tues–Sun 1–4. Adm £1.50, Chd 75p (subject to alteration for special events). Parking and gardens free and open at all times. Guided tours of the Hall every afternoon. Day and evening tours for parties by arrangement.
Refreshments: The Stables cafe serves lunches and teas, and is available for functions. Cafe open Apr–Sept daily 11–4.30. Oct–Dec: Tues–Sun 11–4; Jan: Sat & Sun 11–4; Feb–Mar: Sun 11–4.

LYME HALL AND PARK *(Metropolitan Borough of Stockport)*
Disley, 7 m. from town centre. Tel: (0663) 62023.
Fine house dating from the 16th century, remodelled in early 18th century in Palladian style. Extensive gardens and 1,320 acre park. Maintained by Stockport Metropolitan Borough Council on behalf of the National Trust. Apr–Sept: Tues to Sat 2–4.30; Sun and Bank Holiday 1–6; Oct–Nov: Sun only 1–4.30; *Closed* Mon. Adm per car and occupants £2 (Park and Gardens), £6 (Hall, Park and Gardens).

STOCKPORT MUSEUM
Vernon Park, Turncroft Lane. Tel: 061-474 4460.
Displays on the history of Stockport from Pre-historic times to the present. Apr–Sept: daily 1–5. Open Bank Holiday Mon. Schools and organised parties all year, by appointment.

STOCKPORT WAR MEMORIAL BUILDING ART GALLERY
Wellington Road South. Tel: 061-480 9433.
Changing exhibitions of contemporary art, photography and craft with emphasis on complementary events – practical workshops for children and adults, lectures etc. 'Art Link' loan scheme for contemporary works of art including paintings, sculpture, photographs and craft work. Small permanent collection of 19th and 20th century British paintings. Mon to Fri 11–5; Sat 10–5. *Closed* Sun and Bank Hols.

WIGAN

WIGAN PIER *(Wigan Metropolitan Borough Council)*
Wigan Pier, WN3 4EU. Tel: (0942) 323666.
Canalside Heritage Centre with live interpretation of local life and industry c. 1900. Steam engine with working mill/colliery/ropemaking machinery. Waterbus service. Full educational service. Wigan Pier Festival each Sept. 7 days per week, 10–5 except Christmas Day and Boxing Day, Adm: Day Pass to all attractions £2, concessions £1. Generous group discount. 600 free parking spaces. Suitable for disabled persons. Refreshments. Piermaster: John Swarbrooke.

Stockport Art Gallery: Arts Council Touring Exhibition

*Bramall Hall: Heraldic Glass
(The Davenport/de Bromale Coat of Arms)*

STOCKPORT MUSEUMS AND ART GALLERY SERVICE

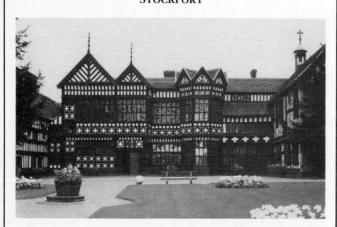

Hampshire

ALDERSHOT

ALDERSHOT MILITARY MUSEUM
(Aldershot Military Historical Trust)
Queens Avenue. Tel: (0252) 314598.
Tells the story of the Home of the British Army from its creation in 1854 to the present day, with photographs, models and displays depicting the daily life of the soldier. Features an original Victorian barrack room with period uniforms and equipment. Diorama of pioneer flying machines, balloons and airships depict the birth of British aviation at Farnborough. Canadian gallery recalls the Canadian Army's long association with Aldershot from Queen Victoria's Diamond Jubilee Review to their takeover of the camp as their main UK base for the whole of World War 2. External exhibits. Ample parking. Open daily Mar–Oct, 10–5; Nov–Feb, 10–4.30. *Closed* 18–26 Dec. Adm £1, Chd 25p. Reductions for OAP and parties. Curator: J. Iveson.

ALRESFORD

ALRESFORD HOUSE
Telephone: (096 273) 2843
(Mr & Mrs P Constable Maxwell)

Georgian country house built by Admiral Lord Rodney 1750.
Location: 8 m E of Winchester off A31 Winchester/Alton Road.
Opening Times: All Aug, parties at other times by arrangement, Wed to Sun 2.30–6. Adm £1.50. Fruit & vegetables—'Pick Your Own' throughout the summer. Catering facilities available for parties, receptions, etc by arrangement.
Refreshments: Teas in walled garden throughout August.

ALTON

THE CURTIS MUSEUM AND ALLEN GALLERY
(Hampshire County Museum Service)
High Street. Tel: (0420) 82802.
The Curtis Museum contains the new 'Story of Alton' display and includes an aquarium and a fascinating collection of children's toys, dolls and games. The Allen Gallery displays a comprehensive collection of English pottery, paintings from the W.H. Allen bequest, and an exciting programme of temporary exhibitions. There is also a garden for visitors to enjoy. Open Tues–Sat, 10–5. *Closed* Sun and Mon. Parties welcome. Curator: T. Cross.

AMPFIELD

THE HILLIER GARDENS AND ARBORETUM
(Hampshire County Council)

Begun by the famous nurseryman Sir Harold Hillier in 1953, and gifted to Hampshire County Council in 1977, the Gardens and Arboretum now extend to some 160 acres and contain the largest collection of different hardy plants in the British Isles. With this diversity in plants, the Gardens provide something of interest throughout the seasons, from the magnificent floral displays in the spring, followed by the pastel shades of summer which become overwhelmed by the riot of autumnal hues in October to the highly scented winter flowering Witch Hazels.
Location: 3 m north east of Romsey, off A31.
Opening Times: Mon to Fri 10–5 (all year round). Sats, Suns and Bank Hols 1–6 (Mar to mid Nov). Adm £1.50, Chd (under 16 years) Free on weekdays, 50p at weekends and Bank Holidays. Groups over 30 £1.20. Regret NO DOGS.
Refreshments: Attractive picnic area.

ANDOVER

THE ANDOVER MUSEUM AND ART GALLERY
(Hampshire County Museum Service)
Church Close. Tel: (0264) 66283.
Accumulating collections relating to the Andover area. Displays of recent accessions, Tasker Gallery, National History Gallery and Aquaria. Temporary exhibitions changed monthly. Archaeology and Geology galleries, Tues to Sat 10–5. Museum of the Iron Age of Southern Britain also open Sun 2–5 Apr to Oct. Parties by arrangement. Curator: D.W.H. Allen, Bsc., FSA.

BASINGSTOKE

STRATFIELD SAYE HOUSE
Telephone: Basingstoke (0256) 882882   &
(The Duke of Wellington)

This Stuart house is filled with the Great Duke's possessions and personality. Wellington Exhibition. State Coach. Great Duke's Funeral Carriage, Grounds, gardens, wildfowl sanctuary and Copenhagen's grave.
Location: 1 m W of A33 between Reading & Basingstoke (turn off at Wellington Arms Hotel); signposted. Close to M3 & M4.
Opening Times: House and Gardens; open daily (except Fris) from May 1 to last Sun in Sept 11.30–5. Wellington Country Park (3 m from House)—Nature trails, adventure playgrounds, animals, boating, windsurfing, fishing, deer park miniature steam railway. National Dairy Museum, Thames Valley Time Trail—Mar to Oct daily 10–5. Nov–Feb Sats & Suns only. Adm charges House: £3, Chd £1.50. Park: £2, Chd £1. Combined House and Park: £3.60, Chd £1.70.
Refreshments: Tea and snacks, licensed restaurant.

THE VYNE, The National Trust
Telephone: Basingstoke 881337   &

An important early 16th century house with classic portico added 1654. Tudor panelling, 18th century ornamented staircase. Extensive lawns, lake, trees, herbaceous border.
Location: 4 m N of Basingstoke between Bramley & Sherborne St John (1½ m from each).
Station: Bramley (2½ m).
Opening Times: Mar 24 to Oct 15—Tues, Weds, Thurs, Sats & Suns 1.30–5.30. Open Bank Hol Mons 11–5.30. Last adm 5. *Closed Tues, following Bank Hol Mons.* Adm HOUSE AND GARDEN: Suns & Bank Hol Mons £2.60, other open days £2.30. GARDEN ONLY: £1.30/£1.10. Chd half price. *Reduced rates for pre-booked parties Tues, Weds & Thurs only.* Shop. Dogs in car park only. Wheelchair provided.
Refreshments: Light lunches and teas in the Old Brewhouse (12.30–5.30).

WILLIS MUSEUM AND ART GALLERY
(Hampshire County Museum Service)
Old Town Hall, Market Place. Tel: (0256) 465902.
Opened 1931. Local collections of archaeology, natural history, geology, embroideries and toys; Basingstoke Canal; horology and watch and clockmakers' tools. Displays of recent accessions and temporary exhibitions in the art gallery. The Town Gallery traces the town's development. Tues to Fri 10–5; Sat 10–4. Parties by arrangement. *Closed* Sun and Mon. Curator: P.R. Russell-Jones.

BEAULIEU

BEAULIEU
Telephone: Beaulieu (0590) 612345
(The Lord Montagu of Beaulieu)

Palace House and Gardens; Beaulieu Abbey and Exhibition of Monastic Life; The National Motor Museum featuring more than 200 exhibits including motor cars, commercial vehicles and motorcycles; 'Wheels' – a fantastic ride on 'space age' pods through 100 years of motoring from 1895 to the present day. Monorail, veteran bus and miniature veteran car rides, 'Transporama' – an audio-visual presentation of the history of motoring; model railway, radio-controlled cars, mini racing car and motorcycle rides. Daily cavalcades of historic vehicles during peak summer season and many other events throughout the year.
Location: In Beaulieu 7 m SE of Lyndhurst; 14 m S of Southampton; 6 m NE of Lymington.
Opening Times: All facilities open throughout the year. May to Sept—Daily 10–6; Oct to May—Daily 10–5. *Closed Christmas Day.* Inclusive adm charge. Reduced rates for Children & OAPs. *Parties at special rates.*
Refreshments: Lunches and teas at licensed Brabazon Restaurant.

MARITIME MUSEUM
Buckler's Hard. 87 miles from London. Tel: (059 063) 203.
Collection of models and exhibits of ships built at Buckler's Hard for Nelson's Fleet. Also the 18th century homes of a master shipbuilder, Shipwright and labourer and an Inn Scene have been re-created in the village in the original cottages. This open to the public as part of the Buckler's Hard restoration programme. Daily: Easter to May, 10–6; June to Sept, 10–9; Oct to Easter, 10–4.30. Adm charge.

BENTLEY

JENKYN PLACE
(Mr & Mrs G E Coke)

Beautifully designed garden with large collection of rare plants, roses, double herbaceous borders.
Location: In Bentley 400 yds N of cross roads (sign to Crondall). Signposted on A31.
Station: Bentley (1 m).
Opening Times: GARDEN ONLY. Apr 13 to Sept 10—Thurs, Fris, Sats, Suns & Bank Hol Mons 2–6. Coaches only by prior arrangement. Adm £1.50, Chd (5–15) half price. Open on certain Suns in aid of the National Gardens Scheme. No dogs. Car park free.

BISHOP'S WALTHAM

BISHOP'S WALTHAM PALACE
Telephone: (048 93) 2460

The Bishops of Winchester held Waltham since Saxon times, but they did not build here until about 1135. Heavily fortified, this was more castle than palace, and was dismantled by Henry II. Most of the present remains are from the spacious 15th century palace with its walled garden, all within this vast moated site. Forfeited by the bishops at the Reformation, the palace was reduced to a ruin in the Civil War, when it was held for the King against Parliament.
Location: Bishop's Waltham. OS map ref SU552173.
Opening Times: Good Friday to Sept 30, daily 10–6; Oct 1 to Maundy Thursday, daily 10–4. *Closed Mons, Christmas and New Year.* Adm £1.10, OAPs 80p, Chd 55p.

BOTLEY

THE HAMPSHIRE FARM MUSEUM
Upper Hamble Country Park, near Botley off Junction 8 M27.
Tel: Botley (048 92) 87055.
The Hampshire Farm Museum has been developed to show, explain and demonstrate the development of agriculture in Hampshire during the last 150 years. Farming was and is the major industry in the county and a wide range of tools, artefacts, implements and machinery are used to display the many aspects of this. The livestock also reflects the changes over the years. Dairy shorthorn cows were once common in the Botley area but are now a rare breed. Similarly, the Wessex Saddleback pig was popular in South Hampshire at the turn of the century but is scarcely heard of nowadays. The buildings at Manor Farm have changed in function and use over the years as farming needs and storage requirements altered. Four buildings, the Staddle Barn, the Wheelwright's Workshop and the Forge, have been saved from demolition and re-erected at the farm. Each is appropriate for the story being told. Open Summer: daily 10–6; Winter: daily 10–5, but *closed* during Jan & Feb except weekends. (Last adm 1 hour before closing.) Adm. charge.

BRAMDEAN

BRAMDEAN HOUSE
Telephone: 096 279 214
(Mrs H. Wakefield)

Carpets of Spring bulbs. Walled garden with famous herbaceous borders, working kitchen garden and large collection of unusual plants.
Location: Bramdean. On A272 midway between Winchester & Petersfield.
Opening Times: Suns Mar 26, Apr 16, May 21, July 16, Aug 20, Mon Mar 27 2–5. Adm £1, Chd free. Car park. Not suitable for disabled.

HINTON AMPNER, The National Trust   &

The house was remodelled in the Georgian style in 1934 by Ralph Dutton but decimated by fire in 1960. Rebuilt and re-furnished with fine regency furniture, pictures and porcelain. The gardens juxtapose formality of design and informality of planting, producing delightful walks and unexpected vistas.
Location: 1 m W of Bramdean Village on A272; 8 m E of Winchester.
Opening Times: Mar 24 to end Sept. Garden: Wed to Sun 1.30–5.30. House: Wed only 1.30–5.30 (last adm 5). Admission: Garden £1.30, House £1 extra. Children half-price. No dogs. Most of garden accessible by wheelchair. Party reductions (£1.50 House & Garden) Wed only by prior booking with Southern Region Office, Polesden Lacey, Dorking, Surrey. (Tel: Dorking (0372) 53401.)
Refreshments: Teas.

BRANSGORE

MACPENNY'S
Telephone: Bransgore (0425) 72348
(Tim Lowndes, Esq)

Large woodland garden. Nurseries, camellias, rhododendrons, azaleas, heathers.
Location: 4 m NE of Christchurch; 1½ m W of A35.
Opening Times: Garden and nurseries open all year daily (except Christmas Hols). Mons to Sats 9–5; Suns 2–5. *Collecting box in aid of National Gardens Scheme.*

BURGHCLERE

SANDHAM MEMORIAL CHAPEL, The National Trust
Telephone: Burghclere 394 or 292   &

Walls covered with paintings by Stanley Spencer depicting war scenes in Salonica.
Location: In village of Burghclere 4 m S of Newbury ½ m E of A34.
Opening Times: All the year—Daily 11–6 (or dusk if earlier). Open Good Friday, but closed Christmas Day & New Year's Day. Adm 70p, Chd half-price. Parties must book. No reduction for parties. No dogs. Wheelchair access.

CHAWTON

JANE AUSTEN'S HOUSE
(Jane Austen Memorial Trust)

Jane Austen's home with many interesting personal relics of herself and her family.
Location: 1 m SW of Alton off A31 and B3006, sign post Chawton.
Station: Alton (1¾ m).
Opening Times: Daily Apr–Oct; Nov, Dec & Mar: Weds to Suns. Jan & Feb: Sats & Suns only, 11–4.30. *Closed Christmas Day & Boxing Day.* Adm £1, Chd (under 14) 50p.

EASTLEIGH

EASTLEIGH MUSEUM & ART GALLERY
(Hampshire County Museums Service)
High Street. Tel: (0703) 643026.
Displays reflecting the history, life and culture of the Eastleigh area from the arrival of the railway in about 1840. Video presentations including archive film. Temporary exhibitions changed regularly. Museum shop selling local gifts and publications. Tues to Fri 10–5; Sat 10–4. Free admission. Fully accessible to disabled. Parties welcome by arrangement. Curator: G. G. S. Bowie, BA, MA, PhD.

ELSON

FORT BROCKHURST
Telephone: (070 17) 81059

One of five forts known as the Gosport Advanced Line, Brockhurst was built in the mid-19th century to protect Portsmouth Dockyard. The traditional star shape was abandoned for a polygonal plan. Norman castles had become obsolete with the use of gunpowder, but some features were retained. Brockhurst has a moat and a drawbridge. It also has a keep, traditionally the point of last defence. There is an exhibition on the history of Portsmouth's defences.
Location: Off the A32 in Elson on the north side of Gosport. OS map ref SU596020.
Opening Times: Good Friday to Sept 30, daily 10–6; Oct 1 to Maundy Thursday, daily 10–4. *Closed Mons, Christmas and New Year.* Adm £1.10, OAPs 80p, Chd 55p.

EXBURY

EXBURY GARDENS
(E L de Rothschild, Esq)

Unique 200 acre woodland garden created by Lionel de Rothschild, with a superb display of Rhododendrons, Azaleas, Camellias, Magnolias, other fascinating flora and new plantings. Well stocked Plant Centre and Gift Shop, artist's studio, licensed tea rooms.
Location: Exbury village, 15 m SW of Southampton close to New Forest. Turn S off B3054 between Beaulieu & Dibden Purlieu.
Opening Times: Daily Mar 18 to July 9, 10–5.30. Adm; early and late season discounts – please telephone. **Spring:** main flowering season £2.20, OAPs, Parties & Chd (12–15) £1.70; Bank Hol weekends and May weekends all charges 50p more. **Autumn:** Sept 9 to Oct 22. Adm OAPs £1, all others £1.50. **Plant Centre:** Daily Feb 25 to Dec 21. 10–5.30 or dusk if earlier.
Refreshments: Tearooms. Ample parking. Toilets.

FAWLEY

CALSHOT CASTLE
Telephone: (0703) 892023

Part of the chain of Henry VIII's coastal defences against the Catholic powers of Europe. Completed in 1540 and still virtually intact, the Castle has played an important role in England's defence from the 16th Century until World War II. From 1912 to the mid 1950's it formed part of a flying boat base, initially a Royal Naval Air station, then RAF Calshot. Site exhibition in restored WWI barrack room.
Location: On Spit 2 m (3.2 km) south west of Fawley off B5053, 15 m (24 km) south east of Southampton. OS map 196, ref SU488025.
Opening Times: Good Friday to Sept 30, daily 10–6. Adm £1.10, OAPs 80p, Chd 55p.

FORDINGBRIDGE

BREAMORE HOUSE
Telephone: Downton (0725) 22468
(Sir Westrow Hulse, Bt)

Elizabethan Manor House (1583) with fine collection of paintings, tapestries, furniture. Countryside Museum. Carriage Museum.
Location: 3 m N of Fordingbridge off the main Bournemouth Road (A338) 8 m S of Salisbury.
Opening Times: Mar 25, 26, 27; Apr—Tues, Weds, Suns; May, June, July & Sept—Tues, Weds, Sats, Suns and all Bank Hols; Aug—Daily, 2–5.30. Adm: Combined ticket £3, Chd £1.50. Reduced rates for parties & OAPs. *Other times by appointment.*
Refreshments: Home-made Teas. Food available. Bat and Ball, Breamore.

ROCKBOURNE ROMAN VILLA
(Hampshire County Museum Service)
Rockbourne, near Fordingbridge. Tel: Rockbourne (072 53) 541
Site Museum displaying finds from the Roman Villa, totally refurbished in 1988. Foundations with mosaics, open to view. Early Apr to early Oct: Mon to Fri 2–6; Sat, Sun and Bank Hols 10.30–6; July and Aug daily 10.30–6. Parties by arrangement. Adm 80p; Chld and OAP 40p.

GOSPORT

GOSPORT MUSEUM *(Gosport Borough Council)*
Walpole Road. Tel: (0705) 588035.
An interesting and unusual Art Nouveau building (1901) housing a permanent exhibition of local archaeology, geology, maritime crafts and local history. Displays of recent acquisitions and regular temporary exhibitions. Adm free. Tues to Sat 9.30–5.30. Suns (May–Sept only) 1–5. *Closed* Mon.

SUBMARINE MUSEUM AND HMS ALLIANCE
Tel: (0705) 529217. Museum office: (0705) 510354.
Underwater warfare yesterday and today displayed in the world's most comprehensive Submarine Museum, featuring Britain's last World War II submarine, HMS Alliance and the Royal Navy's first submarine Holland I, recovered from the seabed in 1982. Daily Apr to Oct, 10 – last tour starting 4.30; Nov to Mar, 10 – last tour starting 3.30. *Closed* Dec 24–Jan 2 incl. Adm charge. *Special rates for Groups.*

GREATHAM

GREATHAM MILL
Telephone: Blackmoor 219
(Mrs Frances Pumphrey)

Attractive garden of 1½ acres bordered by small river and intersected by Mill waterways. Many unusual plants. Also nursery garden with plants for sale.
Location: 5 m from Petersfield. Take A325 towards Farnham and turn L to B3006. After 500 yds fork L into NTR lane to garden.
Opening Times: Suns & Bank Hols Apr 16 to Sept 24, 2–7. Adm £1, Chd free. Parties by arrangement on weekdays. Ample car parking space on grass. Coaches must disembark and park at lane head, 200 yds from garden. Not suitable for disabled persons. On Suns and Bank Hols follow yellow signs from Greatham.
Refreshments: None at garden, Queens Hotel and Teashop in Selborne, 2½ miles.

HARTLEY WINTNEY

WEST GREEN HOUSE, The National Trust

Small early 18th century house of great charm in a delightful garden.
Location: 1 m W of Hartley Wintney, 1 m N of A30; 10 m NE of Basingstoke.
Station: Winchfield (2 m).
Opening Times: Mar 26–end Sept. Garden: Wed, Thurs & Sun 2–6; House: (three rooms and staircase) *by written appointment only Wed 2–6..* Adm Garden only £1.30, House 50p extra, Chd half price. No reductions for parties. Apply: Lord McAlpine of West Green, 40 Bernard Street, London WC1N 1LG. Last adm 5.30.

HAVANT

THE HAVANT MUSEUM *(Hampshire County Museum Service)*
East Street. Tel: (0705) 451155
Building up collections which relate to the Havant area. Displays of recent accessions and temporary exhibitions in the Art Gallery. The Vokes Collection of firearms is on display in three 1st floor galleries. Tues to Sat 10–12, 1–5. *Closed* Sun and Mon. Parties by arrangement. Curator N. Hall, B.A.

HIGHCLERE

HIGHCLERE CASTLE
Telephone: (0635) 253210
(The Earl of Carnarvon KCVO, KBE)

Highclere Castle is the ultimate in high Victorian exuberance. Designed by Charles Barry in the 1830s at the same time as he was building the Houses of Parliament, this soaring pinnacled mansion provided the perfect social setting for the 3rd Earl of Carnarvon, one of the great hosts of Queen Victoria's reign. Several prominent Victorian architects, including Barry, George Gilbert Scott and Thomas Allom, are responsible for the extravagant interiors in styles which range from church Gothic through Moorish flamboyance and rococo revival to the solid masculinity in the long library. Old master paintings mix with portraits by Van Dyck and 18th Century painters. Napoleon's desk and chair rescued from St. Helena sits with other 18th and 19th Century furniture.
The 5th Earl of Carnarvon, passionate archaeologist and Egyptologist, was the discoverer of the tomb of Tutankhamun and a special display shows some of his early finds in Egypt which had laid hidden for over 60 years and have only recently been rediscovered.
GARDENS – The parkland with its massive cedars was designed by Capability Brown. The walled gardens also date from the earlier house at Highclere but the dark yew walks are entirely Victorian in character. The glass Orangery and Fernery add an exotic flavour and an impression of the complexity of the gardens at their peak. Walking through to the Secret Garden, the walled walks unexpectedly open up into a curving, densely planted herbaceous garden laid out in this Century with ornamental trees and flowering plants and shrubs.
Location: 4½ m S of Newbury on A34, junction 13 of M4 about 2 m from Newbury. M3. Basingstoke junction about 15 m. Heathrow via M4 1 hour. Rail from London (Paddington station) 1 hour. Taxi W. Martin (0635) 253561 from Newbury.
Opening Times: Sun July 2 – Sun Oct 1 1989, 2–6 (last entry 5). Adm £3, OAP/Chd (under 16) £2. Special reductions for parties of 50 or more by application. Car park and picnic area adjacent to Castle. Suitable for disabled persons on ground floor only. One wheelchair available. Visitors can buy original items in Castle Gift Shop and visit the Plant Centre only a short distance away in the Park.
Refreshments: Traditional country cream teas, ices, soft drinks, etc.

KEYHAVEN

HURST CASTLE
Telephone: (0590) 2344

Built by Henry VIII to defend the Solent, Hurst Castle was completed in 1544, and had a garrison of 23 men. During the Civil War it was occupied by Parliamentary forces and Charles I was imprisoned here for a short time. A longer incarceration was that of an unfortunate priest called Atkinson, who was a prisoner here for 29 years in the 18th century. The castle was considerably modernised in the mid-19th century, under the fear of a French invasion, and was still useful in the Second World War.

Location: Approach by ferry from Keyhaven. OS map ref SZ319898.
Opening Times: Good Friday to Sept 30, daily 10–6; Oct 1 to Maundy Thursday, weekends only 10–4. *Closed Christmas and New Year.* Adm £1.10, OAPs 80p, Chd 55p.

LYMINGTON

SPINNERS
Telephone: Lymington 73347
(Mr & Mrs P G G Chappell)

Garden entirely made by owners; azaleas, rhododendrons interplanted with primulas, blue poppies and other choice woodland and ground cover plants.
Location: 1½ m N of Lymington.
Station: Lymington Town (2 m).
Opening Times: GARDEN ONLY. Apr 22 to Sept 1 – Daily 10–6. Other times by appointment. Large nursery for choice and rare plants open all the year. Adm 75p. *For National Gardens Scheme on certain days. No dogs.* Many rare plants for sale.

MIDDLE WALLOP

MUSEUM OF ARMY FLYING
Stockbridge. Tel: (0264) 62121, Ext. 421/428.
On the A343 between Andover and Salisbury. The Story of Army Flying from the 19th Century to the present day; Balloons, Kites and Airships, World War I and II Aircraft, unique collection of Military Gliders and Experimental Helicopters. More recent campaigns also represented including Northern Ireland and the Falklands. Open daily throughout the year except Christmas period, 10–4.30. Admission Adult £2, Chld/OAP £1 (1988 rates). Group reductions on application. Ample parking, refreshments, shop and free cinema, full disabled facilities.

MINSTEAD

FURZEY GARDENS
Telephone: Southampton (0703) 812464   &

Lovely gardens in nearly eight acres of peaceful glades. There are many main attractions including Heathers throughout the year and Azaleas, Rhododendrons, Bluebells, Peonies and Irises in season, plus many other attractive plants to extend the beauty.
Location: Southampton 10 m, Ringwood 8 m, Lyndhurst 3½ m.
Opening Times: All the year – Daily 10–5. *Closes at dusk in winter.* Adm Mar–Oct £1.75, Chd (5-14 years) 90p; Nov–Feb £1, Chd (5-14 years) 50p.
Refreshments: Trusty Servant; Honeysuckle Restaurant.

MOTTISFONT

MOTTISFONT ABBEY, The National Trust
Telephone: Lockerley 40757   &

Originally a 12th century Augustinian Priory. South front 18th century. Drawing room by Rex Whistler. Fine lawns and trees. Walled garden with Trust's collection of old fashioned roses.
Location: 4½ m NW Romsey ¾ m W of A3057.
Station: Dunbridge (¾ m).
Opening Times: Apr to end Sept: GROUNDS (including Rose Garden) daily except Fri and Sat, 2–6 (last adm 5); ROSE GARDEN only also open 7–9 Tues, Wed, Thurs and Sun during rose season (check with property before making special visit) (last adm 8.30). HOUSE: (Whistler Room and Cellarium only) Weds 2–6. Adm: Grounds £1.50; Chd half-price. Whistler Room & Cellarium 40p extra, Chd half-price; no reduction for parties. Owing to difficulties with opening arrangements, it is not always possible to view rooms in the house (please check in advance). Visits to the house are by guided parties. Numbers are restricted and access may not be possible for all at peak times. Timed tickets should be obtained at entrance kiosk on arrival. Shop. Dogs in car park only. Wheelchairs – grounds and cellarium only. Special parking area for disabled people, please ask at kiosk on arrival.

NETLEY

NETLEY ABBEY
Telephone: (0703) 453076

Extensive picturesque remains of a Cistercian abbey on the east bank of the Southampton Water. Netley Abbey was founded in 1239 by monks from Beaulieu. Remains include the church and cloister buildings.
Location: In Netley, 7 m SE of Southampton, facing Southampton Water.
Opening Times: Good Friday to Sept 30, daily 10–6; Oct 1 to Maundy Thursday, weekends only 10–4. *Closed Christmas and New Year.* Adm 80p, OAPs 60p, Chd 40p.

PORTCHESTER

PORTCHESTER CASTLE
Telephone: (0705) 378291

A Roman fortress, a Norman castle and a Romanesque church share this same site on the north shore of Portsmouth harbour. The outer walls were built in the 3rd century when Britain was the vulnerable north-west frontier of a declining Roman Empire. Today they are among the finest Roman remains in northern Europe. Eight centuries – and very little repair work – later, the walls were sound enough to encompass a royal castle. Portchester was popular with the medieval monarchs but by the 15th century royal money was being spent on Portsmouth instead. The last official use of the castle was as a prison for French seamen during the Napoleonic wars.
Location: South side of Portchester. OS map ref SU625046.
Opening Times: Good Friday to Sept 30, daily 10–6; Oct 1 to Maundy Thursday, daily 10–4. *Closed Mons, Christmas and New Year.* Adm £1.10, OAPs 80p, Chd 55p.

PORTSMOUTH

CHARLES DICKENS' BIRTHPLACE MUSEUM
(Portsmouth City Council)
393 Old Commercial Road. Tel: (0705) 827261.

CITY MUSEUM AND ART GALLERY *(Portsmouth City Council)*
Museum Road, Old Portsmouth PO1 2LJ. Tel: (0705) 827261

EASTNEY ENGINE HOUSE *(Portsmouth City Council)*
Henderson Road, Eastney.

FORT WIDLEY *(Portsmouth City Council)*
Portsdown Hill Road.

HMS VICTORY
HM Naval Base. Tel: (0705) 819604. (Group visits: 839766).
Nelson's flagship *HMS Victory* has been displayed in the Naval Base since the 1920's when it was brought into a dry dock after about 150 years at sea. *HMS Victory* is presented as the world's oldest surviving ship of the line. Laid down in Chatham in 1759 she has been in continuous commission since 1778 and is still manned by serving Royal Navy and Royal Marines personnel. Preservation work has also been non-stop; she is maintained in the configuration she held at the Battle of Trafalgar in 1805, the famous naval encounter in which Nelson lost his life. Open daily (except Christmas Day), Mon to Sat 10.30–5, Sun 1–5. Adm. charge.

HMS WARRIOR 1860 *(Warrior Preservation Trust)*
HM Naval Base. Tel: (0705) 291379 (Group Visits: 839766)
(*Mailing Address* – HMS Warrior 1860, Victory Gate, HM Naval Base, Portsmouth PO1 3QX)
HMS Warrior, launched in 1860, was the ultimate deterrent of her day. Yet, so revolutionary was she that within 10 years she was obsolete. In the next hundred years she was used as a depot ship, a storage hulk and then formed part of the Royal Naval Torpedo Training School at Portsmouth. Finally, after 50 years as an oil jetty at Milford Haven, she was rescued and towed to Hartlepool. Now fully restored, *Warrior* is proudly on display in Portsmouth's historic Naval Base for generations more to see and enjoy. Every detail, however minute has been perfectly re-created. Visitors are given a unique glimpse of life onboard a 19th-century warship as they explore at their leisure. They can sit at the mess tables in the Main Gun Deck; examine *Warrior's* formidable firepower and compare the spartan existence of the ordinary seamen with the spacious luxury and furnishings of the Captain and officers. The magnificent Penn horizontal trunk steam engine, reproduced in every detail, is demonstrated regularly. Open daily Mar to Oct: 10.30–5.30; Nov to Feb: 10.30–5. *Closed* Christmas Day. Adm (1988 rates) £3, Chd £1.50, OAP £2.50. For group visits please telephone (0705) 839766 for discounts and availability. Access for the disabled to the Jetty and Upper Deck.

MARY ROSE SHIP HALL AND EXHIBITION *(Mary Rose Trust)*
H.M. Naval Base. Tel: (0705) 750521. (Group visits: 839766).
(*Mailing Address* – College Road, HM Naval Base, Portsmouth PO1 3LX
In October 1982, thousands watched as Henry VIII's favourite warship, *Mary Rose*, was recovered from the Solent seabed, where she had lain for 437 years. Now the hull is on show in a special dry dock workshop in Portsmouth Naval Base. Nearby, in an historic boathouse, an Exhibition features many of the 13,000 objects recovered during the excavations. It includes an audio-visual presentation and background displays re-creating scenes of life on board and from Tudor social and maritime history. Daily 10.30–5. *Closed* Christmas Day. Adm charge. Gift shop adjacent to Exhibition features exciting range of souvenir items. No car parking in Naval Base. Multi-storey car park nearby. Suitable for disabled persons.* Wheelchairs are available. Refreshments in the Naval Base, Victory Buffet, hot and cold snacks and drinks. Seats 125.
* NB. In the Ship Hall, access for wheelchairs is limited to a single gallery.

NATURAL SCIENCE MUSEUM *(Portsmouth City Council)*
Eastern Parade. Tel: (0705) 827261.

ROYAL MARINES MUSEUM
Eastney (entry via main gate of Barracks). Tel: (0705) 819385.
The history of the Royal Marines from 1664 to the present day displayed in the magnificent setting of the original R.M. Artillery Officer's Mess.

THE ROYAL NAVAL MUSEUM, PORTSMOUTH
H.M. Naval Base. Tel: (0705) 733060. (Group visits: 839766).
YOU'VE SEEN THE SHIPS, NOW MEET THE MEN. Alongside *HMS Victory*, the *Mary Rose* and *HMS Warrior 1860* stands the Royal Naval Museum, the only museum in Britain devoted to the overall history of the Royal Navy. Here the ghosts of past seamen are brought vividly to life in a series of exciting, modern displays that tell the story of our Senior Service from earliest times right up to the present day. Exhibits include figureheads, ship models, uniforms, medals, relics of personnel and ships, paintings and prints, and commemorative silverware and pottery. Pride of place is given to the possessions of ordinary officers and seamen and the displays concentrate on the social history of the Royal Navy. Within the Museum complex there is a Buffet and a well-stocked souvenir and book shop. Daily: 10.30–5 (some seasonal variations). Adm charge.

SOUTHSEA CASTLE AND MUSEUM *(Portsmouth City Council)*
Clarence Esplanade. Tel: (0705) 827261

SQUARE TOWER
City Museums Department, Broad Street, Old Portsmouth.
Tel: (0705) 832144.

ROMSEY

BROADLANDS
Telephone: Romsey (0794) 516878
(Lord and Lady Romsey)

Famous in recent times as the home of Lord Mountbatten, Broadlands was also the country residence of Lord Palmerston, the great Victorian Prime Minister. Fine example of Palladian architecture set in Capability Brown parkland by the banks of the River Test. Visitors may view interior of house containing many fine works of art including "The Iron Forge" by Joseph Wright of Derby, several Van Dycks and furniture by Ince and Mayhew. Visitors may also relive Lord Mountbatten's life and times in the Mountbatten Exhibition and audio-visual display housed in William and Mary stable block.
Location: 8 m N of Southampton (A3057); entrance from by-pass immediately S of Romsey (A31).
Station: Romsey (1 m).
Opening Times: Mar 23 to Oct 1. Daily 10–4. *Closed* Mons, except Bank Hols, until Aug. Adm £3.95, Chd 12–16 £2.25, Chd under 12 accompanied by parent/guardian free, OAPs £2.95. Disabled £2.95, Students £2.95. Reduced rates for parties of 15 or more. Free coach and car park.
Refreshments: Self-service restaurant. Kiosk in picnic area.

PAULTONS ROMANY MUSEUM
Paultons Park and Bird Gardens, Ower; Exit 2 M27. Tel: (0703) 814442.
A large, unique collection of beautifully carved and decorated Romany wagons and carts together with cameo displays depicting Romany life, their crafts and history. Open Apr–Oct. Adm included in overall charge to Paultons Park, £3, Chld £2.50, Groups (over 20) £2.70, Chld £2.20 (1988 rates). Self service restaurants.

PAULTONS VILLAGE LIFE MUSEUM
Paultons Park and Bird Gardens, Ower; Exit 2 M27. Tel: (0703) 814442.
Depicts many craft workshops set up as they were 80 years ago, together with numerous other items appertaining to village and domestic life. Open Apr to Oct. Adm included in overall charge to Paultons Park, (1988 rates) £3, Chld £2.50, Groups (over 20) £2.70, Chld £2.20. Self service restaurants.

SELBORNE

OATES MEMORIAL LIBRARY AND MUSEUM AND THE GILBERT WHITE MUSEUM
Telephone: Selborne 275
(Rev Gilbert White, 1720–1793)

'The Wakes', home of the Rev Gilbert White, pioneer English naturalist and author of *The Natural History of Selborne*, a classic published nearly 200 years ago and still in print. Historic house, two furnished rooms and museum displays on Gilbert White and Selborne, together with 5 acres of historic garden, the subject of White's *Garden Kalendar*. Also including The Oates Memorial Museum with exhibitions on Frank Oates, 19th century explorer and naturalist in southern Africa and Capt Lawrence Oates of Antarctic fame.
Location: In Selborne.
Opening Times: Mar 23 to Oct 30, Wed to Sun 11–5.30. (Last adm 5). *Closed* Nov to Feb, also Mon & Tues, except Bank Holidays. Parties by arrangement. Adm £1, Chd (under 16) 50p, OAPs 75p (1988 rates). Special rates for parties booked in advance. Parking nearby.
Refreshments: available nearby.

SILCHESTER

CALLEVA MUSEUM
Rectory Grounds, Silchester Common. Tel: (0734) 700322 or 700362.
Completely redesigned in 1976. Providing a pictorial graphical display of life in Roman Silchester. Daily 10–dusk. Voluntary donations.

SOUTHAMPTON

BARGATE GUILDHALL MUSEUM *(Southampton Corporation)*
High Street. Tel: (0703) 22544.
Local historical exhibits and changing exhibitions. Museum is housed in the former Hall of Guilds above the Medieval north gate. Tues to Fri 10–12, 1–5; Sat 10–12, 1–4; Sun 2–5. *Closed* Mon.

GOD'S HOUSE TOWER MUSEUM *(Southampton Corporation)*
Town Quay. Tel: (0703) 20007.
Early 15th century fortification now a museum of local archaeology. Tues to Fri 10–12, 1–5; Sat 10–12, 1–4; Sun 2–5. *Closed* Mon.

JOHN HANSARD GALLERY
The University.

MARITIME MUSEUM *(Southampton Corporation)*
Wool House, Bugle Street. Tel: (0703) 23941.
Fourteenth century wool store now a museum of shipping. Tues to Fri 10–12, 1–5; Sat 10–12, 1–4; Sun 2–5. *Closed* Mon.

MEDIEVAL WINE MERCHANTS HOUSE
Telephone: (0892) 48166

A medieval merchant's house, built in the 1290s is now fully restored to its 14th century appearance. On the ground floor is the restored medieval shop stocked with traditional wines and other produce. The house is furnished with medieval reproductions based on contemporary illustrations.

Location: In Southampton City centre between Castle Way and Town Quay.
Opening Times: Good Friday to Sept 30, daily 10–6; Oct 1 to Maundy Thursday, daily 10–4. *Closed Mons, Christmas and New Year.* Adm £1.10, OAPs 80p, Chd 55p.

SOUTHAMPTON CITY ART GALLERY *(Southampton Corporation)*
Civic Centre. Tel: (0703) 832769.
Specialising in British painting, particularly 20th century; a good collection of Old Master paintings and Impressionist and Post-Impressionist works. Tues to Fri 10–5; Sat 10–4; Sun 2–5. (**Thurs open to 8**). *Closed* Mon.

TUDOR HOUSE MUSEUM *(Southampton Corporation)*
St. Michael's Square. Tel: (0703) 24216.
Tudor mansion, built in the 16th century, containing historical and antiquarian exhibits. Tues to Fri 10–12, 1–5; Sat 10–12, 1–4; Sun 2–5. *Closed* Mon.

STOCKBRIDGE

HOUGHTON LODGE   &
(Captain & Mrs M W Busk)
Starred Grade II in the Register of Parks and Gardens of Special Historic Interest in England. From the terrace of this 18th century 'cottage orne' the lawns lead down to the River Test with fine views over the unspoilt valley. Rare chalkcob walls surround the Kitchen Garden. Extensive greenhouses and vinery. Over 100 varieties of fuchsia. 18th century Folly.
Location: 1½ m S of A30 at Stockbridge on minor road to Houghton village.
Opening Times: GARDEN ONLY. Mar to Aug inclusive—Weds & Thurs, Easter Sun & Mon and Bank Hols in May, and Sun Sept 3 2–5 or by appointment. Adm £1, Chd 50p. *No dogs.* Plants & produce for sale every weekday.

TITCHFIELD

TITCHFIELD ABBEY
Telephone: (0329) 43016

Founded in 1232 for the Premonstratensian Order or 'White Canons'. Several royal visits are recorded in the Middle Ages. On its dissolution in 1537, the abbey was converted into a mansion for the Earl of Southampton. The third earl is best known as Shakespeare's patron. Much of the Tudor building was demolished in the 18th century, to reveal the 13th century stonework.
Location: ½ m (0.8 km) north of Titchfield. OS map ref SU541067.
Opening Times: Good Friday to Sept 30, daily 10–6. Adm 80p, OAPs 60p, Chd 40p.

WEYHILL

THE HAWK CONSERVANCY
Telephone: Weyhill 2252
(R., H. and A. Smith)

The Hawk Conservancy is a specialist centre for birds of prey from all over the world, created in a wild garden setting on the edge of Salisbury plain. Using traditional methods to train our birds, Hawks, Falcons, Eagles and Owls are flown daily at 12 noon, 2, 3, and 4 (weather permitting), and this really is a unique opportunity to appreciate the beauty and splendour of the birds in flight. At these demonstration times you will have the chance to hold a Bird of Prey and to take photographs.
Location: 4 miles west of Andover, just off the A303.
Opening Times: Open daily from Mar 1 to last Sun in Oct 10.30–last adm 4 (Spring and Autumn) 5 (Summer). Adm not available at time of going to press. Reduction for pre-booked parties of 20 and over. Large free car park. Suitable for disabled persons but no toilets for disabled.
Refreshments: Cafe offering a wide variety of snacks and hot and cold meals.

WINCHESTER

AVINGTON PARK
Telephone: 0962-78 202
(Mr and Mrs J B Hickson)

William Cobbett wrote of Avington that it was 'one of the prettiest places in the County' and indeed it is true today. Avington Park, where Charles II and George IV both stayed at various times, is an old house enlarged in 1670 by the addition of two wings and a classical Portico surmounted by three Statues. The State Rooms on view include the Ballroom with its magnificent ceiling, the Red Drawing Room, Library etc. Avington Church, one of the most perfect Georgian Churches in Hampshire, is in the grounds close by and may be visited.
The facilities are available for filming or still photography.
The Library is also available for Wedding Receptions, Conferences etc.
Location: 4 m NE of Winchester, just S of B3047 in Itchen Abbas.
Opening Times: May to Sept—Sats, Suns & Bank Hols 2.30–5.30 (last tour begins 5). *Occasionally closed Sats or Suns for wedding receptions.* Adm £1.50, Chd (under 10) 75p. *Other times for large parties by prior arrangement.*
Refreshments: Tea at the House *(Suns & Bank Hols only).*

GUILDHALL GALLERY *(Winchester City Council)*
Broadway. Tel: (0962) 840222, Ext. 2289.
Programme of changing exhibitions. Tues to Sat 10–5; Mon and Sun 2–5 (summer). *Closed* Mon in winter.

WOLVESEY: OLD BISHOP'S PALACE
Telephone: (0962) 54766

Ruins of an extensive palace of the Bishops of Winchester, built round a quadrangular courtyard.
Location: ¼ m (0.5 km) south east of Winchester Cathedral, next to the Bishop's Palace. OS map ref SU484291.
Opening Times: Good Friday to Sept 30, daily 10–6. Adm 80p, OAPs 60p, Chd 40p.

THE PILGRIMS' HALL
(The Dean & Chapter, Winchester Cathedral)

Late 13th century hall with fine hammer-beam roof.
Location: In the Cathedral Close.
Station: Winchester (5 mins walk).
Opening Times: All the year—Daily (except when booked for private meetings, functions, etc). *Parties must give notice in advance.* Adm free.

THE WESTGATE MUSEUM *(Winchester City Council)*
High Street. Tel: (0962) 840222, Ext. 2269.
Medieval west gate of the city. Sixteenth century painted ceiling from Winchester College. Mon to Sat 10–5; Sun 2–4 (winter), 2–5 (summer). *Closed* Mon in winter. Adm 20p, Chld 10p.

WINCHESTER CITY MUSEUM *(Winchester City Council)*
The Square. Tel: (0962) 840222, Ext. 2269.
Archaeology and history of Winchester and central Hampshire. 19th century shops. Mon to Sat 10–5; Sun 2–4 (winter), 2–5 (summer). *Closed* Mon in winter.

THE WINCHESTER GALLERY *(Winchester School of Art)*
Park Avenue. Tel: (0962) 842500.
Changing exhibitions of contemporary painting, sculpture, printmaking, crafts, design. Mon to Thur 10–5; Fri 10–4.30; Sat 9–12 (during term time). *Closed* Sun and Bank Hols.

JENKYN PLACE GARDEN
Bentley, Hants

ADMISSION – SEE EDITORIAL REFERENCE

Visit
BROADLANDS
THE MAGNIFICENT STATELY HOME OF LORD MOUNTBATTEN

'One of the finest houses in all England.'
Lord Palmerston

With the Palladian architecture and ornate room interiors, the furniture, the Van Dyck collection, the family portraits, and the Wedgwood porcelain.

'The Mountbatten Exhibition is intensely memorable.' *Opened by HRH The Prince of Wales.*

It's a fascinating insight into the eventful lives of Lord and Lady Mountbatten. Featuring Lord Mountbatten's state occasions, command in S.E. Asia, diplomacy in India, the drama of the Kelly in his highly successful career in the Royal Navy.

'The views across the river are breathtaking.' *'Capability' Brown*

Ideal for picnicking on the riverside.

1989 opening dates: 23 March -1 October (closed Mondays – except Bank Holidays – until August). Times of admission: 10am - 4pm. All inclusive admission charge. Children under 12 accompanied by parent/guardian admitted free. Free car parking. Self-service restaurant. Gift shop. For further details **telephone Romsey (0794) 516878.**

20 MINUTES FROM THE NEW FOREST ON THE A31 AT ROMSEY (JUNCTION 3 OFF THE M27).

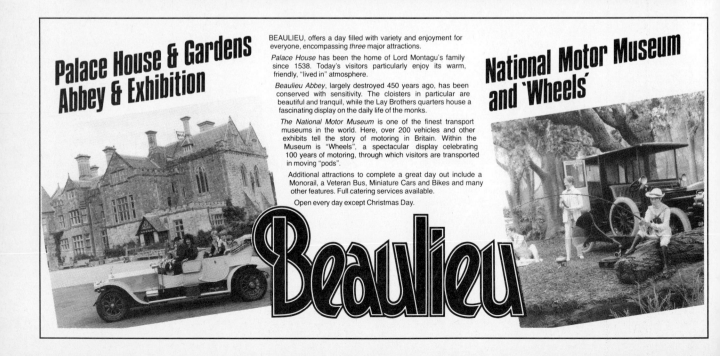

Palace House & Gardens Abbey & Exhibition

BEAULIEU, offers a day filled with variety and enjoyment for everyone, encompassing *three* major attractions.

Palace House has been the home of Lord Montagu's family since 1538. Today's visitors particularly enjoy its warm, friendly, "lived in" atmosphere.

Beaulieu Abbey, largely destroyed 450 years ago, has been conserved with sensitivity. The cloisters in particular are beautiful and tranquil, while the Lay Brothers quarters house a fascinating display on the daily life of the monks.

The National Motor Museum is one of the finest transport museums in the world. Here, over 200 vehicles and other exhibits tell the story of motoring in Britain. Within the Museum is "Wheels", a spectacular display celebrating 100 years of motoring, through which visitors are transported in moving "pods".

Additional attractions to complete a great day out include a Monorail, a Veteran Bus, Miniature Cars and Bikes and many other features. Full catering services available.

Open every day except Christmas Day.

National Motor Museum and 'Wheels'

Beaulieu

AVINGTON PARK
WINCHESTER

Red brick house in the Wren tradition with facilities available for filming or still photography. The Library is also available for Wedding Receptions, Conferences etc. Enquiries to the Secretary, Avington Park, Winchester, Hants. Tel.: Itchen Abbas (0962 78) 202.

ADMISSION—SEE EDITORIAL REFERENCE

THE OATES MEMORIAL LIBRARY AND MUSEUM AND GILBERT WHITE MUSEUM
SELBORNE, ALTON, HAMPSHIRE

The Wakes, home of The Rev. Gilbert White, author of The Natural History of Selborne
* Historic house and 5-acre garden
* Gilbert White Museum
* Oates Memorial Museum
Come and enjoy a day out in Selborne

Hereford & Worcester

ABBERLEY

ABBERLEY HALL
Telephone: (0299) 896634 (office hours only)
(Mrs Atkinson)

Five principal rooms show ornate decoration of mid-Victorian period.
Location: 12 m NW of Worcester on A443.
Opening Times: HOUSE ONLY. May 29; July 18–21 and 24–28; Aug 1–4, 7–11, 14–18, 21–25, 28; 1.30–4.30. Adm £1. Unsuitable for wheelchairs. No dogs.

ASHTON UNDER HILL

BREDON SPRINGS
(Ronald Sidwell, Esq)

1¾ acre garden. Large plant collection in natural setting.
Location: 6 m SW of Evesham, turn off A435; in Ashton turn right then 1st left.
Opening Times: GARDEN ONLY. Apr 1 to Oct 29 — Sats, Suns, Weds, Thurs, Bank Hol Mon & Tues, 10–dusk. Adm 50p (Chd free). *In aid of National Gardens Scheme.* Coach parties alight at church — 6 mins walk through church-yard and over 2 fields. Limited parking at house. Plants for sale. Dogs welcome.

BEWDLEY

BEWDLEY MUSEUM *(Wyre Forest District Council)*
The Shambles, Load Street. Tel: (0299) 403573.
The town's 18th century market converted to a folk museum of Bewdley and the Wyre Forest. Mar to Nov: Mon to Sat (and Bank Hols) 10–5.30; Sun 2–5.30. At other times by appointment. Adm 40p, Chld/OAPs 15p.

BROMSGROVE

AVONCROFT MUSEUM OF BUILDINGS
Telephone: Bromsgrove 31886 or 31363
(Council of Management)

An open-air Museum containing buildings of great interest and variety. Exhibits include a working windmill, a 15th century timber-framed house, a cockpit theatre, two great 14th century roofs, a 1946 prefab and an ice house and earth closet from the 18th century. New exhibit – a toll house.
Location: At Stoke Heath 2 m S of Bromsgrove off A38 between junctions 4 & 5 of M5 and 3½ m S of M42 junction 1.
Opening Times: Mar & Nov 11–4.30, closed Mons & Fris; Apr, May, Sept & Oct 11–5.30, *closed Mons;* June, July & Aug daily 11–5.30. Open Bank Holidays. *Closed Dec to Feb.* Adm £2, Chd £1, OAPs £1.20. Parties at reduced rates by arrangement. Free car park & picnic site.
Refreshments: Available at Museum tea room. Souvenir and Bookshop.

BROMSGROVE MUSEUM *(Dennis Norton)*
26 Birmingham Road. Tel: (0527) 77934.
Past industries and crafts; Victorian and Edwardian Shops displaying Costume, Haberdashery, Toys, Chemists, Hairdressing, Radios, Millinery, Shoes etc. Craft Workshops. Open Mon to Sat 10–5; Sun 2–5. Adm (1988 charges) 70p, OAPs and Students 35p, Chld 25p. Public car park opposite.

BROMYARD

LOWER BROCKHAMPTON, The National Trust
Telephone: Bromyard 88099

Small half-timbered manor house c. 1400 with unusual detached 15th century gate house and ruins of 12th century chapel.
Location: 2 m E of Bromyard N of A44 Bromyard/Worcester Road.
Opening Times: Medieval Hall and Parlour only: Mar 25 to end of Sept (closed Good Fri) — Weds, Thurs, Fris, Sats, Suns & Bank Hol Mons 10–1, 2–6. Oct – Wed to Sun 10–1, 2–4. Other months by previous written appointment only. Adm £1, Chd 50p; Parties by prior written arrangement only. N.B. Hall reached by rough narrow road through 1½ m woods & farmland. No dogs in Hall. Wheelchair access.

DROITWICH

CLACK'S FARM
Telephone: Worcester (0905) 620250
(Mr & Mrs Arthur Billitt)

Well known to television viewers, featured in BBC2 'Gardener's World' programmes from 1969 till 1981 and more recently in Central T.V. 'Gardening Time' programmes. A 2½ acre garden created from zero since 1965 without any paid labour, Arthur and Riet Billitt are the caring gardeners. The ornamental garden with its shrubs and trees, plus its alpine and peat areas, is supplemented during the season with many different bedding plants and is at all times colourful. There is also a water garden with small and medium sized pools. The television area with its 8 amateur greenhouses of varying sizes demonstrate how the home gardener can grow melons, cucumbers, tomatoes, houseplants, etc. There are demonstration plots for growing vegetables, soft fruit and tree fruits, with the emphasis on varieties of quality and with flavour. The demonstration rose gardens illustrate the control of pest and diseases on a number of old and new varieties. The two patio areas show the use of container growing and a display of hanging baskets. On open days there are experts available to answer your questions.
Location: 8 miles from Worcester and Kidderminster. A449 Worcester–Kidderminster Road, turn into Woodfield Lane, then follow signs.
Opening Times: Sat & Sun May 13 and 14, June 10 and 11, June 17 and 18 (Special Fuchsia Week-end), July 8 and 9, Aug 12 and 13, Sept 9 and 10. By previous arrangement only, coach parties at any time during the season. Adm 50p, Chd 25p. Parties £1 per person including coffee or tea and biscuits. *In aid of National Gardens Scheme,* R.N.L.I., Stars Organisation for Spastics, Horticultural Therapy, and The Blue Cross. Car park free (room for 500 cars). Suitable for disabled persons, no wheelchairs available.
Refreshments: Several pubs/restaurants in Ombersley (3 miles), The Mitre Oak, Crossway Green, on the A449 (2½ miles). Clack's Farm itself has a tea garden serving coffee, tea, soft drinks, etc. and biscuits (no food available).

DROITWICH HERITAGE CENTRE
Heritage Way. Tel: (0905) 774312 (24 hours).
Originally a Victorian Methodist chapel, the building has been carefully converted into a local history museum, exhibition hall and tourist information centre. The town's history display depicts the fascinating development of Droitwich from iron age salt town to present day luxury spa resort. Incorporated in the display are finds from some of the most significant archaeological excavations of recent times, including iron age salt making containers, Roman salt barrel, skeleton, mosaic floor and other Roman artifacts, an Elizabethan salt bushel and many items connected with the salt and spa industries of the town.

The centre also has an extensive programme of temporary exhibitions and is also an established brass rubbing centre offering a wide selection of brasses. Open summer: Mon to Fri 10–5. Winter: Mon to Fri 10–4; Sat 10–4. Admission is free, parties welcome, information sheets and guides available. Free car parking space, suitable for disabled visitors.

HANBURY HALL, The National Trust
Telephone: Hanbury 214   &

Wren style red brick house c. 1700 built for a wealthy lawyer. Outstanding painted ceilings and staircase by Sir James Thornhill. The Watney Collection of porcelain; Orangery c. 1730.

Location: 3½ m E of Droitwich, 1 m N of B4090.
Opening Times: Easter Sat, Sun, Mon 2–6. Mar 29–31, 2–5. Apr and Oct, Sat, Sun 2–5. May to end Sept, Wed to Sun and Bank Holiday Mon 2–6. Adm £1.90, Chd 95p. *Parties by prior written arrangement only.* Evening visits for pre-booked parties, 7.30–9.30, third Wed each month. Full price for evening visits (including National Trust members). Shop. No dogs. Wheelchairs provided. Braille guidebook available. Last admission 30 mins before closing.
Refreshments: Teas in the house.

EARDISLAND

BURTON COURT
Telephone: Pembridge 231   &
(Lt-Cmdr & Mrs R. M. Simpson)

14th century Great Hall. European and Oriental Costume. Working model fairground.

Location: 5 m W of Leominster between A44 & A4112.
Opening Times: Spring Bank Hol to end Sep—Weds, Thurs, Sats, Suns & Bank Hol Mons 2.30–6. Adm £1.25, Chd 60p. Coach parties £1.
Refreshments: Coach parties catered for. Teas.

EVESHAM

ALMONRY MUSEUM
Abbey Gate. Tel: (0386) 6944.
Romano-British, Anglo-Saxon, Medieval and monastic remains. Agricultural implements and exhibits of local historic interest. Good Friday to Sept: Mon–Sat 10–5; Sun 2–5; Bank Holiday 10–5. Adm 40p, OAPs 25p, Chld free.

EYTON

EYTON OLD HALL
Telephone: (0568) 2418
(Ronald Rolf)

Early Victorian House with Regency additions. Gardens approached by 300 yard drive, with lawns and woodland. Special display of spring flowering bulbs.

Location: Village of Eyton 2 m NW Leominster, Herefordshire.
Opening Times: By appointment only between the period of Easter to mid Sept. Adm charges will be given on telephoned appointment.

GREAT MALVERN

LITTLE MALVERN COURT
Telephone: Malvern (0684) 892988
(Mr and Mrs T M Berington)

14th century Prior's Hall once attached to 12th-century Benedictine Priory, and principal rooms in Victorian addition by Hansom. Family and European paintings and furniture. Collection of 18th and 19th century needlework. Home of the Berington family by descent since the Dissolution.

Location: 3 m S of Great Malvern on Upton-on-Severn Road (A4104).
Opening Times: Apr 12 to July 13—Weds and Thurs 2.30–5.00. Parties by prior arrangement. Adm £1.60, Chd 80p. No concession for OAPs. Parties at other times £2 by arrangement per head. Unsuitable for wheelchairs. Garden open only in aid of National Gardens Scheme Sun Apr 9, June 25. Adm £1.

HEREFORD

CHURCHILL GARDENS MUSEUM *(Hereford County Council)*
Venn's Lane. Tel: (0432) 267409.
Part of the extensive costume collection is always on show, also fine furniture, choice water-colours and paintings by local artists. Period Rooms: Room of corn dollies and straw work. The Brian Hatton Gallery is an extension of the museum and is devoted to the work of this local artist. Tues to Sat 2–5; Sun (Apr to Oct) 2–5. *Closed* Mon but open Bank Hol Mons. Adm 50p; Chld/OAPs 25p. Party visits welcome by appointment. Joint adm to The Old House: 80p, Chld/OAP 40p.

CIDER MUSEUM AND KING OFFA CIDER BRANDY DISTILLERY
(Hereford Cider Museum Trust)
Pomona Place, off Whitecross Road (A438 to Brecon) HR4 0LW.
Tel: (0432) 354207.
Originally a cider works, where the story of traditional farm cidermaking is told up to the growth of modern factory methods. Displays include a huge 17th century beam press from Normandy, a cooper's shop, an old farm ciderhouse, original champagne cider cellars with their tiers of bottles and great oak vats of the Napoleonic period. In the distillery can be seen the beautiful copper calvados stills which are used to produce King Offa cider brandy. Gift shop and off licence. Free coach and car park. Apr–Oct: seven days a week 10–5.30. Nov–Mar: Mon to Sat 1–5. Parties of 20 or more, at any time by appointment. Adm £1.20, Chld/OAP 90p. Parties 90p and 70p.

DINMORE MANOR   &
(R.G. Murray)

14th century Chapel also cloisters, "Music Room" and rock garden.
Location: 6 m N of Hereford on Leominster Road (A49).
Opening Times: All the year—Daily (except Christmas Day & Boxing Day) 2–6. Adm £1.50, OAPs 75p, children under 14 admitted free when accompanied. *Garden, Chapel & Music Room only open.*
Refreshments: Occasional teas served during summer. Also café at Dinmore Hill, Little Chef 2 m N on A49.

HEREFORD CITY MUSEUM AND ART GALLERY
(Hereford County Council)
Broad Street. Tel: (0432) 268121, Ext. 207.
Collections of archaeology and natural history, embroidery, textiles, military equipment and agricultural bygones. Pictures by local artists and examples of applied art, silver, pottery and porcelain in the Art Gallery. Changing Exhibitions monthly. Tues, Wed and Fri 10–6; Thurs and Sat 10–5 (winter *closes* at 4 on Sat). *Closed* Mon but open Bank Hol Mons. Adm free. Party visits welcome by appointment.

KENTCHURCH COURT
Telephone: Golden Valley 240228
(J E S Lucas-Scudamore, Esq)

Fortified border manor house altered by Nash. Gateway and part of the original 14th century house still survives. Pictures and Grinling Gibbons carving. Owen Glendower's tower.

Location: Off B4347, 3 m SE of Pontrilas; 12 m Monmouth; 14 m Hereford; 14 m Abergavenny, on left bank River Monnow.
Opening Times: May to Sept. *Parties only by appointment.* Adm £2, Chd £1.
Refreshments: At Kentchurch Court by appointment.

THE OLD HOUSE *(Hereford City Council)*
High Town. Tel: (0432) 268121, Ext. 207.
The Old House is preserved as a Jacobean period museum and is furnished accordingly. Apr to Sept: Mon to Sat 10–1, 2–5.30. Oct to Mar: Mon 10–1 (*closed* p.m.) Open Bank Hol Mons. Tues to Fri 10–1, 2–5.30; Sat 10–1 (also 2–5.30, Summer only). Adm 50p, Chld/OAPs 25p. Parties welcome by appointment. Joint adm to Churchill Gardens Museum: 80p, Chld/OAP 40p.

HOW CAPLE

HOW CAPLE COURT GARDENS
Telephone: How Caple 626
(Mr & Mrs P L Lee)

11 acres overlooking the river Wye. Formal terraced Edwardian gardens, extensive plantings of mature trees and shrubs, water features and a sunken Florentine garden undergoing restoration. Norman church with 16th century Diptych. Specialist nursery plants for sale. Fabrics shop.
Location: B4224, Ross on Wye (4½ m) to Hereford (9 m).
Opening Times: April to Nov Mons to Sats 9.30–4.30. May to Oct also Suns 10–5. Adm £1.50, Chld 75p. Parties by appointment. Car parking. Toilets.
Refreshments: Afternoon teas available Suns & Bank Hols.

KEMERTON

THE PRIORY
(Mr & The Hon Mrs Peter Healing)

4 acre garden; main features are long herbaceous borders planned in colour groups; stream and sunken garden; many interesting and unusual plants and shrubs.
Location: NE of Tewkesbury, turn off A435 (Evesham/Cheltenham) at Beckford.
Opening Times: GARDEN ONLY. May to Sept—Thurs; also Suns May 21, June 18, July 9, Aug 6, 27 & Sept 10: 2–7. Adm £1. Accompanied chd free. *In aid of National Gardens Scheme & other charities.* Plants for sale.

KIDDERMINSTER

ART GALLERY *(Wyre Forest District Council)*
Market Street. Tel: (0562) 66610.
Loan exhibitions (from National Collections and by individual artists). Brangwyn etchings, small permanent collection. Mon to Sat 11–4. *Closed* Wed and Sun.

HARTLEBURY CASTLE
Telephone: Hartlebury (0299) 250410
(The Church Commissioners)

Historic home of the Bishops of Worcester for over 1,000 years. Fortified in 13th century, rebuilt after sacking in the Civil War and Gothicised in 18th century. State Rooms include medieval Great Hall, Hurd Library and Saloon. Fine plaster-work and interesting portraits. Also County Museum in North Wing.
Location: In village of Hartlebury, 5 m S of Kidderminster, 10 m N of Worcester off A449.
Opening Times: State Rooms Easter Sunday to Sept 4—First Sun in every month. Every Wed Easter to end of August Bank Hol Sun & Mon 2–4. Adm 60p, Chd 25p, OAPs 25p. Guided tours for parties of 30 or more on weekdays by arrangement. **County Museum** Mar to Nov—Mons to Fris 2–5. Suns 2–6. Bank Hols 11–5. Closed Good Friday. Adm 40p, OAPS, Students & Chd 20p. Family tickets (2 adults and up to 3 children) £1 (all 1987 rates). School parties free. Picnic area.
Refreshments: Available.

HARVINGTON HALL
Telephone: Chaddesley Corbett (056 283) 267
(The Roman Catholic Archdiocese of Birmingham)

Moated medieval and Elizabethan manor-house containing secret hiding-places and rare wall-paintings. Georgian Chapel in garden with 18th century altar, rails and organ. Harvington Festival 14, 15 & 16 July 1989. Other events throughout the summer.
Location: 3 m SE of Kidderminster, ½ m from the junction of A448 and A450 at Mustow Green.
Opening Times: Mar 1 to Oct 31 daily except Good Friday, 11.30–5.30. *Closed Nov to Feb except by appointment.* Adm £1.75, Chd 80p, OAPs £1.25. (Correct at time of going to press.) Parties by arrangement with the custodian. Free car parking.
Refreshments: Licensed restaurant in the medieval wing overlooking the moat, open Easter to end Sept daily, except Mons and Fris and on Suns in Oct. Light refreshments in the dairy on other afternoons. Bookings taken for Sunday lunch and evening functions.

MUSEUM *(Wyre Forest District Council)*
Local studies and archaeology. Official repository for the Kidderminster and District Archaeological and Historical Society. Opening times as Art Gallery.

STONE HOUSE COTTAGE GARDENS
Telephone: Kidderminster 69902
(Major & The Hon Mrs Arbuthnott)

Sheltered wall garden with towers. Rare wall shrubs and climbers also interesting herbaceous plants, all labelled. Adjacent Nursery.
Location: 2 m SE of Kidderminster on A448 to Bromsgrove; next to Stone Church.
Station: Kidderminster (2 m).
Opening Times: GARDEN & NURSERY ONLY. Mar to Nov: Weds, Thurs, Fris, Sats 10–6; Suns, May and June, 2–6. Adm £1, accompanied Chd free. Coaches by appointment only. *In aid of National Gardens Scheme and Mother Teresa.*
Refreshments: Food & drink available at Harvington Hall.

KINGTON

HERGEST CROFT GARDENS
Telephone: Kington (0544) 230160
(W L & R A Banks, Esq)

50 acres of trees, shrubs and many other plants from all over the temperate world. Excellent autumn colour, a working kitchen garden and fine herbaceous borders.
Location: On outskirts W of Kington off Rhayader Road (A44) *(signposted to Hergest Croft at W end of bypass).*
Opening Times: Daily—Apr 30 to Oct 29, 1.30–6.30. Adm £1.40, Chd 70p. Reduced rates for pre-booked parties of over 20 by appointment at any time.
Refreshments: Home-made teas on most Suns and for parties of over 20 by arrangement.

LEDBURY

EASTNOR CASTLE
Telephone: Ledbury (0531) 2305

Excellent specimen of 19th century castellated architecture containing armour, pictures, etc. Arboretum, extensive park with red deer.
Location: 5 m from M50 (exit 2) 2 m E of Ledbury on Hereford/Tewkesbury Road A438.
Station: Ledbury (2 m).
Opening Times: Bank Hol Mons. May 21 to Sept 17: Suns. July and Aug: Weds and Thurs. 2.15–5.30. Parties by appointment on any day, Easter to Sept. Adm £2, Chd & OAPs £1. Reduced rates for parties of 20 or more.
Refreshments: At the castle.

LEOMINSTER

BERRINGTON HALL, The National Trust
Telephone: Leominster 5721   &

Built 1778–1781 by Henry Holland, the architect of Carlton House. Painted and plaster ceilings. "Capability" Brown laid out the park.
Location: 3 m N Leominster W of A49.
Opening Times: Easter Sat–Mon: 2–6; Apr and Oct Sat & Sun 2–5; May to end of Sept—Weds to Suns & Bank Hol Mons 2–6. Grounds & tea room open from 12.30. Adm £1.80, Chd half-price. Parties by prior written arrangement only. Joint ticket with Croft Castle £3.20, Chd half-price; Parties by prior written arrangement only; this refers to joint ticket with Croft Castle. No dogs. Wheelchairs provided. Wheelchair access grounds only. Indoor photography by prior written arrangement only. Last admission 30 mins before closing.
Refreshments: Tea room at Hall.

CROFT CASTLE, The National Trust
Telephone: Yarpole 246   &

Welsh Border castle mentioned in Domesday. Inhabited by the Croft family for 900 years. Fine 18th century Gothic interior. Extensive wooded parkland.
Location: 5 m NW of Leominster just N of B4362 signposted from Ludlow Road (A49).
Opening Times: Easter Sat, Sun & Mon: 2–6; Apr & Oct Sat & Sun 2–5; May to Sept—Weds to Suns & Bank Hol Mons 2–6. Adm £1.80, Chd 90p; Parties by prior written arrangement. Joint ticket with Berrington Hall £3.20, Chd £1.60; Parties by prior written arrangement. Access for disabled to ground floor and part of grounds. Wheelchairs provided. Last admission 30 mins before closing.

LEOMINSTER FOLK MUSEUM
Etnam Street.

MORTIMER'S CROSS WATER MILL, LUCTON
Erected in the 18th century, this small and compact watermill was still in use in the 1940s. The outer housing is of sandstone rubble and the mechanism, which could be worked by one man, is located on three floors.
Location: 4½ m (7.2 km) north west of Leominster. OS map ref SO426637.
Opening Times: Apr 1 to Sept 30, Thurs, Suns and Bank Holidays only 2–6. Adm 55p, OAPs 40p, Chd 25p.

LITTLE WITLEY

EASTGROVE COTTAGE GARDEN NURSERY
Telephone: (0299) 896389
(Mr & Mrs J. Malcolm Skinner)

A peaceful old world country flower garden displaying a specialist collection of hardy plants maintained by the owners since 1970. This cottage garden is sensitively arranged with great emphasis laid on colour and form, and with the 17th century cottage and timber framed barn, it blends into the unspoiled country of meadow and woodland. The owners are on hand to offer advice and a wide range of good quality and unusual plants are grown at the nursery.
Location: Near Shrawley—4 m SW of Stourport; 8 m NW of Worcester on road between Shrawley (on B4196) and Great Witley (on A443).
Opening Times: Open Daily, afternoons—Apr 1 to Oct 30, 2–5; except Tues & Weds; *closed throughout Aug.* Adm 80p, Chd 20p in aid of National Garden Scheme. Parties by arrangement – mornings & evenings. Suitable for disabled (wheelchairs not provided).

LLANGARRON

BERNITHAN COURT
Telephone: Llangarron 477
(M.J. Richardson)

William & Mary house built for Hoskyns family in 1692: some surviving panelling, fine staircase, walled gardens.
Location: 4 m Ross on Wye, 1½ m from A40 Ross–Monmouth road.
Opening Times: By prior appointment, telephone Mrs James (0989 84) 477. Adm £1.

MOCCAS

BROBURY GARDEN & GALLERY
Telephone: Moccas (09817) 229
(Eugene Okarma, Esq)

6 acres of garden around a 100 years' old house on the banks of the River Wye. Spacious lawns, rock gardens, terraces, herbaceous borders; mature conifers. The Gallery specialises in old prints and 19th and 20th century watercolours.
Location: 11 m W of Hereford, off A438; signposted Brobury Bredwardine.
Opening Times: GARDEN. June 1 to Sept 30—Mons to Sats 9–4.30. Adm £1, Chd 50p. GALLERY: Open all the year—Mons to Sats 9–4.30 (closes at 4 in winter). Adm free.

Hereford & Worcester – *continued*

MOCCAS COURT

Telephone: Moccas (098 17) 381
(R T G Chester-Master, Esq)

Designed by Adam, built by Keck in 1775 and has been in the ownership of the Cornewalls, and the present owner, for three centuries. The House stands in 'Capability' Brown parkland on the south bank of the River Wye.
Location: 13 m W of Hereford by River Wye. 1 m off B4352.
Opening Times: House & Gardens. Apr to Sept—Thurs 2–6. Adm £1.20. Picnics in garden allowed.
Refreshments: Food and drink available at the Red Lion Hotel, Bredwardine, by prebooking only.

MUCH MARCLE

HELLEN'S

(The Pennington-Mellor-Munthe Trust)

Manorial house lived in since 1292. Visited by Black Prince and Bloody Mary.
Location: In village of Much Marcle on Ledbury/Ross Road. Entrance opp church.
Opening Times: Easter to Oct 1—Weds, Sats & Suns 2–6 (guided tours each hour). *Other times by written appointment with the Custodian*. Adm £2, Chd (must be accompanied by adult) 75p.
Refreshments: Teas by prior arrangement.

REDDITCH

THE NATIONAL NEEDLE MUSEUM

Forge Mill, Needle Mill Lane, B97 6RR. Tel: (0527) 62509.

Opened by the Queen in 1983, Forge Mill commemorates the world famous Redditch needle and fishing tackle industries. The Museum is housed in a former needle scouring mill. The machinery (installed in 1730) has been restored to full working order and is powered by a water-wheel. Life-like models, original machines and audio-visual aids transport the visitor back to the 1800s and provide a unique insight into 19th century working conditions. The Museum is set within the Bordesley Abbey Meadows, site of the best preserved monastic precinct in Europe. A free archaeological exhibition has recently been opened. Easter to Oct: Mon to Fri 11–4.30; Sat 1–5; Sun & Bank Hols 11.30–5. Nov to Mar: Weekdays only.

ROSS ON WYE

GOODRICH CASTLE

Telephone: (0600) 890538

The castle was built to command the ancient crossing of the Wye by the Gloucester/ Caerleon road. Among the extensive remains of the original castle the keep survives, which largely dates from the late 13th century. For almost 300 years from the mid-14th century it was held by the Earls of Shrewsbury.
Location: 3 m (4.8 km) south west of Ross-on-Wye. OS map ref SO579199.
Opening Times: Good Friday to Sept 30, daily 10–6; Oct 1 to Maundy Thursday, daily 10–4. *Closed Mons, Christmas and New Year*. Adm £1.10, OAPs 80p, Chd 55p.

HILL COURT GARDENS & GARDEN CENTRE

Telephone: Ross 763123 &
(Mr J C Rowley)

Set in the beautiful grounds of a William and Mary Mansion. An avenue of white limes line the drive up to the house, gardens, and garden centre. The two and a half acres of ornamental gardens include an 18th century Yew Walk, colourful herbaceous borders, water garden with gazebo, rose gardens and monthly shrub borders. Set in one of the walled gardens these borders are designed to assist the visitors in their choice of shrubs for their own gardens throughout the year. The garden centre offers the gardener excellent choice in plants and products, professional advice from horticulturally trained staff, a relaxing environment and the pleasure of strolling through the gardens too. There is a tea garden serving light lunches and afternoon teas within another of the lovely walled gardens.
Location: B4228 from Ross on Wye, fork right at the Prince of Wales public house, drive for 2½ miles.
Opening Times: Open daily 9.30–5.30, open all Bank Holidays. Adm free. All parties by appointment only, particularly coach parties. Ample car parking. Suitable for disabled, although shingled ground does sometimes cause problems.
Refreshments: A delightful tea garden set in one of the walled gardens with indoor and patio seating. Open Spring & Summer season, weekends only during early Spring season. Light lunches and afternoon teas available, all cakes homemade. Special group bookings possible. The house is not open to the public.

SWAINSHILL

THE WEIR, The National Trust

Spring garden with fine views of the river Wye and the Welsh and Monmouthshire hills from the cliff garden walks.
Location: 5 m W of Hereford on A438.
Opening Times: Mar to Oct—Wed to Sun & Bank Hol Mon 2–6. (*Closed Good Fri*). Adm 50p. No reduction for parties. No coach parties. No dogs. Unsuitable for wheelchairs or visually handicapped.

TENBURY WELLS

BURFORD HOUSE GARDENS

Telephone: (0584) 810777
(Treasures of Tenbury Ltd.)

The gardens at Burford were created by John Treasure over a period of 35 years and are filled with a wealth of rare and interesting plants many of which are grown by the adjoining world famous nursery which bears his name.
Location: 1 m W of Tenbury Wells on the A456.
Opening Times: Mar 18 to Oct 22, Mon to Sat 11–5, Sun 2–5. At other times by prior arrangement. Adm £1.95, Chd 80p. Parties of 25 or more by prior arrangement – Adm £1.60 each. No wheelchairs available.
Refreshments: Tea Rooms situated near entrance, serving morning coffee, light lunches and teas with locally baked cakes and scones.

WHITNEY-ON-WYE

CWMMAU FARMHOUSE, BRILLEY, The National Trust

Early 17th century timber-framed and stone tiled farmhouse.
Location: 4 m SW of Kington between A4111 and A438. Approached by a long narrow lane.
Opening Times: Easter, Spring, May & Summer Bank Hol weekends only—Sats, Suns & Mons 2–6. *At other times by prior written appointment with the tenant Mr S M Joyce*. Adm £1.10, Chd 55p. *No reduction for parties*. No dogs. Unsuitable for wheelchairs & coaches. Picnics only by prior arrangement with the tenant.

WORCESTER

CITY MUSEUM AND ART GALLERY *(Worcester City Council)*

Foregate Street WR1 1DT. Tel: (0905) 25371.

Displays of Worcester archaeology, geology and natural history, with the museum of the Worcestershire Regiment and Worcestershire Yeomanry Cavalry. Programme of contemporary art exhibitions in the art gallery plus regular displays from the permanent collections. Adm free. Details of educational programme advertised locally.

THE COMMANDERY

Telephone: Worcester (0905) 355071

Founded late in the 11th century as the Hospital of St. Wulstan, the Commandery became in 1545 the country home of the Wylde family. During their 200 year stay, Charles II came here and held his Council of War before the Battle of Worcester.
The building itself dates mainly from 1500 – an excellent Tudor construction where Monks once ministered to the sick and poor. Mediaeval wall paintings of the saints can still be seen in the room where dying patients were laid. The Great Hall has a superb hammer-beam roof and a minstrels gallery.
Location: Centre of Worcester.
Opening Times: Mon to Sat 10.30–5, Sun 2–5. Adm £1.50, Chd/OAPs 75p (1988 rates).
Refreshments: Snacks, lunches, cream teas available at the canalside tearooms.

THE DYSON PERRINS MUSEUM OF WORCESTER PORCELAIN

(Dyson Perrins Museum Trust)
Worcester Royal Porcelain Works, Severn Street. Tel: (0905) 23221.
The finest and most comprehensive collection of old Worcester in the world.

THE ELGAR BIRTHPLACE

Crown East Lane, Lower Broadheath.

THE GREYFRIARS, The National Trust

Telephone: Worcester 23571

A richly timber-framed house built c. 1480, sympathetically furnished with tapestries, crewel work hangings etc.
Location: In Friar Street, Worcester.
Station: Worcester, Foregate Street (½ m).
Opening Times: Mar 27 to Oct—Weds & Thurs and Bank Holiday Mons 2–6. Other times adult parties by written application only. Adm £1.10, Chd 55p. Parties of children (inc schools) not admitted. No dogs. Unsuitable for wheelchairs.

SPETCHLEY PARK

(Mr & Mrs R J Berkeley)

This garden, extending over nearly 30 acres, is a plantsman's delight, and it contains many fine trees and rare shrubs and plants. Particularly beautiful in April, May and June but also a show of colour throughout the summer. The park contains Red and Fallow Deer.
Location: 3 m E of Worcester on Stratford-upon-Avon Road (A422).
Opening Times: Gardens & Garden Centre: Mar 24 to Sept 30—Daily (except Sats) 11–5; Suns 2–5; Bank Hol Mons 11–5. Adm £1.40, Chd 70p. Regret no dogs. Plants and shrubs for sale. House not open.
Refreshments: Tea in the garden *(Suns & Bank Hols)*.

TUDOR HOUSE MUSEUM *(Worcester City Council)*

Friar Street. Tel: (0905) 25371.
A 15th century timber-framed building with displays illustrating the social, domestic and agricultural history of Worcester. Period rooms, Victorian bedroom, schoolroom, kitchen, bathroom, bar and 1920's office. Temporary exhibitions. Adm free. Limited parties, public car park nearby.

WORCESTER CATHEDRAL

Telephone: Worcester (0905) 28854   ♿
(The Dean and Chapter of Worcester)

Beside the River Severn opposite the Malvern Hills. Built between 1084 and 1375. Norman Crypt and Chapter House. Early English Quire, Perpendicular Tower. Monastic buildings include refectory (now College Hall and open on request during August), cloisters, remains of guesten hall and dormitories. Tombs of King John and Prince Arthur. Cloister herb garden, Elgar memorial window, misericords. Edgar Tower gatehouse.

Location: Centre of Worcester. Main roads Oxford and Stratford to Wales. 3 m junction 7 (M5).

Opening Times: Every day 7.30–6 (June to early Sept, 7.30–7). Choral Evensong daily (except Thurs and school hols). Tower open on Sats and Public Hols. Appointments for parties and coach groups. No admission charge but donations accepted. Parties: suggested minimum donation of £2 (Chd 50p) per head for guided tours. No cathedral car parking—City centre parking. Disabled visitors most welcome—some steps, but help and wheelchair available. Bookstall, shop and toilets, including toilet for disabled.

Refreshments: Light refreshment in Cloister Tea Room. Special arrangements made for parties.

Hertfordshire

ASHWELL

ASHWELL VILLAGE MUSEUM (Trustees)
Swan Street.
Illustrates life and work in the village from the Stone Age to the present day.

AYOT ST. LAURENCE

SHAW'S CORNER, The National Trust
Telephone: Stevenage (0438) 820307

Home of George Bernard Shaw from 1906–1950. The rooms downstairs remain as in his lifetime. Upstairs rooms (Shaw's bedroom and bathroom) open on weekdays.
Location: SW end of village of Ayot St Lawrence. 3 m NW Welwyn; 2 m NE of Wheathampstead.
Opening Times: Mar 25 to end Oct—Wed to Sat 2–6; Suns & Bank Hol Mons 12–6. *Closed Good Friday & Mons & Tues.* Group visits by written appointment only. Mar to Nov. Last adm 5.30. Adm £1.80, Chd 90p. Parties must book. *On busy days adm may be by timed ticket. Dogs in car park only. Unsuitable for wheelchairs.*

BENINGTON

BENINGTON LORDSHIP GARDENS
Telephone: Benington (043 885) 668
(Mr & Mrs C. H. A. Bott)

Terraced hill-top garden overlooking lakes. Includes old and modern roses, Victorian folly, Spring rock and water garden. Spectacular herbaceous borders. Woodland walk and Norman defences. Interesting all the year.
Location: 4 m E of Stevenage in village of Benington between Walkern (B1037) & Watton-at-Stone (A602).
Opening Times: GARDEN ONLY. Easter Mon, Spring and Summer Bank Hols 12–5, and every Wed May to end Oct 12–5. Suns Apr 24, May 8, 15, 22 and every Sun June, July and Aug to 7th, other days shown 2–5. Parties please book. Open by appointment for parties all the year. Adm £1.20 Weds and Suns, accompanied Chd free, 12–18 60p. No facilities for wheelchairs or disabled. *No dogs please.*
Refreshments: Teas (Suns and Bank Holidays only).

BERKHAMSTED

ASHRIDGE
Telephone: Little Gaddesden (044 284) 3491
(Governors of Ashridge Management College)

Early Gothic revival. Begun 1808 by James Wyatt for 7th Earl of Bridgewater. 13th century Crypt. Tudor barn. Gardens landscaped by Repton.
Location: 3½ m N of Berkhamsted (A41), 1 m S of Little Gaddesden.
Opening Times: Gardens open Apr to Oct—Sats & Suns 2–6. Adm £1, Chd/OAPs 50p. House fully open some weekends & partially on others during the summer; please telephone for further information. Adm House & Garden £2, Chd/OAPs £1.

HATFIELD

HATFIELD HOUSE
(The Marquess of Salisbury)

Noble Jacobean house and Tudor palace, childhood home of Queen Elizabeth I. House built by Robert Cecil, first Earl of Salisbury in 1611. Fine portraits, furniture and relics of Queen Elizabeth I. Fine gardens and large park. TWO EXHIBITIONS FOR 1989. THE TONY DUROSE VEHICLE COLLECTION—*A splendid display of veteran, vintage, classic and specialist vehicles together with a large variety of accessories and vehicle memorabilia spanning more than 60 years. Open one hour before the House plus the NATIONAL COLLECTION OF MODEL SOLDIERS.*
Location: In Hatfield, 21 m N of London. Close to M1 & A1(M).
Station: Hatfield (opposite house).
Opening Times: House & West Gardens. Mar 25 to Oct 8—Daily (except Mons but open on all Bank Hol Mons). *Closed Good Friday.* Hours—Weekdays 12–5 (guided tours); Suns 1.30–5; Bank Hols 11–5 (Suns & Bank Hols no guided tours—guides in each room). Adm £3.20, Chd £2.25. Reductions for pre-booked parties of 20 or more. Coach & car park free. A guided tour of State rooms (weekdays) takes 1 hr. Dogs not adm to House or Gardens. Park & West Gardens: Mar 25 to Oct 8. Park—Daily 10.30–8; West Gardens open at House times (also Mons 2–5). *Closed Good Friday.* Park, East & West Gardens: Mons only (except Bank Hols)—Park 10.30–8; Gardens 2–5.
Refreshments: Available in adjacent restaurant—cafeteria. ELIZABETHAN BANQUETING IN THE OLD PALACE THROUGHOUT THE YEAR.

MILL GREEN MUSEUM AND MILL
(Welwyn Hatfield District Council)
Mill Green. Tel: (070 72) 71362.
Working Mill producing flour. Adjoining former Miller's house has local history displays and a small temporary exhibition gallery. Tues to Fri 10–5; weekends and Bank Hols 2–5. Adm free. Suitable for the disabled. Car parking.

HERTFORD

HERTFORD MUSEUM (Trust)
18 Bull Plain. Tel: (0992) 582686.
The geology, archaeology, natural history and social history of the county town and the County. Changing exhibition programme. Tues to Sat 10–5. *Closed Mon.*

HITCHIN

HITCHIN MUSEUM AND ART GALLERY
(North Herts. District Council)
Paynes Park. Tel: (0462) 34476.
Displays of social history, natural history, costume. Hertfordshire Yeomanry Regimental Museum. Art exhibitions changed monthly. Mon to Sat 10–5. *Closed* Bank Hols. Adm free.

HODDESDON

LOWEWOOD MUSEUM (Borough of Broxbourne)
High Street. Tel: Hoddesdon 445596.
Lowewood Museum contains a fascinating cross section of artefacts and pictures which bring the local history of the Borough to life. Two rooms contain permanent displays which portray the town life, early history and geology of the Borough. A third room is set aside for changing exhibitions of local and general interest. Open Wed and Sat 11–5. School parties and organised groups welcome any day Mon to Fri, and evenings by prior arrangement with the Museum.

HUNSDON

HUNSDON HOUSE
Telephone: Estate Office: (0920) 871445

A house was first built on the site in 1447 and later used as a hunting lodge by Henry VIII and nursery for the Tudor Princesses and Edward VI. It was greatly altered in the early 19th C. Today the grounds and mainly Victorian house are the subject of a continuing programme of conservation and restoration.
Opening Times: HOUSE: open by written appointment. GARDEN: open in June, Mon–Fri 10–2 only. Adm HOUSE: £1.50; GARDEN: 50p. Parties (Max 20) by written appointment. Free car parking close to house. Most of the guided tour suitable for disabled persons (no wheelchairs available).
Refreshments: No refreshments available, but full catering facilities at Briggens House Hotel, 1 mile away.

KNEBWORTH

KNEBWORTH HOUSE
Telephone: Stevenage 812661
(The Lord Cobbold)

Family home of the Lyttons since 1490, it was transformed 150 years ago by the spectacular high gothic decoration of Sir Edward Bulwer-Lytton the Victorian novelist and statesman. Lutyens gardens currently being restored and include a Jekyll herb garden. Delhi Durbar Exhibition. Large adventure playground with Fort Knebworth.
Location: 28 m N of London. Own direct access off A1(M) Junction 7 (Stevenage South A602).
Stations: Stevenage (2 m).
Opening Times: HOUSE, GARDENS AND PARK, weekends, Bank Hols and School Hols from Mar 22 to May 21; then daily (except Mons) May 27 to Sept 10, plus weekends only to Oct 1 (subject to special events). Open Park: 11–5.30; House & Gardens 12–5. House, Garden and Park: £3.30, Chd/OAPs £2.80; Park only: £1.80. (No reductions for Chd/OAPs.) Reductions for pre-booked parties of 20 or more (Mar 22 to Oct 1). Coach and Car Park free. Dogs admitted to Park only on leads. Telephone above number for further details.
Refreshments: Catering in 16th century Tythe Barns, Tel: Stevenage 813825.

LETCHWORTH

FIRST GARDEN CITY HERITAGE MUSEUM
(Letchworth Garden City Corporation (Enterprises))
296 Norton Way South. Tel: (0462) 683149.
Exhibition of items relating to the Garden City movement and social history of Letchworth, displayed in the former office and home of the architect Barry Parker. Temporary exhibitions. Mon to Fri 2–4.30; Sat 10–1, 2–4. *Closed* Sun, Christmas and Boxing Day. Adm free.

MUSEUM AND ART GALLERY (North Herts. District Council)
Broadway. Tel: (0462) 685647.
Displays of N. Herts archaeological material, new natural history gallery. Special exhibitions changed monthly. Mon to Sat 10–5. *Closed* Bank Hols. Adm free.

LONDON COLNEY

THE MOSQUITO AIRCRAFT MUSEUM
Salisbury Hall. Tel: Bowmansgreen 22051.
The prototype of the historic de Havilland Mosquito aircraft designed and built at Salisbury Hall during the Second World War.

RICKMANSWORTH

MOOR PARK MANSION
Telephone: Rickmansworth (0923) 776611
(Three Rivers District Council)

Palladian house reconstructed in 1720 by Sir James Thornhill and Giacomo Leoni incorporating house built in 1678/79 for James, Duke of Monmouth. Magnificent interior decorations by Verrio, Sleker and others. Club House of Moor Park Golf Club. Being restored by the District Council.

Location: 1 m SE of Rickmansworth.
Stations: Rickmansworth or Moor Park.
Opening Times: All the year—Mons to Fris 10–4; Sats 10–12 noon. *Restricted viewing may be necessary on occasions.* Visitors are requested to report to reception. Adm free. Descriptive leaflet available. Guided tours during summer months.
Information from Information Centre or Prestel page 28800741.

ROYSTON

MUSEUM *(Royston Town Council)*
Lower King Street. Tel: (0763) 42587.
Local and social history and paintings by E.H. Whydale. Temporary exhibitions (changing every 4–5 weeks). Postal history collection. Open: Wed & Sat 10–5, other times by appointment. Adm free. Parties by arrangement. Parking at Town Hall, 5 mins walk. Ground floor suitable for disabled.

ST. ALBANS

CITY MUSEUM – THE MUSEUM OF ST. ALBANS
(St. Albans District Council)
Hatfield Road. Tel: (0727) 56679 or 66100.
New displays opening early 1989 will tell the 'Story of St. Albans' from the end of Roman Verulamium until modern times. The impressive Salaman collection of craft and trade tools. Mon to Sat 10–5. Adm free.

CLOCKTOWER *(St. Albans District Council)*
Market Place.
Erected in 1402–11; restored by Sir Gilbert Scott in 1866. The tower stands 77 ft. high with five storeys. Adm 20p, Chld 10p.

THE GARDENS OF THE ROSE
Telephone: St Albans (0727) 50461   ♿
(Royal National Rose Society)

The Showgrounds of the R.N.R.S. containing some 30,000 roses of over 1,650 different varieties.
Location: Off B4630 (formerly A412) St Albans/Watford Road.
Stations: St Alban's City (2 m).
Opening Times: Mid-June to Oct—Mons to Sats 9–5; Suns & Bank Holidays 10–6. Adm £1.80, Chd (under 16) free. British Rose Festival—July 8 & 9, increased admission charge. Facilities for the disabled.
Refreshments: Licensed cafeteria.

GORHAMBURY
Telephone: St Albans (0727) 54051
(The Earl of Verulam)

Mansion built 1777-84 in modified classical style by Sir Robert Taylor. 16th century enamelled glass and historic portraits.
Location: 2 m W of St Albans. Entrance off A4147.
Opening Times: May to Sept—Thurs 2–5. Adm £2, Chd & OAPs £1. Guided tours only. Parties by prior arrangement.

HERTFORDSHIRE COLLEGE OF ART AND DESIGN, MARGARET HARVEY GALLERY
7 Hatfield Road, AL1 3RS. Tel: (0727) 64414.
Various exhibitions of contemporary painting, drawing, sculpture, design, crafts. Tel the above number, or write, for further details.

ST. ALBANS ORGAN MUSEUM
320 Camp Road. Tel: (0727) 51557/73896.
A permanent exhibition of mechanical musical instruments. Organs by Decap, Bursens, and Mortier; Mills Violano-Virtuoso; reproducing pianos by Steinway and Weber; musical boxes, Wurlitzer and Rutt theatre organs. Every Sun (except Christmas Day) 2.15–4.30. Adm £1, Chld 60p. Parties by arrangement. Light refreshments. Souvenirs. Shop.

THE VERULAMIUM MUSEUM *(St. Albans District Council)*
St. Michael's. Tel: (0727) 54659, 59919 or 66100.
Stands on the site of the Roman City of Verulamium and houses material from the Roman and Belgic cities including several of the finest mosaics in Britain, one of which is preserved *in situ* in the 'Hypocaust annexe'. Summer: Mon to Sat 10–5.30; Sun 2–5.30. Winter: Mon to Sat 10–4; Sun 2–4. Adm (incl. Hypocaust) £1, Chld, Students, OAPs 50p, Family ticket (2 Adults, 2 Chld) £2 (residents free).

STEVENAGE

STEVENAGE MUSEUM
St. George's Way, New Town Centre SG1 1XX. Tel: (0438) 354292.
A local museum which tells the story of Stevenage through its displays. There is also a Natural History and Geology display. Two temporary exhibition areas house up to twenty exhibitions each year. A comprehensive education service provides talks and loans material to Hertfordshire schools. Mon–Sat 10–5. *Closed* Sun and Bank Hols. Adm free. Multi-storey car park 100 yds. Suitable for disabled.

TRING

ZOOLOGICAL MUSEUM, BRITISH MUSEUM (NATURAL HISTORY)
Akeman Street. Tel: (044 282) 4181.
Mounted specimens of animals from all parts of the world. Mon to·Sat 10–5; Sun 2–5. *Closed* Jan 1, Good Friday, May 2 and Dec 24 to 26. Adm £1, Chld and concessions 50p. Free adm 3.30–5 Mon–Fri, 4.30–5 Sat, Sun and Bank Hols.

WALTHAM CROSS

CAPEL MANOR
Telephone: Lea Valley (0992) 763849
(London Borough of Enfield)

The extensive grounds of this Horticultural College offer a comprehensive collection of hardy outdoor and glasshouse plants. Many fine trees including one of the largest surviving Copper Beeches in the country. Shrub borders containing old fashioned Roses, herbaceous plants. Attractive bedding schemes. Large rock and water garden. 17th century garden containing culinary, aromatic and medicinal plants. Also knot hedges and contemporary plants. 5 acre trials and demonstration garden. Facilities for physically handicapped persons. A sensory garden for the blind is just one of the many theme gardens which are on show for the public to enjoy.
Location: 2½ m NE of Enfield; ¼ m W of A10 at Bullsmoor Lane traffic lights; junction 25/M25/A10.S ¼ m W off A10 traffic lights.
Station: Turkey Street (1¼ m).
Opening Times: Apr to Oct—Mons to Fris 10–4.30, Sat & Sun 10–5.30. Adm £1, under 18 & OAPs 50p. Several Open weekends throughout the year. Adm £1.50, under 18 & OAPs 75p. Special rates for season tickets and coach parties or visiting groups. Further details on request from the Resources Officer, Capel Manor, Bullsmoor Lane, Waltham Cross, Herts. EN7 5HR.

WATFORD

WATFORD MUSEUM *(Watford Borough Council)*
194 High Street. Tel: (0923) 32297.
Local history with special emphasis on printing, brewing and wartime, plus an art gallery and a temporary exhibition gallery with displays changing monthly. Mon to Sat 10–5. *Closed* Sun. Adm free.

WELWYN

WELWYN ROMAN BATHS *(Welwyn Hatfield District Council)*
Welwyn By-pass. Tel: (070 72) 71362.
Remains of a c. 3rd AD suite of Roman Baths in a specially constructed vault under the A1(M). Sun and Bank Hols 2–5 (or dusk if earlier). Parties at other times by arrangement. Adm 25p; Chld free. Suitable for the disabled.

WHITWELL

ST. PAUL'S WALDEN BURY
(Simon Bowes Lyon)

Formal woodland garden with temples, statues, lake, ponds. Laid out about 1730, covering about 40 acres. There are also rhododendron and flower gardens.
Location: 5 m S of Hitchin; ½ m N of Whitwell on B651.
Opening Times: GARDEN ONLY. Telephone Whitwell 229 or 218 for information on dates. Adm £1, Chd and OAPs 50p. *Opened in aid of National Gardens Scheme and other charities.*
Refreshments: Tea at the garden on open days.

Tring Zoological Museum

HERTFORDSHIRE'S GREATEST DAY OUT!

Times of opening
Monday–Saturday 10.00–17.00 Sunday 14.00–17.00
The Museum is closed on 1 January, Good Friday,
May Day, and 24–26 December

Museum Shop
The shops sells postcards, souvenirs, models, toys,
pottery, jewellery and many more gifts relating to
natural history. It also contains a wide range of natural
history books.

For information please write to the Press Office (ZM),
British Museum (Natural History), Cromwell Road,
London SW7 5BD or Telephone 044 282 4181

Admission Charged

Humberside

BARTON ON HUMBER

BAYSGARTH MUSEUM *(Glanford Borough Council)*
   Baysgarth Park, Caistor Road.
An 18th century town house and park with displays of porcelain, local history,
archaeology and geology. Changing exhibitions. Thurs to Sun 10–4. Open Bank
Hols. Adm free.

BEVERLEY

BEVERLEY ART GALLERY AND MUSEUM
   (Beverley Borough Council)
   Champney Road. Tel: (0482) 882255.
Art Gallery includes paintings by the Beverley artist F.W. Elwell, R.A. Museum
of local antiquities. Weekdays 10–12.30, 2–5.30 (Thurs 10–12 noon; Sat 10–4).

THE GUILDHALL
Telephone: 0482 882255
(East Yorkshire Borough of Beverley Borough Council)

The Guildhall, Beverley, established in 1500, in original medieval house,
rebuilt 1762, when served as Town Hall. Currently used as the Mayor's Parlour.
Houses Magistrates' Room, formerly Council Chamber, containing 15th century
furniture and 16th century pewter collection. Also Mayor's Parlour, built 1830
and used as Council Chamber until 1896 when Court Room altered to
accommodate meetings. Exhibits of civic regalia, ancient charters, records,
paintings and mayoral historic items. Courtroom reveals medieval wall, a
particularly beautiful all-seeing figure of Justice riding the clouds; an outstanding example of work of Italian stuccoist Cortese; also town's and Kings Arms,
executed by Cortese.
Location: In Town Centre, off pedestrianised zone, Register Square.
Opening Times: Easter to Oct on Tues 10–4.30. Also Bank Holidays 10–4.30.
Adm free. Parties welcomed by appointment – small charge applies only on
days other than Tues. Car parking very limited. Free car parks in near vicinity.
Ground floor only suitable for disabled.
Refreshments: Facilities in near proximity.

SKIDBY WINDMILL AND MUSEUM *(Beverley Borough Council)*
   Skidby. Tel: (0482) 882255.
Restored windmill and museum relating to milling and corn production. May
to Sept: Tues to Sat 10–4; Sun 1.30–4.30. Operated alternate Suns commencing
first Sun in May.

BRIDLINGTON

BRIDLINGTON ART GALLERY AND MUSEUM
   (Borough of East Yorkshire)
   Sewerby Hall. Tel: (0262) 678255.
Amateur artists' exhibition. July–Aug. Permanent Amy Johnson exhibition.
Local and natural history and archaeology. Old farm implements. Easter to end
Sept: Sun to Fri 10–12.30, 1.30–6; Sat 1.30–6. Enquiries tel above number.

SEWERBY HALL
(Borough of East Yorkshire)

Built 1714–20 by John Greame with additions 1803. Gardens of great botanical
interest.
Location: In Bridlington on the cliffs, 2 m NE from centre town.
Stations: Bridlington (2½ m); Bempton (2 m).
Opening Times: Park open all year—Daily 9–dusk. Art Gallery open Easter to
Sept—Suns to Fris 10–12.30, 1.30–6; Sats 1.30–6. Provisional adm £1, Chd 50p
(including zoo and art gallery). Pay and Display car park.
Refreshments: Self-service snack bar in the Hall (summer season only).

BRIGG

ELSHAM HALL COUNTRY PARK
Telephone: Barnetby 688698
(Capt J Elwes, DL)

Beautiful English park with lakes and wild gardens. Waterfowl and giant Carp.
Domestic animals, Chinese Muntjac Deer and Bird garden. Nature trails.
Adventure playground. Arts and Craft Centre, Granary Tearooms, Wrawby
Moor Art Gallery, Blacksmith (weekends only). Caravan Club site. Wild
Butterfly Garden. Six National Awards for Catering and Conservation.
Location: 4 m from Brigg on Barton-on-Humber Road A15.
Stations: Elsham (1½ m); Barnetby (2½ m); Kirmington Airport 3½ m.
Opening Times: PARK. Easter to Oct—Mons to Sats 11–5.30; Suns & Bank Hols
11–6.30. *Park closes 8 pm or dusk.* Oct to Easter—Suns & Bank Hols only 11–4
or dusk. *Park closes early in bad weather.* Closed Good Friday & Christmas Day.
Admission: Price subject to review. Please telephone for Party bookings and
winter discount. Schools party discount and Guided Natural History Trails
available on request.
Refreshments: The Granary Tea Room—lunches & fresh teas daily in summer &
Suns & Bank Hols in winter. Parties by arrangement. Special menus available.
Winter conferences and wedding catering. Coach parties welcome by arrangement with Administrator.

BURTON AGNES

BURTON AGNES HALL
Telephone: Burton Agnes (0262 89) 324
(Preservation Trust Ltd)

One of the least altered of Elizabethan country houses. Fine collection of old
and French impressionist paintings, carved ceilings and overmantels.
Location: In village of Burton Agnes, 6 m SW of Bridlington on Driffield/
Bridlington Road (A166).
Opening Times: Mar 24 to Oct 31—Daily 11–5. Hall and Gardens: Adm £1.75,
Chd & OAPs £1.25. *The management reserves the right to close the house or
part thereof without prior notice; adm charges will be adjusted on such days.*
Refreshments: Licensed cafeteria. Teas, light lunches & refreshments. Gift
shop. Toilet for the disabled.

BURTON CONSTABLE

BURTON CONSTABLE
Telephone: (0964) 562400
(J Chichester Constable, Esq)

Magnificent Elizabethan House, built c1570. Outstanding collection of furniture, pictures and works of art. Unique collection of eighteenth century scientific instruments. Carriage display in stables, parkland by 'Capability' Brown.
Location: At Burton Constable; 1½ m N of Sproatley; 7½ m NE of Hull (A165); 10 m SE of Beverley (A1035).
Opening Times: Apr 1 to Sept 30. Apr, May, June & Sept – Suns & Bank Holiday Mons only 1–5.30: July & Aug – Suns to Thurs inclusive 1–5.30. Grounds open at noon. Parties at any time by arrangement. For further details write to: The Administrator, Burton Constable Hall, Hull, HU11 4LN, or Tel: (0964) 562400.
Refreshments: Cafeteria. Gift shop.

EPWORTH

EPWORTH
Telephone: Epworth (0427) 872268
(Trustees of the World Methodist Council)

Built 1709. Restored 1957. Childhood home of John & Charles Wesley, oldest Methodist shrine.
Location: In Epworth, 3 m N of Haxey on A161, 18 m E of Doncaster M180 exit 2.
Opening Times: Mar to Oct—Weekdays 10–12, 2–4; Suns 2–4. Adm £1, Chd 50p. A/V presentation. Coaches by arrangement only. Accommodation by arrangement.
Refreshments: At the House *by arrangement only.*

GOOLE

CARLTON TOWERS
Telephone: (0405) 861662
(Duke of Norfolk)

The most complete Victorian Gothic House, still a family home and includes beautiful china, silver, carved woodwork, etc and a Priest's Hiding Hole.
Location: 20 m S of York; 6 m S of Selby and 1 m N of Snaith (A1041) and 6 m from M62 exits 34 & 36.
Station: Snaith (1 m).
Opening Times: Easter Sat to Tues incl; Early May Bank Hol Sun & Mon; Spring Bank Hol Sat to Tues incl; Aug Bank Hol Sat to Tues incl. All Suns from the beginning of May to end of Sept. House open 1–5 (last adm 4.30), Parkland and Rose Garden, 12.15–6. Adm £2, Chd £1, OAPs £1.50. Party bookings on any day, by appointment (minimum of 20); a guided tour given from beginning of May to end of Sept and also on Thurs evenings, £2 per person. Enquiries to The Comptroller, Carlton Towers, Nr Goole.
Refreshments: Tea room (open 12.30–5.30).

GOOLE MUSEUM AND ART GALLERY
(Humberside County Council)
Goole Library, Market Square, DN14 5AA. Tel: (0405) 2187.
Collections illustrating the early history of the area and the formation and development of Goole as a port. Maritime paintings. Temporary exhibitions. Mon to Fri 10–5; Sat 9.30–12.30. Adm free.

GREAT GRIMSBY

WELHOLME GALLERIES *(Great Grimsby Borough Council)*
Welholme Road. Tel: (0472) 242000.
Model ships, marine paintings, costume, folk life. Unique Hallgarth Collection of Lincolnshire photographs. Tues to Sat 10–5.

HESSLE

CLIFF MILL *(Beverley Borough Council)*
Hessle Foreshore. Tel: (0482) 882255.
Renovated whiting mill, close to the Humber Bridge with adjacent car parking and picnic areas. May to Sept: Sun 2–4.30.

HORNSEA

NORTH HOLDERNESS MUSEUM OF VILLAGE LIFE (HORNSEA MUSEUM)
11 Newbegin. Tel: (0964) 533443.
Period rooms; small varied displays reflecting trades and development of the area. Easter to Oct: Daily (afternoons only). Parties by arrangement all year. Small adm charge. Small Museum of the Year 1980. H.E.T. Sandford Award 1987.

HULL

BLAYDES HOUSE
Telephone: Hull (0482) 26406
(The Georgian Society for East Yorkshire)

Mid-Georgian merchants house, fine staircase and panelled rooms. Restored by the Society in 1974-5.
Location: 6 High Street, Hull.
Station: Hull.

Opening Times: Staircase, Blaydes and Partners' Rooms—all the year Mons to Fris (except Bank Hols) 10.30–1, 2–4. By appointment only with Blackmore Son & Co, Chartered Architects at Blaydes House. Adm 50p.

THE CHARTERHOUSE
Telephone: (0482) 20026
(Charterhouse Trustees)

God's House Hospital, commonly called The Charterhouse, was founded in 1384 by Michael de la Pole, Earl of Suffolk. The Charterhouse is an almshouse which provides accommodation for the elderly, and visitors are requested not to enter areas other than the Chapel and Gardens.
Location: Charterhouse Lane, Hull.
Opening Times: CHAPEL & GARDENS open daily during July and on Good Friday, Easter Day, Easter Monday, Spring and Summer Bank Holidays 10–8. No adm charge but prior notice should be given for parties of 10 or more. Children should be accompanied by an adult. Dogs not permitted. Limited car parking available.
Refreshments: Facilities in nearby City centre.

FERENS ART GALLERY *(Hull City Council)*
Queen Victoria Square. Tel: (0482) 222750.
Permanent collection of Old Masters; English 18th to 20th century portraits; Humberside marines; a modern gallery struggling for space with frequent visiting exhibitions. Mon to Sat 10–5; Sun 1.30–4.30. Café 10.30–3.30 daily (4 Fri and Sat).

MAISTER HOUSE, The National Trust
Telephone: Hull (0482) 24114
Rebuilt 1744 with a superb staircase-hall designed in the Palladian manner.
Location: 160 High Street, Hull.
Station: Hull (¾ m).
Opening Times: Staircase and entrance hall only. All the year—Mons to Fris 10–4. *Closed Bank Hols.* Adm by guide book 50p. No dogs. Unsuitable for wheelchairs & parties.

OLD GRAMMAR SCHOOL *(Hull City Council)*
South Church Side. Tel: (0482) 222737.
Hull's oldest secular building, 1583–5, changing and permanent displays: The Story of Hull and its People. Open Mon–Sat 10–5, Sun 1.30–4.30.

POSTERNGATE ART GALLERY
(Hull City Council, sponsored by Lincolnshire & Humberside Arts)
6 Posterngate. Tel: (0482) 222745.
Programme of temporary exhibitions, mainly works by young artists and photographers. Coffee. Books, cards and prints. Tues to Sat 9.30–5.30. *Closed Sun and Mon.*

SPURN LIGHTSHIP *(Hull City Council)*
Hull Marina. Tel: (0482) 222737.
Built 1927 and restored 1985/6, visitors can see the master's cabin, crew's quarters and light mechanism etc. Open Mon–Sat 10–5, Sun 1.30–4.30. *Closed Mon and Tues Winter months.*

TOWN DOCKS MUSEUM *(Hull City Council)*
Queen Victoria Square. Tel: (0482) 222737.
Whales and Whaling with collection of Scrimshaw; Fishing and Trawling; Court Room of the former Docks Board; Hull and the Humber; Ships and Shipping. Mon to Sat 10–5; Sun 1.30–4.30. Café 11–4 (Mon to Sat).

TRANSPORT AND ARCHAEOLOGY MUSEUM *(Hull City Council)*
36 High Street. Tel: (0482) 222737.
Collection of horse-drawn vehicles and early motorcars. Archaeology of East Yorkshire including the Hasholme Boat and spectacular Roman mosaics. Mon to Sat 10–5; Sun 1.30–4.30.

UNIVERSITY OF HULL ART COLLECTION *(University of Hull)*
The Middleton Hall, University of Hull, Cottingham Road.
Tel: (0482) 465192.
Specialising in art in Britain 1890–1940. Painting, sculpture and drawings including work by Sickert, Steer, Lucien Pissarro, Augustus John, Stanley Spencer, Gill, Epstein and Moore. Also the Thompson Collection of Chinese Ceramics (chiefly 17th century) and temporary exhibitions. Open term time only: Mon–Fri 2–4; (Wed 12.30–4). No adm charge. Parties welcome. Limited car parking. Suitable for disabled persons, though not ideal. Hon. Curator: John G. Bernasconi.

WILBERFORCE HOUSE
Telephone: Hull (0482) 222737
(Hull City Council)

17th century mansion. Birthplace of William Wilberforce, the slave emancipator.
Location: 25 High Street, Hull.
Station: Hull.
Opening Times: All the year—Weekdays 10–5; Suns 1.30–4.30. *Closed Good Friday, Christmas Day, Boxing Day & New Year's Day.* Adm free.

POCKLINGTON

BURNBY HALL GARDENS
Telephone: Pocklington (0759 30) 2068   ♿
(Stewart's Burnby Hall Gardens & Museum Trust)

Large gardens with 2 lakes. Finest display of hardy water lilies in Europe – 45 varieties, designated Supplementary National Collection. Museum housing Stewart Collection—sporting trophies, ethnic material. Picnic area.

Location: 13 m E of York on A1079.
Opening Times: Easter to mid Oct—daily 10–6. Adm 80p, Chd (under 5) free, (5–16) 30p, OAPs & Parties 60p. Free coach and car park. Disabled facilities.
Refreshments: Teas in the garden.

SCUNTHORPE

BOROUGH MUSEUM AND ART GALLERY
(Scunthorpe Borough Council)
Oswald Road. Tel: (0724) 843533.

The Regional Museum for South Humberside. Local history and industry; video room features film on iron and steelmaking; social history collections; geology and countryside gallery; important collections of pre-historic, Roman and later archaeology. Temporary exhibitions. Mon to Sat 10–5; Sun 2–5; Bank Hols 10–5.

NORMANBY HALL AND COUNTRY PARK
Telephone: Scunthorpe (0724) 720215
(Scunthorpe Borough Council)

A Regency mansion set in 350 acres of beautiful parkland and gardens. Normanby Hall was designed by Sir Robert Smirke (architect of the British Museum) and completed in 1830. It is now leased from the Sheffield family, formerly Dukes of Buckingham and owners of Buckingham Palace, and has been decorated and furnished in period by Scunthorpe Museums and Art Gallery. The spacious Country Park surrounding the Hall provides interest for all the family, with herds of red and fallow deer, wild and exotic birds, lakeside and woodland nature trails, a Craft and Countryside Centre, picnic areas, riding stables and a golf club. The Normanby Park Farming Museum is due to open in 1989.

Location: 4 m N of Scunthorpe on B1430, turn right at Normanby village. Car Park off Thealby Lane.
Opening Times: HALL: Easter to Oct—Mons to Fris 11–5, Suns 2–5, Nov to Mar—by appointment only. *Closed Sats all year.* Adm 65p, Chd/OAPs 35p. (1988 rates.) Wheelchairs—ground floor only. Guided tours and parties by appointment.
PARK: Open during daylight hours, daily throughout the year.
Refreshments: Café in grounds, summer only.

SLEDMERE

SLEDMERE HOUSE
(Sir Tatton Sykes, Bart)

A Georgian house begun in 1751 with important additions attributed to Samuel Wyatt in conjunction with Sir Christopher Sykes, containing superb library 100ft long. The entire building was burnt to the ground in 1911 and splendidly restored with an Edwardian feeling for space by York architect Walter Brierley during the first world war. The latter copied Joseph Rose's fine ceilings and inserted a magnificent Turkish room. The House contains much of its original furniture and paintings. An unusual feature is the great organ, which is frequently played on open days. Capability Brown Park. 18th century walled rose garden. Main garden under reconstruction.

Location: 24 m E of York on main York/Bridlington Road; 8 m NW of Driffield at junction of B1251 & B1253.
Opening Times: Easter weekend, all Suns in Apr; Apr 30 to Oct 1—Daily (except Mons and Fris); open all Bank Hols. 1.30–5.30 (last adm 5). Adm £2, Chd £1, OAPs and Coach Parties £1.70; grounds only £1, Chd 60p. Private parties arranged by appointment only on Weds evenings. Free Car Park and Coach Parks. Illustrated brochure from The House Secretary, Sledmere House, Driffield, East Yorkshire.
Refreshments: Self service restaurant. Licensed restaurant for booked meals, Driffield (0377) 86208.

THORNTON CURTIS

THORNTON ABBEY
Telephone: (0469) 40357

The great crenellated gatehouse demonstrates that Thornton was one of the richer monasteries of the Augustinian Order. It was founded about 1139 by William le Gros, Earl of Albemarle, who is buried here. The dissolution of the monastery in the 16th century gave rise to a macabre legend—that the remains of a monk had been found walled up in a room, seated at a table with a book, pen and ink.

Location: 2 m (3.2 km) north east of Thornton Curtis. OS map ref TA115190.
Opening Times: Good Friday to Sept 30, daily 10–6; Oct 1 to Mar 23, weekends only 10–4. Adm 80p, OAPs 60p, Chd 40p.

Isle of Man

CASTLETOWN

THE NAUTICAL MUSEUM *(Branch of Manx Museum)*
Bridge Street, Castletown.

Contains the schooner-rigged armed yacht 'Peggy', built 1791, preserved in her original boathouse; personalia of the Quayle family (her builders), a sailmaker's loft, ship models, nautical gear. Early photographs of Manx maritime trade and fishing. Small adm charge. Open early May to late Sept.

DOUGLAS

THE MANX MUSEUM
Tel: (0624) 75522.

Displays and conserves collections illustrating Manx archaeology, folk life and natural history. Art Gallery devoted to Manx paintings and works by Manx artists. Reference Library of Manx studies. Memorial room to T.E. Brown, the Manx poet. Reconstructed 19th century farmhouse, barn, dairy etc. Mon to Sat 10–5. *Closed* Sun, Christmas Hols, New Year's Day, Good Friday and the morning of Tynwald Day.

PORT ERIN

MARINE BIOLOGICAL STATION
A department of the University of Liverpool for teaching and research in marine biology. An aquarium containing local fishes and invertebrates. Photographic displays on a variety of marine topics. Apr–Oct incl. weekdays 10–5. Sat 10–1.

PORT ST. MARY

THE CREGNEASH VILLAGE FOLK MUSEUM
(Branch of Manx Museum) Near Port St. Mary.

Group of thatched buildings in Cregneash village. Includes traditionally furnished crofter-fisherman's cottage, weaver's shed, turner's shop, smithy and a farmstead. Small adm charge. Open early May to late Sept.

RAMSEY

THE GROVE RURAL LIFE MUSEUM
(Branch of Manx Museum) Near Ramsey

Early Victorian house of some social standing with associated out-buildings and garden. Horse-driven threshing mill, agricultural gear and vehicles. Small adm charge. Open early May to late Sept. For full details of opening hours of the Branch Museums see the full page advertisement.

The Manx Museum
and National Trust

ISLE OF MAN

THE MANX MUSEUM, DOUGLAS

The National Museum of the Island, with attractive modern displays on Manx history and archaeology, natural history and folk life and an Art Gallery with work of Manx interest. The building also houses the Island's national reference library.

Hours: Monday–Saturday 10–5
Closed Sundays, Christmas holidays, New Year's Day, Good Friday and the morning of Tynwald Day.
Admission free.

The Manx Museum has three branch museums which are open during the summer season (early May to late September). These are:

THE CREGNEASH VILLAGE FOLK MUSEUM, near Port St. Mary and Port Erin in the south of the Island. Established in 1938, this illustrates, in situ, the life of a typical Manx upland crofting/fishing community at the turn of the century. Most of the buildings (at the south end of the village) are thatched and include a crofter-fisherman's home, a weaver's shed with handloom, a turner's shed with treadle lathe, a thatched farmstead and a smithy. Spinning demonstrations are given on certain days each week and a blacksmith works from time to time in the smithy, and if you are lucky you might get a taste of fresh baked bonnag in Harry Kelly's cottage. The property adjoins the Manx National Trust lands of the Spanish Head area.
Hours: Monday–Saturday 10–1, 2–5; Sundays 2–5.
Small admission charge.

THE NAUTICAL MUSEUM, in Castletown. Across the harbour from Castle Rushen, the displays centre on the late 18th century armed yacht 'Peggy' in her contemporary boat-house. Part of the original building is constructed as a Cabin Room of the Nelson period and the museum also displays many nautical exhibits, ship models etc., a fine range of photographs of Manx vessels in the days of sail and a reconstruction of a sailmaker's loft.
Hours: Monday–Saturday 10–1, 2–5; Sundays 2–5.
Small admission charge.

THE GROVE RURAL LIFE MUSEUM, near Ramsey. On the outskirts of Ramsey – on the Andreas Road – this newest branch of the Manx Museum centres on a small, pleasantly-proportioned early Victorian house with associated range of outbuildings. The house displays a series of Victorian period rooms, a costume room and general museum displays. The outbuildings contain early agricultural equipment and vehicles include a horse-drawn threshing mill restored to a working condition. The pleasant garden is being brought back to its Victorian state, with ornamental pool and fish pond, and waterfowl on the duck-pond. Watch out for Manx cats!
Hours: Monday to Friday 10–5; Sundays 2–5.
Closed Saturday.
Small admission charge.

Isle of Wight

BEMBRIDGE

BEMBRIDGE MARITIME MUSEUM *(Martin J. Woodward)*
Sherborne Street. Tel: (0983) 872223 or 873125.
Six galleries plus a shop. Ship models, wreck items. Our discovery of the missing WW2 submarine HMS Swordfish.

THE RUSKIN GALLERY
Bembridge School. Tel: (0983) 872101.
Large collection of pictures and manuscripts by Ruskin and his contemporaries. By appointment only.

BRADING

LILLIPUT MUSEUM OF ANTIQUE DOLLS AND TOYS
High Street.

NUNWELL HOUSE AND GARDENS
Telephone: Isle of Wight (0983) 407240
(Colonel & Mrs J A Aylmer)
Nunwell with its historic connections with King Charles I is set in beautiful gardens and parkland with channel views. A finely furnished family house with Jacobean and Georgian wings. Home Guard museum and family military collection.
Location: 1 m from Brading, turning off A3055; 3 m S of Ryde.
Station: Brading.
Opening Times: House and Gardens: May Bank Holidays Apr 30 to May 1, and May 28, 29, Sun July 9 to Thurs Sept 28, Suns to Thurs 10–5. Adm £1.80, Chd 60p. Gardens only: June 1 to June 30 – 1.30–5. Adm £1, Chd 50p. *Closed* Fri and Sats. Coach and School parties welcome all year by appointment. No dogs.
Refreshments: Light refreshments when House open; large parties book catering in advance.

OSBORN-SMITH'S ANIMAL WORLD
Probably the finest collection in Great Britian of animals, birds and reptiles from all over the world displayed in large, colourful dioramas depicting their natural surroundings. Superb natural history museum. Open all year – May to Sept: Daily 10–10; Oct to Apr: Daily 10–5. Special party rates.

OSBORN-SMITH'S WAX MUSEUM
Cameos of Island history with authentic costume, wax figures, period furniture and harmonious settings cleverly brought to life with the added realism of sound, light and motion. Artistically set in the Ancient Rectory Mansion, part dating from 1066 A.D. Open all the year – May to Sept: Daily 10–10; Oct to Apr: Daily 10–5. Special party rates.

THE ROMAN VILLA
Tel: (0983) 614623.
The remains of a Roman villa with exquisite mosaic pavements *in situ*, hypocaust and Roman objects. Apr to end of Sept: Weekdays 10–5.30; Sun 10.30–5.30. Winter months by appointment only. Adm charge.

COWES

COWES MARITIME MUSEUM *(Isle of Wight County Council)*
Beckford Road. Tel: Cowes (0983) 293341.
Open all year except Thurs and Bank Holidays.

SIR MAX AITKEN MUSEUM
The Prospect, 83 High Street. Tel: (0983) 293800.
The Museum is a collection of fine marine paintings, nautical instruments and yachting memorabilia which Sir Max Aitken had gathered over the past fifty years. Open June, July, Aug: Mon to Fri, 10–2. Other times by appointment for groups. Suitable for disabled (no wheelchairs available). Adm free.

EAST COWES

OSBORNE HOUSE
Telephone: (0983) 200022
(English Heritage)
This was Queen Victoria's seaside residence built at her own expense, in 1845. The Prince Consort played a prominent part in the design of the house—it was his version of an Italian villa—and the work was carried out by Thomas Cubitt, the famous London builder. The Queen died here in 1901 and her private apartments have been preserved more or less unaltered. Crowded with furniture and bric-a-brac they epitomise the style we call 'Victorian'. Also see Queen's bathing machine.
Location: 1 m SE of East Cowes. OS map ref SZ 516948.
Station: Ferry terminal East Cowes (1 m).
Opening Times: Good Friday to Sept 30, daily 10–6; Oct 1–31, daily 10–5. Last Adm 1 hour before closing. Adm £3, OAPs £2, Chd £1.50.

NEWPORT

CARISBROOKE CASTLE
Telephone: (0983) 522107
Here are seven acres of castle and earthworks to explore. The oldest parts of the castle are 12th century, but the great mound—71 steps high—bore a wooden castle before that, and there are fragments of Roman wall at its base. Fortified against the French, then the Spaniards, the castle is best known as the prison of Charles I in 1647/8. A bold escape plan failed when the King became wedged between the bars of the great chamber window. The castle contains the island's museum.
Location: 1¼ m (2 km) south west of Newport. OS map ref SZ486877.
Opening Times: Good Friday to Sept 30, daily 10–6; Oct 1 to Maundy Thursday, daily 10–4. *Closed Mons, Christmas and New Year.* Adm £2.20, OAPs £1.65, Chd £1.10.

COTHEY BOTTOM HERITAGE CENTRE
(Industrial Archaeology)
Westridge, Ryde. Tel: (0983) 68431

ROMAN VILLA
Cypress Road, Newport. Tel: (0983) 529720
Open Easter–Sept: 10–4.30 Sun–Fri. Adm charge.

NEWTOWN

NEWTOWN OLD TOWN HALL, The National Trust
18th century building of brick and stone. One of the buildings surviving from the island's former ancient borough.
Location: In Newtown, midway between Newport and Yarmouth.
Opening Times: Mar 24 to end Sept: Mons, Weds & Suns 2–5; July & Aug daily except Fri & Sat 2–5 (last adm 4.45). Also open Good Friday & Easter Saturday. *Closed Oct to end March.* Adm 50p, Chd 25p. No reduction for parties. No dogs. Unsuitable for wheelchairs.

RYDE

NATIONAL WIRELESS MUSEUM
"Lynwood", 52 West Hill Road.

SANDOWN

MUSEUM OF ISLE OF WIGHT GEOLOGY
(Isle of Wight County Council)
High Street. Tel: (0983) 404344.
Open all year except Wed, and Bank Holidays.

TOTLAND BAY

THE NEEDLES OLD BATTERY, The National Trust
Telephone: Isle of Wight 754772
A former Palmerstonian fort built in 1862, 250 ft above sea level; 200 ft tunnel to spectacular view of the Needles. Exhibition on history of the Needles Headland.
Location: West Highdown, Totland Bay.
Opening Times: Mar 24 to Nov 5—Daily, except Fris & Sats but open Good Fri & Easter Sat; also Fris & Sats in July & Aug; 10.30–5 (last admission 4.30). Adm £1, Chd 50p. No reduction for parties.

WROXALL

APPULDURCOMBE HOUSE
Telephone: (0983) 852484
The only house in the 'grand manner' on the Island, Appuldurcombe (pronounced 'Applercombe') was a status symbol and not a home. Sir Robert Worsley started the house in 1701 but ran out of money. The east façade, a beautiful example of English baroque, dates from this year. The house was not completed until the end of the century. The house is now an empty shell but still stands in its fine park, moulded by 'Capability' Brown.
Location: ½ m (0.8 km) west of Wroxall. OS map ref SZ543800.
Opening Times: Good Friday to Sept 30, daily 10–6; Oct 1 to Maundy Thursday, daily 10–4. *Closed Mons, Christmas and New Year.* Adm 80p, OAPs 60p, Chd 40p.

YARMOUTH

YARMOUTH CASTLE
Telephone: (0983) 760678
Part of the coastal defences of Henry VIII, Yarmouth embodied the very latest fashion in military engineering. Completed in 1547, it is square in plan, and washed on two sides by the sea. During the Civil War the island was strongly royalist and throughout the Commonwealth Cromwell kept a large garrison here. When Sir Robert Holmes was appointed Captain of the Island in 1667, the castle was already outmoded and ineffective. He reduced it in size, filled in the moat and built himself a house—now the hotel—on the site.
Location: Yarmouth. OS map ref SZ354898.
Opening Times: Good Friday to Sept 30, daily 10–6. Adm 80p, OAPs 60p, Chd 40p.

Kent

ASHFORD

ASHFORD LOCAL HISTORY MUSEUM *(Kent County Council)*
Central Library, Church Street. Tel: (0233) 20649.
A museum display of local history material which forms the beginning of a museum for Ashford and the surrounding area. Mon, Tues 9.30–6; Weds, Sats 9.30–5; Thurs, Fri 9.30–7. *Closed* on public holidays. Adm free. Small car park. Unsuitable for disabled persons.

GODINTON PARK
(Alan Wyndham Green, Esq)

House belongs mostly to Jacobean times, interior contains wealth of panelling and carving, portraits, furniture and china. Formal gardens.
Location: 1½ m W of Ashford off Maidstone Road at Potter's Corner (A20). *Station: Ashford (2 m).*
Opening Times: Easter Sat, Sun & Mon; then June to Sept—Suns & Bank Hols only 2–5. Adm House & Gardens £1.50, Chd (under 16) 70p. Weekdays by appointment only. Parties of 20 or more £1.20 per person.

BENENDEN

BENENDEN WALLED GARDEN
Telephone: Cranbrook (0580) 240749
(Richard & Diane Cotter)

An 18th century walled garden with large collection of old fashioned, fragrant plants, specie salvias and herbs. Picnic lawn. Ladies garden, Gourmet garden, plants for sale. No dogs in garden. Richard & Diane Cotter are available for illustrated lectures.
Location: Benenden, nr Cranbrook, Kent. In the grounds of Benenden School, entrance on Benenden to Sissinghurst Road 1 mile from Benenden cross road.
Opening Times: Mar 18 to Apr 17, May 27 to June 1, July 9 to Sept 6, 10–Dusk. Adm £1, OAP 75p, Disabled 75p, Chld under 16 free. Parties of 10 or more 75p by appointment. Conducted tours can be arranged. Hard standing and grass car park areas. No coaches in school grounds. Suitable for disabled persons.
Refreshments: Morning coffee, light lunches, cream teas.

BIRCHINGTON

THE POWELL-COTTON MUSEUM AND QUEX HOUSE
Quex Park. Tel: Thanet (0843) 42168.
A28 12 miles east of Canterbury; signposted St. Nicholas-at-Wade and Prospect Roundabouts and Birchington Square. Combine a morning visit to Canterbury with a never to be forgotten afternoon at Quex House, set in 250 acres of beautiful gardens & woodland. The fine Regency house was built in 1805 by John Powell, High Sheriff of Kent and is still the Powell-Cotton family home. Seven of the rooms are on view with superb Family collections – fine furniture, porcelain, pictures, silver, clocks etc. Of unique importance is the Museum built adjoining the House by Maj. P.H.G. Powell-Cotton, Naturalist, Explorer, Photographer, Author and Collector Extraordinary. Words cannot do justice to the amazing collections housed in this remarkable private museum of nine large galleries. The African and Asian animals in their huge natural landscape dioramas look so alive that visitors have claimed to have seen them move; one of the most important ethnographical collections is housed here together with a very large weapons and cannon collection, African butterflies, local archaeological material, treasures from the Orient, including a unique series of Chinese Imperial and Export porcelain and Family Bygones. Tea room open in season; free parking for cars & coaches. **House and Museum:** open 2.15–6 April 1 to Sept 30: Weds, Thurs and Sun, Bank Hols and Fri in Aug. **Museum only:** Oct to Mar: Sun only. Pre-booked parties at other times; contact Curator (0843) 42168. After hours (0843) 45088.

BOROUGH GREEN

GREAT COMP
Telephone: Borough Green 882669
(The Great Comp Charitable Trust)

Outstanding garden of seven acres, very wide variety of trees, shrubs, heathers and herbaceous plants. Old brick walls, much new stone work, paving and ornaments.
Location: 2 m E of Borough Green B2016 off A20. First right at Comp crossroads ½ m on left.
Station: Borough Green & Wrotham (1½ m).
Opening Times: GARDEN ONLY. Apr 1 to Oct 31—Daily 11–6. *Parties by prior arrangement.* Adm £1.50, Chd 70p. *No dogs.*
Refreshments: Tea for parties by arrangement.

BOUGHTON MONCHELSEA

BOUGHTON MONCHELSEA PLACE
Telephone: Maidstone (0622) 43120
(M B Winch, Esq)

Grey stone, battlemented Elizabethan manor house with breathtaking views over the 18th century landscaped park with fallow deer.
Location: On B2163. In village of Boughton Monchelsea 5 m S of Maidstone. Turn off Maidstone/Hastings Road (A229) at Linton.

Opening Times: Good Fri to early Oct—Sats, Suns & Bank Hols (also Weds during July & Aug) 2.15–6. House & Grounds Adm £1.80, Chd £1. Grounds only Adm £1, Chd 50p (1989 prices). *Parties welcome any day, at special rates, but only by previous engagement.*
Refreshments: Tea rooms at the House. For parties lunch & supper can be ordered in advance.

BRASTED

EMMETTS GARDEN, The National Trust
Telephone: Ide Hill 429 &

Hillside shrub garden of 5 acres. Lovely spring and autumn colours, formal garden and roses. Further areas of garden being restored and re-planted.
Location: 1½ m S of A25 on Sundridge/Ide Hill Road.
Opening Times: GARDEN ONLY. Mar 24 to end Oct—Wed to Sun, Good Fri, Bank Hol Mon 2–6. Last adm 5. Adm £1.50, Chd 80p. Pre-booked parties: £1.10, Chd 60p (15 or more). Dogs admitted on lead. Wheelchair access to level parts of garden only. Tearoom.

BROADSTAIRS

CRAMPTON TOWER MUSEUM
High Street. Tel: (0843) 62078.
Dedicated to the work of Broadstairs resident, Thomas Russell Crampton, eminent Victorian railway engineer. Open (1988) Apr–Sept: 2.30–5 (*Closed* Wed and Weekends except Bank Holiday Suns). Adm charge, discount for chd and school parties. Souvenirs available.

DICKENS' HOUSE MUSEUM *(Thanet District Council)*
Victoria Parade.
Dickens' letters and personal belongings. Local and Dickensian prints, Costume and Victoriana. Apr to Oct: Daily 2.30–5.30. Adm charge.

CANTERBURY

THE CANTERBURY CENTRE
(The Canterbury Urban Studies Centre)
St. Alphege Lane, CT1 2EB. Tel: (0227) 457009.
Converted medieval church housing historical and contemporary exhibitions, urban environmental reference collection, video, A/V, cafe and bookshop. Tues–Sat, 10.30–5. Contact Director.

CANTERBURY HERITAGE – TIME WALK MUSEUM
(Canterbury City Council)
Poor Priests' Hospital, Stour Street. Tel: (0227) 452747.
See the best of the city's treasures set in one of the country's medieval interiors.

CANTERBURY PILGRIMS WAY *(Heritage Products Ltd)*
St. Margaret's Street CT1 2TG. Tel: (0227) 454888.
The Canterbury Pilgrims Way offers an experience like no other. Modern travellers step back into the Middle Ages and breathe again the air that ruffled the cloaks and wimples of Chaucer's immortal medieval band. As your journey unfolds you experience authentic, unforgettable sights, sounds and smells of 14th century life. Along the dusty stretches of road, five of your Chaucerian companions the bawdy Miller, the courtly Knight, the Wife of Bath, the Nun's Priest and the Pardoner will recount their colourful stories of chivalry, romance, jealousy, pride and avarice. Open daily (except Christmas Day) from 9. Adm £3, Chld £1.50. Reductions for OAP, students and families. Parties of more than 20 may book in advance to avoid queues. Suitable for disabled persons. Gift shop.

GOODNESTONE PARK
(The Lord & Lady FitzWalter)

Large garden. Old walled rose garden. Fine trees; good views. Connections with Jane Austen.
Location: 8 m SE of Canterbury; 4 m E of A2; ¼ m SE of B2046; S of A257. *Station: Adisham (2 m).*
Opening Times: GARDEN ONLY. Apr 10 to July 14, Mons to Fris 11–5; Aug 21 to Sept 29, Mons to Fris 11–5 (including Bank Hols); also Suns—Apr 16, 23, May 21 and every Sun to July 9, and Aug 27 2–6. *Closed Sats.* Adm £1.30, Chd (under 12) 20p, OAP £1.10. Disabled in wheelchairs 90p. Parties over 25 £1. **No dogs.**
Refreshments: Teas Suns only *but not in April.*

THE ROMAN MOSAIC *(Canterbury City Council)*
Butchery Lane. Tel: (0227) 452747.
Foundations of Roman house.

THE ROYAL MUSEUM & ART GALLERY AND BUFFS REGIMENTAL MUSEUM
(Canterbury City Council)
High Street. Tel: (0227) 452747.
Collections of medals, weapons, uniforms, pictures and trophies. Pottery and porcelain.

ST AUGUSTINE'S ABBEY
Telephone: (0227) 67343

This was founded in 598 by St Augustine, the first Archibishop of Canterbury. The excavated finds from this early building are rare memorials of the Anglo-Saxon church. The remains we see today are from the later Norman church, its well-preserved crypt, and the medieval monastery.
Location: Canterbury, near the Cathedral. OS map ref TR154578.
Opening Times: Good Friday to Sept 30, daily 10–6; Oct 1 to Maundy Thursday, daily 10–4. *Closed Mons, Christmas and New Year.* Adm 80p, OAPs 60p, Chd 40p.

THE WEST GATE *(Canterbury City Council)*
Tel: (0227) 452747.
Museum of arms and armour housed in the 14th century city gate-house.

WHITSTABLE MUSEUM *(Canterbury City Council)*
Oxford St. Tel: (0227) 276998.

CHATHAM

CHATHAM HISTORIC DOCKYARD
(Chatham Historic Dockyard Trust)
Chatham Historic Dockyard ME4 4TE. Tel: (0634) 812551.
The former Royal Dockyard, is now open to the public as a living museum. Provides a journey through time into Britain's naval history with impressive displays, audio-visual presentations and exhibits. Working eighteenth century Ropery. Craft workshops, ship restoration, sail and flag making. Open **Summer season:** Wed to Sun and Bank Holidays 10–6. **Winter season:** Wed, Sat and Sun 10–4.30. Adm (1988/89) £1.75, Chld, OAP, Student 75p, Chld under 5 free, (guided tours extra). Coach parties welcome, guided tours for groups. Car parking free. Suitable for disabled persons, no wheelchairs available. Toilet facilities available. Special tours for schools – teachers packs and school rooms available (contact Jane Middleton, Education Officer). Gift shops and cafe.

FORT AMHERST
off Dock Road.

MEDWAY HERITAGE CENTRE
Dock Road.

CHIDDINGSTONE

CHIDDINGSTONE CASTLE
Telephone: Penshurst (0892) 870347   ♿
(Trustees of the Denys Eyre Bower Bequest)

Royal Stuart and Jacobite collection; superb Japanese lacquer and swords; Egyptian antiquities, displayed in gracious country house setting.
Location: In Chiddingstone off Edenbridge-Tonbridge road B2027 at Bough Beech Turning. *Bus Service:* Tunbridge Wells–Edenbridge via Bough Beech. *Station:* Penshurst (2½ m).
Opening Times: Mar 26 to Oct 31 – All public holidays. Mar and Apr – Suns and Easter holiday. May 1 to Sept 30 – Weds to Suns, also Tues from mid June to mid Sept. Oct – Weds and weekends only. Hours: weekdays 2–5.30, Suns and Public Holidays 11.30–5.30. Other times also available for booked parties. Adm £2.50, chld 5–15 £1.30, under 5 free. Booked parties of 20 and over £2.25. Coarse fishing in lake in season £6 daily (one onlooker permitted per fisherman £2.50).
Refreshments: Home-made teas, organised by Friends of Chiddingstone Castle. Catering for parties by arrangement. Shop. The courtyard wing of the Castle may be hired for conferences, dinners, weddings etc. A useful stopping place for parties going to and from Gatwick airport.

CHILHAM

CHILHAM CASTLE GARDENS
Telephone: Canterbury 730319
(Viscount Massereene & Ferrard DL)

25 acre garden with formal terraces first made by Tradescant when the Jacobean house was built by the side of the old Norman Castle Keep Informal lake garden. Magnificent views and many fine trees. Park reputedly laid out by Capability Brown. Birds of Prey on display and flying free, afternoons daily except Mon and Fri. Gift shop. Jousting display Sundays & Bank Holidays. Medieval banquets, dinners, wedding receptions in Gothic Hall.
Location: In Chilham village, 6 m W of Canterbury (A252); 8 m NE of Ashford (A28); 22 m NW of Dover, Faversham turn off M2.
Station: Chilham (1 m).
Opening Times: Apr to mid-Oct–Daily (inc Bank Hols). Open from 11 am. Adm weekdays £2, Sun £3, Chd half-price (1987 rates). Free parking. Coaches welcome. Special rates for parties on application.
Refreshments: Jacobean tea room.

COBHAM

NEW COLLEGE OF COBHAM
Telephone: Meopham (0474) 814280   ♿
(Presidents of the New College of Cobham)

Almshouses based on medieval chantry built 1362, part rebuilt 1598. Originally endowed by Sir John de Cobham and descendants.
Location: 4 m W of Rochester; 4 m SE of Gravesend; 1½ m from junction Shorne/Cobham (A2). In Cobham rear of Church of Mary Magdalene.
Station: Sole St (1 m).

Opening Times: Apr to Sept–Daily (except Thurs) 10–7. Oct to Mar–Mons, Tues, Weds, Sats & Suns 10–4.
Refreshments: Afternoon teas by prior arrangement.

OWLETTS, The National Trust

A red-brick Carolean house with contemporary staircase and plasterwork ceiling. Small gardens.
Location: 1 m S of A2 at W end of village, at junction of roads from Dartford & Sole Street.
Station: Sole Street (1 m).
Opening Times: Mar 29 to end of Sept–Weds & Thurs 2–5 (last adm 4.30). Adm 60p. *No reduction for parties or children. No indoor photography. No dogs.* Wheelchair access to ground floor only.

DARTFORD

DARTFORD BOROUGH MUSEUM *(Dartford Borough Council)*
Market Street. Tel: (0322) 343555.
A lively and interesting 'local' museum. Archaeology, natural and local history, geology, 'The Darenth Bowl' (c.450 A.D.), reconstruction Draper's Shop with working 'Cash Railway'. Temporary exhibitions. School Loans Service. Mon, Tues, Thur and Fri 12.30–5.30; Sat 9–1, 2–5. *Closed* Wed and Sun.

DEAL

DEAL AND WALMER CASTLES
Telephone: Deal Castle (0304) 372762 or
Walmer Castle (0304) 364288

When Henry VIII divorced Catherine of Aragon he defied the Pope and broke with Catholic Europe. Deal and Walmer were built under the threat of a 'crusade' against Henry—an invasion which never came. Deal contains an exhibition on the coastal defences of Henry VIII. At Walmer the atmosphere is country house rather than martial, for this has long been the official residence of the Lords Warden of the Cinque Ports. One of the best remembered is the Duke of Wellington (the original 'Wellington boot' may be seen here), and one of the best loved, Queen Elizabeth the Queen Mother.
Location: Deal Castle is near the town centre. OS map ref TR378521.
Opening Times: Deal: Good Friday to Sept 30, daily 10–6; Oct 1 to Maundy Thursday, daily 10–4. *Closed Mons, Christmas and New Year.* Adm £1.10, OAPs 80p, Chd 55p.
Location: Walmer is south of Deal. OS map ref TR378501.
Opening Times: Walmer: Good Friday to Sept 30, daily 10–6; Oct 1 to Maundy Thursday, daily 10–4. *Closed Mons, Christmas and New Year and when Lord Warden is in residence.* Adm £1.60, OAPs £1.20, Chd 80p.

DEAL ARCHAEOLOGICAL COLLECTION *(Kent County Council)*
Deal Library, Broad Street. Tel: (0304) 374726.
Some of the most interesting archaeological finds that have been made in the Deal area, spanning a period of some 5,000 years. They include objects from prehistoric, Roman and Anglo-Saxon burials and from the deserted medieval port of Stonor. Mon, Tues, Thurs 9.30–6; Wed 9.30–1; Fri, Sat 9.30–5. *Closed* on public holidays. Adm free. Public car park near by. Unsuitable for disabled persons.

NORTHBOURNE COURT GARDENS
Telephone: (0304) 611281
(The Lord Northbourne)

Northbourne Court is on the site of a palace which belonged to Eadbald, son of Ethelbert Saxon King of Kent. In 618 he gave it to the monks of St Augustines Abbey who used the produce from the farms and fish ponds for the support of the poor. After the dissolution it reverted to the crown and finally King James I gave it to Sir Edwyn Sandys. Sir Edwyn built a large house facing three tiers of terraces, which were probably built by Edwin Saunders. These terraces and their high flanking walls are still standing and provide the principal architectural feature of the gardens. The terrace forms a mount which is a rarely surviving characteristic of Tudor Gardens. These gardens are planted with a wide range of old fashioned and grey foliage plants on chalk soil to provide interest and colour all year round.
Location: A256 (Dover to Sandwich). Turn right towards Deal/Mongeham and continue for approximately 2 m.
Opening Times: Suns May 28, June 11, 25, July 9, 23, Aug 13, 27, Sept 17: 2–6. Weds May 31 to Aug 30: 2–5. Adm £1.40, Chd/OAP 50p (reductions for parties) in aid of National Gardens Scheme. Plenty of car/coach parking nearby. Limited access for disabled persons (no wheelchairs available).
Refreshments: Pub in village serves good food. Otherwise contact C James on (0304) 611281.

DOVER

DOVER CASTLE
Telephone: (0304) 201628

Castle Hill dominates the shortest passage between Britain and the Continent, and has been the scene of military activity from the Iron Age to the present day. Here is extensive proof from every age of man's ingenuity in devising ways to repel invaders. Dover Castle had its narrowest escape in 1216 when—in a heroic siege—it just managed to hold out against the French. There is much to see, including the underground works, the Roman lighthouse (now the bell tower of a fine Saxon church) and the great keep itself and a spectacular exhibition "All the Queen's Men".
Location: East side of Dover. OS map ref TR326416.
Opening Times: Good Friday to Sept 30, daily 10–6; Oct 1 to Maundy Thursday, daily 10–4. *Closed Christmas and New Year.* Adm £2.50, OAPs £1.80, Chd £1.30. Refreshments in the Keep Yard.

Kent – *continued*

DOVER MUSEUM *(Dover District Council)*
Ladywell CT16 1DQ. Tel: (0304) 201066.
Dover's history and natural history with other items of interest. Monthly programme of temporary exhibitions. Tues–Sat 10–5; Sun 2–5 (Summer only). *Closed* Mon. Entrance fee.

DOVER OLD TOWN GAOL *(Dover District Council)*
Biggin Street. Tel: (0304) 201066
Courtroom, cells and Victorian prison life. Open Tues to Sat 10–5; Sun 2–5 (Summer only). *Closed* Mon. Adm £1.50, Chld/OAP 75p.

GRAND SHAFT *(Dover District Council)*
Snargate Street. Tel: (0304) 201066.
Unique Napoleonic staircase cut through the cliffs of Dover. Open May 30 to Sept 11: Wed to Sun 2–5. Adm 50p, Chd 25p, booked school parties free. Also open Sun during Aug 2–5. 40p, Chld 20p, booked schools free.

ROMAN PAINTED HOUSE
New Street. Tel: (0304) 203279.
Roman town house with extensive wall paintings; part of late-Roman defences; finds and displays on Roman Dover. Apr to Oct: Daily 10–5. *Closed* Mon; also Nov to Mar inclusive. Adm 80p, Chld and OAPs 40p.

TIME-BALL TOWER
Beach Street. Tel: (0304) 201066.
Nineteenth century Semaphore House converted to a Time-ball Tower in 1855. Displays on signalling and time. May 30 to Sept 11: Tues to Sun 10–5, and Bank Holiday Mon. Adm 50p, Chld 25p, booked school parties free.

▣ DOWNE

DOWN HOUSE
Telephone: Farnborough (0689) 59119   ♿
(Royal College of Surgeons of England)
The home of Charles Darwin for 40 years—now his memorial and museum. House, garden and Sandwalk Wood.
Location: In Downe, 5½ m S of Bromley off A233.
Opening Times: Mar 1 to following Jan 31—Daily (except Mons & Fris but open Bank Hol Mons) 1–6. Last adm 5.30. Adm £1.50, Chd 30p, OAPs 75p. *Closed Dec 24–26 & Feb.*

▣ DYMCHURCH

DYMCHURCH MARTELLO TOWER (No 24)
Telephone: 0303 873684
Seventy-four Martello towers were built along the coast between 1805 and 1812. The 24 lb gun on the roof was to resist a Napoleonic invasion. To further confound the French there was no doorway at ground level—entry was by a movable external ladder to the first floor.
Location: Dymchurch. OS map ref TR102294.
Opening Times: Good Friday to Sept 30, daily 10–6. Adm 80p, OAPs 60p, Chd 40p.

▣ EYNSFORD

LULLINGSTONE CASTLE
Telephone: Farningham (0322) 862114
(Guy Hart Dyke, Esq)
Family portraits, armour, Henry VII gateway. Church.
Location: In the Darenth valley via Eynsford on A225.
Station: Eynsford (½ m).
Opening Times: CASTLE & GROUNDS. Apr to Oct, Sats, Suns, Bank Hols 2–6. Adm £2.50, Chd £1, OAPs £2. Weds, Thurs & Fris 2–6 by arrangement. No dogs. Free car parking. Telephone for enquiries or bookings.
Refreshments: At the gate house on Sun and for booked parties only.

LULLINGSTONE ROMAN VILLA
Telephone: (0322) 863467
(Closed for refurbishment in 1989.)
The ancient Romans understood the art of gracious living. In this country villa they walked on mosaic floors, dined off fine tableware and commissioned elaborate wall paintings to decorate one of the earliest churches in Britain. The museum gives a remarkable picture of what it was like to be wealthy in the 2nd, 3rd and 4th centuries.
Location: ½ m (0.8 km) south west of Eynsford. OS map ref TQ529651.
Opening Times: *Good Friday to Sept 30, daily 10–6; Oct 1 to Maundy Thursday, daily 10–4. Closed Mons, Christmas and New Year.* Tel: 01-211 8828 for details. Adm £1.30, OAPs £1, Chd 65p.

▣ FAVERSHAM

BELMONT
Telephone: 079 589 202
(Harris (Belmont) Charity)
Belmont was built in the late 18th century to the design of Samuel Wyatt, in a splendid elevated position having commanding views over the attractive and unspoilt countryside. It has been the family seat of the Harris family since it was acquired in 1801 by General George Harris, the victor of Seringapatam. The Mansion remains in its original state and contains the finest collection of clocks in any English country house open to the public, superbly presented in an ideal setting.
Location: 3½ m SSW of Faversham.
Opening Times: Easter to end of Sept. Suns, 10–5, Gardens and Park only. Adm £1. Tues, Thurs, Sat and Bank Holiday Mons, Grounds, Mansion and Clock Museum. Visit by telephone appointment only in guided parties. Adm to Mansion and Clock Museum £3, Chd half price. Car parking. To book, contact Curator, Telephone 079-589-202.

FLEUR DE LIS HERITAGE CENTRE *(The Faversham Society)*
Preston Street ME13 8NS. Tel: (0795) 534542.
Audio-visual, bygones and colourful displays on 1,000 years of life in one of Britain's finest Heritage Towns with over 400 listed buildings. Housed in a 15th century inn, where the plot to murder 'Arden of Feversham' was hatched in 1551, this is the first Heritage Centre in the South. Mon to Sat 9.30–1, 2–4.30. Closes at 4, Oct to Easter inc., *closed* Thurs and Bank Hols. Adm 80p, Chld and OAPs 40p.

MOUNT EPHRAIM
Telephone: Canterbury (0227) 751310 or 751496.
(Mrs M N Dawes & Mr & Mrs E S Dawes)
Terraced garden, with beautiful views, leading to small lake. Herbaceous border, topiary, extensive Japanese rock garden. Small woodland area with rhododendrons. Wide variety of plants and shrubs. Fine trees. Rose terraces.
Location: 6 m W of Canterbury, 3 m E of Faversham; ½ m N of A2 at Boughton.
Opening Times: GARDENS ONLY. May, June, Aug & Sept 2–6. Adm £1.25, Chd 25p. Parties by prior arrangement.
Refreshments: Teas available. Suns only.

▣ FOLKESTONE

FOLKESTONE MUSEUM AND ART GALLERY
(Kent County Council)
Grace Hill. Tel: (0303) 57583.
Museum: local history, archaeology and natural science. Art Gallery: temporary loan exhibitions. Mon, Tues, Thurs and Fri 9–5.30; Wed 9–1; Sat 9–5. *Closed* on public holidays. Adm free.

METROPOLE ARTS CENTRE
The Leas. Tel: (0303) 55070.
Art exhibitions, chamber/jazz/piano recitals, lectures, workshops, children's events. Kent Literature Festival – Oct. Paintings, cards, books and craft works for sale. Coffee shop open daily. Mon–Sat 10–5; Sun 2.30–5. Telephone the Gallery reception on 55070 for further information.

▣ GILLINGHAM

GILLINGHAM MUSEUM
Church Walk.

▣ GOUDHURST

BEDGEBURY NATIONAL PINETUM
Telephone: (0580) 211044
(Forestry Commission Research Station)
Has the most comprehensive collection of conifers in Europe. Conifers from all continents are planted in generic groups within 160 acres. Landscaped with grass avenues, paths, stream valleys, ridges and a lake. Rhododendrons, azaleas, maples and uncommon oak species add colour in spring and autumn.
Location: On B2079, 1 m from A21 London to Hastings travelling towards Goudhurst.
Opening Times: Daily 10 till dusk. Adm charge. Visitor centre: open Easter to Sept. Car parking. Difficult for wheelchairs.
Refreshments: In nearby villages.

FINCHCOCKS, LIVING MUSEUM OF MUSIC
(Mr & Mrs Richard Burnett)
Nr. Cranbrook. Tel: Goudhurst (0580) 211702.
Finchcocks is a fine early 18th century house set in beautiful gardens & parkland, containing a magnificent collection of historical keyboard instruments, most of which are restored to concert condition. These are played whenever the house is open. Open: Easter to end of Sept; daily in Aug (except Mon & Tues) 2–6. Groups by appointment most days Apr–Oct. Approx £3 including music. Students & schoolchildren at reduced rates. Parties approx £3 for private visits. Car parking free. Suitable for disabled persons but toilets and restaurant awkward. Recitals & demonstration tours included in open days and private visits. Fully licensed restaurant.

LADHAM HOUSE
(Betty, Lady Jessel)
10 acres of rolling lawns, fine specimen trees, rhododendrons, azaleas, camellias, shrubs and magnolias. Newly planted arboretum. Spectacular twin mixed borders. Fountain garden and bog garden. Fine view. Re-planted and tidied up since the hurricane.
Location: 11 m E of Tunbridge Wells off A262 on NE of village.
Opening Times: GARDEN ONLY. Suns May 7, 14: 11–6. Sun July 9: 11–6. *Open other times by appointment and for coaches:* Adm £1, Chd (under 12) 50p. *In aid of National Gardens Scheme.* Free parking.

GRAVESEND

GRAVESHAM MUSEUM
(Kent County Council and Gravesham Borough Council)
High Street. Tel: (0474) 323159.
Local archaeology, including finds from the important Roman site at Springhead, and material illustrating the growth, development and civic life of Gravesend during the last 200 years. Mon, Tues, Thurs, Fri 2–5; Sat 10–1. *Closed* on public holidays. Adm free. Unsuitable for wheelchairs.

MILTON CHANTRY, GRAVESEND
Telephone: (0474) 21520

In the 14th century priests prayed here for the souls of the de Valence and Montechais families, and the building also housed the chapel of a leper hospital. After the Reformation, the building was used as a house, barracks, tavern and museum.
Location: Adjacent to the Fort in Milton. OS map ref TQ652743.
Opening Times: Good Friday to Sept 30, daily 10–6. Adm 55p, OAPs 40p, Chd 25p.

HAXTED

HAXTED MILL & MUSEUM
Telephone: Curator, Summer months Edenbridge (0732) 862914. Mr. D.G. Neville. Dorking (0306) 887979 during winter months.

Working Water Mill & Museum.
Location: 1½ m W of Edenbridge beside road joining B2029 at Lingfield Common with B2026 at Edenbridge.
Opening Times: April to May: Sat, Sun & Bank Hols, 12–5; June to end Sept: daily including Sun. Guides parties at any time by prior appointment. Adm £1.50, Chd 75p, OAPs £1. Reductions for parties booked in advance.
Refreshments: Licensed restaurant open daily *except Mon.*

HERNE BAY

HERNE BAY MUSEUM *(Kent County Council)*
High Street. Tel: (0227) 360151.
New displays telling the story of Herne Bay. Mon, Tues and Fri 9.30–7; Wed 9.30–1; Thurs and Sat 9.30–5. *Closed* on public holidays. Adm free.

RECULVER TOWERS AND ROMAN FORT
Telephone: (022 73) 66444

Some of the Roman walls remain—after seventeen centuries. But more striking are the twin towers, 'The Reculvers'. Long after most of the Saxon and Norman church was demolished the Towers have been preserved as a famous landmark and guide to sailors.
Location: 3 miles (4.8 km) east of Herne Bay. OS map ref TR228694.
Opening Times: Good Friday to Sept 30, daily 10–6. Adm 80p, OAPs 60p, Chd 40p.

HEVER

HEVER CASTLE & GARDENS
Telephone: Edenbridge (0732) 865224; Fax (0732) 866796
(Broadland Properties Limited)

Enchanting 13th century double-moated castle, childhood home of Queen Anne Boleyn, set in magnificent gardens of 30 acres. The gardens feature fine topiary including a maze, the magnificent Italian garden with statuary and sculpture dating back 2000 years, and the 35 acre lake alongside which visitors can walk and picnic. The Castle was restored and filled with treasures by William Waldorf Astor in 1903.
Location: Mid-way between London and S coast, between Sevenoaks and East Grinstead, 3 m SE Edenbridge off B2026. M25—junction 6, 20 mins. M23—junction 10, 20 mins.
Station: Hever (1 m walk, taxis available), Edenbridge Town (3 m).
Opening Times: CASTLE & GARDENS open daily—Mar 21–Nov 5. GARDENS: 11–6 (last entry 5pm). CASTLE: opens 12 noon. Dogs on leads gardens only. Adventure playground. Facilities for disabled visitors. Special pre-booked private tours available all year. Special rate for groups.
Refreshments: Large self-service cafeteria (licensed). Picnics welcome.

HORSMONDEN

SPRIVERS GARDEN, Mrs G C Dibben (The National Trust)

Garden with some unusual plants and shrubs, herbaceous borders, architectural temples and ornaments. Parts of the garden under restoration and replanting. Small collection of Waterfowl. Woodland walks and avenues being re-opened and planted.
Location: 3 m N of Lamberhurst on B2162; 10 m SE of Tonbridge.
Opening Times: May to Sept 27—Weds only 2–5.30 (last adm 5). Adm 70p. No reductions for parties or Chd. No dogs. Wheelchair access. No lavatories.

HYTHE

HYTHE LOCAL HISTORY ROOM
(Hythe Town Council and Kent County Council)
Oaklands, Stade Street. Tel: (0303) 66152.
Local history. Open Mon to Sat when Library is open.

SALTWOOD CASTLE
Telephone: Hythe (0303) 67190 (Secretary)
(The Hon Alan Clark, MP & Mrs Clark)

Norman castle, subject of quarrel between Thomas à Becket and Henry II. Grounds and parts of Castle including battlement walk, undercroft, armoury.
Location: 2 m NW of Hythe; from A20 turn S at sign to Saltwood.
Station: Sandling (1½ m).
Opening Times: *Saltwood Castle is closed to the general public in 1989.* Private parties of 20 or more can be accommodated *(on weekdays only)* following an appointment confirmed in writing.

IVY HATCH

IGHTHAM MOTE, The National Trust
Telephone: Plaxtol 810378

One of the most complete remaining examples of a medieval moated manor house.
Location: 3 m S of Ightham, off A227, 4½ m E of Sevenoaks off A25.
Opening Times: Mar 24 to end Oct—Mons, Weds, Thurs, Fris 12–5.30; Suns and Bank Hol Mons 11–5.30 (last adm 5); pre-booked tours 11–12 weekdays. Open Good Friday. Adm £2.50, Chd £1.20. Parties: £2.20, Chd £1.
Refreshments: Tea bar in car park.

LAMBERHURST

MR. HEAVER'S MODEL MUSEUM AND CRAFT CENTRE
Forstal Farm. Tel: (0892) 890711.
Located on A262 between Goudhurst and Pembury. Model scenes and dioramas, ranging from nursery themes and Rome to Victorian London and science fiction.

OWL HOUSE GARDENS
(Maureen, Marchioness of Dufferin & Ava)

16th century half-timbered, tile-hung wool smuggler's cottage. Beautiful gardens, magnificent roses, daffodils, rhododendrons. Woodland walks.
Location: 8 m SE of Tunbridge Wells; 1 m from Lamberhurst off A21.
Opening Times: GARDENS ONLY. All the year—daily and weekends including all Bank Hol weekends 11–6. Adm £1.50, Chd 75p. (Proceeds towards Lady Dufferin's charity, Maureen's Oast House for Arthritics.) Dogs on lead. Free parking. Coach parties welcome.

SCOTNEY CASTLE GARDEN, The National Trust
Telephone: Lamberhurst (0892) 890651

Romantic landscape garden framing moated castle.
Location: 1½ m SE of Lamberhurst (A21).
Opening Times: Garden: Mar 25 to Nov 12—Weds to Fris 11–6 or sunset if earlier *(closed Good Fri)*; Sats, Suns & Bank Hol Mons 2–6 or sunset if earlier. Last adm half-hour before closing. Old Castle: May to end Aug—days & times as for Garden. Adm £2, Chd £1. Parties by prior appointment £1.60. *No reduction on Sats, Suns or Bank Hol Mons. No dogs.* Shop. Wheelchairs available. (Steep entrance to garden.)

LYMPNE

LYMPNE CASTLE
Telephone: Hythe (0303) 67571
(Harry Margary, Esq)

14th century building restored in 1905. Once owned by the Archdeacons of Canterbury. Terraced gardens with magnificent views out to sea and across Romney Marshes to Fairlight.
Location: 3 m NW of Hythe off B2067, 8m W of Folkestone.
Station: Sandling (2½ m).
Opening Times: May to Sept & Bank Hol weekends—Daily 10.30–6. *Open most days Easter to May 31, but please check, and to parties by appointment.* Adm £1.25, Chd 30p.

PORT LYMPNE
ZOO PARK, MANSION & GARDENS
Telephone: Hythe (0303) 264646
(John Aspinall, Esq)

Described as the "last historic house built this century", Port Lympne encompasses the essence of Roman villas and the English country house. Overlooking the Channel and set in ornamental gardens, the interior of the house features a Moorish patio, marble columns, an intriguing hall floor plus the exquisitely painted Tent Room by Rex Whistler and another, South Asian in concept, currently being painted by wildlife artist Spencer Roberts. Wildlife Art Gallery, exhibitions of photography and bronzes. 270 acre zoo park. Safari trailer. Gift shop. Picnic areas.
Location: 3 m W of Hythe; 6 m W of Folkestone; 7 m SE of Ashford off A20.
Opening Times: All the year—Daily. Summer 10–5*; Winter 10–one hour before dusk* (*last admissions). *Closed Christmas Day.* Reduced prices for OAPs and Chld 4–14 (3 and under free). Special party rates. Free car park.
Refreshments: Cafeteria.

MAIDSTONE

LEEDS CASTLE
Telephone: Maidstone (0622) 765400. Telex: 965737
(Leeds Castle Foundation)

Fairytale Castle of the medieval Queens of England. Built in the middle of a lake in romantic setting of landscaped parkland. Dating back to 9th century, rebuilt in 1119 as a Norman fortress, it was later converted to a royal palace by Henry VIII. Superb collection of medieval furnishings, tapestries and Impressionist paintings. Museum of medieval Dog Collars. Water and woodland garden. Culpeper flower garden, Greenhouses, Vineyard. Duckery, new Aviaries, Maze and Grotto. 9 hole public golf course open daily all year. Castle gift shop and plant shop. Regret no dogs.

Location: 4 m E of Maidstone; access on B2163 A20 at junction 8 of the M20. *Station: Bearsted or Hollingbourne (2 m). Inclusive rail/admission tickets from British Rail.*
Opening Times: Mar 24 to Oct 31 – Daily 11–5*. Nov to Mar – Sats & Suns only 12–4* (*last admission to grounds). Winter – Sunday Lunches with tours of Castle. Special events programme. Kentish Evening Dinners every Saturday throughout year. Reduced prices for Chd (under 16) Students & OAPs, also for Groups and School Parties who are welcomed at any time all year round, by appointment. Picnic area. Car park. Passenger trailer takes elderly visitors from car park to Castle. Facilities for the disabled.
NB The Trustees reserve the right to close all or parts of the Castle for Government seminars. Closed July 1 & Nov 4 for Open Air Concert & Fireworks Display.
Refreshments: Lunch and refreshments available in licensed restaurants and the Park Gate Inn.

MUSEUM AND ART GALLERY *(Maidstone Borough Council)*
St. Faith's Street. Tel: (0622) 54497.
House in 16th century Chillington Manor, the museum (extended considerably in the 19th century) contains outstanding collections, some of national importance. These include Ceramics, Natural History, Costume, Furniture, Local History and, in the recently refurbished Art Gallery, 17th & 18th century Dutch & Italian oil paintings. Also on display is the museum of the Queen's Own Royal West Kent Regiment. Following redisplay work, galleries of Pacific Ethnography, Japanese Decorative Art and Kentish Archaeology will be opened. Mon to Sat 10–5.30; Sun 2–5; Bank Hol Mon 11–5.

MUSEUM OF KENT RURAL LIFE
(Kent County Council/Maidstone Borough Council)
Lock Lane, Sandling. Tel: (0622) 63936.
The history of the Kent Countryside explained through displays on farming history, exhibits of agricultural tools and machinery and outside planting of crops important to Kent, including orchard fruits, hops, arable, pasture and market garden crops, and livestock typical to the county, especially Romney Marsh Sheep. Inside displays are housed in a picturesque oast house and dairy courtyard set in twenty seven acres of land bordering the River Medway. New developments include an aisled barn, village and craft displays. Open Mar 23 to Oct 10: Mon, Tues, Thurs, Fri 10–5, Sat 12–5, Sun 12–6. Adm 80p, Chd 40p. Reductions for booked parties. Farmhouse cafeteria. Car Park. Keeper: Dr Annie Hood.

TYRWHITT-DRAKE MUSEUM OF CARRIAGES
(Maidstone Borough Council)
Archbishop's Stables, Mill Street. Tel: (0622) 54497.
Housed in the stable block of the nearby Archbishops Palace, the Carriage Collection is thought to be the finest and most wide-ranging in Britain. Most types of carriages are represented, all in superbly original condition, alongside a number of Royal vehicles. Mon to Sat 10–1, 2–5. Also open afternoons on Sun and Bank Hols (Apr to Sept). Adm 60p, Chld and OAPs 30p.

MARGATE

OLD TOWN HALL LOCAL HISTORY MUSEUM
(Thanet District Council)
Market Place. Tel: (0843) 225511 ext. 2520.
18th–19th century local history including old court-room, Council chamber and Victorian police cells. Open (1988) May–Sept: Tues–Sat 10–1, 2–4. Adm charge. Discounts for Chd, groups and school parties. Combined adm ticket available for Old Town Hall Museum and Tudor House Museum. Small selection of souvenirs.

TUDOR HOUSE AND MUSEUM *(Thanet District Council)*
King Street. Tel: (0843) 225511 ext. 2520.
16th century timbered building. Human occupation of Thanet from Neolithic to Tudor times. Open (1988) May–Sept: Tues to Sat, 10–1, 2–4. Adm charge. Discounts for Chd, groups and school parties. Combined adm ticket for Tudor House Museum and Old Town Hall Museum available.

MATFIELD

CRITTENDEN HOUSE
(B P Tompsett, Esq)
Garden completely planned and planted since 1956 on labour-saving lines. Spring shrubs, roses, lilies, foliage, waterside planting of ponds in old iron workings. Of interest from the early Spring bulbs to Autumn colour.
Location: 5 m SE of Tonbridge off B2160.
Opening Times: GARDENS ONLY. Sun, Mon, Mar 26, 27; Sun Apr 30; Mon May 1 *National Gardens Scheme;* Sun May 7; Sun, Mon, May 28, 29, RSPCA; Sun June 11 2–6. Adm £1, Chd 20p. Cars free.

OSPRINGE

MAISON DIEU, OSPRINGE
Telephone: (0795) 76204

Maison Dieu (God's House) was the medieval name for a hospital. A hospital was also part hotel, and Maison Dieu gave shelter to travellers, from the poorest pilgrim to the King himself. Only fragments of the medieval building survive, but some fine 16th century beamed ceilings may be seen, and a collection of Roman burial objects – pottery, glass and jewellery.
Location: ½ m (0.8 km) west of Faversham. OS map ref TR002608.
Opening Times: Good Friday to Sept 30, weekends only 10–6. Adm 80p, OAPs 60p, Chd 40p.

OTHAM

STONEACRE, The National Trust
A half-timbered small manor house, c. 1480. Small garden.
Location: In Otham, 3 m SE of Maidstone; 1 m S of A20.
Station: Bearsted (2 m).
Opening Times: Apr to end Oct – Weds & Sats 2–6 (last adm 5). Adm £1, Chd 50p. No reduction for parties. No dogs. Unsuitable for wheelchairs. Narrow access road.

PADDOCK WOOD

WHITBREAD HOP FARM *(Whitbread & Co, plc)*
Beltring. Tel: Maidstone (0622) 872068.
Award winning museum housed in the world's largest group of Victorian Oasts. Rural Crafts (Wheelwright, Blacksmith, Dairy, cricket ball maker, stationery engine and other displays) – home of the famous Whitbread Shire Horses. Farm Machinery – horse drawn vehicles – harness wear – hop farming and Queen Victoria's Rifles display. Nature trails, craft centre, pets, play area. Various special events held each year. Opening dates and times on request. Courier assisted tour for party bookings. Adm charge. Certain areas suitable for disabled persons. Tea room. Curator: Peter G. Leslie, Leisure Manager.

PENSHURST

PENSHURST PLACE
Telephone: Penshurst (0892) 870307
(The Rt Hon Viscount De L'Isle, VC, KG)

The early house, including the Great Hall, dates from 1340. There were later additions but the whole house conforms to the English Gothic style in which it was begun.
Location: In Penshurst village on B2176, W of Tonbridge & Tunbridge Wells. *Station: Penshurst (2 m).*
Opening Times: Penshurst Place is open every afternoon (except Mons) from Apr 1 to Oct 1. Open Bank Hol Mons & Easter Bank Hols.
Grounds 12.30–6. House 1–5.30 (last entry to House is 5). Reduced adm rates for groups, OAPs and Chd. Free car park for visitors. No dogs admitted.
Refreshments: Light luncheons and teas available in Endeavour Restaurant.

RAMSGATE

MARITIME MUSEUM COMPLEX *(East Kent Maritime Trust)*
Pier Yard. Tel: (0843) 587765.
National and local maritime history including wreck relics; adjacent dry-dock and old vessels. Open (1988) Oct–Mar: Mon–Fri 11–3.30. Apr–Sept: Mon–Fri 11–4; Sat & Sun 2–5. Adm charge. Discounts for Chd, groups and school parties. Car parking on road nearby. Ground floor only suitable for disabled persons. Souvenirs and books available. AV presentations for groups by arrangement.

RAMSGATE MOTOR MUSEUM *(The Gables Service Station)*
Westcliff Hall, The Paragon. Tel: (0843) 581948.
Exotic and exciting vintage and classic cars plus motorcycles, bikes and related memorabilia. Open (1988) Easter–end Sept: Daily 10 to one hour prior to sunset. Winter: Sun only. Adm charge. Reduction for Chd, groups and school parties. Suitable for disabled persons once inside but access involves a short flight of steps down. In-house cinema shows original black and white transportation films. Souvenirs available.

RAMSGATE MUSEUM *(Kent County Council)*
Ramsgate Library, Guildford Lawn. Tel: (0843) 593532.
Displays are being renewed to tell the history of Ramsgate. Mon to Thurs 9.30–6; Fri 9.30–8; Sat 9.30–5. *Closed* on public holidays. Adm free. Limited car parking nearby. Suitable for disabled persons.

SPITFIRE MEMORIAL PAVILION *(R.A.F. Manston)*
R.A.F. Manston. Tel: (0843) 823351.
Well preserved Spitfire, English Electric Canberra, Gloster Javelin. Second World War memorabilia. Open all year 10–5. Adm free (donations gratefully received). Car parking available. Wide selection of souvenirs. Suitable for disabled.

RICHBOROUGH

RICHBOROUGH CASTLE
Telephone: (0304) 612013

The sea has deserted Richborough, but as Rutupiae it was well-known in Roman times as a seaport. It was here that the conquering Roman army landed in AD 43. The massive stone walls were built in the 3rd century to combat the ferocious attacks of Saxon sea-raiders.
Location: 1½ m (2.4 km) north of Sandwich. OS map ref TR324602.
Opening Times: Good Friday to Sept 30, daily 10–6; Oct 1 to Maundy Thursday, daily 10–4. *Closed Mons, Christmas and New Year.* Adm 80p, OAPs 60p, Chd 40p.

ROCHESTER

COBHAM HALL
Telephone: Shorne 3371
(Westwood Educational Trust Ltd)

Charming mixture of Gothic and Renaissance architecture in 50 acres of grounds. Fine example of work of James Wyatt. Now a girls' public school.
Location: 4 m W of Rochester on Watling Street & Rochester Way (B2009 off A2). 27 m from London.
Station: Sole Street (1½ m).
Opening Times: Easter, Mar 23, 24, 26, 27, 29, 30; Apr 5, 6; July 16, 19, 20, 30; Aug 6, 9, 10, 13, 16, 17, 20, 23, 24, 28, 30, 31. 2–5.30 (last tour 5). Adm £1.50 Chd & OAPs 75p, disabled 30p. No reduction for parties.
Refreshments: Teas and light refreshments, enquiries (0474 82) 3371.

GADS HILL PLACE
(Gads Hill Place School Ltd)

Grade 1 listed building, built 1780. Home of Charles Dickens from 1858 to 1870.
Location: On A226; 3 m from Rochester; 4 m from Gravesend.
Station: Higham (1 m).
Opening Times: By prior appointment only. Apply to the Bursar, Gads Hill Place School, Higham, Rochester. Adm free.
Refreshments: Food & Drink available at Sir John Falstaff Hotel opposite House.

GUILDHALL MUSEUM *(Rochester-upon-Medway City Council)*
Guildhall, High Street. Tel: (0634) 48717.
Local history, archaeology, arms and armour, costumes, Victoriana, models of ships and aircraft. Daily 10–5.30.

KENNETH BILLS ROCHESTER MOTOR CYCLE MUSEUM
(Ken Bills)
144 High Street. Tel: (0634) 814165.
The museum consisting of over 100 British bikes including many classic racers. Adm £1.25. Children free provided they are accompanied. Car parking East Gate.

ROCHESTER CASTLE
Telephone: (0634) 402276

The great square keep of Rochester Castle has resisted destruction for 900 years. Besieged many times, it held out in 1215 for two months against King John. Battering the castle from huge stone-throwing engines, the King finally breached the keep by mining under it and setting fire to the pit props with the fat of 40 pigs.
Location: Just south of Rochester Bridge. OS map ref TQ742686.
Opening Times: Good Friday to Sept 30, daily 10–6; Oct 1 to Maundy Thursday, daily 10–4. *Closed Mons, Christmas and New Year.* Adm £1.10, OAPs 80p, Chd 55p.

ROLVENDEN

THE C.M. BOOTH COLLECTION OF HISTORIC VEHICLES
Falstaff Antiques, 63–67 High Street. Tel: Cranbrook (0580) 241234.
Specialising in Morgan 3-wheel cars, other exhibits include 1904 Humber tri-car, 1929 Morris Van, 1936 Bampton Caravan, Motorcycles, Bicycles, Toy and model cars, and much motoring memorabilia.

GREAT MAYTHAM HALL
(Country Houses Association Ltd)

Built in 1910 by Sir Edwin Lutyens.
Location: ½ m W of Rolvenden village.
Opening Times: May to Sept—Weds & Thurs 2–5. Adm £1, Chd 50p. Free car park. No dogs admitted.

SANDWICH

THE GUILDHALL MUSEUM *(Sandwich Town Council)*
Collection of ancient and interesting items. Open Tues to Fri.

THE PRECINCT TOY COLLECTION
38 Harnet Street.
Dolls' houses, Noah's Arks, dolls, clockwork toys etc. Easter to end Sept: Mon to Sat 10–5; Sun 2–5. Oct: Sat and Sun only 2–5. Adm 30p, Chld/OAPs 15p.

SEVENOAKS

BLACK CHARLES
Telephone: Hildenborough (0732) 833036
(Mr & Mrs Hugh Gamon)

Charming 14th century home of John de Blakecherl and his family. A hall house with beautiful panelling, fireplaces and many other interesting features.
Location: 3 m S of Sevenoaks off A21; 1 m E in the village of Underriver.
Opening Times: Open to groups by appointment (minimum of 10).

KNOLE, The National Trust
Telephone: Sevenoaks 450608

One of the largest private houses in England, dating mainly from 15th century, with splendid Jacobean interior and fine collection of 17th century furniture.
Location: At the Tonbridge end of Sevenoaks, just E of A225; 25 m from London.
Station: Sevenoaks (1½ m)
Opening Times: Mar 24 to end of Oct—Weds to Sats (inc Good Fri) & Bank Hol Mons 11–5; Suns 2–5. Last Adm 4. Guided tours Tues only, for pre-booked parties of 25 or more. Garden: May to Sept, first Wed in every month. Adm: £2.50 (£3 Fri – extra rooms shown). Chd £1.30 (£1.50 Fri). Garden only: 50p. Pre-booked parties of 25 or more £1.80, Chd £1. Wheelchairs park and gardens only. Parking £5 (£5.50 Fri) includes one admission.

RIVERHILL HOUSE
Telephone: Sevenoaks (0732) 452557/458802
(John Rogers Esq)

Small country house, home of the Rogers family since 1840. Panelled rooms, portraits and interesting memorabilia. An historic garden with rare trees and shrubs. Fine collection of mature trees. Sheltered terraces and rhododendrons and azaleas in woodland setting. Good hydrangeas. Ancient trackway known as "Harold's Road".
Location: 2 m S of Sevenoaks on road to Tonbridge (A225).
Station: Sevenoaks (2 m).
Opening Times: Easter to end of Aug. GARDEN every Sun in above period, also Sats & Mons of all Bank Hol weekends, 12–6. Picnics allowed. No dogs. Adm £1, Chd 30p. HOUSE **only** open Sat, Sun & Mon of Bank Hol weekends. Adults only inside. Adm £2, 2–5. Party bookings for House and Garden or Garden only (20 upwards) any day except Bank Hol weekends from Easter until Oct 18.
Refreshments: Home-made teas in the Old Stable from 2.30. Catering for booked parties—Ploughman's Lunches and Teas—by arrangement. All enquiries to Mrs Rogers.

SEVENOAKS MUSEUM *(Kent County Council)*
Buckhurst Lane. Tel: (0732) 452384 & 453118.
Reopened in 1986 in the new Library and Museum building, with displays telling the history of Sevenoaks and its neighbourhood from prehistoric times onwards including local trade and industry during the last hundred years. Mon to Weds, Fri 9.30–5.30; Thurs 9.30–7; Sat 9–5. *Closed* on public holidays. Adm free. Public car parks nearby. Suitable for disabled persons.

SISSINGHURST

SISSINGHURST CASTLE GARDEN, The National Trust
Telephone: Cranbrook 712850

The famous garden created by the late Vita Sackville-West and Sir Harold Nicolson between the surviving parts of an Elizabethan mansion.
Location: 2 m NE of Cranbrook; 1 m E of Sissinghurst village (A262).
Opening Times: Mar 24 to Oct 15—Tues to Fris 1–6.30; Sats, Suns & Good Fri 10–6.30. (Last adm 6.) *Closed Mons, incl Bank Hol Mons.* The garden may be overcrowded at around 3pm. Visitors may be asked to wait. Adm Tues to Sats £3, Suns £3.50; Chd £1.50, Suns £1.80. Parties by appointment only; reductions on weekdays only. No dogs. Shop. No picnics in garden. Adm to wheelchair visitors is restricted to 2 at any one time.
Refreshments: In the Granary Restaurant. Mar 24 to Oct 15—Tues to Fri 12–6, Sat & Sun 10–6. Closed Mons.

SITTINGBOURNE

DODDINGTON PLACE GARDENS
Telephone: Doddington (079585) 385
(Mr Richard and The Hon. Mrs Oldfield)

10 acres of landscaped gardens set in the grounds of a large Victorian house built by Charles Trollope in 1860. A Wellingtonia avenue dates from that period. The rest of the garden was laid out in the early 1900s by a forebear of the present owner. The main features are a large rock garden with a series of pools, a formal sunk garden and terraces, and wide lawns with fine trees bordered by yew hedges. A woodland rhododendron and azalea garden was added in the 1960s. There are excellent views over the Syndale valley and surrounding countryside.
Location: 4 m from A2 and A20. 5 m from Faversham. 6 m from Sittingbourne. 12 m from Canterbury.
Opening Times: Weds and Bank Holiday Mons, May to Sept 11–6. Adm £1, Chd 25p. 20% discount for groups of more than 20 by prior arrangement. Car parking free. Suitable for disabled (no wheelchairs available). Present shop.
Refreshments: Restaurant serving morning coffee, light lunches, afternoon teas; supper parties by arrangement.

Kent — *continued*

DOLPHIN SAILING BARGE MUSEUM
Crown Quay Lane.

STROOD

UPNOR CASTLE
Telephone: (0634) 718742

The Castle was built in 1559 on the orders of Elizabeth I, to protect her warships moored in the Medway alongside the new dockyards at Chatham. Within a century the castle was out of date, and was used as a magazine for gunpowder and munitions.

Location: 1¾ m (2.8 km) north east of Strood. OS map ref TQ758706.
Opening Times: Good Friday to Sept 30, daily 10–6. Adm 80p, OAPs 60p, Chd 40p.

SUTTON-AT-HONE

ST JOHN'S JERUSALEM GARDEN, The National Trust &

Large garden, moated by River Darent. The house, the main walls of which formed the church of a Commandery of the Knights Hospitallers, was altered in later centuries. Only the former chapel and the garden are open to the public.

Location: 3 m S of Dartford at Sutton-at-Hone on E side of A225.
Station: Farningham Road (¾ m).
Opening Times: GARDEN & FORMER CHAPEL ONLY. Mar 29 to end Oct — Weds 2–6 (last adm 5.30). Adm 40p. *No reduction for parties or children. No dogs.* Wheelchair access to garden only.

TENTERDEN

SMALLHYTHE PLACE, The National Trust
Telephone: Tenterden 2334

The Ellen Terry Memorial Museum. Half-timbered 16th century yeoman's home. Mementoes of Dame Ellen Terry, Mrs Siddons, etc.

Location: 2½ m S of Tenterden on E side of Rye Road (B2082).
Opening Times: Mar 24 to end of Oct — Daily (except Thurs & Fris) 2–6 or dusk if earlier. Open Good Fri. Last adm half-hour before closing. Adm £1.40, Chd 70p. *Parties should give advance notice — no reduction. No parties in August. No indoor photography. No dogs. Unsuitable for wheelchairs. Can only take 25 at a time in house.*
Refreshments: Tea available at The Spinning Wheel & the Tudor Rose, Tenterden.

TENTERDEN AND DISTRICT MUSEUM
Station Road. Tel: (058 06) 3350 and 4310.

Townscape and history of Tenterden, Limb of the Cinque Ports. Local trades and industries, building materials; bygones, agricultural implements, hop gardens. The Col. Stephens Railway Collection. Easter to Oct: Daily 2–5 (Fri and Sat, June to Sept, 10–5). Winter months: Sat and Sun 2–4. Adm charge. Special arrangements for groups.

TONBRIDGE

THE MILNE MUSEUM *(South Eastern Electricity Board)*
The Slade. Tel: (0732) 364726.

Former generating station housing large collection of exhibits illustrating the history of electricity. Some working exhibits. Many domestic appliances. Items to interest both young and old. Open to the general public Tues 2–5. Visits at other times (including organised groups) by appointment. Adm free. Please telephone before visiting, as a move to the *Amberley Chalk Pits Museum* is in prospect.

TUNBRIDGE WELLS

TUNBRIDGE WELLS MUNICIPAL MUSEUM AND ART GALLERY
(Tunbridge Wells Borough Council)
Civic Centre, Mount Pleasant. Tel: (0892) 26121, Ext. 3171.

Local history, Tunbridge ware, dolls, toys, bygones, natural history. Mon to Fri 10–5.30, Sat 9.30–5. *Closed* Bank Hols.

WESTERHAM

CHARTWELL, The National Trust
Telephone: Edenbridge 866368 &

The home for many years of Sir Winston Churchill.

Location: 2 m S of Westerham off B2026.
Opening Times: House. Mar to end Nov: Mar 1–22, & Nov — Sats, Suns & Weds only 11–4; Mar 25 to end Oct — Tues, Weds, Thurs 12–5; Sats, Suns & Bank Hol Mons 11–5. Closed Good Fri and Tues following Bank Hol. All Tues mornings (except after Bank Hols) reserved for pre-booked parties and guided tours. Garden & Studio: Mar 25 to end Oct — Same times as house. Adm House & Garden £3, Chd £1.50. Garden only £1.20, Chd 60p. Studio 40p extra (Chd no reduction). Prebooked parties, Tues mornings only, £2.50, Chd £1.30. Guided tours for parties (15 or more) Tues mornings only. Write to the Administrator, Chartwell, Westerham, Kent. Car Park. Lavatory for disabled.
Refreshments: Restaurant open from Mar 25 to end Oct — 10.30–5 (Mar 1–22 & Nov: 10.30–4) on days when house is open. Self-service, licensed (no spirits).

QUEBEC HOUSE, The National Trust
Telephone: Westerham 62206

Probably early 16th century in origin, now mainly 17th century. Mementos of General Wolfe, and colourful exhibition about the Battle of Quebec.

Location: At junction of Edenbridge & Sevenoaks Roads (A25 & B2026).
Opening Times: Mar 24 to end Oct — Daily (except Thurs & Sats), inc Good Fri and Bank Holiday Mon 2–6. Last adm 5.30. Adm £1.40, Chd 70p. *Pre-booked parties £1, Chd 50p.* No dogs. Unsuitable for wheelchairs.

SQUERRYES COURT
Telephone: Westerham (0959) 62345 or 63118
(J St A Warde, Esq)

William and Mary manor house. Period furniture, paintings, tapestries and china. Objects of interest connected with General Wolfe. Attractive grounds with lake, fine display of spring bulbs, rhododendrons and azaleas.

Location: Western outsirts of Westerham on A25.
Opening Times: Mar Suns and Bank Hol only 2–6. Apr–Sept, Weds, Sats, Suns and Bank Hol Mons 2–6 pm (last adm 5.30). Adm House & Grounds £2.20, Chd (under 14) £1.20; Grounds only £1.20, Chd (under 14) 60p. Parties over 20 (any day except Suns) by arrangement at reduced rates. Dogs on leads in grounds only. Free parking at house.
Refreshments: Homemade teas at weekends & for booked parties.

WYE

AGRICULTURAL MUSEUM *(University of London)*
Wye College, Court Lodge Farm, Brook.

Exhibition of agricultural implements, machinery, hand tools and other farming equipment. May to Sept: Wed 2–5; also Sat 2–5 during Aug and by written appointment with the Hon. Curator.

BOUGHTON MONCHELSEA PLACE
near MAIDSTONE, KENT

Battlemented Elizabethan Manor of Kentish ragstone built in 1567, with interesting Regency alterations. Dramatically situated with breathtaking view over its own landscaped park, in which fallow deer have roamed for at least 300 years, and beyond it to the whole Weald of Kent. Its beautiful interior is still that of an intimate and inhabited 'home' to which successive generations have added new treasures. Dress display. Ancient vehicles and early farm implements. Manor records. Walled flower gardens with interesting plants. Tudor Kitchen and Garden Tea Rooms.

Good Friday to early October on Saturdays, Sundays and Bank Holidays (also Wednesdays in July and August). 2.15 to 6 pm.

Parties welcome any day, at special rates, but only by previous arrangement.

Telephone Maidstone 43120. Free Car Park.

CHILHAM CASTLE GARDENS
CANTERBURY, KENT

For the lover of gardens, trees and fine views. For the excitement of medieval jousting (on Sundays) and the grace of flying birds of prey and a peaceful lakeside walk.

COBHAM HALL
COBHAM, Kent
Mid-way between London and Canterbury

'Country Life' photograph

AN INDEPENDENT PUBLIC SCHOOL FOR GIRLS

A combination of a spacious house, dating from 1587 and magnificent grounds. Interior by James Wyatt. Family gilded State Coach built in 1715.

The 50 acres of grounds with giant cedars, other specimen trees and 100-year-old lawns provide a good example of Reptons landscape gardening.

Teas are available for visitors.

Further particulars from The Bursar, Cobham Hall, Cobham. Telephone Shorne 3371.

ADMISSION – SEE EDITORIAL REFERENCE

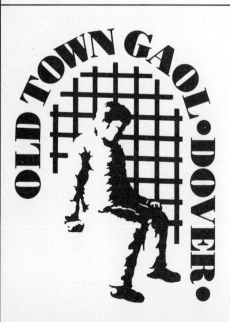

ENTER THE FASCINATING WORLD OF

THE OLD TOWN GOAL • DOVER

Brought to life by the latest animation and audio-visual techniques

OPEN
Summer Daily 10am–5pm
Winter Tuesday to Saturday 10am–5pm

GUIDED TOURS ONLY
Last Tour 4.30pm

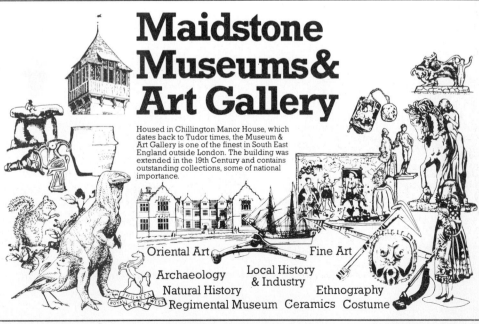

Lancashire

ACCRINGTON

HAWORTH ART GALLERY *(Hyndburn Borough Council)*
Haworth Park Tel: (0254) 33782.
Collection of works of the early English watercolour period. One of the finest collections of Tiffany glass in the world. Special exhibitions throughout the year.

BACUP

BACUP NATURAL HISTORY SOCIETY'S MUSEUM
24 Yorkshire Street.
Collection of natural history subjects; a local geology collection and domestic bygones.

BARROWFORD

PENDLE HERITAGE CENTRE
Park Hill, Nelson, BB9 6JQ. Tel: Nelson (0282) 695366.
A Regional Centre for Heritage Education and Interpretation. Permanent displays and changing exhibitions about traditional buildings and conservation projects. The Centre is based in an historic house with adjacent Barn and Toll House. Other attractions include an 18th century Walled Garden, audio-visual presentation and shop. Refreshments available. Guided tours by arrangement party visits welcomed. Easter to 30 Nov; Tues to Thur, Sat, Sun and Bank Hols from 2–4.30 and at other times by appointment. Adm charge. Study Centre open 9–5 weekdays throughout the year.

BLACKBURN

BLACKBURN MUSEUM AND ART GALLERY
(Blackburn Borough Council)
Museum Street. Tel: (0254) 667130.
The R.E. Hart collection of coins, illuminated manuscripts, and printed books, Japanese prints, oil paintings, English watercolours, British and Oriental ceramics and decorative art, icons in a newly opened gallery, local history, archaeology, ethnography, natural history, children's corner, and 'time tunnel'. The museum also houses the museum of the East Lancashire Regiment, including material from the regiment's predecessors the 30th and 59th Foot, the 5th Royal Lancashire Militia and East Lancashire units of the Rifle Volunteers. Children's activity, questionnaire and colouring sheets are available on request. Tues to Sat 10–5.

LEWIS TEXTILE MUSEUM *(Blackburn Borough Council)*
Exchange Street. Tel: (0254) 667130.
Ideal for visits by groups who can be shown in action the inventions of Kay, Hargreaves, Arkwright and Crompton by a member of the Museum staff. Constantly changing art exhibitions in first-floor gallery. Tues to Sat 10–5.

SUNNYHURST WOOD VISITOR CENTRE
(Blackburn Borough Council)
Sunnyhurst Wood, Darwen. Tel: (0254) 71545.
Changing displays on the history of Darwen; a full programme of changing art exhibitions. Tues, Thur, Sat, Sun and Bank Hol Mons 2–4.30.

TURTON TOWER
Telephone: Bolton (0204) 852203
(Lancashire County Council)

15th century pele tower with Elizabethan farmhouse attached, standing in 8 acres of grounds. Owned by Humphrey Chetham of Manchester in the Civil War. Period furnishings, paintings, weaponry and local history room.
Location: Chapeltown Road, Turton. 5 m N of Bolton on B6391.
Station: Bromley Cross.
Opening Times: Gardens open throughout the year—Adm. Tower Mar, Apr, Oct: Sat to Wed 2–5; May to Sept: Mon to Fri 10–12, 1–5, Sat & Sun 1–5. Nov and Feb: Suns 2–5; Dec & Jan: *Closed.* Adm 70p, OAPs 50p, Chd 35p. Family ticket £1.70.

WITTON COUNTRY PARK VISITOR CENTRE
(Blackburn Borough Council)
Witton Country Park, Preston Old Road. Tel: (0254) 55423.
Located in the stables with displays of harness and agricultural machinery and a natural history room. A fresh section is the newly opened wildlife centre. Thurs, Fri and Sat 1–5; Sun and Bank Hol Mons 11–5.

BLACKPOOL

GRUNDY ART GALLERY *(Blackpool Borough Council)*
Queen Street. Tel: (0253) 23977.
Permanent collection of paintings and drawings by outstanding 19th and 20th century British artists, also regular one man shows and travelling exhibitions. Mon to Sat 10–5.

BRIERFIELD

THE NEVILLE BLAKEY MUSEUM OF LOCKS, KEYS AND SAFES
(Wm Neville Blakey and Wm Norman C. Blakey)
Church Street. Tel: (0282) 63593.
An outstanding rare collection of locks, keys, safes and other security items from the earliest times to the present.

BURNLEY

TOWNELEY HALL ART GALLERY & MUSEUM and MUSEUM OF LOCAL CRAFTS & INDUSTRIES
Telephone: Burnley 24213
(Burnley Borough Council)
House dates from 14th century with 16th, 17th and 19th century modifications. Fine entrance hall.
Location: ½ m SE of Burnley on the Burnley/Todmorden Road (A671).
Station: Burnley Central (1¾ m).
Opening Times: All the year—Mons to Fris 10–5, Suns 12–5. *Closed Sats throughout year.* Adm free. *Closed Christmas–New Year.*
Refreshments: At café in grounds.

WEAVERS' TRIANGLE VISITOR CENTRE
Wharfmaster's House, 85 Manchester Road.
Textile Heritage Centre in a Victorian industrial area astride Leeds & Liverpool Canal. Apr to Sept. Tues, Wed, Sat, & Sun 2–4. Parties by arrangement.

CARNFORTH

LEIGHTON HALL
Telephone: 0524 734474
(Mr & Mrs R. G. Reynolds)
Mid 12th century House rebuilt in the late 18th century with a neo Gothic façade added in 1800. Home of the Gillow family containing early and prototype Gillow furniture. Extensive grounds and garden. **Displays with trained eagles and falcons at 3.30 pm unless raining.**
Location: 2 m W of A6 through Yealand Conyers; signposted from M6, exit 35 junction with A6.
Stations: Silverdale (1½ m, bridlepath only); Carnforth (2½ m).
Opening Times: May to Sept—Suns, Bank Hol Mons & Tues to Fris 2–5 (last tour of House 4.30). Other times by appointment for parties of 25 or more. Special Educational Programme for Schools—mornings from 10 am. Adm House & Grounds £2, Chd £1.10 – family ticket 2nd child free. Teachers with schools free. Inquiries: Mrs Reynolds at the Hall. Schools Programme—Mr A Oswald Tel: 0524 701353. Disabled visitors welcome.
Refreshments: Teas at the Hall. Salad lunches/high teas for booked parties.

CHORLEY

ASTLEY HALL ART GALLERY AND MUSEUM
Astley Park. Tel: (025 72) 62166.
Mostly antique furniture, with collections of old glass, Leeds pottery and pictures. Apr to Sept: Daily 12–6. Oct to Mar: Mon to Fri 12–4; Sat 10–4; Sun 11–4. Last adm half hour before closing. Adm 75p; Chld accompanied by adult 35p, unaccompanied 50p; OAPs and Registered Unemployed 50p. Party rates: Adults 70p, Chld 25p, OAPs and Registered Unemployed 25p. Free car park at rear of the Hall.

CLITHEROE

BROWSHOLME HALL
Telephone: Stoneyhurst 330
Home of the Parker family, Bowbearers of the Forest of Bowland. Tudor with Elizabethan front, Queen Anne Wing and Regency additions. Portraits furniture and antiquities. Guided tours by members of the family.
Location: 5 m NW of Clitheroe; off B6243; Bashall Eaves—Whitewell signposted.
Opening Times: Easter Sat, Sun & Mon and following Sat & Sun. Late May Bank Hol weekend. Every Sat in June, July & Aug. Summer Bank Hol & preceding week 2–5. Reductions for booked parties at other times by appointment with Mrs Parker, Tel. as above.

COLNE

BRITISH IN INDIA MUSEUM
Sun Street.
Paintings, photographs, coins, stamps, medals, diorama, model railway and other items. Open first Sat and Sun in each month May 1 to Sept 30 incl 2–5.

GOOSNARGH

CHINGLE HALL
Telephone: (0772) 861082
Built by Adam de Singleton in 1260 almost certainly on a Viking or earlier site adjacent to the Viking village of Goosnargh, the Hall is the earliest surviving brick built house in the British Isles; this small moated Manor House is currently an undisturbed enigma but now subject to 5 areas of serious ongoing Research: **Archaeological:** Excavation in progress, moat and drawbridge being reconstructed. **Architectural:** Subject of several renovations its Great Hall is Viking beamed (circa 700 AD). **Historical:** Part of the running skirmish of the Battle of Preston occurred on the grounds, etc. **Religious:** A Reformation Mass Centre (undiscovered by Lord Birley in 1580). Hides by Nicholas Owen (Martyred). Birthplace of St. John Wall (Martyred) Franciscan. Modern Ecumenical movement founded in a meeting between Bishop Hoskins Abrahall and Cardinal Heenan in 1962 on re-discovery of the Chingle Cross. Catholic Shrine. **Paranormal:** Reputed to be one of the most haunted houses in the British Isles monks among other sightings and manifestations. Garden, play area, picnic area.

Location: Leave M6 at Junction 32 on to M55 to Blackpool, leave M55 at Junction 1 on to A6 to Garstang. Turn right at first set of traffic lights, continue for 2 miles, turn right at Whittingham/Goosnargh signpost.
Opening Times: Open all year. (Booked parties only between Dec 20 and Jan 31.) Tour (1 hour) – Adults £2.50, Students and OAPs £2, Chd (7–12) £1.50. Coaches (day or evening) by appointment.
Refreshments: Available. Stay the night in St John Wall's or the Priest's Room, by prior arrangement only for paranormal and charity 'sit ins'. Telephone above no. for details.

GREAT HARWOOD

MARTHOLME
(Mr & Mrs T H Codling)

Screens passage and service wing of medieval manor house altered 1577 with 17th century additions. Gatehouse built 1561, restored 1969.
Location: 2 m from Great Harwood off A680 to Whalley.
Opening Times: Exterior: all the year—Fri & Sat. Interior: by appointment only. Adm: Exterior: £1. Interior: £2.

HELMSHORE

HELMSHORE TEXTILE MUSEUMS *(Lancashire Council)*
Holcombe Road.
Two mill museums showing many aspects of the history of Lancashire's textile industry.

LANCASTER

ASHTON MEMORIAL
Telephone: (0524) 33318
(Lancaster City Council)

Described by Sir Nikolaus Pevsner as 'The Grandest Monument in England', the Ashton Memorial stands in a superb site overlooking the city. The design is in the style of the Edwardian revival of the English Baroque, typical of the late Wren, Vanbrugh and Hawksmoor 200 years earlier. Architect John Belcher RA, PRIBA. The Old Palm House, near the Ashton Memorial, has been restored and transformed into a Butterfly House for rare and exotic tropical butterflies. A British Butterfly House will be opening early in 1989.
Opening Times: Open all year except Christmas Day, Boxing Day and New Year's Day. Winter opening 10–3. Summer opening 10–5. Adm charge. Party rate available for prior bookings.

CITY MUSEUM *(Lancaster City Council)*
Market Square. Tel: (0524) 64637.
Prehistoric, Roman and Medieval archaeology and local history. Museum of the King's Own Royal Regiment. Mon to Fri 10–5; Sat 10–3.

JUDGES' LODGINGS – GILLOW AND TOWN HOUSE MUSEUM AND MUSEUM OF CHILDHOOD
Telephone: (0524) 32808
(Lancaster County Council)

17th century town house, built by Thomas Covell, Keeper of the Castle during the notorious Pendle Witches Trial. Used as a lodging for visiting judges from 1826 to 1975. Period rooms, Gillow furniture, turn of the century classroom, children's dolls, toys and games from 18th century to present day.
Location: Church Street, Lancaster
Station: Lancaster Castle
Opening Times: Apr to Oct: Mon to Sat 2–5. Also mornings in July to Sept 10–1. **Gillow and Town House Museum & Museum of Childhood:** Open Good Fri to Oct 31.

MARITIME MUSEUM *(Lancaster City Council)*
St. George's Quay. Tel: (0524) 64637.
Ship models, the Port of Lancaster, inshore fishing, the Lancaster canal. Apr to Oct: Daily 11–5; Nov to Mar: Daily 2–5; large new extension opened spring 1987. Adm charge.

PERIOD COTTAGE *(Lancaster City Council)*
15 Castle Hill. Tel: (0524) 64637.
Artisan furnished dwelling. Easter, then May to Sept: Daily 2–4.45. Adm charge.

LEYLAND

SOUTH RIBBLE MUSEUM AND EXHIBITION CENTRE
(South Ribble Borough Council)
The Old Grammar School, Church Road. Tel: (0772) 422041.
Timber framed Tudor Grammar School housing Borough's Museum collection. Local history and archaeology. Monthly exhibitions by local artists. Tues 10–4; Thurs 1–4; Fri 10–4; Sat 10–1. *Closed* Bank Hols. Adm free. Car parking 200m from main town centre car park. Not suitable for disabled persons.

PADIHAM

GAWTHORPE HALL, The National Trust
Telephone: Padiham (0282) 78511

House built in 1600-1605, restored by Barry in 1850; Barry's designs newly re-created in principal rooms. Display of Rachel Kay-Shuttleworth textile collections, private study by arrangement. Major display of late 17th century portraits on loan from the National Portrait Gallery. Estate building, recently restored, houses a broad programme of craft and management courses.
Location: On E outskirts of Padiham (¾ m drive to house is on N of A671).
Station: Rose Grove (2 m).
Opening Times: Mar 24 to end Oct. HALL: Tues, Weds, Thurs, Sats & Suns, 2–6, last also 5.30. Open Good Fri & Bank Holiday Mons. GARDEN: Open daily all year 10–6. GALLERY and SHOP: Daily Feb to Dec 20, 10.30–12.30, 2–5 (Sat & Sun 2–5). Adm House and Garden: £1.50, Chd 75p. Reductions for pre-booked parties of 15 or more (except Bank Holidays). No dogs. Access for disabled: Ground floor of Hall, Shop & Gallery. W.C.
Refreshments: Refectory in Estate Building open as shop, but 11–5 weekdays.

PRESTON

HARRIS MUSEUM AND ART GALLERY *(Borough of Preston)*
Market Square, PR1 2PP. Tel: (0772) 58248.
The magnificent Greek Revival building houses fine collections of British paintings, ceramics, glass and costume. The new **Story of Preston** gallery traces the development of the town over 12,000 years and there is a lively programme of temporary exhibitions of local history and of some of the most exciting developments in contemporary art. Events and activities; museum shop and cafe. Open weekdays 10–5.

HOGHTON TOWER
Telephone: Hoghton (025 485) 2986
(Sir Bernard de Hoghton, Bt)

Dramatic 16th century fortified hill-top mansion with the magnificent Banqueting Hall where James I knighted the 'Loin of Beef' in 1617. Permanent collection of dolls' houses. Walled gardens and Old English Rose Garden.
Location: 5 m E of Preston on A675.
Station: Pleasington (2¾ m).
Opening Times: Easter Sat. Sun & Mon, then Suns to end of Oct, also Sats in July & Aug & all Bank Hols: 2–5. Adm £2, Chd 50p. School parties—Chd 50p. Private visits welcome (minimum 25 persons) at any time throughout week. Apply Administrator, Hoghton Tower, Preston PR5 0SH. Souvenir & Craft Shop.
Refreshments: Tea rooms.

LANCASHIRE COUNTY & REGIMENTAL MUSEUM
(Lancashire County Council)
Stanley Street PR1 4YP. Tel: (0772) 264075.
This large new museum is housed in Old Sessions House, Preston, and contains displays on the history of Lancashire from Domesday onwards; also the combined Military Museums of the 14th/20th King's Hussars, Duke of Lancaster's Own Yeomanry and the Queen's Lancashire Regiment. Recreated scenes, sound, light and smell effects(!) are used throughout. Temporary exhibitions on a wide range of topics, including fine and decorative arts, crafts and social history. School parties welcome. ADM FREE. Car parking free. Suitable for disabled ground floor only (wheelchair ramps and disabled toilets). No wheelchairs available. Open daily 10–5 except *closed* Thurs, Sun and Bank Hols.

SAMLESBURY HALL
(Samlesbury Hall Trust)

14th century Manor House owned and administered by private trust.
Location: On A677; 6 m E of Preston; 5 m W of Blackburn.
Opening Times: All the year—Tues to Suns 11.30–5 (summer), 11.30–4 (winter). *Closed Mons.* Adm £2, Chd (under 16) 80p. Coach & organised parties by appointment Tues to Fris only. Ongoing sales of antiques and collectors' items. Also various craft, at work and other exhibitions.
Refreshments: Tea-room open 12–4 (coffee etc).

RIBCHESTER

MUSEUM OF CHILDHOOD
Church Street. Tel: (025484) 520.
A museum of childhood, comprising a private collection of toys, models, dolls, miniatures, curios, 54 dolls houses and a 20 piece Model Fairground. Museum shop, with collector's items, miniatures etc. Open daily 11–5, Tues–Sun incl. and Bank Hols. *Closed* Mon. Open Bank Hols. Adm charge.

THE RIBCHESTER MUSEUM
near Preston. Tel: Ribchester (025 484) 261.
Remains from the Roman site of Bremetennacum including an excavated area adjoining the museum revealing part of the Granaries. Mar to Oct: Daily 2–5. June, July and Aug: Daily 11.30–5.30. Nov to Feb: Sun only 2–4. Adm charge. Parties by prior arrangement with Curator, Museum, Ribchester.

ROSSENDALE

ROSSENDALE MUSEUM *(Rossendale Borough Council)*
Whitaker Park, Rawtenstall. Tel: (0706) 217777; after hours 226509.
Fine arts, natural history, Rossendale Collection, temporary exhibitions. Mon to Fri 1–5; Sat 10–12, 1–5. Sun Nov to Mar 1–4; Apr to Oct: 1–5.

Lancashire – *continued*

RUFFORD

RUFFORD OLD HALL, The National Trust
Telephone: Rufford (0704) 821254

One of the finest buildings of the 15th century in Lancashire. The Great Hall is remarkable for its ornate hammer-beam roof and unique screen. Fine collections of 17th century oak furniture and 16th century arms and armour and tapestries.

Location: 7 m N of Ormskirk at N end of Rufford village on E side of A59.
Stations: Rufford (½ m) (not Suns); Burscough Bridge (2½ m).
Opening Times: Mar 24 to Nov 5—Daily (except Fris) 1–5, Suns 2–5. Last adm 4.30. Garden, Cafe and shop: open 11–5 on same days, Suns 2–5. Adm Hall & Garden £1.50, Chd 75p. Reduced rate for parties of 15 or more by arrangement. Access for disabled garden only. Guide dogs.
Refreshments: At the Hall (parties should book).

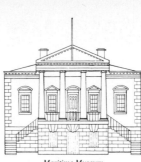
Maritime Museum

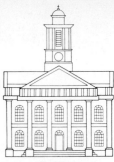
City Museum

Lancaster City Museums

Cottage Museum

CHINGLE HALL
Nr PRESTON

Small moated Manor House

Earliest domestic brick built structure in the British Isles 1260

Archeological excavation in progress

Birthplace of St John Wall (1620–1679)

Site of foundation meeting of modern Ecumenical movement

The most haunted house in the British Isles

ADMISSION – SEE EDITORIAL REFERENCE

TOWNELEY HALL
ART GALLERY & MUSEUMS
Burnley, Lancashire

The former home of the Towneley family, dating originally from the 14th Century, has been an Art Gallery & Museum since 1903. A separate Museum of Local Crafts & Industries is housed in the brew-house, and there is a Natural History Centre with Nature Trails in the grounds.

BLACKBURN MUSEUMS & ART GALLERIES
Enquiries Telephone (0254) 667130

Buddhist stone sculptures of the 1st to 5th Centuries AD from the surroundings of Peshawar

Leicestershire

ASHBY DE LA ZOUCH

ASHBY DE LA ZOUCH CASTLE
Telephone: (0530) 413343

In 1464 Edward IV granted the Norman manor house of Ashby to his Lord Chamberlain, Lord Hastings, who built the impressive four-storey tower. His enjoyment of it was short-lived, alas, for in 1483 he was beheaded by Richard III. His successors fared better and among royal visitors were Henry VII, Mary Queen of Scots, James I and Charles I. In 1649 the tower was partially destroyed by Parliamentary forces.

Location: In Ashby de la Zouch. OS map ref SK363167.
Opening Times: Good Friday to Sept 30, daily 10–6; Oct 1 to Maundy Thursday, daily 10–4. *Closed Mons, Christmas and New Year.* Adm 80p, OAPs 60p, Chd 40p.

BELVOIR

BELVOIR CASTLE
Telephone: Grantham (0476) 870262
(His Grace the Duke of Rutland)

Seat of the Dukes of Rutland since Henry VIII's time, rebuilt by Wyatt 1816. Notable pictures, furniture, objets d'art. Special Events most Sundays.

Location: 7 m WSW of Grantham, between A607 (to Melton Mowbray) and A52 (to Nottingham).
Opening Times: Mar 18 to Oct 8—Tues, Weds, Thurs & Sats 11–6; Suns 11–7; Bank Hol Mons only 11–7; Good Friday and also Fri during June, July, Aug, Sept 11–6; also Sats & Suns only in Oct, 11–6. Last adm 40 mins before closing. Adm £2.60, Chd £1.50. *No extra charges in Castle.* Parties of 30 or more OAPs £1.50 (organiser free); 30 or more adults £2; 30 or more School children £1.50 (accompanying teachers free). All Coach Excursion passengers £2. No dogs.
Refreshments: Café at Castle.

CASTLE DONINGTON

THE DONINGTON MOTOR MUSEUM
Donington Park. Tel: (0332) 810048.
The Donington Motor Museum. Donington Park Racing Circuit, Castle Donington Derby (3 miles from junction 24 M1 motorway and M42/A453 Birmingham Nottingham. The world's largest collection of Grand Prix Racing Cars tracing the history of motor sport from pre-war to the present day complimented by a growing collection of Grand Prix motorcycles including machines used by the legendary Mike Hailwood and Barry Sheene. Open daily (except Christmas week) 10–5. Adm £4, OAPs £1.50, Chld 50p. Concessions for group bookings prior to the day. Free ample parking for cars and coaches.

COALVILLE

MANOR HOUSE
Telephone: Coalville (0530) 31259
(Leicestershire Museums, Art Galleries & Records Service)

Early 14th century Manor house with furniture. Herb garden.
Location: 1 m SW of Coalville; 13 m NW of Leicester off A50; 4 m from M1 at exit 22.
Opening Times: Mar 22 to Oct 1 Bank Hol Mons & Tues 2–6. Adm free.
Refreshments: Cream teas available in the Barn.

KIRBY MUXLOE

KIRBY MUXLOE CASTLE
Telephone: (0533) 663230

William, Lord Hastings, was a very wealthy man, so he was able to indulge his passion for building. He developed his moated brick mansion from a fortified manor house, but it was never completed. A striking feature is the patterned brickwork, clearly visible on the gatehouse walls.

Location: 4 m (6.4 km) west of Leicester. OS map ref SK524046.
Opening Times: Good Friday to Sept 30, daily 10–6; Oct 1 to Maundy Thursday, daily 10–4. *Closed Mons, Christmas and New Year.* Adm 80p, OAPs 60p, Chd 40p.

LEICESTER

BELGRAVE HALL
Telephone: Leicester (0533) 554100 &
(Leicestershire Museums, Art Galleries & Records Service)

A small Queen Anne house and garden with furniture of 18th and early 19th century.
Location: Off Thurcaston Road, Belgrave 2 m from City centre on Loughborough Road (A6).
Station: Leicester (2½ m).
Opening Times: All the year—Weekdays 10–5.30; Suns 2–5.30. Adm free. *Closed Good Friday, Christmas Day & Boxing Day.*

GAS MUSEUM *(British Gas East Midlands)*
Aylestone Road. Tel: (0533) 549414, Ext. 2192 or 535608 (outside opening hours).
Museum devoted to the history of the gas industry, mainly in the East Midlands, with a wide range of exhibits, reflecting all aspects of the industry's heritage. Tues to Fri 12.30–4.30. *Closed* Sat to Mon, Bank Hols and Tues following.

GUILDHALL
Telephone: Leicester (0533) 554100 &
(Leicestershire Museums, Art Galleries & Records Service)

A medieval timber building dating from 14th to 17th centuries. Mayor's Parlour, Library and old police cells.
Location: Guildhall Lane.
Station: Leicester.
Opening Times: All the year—Weekdays 10–5.30; Suns 2–5.30. Adm free. *Closed Good Friday, Christmas Day & Boxing Day.*

JEWRY WALL MUSEUM
St. Nicholas Circle. Tel: (0533) 544766.
Museum of archaeology from prehistoric times to 1500. Roman Jewry Wall and Baths. Weekdays 10–5.30; Sun 2–5.30. *Closed* Christmas, Boxing Day and Good Friday.

THE LEICESTERSHIRE MUSEUM AND ART GALLERY
New Walk. Tel: (0533) 554100.
Collections of 18th to 20th century English paintings, drawings and water-colours; unique collection of 20th century German art, especially of Expressionism; Old Masters and modern prints. Small Egyptology gallery, The Rutland Dinosaur, geology displays and natural history galleries. Temporary exhibitions. Extensive reference and study collections in Art and Natural Sciences. Active educational programme including holiday activities. Weekdays 10–5.30; Sun 2–5.30. *Closed* Christmas, Boxing Day and Good Friday.

LEICESTERSHIRE MUSEUM OF TECHNOLOGY
Abbey Pumping Station, Corporation Road. Tel: (0533) 661330.
Giant beam engines 1891. Steam shovel and other engines. Transport; knitting gallery; special events as advertised. Weekdays 10–5.30; Sun 2–5.30. *Closed* Christmas, Boxing Day and Good Friday.

LEICESTERSHIRE RECORD OFFICE
57 New Walk. Tel: (0533) 544566.
Extensive collection of official and private archives, both rural and urban, relating to the County of Leicestershire. Mon to Thurs 9.15–5; Fri 9.15–4.45; Sat 9.15–12.15. *Closed* Christmas Day, Boxing Day, Good Friday and Bank Holiday weekends, Sat to Tues.

MUSEUM OF THE ROYAL LEICESTERSHIRE REGIMENT
The Magazine, Oxford Street. Tel: (0533) 554100.
Mementoes, battle trophies and relics. Weekdays 10–5.30; Sun 2–5.30. *Closed* Christmas, Boxing Day and Good Friday.

NEWARKE HOUSES MUSEUM
The Newarke. Tel: (0533) 554100.
Social history of the city and county from 1500 to the present day. 19th century street scene, 17th century room, local clocks, musical instruments. Weekdays 10–5.30; Sun 2–5.30. *Closed* Christmas, Boxing Day and Good Friday.

WYGSTON'S HOUSE
Telephone: Leicester (0533) 554100
(Leicestershire Museums, Art Galleries & Records Service)

Museums of Costume (1769-1924) in a medieval house with Georgian additions. Shop reconstructions.
Location: Applegate St Nicholas Circle nr City centre.
Station: Leicester.
Opening Times: All the year—Weekdays 10–5.30; Suns 2–5.30. Adm free. *Closed Good Friday, Christmas Day & Boxing Day.*

LOUGHBOROUGH

THE BELL FOUNDRY MUSEUM
(John Taylor & Co (Bell Founders) Ltd)
Freehold Street. Tel: (0509) 233414.
Unique exhibition of the bellfounder's craft. Original material relating to bells, their history and fittings. Industrial archaeology and historic furnace area. Open all year Tues to Sat and Bank Hol Mons 9.30–4.30. Tours of the working bell foundry by arrangement. Ample free parking. Museum only 75p, Chld 50p. Combined museum visit and bell foundry £2, Chld £1. Supervising teachers free with school parties.

LOUGHBOROUGH CARILLON AND WAR MEMORIAL TOWER
(Charnwood Borough Council, Leisure Services Department)
c/o Queens Park. Tel: (0509) 263151
On three levels a collection of militaria and associated memorabilia relating to service of the crown since 1900 to the present. Housed in a unique carillon bell tower where 47 bells are played via a clavier keyboard. Recitals twice weekly – Easter to Sept 30, Thur and Sun. Open Good Friday to Sept 30: daily 2–6. Adm 30p, Chd 15p.

LUTTERWORTH

STANFORD HALL
Telephone: Rugby (0788) 860250
(The Lady Braye)

A William and Mary House built in the 1690's containing a fine collection of pictures (including the Stuart Collection), antique furniture and family costumes dating from Queen Elizabeth I's time. There is a full-size replica of the 1898 Flying Machine of Percy Pilcher who is officially recognised as England's Pioneer Aviator. He experimented at Stanford where he was killed whilst flying in 1899. The Motorcycle Museum contains an outstanding collection of Vintage and historic motorcycles. Walled Rose Garden leading to Old Forge. Nature Trail. Craft Centre most Sundays.

Location: 7½ m NE of Rugby; 3½ m from A5; 6 m from M1 at exit 18; 5 m from M1 at exit 20; 6 m from M6 at exit 1; 1¼ m from B5414 at Swinford.
Opening Times: Easter Sat to end of Sept—Thurs, Sats & Suns also Bank Hol Mons & Tues following 2.30–6. Adm House & Grounds, etc, £2.10, Chd £1. Grounds, Rose Garden, Flying Machine, Old Forge, Craft Centre (most Suns) £1.10, Chd 50p. Parties of 20 or more (min £36) £1.80, Chd 80p. OAP parties of 20 or more £1.70. School parties of 20 or more (one teacher adm free) £1.80, Chd 80p. Adm prices subject to increase on occasional Event Days. Motor cycle Museum £1, Chd 25p.
NB On Bank Hols and Event Days open 12–6 (House 2.30).
Refreshments: Home-made teas. Light lunches most Suns. Lunches, High Tea or Suppers for pre-booked parties any day during season.

LYDDINGTON

LYDDINGTON BEDE HOUSE
Telephone: (057 282) 2438
(English Heritage)

The building is the only surviving part of a grand medieval palace of the Bishops of Lincoln. After the Reformation it passed to Thomas, Lord Burghley, who turned it into an almshouse. It was used as such until the present century.
Location: In Lyddington 6m (9.6 km) north of Corby. OS map ref SP875970.
Opening Times: Good Friday to Sept 30 – daily 10–6. Adm 80p, OAPs 60p, Chd 40p.

MARKET BOSWORTH

BOSWORTH BATTLEFIELD VISITOR CENTRE & COUNTRY PARK
Telephone: Market Bosworth (0455) 290429   &
(Leicestershire County Council)

Site of the famous Battle of Bosworth Field (1485) with extensive Visitor Centre including exhibitions, models, film theatre, book and gift shops and cafeteria; and outdoor interpretation of the Battle. Series of special mediaeval attractions during summer months.
Location: 15 m W of Leicester; 2 m S of Market Bosworth (sign posted off A5, A447, A444 and B585).
Opening Times: BATTLEFIELD VISITOR CENTRE. Mar 22 to Oct 31—Mons to Sats 2–5.30; Suns and Bank Hols 1–6. July 1 to Aug 31: open from 11a.m. Admission £1.20, Chd (under 16 years) and OAPs 80p. (Special charges apply on main Special Event days.) Parties at any time by appointment at reduced rates. COUNTRY PARK & BATTLE TRAILS: All year during daylight hours.
Refreshments: Bosworth Buttery Cafeteria.

SHACKERSTONE RAILWAY MUSEUM
(Shackerstone Railway Society Ltd)
Shackerstone Station CV13 6NW. Tel: Tamworth 880754.
Museum of RAILWAYANIA, much of it 19th century with special emphasis on railways of WEST LEICESTERSHIRE. Adm 60p, Chld 30p (Suns and Bank Hols); when trains are not running (Sats) 40p, Chld 20p. No reductions for parties. Free car parking. Suitable for disabled.

MARKET HARBOROUGH

HARBOROUGH MUSEUM *(Leicestershire County Council)*
Council Offices, Adam and Eve Street. Tel: Market Harborough (0858) 32468.
Museum illustrating local history of Harborough area, particularly the town's role as a marketing and social focus. Mon to Sat 10–4.30; Sun 2–5. *Closed* Christmas Day, Boxing Day and Good Friday.

MELTON MOWBRAY

MELTON CARNEGIE MUSEUM *(Leicestershire County Council)*
Thorpe End. Tel: (0664) 69946.
Museum illustrating the past and present life of the area. Special displays on Stilton cheese and Melton pies. Easter to Sept: Mon to Sat 10–5; Sun 2–5. Oct to Easter: Mon to Fri 10–4.30; Sat 10.30–4. *Closed* Christmas Day, Boxing Day, and Good Friday.

OAKHAM

OAKHAM CASTLE
Telephone: Oakham (0572) 3654   &
(Leicestershire Museums, Art Galleries & Records Service)

Late 12th century Norman hall with collection of horseshoes given by peers of the realm.
Location: N of Market Place nr town centre. Off A605.
Station: Oakham (5 mins walk).
Opening Times: Grounds. Apr to Oct—Daily 10–5.30. Nov to Mar—Daily 10–4. Castle, Apr to Oct—Suns 2–5.30; Tues to Sats & Bank Hols 10–1, 2–5.30; Nov to Mar—as above but closing at 4. Adm free. *Closed Good Friday, Christmas Day & Boxing Day.*

RUTLAND COUNTY MUSEUM *(Leicestershire County Council)*
Catmos Street. Tel: (0572) 3654.
Extended displays on agricultural life. Courtyard with farm wagons and machinery. Volunteer Soldier Gallery. Local archaeology, particularly Anglo-Saxon finds, Rural trades-men's tools and domestic life. Tues to Sat and Bank Hol Mons 10–1, 2–5; Sun (Apr to Oct) 2–5. *Closed* Christmas Day, Boxing Day and Good Friday.

RUTLAND WATER

NORMANTON CHURCH WATER MUSEUM
(Anglian Water)
Nr. Oakham. Tel: Empingham (0780 86) 321.
A chance to visit the only Water Museum in a church! Originally part of the Normanton Manor Estate, Normanton Church was deconsecrated when Rutland Water was built, and now houses a splendid museum depicting the history of the Water Industry and the local area before the existence of the reservoir. Open Easter to end Sept: Sat & Sun 11–5; Mon–Fri 11–4. Adm 30p, Chld/OAPs 10p.

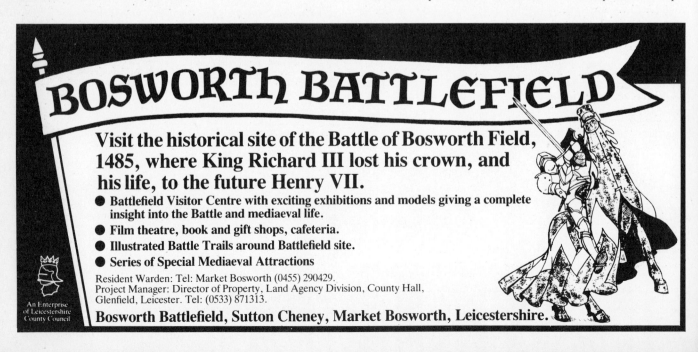

Lincolnshire

ALFORD

MANOR HOUSE FOLK MUSEUM
West Street.

BOSTON

GUILDHALL MUSEUM (Boston Borough Council)
South Street. Tel: (0205) 65954.

The museum houses the original prison cells in which the early Pilgrim Fathers were imprisoned in 1607 after their abortive attempt to leave England for religious freedom in Holland. Pictures and prints of local interest. Local archaeological material. Collection of firemarks and maritime exhibits. Open all year: Mon to Sat 10–5; Sun (*Apr to Sept only*) 1.30–5. Adm 40p, OAPs 20p, Chd free.

SIBSEY TRADER MILL
Telephone: (0205) 750036

Near the Stone Bridge Drain stands this cornmill, built in 1877 on the site of an older mill. One of the last to be erected in Lincolnshire, it is notable for having six sails. The Trader Mill was still working in 1953. It has since been completely restored.

Location: ¾ m (1 km) west of Sibsey, north west of Boston. Os map ref TF345511.
Opening Times: Good Friday to Sept 30, daily 10–6. Adm 55p, OAPs 40p, Chd 25p.

BOURNE

GRIMSTHORPE CASTLE AND GARDENS
(Grimsthorpe & Drummond Castle Trust)

The home of the Willoughby de Eresby family since 1516. Examples of early 13th century architecture, the Tudor period of the reign of Henry VIII and work by Sir John Vanbrugh. State Rooms and Picture Galleries open to the Public.

Location: 4 m NW of Bourne on A151 Colsterworth/Bourne Road, SE of Grantham.
Opening Times: Castle, Garden & Grounds—July 30 to Sept 3—daily except Mons & Fris, but including Aug 28—2–6. Adm £2.30, Students £1, Chd under 5 free. Nature Trails.
Refreshments: Afternoon teas.

BURGH-LE-MARSH

GUNBY HALL, The National Trust

Built by Sir William Massingberd in 1700. Reynolds' portraits, contemporary wainscoting. Ground floor only open to the public. Walled gardens full of flowers and roses.

Location: 2½ m NW of Burgh-le-Marsh; 7 m W of Skegness on S side of A158.
Opening Times: House & Garden. Mar 25 to end of Sept—Thurs 2–6; Tues, Weds & Fris by prior written appointment only to J. D. Wrisdale, Esq., Gunby Hall, nr Spilsby, Lincs. Gardens only also on Weds 2–6. Adm House & Gardens £1.30, Chd 60p. Garden only: 90p, Chd 40p. No reduction for parties. Dogs in garden only, on leads. Wheelchairs in garden only.

COLSTERWORTH

WOOLSTHORPE MANOR, The National Trust
Telephone: Grantham (0476) 860338

17th century farm house, birthplace of Sir Isaac Newton. Traditionally it was under an apple tree in this garden that Newton was struck with the theory of gravity.

Location: 7 m S of Grantham, ½ m NW of Colsterworth; 1 m W of A1 (not to be confused with Woolsthorpe, nr Belvoir).
Opening Times: Mar 25 to end—Weds to Suns 1–5.30, last adm 5. *Closed Mons and Tues (except Bank Hol Mons).* Adm £1.50, Chd £1.40. No reduction for parties. *Closed Good Friday.* No dogs. Wheelchair access to garden & ground floor only. Parking for coaches limited to one at a time—please book. *NB In the interests of preservation numbers admitted to rooms at any one time must be limited; liable to affect peak weekends & Bank Hols.*

DODDINGTON

DODDINGTON HALL
Telephone: Lincoln (0522) 694308
(Mr & Mrs A. G. Jarvis)

Elizabethan mansion, furniture. Spring bulbs, rose garden; Schools project.

Location: 5 m W of Lincoln on the B1190 & signposted off the A46 Lincoln by-pass.
Opening Times: Easter Mon then May to Sept—Weds, Suns & Bank Hol Mons 2–6. Adm £2.50, Chd £1.25. Party rates £2.25, Chd £1.25. Gardens only: £1.25, Chd 60p. Minimum charge per booked party, 20 people, £45.

FULBECK

FULBECK HALL
Telephone: Loveden (0400) 72205
(Mrs M. Fry)

Home of the Fane family since 1632. House mainly 18th century – older service wing, later additions to main block. Family collection furniture, pictures and items from India and the Far East. 11 acres garden. Plants for sale. Nature trail with free leaflet.

Location: On A607. Lincoln 14 m, Grantham 11 m. 1 m S of A17.
Opening Times: Easter and May Bank Holiday Mons. Daily from Aug 3 to Aug 29 incl. 2–5. Adm £2, OAPs, £1.50, Chd 50p. Members HHA Free. Parties by agreement. Car parking free. Suitable for disabled persons (no wheelchairs available).
Refreshments: None at house. Village pub does lunches and dinners. Coffee shop at local craft centre.

GAINSBOROUGH

THE OLD HALL
Telephone: 0427 2669.
(Lincolnshire County Council and English Heritage)

An unspoilt 15th century timber framed manor house, built between 1460 and 1480 by Thomas Burgh. Superb medieval kitchen and great hall. Kitchen displayed to portray its use in 1483, on the eve of Richard III's visit. Henry VIII held court here in 1541. Manor house sold to William Hickman in 1597 who allowed the early Dissenters to worship here. They were later the core of the Mayflower Pilgrims. John Wesley preached at the Hall several times. 17th and 18th century Hickman portraits and furniture. Medieval, Tudor, and Stuart room settings. Displays on Richard III, Henry VIII's Lincolnshire, and the history of the building. Soundalive sound tour. Regular living history events, and school re-enactments.

Location: In centre of Gainsborough.
Stations: Gainsborough Lea Road and Gainsborough Central.
Opening Times: All the year—Mons to Sats 10–5; Suns (Easter to Oct) 2–5. *Closed Christmas Day, Boxing Day, New Year's Day & Good Friday.* Adm charge. Organised parties welcome outside normal opening hours.
Refreshments: Tea shop open daily. Meals by arrangement. We look forward to seeing you!

RICHMOND PARK EXHIBITION CENTRE
Richmond Park.

GRANTHAM

BELTON HOUSE, The National Trust
Telephone: Grantham (0476) 66116

The crowning achievement of Restoration country house architecture, built 1684–1688 for Sir John Brownlow, heir to the fortunes of a successful Elizabethan lawyer; alterations by James Wyatt 1777, plasterwork ceilings by Edward Goudge, fine wood carvings of the Grinling Gibbons school. Family portraits, furniture, tapestries, Speaker Cust's silver and silver-gilt, Duke of Windsor memorabilia. Formal gardens, orangery by Jeffrey Wyattville, 17th century stables, magnificent landscape park. Extensive Adventure Playground for children.

Location: 3 m NE of Grantham on A607 Grantham/Lincoln Road; easily accessible from A1.
Opening Times: Mar 25 to end of Oct—Weds to Suns & Bank Hol Mons 1–5.30. Closed Good Friday. Gardens open 12. Parkland opens daily with free access on foot (may be closed for special events). Last adm 5. Adm House £3. Party rate £2.40. School parties contact the Administrator for details. 1989 Events—details from the Administrator.
Refreshments: Counter service licensed restaurant open 12–5.30 for lunches and teas.

GRANTHAM HOUSE, The National Trust

Dating from 1380 but extensively altered and added to throughout the centuries. Ground floor only open to the public. The grounds run down to the river.

Location: In Castlegate, immediately E of Grantham Church.
Station: Grantham (1 m).
Opening Times: Apr to end of Sept, Weds only—2–5 by written appointment only with Maj-Gen Sir Brian Wyldbore-Smith, Grantham House, Castlegate, Grantham NG1 6SS. Adm £1, Chd 50p. No reduction for parties. No dogs. Unsuitable for wheelchairs. No lavatories.

MARSTON HALL
Telephone: Loveden (0400) 50225
(Rev Henry Thorold, FSA)

16th century manor house. Interesting pictures and furniture. Held by Thorolds since 14th century. Ancient garden with notable trees. Gothick gazebo.

Location: 6 m NW of Grantham; 1½ m off A1.
Opening Times: Open on certain Sundays for local charities (details to be announced in local press) and at other times by appointment. Adm House & Garden £1.

MUSEUM *(Lincolnshire County Council)*
St. Peters Hill. Tel: Grantham (0476) 68783.

Collection of local prehistoric, Roman and Saxon archaeology, Grantham local history, trades and industries and a collection devoted to Isaac Newton. May to Sept: Mon to Sat 10–5, Sun 2–5; Oct to Apr: Tues to Sat 10–12.30, 1.30–5. Adm charge.

LINCOLN

LINCOLN: BISHOP'S PALACE
Telephone: (0522) 27468

When James I visited Lincoln in 1617 the palace was a ruin. It was not until the 1880s that it was partially restored by Bishop King. Excavations have revealed most of the medieval layout which largely dates from the 12th, 13th and 15th centuries.
Location: South side of Lincoln cathedral. OS map ref SK981717.
Opening Times: Good Friday to Sept 30, daily 10–6. Adm 55p, OAPs 40p, Chd 25p.

CITY AND COUNTY MUSEUM *(Lincolnshire County Council)*
Broadgate. Tel: (0522) 30401.
Shows the natural history and geology of the county and the Story of man in Lincolnshire from prehistoric times to 1750. Weekdays 10–5.30, Sun 2.30–5. Adm charge.

LINCOLN CASTLE
Telephone: Lincoln (0522) 511068
(Recreational Services Dept, Lincolnshire County Council)

Visitors can enjoy the impressive walls, towers and gatehouses that enclose beautiful and peaceful lawns and gardens. There are fine views of Lincoln and the surrounding countryside from the walls, and particularly from the Observatory Tower. The Castle, built in 1068, also houses a unique Victorian Prison Chapel which is open to visitors. During the summer the Castle is the ideal setting for a wide range of special events, including historical reconstructions, jousting tournaments, rallies and concerts. Further details regarding this year's special events can be obtained from the Manager, Lincoln Castle, or Recreational Services Department, Lincolnshire County Council, Telephone Lincoln (0522) 552222.
Location: Above Hill, Lincoln.
Opening Times: Open Bank Hols, except Christmas, British Summer Time: Mons to Sats 9.30–5.30, Suns 11–5.30. Winter Time: Mons to Sats 9.30–4, *Closed Suns.* Adm 50p concessionary 30p. Reduced rates for parties of 20 or more. No public car parking inside Castle, adequate parking in car parks close to walls. Suitable for disabled persons but not on walls and towers. The Castle has a well stocked gift shop and is close to Lincoln Cathedral and other museums run by the Recreational Services Department.
Refreshments: Available at Castle. Picnicking is encouraged within the grounds.

LINCOLN CATHEDRAL LIBRARY
Tel: (0522) 44544 or 25158.
Medieval MSS and early printed books. Wren Library by appointment only.

LINCOLN CATHEDRAL TREASURY
The Cathedral. Tel: (0522) 36458.
Gold and Silver plate from the Diocese. Easter to Sept: Weekdays 2.30–4.30. Adm by donation.

MUSEUM OF LINCOLNSHIRE LIFE *(Lincolnshire County Council)*
Burton Road. Tel: (0522) 28448.
Displays illustrate the social, domestic, commercial, agricultural and industrial life of Lincolnshire over the last 200 years. New display of the Royal Lincolnshire Regiment. Mon to Sat 10–5.30; Sun 2–5.30. Parties by appointment. Adm charge.

USHER GALLERY *(Lincolnshire County Council)*
Lindum Road. Tel: (0522) 27980.
Collections include the Usher Collection of fine antique watches, miniature portraits and porcelain. Gallery of works by the famous English watercolourist, Peter de Wint. Tennyson collection. Topographical collections relating to the County and the City. Large coin and medal display. Mon to Sat 10–5.30; Sun 2.30–5. Adm charge.

LOUTH

LOUTH MUSEUM
(Louth Naturalists, Antiquarian and Literary Society)
4 Broadbank, LN11 0EQ.
Local bygones; butterflies and moths; 6th century cremation urns, last century Louth-made carpets and old Louth blunderbuss on view, also Tennyson material and local photos. Wed, Sat and Sun afternoons (additional afternoon openings during July, Aug and early part of Sept). Adm charge (adults).

SKEGNESS

CHURCH FARM MUSEUM *(Lincolnshire County Council)*
Church Road. Tel: (0754) 66658.
Houses the Bernard Best collection of agricultural and domestic equipment in a 19th century farm complex. Reconstructed timber-framed cottage and brick barn now open. Apr to Oct: Daily 10.30–5.30. Adm charge.

SPALDING

AYSCOUGHFEE HALL AND GARDENS
(South Holland District Council)
Churchgate. Tel: (0775) 5468.
First phase of a new museum opens in May. Displays on land reclamation, agriculture and horticulture. Gardens open all year. Museum: Apr–Sept daily, Oct–Mar weekends only. Adm free.

SPALDING MUSEUM *(Spalding Gentlemen's Society)*
Broad Street. Tel: (0775) 4658.
Good collection of bygones, ceramics, glass, coins, medals and prehistoric relics. By appointment with Curator.

SPRINGFIELDS GARDENS
Telephone: Spalding (0775) 4843
(Springfields Horticultural Society)
Centre of the British Bulb Industry. 25 acres of landscaped gardens with over 1,000,000 Spring flowers in bloom. In Summer over 5,000 roses together with 250,000 bedding plants. Glasshouses etc. SPECIAL ATTRACTIONS — FLOWER PARADE WEEKEND MAY 6, 7, 8. COUNTRY FAIR MAY 6, 7. GARDENER'S AND FLOWER ARRANGER'S WEEKEND AUGUST 12, 13.
Location: 1½ m from centre of Spalding on A151.
Station: Spalding (2 m).
Opening Times: Apr 1 to Sept 30—Daily 10–6. Adm £1.80. Special events £2. Reduction of 15% for pre-booked parties of 30 and over. Shops. Free Wheelchairs, etc.
Refreshments: Cafeteria/tea shop. Licensed Restaurant open all year.

STAMFORD

BROWNE'S HOSPITAL
Broad Street PE9 1PD. Tel: (0780) 63746 and 51226
Ancient almshouses founded c. 1483 by William Browne, Wool Merchant. Historical display and fine medieval stained glass in Chapel and Audit Room. Open May to Sept 30: daily except Fri, 11–5. (Other times by appointment.) Adm £1, Chd/OAPs 50p. Reduced rates for families and parties.

BURGHLEY HOUSE
Telephone: Stamford (0780) 52451
(Burghley House Trustees)

The finest example of later Elizabethan architecture in England. Eighteen State rooms open containing fine furniture, porcelain, silver and the largest private collection of Italian art. Also magnificent painted ceilings by Verrio and Laguerre. Special exhibition for 1989 of the large collection of clocks and timepieces, many of which will be exhibited for the first time. The deer park is open to the public at no extra charge.
Location: 1 m SE of Stamford just off A1.
Station: Stamford (1m).
Opening Times: Good Friday to Oct 1—Daily 11–5. Good Friday 2–5. *Closed Sept 9.* Adm £3. Chld £1.70. Party rates available.
Refreshments: Lunches and teas in the Orangery. Enquiries for party rates & menus tel: (0780) 52451.

MUSEUM *(Lincolnshire County Council)*
Broad Street. Tel: (0780) 66317.
A museum of local archaeology and history. Exhibits include Daniel Lambert's clothing. May to Sept: Mon to Sat 10–5, Sun 2–5. Oct to Apr: Tues to Sat 10–12.30, 1.30–5. Adm charge.

STAMFORD BREWERY MUSEUM
All Saints Street.
Set in attractive stone buildings the Museum is a complete Victorian steam brewery with steam engine, coppers, coopered vats, boiler, boot and flogger and welly warmer. Displays features Victorian working life in a cooperage, brewer's office, laboratory and in home brewing. Refreshment room serving beer from the wood. Souvenir shop.

TATTERSHALL

TATTERSHALL CASTLE, The National Trust
Telephone: Coningsby (0526) 42543

The Keep is one of the finest examples of a fortified brick dwelling, although built more for show than defence, c. 1440, for Ralph Cromwell. Museum and shop in Guardhouse.
Location: 12 m NE of Sleaford on Louth Road (A153); 3½ m SE of Woodhall Spa.
Opening Times: Daily—Mar 25 to end of Oct, 10.30–6. Nov to Apr 1990: 12 noon–4.30 *Closed Christmas Day & Boxing Day.* Adm £1.50, Chd 70p. Parties of 15 or more £1.50, Chd 70p. Dogs in grounds only, on leads. Wheelchair access.
Refreshments: Fortescue Arms Hotel, Tattershall.

DODDINGTON HALL
A SUPERB ELIZABETHAN MANSION SET IN ROMANTIC GARDENS

This lovely house was completed in 1600 during the reign of Queen Elizabeth I. Its fascinating contents reflect continuous occupation by four families over nearly 400 years, and the Hall is still a family home.

Delicious meals in the licensed Garden Restaurant are available from 12 noon on open days. For information ring (0522) 690980.

Schools Project. Doddington Hall has twice received the Sandford Award for Heritage Education, and is a pioneer in the imaginative use of historic houses as a teaching resource. For information ring (0522) 694308.

ADMISSION – SEE EDITORIAL REFERENCE

Central & Greater London

BARNET

BARNET MUSEUM *(Barnet and District Local History Society)*
  31 Wood Street, Barnet, Herts. Tel: 01449 0321, Ext. 4
Archaeological and historical exhibits relating to the area. Dec 1 to end Feb: Tues, Wed, Thurs and Sat 2–4; Mar 1 to end Nov: Tues, Wed and Thurs 2.30–4.30; Sat 10–12 and 2.30–4.30; Mar 1 to end Nov.

CHURCH FARM HOUSE MUSEUM *(London Borough of Barnet)*
  Greyhound Hill, Hendon, NW4 4JR. Tel: 01-203 0130.
Local history, furnished rooms in period style. Special exhibitions throughout the year. Mon to Sat 10–1, 2–5.30 (Tues 10–1); Sun 2–5.30.

THE LONDON MUSEUM OF JEWISH LIFE
  (The Sternberg Centre)
  80 East End Road, N3 2SY. Tel: 01-346 2288/349 1143.
Small permanent display on Jewish immigration and settlement. Reconstruction of tailoring workshop, immigrant home, Workers' Circle office and east London bakery. Changing exhibitions, travelling displays, walking tours, research group, archives and family history workshops. Open Mon to Thurs 10.30–5; Sun 10.30–4.30. *Closed* Fri and Sat, Jewish and Bank Hols and throughout Aug. Curator: Rickie Burman, MA, M.Phil.

BEXLEY

BEXLEY MUSEUM
  Hall Place, Bourne Road, Bexley. Tel: Crayford (0322) 526574.
Historic House, permanent and temporary exhibitions, general and local. Local Studies Centre. Mon to Sat 10–5 (dusk in winter); Sun (in summer) 2–6. Beautiful gardens open daily.

ERITH MUSEUM
  Erith Library, Walnut Tree Road, Erith. Tel: Crayford (0322) 526574.
Local history including archaeology, industry and famous events. Mon, Wed and Sat 2–5.

HALL PLACE
(Bexley London Borough Council)
Historic mansion (1540). Outstanding Rose, Rock, Water, Herb, Peat gardens and Floral bedding displays, Conservatories, Parkland, Topiary designed in the form of the Queen's Beasts.
Location: Near the junction of A2 and A223.
Station: Bexley (½ m).
Opening Times: MANSION. Weekdays 10–5; Suns 2–6 (except from Nov to Mar). Museum & other exhibitions. PARK & GROUNDS. Daily during daylight throughout the year. Adm free.
Refreshments: At café.

BRENT

GRANGE MUSEUM *(London Borough of Brent)*
  Neasden Lane, N.W.10 (on roundabout). Tel: 01-908 7432.
Local history museum housed in the stable block of a large farm built in the early 1700s and converted into a gothick cottage in about 1810. The permanent display covers aspects of life in the area and includes a Victorian Parlour, a 1930s Lounge and an Edwardian draper's shop as well as a display of souvenirs of the British Empire Exhibition held at Wembley in 1924–5. The museum also has a programme of temporary displays during the year. The Grange houses the borough's archives and local history library collection. Tues, Thurs, 12–5; Wed 12–8; Sat 10–5. *Closed* Sun and Bank Hols. Adm free. Parties by arrangement only. Parking available on roundabout. Garden open for picnics. Nearest Station: Neasden (Jubilee Line).

BROMLEY-BY-BOW

THE LONDON GAS MUSEUM
  Bromley-By-Bow.
The London Gas Museum, Bromley-By-Bow is a small Museum illustrating the history of the gas industry with particular emphasis on London. It contains many examples of gas memorabilia and items of interest are constantly being discovered and sent to the museum for classification and display. The Museum was created by British Gas North Thames in 1982, 170 years after the establishment of a gas supply in London. On this large site a gasworks was constructed in 1870 by the Imperial Gas Light Company in an attempt to maintain its commercial position against the competition from an even larger gasworks at Beckton established by the Gas Light and Coke Company which commenced gas production the same year. Parking available. Organised parties are welcome by arrangement with the museum. Telephone 01-987 2000.

CAMDEN

THE BRITISH LIBRARY
  Great Russell Street, W.C.1.
The national library has its own exhibition galleries where you can see the Magna Carta, the First Folio edition of Shakespeare's Works (1623) and many other treasures – books, manuscripts, music and maps. Temporary exhibitions on specific topics are regularly mounted. Mon to Sat 10–5; Sun 2.30–6.

BRITISH MUSEUM
  Great Russell Street, WC1B 3DG. Tel: 01-636 1555.
Comprising the National Collection of Antiquities and Prints and Drawings. The museum departments are: Greek and Roman, Egyptian, Pre-historic and Romano-British, Western Asiatic, Oriental, Coins and Medals, Medieval and later, Prints and Drawings and Ethnography (see under Museum of Mankind). Weekdays 10–5; Sun 2.30–6. (Underground stations: Tottenham Court Road, Russell Square, Holborn.)

BURGH HOUSE

Telephone: 01-431 0144   ♿
(Burgh House Trust)

Built 1703. Now used for art exhibitions, concerts. Hampstead Museum. Terrace Garden.
Location: New End Sq E of Hampstead Underground Station.
Station: Hampstead (Underground). Hampstead Heath (BR North London Link).
Opening Times: Weds to Suns 12–5; Bank Hol Mons 2–5. Adm free.
Refreshments: Coffee, lunches and Teas. Licensed Buttery (for bookings Tel: 01-431 2516).

COURTAULD INSTITUTE GALLERIES

Woburn Square, W.C.1. Tel: 01-580 1015 and 01-636 2095.
The Galleries of the University of London; including the Lee Collection, the Gambier-Parry Collection, the important Princes Gate Collection of Old Master paintings and drawings, the famous Courtauld Collection of Impressionist and Post-Impressionist paintings, and the Fry Collection. Weekdays 10–5; Sun 2–5. *Closed* Bank Hols.
IMPORTANT NOTICE: The Courtauld Institute Galleries will be moving to Somerset House, The Strand, WC2, during the Summer of 1989. **Intending visitors should check that the Woburn Square premises are still in use after June 1 1989.**

THE DICKENS HOUSE, WC1N 2LF

Telephone: 01-405 2127
(The Trustees of the Dickens House)

House occupied by Dickens and his family 1837-39. Relics displayed include manuscripts, furniture, autographs, portraits, letters and first editions.
Location: 48 Doughty Street, near Grays Inn Road/Guilford Street.
Opening Times: All the year—Mons to Sats 10–5. *Closed Suns, Bank & Public Hols.* Adm £1.50, Students £1, Chd 75p; Families £3 (subject to alteration). Parties by appointment. Ground floor only (2 rooms) suitable for disabled—reduced adm charge.
For further details see advertisement.

FENTON HOUSE, The National Trust

Hampstead   *map K4*
Telephone: 01-435 3471

Collection of porcelain, pottery and Benton Fletcher collection of early keyboard musical instruments.
Location: On W side of Hampstead Grove, 300 yards N of Hampstead.
Stations: Hampstead (Underground 300 yards); Hampstead Heath (BR 1 m).
Opening Times: Mar 4–19—Sat & Sun only 2–6; Easter Sat to end Oct—Sats to Weds (inc Bank Hol Mons) 11–6. Last adm 5 pm. *Closed Good Friday.* Adm £2, Chd half price. *Reduction for parties on application to Custodian.* No dogs. Unsuitable for wheelchairs.

FREUD MUSEUM

20 Maresfield Gardens, Hampstead. Tel: 01–435 2002.
The museum contains Sigmund Freud's extraordinary collection of antiquities, his library and furniture, including the famous couch. The founder of psycho-analysis transferred his entire domestic and working environment here from Nazi-occupied Vienna, and resumed work. Interpretive displays; tours; archive films; shop. Open Wed–Sun 12–5 all year except Christmas, New Year and Easter. Adm £2, OAPs and students £1.

HAMPSTEAD MUSEUM *(Burgh House Trust (Registered Charity))*

Burgh House, New End Square, NW3 1LT. Tel: 01-431 0144.
Queen Anne house, includes the Museum of local history. Licensed Buttery. Wed to Sun 12–5; Bank Hols, 2–5. Adm Free.

HIGHGATE CEMETERY

Telephone: 01-340 1834
(Highgate Cemetery Charity)

The Western Cemetery: burial place of Jacob Bronowski, Michael Faraday and the Dickens family and many famous Victorians. A place of tranquility set in managed woodland with rare wild flowers and bizarre buildings.
The Eastern Cemetery: burial place of George Eliot, Ralph Richardson and Karl Marx is open for unrestricted access every day of the year but closed during funerals and on Christmas Day. 10–4 Nov to Mar; 10–5 Apr to Oct. Donations requested at sales point where there are numerous publications.
Location: Swains Lane, Highgate.
Station: (Underground) Archway.
Opening Times: (Western Cemetery only) – Guided tours are essential and held every hour (10–4) each weekend of the year. Special tours for groups by appointment at any time (s.a.e. please). Midweek tours planned for 12, 2 and 4 from Apr to Oct only. Generous donations, please, to help Friends of Highgate Cemetery (Charity No. 282220) who are responsible for management.
Special arrangements for photography and other facilities on application.

HUNTERIAN MUSEUM

Royal College of Surgeons, Lincoln's Inn Fields, WC2A 3PN.
Tel: 01-405 3474.
Comparative and morbid anatomy collection, mainly 18th century material. By written application to the Curator.

JEWISH MUSEUM

Woburn House, Tavistock Square WC1H 0EP. Tel: 01-388 4525.
Collection of antiquities illustrating Judaism and Jewish history. Open Sun, Tues to Thurs (and Fri during the summer) 10–4; Fri during the winter 10–12.45. *Closed* Mon, Sat, Bank and Jewish Hols. Group visits by arrangement with the Secretary.

KEATS HOUSE

Telephone: 01-435 2062
(London Borough of Camden)

Built in 1815-16 and completely restored in 1974-75. Poet John Keats wrote his famous odes here.
Location: S end of Hampstead Heath nr South End Green.
Station: (BR Hampstead Heath). Underground: Belsize Park or Hampstead. Bus: 24, 46, 168, C11 (alight South End Green). 268 (alight Downshire Hill).
Opening Times: All the year—Apr to Oct: Mon–Fri 2–6, Sat 10–5, Sun and Bank Holiday 2–5. Nov to Mar: Mon–Fri 1–5, Sat 10–5, Sun 2–5. Adm free. *These times are not confirmed. You are advised to telephone for up-to-date information before your visit. Closed Christmas Day, Boxing Day, New Year's Day, Good Friday, Easter Eve & May 4.*

KENWOOD, THE IVEAGH BEQUEST

Telephone: 01-348 1286
(English Heritage)

Adam mansion, once the seat of Lord Mansfield. The Iveagh Bequest of Old Master and British paintings, including works by Rembrandt, Vermeer, Hals, Gainsborough, Turner and Reynolds. Fine collection of neo-classical furniture.
Location: Hampstead Lane, NW3.
Station: Archway or Golders Green Underground (Northern Line), then Bus 210.
Opening Times: Good Friday to Sept 30, daily 10–6; Oct 1 to Maundy Thurs, daily 10–4. *Closed* Dec 24, 25. Adm free.
Refreshments: At the Coach House.

NATIONAL FILM ARCHIVE   *(British Film Institute)*

21 Stephen Street W1P 1PL. Tel: 01-255 1444.
Collection of cinematograph films and recorded television programmes, both fiction and non-fiction, illustrating history of cinema and television as art and entertainment and as a record of contemporary life and people, ethnography, transport, exploration etc. Also a large collection of film stills, posters and set designs. Open daily (by appointment only) 10–5.30.

PENTONVILLE GALLERY   *(Geoff Evans)*

4 Whitfield Street, W1P 5RD. Tel: 01-631 0852.
London home to radical issue-based fine art. Framing service, bookshop, meeting room. Mon to Fri 10–5.30; Sat 10–2.

PERCIVAL DAVID FOUNDATION OF CHINESE ART

(University of London, School of Oriental and African Studies)
53 Gordon Square, WC1H 0PD. Tel: 01-387 3909.
The Foundation comprises the collection of Chinese ceramics and a library of Chinese and other books dealing with Chinese art and culture presented by Sir Percival David to the University of London in 1950. Mon to Fri 10.30–5. *Closed* Bank Holidays and weekends.

PETRIE MUSEUM OF EGYPTIAN ARCHAEOLOGY

University College, Gower Street, WC1E 6BT. Tel: 01-387 7050, Ext. 2884.
Contains the collections of the late Miss Amelia Edwards and of the late Professor Sir Flinders Petrie. Parties are requested to make an appointment.

POLLOCK'S TOY MUSEUM

1 Scala Street, W1.

SIR JOHN SOANE'S MUSEUM

Telephone: 01-405 2107

Built by Sir John Soane, RA, in 1812–13 as his private residence. Contains his collection of antiquities and works of art. Tues to Sat 10–5 (lecture tours Sat 2.30, maximum 22 people, no groups). Groups welcome at other times, but must book in advance. Also library and architectural drawings collection: access by appointment. *Closed* Bank Holidays.

THE THOMAS CORAM FOUNDATION FOR CHILDREN

(Foundling Hospital Art Treasures)
40 Brunswick Square, W.C.1. Tel: 01-278 2424.
About 150 paintings, prints etc., including works by Hogarth, Gainsborough and Reynolds; historical records; musical scores by Handel; furniture and clocks; mementoes from the Foundling Hospital (founded 1739 and celebrating its 250th anniversary in 1989). Mon to Fri 10–4. *Closed* at weekends, Public Hols and when the rooms are in use for conferences etc. Before visiting, it is advisable to check by telephone that the rooms are open. Adm 50p, OAPs, registered art students and Chld 25p. Underground stations: Russell Square, King's Cross. Buses to Russell Square.

UNITED GRAND LODGE OF ENGLAND LIBRARY & MUSEUM

Freemason's Hall, Great Queen St., WC2.

UNIVERSITY COLLEGE MUSEUM OF ZOOLOGY AND COMPARATIVE ANATOMY

Gower Street,
WC1E 6BT. Tel: 01-387 7050, Ext. 3564.
Specialised teaching collection of Zoological material. By arrangement only.

THE CITY

BARBICAN ART GALLERY
(Corporation of the City of London (Libraries, Art Galleries Department))
Level 8, Barbican Centre, EC2Y 8DS.
Tel: 01-638 4141 Extension 306.
Large temporary exhibition gallery with a varied programme of changing exhibitions. Telephone for details of current exhibitions. Open Mon to Sat 10–6.45, Sun and Bank Hols 12–5.45. Telephone for Christmas closure details. Adm charges vary with each exhibition. Half price for Chld, Students, OAPs, Registered Disabled and Unemployed. Reduced rates for pre-booked parties. National Car Park in Barbican Centre; further parking in NCP car parks, London Wall and Finsbury Square. Suitable for disabled persons. Wheelchairs available from Red Cross. Restaurants in Barbican Centre.

CHARTERED INSURANCE INSTITUTE'S MUSEUM
20 Aldermanbury, EC2V 7HY. Tel: 01-606 3835.
Collection of Insurance Companies' firemarks, firefighting equipment, helmets, medals indicating the part played by insurance companies in lessening the dangers of fire. Open during office hours, Mon to Fri.

CLOCKMAKERS' COMPANY MUSEUM
Guildhall Library, Aldermanbury.

COLLEGE OF ARMS
Telephone: 01-248 2762
(The Corporation of Kings, Heralds & Pursuivants of Arms)
Mansion built in 1670s to house the English Officers of Arms and their records, and the panelled Earl Marshal's Court.
Location: On N side of Queen Victoria Street; S of St Paul's Cathedral.
Opening Times: EARL MARSHAL'S COURT ONLY. Open all the year (except Public holidays & on State & special occasions) Mons to Fris 10–4. Group visits (up to 10) by arrangement only. RECORD ROOM open for tours (groups of up to 20) by special arrangement in advance with the Registrar. Adm free (parties by negotiation). *No coaches, parking, indoor photography or dogs.* Shop—books, souvenirs.

DR. JOHNSON'S HOUSE
17 Gough Square, E.C.4. Tel: 01-353 3745.
Where he lived 1749–59 and compiled his Dictionary. Relics and prints. Mon to Sat 11–5.30 (Oct to Apr, 11–5). *Closed* Sun and Bank Hols. Adm charge.

GOLDSMITHS' HALL
Foster Lane, EC2.

THE MUSEUM OF LONDON
London Wall, EC2Y 5HN. Tel: 01-600 3699.
Opened in December 1976 (Museum of the Year – 1978) – presents the visual biography of the London area from 250,000 years ago. Exhibits (based on collections of former Guildhall and London Museums) arranged chronologically include the Lord Mayor's Coach, models and room reconstructions, everyday tools and rich men's extravagances, Mithraic treasure, the Great Fire experience, 18th century prison cells, 19th century shops, Selfridge's lifts. Education Department, Print Room, Library, by appointment. Restaurant. Tues to Sat 10–6; Sun 2–6. *Closed* Mons, including Bank Hols, Dec 24–26 incl, and New Year's Day. Parties must book in advance. Adm free.

THE MUSEUM OF METHODISM
in the crypt of Wesley's Chapel, with John Wesley's house, 49 City Road, EC1Y 1AU.
The house in which John Wesley lived and died.

NATIONAL POSTAL MUSEUM
King Edward Building, King Edward Street, EC1A 1LP. Tel: 01-432 3851.
Reginald M. Phillips and Post Office Collections of British postage stamps. and related material. Frank Staff collections of postal history. UPU collection of world stamps since 1878. Special exhibitions each year. Philatelic correspondence archives of Thos. de la Rue and Co., covering postage and/or revenue stamps of 200 countries or states 1855–1965. Research facility available by prior arrangement. Mon to Thurs 9.30–4.30; Fri 9.30–4. Adm free.

ROYAL BRITAIN
Aldersgate Street, Barbican EC2 (immediately opposite Barbican tube).
Tel: 01-588 0588.
Royal Britain is a unique and evocative entertainment where 20th century technology unfolds the story of British monarchy spanning more than one thousand years of kings and queens from Edgar to Elizabeth II. Visitors 'walk through' living history, experiencing sights, sounds, atmosphere and ambience as though they are actually present at specific episodes in royal history from AD 973 to 1988. Restaurant; Gift Shop (also specialising in books on royalty); Exhibition and restaurant available for evening functions. Open daily (except Christmas Day) 9–5.30. Adm £5, Chld (under 16) & OAPs £3, Students £4.50. Parties (15 or more) Adults £4, Chld (under 16) & OAPs £2.50. Suitable for disabled persons (wheelchairs available).

ST BARTHOLOMEW'S HOSPITAL PATHOLOGICAL MUSEUM
West Smithfield, E.C.1. Tel: 01-601 8537.
Pathological specimens. Sherlock Holmes connection. Available for meetings. Visitors welcome by appointment.

ST. BRIDE'S CRYPT MUSEUM
(Rector and Churchwardens of St. Bride's Church)
St. Bride's Church, Fleet Street E.C.4. Tel: 01-353 1301.
During excavations made prior to rebuilding over 1,000 years of unrecorded history were revealed. Roman pavement and remains of seven previous churches (dating from 6th century) on site can be seen together with permanent display of history of print etc. Daily 9–5.

TELECOM TECHNOLOGY SHOWCASE
135 Queen Victoria Street, EC4V 4AT. Tel: 01-248 7444.
Information Line: 0800 289 689.
Near Blackfriars Underground. A unique, permanent exhibition tracing over 200 years of telecommunications history. From the first telegraph machine through to the people and their inventions which created today's digital communications equipment. Major exhibits include Victorian exchanges, wartime reconstructions and displays showing the digital revolution, fibre optics and satellite technology. Mon to Fri 10–5, except Bank Hols. Special opening each year on Lord Mayor's Show day.

CROYDON

THE OLD PALACE
Telephone: 01-680 5877
(Old Palace School (Croydon) Ltd)
Seat of Archbishops of Canterbury since 871. 15th century Banqueting Hall and Guardroom. Tudor Chapel, Norman undercroft.
Location: In central Croydon. Adjacent to Parish Church. A212 & A213.
Stations: East Croydon or West Croydon (few mins walk).
Opening Times: Conducted Tours Only. Doors open 2, all tours commence promptly at 2.30. Mon Apr 3 – Sat Apr 8; Tues May 30 – Fri June 2; Mon July 17 – Sat July 22; Mon July 24 – Sat July 29. Adm £2, Chd & OAPs £1.25, this includes home made tea served in the Undercroft. Car park. Souvenir shop. Parties catered for, apply Bursar. Unsuitable for wheelchairs.

DAGENHAM

VALENCE HOUSE MUSEUM
(London Borough of Barking and Dagenham)
Becontree Avenue, Dagenham, Essex. Tel: 01-592 4500, Ext. 4293.
A 17th century manor house still partly moated, devoted exclusively to local history, including Fanshawe portraits. Open Mon to Fri, 9.30–1, 2–4.30.

EALING

GUNNERSBURY PARK MUSEUM
(London Boroughs of Ealing and Hounslow)
Gunnersbury Park, W3 8LQ. Tel: 01-992 1612.
Local history museum for the London Boroughs of Ealing and Hounslow. Collections cover archaeology, social history, local views, domestic life, toys and dolls, costume, transport (including Rothschild carriages), crafts and industries, especially laundry. Housed in part of an early 19th century former Rothschild country house set in a large park. Programme of temporary exhibitions. Victorian kitchens under restoration, open on selected weekends during the summer. Special facilities for schools by arrangement. Mar to Oct (to end BST): Mon to Fri 1–5; Sat, Sun and Bank Hols 2–6. Oct (from end BST) to Feb. Mon to Fri 1–4; Sat, Sun and Bank Hols 2–4. *Closed* Christmas Eve (variable), Christmas Day and Boxing Day. Adm free. Underground: Acton Town. Bus: E3 (daily), 7 (Suns only).

MARTIN WARE POTTERY COLLECTION
(London Borough of Ealing)
Southall Public Library, Osterley Park Road, Southall, Middlesex.
Tel: 01-574 3412.
Martinware Pottery was made by the Martin brothers at their factory in Southall from 1877–1915. The display is open on request during Library hours, Tues–Sat. Please telephone for an appointment. Adm free.

PITSHANGER MANOR MUSEUM
Telephone: 01-579 2424 ext 42683
(London Borough of Ealing)
Set in an attractive park, Pitshanger Manor was built 1800-04 by the architect Sir John Soane (1753-1837) as his family home. The house incorporates a wing of the late 1760s by George Dance. The interiors are being restored. *Please enquire in advance as to which of these rooms are open to the public.* A Victorian room holds a changing and extensive display of Martinware pottery including a unique chimney-piece of 1891. Exhibitions are held from time to time. Adm free. Parties by arrangement in advance. Limited disabled access – further details available on request.
Location: 1/3 m from Ealing Broadway Tube Station (Central and District Lines). On the A3001 (Ealing Green). No parking.
Opening Times: Tues to Sat 10–5. *Closed Sun & Mon. Also closed Christmas, Easter and New Year.*
Refreshments: Tea and coffee vending machine.

EAST MOLESEY

HAMPTON COURT PALACE
(Dept of the Environment)

The splendour of Cardinal Wolsey's country house began in 1514, surpassed that of many a royal palace, so it is not surprising that Henry VIII at first coveted and then obtained it prior to Wolsey's fall from power. Henry enlarged it; Charles I lived in it as King and as prisoner; Charles II repaired it; and William and Mary largely rebuilt it to a design by Sir Christopher Wren. The beauty of Wren's buildings is combined with some of the finest Tudor architecture in Britain.
Note: This historic property is in the care of the Department of the Environment.
Location: North side of Thames by Hampton Court Bridge.
Opening Times: State Apartments open Apr to Sept—Mons to Sats 9.30–6; Suns 11–6; Oct to Mar—Mons to Sats 9.30–5, Suns 2–5. Last admissions half an hour before closing time. *Closed* Dec 24–26, Jan 1. Great Kitchens and Cellars. Tudor Tennis Court. Apr to Sept only, times as above. Mantegna Paintings Gallery, as above, except in winter when closing time is either 5 or half an hour before dusk.
Gardens: Great Vine, King's Privy Garden, Great Fountains Gardens, Tudor and Elizabethan Knot Gardens, Broad Walk and Wilderness are open, free of charge, every day until dusk (9).
Maze: open daily, Mar to Oct, 10–5. Inquiries: 01-977 8441.
Refreshments: In the Grounds.

ENFIELD

BROOMFIELD MUSEUM *(London Borough of Enfield)*
Broomfield Park, Palmers Green, N13 4HE.
Closed, due to fire, from April 25th 1984.

FORTY HALL MUSEUM *(London Borough of Enfield)*
Forty Hill, Enfield, EN2 9HA. Tel: 01-363 8196.
Built in 1629 for Sir Nicholas Raynton, Lord Mayor of London. 17th and 18th century furniture and pictures. Local history. Exhibitions. 1 Oct to Easter: Tues to Sun 10–5; Easter to 30 Sept: Tues to Sun 10–6. *Closed* Mons.

GREENWICH

CUTTY SARK CLIPPER SHIP *(Cutty Sark Society)*
King William Walk, Greenwich, SE10. Tel: 01-858 3445.
The last of the China Tea Clippers built 1869. New and improved exhibition on board including famous Long John Silver figurehead collection. Mon to Sat 10.30–5.30, Sun 12–5.30. Winter close 4.30. Adm £1.30, Chld (under 16)/OAPs 60p, handicapped free. Parties 70p, Chld 40p booked in advance Mon to Fri. Also Gipsy Moth IV, Sir Francis Chichester's Round the World Yacht. Adm 20p. Car park and coach parking alongside. Only partly suitable for disabled persons. Curator: Capt. Frank Bell.

THE FAN MUSEUM
10–12 Crooms Hill SE10 Tel: The Fan Museum Trust 01-305 1441.
Proposed opening late 1989.

GREENWICH BOROUGH MUSEUM *(London Borough of Greenwich)*
232 Plumstead High Street, S.E.18. Tel: 01-855 3240.
Exhibitions of prehistory, history and natural history relating to the environment of Greenwich. Mon 2–8; Tues, Thurs, Fri and Sat 10–1, 2–5. *Closed* Wed & Sat.

LOCAL HISTORY LIBRARY *(London Borough of Greenwich)*
90 Mycenae Road, Blackheath, S.E.3. Tel: 01-858 4631.
Mon, Tues and Thurs 9–8; Sat 9–5. *Closed* Wed and Fri.

NATIONAL MARITIME MUSEUM *(A National Museum)*
Romney Road, Greenwich SE10 9NF. Tel: 01-858 4422.
Galleries here and in the Old Royal Observatory in Greenwich Park, now part of the Museum, show many aspects of maritime history in paintings and prints, ship models, relics of distinguished sailors and events, navigational instruments and charts, history of astronomy, medals, a large library with a reference section and information service and a fine collection of manuscripts. See the Neptune Hall with the paddle tug *Reliant*, boat-building shed, Barge House and collection of boats. West Wing galleries on Nelson and Cook, boat archaeology, yachting etc. Mon to Sat 10–6 (closes at 5 in winter); Sun 2–6 (closes at 5 in winter). Adm £2.20, Chld/OAPs £1.10 (1988 prices). The Planetarium gives educational and public performances at stated times. *Closed* Christmas Eve, Christmas Day, Boxing Day, New Year's Day, Good Friday and May Day. Licensed restaurant. For NMM Outstations see Bath, Brixham, Saltash, Poole, Tresco (Isles of Scilly).

OLD ROYAL OBSERVATORY
(National Maritime Museum)

Part of the National Maritime Museum it includes Flamsteed House, designed by Sir Christopher Wren, the Meridian Building and the Greenwich Planetarium.
Location: In Greenwich Park, N side of Blackheath.
Station: Maze Hill (short walk).
Opening Times: Weekdays—summer 10–6; winter 10–5. Suns—summer 2–6; winter 2–5. *Closed Good Friday, Christmas Eve, Christmas Day, Boxing Day, New Year's Day & May Day Bank Holiday.* Adm charge.
Refreshments: In Park cafeteria and museum main buildings.

PLUMSTEAD MUSEUM
232 Plumstead High Street, SE18.

RANGER'S HOUSE
Telephone: 01-853 0035
(English Heritage)

A Gallery of English Portraits in the 4th Earl of Chesterfield's house, from the Elizabethan to the Georgian period. Dolmetsch Collection of musical instruments in period rooms on newly restored first floor.
Location: Chesterfield Walk, SE10.
Stations: Greenwich or Blackheath (15 mins walk).
Opening Times: Good Friday to Sept 30, daily 10–6; Oct 1 to Maundy Thurs, daily 10–4. *Closed* Dec 24, 25. Adm free.

ROYAL ARTILLERY REGIMENTAL MUSEUM
Royal Military Academy, Academy Road, Woolwich, S.E.18.
Tel: 01-854 2242, Ext 3128.
Bus: 161, 161a, 122.

THAMES BARRIER VISITORS' CENTRE
Unity Way, Woolwich, SE18 5NJ. Tel: 01-854 1373.
A multi-media exhibition of photographs, models, video film and information display tubes about the history of the Thames Barrier. Daily Mon to Fri 10.30–5; Sat and Sun 10.30–5.30. Open Bank Hols. *Closed* Christmas Day, Boxing Day, New Year's Day. Special boat trips around Barrier. (Tel: 01-854 5555.) Access for disabled persons.

WOODLANDS ART GALLERY *(London Borough of Greenwich)*
90 Mycenae Road, Blackheath, S.E.3. Tel: 01-858 4631.
Mon, Tues, Thurs and Fri 10–7.30; Sat 10–6; Sun 2–6. *Closed* Weds.

HACKNEY

GEFFRYE MUSEUM *(Inner London Education Authority)*
Kingsland Road, Shoreditch, E2 8EA. Tel: 01-739 9893.
The permanent display of period rooms shows the development of the middle-class English home from about 1600. Reference library of books and periodicals on the decorative arts. Temporary exhibitions. Special arrangements for group visits which must be booked in advance. Tues to Sat 10–5; Sun 2–5. *Closed* Mon (except Bank Hols), Christmas Day, Boxing Day and Good Friday. Stations: Liverpool Street or Old Street. Buses: 22B, 48, 67, 149, 243.

HAMMERSMITH & FULHAM

FULHAM PALACE
Telephone: 01-736 5821, 01-385 3723
(London Borough of Hammersmith and Fulham)

Former residence of the Bishops of London since the 8th century. Buildings now date from 15th century and stand on the site of a Roman Settlement.
Location: In Bishop's Ave, ½ m N of Putney Bridge.
Opening Times: Tours of principal rooms and grounds are conducted by the Fulham Archaeological Rescue Group on certain Sunday afternoons throughout the year at 2pm in winter and 2.30pm in summer. Adm £1.50, includes historical notes and tea and biscuits, Chd 75p. **Grounds** open daily as usual, adm free.

HARINGEY

BRUCE CASTLE MUSEUM
Lordship Lane, Tottenham, N17 8NU. Tel: 01-808 8772.
Local history. Postal history. Mon to Sun: 1–5. Museum of the Middlesex Regiment. Tues–Sat 1–5. *Closed* winter Bank Hols and Good Friday.

MARKFIELD BEAM ENGINE AND MUSEUM
(Markfield Beam Engine and Museum Ltd, Charitable Company, Limited by Guarantee)
Markfield Road, South Tottenham, N15 4RB. Tel: 01-800 7061.
1886 Compound beam pumping engine in listed engine house. Restored to working order. Steaming certain weekends and by arrangement. Small exhibition illustrating aspects of the role of the pumping engine in public health engineering in 19th and 20th centuries. Steam weekends on dates to be announced. Apr to Oct. Parties by arrangement – can include special steaming on weekdays. Car parking not on site. London transport, trains and buses, Seven Sisters station. Suitable for disabled persons. Technical Director: A.J. Spackman, MSc, DIC, CEng, FRSA.

SILVER STUDIO COLLECTION
Middlesex Polytechnic, Bounds Green, N11.

HARROW

HARROW MUSEUM AND HERITAGE CENTRE
(Harrow Arts Council)
Headstone Manor. Tel: 01-861 2626 or 1818.
Based in 16th century Tithe Barn, with associated moated manor house dating back to 14th century. Purpose to reflect the history and heritage of Harrow. Open Wed to Fri 12.30–5, Sat, Sun and Bank Holidays 10.30–5. *Closed* Mon, open Tues afternoons for lectures. Parties by arrangement, morning and evening. Car parking. Easy access and toilet for disabled persons. Catering, books and souvenir shop.

OLD SPEECH ROOM GALLERY, HARROW SCHOOL
(Governors of Harrow School)
High Street, Harrow-on-the-Hill. Tel: 01-422 2196, Ext 225.

Situated in the Old Schools at Harrow School, Old Speech Room Gallery was designed by Alan Irvine in the mid '70s, and is now completed; it houses the School's collections and treasures: watercolours, antiquities, manuscripts, natural history, Harroviana. Exhibitions average 2 a year. Open on most days during term (except Wed), weekdays at other times. Times of opening and enquiries telephone the above number. Adm free. Tour parties can be arranged. Curator: Miss K. M. Hutton BA, M.Litt.

HENDON

ROYAL AIR FORCE MUSEUM   *(a National Museum)*
Hendon, NW9 5LL. Tel: 01-205 2266.

The only National Museum to be devoted to aviation and to telling the complete story of a Service, including its predecessors, from its start to the present. Some 60 aircraft are on show, with galleries depicting aviation history from the Royal Engineers of the 1870s up to the RAF of the 1980s. The uniforms of the RE, RFC, RNAS and RAF are shown; also a unique range of personalia, medals, orders, navigational and other equipment, bombs, missiles and weapons, paintings and drawings, model aircraft and dioramas. Service cars and transport, escape aids, early workshop scenes, WRAF huts etc. The Battle of Britain Hall houses a unique collection of aircraft and other memorabilia which serve as a permanent memorial to the men, women and machines involved in the great Air Battle of 1940. Also in the same complex is the massive Bomber Command Hall with its striking display of famous bomber aircraft including the Lancaster, Wellington and Vulcan. There is a restaurant, a cinema with frequent free shows and a research centre. Daily, including Sun 10–6. *Closed* Christmas Eve, Christmas Day, Boxing Day, New Year's Day. Free car park. Nearest Underground: Colindale on the Northern Line. Adm charge.

HILLINGDON

HAYES AND HARLINGTON MUSEUM
(Hayes and Harlington Local History Society and London Borough of Hillingdon)
Golden Crescent, Hayes, Middlesex. Tel: 01-573 2855.
A small museum of local history.

HOUNSLOW

BOSTON MANOR
Telephone: 01-570 7728 ext 3974
(London Borough of Hounslow)

Jacobean house (1622) with elaborate plaster ceiling in the State Room which also contains a fireplace and mantelpiece dating from 1623. Original oak staircase. The house is set in a small park.
Location: In Boston Manor Road.
Opening Times: May 20 to Sept 23 — Sat afternoons only 2–4.30. Adm free.

CHISWICK HOUSE
Telephone: 01-995 0508
(English Heritage)

Architect and patron of the arts, the third Earl of Burlington set a fashion with this Italian-style villa, built to house his library and art collections. The gardens were landscaped by William Kent.
Location: Burlington Lane (½ m) NE of Chiswick Station.
Opening Times: Good Friday to Sept 30, daily 10–6; Oct 1 to Maundy Thurs, daily 10–4. *Closed* Dec 24, 25, Adm £1.30, OAPs £1, Chd 65p.

HERITAGE MOTOR MUSEUM
(The British Motor Industry Heritage Trust)
Syon Park, Brentford. Tel: 01-560 1378.
The finest collection of uniquely British cars on display. 100 vehicles covering the history of the British Motor Industry. Open daily 10–5.30 (except Christmas Day and Boxing Day): Nov to Mar, 10–4. Discounts for Group Bookings by arrangement. Free car parking. Suitable for disabled persons. Refreshments within 100 yards. Curator: Mr. R. Westcott.

HOGARTH'S HOUSE
Telephone: 01-994 6757
(London Borough of Hounslow)

The artist's country house for 15 years containing many prints and some relics associated with the artist.
Location: In Hogarth Lane, Great West Road, Chiswick W4 2QN (200 yards Chiswick House).
Stations: Chiswick (½ m) (Southern Region); Turnham Green (1 m) (District Line).
Opening Times: Apr to Sept — Mons to Sats 11–6; Suns 2–6. Oct to Mar — Mons to Sats 11–4; Suns 2–4. *Closed Tues, Good Friday, Sept 4–17, last 3 weeks in Dec & New Year's Day.*

KEW BRIDGE STEAM MUSEUM   *(Kew Bridge Engines Trust)*
Green Dragon Lane, Brentford. Tel: 01-568 4757.
Giant beam engines (the earliest built 1820) operating under steam (at weekends only) the largest of their kind in the world. Working forge, steam railway, models. Open daily and Bank Hol Mons from 11, last adm 5. Adm charge. Family and party rates. Suitable for the disabled.

THE MUSICAL MUSEUM
(A Charitable Trust, registered as The British Piano Museum)
368 High Street, Brentford. Tel: 01-560 8108.
Proclaimed now the finest collection of its kind in the world, with 10 reproducing piano systems and 3 reproducing pipe organ systems playing back ON THE INSTRUMENTS recordings made earlier in this century by famous musicians. Surrounded by orchestrions, street pianos, barrel organs, phonographs, music boxes etc. Usually ably and wittily introduced by Frank Holland MBE. Sat and Sun 2–5, Apr to Oct inclusive, additional days during school holidays. Adm £1.50. Send SAE for Party Visit Form PV15 or Concert List. Director: Frank W. Holland, MBE, FIMIT.

OSTERLEY PARK HOUSE
Telephone: 01-560 3918   ♿
(Administered by the Trustees of the Victoria & Albert Museum on behalf of The National Trust)

Splendid State Rooms furnished by Robert Adam, including a Gobelins Tapestry Room. Garden houses and Tudor stable block.
Location: ½ m N of Great West road (turn off at traffic lights, Thornbury Road, near Osterley Station).
Stations: Syon Lane (½ m); Brentford (1¾ m).
Opening Times: House: all year daily (except Mons) 11–5, Open Bank Holiday Mons (except May 1), closed Good Friday, Dec 24–28 and Jan 1. Adm £2, Chd (under 16) & OAPs £1. Chd under 12 must be accompanied by an adult. Park: open daily 10–8 (or sunset if earlier). Adm free.
Refreshments: In the Stables (summer months).

SYON HOUSE
Telephone: 01-560 0881/3
(His Grace the Duke of Northumberland)

Noted for its magnificent Adam interior and furnishings, famous picture collection, and historical associations dating back to 1415, 'Capability' Brown landscape.
Location: On N bank of Thames between Brentford & Isleworth.
Stations: Brentford (BR 1 m); Syon Lane (BR 1 m).
Opening Times: Apr 1 to Sept 29 — Daily (except Fris & Sats) 12–5. Last adm 4.15. Also Suns in Oct, 12–5. Adm charges not available at time of going to press.

SYON PARK GARDENS
Telephone: 01-560 0881/3
(His Grace the Duke of Northumberland)

Includes the Great Conservatory by Dr Fowler. Within the Estate is the London Butterfly House and the British Heritage Motor Museum (telephone details below); also the Syon Art Centre.
Location: On N bank of Thames between Brentford & Isleworth.
Stations: Brentford (1 m); Syon Lane (¾ m).
Opening Times: All the year — Mar to Oct — Daily 10–6. Oct to Feb — Daily 10–dusk; Last adm 1 hour before closing. *Closed Christmas Day & Boxing Day.* Adm charges not available at time of going to press. Winter — reduced rates. Free car park. Telephone 01-560 0881/3.
London Butterfly House — opening times & adm charges: Telephone 01-560 7272.
British Heritage Motor Museum — opening times & adm charges: Telephone 01-560 1378.
Syon Art Centre — free admission: Telephone 01-568 6021
Refreshments: Light refreshments and meals in Bars & Restaurant. Telephone 01-568 0778/9.

ISLINGTON

ST JOHN'S GATE
Telephone: 01-253 6644, Ext 35
(The Order of St John)

Headquarters of the Order in England, the 16th gatehouse contains the most comprehensive collection of items relating to the Order of St John outside Malta.
Location: In St John's Lane, EC1M 4DA.
Station: (Underground) Farringdon.
Opening Times: MUSEUM. Tues, Fris 10–6; Sats 10–4. Tours of the building, including the Grand Priory Church and Norman crypt, 11 & 2.30 on these days.

WESLEY'S CHAPEL
Tel: 01-253 2262.
Built 1778, completely restored 1978, open each day. Sunday Service at 11am followed by light lunch (prior notice for parties) and 'Wesley Walkabout'. Minister: The Rev. Dr. Ronald C. Gibbins.

KENSINGTON

BADEN-POWELL HOUSE   *(The Scout Association)*
Queen's Gate, SW7 5JS. Tel: 01-584 7030.
Mementoes of Baden-Powell and historical records. Daily 9–5.

CARLYLE'S HOUSE, The National Trust
Telephone: 01-352 7087

Home of Thomas and Jane Carlyle 1834/1881. *Note: Certain rooms have no electric light, visitors wishing to make a close study of the interior should avoid dull days.*

Location: At 24 Cheyne Row, Chelsea SW3 (off Cheyne Walk on Chelsea Embankment).
Stations: Sloane Sq (Underground 1 m); Clapham Junction (BR 1½ m).
Opening Times: Mar 25 to end of Oct – Weds to Suns & Bank Hol Mons 11–5. Last adm 4.30. *Closed Good Friday.* Adm £1.60, Chd 80p. No reduction for parties, which should not exceed 20. No dogs. Unsuitable for wheelchairs.

CHELSEA PHYSIC GARDEN

The second oldest Botanic garden in the country, founded 1673 and only recently opened to the public, comprises 4 acres densely packed with c. 5,000 plants, many rare and unusual.
Location: 66 Royal Hospital Road, Chelsea; nr junction of Royal Hospital Road & Chelsea Embankment; entry via Swan Walk.
Station: Sloane Square (Underground).
Opening Times: Apr 2 to Oct 22 – Suns and Weds, 2–5. Also Tues 23 to Fri May 26 (Chelsea Flower Show Week) 12–5. Adm (1988 prices) £1.50, Chd & students (with cards) £1. Open at other times for groups by appointment. No dogs. Garden accessible for disabled & wheelchairs. Parking in street Suns, other days across Albert Bridge in Battersea Park, free.

CHELSEA SCHOOL OF ART (THE LONDON INSTITUTE)
Summer Shows
Foundation, B'TEC National Diploma, B'TEC Higher National Diploma and BA Degree shows are held in late June/early July. MA Degree shows are held in the first week of September. Please telephone college for details. Tel: 01-351 3844.

COMMONWEALTH INSTITUTE
Kensington High Street, W8 6NQ.
Tel: 01-602 3257 for 24 hour recorded information service.
Tel: 01-603 4535 for free What's On leaflet.
Underground: High Street Kensington. Bus: C1, 9, 27, 28, 33, 49, 73 and 31. Coach: Green line 701, 704, 714. A cultural and educational centre for spreading knowledge and understanding of the Commonwealth. Three floors of exciting exhibitions about the history, culture and peoples of the 48 countries which make up today's Commonwealth. A changing programme of art shows, performances, conferences and workshops for schools and general public. Licensed Restaurant. Mon to Sat 10–5.30; Sun 2–5. *Closed* Christmas Eve, Christmas Day, Boxing Day, New Year's Day, Good Friday and May Day. Adm free. Visitor's car park. Leaflet available about facilities for the disabled.

GEOLOGICAL MUSEUM
(part of the British Museum – Natural History)
Exhibition Road, South Kensington SW7 2DE. Tel: 01-938 9123.
Illustrates earth history and the general principles of geological science; the regional geology of Great Britain and the economic geology and mineralogy of the world. Famous collection of gemstones. Major exhibitions include Story of the Earth, Treasures of the Earth, Britain before Man and British Fossils. Programme of talks, demonstrations and films. Details on request. Mon to Sat 10–6; Sun 1–6. Adm £1 adults, Chld and concessions 50p. Free admission 4.30–6 Mon to Fri, 5–6 Sat, Sun and Bank Hols. Recorded information on events and activities (24 hr) 01-725 7866.

GOETHE-INSTITUT LONDON
50 Princes Gate, Exhibition Road, S.W.7. Tel: 01-581 3344.
Exhibitions of German Art. Open (usually) Mon to Thurs 12–8; Fri 12–6; Sat 10–1; please check first. Adm free. Underground: South Kensington.

KENSINGTON PALACE
(Dept of the Environment)
Bought by William III, 1689. Altered and added to by Wren and later alterations. Court Dress Collection.
Location: W side of Kensington Gardens.
Station: (Underground) Kensington High Street (½ m).
Opening Times: Open all year Mon–Sat 9–5; Sun 1–5. *Closed* Good Friday, Dec 24–26, Jan 1. Enquiries 01-937 9561.

LEIGHTON HOUSE MUSEUM
Telephone: 01-602 3316
(Royal Borough of Kensington and Chelsea)
Adjacent to Holland Park in Kensington lies the Artists' Colony, a group of remarkable Studio Houses, built by some of the leading figures of the Victorian art world. Leighton House Museum was the first of these to be built, and is today a museum of high Victorian art. The opulent fantasy of Frederick Lord Leighton, President of the Royal Academy, the house was designed by George Aitchison. Leighton lived here from 1866 until his death in 1896. His unique collection of Islamic tiles is displayed in the walls of the Arab Hall, and the Victorian interiors, now being restored to their original splendour, are hung with paintings by Leighton, Millais, Watts, Burne-Jones and others. Fine 'New Sculpture' by Leighton, Brock and Thornycroft is displayed in the house and garden. The study collection of Leighton drawings may be seen by appointment. Temporary exhibitions of modern and historic art throughout the year.
Location: Kensington.
Opening Times: All year. Mon–Sat 11–5 *(During exhibitions 11–6)* **Garden:** Apr–Sept *(Closed Bank Holidays).* Parties by arrangement with the Curator. Chd under 16 must be accompanied by an adult.

LINLEY SAMBOURNE HOUSE, W8
Telephone: 01-994 1019
(The Victorian Society)
The home of Linley Sambourne (1844–1910), chief political cartoonist at 'Punch'. A unique survival of a late Victorian town house. The original decorations and furnishings have been preserved together with many of Sambourne's own cartoons and photographs, as well as works by other artists of the period.
Location: 18 Stafford Terrace.
Station: (Underground) Kensington High Street.
Opening Times: 1 Mar to 31 Oct – Weds 10–4, Suns 2–5. Parties at other times by prior arrangement. Apply to The Victorian Society, 1 Priory Gardens, London W4. Adm £2.

NATIONAL ARMY MUSEUM   *(a National Museum)*
Royal Hospital Road, SW3 4HT. Tel: 01-730 0717.
The only museum dealing with the British Army in general during the five centuries of its existence, it includes the story of the Indian Army to 1947. Paintings, uniforms, weapons, equipment, regimental and personal mementoes and colours. Mon to Sat 10–5.30; Sun 2–5.30. The reference collections of prints, photographs, books and archives are open Tues to Sat (except Sats of Bank Hol weekends) 10–4.30. For Christmas closures see Press. Also *closed* Jan 1, Good Friday and May 1. At the Royal Military Academy, Sandhurst, items from the museum's collections are displayed in the Indian Army Memorial Room. They may normally be viewed by appointment, Mon to Fri. Written applications giving at least seven days' notice to National Army Museum, RMA, Sandhurst, Camberley, Surrey GU15 4PQ. Tel: (0276) 63344 Ext. 457.

NATURAL HISTORY MUSEUM
(Part of the British Museum – Natural History)
Cromwell Road, South Kensington, SW7 5BD. Tel: 01-938 9388.
Eight exciting exhibitions invite visitors to discover a new way of looking at natural history – The Hall of Human Biology, Introducing Ecology, Man's Place in Evolution, Dinosaurs and their living relatives, Origin of Species, Discovering mammals, Classification and British Natural History. Also many other displays of living and fossil plants and animals, minerals, rocks and meteorites from the national collections. Mon to Sat 10–6; Sun 1–6. *Closed* Jan 1, Good Friday, May 2 and Dec 24 to 26. Adm £2, Chld £1, Free adm 4.30–6 Mon to Fri, 5–6 Sat and Sun and Bank Hols. Recorded information on events and activities (24 hrs) 01-725 7866.

ROYAL GEOGRAPHICAL SOCIETY
Map Room open to public 10–5 weekdays, only for serious enquiries about maps preferably by appointment with Map Curator.

ROYAL HOSPITAL MUSEUM   *(Commissioners Royal Hospital)*
Royal Hospital Road, Chelsea, SW3 4SL.
Pictures, plans and maps, medals and uniforms, connected with Royal Hospital. Daily 10–12, 2–4. *Closed* Bank Hol weekends (Sat to Mon) and Sun from Oct to Mar.

SCIENCE MUSEUM
Exhibition Road, South Kensington. Tel: 01-938 8000.
Historical collections portraying the sciences of mathematics, physics and chemistry and their applications. The development of engineering, transport, communications and industry from early times to the present day. Study the history of medicine on the fourth and fifth floors, or visit the newly opened galleries on Plastics, Chemical Industry, the Exploration of Space and an interactive gallery for children of all ages – Launch Pad. Mon to Sat 10–6; Sun 11–6. *Closed* Christmas Eve, Christmas Day, Boxing Day and New Year's Day. The Science Museum Library is open on weekdays 10–5.30. Adm free.

VICTORIA AND ALBERT MUSEUM
Cromwell Road, South Kensington, SW7 2RL. Tel: 01-938 8500.
Recorded information on 01-938 8441.
The National Museum of Art and Design. One of the world's greatest museums of decorative and fine arts, the V&A's collections date from early Christian times to the present. They include paintings, sculpture, jewellery, costume and textiles, furniture, ceramics and glass, and metalwork. Special galleries display objects from the Middle and Far East and India. Paintings, prints, drawings and photographs are to be seen in the Henry Cole Wing. There is also an exciting programme of temporary exhibitions. (Recorded information on exhibitions 01-938 8349). Mon to Sat 10–5.50; Sun 2.30–5.50. *Closed* Christmas Eve, Christmas Day, Boxing Day, New Year's Day and May Day Bank Holiday. Restaurant available daily until 5.30 (Licensing hours 11–3, except Sun); Craft shop open as for Museum.

ZAMANA GALLERY LTD.
1 Cromwell Gardens, SW7 2SL. Tel: 01-584 6612.
Dedicated to the arts, architecture and culture of developing countries, with an emphasis on Islamic cultures, the gallery intends to contribute to a public awareness of a broad range of non-western societies.

KINGSTON-UPON-THAMES

KINGSTON UPON THAMES MUSEUM AND HERITAGE CENTRE
Wheatfield Way, Kingston upon Thames, Surrey. Tel: 01-546 5386.
Eadweard Muybridge photographic exhibition; local history displays; temporary exhibitions and tourist information. Mon to Sat 10–5.

LAMBETH

HAYWARD GALLERY SOUTH BANK CENTRE
Belvedere Road, South Bank, S.E.1. Tel: 01-928 3144.
Tel: 01-261 0127, Recorded Information.
Temporary exhibitions of British and foreign art. Opening times during exhibitions: Mon to Wed 10–8; Thurs, Fri and Sat 10–6; Sun 12–6. Adm charge. For Bank Hols openings check with gallery. *Closed* between exhibitions. Underground: Bakerloo and Northern to Waterloo; or District, Circle and Jubilee to Embankment (and by foot across Hungerford Bridge). Bus: to Waterloo Bridge, 1, 4a, 68, 171, 176, 188, 196, 501, 502, 505, 513 (Sun 1a, 171a); to York Road, 76, 149, 166a.

IMPERIAL WAR MUSEUM *(a National Museum)*
Lambeth Road, SE1 6HZ. Tel: 01-735 8922.
In June 1989 the Imperial War Museum will complete the first stage of its major redevelopment scheme which creates an entirely new Museum in the walls of the existing building, providing an exciting setting for innovative displays and improved visitor facilities designed for the 1990's and beyond. The exhibitions include items never previously on public display and have been organised to be readily accessible to the visitor, and the visitor can follow displays which tell the story of war in our century. *Triple height large exhibition hall* offering spectacular views of more than forty historic exhibits including: Sopwith Camel, Spitfire, P51D Mustang; Focke Wulf 190 aircraft; Mark V, Churchill, Sherman and Jagdpanther tanks; 13 pdr and 5.5″ field guns; 9.2″ and 122mm howitzers; Biber submarine; Italian human torpedo; 5.5″ gun from HMS *Chester*; V1 flying bomb; V2 rocket and Bloodhound and Polaris missiles. *Second World War exhibition, Blitz Experience, The Post-War World. Special inter-active A/V stations, New suite of art galleries. Access for the disabled, Licensed restaurant, Shop.* Weekdays 10–5.50; Sun 2–5.50. *Closed* New Year's Day, Christmas Eve, Christmas Day, Boxing Day. **Note:** The Museum galleries will be closed until mid-Mar 1989 to allow contractors to install the new displays. The Museum's reference departments will remain open as usual, but by appointment only. For further information ring Christopher Dowling 01-735 8922, Ext. 310.

MUSEUM OF GARDEN HISTORY
Telephone: 01-373 4030 (between 7 and 9 am)
and 01-261 1891 (between 11 and 3)
(The Tradescant Trust)

The former church of St Mary-at-Lambeth has been converted into the first museum of its kind in the world. The tomb of John Tradescant, gardener to Charles I, lies in the churchyard where the Tradescant Garden has been created, planted with species shrubs and flowers of the period. Lectures, exhibitions, shop.
Location: At the gates of Lambeth Palace.
Station: Waterloo or Victoria, then 507 Red Arrow bus, alight Lambeth Palace.
Opening Times: Mons to Fris 11–3; Suns 10.30–5. At other times by appointment. *Closed from second Sun in Dec to first Sun in Mar.* Further information from: The Tradescant Trust, 74 Coleherne Court, London SW5 0EF. Adm free. Donation requested.
Refreshments: Tea, coffee, light lunches; parties catered for if pre-booked.

MUSEUM OF THE MOVING IMAGE
South Bank, SE1 8XT.
Exciting, informative and fun, the Museum traces the story of the moving image from early Chinese shadow theatre through to future film and television technologies. Opening Sept 16 1988, MOMI's exhibits offer hands-on involvement as they take you from the earliest cinematic experiments to the coming of sound, Charlie Chaplin to a modern TV studio. Cafe and shop. Open Tues–Sat 10–8, Sun 10–6. Adm charge. Location: right underneath Waterloo Bridge on London's South Bank (between the National Theatre and Hayward Gallery).

PHARMACEUTICAL SOCIETY'S MUSEUM
1 Lambeth High Street, SE1 7JN. Tel: 01-735 9141.
Collection of crude drugs of vegetable and animal origin used in the 17th century; early printed works, manuscripts and prints relating to pharmacy; English delft drug jars, leech jars, bell-metal mortars, medicine chests, dispensing apparatus etc. By appointment.

LEWISHAM

HORNIMAN MUSEUM *(Inner London Education Authority)*
London Road, Forest Hill, SE23 3PQ. Tel: 01-699 1872/2339/4911.
An ethnographical museum dealing with the study of man and his environment. Natural history collections and aquarium. There is a large collection of musical instruments from all parts of the world. Special exhibitions throughout the year. Extensive library. Education centre for schools and children's leisure activities. Free lectures and concerts (autumn and spring). Weekdays 10.30–6; Sun 2–6. Open Good Friday. *Closed* Christmas Eve, Christmas Day and Boxing Day. Tea room open Mon to Fri 11–4.30, Sat 11–5.30, Sun 2.30–5.30. Pleasantly located with gardens, picnic area, nature trails and animal enclosures. Free parking in Sydenham Rise (opp. museum).

MERTON

SOUTHSIDE HOUSE
(Pennington–Mellor–Munthe Trust)
The Kemeys-Pennington-Mellor-Munthe family built the house after the great plague of London in 1665 and still live here. Furniture and pictures of the 17th

to 19th centuries; vanity case of Anne Boleyn; sword used in a fatal duel of 1608. Home of Hilda Pennington-Mellor, English wife of Axel Munthe, the Swedish doctor and philanthropist.
Location: On S side of Wimbledon Common, opposite 'Crooked Billet' Inn.
Stations: Wimbledon (1 m); Raynes Park (1 m).
Opening Times: Oct 1 to May 31, '89 — Tues, Thurs & Sat 2–5. Guided tours each hour. Adm £2, Chd £1 (must be accompanied by adult). Other times by written appointment only to the Curator. *The house is closed for Christmas & Easter.*

THE WIMBLEDON LAWN TENNIS MUSEUM
All England Club, Church Road, Wimbledon, SW19 5AE. Tel: 01-946 6131.
Fashion, trophies, replicas and memorabilia are on display representing the history of lawn tennis. An audio visual theatre shows films of great matches and the opportunity is now given to observe the famous Centre Court from the museum. The museum shop offers a wide range of attractive souvenirs. Open Tues to Sat 11–5, Sun 2–5. *Closed* Mons, Public and Bank Hols and on the Fri, Sat and Sun prior to the Championships. During the Championships, admission to the museum is restricted to those attending the tournament. Adm £1.50, Chld and OAPs 75p. 10% reduction for parties of 20 or more booked in advance. Car parking. Limited facilities for disabled visitors who are most welcome. Curator Miss Valerie Warren.

WIMBLEDON SOCIETY'S MUSEUM
Village Club, Ridgway, Wimbledon.
History and natural history of Wimbledon. Photographic survey 1900–14 containing 900 prints. Good collection of watercolours and prints. Sat 2.30–5.

WIMBLEDON WINDMILL MUSEUM
Windmill Road, Wimbledon Common, S.W.19. Tel: 01-788 7655.
The history of windmills and windmilling told in pictures, models and the machinery and tools of the trade. Easter to Oct: Sat, Sun and Public Hols 2–5. Adm 30p, Chld 15p. Group visits by arrangement.

NEWHAM

MUSEUM NATURE RESERVE AND INTERPRETATIVE CENTRE
(Administered by the Governors of the Passmore Edwards Museum)
St. Mary Magdalene, Norman Road, East Ham. E6 4HN. Tel: 01-470 4525.
Nine acre churchyard containing many species of birds, animals and plants. Interpretative Centre open Tues, Thurs, Sat and Sun 2–5. Nature Reserve open summer: Mon–Fri 9–5; weekends 2–5; winter: Mon–Fri 9–4; weekends 2–4. Admission Free.

NORTH WOOLWICH OLD STATION MUSEUM
(Administered by the Governors of the Passmore Edwards Museum)
Pier Road, E16 2JJ. Tel: 01-474 7244.
Restored station, Great Eastern Railway exhibits and steam engines. Mon to Sat 10–5; Sun and Bank Hols 2–5. Admission free.

PASSMORE EDWARDS MUSEUM
(Administered by the Governors of the Passmore Edwards Museum)
Romford Road, Stratford, E15 4LZ. Tel: 01-519 4296.
Collections of Essex archaeology, local history, geology and biology. Mon to Fri 10–5; Sat 10–1, 2–5. Bank Hols 2–5. Admission free.

RICHMOND

HAM HOUSE
Telephone: 01-940 1950   &
(Administered by the Trustees of the Victoria and Albert Museum on behalf of The National Trust)

17th century house with superb Charles II and Early Georgian furnishings. Portrait gallery.
Location: On S bank of River Thames opposite Twickenham 1 m S of Richmond.
Stations: Kingston (2 m); Richmond (2 m).
Opening Times: All the year — Daily (except Mons), 11–5. Open Bank Hol Mons (except May 1). Adm £2, Chd (under 16) & OAPs £1, Children under 12 must be accompanied by an adult. Grounds free. *Closed Good Friday, Christmas Eve, Christmas Day, Boxing Day, New Year's Day & May 1.*
Refreshments: In Orangery (summer months).

KEW GARDENS   &
(Royal Botanic Gardens)

300 acres in extent containing living collection of over 50,000 different plant species. Greenhouses. Museums.
Location: On south bank of Thames at Kew 1 m from Richmond.
Station: Kew Gardens (½ m).
Opening Times: All the year — Daily, open at 9.30. *Closed Christmas Day & New Year's Day.* Museums open from 9.30. Closing times vary according to season but not later than 4.30 Mons to Sats & 5.30 Suns. Adm 50p (adults, Chd 10 yrs & over, prams & invalid vehicles). Invalid chairs may be obtained free of charge at the Main Gate. Accompanied children under 10 yrs. adm free (1987 times & rates). Organised school parties issued with free entry vouchers on prior application.
Refreshments: At Pavilion (Mar–Nov); at Tea Bar (all year).

KEW PALACE (Dutch House)
Built 1631 Dutch style. Souvenirs of George III.
Location: In Kew Gardens on S bank of Thames.
Station: Kew Bridge (¾ m). Underground Kew Gardens (¼ m).
Opening Times: Apr to Sept—Daily 11–5.30. Adm 80p, Chd (under 16) & OAPs 40p (1987 rates).
Refreshments: In Kew Gardens *(summer months)*

MARBLE HILL HOUSE
Telephone: 01-892 5115
(English Heritage)

A complete example of an English Palladian villa. Early Georgian paintings and furniture.
Location: Richmond Road.
Stations: St Margaret's (½ m); Twickenham (1 m); Richmond (2 m).
Opening Times: Good Friday to Sept 30, daily 10–6; Oct 1 to Maundy Thurs, daily 1.30–4. *Closed* Dec 24, 25. Adm free.
Refreshments: In Stable Block.

MUSEUM OF RICHMOND
Old Town Hall, Whittaker Ave. Tel: 01-332 1141.
Due to open Oct 1988, this new independent museum deals with Richmond's rich and colourful history in a lively and informative way. Varied collection, models, dioramas and audio visual displays. Tues; 1.30–5. Wed; 1.30–8. Thur & Fri; 1.30–6. Sat; 10–5. (Sun, Jun–Oct; 1–4 and Nov–Dec; 1–3). *Closed* Bank Hols. Adm 80p, annual pass £2. Chld/OAPs and UB40s 40p, annual pass £1. School parties free. Parties welcome weekday mornings by arrangement. Public car park nearby. Suitable for disabled persons, no wheelchairs available.

THE OCTAGON, ORLEANS HOUSE GALLERY
Telephone: 01-892 0221 &
(London Borough of Richmond upon Thames)

The magnificent Octagon built by James Gibbs circa 1720. An outstanding example of the baroque, with adjacent art gallery situated in attractive woodland garden.
Location: Access from Richmond Road (A305).
Stations: St Margaret's (½ m); Twickenham (½ m).
Opening Times: Tues to Sats 1–5.30 (Oct to Mar, 1–4.30); Suns 2–5.30 (Oct to Mar, 2–4.30). Easter, Spring, Summer Bank Hols 2–5.30. *Closed Christmas.* Adm free.

WESTSIDE GALLERY
317 Upper Richmond Road West, East Sheen SW14 8QR. Tel: 01-878 6209.
A distinctively different modern gallery showing contemporary work of the finest quality from many well known British artists and craftsmen. Approximately 8 individual exhibitions a year. Always on show – paintings, etchings, ceramics, jewellery, sculpture, woodwork, metalwork, glass, silks . . . All work is for sale. Open Mon–Sat 9.30–5.30. Adm free. Coffee bar.

SOUTHWARK

BANKSIDE GALLERY
(Blackfriars tube). 48 Hopton Street, Blackfriars, SE1 9JH. Tel: 01-928 7521.
Royal Society of Painters in Water-Colours and the Royal Society of Painter-Etchers and Engravers. Spring and Autumn Exhibitions plus open exhibitions and Contemporary and Historical Exhibitions from Britain and abroad. Tues 10–8; Wed–Sat 10–5; Sun 1–5. *Closed* Mon. For further details telephone the above number.

CUMING MUSEUM *(London Borough of Southwark)*
155–157 Walworth Road, SE17 1RS. Tel: 01-703 3324/5529.
History of Southwark and district. Local collection includes: Roman, medieval and post-medieval objects from archaeological excavations. Dickensian Marshalsea Prison pump and Dog and Pot shop sign, examples of George Tinworth's modelling. Collection of London superstitions. Weekdays 10–5.30 (Thurs 10–7; Sat 10–5). *Closed* Sun.

THE DESIGN MUSEUM AT BUTLER'S WHARF
(The Conran Foundation)
Shad Thames, SE1. Tel: 01-403 6933.
Opening in Summer 1989, the Design Museum will house an international study collection, a review of new products and a gallery for temporary exhibitions. Facilities include a library, lecture theatre and members scheme. Suitable for disabled persons.

DULWICH COLLEGE
Telephone: 01-693 3737

Founded in 1619 Dulwich College is uniquely fortunate in its position, combining the green and spacious surroundings of its estate and excellent communications with Central London. The College offers a new and unusual venue for conferences, receptions, product launches, theatre rehearsals, concerts and filming.
Location: The College grounds are bordered by the South Circular A205, and provide parking for up to 500 cars. West Dulwich main line station is a leisurely ten minute walk from the grounds.
Opening Times: The College is open throughout the year although some facilities are limited during normal school terms. You are cordially invited to see Dulwich College at first hand by telephoning the Bursar's Office (01) 693 3737, for an appointment and any further information you require.
Refreshments: Full catering facilities are available for groups from 20 to 600.

DULWICH PICTURE GALLERY
College Road SE21 7BG. Tel: 01-693 5254.
Recorded Information 01-693 8000.
England's oldest public art gallery. Outstanding collection of Old Masters including paintings by Rembrandt, Rubens, Canaletto, Gainsborough etc. and many Dutch pictures in historic gallery designed by Sir John Soane. *See Diary for special exhibitions.* Tues to Sat 10–1, 2–5; Sun 2–5. *Closed* Mon.

H.M.S. BELFAST
Morgans Lane, off Tooley Street SE1 2JH. Tel: 01-407 6434.
This 11,500 ton cruiser, which is now part of the Imperial War Museum, is permanently moored in the Pool of London as a floating naval museum. During the Second World War the *Belfast* was one of the most powerful cruisers afloat in and took part in the last battleship action in European waters. She is the first warship since H.M.S. *Victory* to be preserved for the nation. Open daily: summer 11–5.50; winter 11–4.30. *Closed* Christmas Eve, Christmas Day, Boxing Day. Adm charge. Special rates for parties, Students, Families, OAPs and Unemployed. Access – Tooley Street. Nearest Underground: London Bridge and Tower Hill. Ferry from Tower Pier in summer (Mar 20 to Oct 31) and at weekends in winter (Nov 1 to Mar 19).

KATHLEEN & MAY *(The Maritime Trust)*
Cathedral Street SE1 9DE. Tel: 01-403 3965.
Britain's last remaining wooden 3-masted topsail schooner (1900) is afloat in St. Mary Overy Dock near Southwark Cathedral. Coastal sailing trade exhibition on board. Open daily throughout the year 10–5. *Closed* Christmas Day and New Year's Day. Adm charge. Party rates.

LIVESEY MUSEUM *(London Borough of Southwark)*
682 Old Kent Road, SE15 1JR. Tel: 01-639 5604.
Changing exhibitions of local and general interest. Mon to Sat 10–5.

ROYAL SOCIETY OF PAINTER-ETCHERS AND ENGRAVERS
Bankside Gallery, 48 Hopton Street, Blackfriars, SE1 9JH. Tel: 01-928 7521
Contemporary Print Exhibitions. Spring (Open Exhibition) and Autumn (Members' Exhibition): Tues 10–8; Wed–Sat 10–5; Sun 1–5. *Closed* Mon.

ROYAL SOCIETY OF PAINTERS IN WATERCOLOURS
Bankside Gallery, 48 Hopton Street, Blackfriars, SE1 9JH. Tel: 01-928 7521
Contemporary Watercolour Exhibitions. Spring and Autumn plus Summer Open Exhibition of Contemporary British Watercolours: Tues 10–8; Wed–Sat 10–5; Sun 1–5. *Closed* Mon.

THE SHAKESPEARE GLOBE MUSEUM
1 Bear Gardens, S.E.1. Tel: 01-620 0202.
Permanent exhibition covering London theatre 1576–1642, including full-size replica 1616 stage and plans for the International Shakespeare Globe Centre's reconstruction of Globe Theatre. May–Oct: Mon to Sat 10–5, Sun 1.30–5.30. Nov–Apr: Mon to Sat 10.30–4.30, Sun 1.30–5.30. Adm charge.

SOUTH LONDON ART GALLERY *(London Borough of Southwark)*
Peckham Road, SE5 8UH. Tel: 01-703 6120.
Temporary exhibitions. Permanent collection not on show. Reference collection of 20th century prints. Tues to Sat 10–6; Sun 3–6. *Closed* Mon.

SUTTON

LITTLE HOLLAND HOUSE
(London Borough of Sutton)

The home of Frank Dickinson (1874–1961), follower of the Arts and Crafts movement: artist, designer and craftsman in wood and metal who built the house himself to his own design and in pursuance of his philosophy and theories. Features his interior design, painting, hand-made furniture and other craft objects.
Location: 40 Beeches Avenue, Carshalton. On B278 (off A232).
Station: Carshalton Beeches.
Opening Times: Mar to Oct—first Sun in the month plus Bank Hol Suns & Mons in that period 12–6. Adm free.

WHITEHALL
Telephone: 01-643 1236
(London Borough of Sutton)

Timber-framed house built c 1500. Features exposed sections of original fabric; and displays including medieval Cheam pottery; Nonsuch Palace; timber-framed buildings; and Cheam School.
Location: 1 Malden Road; on A2043 nr Cheam village crossroads; just N of junction with A232.
Station: Cheam (¼ m).
Opening Times: Apr to Sept—Tues to Fris. Sun 2–5.30. Sat 10–5.30. Oct to Mar—Wed, Thurs, Sun 2–5.30. Sat 10–5.30. Also open Bank Holiday Mons 2–5.30. *Closed Dec 24 to Jan 2 incl.* Adm 50p (under 18 years, 25p). Party bookings & guided tour facilities.
Refreshments: Home-made Refreshments.

TOWER HAMLETS

BETHNAL GREEN MUSEUM OF CHILDHOOD
(A branch of the Victoria and Albert Museum)
Cambridge Heath Road, E2 9PA. Tel: 01-981 1711.
The Museum is notable for its collections of toys, games, dolls and dolls' houses and children's costumes. Also wedding dresses; Spitalfields silks (once a local industry). Mon to Thurs and Sat 10–6; Sun 2.30–6. *Closed* Fri and Christmas Eve, Christmas Day, Boxing Day, New Year's Day and May Day Bank Holiday.

THE HERALDS' MUSEUM AT THE TOWER OF LONDON
Tower of London, E.C.3.
This Museum, first opened in 1980 by the College of Arms Trust, traces the development of heraldry through the ages. On show are manuscripts, a herald in full fig, jewellery, arms, china and paintings – all showing the application of heraldry from medieval times until the present day. Entrance is included in the admission fee to the Tower of London. Apr to Sept: Weekdays 9.30–5.30; Sun 2–5.15. *Closed* Good Friday.

ROYAL ARMOURIES
(The National Museum of Arms and Armour)
HM Tower of London, EC3N 4AB. Tel: 01-480 6358.
Britain's oldest national museum, the Royal Armouries, still in its original home at the Tower of London, houses one of the finest collections of arms and armour in the world. The White Tower houses European armours and weapons from the Dark Ages to the 17th century, including the armours of Henry VIII, Charles I, and Charles II. The Waterloo Barracks houses the Oriental Armoury, including fine Japanese and Indian armours and the famous elephant armour. The New Armouries houses the British Military Armoury, and a new display bringing the story of arms and armour up to the present century. The Bowyer Tower houses the block and axe and other instruments of torture and punishment. Mar to Oct: Mon to Sat 9.30–5.45; Sun 2–5.45. Nov to Feb: Mon to Sat 9.30–5.45; *closed* Sun. Underground: Circle and District lines to Tower Hill. Bus routes: 15, 42, 78. Riverboat: to Tower Pier.

TOWER OF LONDON
(Dept of the Environment)
Dating from Norman times. Historical relics, armouries, dungeons. Crown jewels.
Location: On N bank of Thames above Tower Bridge.
Stations: London Bridge (¾ m); Fenchurch Street (¼ m); Cannon Street (½ m) (Mons to Fris); Liverpool St (¾ m); Moorgate (1 m). (Underground) Tower Hill.
Opening Times: All the year. Mar to Oct—Weekdays 9.30–5, Suns 2–5; Nov to Feb—Weekdays 9.30–4. *Closed Suns Nov to Feb also Good Fri, Dec 24, 25, 26 & Jan 1.* Adm charge. Enquiries 01-709 0765.

WHITECHAPEL ART GALLERY
80–82 Whitechapel High Street, E1 7QX. Tel: 01-377 0107.
A purpose-built gallery opened 1901 to the design of Charles Harrison Townsend and refurbished in 1985. Organises major exhibitions, generally of modern and contemporary art; no permanent collection. An extensive community education programme for adults and children – public tours, lectures, workshops, audio-visual programmes and studio visits. Cafe, lecture theatre, bookshop. *Closed* Mon and Bank Hols. Full access for people with disabilities. Tues to Sun 11–5 (Wed to 8). Adm free.

WALTHAM FOREST

EPPING FOREST MUSEUM *(Corporation of London)*
Queen Elizabeth's Hunting Lodge, Chingford, E.4.
The history of the forest and its wildlife displayed in an ancient timberframed hunting grandstand. Wed to Sun 2–6. Adm 25p, accompanied Chld free.

VESTRY HOUSE MUSEUM *(London Borough of Waltham Forest)*
Vestry Road, Walthamstow, E17 9NH.
Tel: 01-527 5544, Ext. 4391 or 509 1917.
A local history museum housed in an early eighteenth century workhouse in the Walthamstow Village Conservation Area. The permanent displays illustrate aspects of past life in Waltham Forest and include displays of costume and local domestic life, a reconstructed Victorian parlour, a nineteenth century police cell, the Bremer Car, c.1894, etc. Temporary exhibition programme throughout the year. Vestry House also serves as the base for Waltham Forest's Archives and Local History Library. Open Mon to Fri 10–1, 2–5.30; Sat 10–1, 2–5. Adm free. Group visits by prior appointment. Special facilities for schools by arrangement. Nearest station: Walthamstow Central (Victoria Line).

WILLIAM MORRIS GALLERY
(London Borough of Waltham Forest)
Water House, Lloyd Park, Forest Road, Walthamstow, E17 4PP.
Tel: 01-527 5544, Ext. 4390.
Eighteenth century house, the boyhood home of William Morris. Collections include textiles, wallpapers, designs etc. by Morris, the Pre-Raphaelites and contemporaries. The Frank Brangwyn collection of pictures and sculpture by 19th century and other artists and by the donor. Study collection and reference library by appointment. Tues to Sat 10–1, 2–5 (or dusk if earlier). Also first Sun in each month 10–12, 2–5 (or dusk if earlier). *Closed* Mon and all Public Hols. Adm free.

WANDSWORTH

DE MORGAN FOUNDATION
Telephone: 01-788 1341
(De Morgan Foundation)

A substantial part of the De Morgan Foundation collection of ceramics by William De Morgan and paintings and drawings by Evelyn De Morgan (nee Pickering), her uncle Roddam Spencer Stanhope, J. M. Strudwick and Cadogan Cowper are displayed in the ground floor rooms of elegantly restored Old Battersea House – a Wren building. The setting is that of a privately occupied house. The guided tour usually includes a visit to nearby old Battersea Church.
Location: Vicarage Crescent, Battersea.
Opening Times: Admission by appointment only – usually Weds afternoons. Adm 50p, optional catalogue £1. No special reductions. Parties – maximum 30 (split into two groups of 15). Car parking in Vicarage Crescent. Suitable for disabled, (no special facilities for wheelchairs) front steps are the only obstacle. Adm by writing in advance to agent.
Refreshments: No catering at house. Many facilities in Battersea/Wandsworth.

WANDSWORTH MUSEUM *(London Borough of Wandsworth)*
Disraeli Road, Putney SW15 2DR. Tel: 01-871 7074.
Wandsworth's new museum tells the fascinating story of the Thames-side towns of Battersea, Putney and Wandsworth, the water-powered industries of the river Wandle, the farms and country villas of Balham, Tooting and Roehampton – and their transformation into bustling London suburbs. Open Mon, Tue, Wed, Fri and Sat 1–5. Group visits welcomed but please book in advance. Admission free. Nearest stations: Putney (BR) and East Putney (Underground).

WESTMINSTER

APSLEY HOUSE
Telephone: 01-499 5676
(Trustees of the Victoria & Albert Museum)

Built 1771–8, the Iron Duke's London Palace housing his famous collection of paintings, porcelain, silver and personal relics.
Location: At 149 Piccadilly, Hyde Park Corner.
Opening Times: All the year—Daily (except Mons) 11–5. Open Bank Hol Mons (except May 1). Adm £2, Chd (under 16), OAPs £1. *Closed Good Friday also Christmas Eve, Christmas Day, Boxing Day and New Year's Day.*
Refreshments: Coffee shop and new basement gallery opening '89.

BANQUETING HOUSE
Telephone: 01-930 4179
(Department of Environment)

Built 1619–22 to design of Inigo Jones. Painted ceilings by Rubens. Used for Court ceremonies, masques and banquets, and as s chapel from 1724 to 1890.
Location: Whitehall SW1A 2ER.
Opening Times: Open all year, Tues to Sat 10–5, Sun 2–5, *except Jan 1, Dec 24–26, Good Friday and Mons.* Adm 80p, OAPs 60p, Chd 40p (under 5, free). 10% discount for parties of 11 or more. Applications for free educational visits. Parking in NCP Car Park, Trafalgar Square. Unsuitable for disabled persons; no wheelchairs available.

THE BLEWCOAT SCHOOL, The National Trust
Telephone: 01-222 2877

Built in 1709 at the expense of William Green, a local brewer, to provide an education for poor children; in use as a school until 1926, the building was bought by the Trust in 1954; it was restored in 1975 and now houses a National Trust shop and information centre.
Location: No 23 Caxton Street, Westminster, SW1.
Stations: Victoria. ¼ m; Underground St James's Park (Circle and District Lines) less than 100 yards.
Opening Times: All year, Mon to Fri 10–5.30; late night shopping Thurs until 7. *Closed Bank Holiday Mondays, Dec 25–31, Jan 1 & 2 and Good Friday.* Adm free.

BRITISH DENTAL ASSOCIATION MUSEUM
(Smith Turner Historical Collection)
63–64 Wimpole Street, W1M 8AL. Tel: 01-935 0875.
Collection illustrating the history of dental surgery. By appointment only.

BUCKINGHAM PALACE, THE QUEEN'S GALLERY
Buckingham Palace Road, S.W.1.
Special annual exhibition. Tues to Sat and Bank Hol Mons 10.30–5; Sun 2–5. Adm £1.20, Chld, Students, Disabled and OAPs 60p.

CABINET WAR ROOMS
(administered by the Imperial War Museum)
Clive Steps, King Charles Street, SW1A 2AQ. Tel: 01-930 6961.
The Cabinet War Rooms comprise the most important surviving part of the underground emergency accommodation which was provided to protect Winston Churchill, the War Cabinet and the Chiefs of Staff of Britain's armed forces against air attacks during the Second World War. Situated in the basement of the Government Offices, Great George Street, beneath a slab of protective concrete the Rooms were in operational use from August 27 1939 to the Japanese surrender in 1945. The suite of 21 historic rooms include the Cabinet

Room, the Transatlantic Telephone Room from which Churchill could speak directly to President Roosevelt in the White House, the Map Room where information about operations on all fronts was collected and the Prime Minister's Room which served as Churchill's emergency office and bedroom until the end of the war. Daily 10–5.50 Last adm 5.15. *Closed* New Year's Day, Christmas Eve, Christmas Day and Boxing Day. Adm £2.80, Chld (5–16 years)/OAPs, fulltime students and Registered Unemployed £1.50. Organised parties of 20 or more entitled to group reduction. Underground: Westminster. Bus: 3, 11, 12, 24, 29, 53, 70, 77, 77a, 109, 159, 170, 172, 184, T6 (Mon to Sat only).

CANADA HOUSE GALLERY *(Michael Regan – Visual Arts Officer)*
Trafalgar Square, SW1Y 5BJ. Tel: 01-629 9492, Ext 246.
Changing exhibitions of Canadian art, craft and design. Mon to Fri 11–5. *Closed* Bank Hols. Adm free. Suitable for disabled persons.

CHAPTER HOUSE AND PYX CHAMBER
WESTMINSTER ABBEY

Described as 'incomparable' when it was finished in 1253, with some of the finest of English medieval sculpture, the chapter house was one of the largest in England and could seat 80 monks around its walls. It was converted to a record office in the 16th century, but by 1740 the roof had decayed and been removed. Restoration of the whole building took place in 1865 and again after it was bombed in 1941. The 11th century Pyx Chamber now houses the Abbey Treasures. A joint ticket admits to the Abbey Museum.
Location: East side of the abbey cloister.
Opening Times: Good Friday to Sept 30, daily 10–6; Oct 1 to Maundy Thursday, daily 10–4. *Closed Christmas and New Year.* Adm £1.50, OAPs 75p, Chd 40p.

THE CRAFTS COUNCIL
12 Waterloo Place, Lower Regent Street. Tel: 01-930 4811.
Gallery with changing exhibition throughout the year. Tues to Sat 10–5; Sun 2–5. Information Centre provides data on craft courses, shops, publications and craftspeople, Index of makers; and slide library; Bookstall.

THE CRICKET MEMORIAL GALLERY *(Marylebone Cricket Club)*
Lord's Ground, NW8 8QN.
Contains new displays illustrating the history of cricket. Match days (Mon to Sat) 10.30–5. Conducted tours and admission at other times by prior arrangement. Adm charge. Ground adm also payable on match days.

ANTHONY D'OFFAY GALLERY
9 & 23 Dering Street, W1R 9AA. Tel: 01-499 4100.
Exhibitions of International Contemporary Art and 20th century British Art.

FABIAN CARLSSON GALLERY
(Chairman: Fabian Carlsson, M. Director: Clive Adams)
160 New Bond Street, W1Y 0HR. Tel: 01-409 0619.
Private gallery currently dealing in Contemporary and Modern Art by important British, European and American artists and representing the work of Hughie O'Donoghue, Michael Porter, Lance Smith, Andy Goldsworthy, Vincent Woropay, Mon to Fri 10–6; Sat 10–1. *Closed* Bank Hols. Suitable for disabled persons.

THE GUARDS MUSEUM
Wellington Barracks, Birdcage Walk, next to Buckingham Palace.
Tel: 01-930 4466. Ext 3271.
The story of the five Regiments of Foot Guards over three hundred years. Open daily except Friday from 10 to 4. Adm £2, Chld, OAPs and ExGuardsmen (and groups of 10 or more on application) £1. School groups on application 50p; family ticket (2 adults and 2 chld) £4.

'GUINNESS WORLD OF RECORDS'
The Trocadero Centre, Piccadilly Circus, W.1. Tel: 01-439 7331.
The unique exhibition that brings to life thousands of the spectacular facts and feats from the world famous book. Superlative achievements are re-created through breath-taking displays, life-size models, video and multi-screen computers. Open 10–10 seven days a week except Christmas Day.

THE LONDON TOY AND MODEL MUSEUM
23 Craven Hill, W2. (entrance 21 Craven Hill). Tel: 01-262 9450/7905.
Extensive permanent display of commercially made model trains, mechanical toys and nursery items based on two world famous collections and housed in a fine Victorian building. Working trains including garden railway. Bookshop and cafeteria. Changing exhibitions. Tues to Sat 10–5.30; Sun 11–5.30. *Closed* Mon (except Bank Hols). Adm charge. Party rates by arrangement.

LONDON TRANSPORT MUSEUM
Covent Garden, WC2E 7BB. Tel: 01-379 6344.
Horse buses, motor buses, trams, trolleybuses and Underground rolling stock plus unique working exhibits illustrate the fascinating story of the development of London's urban transport systems and their impact on the people who travel in the capital. Daily 10–6 (last admission 5.15). *Closed* Dec 24, 25 and 26. Free admission to Museum Shop. Adm charge. Reduced prices for Chld (5–16 years), OAPs, UB40s, Party rates for groups of 20 or more. Underground stations: Covent Garden, Leicester Square, Charing Cross or Holborn. Bus: to Aldwych or Strand.

MALL GALLERIES *(Federation of British Artists)*
The Mall, SW1Y 5BD. Tel: 01-930 6844.
Annual exhibitions of London'a leading Art Societies and many 'one man' shows. Exhibitions change every 2 to 3 weeks. Daily 10–5.

MARTYN GREGORY
34 Bury Street, St. James's, SW1Y 6AU. Tel: 01-839 3731.
British watercolours and paintings. Pictures relating to China and the Far East.

MATTHIESEN FINE ART
7–8 Mason's Yard, Duke Street, St. James's, SW1. Tel: 01-930 2437.
Specialising in Italian, Spanish and French Old Master paintings, 19th and 20th century paintings and sculpture.

MICHAEL FARADAY'S LABORATORY AND MUSEUM
(The Royal Institution)
The Royal Institution of Great Britain, 21 Albemarle Street, W1X 4BS.
Tel: 01-409 2992.
The Laboratory, where many of the most important discoveries were made, has been restored to the form it was known to have in 1845. An adjacent museum houses a unique collection of original apparatus arranged to illustrate the more significant aspects of Faraday's contribution to the advancement of science. Tues and Thurs 1–4. Parties at other times by arrangement. Adm 40p, Chld 20p.

MUSEUM OF MANKIND
6 Burlington Gardens, W1X 2EX. Tel: 01-437 2224.
(Ethnography Department of the British Museum.) Weekdays 10–5; Sun 2.30–6. Underground stations: Piccadilly Circus, Green Park.

THE NATIONAL GALLERY
Trafalgar Square, WC2N 5DN. Tel: 01-839 3321. Rec. Info: 01-839 3526.
The Nation's outstanding permanent collection of European painting from c. 1200–1900, including works by Leonardo, Rembrandt, Constable and Cézanne. Exhibitions centred on specific aspects of the Collection, plus an excellent Education service offering quizzes, audio-visual shows and lectures for adults and children. Mon to Sat 10–6; Sun 2–6. Adm free. *Closed* Good Friday, May Day, Christmas Eve, Christmas Day, Boxing Day and New Year's Day. Restaurant Mon to Sat 10–5; Sun 2–5. Shop Mon to Sat 10–5.40; Sun 2–5.40.

NATIONAL PORTRAIT GALLERY
St. Martin's Place, Trafalgar Square, WC2H 0EH. Tel: 01-930 1552.
Portraits of the famous in British history and culture: poets and princesses; statesmen and sportsmen; artists and actresses; explorers and astronomers on display in paintings, sculpture drawings, miniatures and photographs. Mon to Fri 10–5; Sat 10–6; Sun 2–6. *Closed* Dec 24–26, Jan 1, Good Friday, May 1. Admission free. Nearest tube: Embankment, Leicester Square.

THE NATIONAL SOUND ARCHIVE OF THE BRITISH LIBRARY
29 Exhibition Road SW7 2AS. Tel: 01-589 6603/4.
The national repository for sound recordings of all kinds from wax cylinders to compact discs. A copy of almost every disc commercially issued in the UK is deposited here and this is the main public access point to the BBC Sound Archives. Also available for reference listening, 25 years of theatre recordings from Britain's major subsidised theatres. Free public listening and video viewing, full reference library – the Archive is essentially a research centre with a permanent display of old gramophones of interest to the casual visitor. Mon to Fri 9.30–4.30. Late opening till 9 on Thurs. Admission free. Car parking in Kensington Gardens.

PUBLIC RECORD OFFICE MUSEUM
Chancery Lane, WC2.

ROYAL ACADEMY OF ARTS
Piccadilly, W1V 0DS. Tel: 01-439 7438.
Major loan exhibitions in 1989 include Italian Art in the 20th century and The Art of Photography, with the annual Summer Exhibition from May to Aug. Open daily 10–6 (including Sun). Restaurant and Gallery Shop open daily to the public. Picture framing service available.

ROYAL COLLEGE OF MUSIC DEPARTMENT OF PORTRAITS
Prince Consort Road, South Kensington, SW7 2BS. Tel: 01-589 3643.
An extensive collection of portraits of musicians, comprising some 200 original portraits and many thousands of prints and photographs. Also houses the College's important collection of concert programmes. During term-time: Mon to Fri *by appointment.* Adm free. Parties by arrangement. Keeper of Portraits: Oliver Davies.

ROYAL COLLEGE OF MUSIC MUSEUM OF INSTRUMENTS
Prince Consort Road, South Kensington, SW7 2BS. Tel: 01-589 3643.
Over 500 keyboard, stringed and wind instruments from c. 1480 to the present, including the Donaldson, Tagore, Hipkins and Ridley Collections. Open on Mon and Wed during term-time, 11–4.30: parties and special visits by appointment with the Curator. Adm charge.

ROYAL COMMISSION ON THE HISTORICAL MONUMENTS OF ENGLAND
(National Monuments Record)
Fortress House, 23 Savile Row, W1X 2JQ. Tel: 01-734 6010.
National archive of photographs, documents and information on archaeological sites and historic buildings in England. Organized in three sections: Archaeological Records, Aerial Photography and Architecture. Arranged topographically for reference and study, it is expanding considerably. Mon to Fri 10–5.

ROYAL MEWS *(Her Majesty The Queen)*
Buckingham Palace Road, SW1W 0QH.
Royal horses and equipages. Wed and Thur 2–4 (not Ascot week in June). Adm charge.

SERPENTINE GALLERY *(Arts Council)*
Kensington Gardens, W2 3XA. Tel: 01-402 6075.
Tel: 01-723 9072, Recorded Information.
Monthly exhibitions of contemporary art. Opening times during exhibitions: Apr to Oct: Mon to Fri 10–6; Sat and Sun 10–7. Nov to Mar: Daily 10 to dusk. Free. *Closed* between exhibitions. Underground: Central to Lancaster Gate; Circle, District and Piccadilly to South Kensington; Piccadilly to Knightsbridge. Bus to the Albert Hall 9, 52, 73.

TATE GALLERY
Millbank, SW1P 4RG. Tel: 01-821 1313, Recorded Information 01-821 7128.
The National collections of British painting (from the 16th century up to about 1900) and 20th century painting and sculpture (British and foreign, from Impressionism to the present day). Special collections of Turner (in the Clore Gallery), Blake, the Pre-Raphaelites and a large collection of contemporary prints. Free lectures, films and guided tours; special activities for children at holiday periods. There is a continuous programme of temporary exhibitions and special displays. Disabled visitors welcomed. Mon to Sat 10–5.50; Sun 2–5.50. *Closed* New Year's Day, Good Friday, May Day, Christmas Eve, Christmas Day and Boxing Day. Licensed Restaurant and Coffee Shop. Gallery Shop.

THEATRE MUSEUM
Old Flower Market, Covent Garden. Tel: 01-836 7891.
The Theatre Museum in the old Flower Market in London's Covent Garden – Britain's first national museum of the performing arts – houses one of the world's richest collections of theatrical material. As well as the permanent gallery which traces the history of theatre, puppetry and pop, ballet and dance, circus and opera from the time of Shakespeare to the present day, there are also two temporary exhibition galleries. The museum has a theatrical paintings gallery, its own studio theatre, a licensed cafe, a shop and its own Box Office where tickets for London shows, concerts and other events may be purchased. Library and study facilities are available by appointment. Galleries Tue to Sun 11–7. Shop, Cafe and Box Office Tues to Sat 11–8. Sun 11–7. *Closed* every Mon. £2.25, Students, OAPs, UB40 holders and Chld aged 5 to 14 £1.25, Chld under 5 and Friends of the V&A free. School parties (pre-booked only) free.

THE TRAVELLERS' CLUB
Telephone: 01-930 8688 *(by prior appointment)*
Built in 1829-33 by Sir Charles Barry. (Roof restored in 1986).
Location: 106 Pall Mall.
Station: Piccadilly Circus Underground.
Opening Times: By prior appointment Mon and Fri only (except from 5th to 30th January when inclusive of Tues to Thurs) from 10–12 and 2–5. *Closed Bank Hols, Aug and Christmas.* Adm £5.

WALLACE COLLECTION
Hertford House, Manchester Square, W1M 6BN. Tel: 01-935 0687.
A National Museum. The collection consists of paintings of the French, Spanish, Italian, Flemish, Dutch and British Schools, Miniatures, sculpture, French furniture, European and Oriental arms and armour, goldsmiths' work, ceramics and other works of art bequeathed to the nation by Lady Wallace in 1897. Mon to Sat 10–5; Sun 2–5. *Closed* Christmas Eve, Christmas Day, Boxing Day, New Year's Day, Good Friday and May 1.

WESTMINSTER ABBEY MUSEUM
(Dean and Chapter of Westminster)
London. Tel: 01-222 5152.
Museum housed in magnificent Norman Undercroft. The Abbey's famous collection of Royal and other effigies forms centrepiece of the exhibition. Other items on display include replicas of Coronation regalia and surviving panels of medieval glass. Open daily 10.30–4. Adm £1.20; students 60p; Chd/OAP 30p *(includes adm to Chapter House and Treasury).*

WHITFORD & HUGHES *(A. A. Mibus/D. W. Hughes)*
6 Duke Street, St. James's. Tel: 01-930 9332.
Fine paintings 1880–1940, Post-impressionist, Symbolist, Modernist, Salon and Academy, Belle Epoque. Mon to Fri 10–6. *Closed* Bank Hols.

LEIGHTON HOUSE
MUSEUM AND ART GALLERY

High Victorian paintings and sculpture by Lord Leighton and his contemporaries, who created the remarkable Artists' Colony of studios centred around Leighton House, the earliest and most opulent aesthetic interior in London, currently the subject of restoration to its original splendour. Open free throughout the year. Monday to Saturday 11 a.m.–5 p.m. (until 6 p.m. Monday to Friday during temporary exhibitions).

Administered by The Royal Borough of Kensington and Chelsea Libraries and Arts Service, 12 Holland Park Road W14 8LZ. Tel. 01-602 3316.

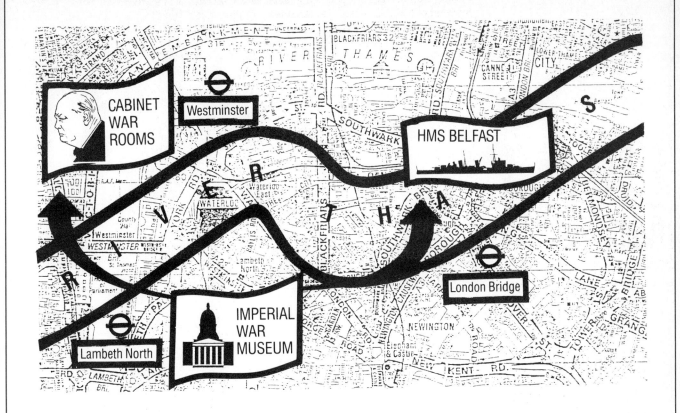

IMPERIAL WAR MUSEUM

IMPERIAL WAR MUSEUM
The story of war in our century
New Museum opens 30 June 1989. Admission charged
Information
01-735 8922   01-820 1683

HMS BELFAST
London's floating naval museum
Information
01-407 6434

CABINET WAR ROOMS
Churchill's secret underground HQ
Information
01-930 6961

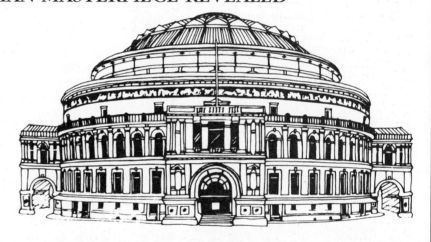

THE *Historical* LONDON CONNECTION

...have you made it?

Nearest tube stations:
St Paul's, Moorgate,
Barbican (closed Sunday)

Buses:
Museum of London: 4, 141,
279a, 502
St Paul's: 6, 8, 9, 9a,
11, 15, 22, 25, 501, 513

Car Park:
NCP in Barbican Centre

Open Tuesday to Saturday
10.00am to 6.00pm
Sunday 2.00pm to 6.00pm.
Closed every Monday

Licensed restaurant

Museum shop

THE MUSEUM OF · LONDON ·

Museum of London
London Wall
London EC2Y 5HN

01-600 3699 x 240/280

Admission FREE

Museum of the Moving Image

Visit the world's most exciting cinema and television museum.

Discover the history and magic of moving images – from Chinese shadow puppets to modern animation; from Charlie Chaplin to newsreading in a television studio – all at the Museum of the Moving Image.

Opening Hours:
Tuesday – Saturday   10am – 8pm
Sunday & Bank Holidays   10am – 6pm
Closed Mondays

Address:
South Bank Centre, Waterloo,
London SE1 8XT
Telephone: 01-401 2636

Nearest Undergrounds:
Waterloo or Embankment

MOMI is a part of the British Film Institute.

BRITISH FILM INSTITUTE
bfi

William III paid £14,000 for Kensington Palace in 1689. Today you can view the property for considerably less.

IF it hadn't been for William III's asthma, Kensington Palace might not have been, because the damp Thames air surrounding Whitehall Palace, combined with the dirt and smell drove William III and Mary II out of central London.

Grinling Gibbons' wood carvings can be seen throughout the panelled William and Mary State Apartments.

King's Gallery

It was at Kensington Palace that Queen Victoria was reputed to have been born, in the North Drawing Room. Many of the rooms have been restored to their Victorian splendour.

Indeed, you can view two of Queen Victoria's formal gowns in the dazzling Court Dress Collection together with the wedding dress worn by Her Royal Highness The Princess of Wales on July 29th, 1981.

So visit Kensington Palace soon. You'll come away thinking it to be exceptionally good value.

William III thought so.

HOW TO GET THERE:
Nearest Tube: High Street Kensington
(District & Circle), Queensway (Central).
Nearest Bus route: 9, 49, 52, 52a, 73, C1.

HOURS OF OPENING:
Open all year Mon-Sat 09.00-17.00.
Sun 13.00-17.00.
Closed 24-26 Dec, 1 Jan, Good Friday.

ADMISSION CHARGE
ROYAL PARKS & PALACES
An experience you'll always treasure

Thanks to Charles I
you can feast your eyes on the Rubens ceiling of the Banqueting House.

THE Banqueting House in Whitehall was commissioned by James I after the previous Banqueting House had burnt down.

Designed by Inigo Jones and started in 1619, the new Hall was part of Whitehall Palace and a favourite building of the King's son, Charles.

And the Great Hall in the Banqueting House was the perfect place for such occasions. The King would preside over the gatherings from his throne set on a platform at one end of the Hall called the Great Neech.

When Charles I came to the

Part of the Rubens ceiling

BANQUETING HOUSE
WHITEHALL

throne he commissioned Rubens, his father's favourite painter, to prepare a fitting tribute to James I at the Banqueting House.

This took the form of nine ceiling panels, a work that Rubens finished in 1634 for the princely sum of

£3000 and a gold chain. Ironically, he was brought back to his beloved Banqueting House to be executed on a scaffold erected outside.

Be sure to visit the Banqueting House soon and feast your eyes on Charles I's stunning legacy.

The Banqueting House

Merseyside

BIRKENHEAD

BIRKENHEAD PRIORY
Priory Street.
Remains of Benedictine Monastery established 1150 AD. Site open Mon to Sat 9.30–12.30, 1–4. Open Bank Holidays.

WILLIAMSON ART GALLERY & MUSEUM
(Wirral Borough Council, Department of Leisure Services & Tourism)
Slatey Road. Tel: 051-652 4177.
Fourteen galleries display valuable collections of British watercolours, British oil paintings including artists of the Liverpool School, Liverpool porcelain, Birkenhead Della Robbia Pottery. Museum displays include maritime and local history. Temporary exhibition programme presents constantly changing displays of all types. Mon to Sat 10–5 (Thurs 10–9); Sun 2–5. *Closed* Good Friday and Christmas Day. Adm free. Car parking. Suitable for disabled persons. One wheelchair available.

LIVERPOOL

CROXTETH HALL & COUNTRY PARK
Telephone: 051-228 5311

500 acre Country Park centred on the ancestral home of the Molyneux family, Earls of Sefton. Hall rooms with character figures on the theme of an Edwardian houseparty. Victorian Home Farm and Walled Garden both with quality interpretive displays; superb collection of farm animals (Approved Rare Breeds Centre). Miniature Railway. Special events and attractions most weekends. Picnic areas and play areas.
Location: 5 m NE of Liverpool City Centre; signposted from A580 & A5088 (ring road).
Opening Times: Parkland open daily throughout the year, adm free. Hall, Farm & Garden open 11–5 daily in main season, please telephone to check exact dates. Inclusive admission to Hall, Farm & Gardens; £2, Chd/OAPs £1 (provisional prices). Reduced rates for parties. Wheelchair access to Farm, Garden and Café but to ground floor only in Hall.
Refreshments: 'The Old Riding School' cafe during season.

DENTAL HOSPITAL MUSEUM
(School of Dental Surgery, Liverpool University)
Pembroke Place. Tel: 051-709 6022, Ext Dental School.
Dental pathology and collections of historical dental items. Available for members of profession and research workers on written application.

LARGE OBJECTS COLLECTION
(National Museums and Galleries on Merseyside)
Princes Dock L3 0AA. Tel: 051-207 0001.
Situated in a large transit shed, the museum has become a treasure house of the Liverpool Museum's largest objects. There are steam vehicles, tractors, lorries, old cars and space rockets as well as telescopes and vintage computers. There is also a Technology Testbed with experiments for children of all ages, and a coffee bar. Open from early Apr to late Oct 1989 daily 10–5. *Closed* Good Friday.

LIVERPOOL MUSEUM
(National Museums and Galleries on Merseyside)
William Brown Street, L3 8EN. Tel: 051-207 0001.
A selection from the magnificent collections presented to the Museum by Joseph Mayer in 1867 is on display, including Egyptian, Roman and Greek antiquities; Anglo-Saxon jewellery, fine porcelain, Limoges enamels, medieval and classical ivories. English silver, Liverpool pottery, Oriental antiquities and African masks and figures are among the other objects on display. Natural history displays, using the founding collections of the Earl of Derby, include a series of world habitats reconstructed with specimens, slides and sound. There is also a large aquarium. The basement gallery is devoted to the land transport of the Merseyside region including locomotives, an overhead railway coach, horse-drawn and steam road vehicles and various cycles. The PLANETARIUM provides a daily programme *(except Mon)* on astronomy and related themes. Associated displays illustrate the history of time-keeping and space exploration and include many outstanding objects. The history of the King's Regiment is featured in another gallery. A coffee bar is open Mon to Fri and special facilities are available for educational groups. Weekdays 10–5; Sun 2–5. *Closed* Christmas Eve, Christmas Day, Boxing Day, New Year's Day and Good Friday. Adm: voluntary contributions welcome; a small charge is made for the Planetarium.

MERSEYSIDE MARITIME MUSEUM
(National Museums and Galleries on Merseyside)
Albert Dock. Tel: 051-709 1551.
The Museum is located on the waterfront at the heart of Liverpool's historic docklands. This multi-acre site includes Albert Dock Warehouses, the Albert Pierhead complex, several small dock buildings and the two Canning Graving Docks. Visitors may tour the dry docked exhibition ship 'Edmund Gardner', a 170ft Liverpool Pilot Cutter. A large Boat Hall contains a variety of full size craft from the North West and workshops where maritime skills such as wooden boat restoration, are demonstrated. The Pilotage Building houses the Fort Belan exhibition of maritime artefacts encompassing 300 years of Liverpool and North Wales history. The Piermaster's house and working cooperage have been returned to their original appearance and function. In the basement of the Albert Dock Warehouse, a fascinating exhibition 'Emigrants to a New World' allows visitors to follow the story of the nine million people who emigrated through the Port of Liverpool between 1830 and 1930. Further exhibitions include Cargoes and Dockers, 'Builders of Great Ships', 'Liverpool – The Evolution of the Port', 'Safe Passage', and 'Art and the Sea'. The Museum has a Smorgasborg restaurant and waterfront café, gift shops and a car park. Open daily 10.30–5.30. Adm charge. *Closed* Dec 24, 25, 26 Jan 1 and Good Friday.

MUSEUM OF LABOUR HISTORY
(National Museums and Galleries on Merseyside)
Islington, Liverpool L3 8EE. Tel: 051-207 0001.
Opened in March 1986, in the former County Sessions House built in 1884, the Museum tells the story of working class life on Merseyside from 1840 to the present day. There is an introductory video programme, 'Merseyside – the People's Story' and displays on Employment, Housing – including a reconstructed Street and Scullery, Education – including a part reconstruction of an Edwardian Classroom, Leisure and Trade Unionism. A display of Trade Union banners can be seen in the main Court Room. Open Mon to Sat 10–5; Sun 2–5. Adm free. *Closed* Dec 24, 25, 26, Jan 1 and Good Friday.

SPEKE HALL, The National Trust
Telephone: 051-427 7231
Richly half-timbered Elizabethan house around a courtyard; features include Great Hall, Priest holes; Jacobean plasterwork and Victorian restoration and decoration. Attractive gardens and extensive woodlands.
Location: On N bank of Mersey 8 m from City centre.
Station: Garston (2 m); Hunts Cross (2 m).
Opening Times: Mar 25 to Nov 5 – daily except Mons, but open Bank Holiday Mons; Tues to Sat 1–5.30; Sun and Bank Holiday Mons 1–6, *closed Good Fri.* Nov 11 to Dec 17 – Sats & Suns 1–5. Adm £1.80. Discount for parties. Guided tours and school visits by prior arrangement with Administrator.
Refreshments: Tea room and shop.

SUDLEY ART GALLERY
(National Museums and Galleries on Merseyside)
Mossley Hill Road, Liverpool L18 8BX. Tel: 051-207 0001 Enquiries.
A fascinating collection of 18th and 19th century English paintings formed by Liverpool merchant George Holt, displayed at his house overlooking the Mersey and Welsh hills. It includes superb works by Gainsborough, Turner, Bonington and the Pre-Raphaelites. Mon to Sat 10–5; Sun 2–5. Adm free. *Closed* Dec 24, 25, 26, Jan 1 and Good Friday.

TATE GALLERY LIVERPOOL
Albert Dock L3 4BB. Tel: 051-709 3223. Information line 051-709 0507.
Open Tues to Sun, 11–7. Adm free.

UNIVERSITY OF LIVERPOOL ART GALLERY
3 Abercromby Square. Tel: 051-709 6022, Ext. 3170.
The Gallery contains a selection from the University's collections: sculpture; paintings, including works by Audubon and Wright of Derby; watercolours, including works by Turner; contemporary prints; furniture; porcelain and silver. Mon, Tues and Thurs 12–2; Wed and Fri 12–4. *Closed* Public Hols and Aug.

WALKER ART GALLERY
(National Museums and Galleries on Merseyside)
Liverpool L3 8EL. Tel: 051-207 0001.
A great collection of European Art from 1300 to the present day. The early Italian and Netherlandish and the British 19th century paintings are outstanding. There are works by Simone Martini, Ercole de Roberti, Poussin, Stubbs, Turner, the Pre-Raphaelites, the High Victorians and important temporary exhibitions are arranged. There is also a weekend coffee bar. Mon to Sat 10–5; Sun 2–5. *Closed* Dec 24, 25, 26, Jan 1 and Good Friday. Adm free.

PORT SUNLIGHT

LADY LEVER ART GALLERY
(National Museums and Galleries on Merseyside)
Port Sunlight Village, Wirral L62 5EQ. Tel: 051-645 3623.
An outstanding collection of English 18th century paintings and furniture, Chinese porcelain, Wedgwood pottery and Victorian paintings, formed by the first Viscount Leverhulme at the turn of the century as the centrepiece of his model village. Of special note is the series of superb carved or inlaid cabinets, some by Chippendale, and paintings by Reynolds, Wilson, Sargent, Burne-Jones and Leighton. Restaurant. Open Mon to Sat 10–5; Sun 2–5. *Closed* Dec 24, 25, 26, Jan 1 and Good Friday. Train services to Bebington.

PRESCOT

PRESCOT MUSEUM OF CLOCK AND WATCH-MAKING
(National Museums and Galleries on Merseyside and Knowsley Metropolitan Borough Council)
34 Church Street, L34 3LA. Tel: 051-430 7787.
Ten miles from the centre of Liverpool. A museum about the craft of clock and watch making in the South Lancashire area. See the tools used to make watches, what the old workshops were like and how the industry has changed. Changing exhibitions on the ground floor. Study facilities on application. Tues to Sat 10–5; Sun 2–5. *Closed* Mon (except Bank Hols), Christmas Eve, Christmas Day, Boxing Day, New Year's Day and Good Friday. Adm free.

ST. HELENS

MUSEUM AND ART GALLERY
*(St. Helens Metroplitan Borough Council. Community
Leisure Department)*
  College Street. Tel: (0744) 24061, Ext. 2959.
Social History and Period Rooms, Natural History, decorative arts, oils and
watercolours from the 19th and 20th centuries, plus changing exhibitions. Mon
to Fri 10–5; Sat 10–1.

PILKINGTON GLASS MUSEUM *(Pilkington P.L.C.)*
  Prescot Road. Tel: (0744) 692014.
The museum shows the evolution of glassmaking techniques. Mon to Fri 10–5;
Wed evening by arrangement; Sat, Sun and Bank Hols 2–4.30. *Closed* Christmas
to New Year. Schools and organised parties by prior arrangement with the
Curator.

SOUTHPORT

ATKINSON ART GALLERY *(Merseyside-Sefton Borough Council)*
  Lord Street. Tel: (0704) 33133, Ext. 2111.
Permanent collections include British art of the 18th, 19th and 20th centuries.
Oils, watercolours and sculpture. Contemporary prints. Old English glass and
Chinese porcelain. Continuous programme of temporary exhibitions. Mon,
Tues, Wed and Fri 10–5; Thurs and Sat 10–1. Adm free.

BOTANIC GARDENS MUSEUM
(Merseyside-Sefton Borough Council)
  Churchtown. Tel: (0704) 27547.
A small museum with interesting displays of local history (The Growth of
Southport), natural history, Victoriana, dolls and Liverpool porcelain. May to
Sept: Tues to Sat 10–6; Oct to Apr 10–5; Sun (all year) 2–5. *Closed* Mon. Open
Bank Hol Mons but *closed* Fri following. Adm free.

MEOLS HALL
(R. F. Hesketh Esq.)

A 17th century house, with subsequent additions, containing an interesting
collection of pictures, furniture, china, etc.
Location: 1 m N of Southport; 16 m SW of Preston; 20 m N of Liverpool; near
A565 & A570.
Stations: Southport (1¾ m); Meols Cop (1 m).
Opening Times: Mon May 29: 2–5; Aug 1–31: 2–5. Adm £1, Chd (accompanied
by adult) free.

STEAMPORT TRANSPORT MUSEUM
  Derby Road.

WALLASEY

WALLASEY MUSEUM & EXHIBITION CENTRE
  Central Library, Earlston Road.

SPEKE HALL
LIVERPOOL, MERSEYSIDE
THE NATIONAL TRUST

Elizabethan manor house including Great Hall, priest's holes, Victorian restoration and decorations. Extensive woodlands and gardens.
ADMISSION – SEE EDITORIAL REFERENCE

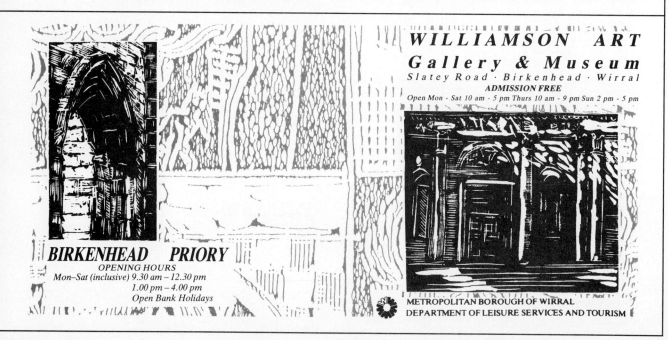

Norfolk

AYLSHAM

BLICKLING HALL, The National Trust
Telephone: Aylsham 733084 &

Great Jacobean house, altered 1765-70. State rooms include Peter the Great Room with fine Russian tapestry, Long Gallery with exceptional ceiling and State bedroom. Textile conservation workshop open to visitors Tues only 2–4. The Formal Garden design dates from 1729. Temple and Orangery, park and lake.

Location: 1½ m NW of Aylsham on N side of B1354 (which is 15 m N of Norwich on A140).
Opening Times: Hall & Gardens—Mar 25 to Oct 29 daily except Mons and Thurs 1–5; Closed Good Fri. Open Bank Hol Mons. Adm House and Garden: £3.50, Chd (with adult) £1.75. Pre-booked parties £3. Free car park. Shop. Dogs in Park & Picnic area only, on leads. Wheelchair access—2 provided. Lift to first floor.
Refreshments: Teas, coffee and lunches. Shop. Open 12–5. (*Parties by arrangement; table licence*). Picnic area in walled orchard. Restaurant, shop and garden open daily in July & Aug, 12–5.
NB Free access to the South Front, shop and restaurant when Hall is open.

BEESTON ST. LAWRENCE

BEESTON HALL
Telephone: (0692) 630771
(*Sir Ronald & Lady Preston*)

18th century 'Gothick' country house with Georgian interiors in picturesque setting.

Location: 2½ m NE of Wroxham on S side of A1151; 11 m NE of Norwich.
Station: Wroxham (2¾ m). Also accessible from Broads at Neatishead.
Opening Times: Principal Rooms, Gardens, Wine Cellars and Woodland Walks. Mar 26 to Sept 17—Fris & Suns, also Bank Hols 2–5.30. Aug also Weds. Adm £1.80, Chd (accompanied by adult) 60p, OAPs £1.50. Parties by arrangement. Free car park.
Refreshments: Teas and light refreshments in the Orangery.

BRANDON

GRIME'S GRAVES
Telephone: (0842) 810656

This is an intricate network of pits and shafts sunk by our neolithic ancestors some 4000 years ago. The purpose of all this industriousness was to find flints for the world's first farmers—flints to make axes to fell trees so that the cleared ground could be sown with seed. Between 700 and 800 pits were dug, some of them to a depth of 30 or 40ft (9–12m). Two of the 16 excavated shafts have been left open; they give an idea of those early miners' working conditions.

Location: 2¾ m (4.4 km) north east of Brandon. OS map ref TL818898.
Opening Times: Good Friday to Sept 30, daily 10–6; Oct 1 to Maundy Thursday, daily 10–4. *Closed Mons, Christmas and New Year*. Adm 80p, OAPs 60p, Chd 40p.

BRESSINGHAM

BRESSINGHAM LIVE STEAM MUSEUM AND GARDENS
(*Bressingham Steam Preservation Co. Ltd*)
Diss IP22 2AB. Tel: Bressingham (0379 88) 386 and 382.
Live Steam Museum. Containing hundreds of steam related exhibits including Standard Gauge locomotives from all over Europe. Footplate rides on Standard Gauge. Three different narrow gauge railways. Road and Static Steam Engines, Victorian Steam Roundabout. Adjoining the internationally famous gardens and nurseries of the Museum's founder, Alan Bloom. Admission prices and open days between Easter and Sept on application. Special reductions Chld, OAPs and Parties. Ample and free car parking. Suitable for disabled persons. Wheelchairs available if advised in advance. 2½ miles west of Diss on the A1066.

CASTLE ACRE

CASTLE ACRE—PRIORY AND CASTLE
Telephone: (076 05) 394

William de Warenne and his wife were so impressed with the great Abbey of Cluny in Burgundy that they determined to found the Order in England. This they did—at Lewes. The priory at Castle Acre was probably established by their son and it survived, not without friction, until 1537 when it was surrendered to Henry VIII. The gaunt ruins span seven centuries and include a 16th century gatehouse, a church of mixed origins and a prior's lodging almost fit to be lived in. The castle, at the other end of the village started as an undefended Norman manor house but later evolved into a conventional keep. Ruins of this keep and outer earthworks can be seen.

Location: 3½ m (5.6 km) north of Swaffham. OS map ref TF814148.
Opening Times: Good Friday to Sept 30, daily 10–6; Oct 1 to Maundy Thursday, daily 10–4. *Closed Mons, Christmas and New Year*. Adm £1.10, OAPs 80p, Chd 55p.

CASTLE RISING

CASTLE RISING CASTLE
Telephone: (055 387) 330

The long and distinguished history of Castle Rising began in 1138. It was then that William de Albini started to build a grand castle to mark the upturn in his fortunes which followed his marriage to Henry I's widow. Later owners were no less notable and included Isabella 'the She-Wolf of France', wife of Edward II, the Black Prince, Prince Hal and the Howard Dukes of Norfolk. The 12th century keep, reached through a handsome, decorated doorway, was—and is—the finest building in the castle. Outside, there is a gatehouse of the same date and the remains of a church.

Location: 4 m (6.4 km) north of King's Lynn. OS map ref TF666246.
Opening Times: Good Friday to Sept 30, daily 10–6; Oct 1 to Maundy Thursday, daily 10–4. *Closed Mons, Christmas and New Year*. Adm 80p, OAPs 60p, Chd 40p.

TRINITY HOSPITAL
(*Trustees*)

Nine 17th century brick and tile Almhouses with court, chapel and treasury.
Location: 4 m NE of King's Lynn on A149.
Opening Times: All the year—Tues, Thurs & Sats. Summer: 10–12, 2–6. Winter: 10–12, 2–4. Adm free.

CROMER

THE CROMER MUSEUM (*Norfolk Museums Service*)
East Cottages, Tucker Street, NR27 9HB. Tel: (0263) 513543.
A museum displaying the rich history, geology and natural history of the Cromer area. Mon to Sat 10–5 (Mon closed 1–2); Sun 2–5. Adm Summer (Spring Bank Hol to Sept): 40p, Chld 10p, Students/UB40s 20p; Winter 25p, 10p, 10p.

FELBRIGG HALL, The National Trust
Telephone: West Runton 444 &

17th century country house with Georgian interiors set in a fine wooded park. Important 18th century Library and Orangery. Traditional walled garden. Woodland and Lakeside walks.

Location: 2 m SW of Cromer on S side of A148.
Station: Cromer (2¼ m).
Opening Times: Hall & Gardens—Mar 25 to Oct 29—Daily (*except* Tues and Fris) open Bank Hol Mons 1.30–5.30. Gardens 11–5.30. Adm £3, Chd (with adult) £1.50. Gardens only £1. Pre-booked parties of 15 or more £2.50. Shop. No dogs. Wheelchair access, 2 provided. Picnic area.
Refreshments: From 12 noon, teas & lunches in old kitchen. Table licence.

FAKENHAM

THE THURSFORD COLLECTION (*J.R. Cushing*)
Tel: (0328 77) 477.
Live musical shows each day from nine mechanical organs and one Wurlitzer cinema organ; there are road rollers, showmen's engines, traction engines, barn/oil engines, and a Savages Venetian Gondola switchback ride. Good Friday to Oct 31: 2–5; Christmas as per programme during Dec. Adm £2.50, Chld £1, OAPs £2.20, Party rate £2.05. Free car parking. Suitable for disabled persons. Self-service dispensing light snacks.

FLORDON

RAINTHORPE HALL & GARDENS &
(*George Hastings, Esq.*)

Rebuilt in 1503 after a fire, and modernised during the reign of Elizabeth, Rainthorpe Hall is one of the very few half-timbered houses of its period in East Anglia. Its chimney breasts are placed in the French manner, at either end of the Great Hall – a pattern rare in this country. It is set in large gardens, with a conservation lake.

Location: 1 m SSW of Newton Flotman (A140) on Flordon Road, 8 m S of Norwich.
Opening Times: GARDENS. May to Sept—Suns & Bank Hol Mons 2–5.30. Adm £1, Chd 50p, OAPs 50p. Car park free. Plants on sale. House open by appointment. Gardens only suitable for disabled.

GREAT YARMOUTH

ELIZABETHAN HOUSE MUSEUM (*Norfolk Museums Service*)
South Quay, NR30 2QH. Tel: (0493) 855746.
16th century merchant's house with period rooms and displaying Victorian domestic life. June to Sept: Daily (except Sat) 10–1, 2–5.30. Oct to May: Mon to Fri 10–1, 2–5.30. Adm Summer (Spring Bank Hol to Sept): 30p, Chld 10p, Students/UB40s 15p; Winter: 15p, 10p, 10p.

EXHIBITION GALLERIES (*Norfolk Museums Service*)
Central Library. Tel: (0493) 858900.
Travelling and local art exhibitions. Mon to Sat 9.30–5.30. (*Closed Sat 1–2*). Adm free. Telephone for further details.

MARITIME MUSEUM FOR EAST ANGLIA
(Norfolk Museums Service)
Marine Parade. Tel: (0493) 842267.
Historic shipwrecked sailor's home with displays illustrating the maritime history of the area. June to Sept: Daily (except Sat) 10–5.30. Oct: Mon to Fri 10–1, 2–5.30; Sun 1–5.30. Nov to May: Mon to Fri 10–1, 2–5.30. Adm Summer (Spring Bank Hol to Sept) 50p, Chld 10p, Students/UB40s 25p; Winter: 25p, 10p, 15p.

NELSON'S MONUMENT   *(Norfolk Museums Service)*
South Beach Parade. Tel: (0493) 858900.
144 ft. monument to Nelson built 1819, 217 steps to the top. Open July and Aug: Mon to Fri and Sun 2–6 and Trafalgar Day (21 Oct). Adm 40p, Chld 10p, Students/UB40s 20p.

OLD MERCHANTS' HOUSE AND THE ROW 111 HOUSES, GREAT YARMOUTH
Telephone: (0493) 857900
Herrings brought prosperity to the town in the mid-16th century and it expanded rapidly to house the growing population. Buildings of wood and reed-thatch were replaced by houses with brick and flint walls, tiled roofs and windows with leaded lights. These distinctive houses were pleasant places to live in until 19th century developers crowded them out. Soon they became cramped, ill lit and insanitary, a decline was hastened by bombing in the Second World War. Fortunately, two fine examples survive with their fittings.
Location: Off South Quay. OS map ref TG525072.
Opening Times: Good Friday to Sept 30, daily 10–6. Adm 55p, OAPs 40p, Chd 25p.

THE TOLHOUSE MUSEUM   *(Norfolk Museums Service)*
Tolhouse Street. Tel: (0493) 858900.
Medieval building. Local history museum and brass rubbing centre. June to Sept: Daily (except Sat) 10–1, 2–5.30. Oct to May: Mon to Fri 10–1, 2–5.30. Adm free.

GRESSENHALL

NORFOLK RURAL LIFE MUSEUM   *(Norfolk Museums Service)*
Beech House, Dereham NR20 4DR. Tel: Dereham (0362) 860563.
A museum of Norfolk Rural Life has been set up at Gressenhall, near East Dereham, to show the history of the County of Norfolk over the past 200 years with particular emphasis on agriculture. Easter to end of Oct: Tues to Sat 10–5; Sun 2–5.30. Open Bank Hol Mons 10–5. Adm 70p, Chld 10p, Students/UB40s 35p. Party rate (10 +) 50p.

KINGS LYNN

THE LYNN MUSEUM   *(Norfolk Museums Service)*
Old Market Street, PE30 1NL (on the Bus Station). Tel: (0553) 775001.
Natural history, archaeology, local history, folk history relating to NW Norfolk. Mon to Sat 10–5. (*Closed* Bank Hols.) Adm Summer (Spring Bank Hol to Sept): 40p, Chld 10p, Students/UB40s 20p; Winter: 20p, 10p, 10p.

MUSEUM OF SOCIAL HISTORY   *(Norfolk Museums Service)*
27 King Street. Tel: (0553) 775004.
Domestic life and dress, toys, dolls. Notable local glass collection. Tues to Sat 10–5. Adm Summer (Spring Bank Hol to Sept): 25p, Chld 10p, Students/ UB40s 10p; Winter: 10p, 10p, 10p.

LODDON

RAVENINGHAM HALL GARDENS
Telephone: (050846) 206
(Sir Nicholas Bacon Bt.)
An extensive garden laid out at the turn of the century surrounding original Georgian house. In the last thirty years there has been considerable designing and planting of new areas including unusual shrubs, plants and old roses, all in the traditional manner. In recent years the large and important Nursery Garden has grown to include many rare and exotic plants that can be seen in the Garden. Catalogue 3 ×18p stamp (refundable on orders over £10).
Location: 4 m from Beccles off the B1136 between Beccles and Loddon.
Opening Times: NURSERY: 9–3 weekdays and at weekends only if Garden is open. GARDEN: 2–5.30 Mar 26, 27; Apr 9, 23, 30; May 1, 21, 28, 29; June 11, 25; July 9, 23; Aug 13, 27, 28; Sept 10 in aid of local Charities. The house is not open. Adm £1, chd free. Car park free. Suitable for disabled persons.
Refreshments: Home made teas served on Garden Open Days only.

NEW HOUGHTON

HOUGHTON HALL
Telephone: East Rudham 569   &
(The Marquess of Cholmondeley)
18th century mansion built for Sir Robert Walpole. State rooms, pictures and china. Pleasure grounds. Shetland ponies. Heavy horses on show in the stables. Private collection of model soldiers and militaria.
Location: 13 m E of King's Lynn; 10 m W of Fakenham off A148.

Opening Times: Easter Sun (Mar 26) to Sept 24—Suns, Thurs & Bank Hols. HOUSE opens 1–5.30. Last adm 5. Gates, Picnic Area. Children's Playground, stables and Model Soldier & Militaria Collection opens Suns, Thurs & Bank Hols 12.30–5. Adm £2.50, OAPs £2, Chd £1 (under 5 free). No additional charges except for special events which will be advertised. Reduction of 10% for pre-booked parties of 20 or more. Car park near House, toilets & lift to State floor for the disabled. Free parking for coaches & cars.
Refreshments: Tea room.

NORWICH

AUGUSTINE STEWARD'S HOUSE
Telephone: (0603) 619056
(Norwich City Council)
Fine timber framed 16th century merchant's house built for Augustine Steward, Sheriff, Mayor and elected member of Parliament who was one of the most interesting historical figures in the Norwich largely responsible for the revival of the city in the 1530s. He also owned the house in Elm Hill which is now Strangers Club. Now converted to a restaurant.
Location: 14 Tombland, Norwich.
Opening Times: Tues – Sat 12–2, 7–9.30. Car parks in central Norwich.

BACON HOUSE
(Norwich City Council)
Fifteenth century merchant's house with 16th and 17th century additions now converted into housing, office, club and shop.
Location: 31 Colegate, Norwich.
Opening Times: Shop at shop hours. Club by prior arrangement with the Secretary, City Club, Bacon House, Colegate, Tel: (0603) 625057. Car parks in central Norwich.
Refreshments: Restaurants and cafes in central Norwich.

BRIDEWELL MUSEUM
Telephone: (0603) 667228
(Norwich City Council/Norfolk Museums Service)
A merchant's house dating from the 15th century, the Bridewell was for 250 years a prison for beggars and tramps. The wall facing St. Andrews Church has been described as the finest flint walling in England. Now a museum, the displays illustrate the trades and industries of Norwich during the past two hundred years.
Location: In Bridewell Alley, off Bedford Street, Norwich.
Opening Times: Mon to Sat 10–5. *Closed Bank Hols.* Adm winter 20p, Chd 10p, concession 15p. Summer (Spring Bank Hol to end Sept) 40p, Chld 10p, concession 20p. Parties by prior arrangement. Car parking in city centre car parks.
Refreshments: Restaurants and cafes in the centre of Norwich.

BRITON'S ARMS
Telephone: (0603) 623367   &
(Norwich City Council/Briton's Arms Coffee House and Restaurant)
A 15th century three storey timber framed building with a decorative arcaded upper floor, it was originally a house for the radical and intellectual group of religious women known as the Béguines. Now a restaurant/coffee house.
Location: 9 Elm Hill, Norwich.
Opening Times: Open as restaurant: Mon to Sat 10–5. *Closed Suns & Bank Hols.* Parties by prior arrangement. Car parking in city centre car parks. Suitable for disabled persons.

CHURCHMAN HOUSE   &
(Norwich City Council)
Built in the mid-18th century this is one of the best provincial houses of its period with fine interior plasterwork, wall paintings and fireplaces.
Location: At junction of St. Giles and Betnel Street, Norwich.
Opening Times: For information apply to the Tourist Information Centre, Guildhall. Parties by prior arrangement. Car parking in city centre car parks. Suitable for disabled persons.
Refreshments: Restaurants and cafes in central Norwich.

NO 18 COLEGATE
Telephone: (0603) 610734
(Norwich City Council/The Broads Authority)
Early 18th century house of seven bays, with good plasterwork ceiling inside, now offices.
Location: 18 Colgate, Norwich.
Opening Times: By prior arrangement with the Broads Authority. Car parking in city centre car parks.
Restaurants: Restaurants and cafes in the centre of Norwich.

COLMAN'S MUSTARD MUSEUM
The Mustard Shop, 3 Bridewell Alley. Tel: (0603) 627889.
Mon to Sat 9–5.30. *Closed* Thurs.

DRAGON HALL (THE OLD BARGE)
Telephone: (0603) 663922   &
(Norwich City Council)

A magnificent large timber framed merchant's hall built about 1480 with a rear wing converted into a house about 1700. In the 15th century part of the building was occupied by Anne Boleyn's grandfather. It is to be used as a Heritage Centre for the study of Norwich.
Location: 115-123 King Street, Norwich.
Opening Times: Mons – Thurs 10–4. Car parking in city centre car parks. Suitable for disabled persons.
Refreshments: Restaurants and cafes in central Norwich.

ELM HILL &
(Norwich City Council)

A narrow cobbled street of mainly timber framed buildings all of which belong to the City Council. Purchased in the early part of the century for the purpose of slum clearance, from which they were saved, the street is an early example of a conservation scheme.
Location: Elm Hill, Norwich.
Opening Times: Interiors of shops and restaurants at normal commercial hours. Car parking in car parks in central Norwich. Suitable for disabled persons.
Refreshments: Briton's Arms (see separate entry).

LAZAR HOUSE (BRANCH LIBRARY)
Telephone: (0603) 45452   &
(Norwich City Council/Norfolk County Libraries)

A Norman Leper Hospital later used as an almshouse, the building was restored in 1906 and is now a branch library.
Location: 219 Sprowston Road, Norwich.
Opening Times: Telephone librarian for current opening hours. Parties by appointment with the librarian. Car parking. Suitable for disabled persons.
Refreshments: Cafe opposite on Sprowston Road.

NORWICH CASTLE
Telephone: (0603) 611277 ext 279   &
(Norwich City Council/Norfolk Museums Service)

Norwich Castle houses one of the finest regional museums in Britain. The castle keep built by the Normans between 1100 and 1130 contains displays of medieval objects and an exhibition illustrating Norfolk's links with Europe. Galleries displaying art (the Norwich School) natural history, archaelogy and ceramics.
Location: In the centre of Norwich.
Opening Times: Mon to Sat 10–5, Suns 2–5, Bank Hols 10–5, *closed Christmas Day*. Adm winter 35p, Chd 10p, concession 20p, Spring Bank Hol to end Sept 70p, Chd 10p, concession 30p. Car parking in central Norwich. Suitable for disabled persons. Wheelchairs available. Museum shop.
Refreshments: Coffees, lunches and teas in Museum cafeteria.

SAINSBURY CENTRE FOR VISUAL ARTS
University of East Anglia, NR4 7TJ. Tel: Norwich (0603) 56060.
The Robert and Lisa Sainsbury collection is wide ranging, remarkable and of international importance and embracing European and Tribal art. There are works by Arp, Bacon, Degas, Epstein, Giacometti, Modiliani, Moore, Picasso and young contemporary artists. The antiquities include Egyptian faience and bronze figures, Greek cycladic sculpture, Etruscan and Roman bronzes as well as medieval and oriental sculpture, Indian and Japanese painting. Also houses the Anderson Collection of Art Nouveau. Three special exhibitions a year. Daily (except Monday). 12–5.

ST. ANDREWS AND BLACKFRIARS' HALLS
Telephone: (0603) 628477   &
(Norwich City Council/Timothy Aldous Manager)

A medieval friary built in the 14th and 15th centuries which has been in the ownership of the City of Norwich since the Reformation. The two halls (former nave and choir of the friars' church) contain part of the extensive collection of civic portraits dating back to the 16th century. With its cloister and other monastic buildings it represents the finest and most complete friary complex in England.
Location: St. Andrews Street, Norwich.
Opening Times: Mon to Sat 10–5 (the halls are sometimes booked for functions). Adm free. Parties by prior arrangement with the Manager. Car parking in city centre car parks. Suitable for disabled persons.
Refreshments: Crypt coffee bar Mon to Sat 10–4.

ST. PETER HUNGATE MUSEUM
Telephone: (0603) 611277 ext 279   &
(Norwich City Council/Norfolk Museums Service)

One of the city's largë ollection of medieval churches St. Peter Hungate is largely 15th century with fine hammer beam roof and painted glass. Now a museum of church art and brass-rubbing centre.
Location: Princes Street, Norwich.
Opening Times: Mon to Sat 10–5, *closed Bank Hols*. Adm free. Parties by prior arrangement. Car parking in city centre car parks. Suitable for disabled.
Refreshments: Restaurants and cafes in central Norwich.

STRANGERS' HALL MUSEUM
Telephone: (0603) 611277 ext 279
(Norwich City Council/Norfolk Museums Service)

A medieval house built around a courtyard with Great Hall, stone vaulted undercroft and interesting 17th and 18th-century additions. The rooms are furnished in styles from the 16th century onwards with exhibits of domestic life.
Location: Charing Cross, Norwich.
Opening Times: Mon to Sat 10–5, *closed Bank Hols*. Adm winter 20p, Chd 10p, concession 15p; Spring Bank Hol to end Sept 40p, Chd 10p, concession 20p. Parties by prior arrangement. Car parking in city centre car parks.
Refreshments: Restaurants and cafes in the centre of Norwich.

REEDHAM
BERNEY ARMS WINDMILL
Telephone: (0493) 200605

At one time the Norfolk and Suffolk marshes were drained entirely by wind-power, a function carried out by this 'tower' mill after it was no longer used for its original purpose of grinding cement clinker. The Mill has seven floors, making it the highest marsh-mill in the area and a landmark for miles around. The whole of the mechanism is in working order.
Location: North bank of River Yare, 3½ m (5.6 km) north east of Reedham. OS map ref TG465051. Accessible only by boat, or ½ m walk.
Opening Times: Good Friday to Sept 30, daily 10–6. Adm 80p, OAPs 60p, Chd 40p.

SANDRINGHAM
SANDRINGHAM HOUSE & GROUNDS
Telephone: King's Lynn (0553) 772675
(Her Majesty the Queen)

House, Grounds and Museum open. *House, Grounds and Museum are NOT open when HM The Queen or any member of the Royal Family is in residence.*
Location: 8 m NE of King's Lynn (off A149).
Opening Times: House & Grounds. Mar 26 to Sept 28—Mons, Tues, Weds & Thurs 11–4.45 (Grounds 10.30–5), Suns 12–4.45 (Grounds 11.30–5). House only closed July 17 to Aug 5 inc. House and Grounds closed July 21 to Aug 2 inc. House & Grounds: £2, Chd £1.20, OAP £1.50. Grounds only: £1.50, Chd 80p, OAP £1.10. No reductions for coach parties. Free coach and car parks. Please check July closing dates with estate office.

WOLFERTON STATION MUSEUM
Sandringham Estate.
Royal Retiring Rooms in which King Edward VII and Queen Alexandra entertained exalted guests arriving for Sandringham House. Queen Victoria's travelling bed. Unusual small railway curios including items from Royal trains and memorabilia of Royal travel.

SAXTHORPE
MANNINGTON HALL GARDENS
Telephone: Saxthorpe (026 387) 284
(Hon Robin & Mrs Walpole)

15th century moated house and Saxon church ruin set in attractive gardens. Outstanding rose gardens. Extensive walks and trails around the estate.
Location: 2 m N of Saxthorpe, nr B1149; 18 m NW of Norwich. 9 m from coast.
Opening Times: GARDEN. Easter Sun 12–5 then Apr to Dec, 12–5 or dusk if earlier. Also Weds, Thurs & Fris June to Aug, 11–6. Adm £1.50, Chd (accompanied children under 16) free, Senior Citizens/Students £1. House open by prior appointment only.
Refreshments: Coffee, salad lunches and home-made teas.

SWAFFHAM
OXBURGH HALL, The National Trust
Telephone: Gooderstone 258   &

Late 15th century moated house. Outstanding gatehouse tower. Needlework by Mary Queen of Scots. Unique French parterre laid out circa 1845. Woodland walk and traditional herbaceous garden. Chapel with fine altar piece.
Location: 7 m SW of Swaffham on S side of Stoke Ferry Road.
Opening Times: Gatehouse, Principal Rooms & Gardens: Mar 25, 26, 27; Sats and Suns in Apr. May 1 to Sept 30—Daily (except Thurs and Fris) 1.30–5.30. Bank Hol Mons 11–5.30. Oct: Sat and Sun 1.30–5.30. Adm £2.50, Chd (with adult) £1.25. Prebooked parties of 15 or more £1.80. Shop. No dogs. Wheelchair access, 2 provided.
Refreshments: In Old Kitchen. Light lunches and teas 12–5.

SWANNINGTON
SWANINGTON MANOR GARDENS
Telephone: Norwich 860700   &
(Mr & Mrs Richard Winch)

East Anglia's most romantic garden. Peaceful 4 acre garden framed by 300-year old yew and box topiary hedge. 17th century house (not open). Fine herbaceous borders with many labelled unusual plants. Colourful 50-yard shrub and herbaceous border. Stream. Woodland walk. Outstanding knot and herb garden. Orchids and green-houses. Many other interesting features.

Location: 10 m NW of Norwich; turn off Norwich–Fakenham Rd (A1067) at Attlebridge.
Opening Times: Easter to End Sept—Weds and Bank Hol Mons 11–6. Adm £1.50, Chd 50p. Parties, by prior arrangement, at special rates. Free parking. Suitable for disabled persons.
Refreshments: Licensed restaurant. Morning coffee, home-made light lunches and afternoon teas.
The Present Shop: One of the most exciting present shops in the country, prices range from very little to indulgent. Everything pretty. Interesting selection of plants for sale.

THETFORD

THE ANCIENT HOUSE MUSEUM *(Norfolk Museums Service)*
   White Hart Street, IP24 1AA. Tel: (0842) 2599.
Early Tudor half-timbered house with collections illustrating Thetford and Breckland life, history and natural history. Mon to Sat 10–5 (*closed* 1–2 on Mon);Sun (Spring Bank Hol to Sept only) 2–5. Adm Summer (Spring Bank Hol to Sept): 25p, Chld 10p, Students/UB40s 10p; Winter: 10p, 10p, 10p.

UPWELL

WELLE MANOR HALL
Telephone: (0945) 773333

Home of Norfolk Punch, the ancient herbal drink, Welle Manor Hall is a rare example of a fortified prebendary manor house, some parts of which date back to 1202. Visitors can see the Hall, the herborium, selenium spa, craft museum, collection of Lafayette photographs and equipment, assembly of historic horse-drawn vehicles, and collection of agricultural implements.
Location: 5 m SE of Wisbech on A1101 next to Church of Upwell, St Peter, in Upwell.
Opening Times: All year by appointment for groups. Special tour on the first Sun of each month. Adm £1.
Refreshments: Wholesome organic refreshments available.

WALSINGHAM

SHIREHALL MUSEUM *(Norfolk Museums Service)*
   Common Place, Little Walsingham, NR22 6BP.
   Tel: Cromer (0263) 513543 or Walsingham (032 872) 510.
The principal exhibit is the Georgian court room which may be seen with its original fittings including the prisoners' lock-up. The museum contains many items illustrating the history of Walsingham including a display on the history of pilgrimage. It also contains a Networked Tourist Information Centre. Maundy Thursday to Sept: Daily11–1, 2–4. Oct: Sat and Sun only 11–1, 2–4. Adm 40p, Chld 10p, Students/UB40s 20p.

WALSINGHAM ABBEY
Telephone: Walsingham 259
(Walsingham Estate Company)

Augustinian Priory and crypt.

Location: On B1105 midway between Wells and Fakenham.
Opening Times: Grounds open 2–5; Apr—Weds; May to July & Sept—Weds, Sats & Suns; Aug—Mons, Weds, Fris, Sats & Suns. Also Bank Hols, Easter to Sept. *Other times by arrangement with Estate Office.* Adm 50p, Chd & OAPs 25p.
Refreshments: Available in the village including Black Lion Hotel; Knight's Gate Hotel and the Old Bakehouse.

WELLS·NEXT·THE·SEA

BYGONES AT HOLKHAM
   Holkham Park (on the A149: Fakenham 10 miles, King's Lynn 30 miles, Norwich 34 miles). Tel: (0328) 710806/710277.
A unique and comprehensive collection of the Victorian and Edwardian era. Housed in the magnificent 19th century stable buildings in Holkham Park the exhibition includes: Fire Engines, Cars, Craft Tools, Harness, a Victorian Cottage Kitchen, Brewery, Dairy, Shoe Shop, Engineerium, Carriages, Veterinary items, Laundry, Sewing Machines. June to Sept: Sun to Thurs 1.30–5. Open Spring and Summer Bank Hol Mons 11.30–5. Adm £1.30, Chld 50p, OAPs £1. Coach parties welcome, discounts given. Also Holkham Hall, Holkham Pottery, Holkham Garden Centre. Teas in a modern complex adjoining the Bygones collection.

HOLKHAM HALL
Telephone: Fakenham (0328) 710227

Fine Palladian mansion. Pictures, Tapestries, Statuary, Furnishings. Nessfield laid out the formal garden.
Location: 2m W of Wells; S of the Wells/Hunstanton Road (A149).
Opening Times: Daily (except Fri/Sat) from May 28 to end Sept 1.30–5, also Spring and Summer Bank Holiday Mons 11.30–5. Adm £1.70, Chd (5–15) 50p, OAPs £1.30. Adm to Park: Cars 50p, Motorcycles 25p, Coaches & Pedestrians free. Pre-paid coach parties of 20 or more 10% reduction.
Refreshments: Served in tea rooms.

WEYBOURNE

THE MUCKLEBURGH COLLECTION
   A149: Cromer 9 miles; King's Lynn 35 miles; Norwich 30 miles.
   Tel: (026 370) 608 or 210.
The largest private collection of armoured fighting vehicles (tanks, etc.) in East Anglia. World War II memorabilia; Diorama Room includes model of part of Weybourne military camp and photographic display of camp life and neighbouring Weybourne village in the 19th century. Working displays of tanks on advertised days. Coach parties welcomed. Open Easter to Oct 10–5 daily including weekends. Winter: weekends only. Adm charge. For details and party discounts telephone above number. Evening parties by arrangement.

RAINTHORPE HALL
NORFOLK

Rainthorpe Hall has appeared in several Television productions. In both 1982 and 1987 it was used for 'Tales of the Unexpected'. It served as the principal location for the six hour murder mystery 'Cover Her Face', which was shown in England in 1985 and in the United States in 1987. Its drive and gates were used in 'The Black Tower' in 1986, and it was the scene of the Hunt Ball in 'Menace Unseen', a three-hour drama shown in 1988.

WELLE MANOR HALL, UPWELL, NORFOLK

A rare example of a fortified prebendary manor house some parts of which date back to 1202. Welle Manor offers also for the visitors interest, its herborium, selenium spa, craft museums and collection of Lafayette photographs and equipment. In the grounds a collection of historic horse drawn vehicles and agricultural equipment. Welle Manor is the home of Norfolk punch. The hall is open all year by appointment for groups and offers a special tour first Sunday of every month. Entrance fee £1.00. Wholesome refreshments available.

TELEPHONE: WISBECH (0945) 773333

Northamptonshire

AYNHO

AYNHOE PARK
(Country Houses Association Ltd)

17th century mansion. Alteration by Soane.

Location: 6 m SE of Banbury on main London/Birmingham Road.
Opening Times: May to Sept—Weds & Thurs 2–5. Adm £1, Chd 50p. Free car park. No dogs admitted.

CANONS ASHBY

CANONS ASHBY HOUSE, The National Trust
Telephone: Blakesley (0327) 860044

The home of the Dryden family since the 16th century; a manor house c. 1580 and altered for the last time in 1710; Elizabethan wall paintings and outstanding Jacobean plasterwork; formal garden with terraces, walls and gatepiers of 1710: medieval Priory Church, privately owned since the Reformation. 70 acre park.
Location: On B4525 Northampton/Banbury Road.
Opening Times: Mar 25 to end of Oct—Weds to Suns & Bank Hol Mons 1–5.30. *Closed Good Friday.* Adm £2.50, Chd £1.20. Parking for cars & coaches which must pre-book (discount for parties). Dogs on leads, in Home Paddock only. 1989 events – details from the Administrator.
Refreshments: Tea room open as House.

CORBY

DEENE PARK
Telephone: Bulwick 278 or 361 (office hours)
(Edmund Brudenell, Esq.)

Mainly 16th century house of great architectural importance and historical interest. Large lake, park, extensive gardens with old fashioned roses, rare trees and shrubs.
Location: 8 m NW of Oundle; 6 m NE of Corby on Kettering/Stamford Road (A43).
Opening Times: Easter, Spring & Summer Bank Hol Suns & Mons, also every Sun in June, July & Aug 2–5. Adm charges not available at time of going to press. Upstairs rooms now usually on view. *Special guided tours to parties of 20 or more may be arranged on application to the House Keeper.*

KIRBY HALL
Telephone: (0533) 663230

Richness and variety of architectural detail distinguish this Elizabethan country house from others. Begun by Sir Humphrey Stafford in 1570, it was completed by Sir Christopher Hatton, a talented courtier to Queen Elizabeth. The fourth Sir Christopher Hatton devoted his energies to the garden. His death in 1706 marked the end of the Hall's golden age.
Location: 2 m (3.2 km) north of Corby. OS map ref SP926927.
Opening Times: Good Friday to Sept 30, daily 10–6; Oct 1 to Maundy Thursday, daily 10–4. *Closed Mons, Christmas and New Year.* Adm 80p, OAPs 60p, Chd 40p.

ROCKINGHAM CASTLE
Telephone: Corby (0536) 770240
(Commander Michael Saunders Watson)

Royal Castle till 1530, since then home of the Watson family. Spans 900 years of English life and culture set amid lovely gardens and fine views.
Location: 2 m N of Corby; 9 m from Market Harborough; 14 m from Stamford on A427; 8 m from Kettering on A6003.
Opening Times: Easter Sun to Sept 30—Suns & Thurs also Bank Hol Mons & Tues following and Tues during Aug: 1.30–5.30. Adm £2.50, Chd £1.30. Gardens only £1.30. OAPs £2. *Any other day by previous appointment for parties.*
Refreshments: Teas—home-made at Castle.

EASTON ON THE HILL

PRIEST'S HOUSE, The National Trust
Telephone: Stamford (0780) 62506

Pre-Reformation priest's house given to the National Trust by The Peterborough Society. Contains a small museum of village bygones.
Location: 2 m SW of Stamford off A43.
Station: Stamford (2 m).
Opening Times: Access only by prior appointment with Mr. R. Chapman, Glebe Cottage, 45 West St., Easton-on-the-Hill, nr Stamford. Adm free. No dogs. Unsuitable for disabled or visually handicapped & Coaches.

HOLDENBY

HOLDENBY HOUSE GARDENS
Telephone: Northampton (0604) 770786 or 770241
(James Lowther, Esq.)

Once the largest house in Elizabethan England, subsequently the prison of Charles I in the Civil War. Original garden remains. Elizabethan garden, fragrant and silver borders. Rare farm animals, falconry centre. Donkeys and train rides. Museum. Pottery.
Location: 7 m NW of Northampton, off A428 & A50; 7 m from M1 exit 18.
Opening Times: GARDENS. Apr to Sept—Suns & Bank Hol Mons 2–6; also Thurs July & Aug, 2–6. Adm Gardens: £1.75, Chd 80p. House and Gardens: £2.75, Chd £1. HOUSE. Open by arrangement to pre-booked parties Mons to Fris Adm £2.50, Chd £1. Enquire for special rates for school parties. Plant & Souvenir shop.
Refreshments: Home-made teas in Victorian Kitchen.

KETTERING

ALFRED EAST GALLERY
Sheep Street. Tel: (0536) 410333.
Regular loan exhibitions throughout the year, and a temporary exhibition programme of art and local history from the permanent collections. Definitive collection of work by Sir Alfred East R.A., always open by appointment. Catalogue published. Car parking. Open Mon to Sat 10–5.

BOUGHTON HOUSE

Telephone: Kettering (0536) 515731 & 82248   ♿
(His Grace the Duke of Buccleuch & Queensberry KT and the Living Landscape Trust)

15th century monastic building enlarged between 1530 and 1695 around 7 courtyards. Celebrated art treasures; lovely grounds, exciting adventure woodland play area and nature trail.

Location: 3 m N of Kettering on A43 at Geddington; 75 m from London by A1 or M1.
Opening Times: House and grounds: July 29–Aug 31. Daily, grounds 12–6; House 2–5. Adm House & Grounds £2.50, (Students, OAPs, Chd £2). Staterooms by prior booking £1 supplement. Grounds (excluding gardens) Apr 29–Oct 1–Daily except Fris, 12–5. Adm 80p, Chd 60p. Stable Yard, Tea Room, Gift Shop and Plant Stall open with House and at most weekends/public holidays. Exhibitions and lecture rooms in Stable Block. Museum and Educational groups by appointment at other times.
Refreshments: Teas in restored Stables during Aug and on some other occasions.

LAMPORT

LAMPORT HALL
(Lamport Hall Trust)

The home of the Isham family from 1560 to 1976. Present house mainly 17th and 18th century. Site of one of the oldest alpine gardens in Britain, which housed the first garden gnomes – introduced by Sir Charles Isham around 1850.

Location: 8 m N of Northampton on A508 to Market Harborough.
Opening Times: House & Gardens. Easter to end of Sept—Suns & Bank Hol Mons 2.15–5.15. Also Thurs in July & Aug, 2.15–5.15. School & private parties any time by appointment. Adm £2.20, OAPs £1.70, Chd £1. Free car park. No dogs please.
Refreshments: Teas at the house.

NORTHAMPTON

ABINGTON MUSEUM   *(Northampton Borough Council)*
Abington Park Tel: (0604) 31454.
Manor House, 15th century, rebuilt in part 1745. Open all year 10–5, Mon to Sat. Apr to Sept also open Sun 2.30–5. Period rooms including 17th century oak panelled room, Victorian school room, nursery, and ladies' drawing room. Also costume and furniture displays.

ALTHORP
(The Earl Spencer)

Built by Sir John Spencer in 1508, altered by Henry Holland in 1790 and entirely redecorated in 1982. Splendid interior containing pictures of many European schools; French furniture; large collection of porcelain. Rooms open in rotation.
NB—*Please respect times when house and grounds are closed. No early arrivals except by appointment.*

Location: 6 m NW of Northampton on Northampton/Rugby Road (A428); 6 m from M1 exit 16.
Opening Times: Sept to June: HOUSE 1–5; July to Aug: HOUSE 11–6, Bank Holidays 11–6. Open all year daily except Christmas Day. Weds – Connoisseurs day throughout the year (extra rooms, longer tour). Adm House and Grounds: £2.75, groups of 8 or more £2.50, Chd £1.75. Connoisseurs day £3.75, Chd £2. Jan, Feb, Mar £2.50. Grounds and Lake only: Adm 50p, Chd 25p. Coach parking fees £10 in advance please, booking essential. Groups of more than 8 people during Jan and Feb £1.50. Cars free. Wine shop & Gift shop. Private morning visits by arrangement at extra cost. Weddings, 21st Birthdays, business or private lunches and dinners our speciality. Ploughman's Platters in Stables Restaurant for groups. For booking (enclosing sae) write to: The Countess Spencer, Althorp, Northampton NN7 4HG. *Information & prices are subject to alteration without notice as details submitted well in advance of printing.*
Refreshments: Tea room; home-made cakes & scones available at counter.
NB—*For security reasons House & Grounds may be closed without notice; Coach parties will be informed.* House unsuitable for small children and frail & disabled people.

CENTRAL MUSEUM & ART GALLERY
(Northampton Borough Council)
Guildhall Road. Tel: (0604) 39415.
Collections of footwear through the ages; cobbler's shop. Local archaeological material and English ceramics. Old Master and modern oil and watercolour paintings. Mon to Sat 10–5 except Thurs, 10–8. *Closed* Sun.

DELAPRE ABBEY
(Northamptonshire Borough Council)

House rebuilt or added to 16th to 19th centuries. Converted for use as The County Record Office.

Location: On London Road (A508) 1 m due S of centre of Northampton.
Station: Northampton (1 m).
Opening Times: All the year—Thurs 2.30–5 (closes 4.30 Oct to Apr). Adm free 'public rooms and passages only'.

MUSEUM OF LEATHERCRAFT   *(Northampton Borough Council)*
The Old Blue Coat School, Bridge Street. Tel: (0604) 39415.
Displays tell the story of leather's use throughout history from ancient Egyptian times to the present day. Many examples of fine craftsmanship include 16th century caskets and missal cases and contemporary saddlery. There are special displays of Costume, Luggage, Sport and Saddlery and Harness Room. Mon to Sat 10–5.

MUSEUM OF THE NORTHAMPTONSHIRE REGIMENT
(Northampton Borough Council)
Abington Park.
Opening hours as for Abington Museum, see above.

MUSEUM OF THE NORTHAMPTONSHIRE YEOMANRY
(Northampton Borough Council)
Abington Park.
Opening hours as for Abington Museum, see above.

NASEBY BATTLE AND FARM MUSEUM
Purlieu Farm.

OUNDLE

LILFORD PARK
Telephone: Clopton (08015) 648
(J. M. Dishington, Esq.)

Country park with extensive aviaries, children's farm, childrens's play area, gift/craft shop. Picnic areas.
Location: On A605 mid-way between Oundle and Thrapston. AA signposted.
Opening Times: Open daily Easter to Oct 10–6 (or dusk). Adm £1.50, Chd 75p. Party discounts by arrangement. Sorry no dogs.
Refreshments: Cafeteria.

LYVEDEN NEW BIELD, The National Trust
Telephone: Benefield (083 25) 358

The shell of an unusual Renaissance building erected about 1600 by Sir Thomas Tresham to symbolize the Passion. He died before the building could be completed and his son was then imprisoned in connection with the Gunpowder Plot. A viewing platform allows visitors to look from the East Window.

Location: 4 m SW of Oundle via A427. 3 m E of Brigstock (A6116) (½ m walk from roadside parking).
Opening Times: All the year— Daily. *Property approached via two fields. Parties by arrangement with Custodian, Lyveden New Bield Cottage, nr Oundle, Northants.* Adm 80p, Chd 40p. *No parking for coaches but which may drop & return to pick up passengers.* Dogs admitted on leads. Unsuitable for disabled or visually handicapped.

SOUTHWICK HALL
Telephone: Oundle (0832) 74064
(Christopher Capron, Esq.)

Manor house, retaining medieval building dating from 1300, with Tudor rebuilding and 18th century additions. Exhibitions:– Victorian and Edwardian life; musical instrument workshop; collections of agricultural and carpentry tools, named bricks and local archaeological finds and fossils.

Location: 3 m N of Oundle 4 m E of Bulwick.
Opening Times: Bank Holidays, Sun & Mon (Mar 26, 27; Apr 30 & May 1; May 28, 29; Aug 27, 28). Weds from May 3 to Aug 23: 2–5. Adm £2, Chd £1, OAPs £1.30. Parties at other times by arrangement with Secretary at Southwick Hall, Peterborough PE8 5BL.
Refreshments: Teas available.

RUSHTON

RUSHTON HALL
(Royal National Institute for the Blind)

Dates from c. 1500, with earlier wing and later additions.
Location: 4 m NW of Kettering, off A6003.
Opening Times: Grounds & exterior of premises only (with a limited inspection of the interior) by prior appointment with the Head Teacher.

RUSHTON TRIANGULAR LODGE
Telephone: (0536) 710761

Three walls with three windows and three gables to each . . . three storeys topped by a three-sided chimney. What is the reason for this triangular theme? The building is the brainchild of Sir Thomas Tresham and every detail is symbolical of the Holy Trinity and the Mass. Tresham's religious beliefs, unpopular in Elizabethan England, earned him many years' imprisonment. The lodge, begun on his return home in 1593, was finished four years later.

Location: ¾ m (1 km) west of Rushton; 4 m (6.4 km) north west of Kettering. OS map ref SP830831.
Opening Times: Good Friday to Sept 30, daily 10–6. Adm 80p, OAPs 60p, Chd 40p.

STOKE BRUERNE

RURAL LIFE MUSEUM
Tel: (0604) 862229.
A compact display of the working crafts and home life of Northamptonshire's farming communities, the village blacksmith, a dairy, and a scullery. Photographs of Stoke Bruerne in the days before the motor car show the relation of the village to its canal. Open Easter to Oct: weekdays 10–5, Sat & Sun 12–5. For further information telephone Waterways Museum on above number. Adm charge (including joint tickets).

STOKE PARK PAVILIONS
(A. S. Chancellor, Esq)

Two pavilions and colonnade. Built in 1630 by Inigo Jones.

Location: Stoke Bruerne village; 7 m S of Northampton just W of Stony/Northampton Road A508.
Opening Times: June, July & Aug—Sats, Suns & Bank Hols 2–6. *Exterior only on view.* Adm £1. Car park free.

THE WATERWAYS MUSEUM
Stoke Bruerne, near Towcester. Tel: (0604) 862229.

The museum displays over 200 years of canal history showing the hard working life of the boat people and the canals on which they lived and traded. The Waterways Museum is on the canalside at Stoke Bruerne with the attraction of canal locks, Blisworth Tunnel and the Waterways Museum Shop. There are privately run boat trips, restaurants and a public house. Easter to Oct: daily 10–6. Oct to Easter: daily (except Mon) 10–4. Adm charge. For details and party discounts telephone above number.

SULGRAVE MANOR
Telephone: Sulgrave (029 576) 205
(The Sulgrave Manor Board)

English home of ancestors of George Washington. The house was completed in 1558 and was lived in by descendants of the Washington family for 120 years.

Location: Sulgrave Village is off Banbury/Northampton Road (B4525); 7 m NE of Banbury; 28 m SE of Stratford-upon-Avon; 30 m N of Oxford; 70 m NW of London.
Opening Times: Mar to Dec 31—Daily (except Weds); Apr to Sept (inc) 10.30–1, 2–5.30. Other months 10.30–1, 2–4. *Closed Christmas Day, Boxing Day, and all January.* February: Groups only by appointment. Adm £2, Chd £1. Free car & coach parking.
Refreshments: At Thatched House Hotel opposite, Tel Sulgrave (029 576) 232.

COTON MANOR GARDENS
Telephone: Northampton (0604) 740219
(Commander & Mrs H. Pasley-Tyler)

An outstanding old English Garden of exceptional charm and beauty. Enchanted by flamingoes, wildfowl and tropical birds at large in the water gardens.

Location: 10 m N of Northampton & 11 m SE of Rugby. Follow tourist signs on A428 and A50.
Opening Times: Easter to end of Sept: Suns and Bank Hol Mons, also Weds in July & Aug, 2–6. Unusual plants for sale.
Refreshments: Home-made teas.

HINWICK HOUSE
Telephone: Rushden (0933) 53624
(R. M. Orlebar)

A Queen Anne house of excellent architecture. Pictures by Van Dyck; Lely, Kneller etc. Lace, tapestries and needlework. Furniture, china, objets d'art. 'A Century of Fashion' clothes from 1840 to 1940 on permanent display. Restaurant and Banqueting facilities for 100 people available. Medieval banquets held monthly. For details contact the Secretary.

Location: 3½ m S of Rushden, 6 m SE of Wellingborough; 3 m from A6 at Wymington.
Opening Times: Mar 26 and 27; Apr 30; May 1, May 2–20, 28 and 29; Aug 27 & 28, 2–4.30 (last tour). Otherwise by appointment. Adm £2. Parties welcome throughout year.
Refreshments: Home-made teas and other catering facilities by arrangement, for parties over 20, otherwise a fully licensed restaurant is available for lunch and dinner. Known as the Flemish House Restaurant, it is situated in the wing of the House.

Northumberland

ALNWICK

ALNWICK CASTLE
Telephone: Alnwick (0665) 510777
(His Grace the Duke of Northumberland, KG)

Important example of medieval fortification restored by Salvin, dating to 12th century. Including the Keep, Armoury, Guard Chamber, Library and other principal apartments, Dungeon, State Coach and Museum of British and Roman antiquities. Pictures by Titian, Canaletto, Van Dyck, and other famous artists.
Location: In the town of Alnwick, 30 m N of Newcastle off the A1.
Opening Times: May–Sept—Daily (except Sats but open Bank Holiday weekends including Sats) 1–5. No admission after 4.30. Adm £2, Chd (under 16) £1, OAPs £1.70. (Organised Party Rates by arrangement.) Free Parking. *No dogs.*

BAMBURGH

BAMBURGH CASTLE
Telephone: Bamburgh 208

Fine 12th century Norman Keep. Remainder of castle considerably restored.
Location: Coastal – 16 m N of Alnwick 6 m from Belford; 3 m from Seahouses.
Opening Times: Easter to last Sun of Oct—Daily (incl Suns) open at 1; Adm £1.70, Chd 60p (1988 prices). *Parties may be booked out of normal hours.* For closing times enquire The Custodian.
Refreshments: Clock Tower tea rooms.

THE GRACE DARLING MUSEUM
(Royal National Life-boat Institution)
Grace Darling relics. Apr to mid-Oct: Daily 11–6 (June, July and Aug, 11–7). Other times by arrangement with Hon. Curator (Mr. D.W.N. Calderwood). Adm free but voluntary donations to R.N.L.I. invited.

BARDON MILL

HOUSESTEADS ROMAN FORT
Telephone: (049 84) 363

This is the best-preserved Roman troop-base on Hadrian's Wall. In the museum, a model shows the layout of barracks, headquarters buildings, commandant's house and granaries. Also displayed are relics from the fort and the settlement that grew up outside the walls in the 3rd and 4th centuries.
Location: 2¾ m (4.4 km) north east of Bardon Mill. OS map ref NY790687.
Opening Times: Good Friday to Sept 30, daily 10–6; Oct 1 to Maundy Thursday, daily 10–4. *Closed Mons, Christmas and New Year.* Adm £1.30, OAPs £1, Chd 65p.

BELSAY

BELSAY HALL CASTLE AND GARDENS
Telephone: (066 181) 636
(English Heritage)

XIX century Neo-Classical mansion lies at the entrance to 30 acres of exciting gardens, which in turn lead on to the XIV century castle and ruined manor. Important collections of rare and exotic flowering trees grow in the meandering, deep ravines of the "picturesque" Quarry Gardens. Massed plantings of rhododendrons. Large heather garden. Spring bulbs. Exhibition of Belsay's architectural and landscape history in stable block.
Location: 14 m (22.4 km) north west of Newcastle upon Tyne. OS map ref NZ088785.
Opening Times: Good Friday to Sept 30, daily 10–6; Oct 1 to Maundy Thurs, daily 10–4. *Closed* Mons, Dec 24–26, Jan 1. Adm £1.60, OAPs £1.20, Chd 80p.

BERWICK

BERWICK BARRACKS
Telephone: (0289) 304493

The barracks were designed in 1717 to accommodate 36 officers and 600 men, first being occupied in 1721. The buildings consist of three blocks of accommodation around a square, the fourth side having a splendidly decorated gatehouse. The barracks' new exhibition, the award winning 'Beat of Drum' traces the history of the British infantryman from 1660 to the end of the 19th century. The regimental museum of the King's Own Scottish Borderers and Borough Museum of Berwick on Tweed are also housed here.
Location: On the Parade, off Church St, Berwick town centre.
Opening Times: Good Friday to Sept 30, daily 10–6; Oct 1 to Maundy Thursday, daily 10–4. *Closed Mons, Christmas and New Year.* Adm £1.30, OAPs £1, Chd 65p.

CAMBO

WALLINGTON HOUSE, WALLED GARDEN and GROUNDS, The National Trust
Telephone: Scots Gap (067 074) 283 (House)

Built 1688, altered 18th century. Central Hall added in 19th century, decorated by William Bell Scott, Ruskin and others. Fine porcelain, furniture and pictures in series of rooms including a late Victorian nursery and dolls' houses. Museum. Coach display in West Coach House. Woodlands, lakes, walled terraced garden and conservatory with magnificent fuchsias.
Location: Access from N, 12 m W of Morpeth on B6343. Access from S, A696 from Newcastle; 6 m NW of Belsay B6342 to Cambo.
Opening Times: HOUSE: Mar 24 to Oct 30, daily 1–5.30. *Closed* Tues. In Apr and Oct on selected days only guided tours may be available. **WALLED GARDEN:** Open all year daily. Easter to end of Sept 10–7 (or dusk if earlier). Oct: 10–6; Nov to Easter 10–4. **GROUNDS:** Open all year during daylight hours. Adm House and Grounds £2.80, Grounds only £1. Party rate £2.40, Chd 70p. No dogs in house; on leads in walled garden. Shop & Information Centre. Wheelchairs provided. *Parties by prior arrangement with the administrators.*
Refreshments: Available at Clock Tower Restaurant. Telephone Scots Gap (067 074) 274.

CHATHILL

PRESTON TOWER
(Major T. H. Baker-Cresswell)

One of the few survivors of 78 Pele Towers listed in 1415. The tunnel vaulted rooms remain unaltered and provide a realistic picture of the grim way of life under the constant threat of 'Border Reivers'. Two rooms are furnished in contemporary style and there are displays of historic and local information.
Location: 7 m N of Alnwick; 1 m E from A1. Follow Historic Property signs. *Station: Chathill (1 m).*
Opening Times: All year—Daily during daylight hours. Adm £1, Chd 50p. Free car park. No dogs (except those left in car).

CHOLLERFORD

CHESTERS FORT
Telephone: (043 481) 379

An impressive bath-house, buildings of great interest inside the fort, the remains of the bridge carrying Hadrian's Wall across the Tyne, a museum full of Roman inscriptions and sculptures, all set in one of the most beautiful valleys in Northumberland—these are among the attractions of Chesters, once garrisoned by a regiment of Roman cavalry.
Location: ½ m (0.8 km) south west of Chollerford. OS map NY913702.
Opening Times: Good Friday to Sept 30, daily 10–6; Oct 1 to Maundy Thursday, daily 10–4. *Closed Mons, Christmas and New Year.* Adm £1.30, OAPs £1, Chd 65p.

CORBRIDGE

AYDON CASTLE
Telephone: (043 471) 2450

Built as a manor house at the end of the 13th century, Aydon Castle fortified almost immediately afterwards as a result of the insecurity of the borders with Scotland. Captured by the Scots in 1315, it was pillaged and burned, and seized again by English rebels two years later. It has survived as a result of its conversion to a farmhouse in the 17th century.
Location: 1 m (1.6 km) north east of Corbridge, on minor road off B6321 or A68. OS map 87, ref NZ002663.
Opening Times: Good Friday to Sept 30, daily 10–6. Adm £1.10, OAPs 80p, Chd 55p.

CORBRIDGE ROMAN SITE
Telephone: (043 471) 2349

For nearly a century this was the site of a sequence of Roman forts, since Corbridge was an important junction of roads to Scotland, York and Carlisle. It developed into a prosperous town and supply base for Hadrian's Wall, with shops, temples, houses, granaries and an elaborate fountain. Among the rich collection of finds in the museum is a remarkable fountainhead—the Corbridge Lion.
Location: ½ m (0.8 km) north west of Corbridge. OS map ref NY983649.
Opening Times: Good Friday to Sept 30, daily 10–6; Oct 1 to Maundy Thursday, daily 10–4. *Closed Mons, Christmas and New Year.* Adm £1.30, OAPs £1, Chd 65p.

EMBLETON

DUNSTANBURGH CASTLE
Telephone: (066 576) 231

Isolated and unspoilt, the ruins stand on a large, rocky cliff top rising steeply from the sea. Begun by Thomas, Earl of Lancaster, in 1313, the castle was attacked by the Scots and besieged during the Wars of the Roses. The keep gatehouse is still impressive and the south wall an enduring memorial to the workmanship of Earl Thomas's masons.
Location: 8 m (13 km) north east of Alnwick. OS map ref NU258220.
Opening Times: Good Friday to Sept 30, daily 10–6; Oct 1 to Maundy Thursday, daily 10–4. *Closed Mons, Christmas and New Year.* Adm 80p OAPs 60p, Chd 40p.

FORD

HEATHERSLAW MILL
near Berwick upon Tweed. Tel: (089 082) 291 or 338.
Restored working water driven corn mill. Museum exhibits of milling and local history. Apr to Sept: 11–6; Oct: weekends only. Adm charge. Cafe. Craft Shop. Rare Breeds.

LADY WATERFORD GALLERY
Ford Village.
19th century murals by Louisa Lady Waterford with villagers as models. Other paintings by her. All year; 10.30–5.30. Adm charge.

HOLY ISLAND

LINDISFARNE CASTLE, The National Trust
Telephone: Berwick (0289) 89244

Built about 1550. Sympathetically restored as a comfortable house by Lutyens in 1903.
Location: 5 m E of Beal across causeway.
Opening Times: Mar 24 to Sept 30—Daily (closed Fris, open Good Fri) 1–5.30; Oct—Weds, Sats & Suns 1–5.30. Last adm 4.30. Adm June, July Aug: £2.50. Other times £1.50. No party rate. No dogs in Castle. Unsuitable for wheelchairs.

LINDISFARNE PRIORY
Telephone: (028 989) 200

Roofless and ruined, the priory is still supremely beautiful, its graceful arches and decorated doorways commemorating the craftsmanship of their Norman builders. This has been sacred soil since 634 when the missionary Bishop Aidan was sent from Iona, to spread Christianity through northern England. New visitor centre with exhibition and shop.
Location: On Holy Island, which can be reached at low tide across a causeway. Tide tables are posted at each end of the causeway. OS map ref NU126418.
Opening Times: Good Friday to Sept 30, daily 10–6; Oct 1 to Maundy Thursday, daily 10–4. *Closed Mons, Christmas and New Year.* Adm £1.10, OAPs 80p, Chd 55p.

HOWICK

HOWICK GARDENS
(Howick Trustees Ltd)

Lovely flower, shrub and rhododendron gardens.
Location: 6 m NE of Alnwick, nr Howick village.
Opening Times: Apr to Sept—Daily 2–7. Adm £1, Chd 50p.

MORPETH

MELDON PARK   ♿
(M. J. B. Cookson, Esq.)

Built in 1832 for the Cookson family and occupied by them up to the present time. Main ground floor rooms only open to the public. Different coloured rhododendrons, especially in the wild garden.
Location: 7 m W of Morpeth on B6343 Morpeth/Hartburn Road; NW of Newcastle-upon-Tyne.
Opening Times: House & Grounds—May 20 to June 18, and Aug 19, 20, 21: daily from 2–5.
Refreshments: Light snacks weekends only.

MORPETH CHANTRY BAGPIPE MUSEUM
The Chantry, Bridge Street. Tel: (0670) 519466.
The collection is one of the largest and best of its kind in the world. The museum has an infra-red sound system which allows each visitor a unique musical experience. Set in a restored 13th century building, which also houses a Tourist Information Centre and thriving Crafts outlet. Open Mon–Sat 9.30–5.30. *Closed* Sun, Christmas Day, Boxing Day, New Year's Day. Adm 50p, chld/OAPs 25p, Museums Ass 25p, parties 10p per person. Wheelchairs available. Free car parking in Morpeth. The museum's unique sound system is available to hearing impaired visitors.

NORHAM

NORHAM CASTLE
Telephone: (028 982) 329

Built in the 12th century by the Bishop of Durham, this massive castle stands on a site of great natural strength. It withstood repeated attacks in the 13th and 14th centuries and was thought to be impregnable. But in 1513 it was stormed by the forces of James IV and partially destroyed. Although later rebuilt, the castle lost its importance as a defensive stronghold by the end of the 16th century.
Location: 8 m (13 km) south west of Berwick. OS map ref NT907476.
Opening Times: Good Friday to Sept 30, daily 10–6; Oct 1 to Maundy Thursday, daily 10–4. *Closed Mons, Christmas and New Year.* Adm 80p, OAPs 60p, Chd 40p.

PRUDHOE

PRUDHOE CASTLE
Telephone: (0661) 32303

Extensive remains of 12th century castle with gatehouse, curtain wall and keep enclosed within surrounding earthworks. In the 19th century a house was built within the ruins, now containing an exhibition on the history of the castle.
Location: In Prudhoe, on minor road off A695. OS map ref NZ092634.
Opening Times: Good Friday to Sept 30, daily 10–6; Oct 1 to Maundy Thursday, daily 10–4. *Closed Mons, Christmas and New Year.* Adm £1.10, OAPs 80p, Chd 55p.

ROTHBURY

BRINKBURN PRIORY
Telephone: (066 570) 628

The priory church stands within a loop of the River Coquet, in beautiful surroundings. Founded about 1130, the priory suffered badly from Scottish raids. In the last century the church was carefully restored by the Newcastle architect, Thomas Austin, and is still in occasional use. It is a fine example of early Gothic architecture.
Location: 5 m (8 km) east of Rothbury. OS map ref NZ116984.
Opening Times: Good Friday to Sept 30, daily 10–6. Adm 80p, OAPs 60p, Chd 40p.

CRAGSIDE HOUSE & COUNTRY PARK, The National Trust
Telephone: Rothbury (0669) 20333   ♿

The House was designed by Richard Norman Shaw for the first Lord Armstrong and built between 1864–95. It contains much of its original furniture and Pre-Raphaelite paintings. It was the first house in the world to be lit by electricity generated by water power. The Country Park is famous for its rhododendrons, magnificent trees and the beauty of the lakes. New in 1988 'The Power Circuit', a three mile circular walk including the restored Ram & Power Houses with their hydraulic and hydroelectric machinery.
Location: ½ m E of Rothbury; 30 m N of Newcastle-upon-Tyne. Entrance off Rothbury/Alnwick Road B6341; 1 m N of Rothbury at Debdon Burn Gate.
Opening Times: COUNTRY PARK, ARMSTRONG ENERGY CENTRE & POWER CIRCUIT: Mar 24 to Oct 30 daily (*closed* Mon) but open Bank Holiday Mon. Easter to end Oct: 10.30–7 (or dusk if earlier). Nov to Easter: 10.30–4, Sat and Sun. HOUSE: Mar 24 to Oct 30 daily 1–5.30 (*closed* Mon) but open Bank Holiday Mon. Last adm 5. In Apr and Oct on selected days only, guided tours may be available. Adm House & Country Park, Museum & Power Circuit £3; Country Park £1.50. Parties £2.50; Country Park £1.20. Parties by prior arrangement only with the Administrator. Armstrong Energy Centre & shop in Visitor centre. Dogs in Country Park only. Wheelchair access to House—lift available (wheelchairs provided). Toilets for disabled. Fishing.
Refreshments: Restaurant in Visitor Centre. Telephone Rothbury (0669) 20134

SEATON SLUICE

SEATON DELAVAL HALL
Telephone: Tyneside (091) 2373040/2371493
(The Lord Hastings)

Splendid English baroque house, regarded by many as Sir John Vanbrugh's masterpiece. An early 18th century feat of architecture, comprising a centre block between two arcaded and pedimented wings.
Location: ½ m from coast at Seaton Sluice, and between Blyth and Whitley Bay (A190). (Northumbria Bus from Newcastle 363, 364.)
Opening Times: May 1–Sept 30: Wed, Sun, and Bank Holidays 2–6. Adm £1, Chd (accompanied by adult) 50p, OAPs 50p.
Refreshments: Lunch and refreshments available at Astley Arms (½ m) on coast.

STOCKSFIELD

CHERRYBURN, BEWICK MUSEUM
(Thomas Bewick Birthplace Trust)
Mickley NE43 7DB. Tel: (0661) 843276.
A new museum, preserving the farm cottage where the famous wood engraver, Thomas Bewick, was born in 1753. Includes displays on Bewick's life and wildlife of the area, which provided much of his inspiration. Open throughout the year 10–5. *Closed* Mon. Adm £1.50, Chld/OAP £1. Schools and other parties at reduced rates. Free car parking. Suitable for disabled persons (no wheelchairs available). Printing demonstrations from time to time.

HUNDAY NATIONAL TRACTOR AND FARM MUSEUM
Newton. Tel: Stocksfield (0661) 842553.
Museum of the Year 1981. Vintage tractors, stationary engines, reaping and threshing machinery; working water wheels; smithy.

WARKWORTH

WARKWORTH CASTLE
Telephone: (0665) 711423

From 1332 the history of Warkworth was the history of the Percy family. In 1399 this became the history of England, when the third Percy lord of Warkworth and his son Harry Hotspur put Henry IV on the throne. Three scenes from Shakespeare's Henry IV Part 1 are set at Warkworth. Norman in origin, the castle has some very fine medieval masonry. The keep was restored and made habitable in the 19th century.

Location: 7½ m (12 km) south of Alnwick. OS map ref NU247057.
Opening Times: Good Friday to Sept 30, daily 10–6; Oct 1 to Maundy Thursday, daily 10–4. *Closed Mons, Christmas and New Year.* Adm 80p, OAPs 60p, Chd 40p.

WARKWORTH HERMITAGE
Telephone: (0665) 711423

The hermitage and chapel of Holy Trinity is situated in a peaceful, retired place, overshadowed and surrounded by trees upon the left bank of the River Coquet half a mile above the castle, in that part of the manor of Warkworth anciently called Sunderland Park. It can be approached by boat up the river from the landing place below the castle or by a pleasant footpath through woods and meadows up the right bank and across by ferry from the upper boat landing.

Location: 7½ m (12 km) south of Alnwick.
Opening Times: Good Friday to Sept 30, open 10–6 weekends only. Adm 55p, OAPs 40p, Chd 25p.

WYLAM

GEORGE STEPHENSON'S BIRTHPLACE, The National Trust
Telephone: Wylam (06614) 3457

A small stone cottage built c. 1750. The birthplace, in 1781, of the inventor.
Location: 8 m W of Newcastle 1½ m S of A69 at Wylam-on-Tyne.
Station: Wylam (½ m).
Opening Times: Mar 24 to Oct 30—Weds, Sats & Suns (open Good Friday & Bank Holiday Mon) 1–5.30 (last adm 5). Other times of the year by appointment only with the tenant. Adm 60p, Chd 30p. Parking facilities 500 yards from cottage by War Memorial in village. No dogs. Wheelchair access.
NB Access to cottage by foot and bicycle only.

Nottinghamshire

CARLTON-ON-TRENT

CARLTON HALL
(Trustees of G H Vere-Laurie dec'd)

George III house built c.1765 by Joseph Pocklington of Newark, banker, 1736–1817. Beautiful drawing room. Magnificent ancient cedar in grounds. Stables attributed to Carr of York.

Location: 7 m N of Newark just off A1.
Opening Times: Any day, telephone (0636) 821421 to be certain of being shown round. Adm House and Garden £1.50.

CLIFTON

CLIFTON HALL
(Trent Polytechnic)

This recently restored Georgian mansion forms part of Trent Polytechnic and houses the School of Education.

Location: Just outside the village, 5 m SW from Nottingham on A453.
Opening Times: Open weekdays, except public holidays. Application for parties to visit the Hall should be made to The Assistant Director (Administration). Trent Polytechnic, Burton Street, Nottingham.

LINBY

NEWSTEAD ABBEY
Telephone: Mansfield (0623) 793557
(Nottingham City Council)

The medieval Priory of Newstead was converted into the Byron family house in the 16th century and restored in the 1820s. It was the home of the poet Byron in the early 19th century and now contains his possessions, furniture, pictures, letters, manuscripts and first editions. Furniture and possessions of the later 19th century owners are also to be seen. The house stands in over 300 acres of beautiful parkland with lakes, waterfalls, a Japanese water garden, rock and rose gardens, a subtropical garden and a Monk's stew pond.

Location: 11 m N of Nottingham on the Mansfield Road (A60).
Station: Nottingham, then by Trent bus no. 63 from Victoria Centre.
Opening Times: House: open Good Friday to Sept 30—Daily 11.30–6 (last adm 5). Adm £1.20, Chd 20p, OAPs & UB40 holders 40p (1988). Also Oct 1 to Easter by arrangement. Gardens open all year—Daily 10–dusk. Grounds & Gardens Adm 85p, Chd 40p (1988). Charges subject to revision.
Refreshments: Tea at tearoom in the grounds. Telephone (0623) 797392.

MANSFIELD

MANSFIELD MUSEUM AND ART GALLERY
(Mansfield District Council)
Leeming Street. Tel: (0623) 663088.
Collections: Natural history display – 'The Nature of Mansfield'; display of William Billingsley porcelain, lustreware and Wedgwood and of watercolours of Old Mansfield. Regular loan exhibitions. Mon to Fri 10–5; Sat 10–1, 2–5.

NEWARK-ON-TRENT

MILLGATE FOLK MUSEUM *(Newark & Sherwood District Council)*
Millgate NG24 4TS. Tel: (0636) 79403.
The three main exhibition floors centre on the social and folk life of Newark from the turn of the century until the second World War. A series of furnished rooms depict domestic scenes, while a street of 19th century shops display the fashions and wares of those times. Tools and implements exhibited relate to the local trades of malting, smithing and farming. Apr–Sept: Mon to Fri, 10–12, 1–5; Sat, Sun, Bank Holidays and day following Bank Holiday 1.30–5.30. Oct: Sun 2–5. Adm free. Parking, Lombard Street (150 yards away). Guided tours of Museum and Newark Castle by appointment. Other times by arrangement.

MUSEUM OF DOLLS & BYGONE CHILDHOOD *(Vina Cooke)*
The Old Rectory, Cromwell. Tel: (0636) 821364.
Fine house built c1685, now home of the Vina Cooke collection of dolls, costumes, toys and items evoking the magic of golden days. Also unique handmade portrait dolls. Open all year but times vary, so appointment necessary. Adm £1, Chld 50p. Parties up to 50 by appointment. Menu by prior arrangement. Car parking free. Unsuitable for disabled persons.

NEWARK AIR MUSEUM
(Registered Charity, run by Committee, Chairman Mr. R. Bryan)
The Airfield, Winthorpe, NG24 2NY. Tel: Newark 707170.
Display of over 30 Aircraft including Avro Vulcan bomber. Extensive collection of engines and aviation related exhibits in the exhibition hall. Apr to Oct: Mon to Fri: 10–5, Sat 1–5, Sun 10–6. Adm £1.50, Chld/OAPs 50p. Parties of 10 or more, 80p, Chld/ OAPs 30p. Free car parking. Suitable for disabled persons. Curator: Mr. M.J. Smith.

NEWARK MUSEUM *(Newark and Sherwood District Council)*
Appleton Gate NG24 1JY. Tel: (0636) 702358.
Collections are of local archaeology and history, some natural history and art. Weekdays 10–1, 2–5; Sun (Apr to Sept) 2–5. *Closed* Thurs.

NOTTINGHAM

BREWHOUSE YARD MUSEUM *(Nottingham City Council)*
Tel: (0602) 483504.
Five 17th and 18th century cottages at the foot of the Castle Rock, containing room settings charting the history of everyday life in Nottingham.

CANAL MUSEUM *(Nottingham City Council)*
Canal Street. Tel: (0602) 598835.
Displays are based on the theme of the River Trent, particularly canal and river transport through the ages.

GEORGE GREEN'S WINDMILL AND SCIENCE CENTRE
(Nottingham City Council)
Tel: (0602) 503635.
Restored working tower mill producing flour for sale.

INDUSTRIAL MUSEUM *(Nottingham City Council)*
Wollaton Park. Tel: (0602) 284602.
Displays in 18th century stable block presenting a history of Nottingham's industries.

THE LACE CENTRE NOTTINGHAM
Severns Building, Castle Road NG1 6AA. Tel: (0602) 413539.
An exhibition of all types of lace manufactured in the Nottingham area. Many articles containing this lace are available to purchase and the idea of the exhibition is to give visitors to the City the opportunity to see and to buy if they wish. Described by Evelyn Laye as "An Alladin's cave of lace". Demonstrations of hand made lace every Thursday afternoon from Easter to the end of Oct. Open daily including Suns and Bank Holidays throughout the year. *Closed* Christmas Day. Adm free. Parties welcome. Parking within 100 yards. Also on road when available.

MUSEUM OF COSTUME AND TEXTILES
(Nottingham City Council)
51 Castlegate. Tel: (0602) 483504.
An elegant row of Georgian terraced houses, built 1788, containing the City's costume, lace and textile collections.

NOTTINGHAM CASTLE MUSEUM *(Nottingham City Council)*
Tel: (0602) 483504.
A 17th century residence built by the Dukes of Newcastle on the site of the medieval royal castle. Now housing collections of fine and decorative art, ethnography, militaria, and a history of Nottingham Gallery. Contemporary Craft shop.

THRUMPTON HALL
Telephone: Nottingham 830333
(George FitzRoy Seymour, Esq)

Jacobean. Magnificent carved staircase. Fine pictures and furniture. Lived in and shown by owners.

Location: 7 m S of Nottingham; 3 m E of M1 at junction 24; 1 m from A453.
Opening Times: By appointment for parties of 20 or more persons. Adm House & Gardens £2, Chd £1. Minimum charge of £40. Open all year including evenings.
Refreshments: By prior arrangement.

UNIVERSITY ART GALLERY
(Dept. of Art History), Portland Building, University Park.
Tel: (0602) 484848 Ext. 2253.
Exhibitions changed two or three times each term. Since 1956 a continuous programme has been arranged (apart from most vacations). Mon to Fri 10–7; Sat 11–5. Refreshments obtained on the premises.

WOLLATON HALL
Telephone: Nottingham 281333
(City of Nottingham)

Fine example of late Elizabethan Renaissance architecture. Natural History Museum – one of the finest in the country.

Location: 2½ m W of City centre.
Station: Nottingham (2¾ m).
Opening Times: All the year. Apr to Sept—Weekdays 10–7, Suns 2–5; Oct to Mar—Weekdays 10–dusk, Suns 1.30–4.30. Adm free (small charge Suns & Bank Hols). *Conducted tours by arrangement 50p, Chd 20p (subject to alteration). Closed Christmas Day.*
Refreshments: Tea at refreshment pavilion *(Apr to Sept).*

OLLERTON

RUFFORD CRAFT CENTRE
Rufford Country Park. Tel: Mansfield (0623) 822944.
Major Craft and Sculpture Exhibitions, Craft Shop, Demonstrations, Café, Sculpture Garden. Open Jan and Feb: weekends only 11–4.30; Mar to Dec: daily 11–5. Adm free.

PAPPLEWICK

PAPPLEWICK HALL
Telephone: (0602) 633491
(Dr R. B. Godwin-Austen)

Fine Adam house built 1784 with park and woodland garden.
Location: 6 m N of Nottingham, 2 m from exit 27 M1.
Opening Times: By appointment only, all year.

RADCLIFFE ON TRENT

HOLME PIERREPONT HALL
(Mr & Mrs Robin Brackenbury)

Medieval brick manor house. Historic Courtyard garden with box parterre, 1875. Regional 17th, 18th, 19th and 20th century furniture, china and pictures. Quiet and free from crowds. Jacob sheep. Shop with Jacob wool products.
Location: 5 m SE from centre of Nottingham off A52 approach past National Water Sports Centre and continue for 1½ m.
Opening Times: Easter Sun, Mon & Tues; May Bank Holiday & Spring & Summer Bank Hol Mons & Tues; June, July & Aug—Suns, Tues, Thurs & Fris 2–6. Adm £1.80, Chd 75p, *subject to alteration. Parties by appointment throughout year.*
Refreshments: Home made teas. Other refreshments by arrangement.

RETFORD

THE BASSETLAW MUSEUM *(Bassetlaw District Council)*
  Amcott House, Grove Street. Tel: Retford (0777) 706741.
Archaeology, local history, bygones, decorative arts. Opened Dec 1986. Opening hours Mon to Sat 10–5, *closed* Sun. (See also Worksop, Nottinghamshire.)

RUDDINGTON

FRAMEWORK KNITTERS' MUSEUM
  Chapel Street. Tel: (0602) 846914.
Unique complex of frameshops and cottages, purpose-built 1829; working handframes and allied machinery; two exhibitions; lecture room; slide/tape sequences and video; period cottages 1850 & 1900. Shop: knitted goods made on site, publications, etc. Open Apr to Oct Tues, Wed & Thurs 10–4. By appointment throughout the year. Adm £1.50, Student/Chld 50p. A Museum of the Year Award and AIA Dorothea Award for Conservation – 1984.

WORKSOP

CLUMBER PARK, The National Trust
Telephone: Worksop (0909) 476592   &

4,000 acre landscaped park with lake and woods. Classical bridge, temples, lawned Lincoln Terrace and pleasure grounds. Kitchen garden exhibition.
Location: Clumber Park 4½ m SE of Worksop; 6½ m SW of East Retford.
Opening Times: Open daily all year. The Estate Office, Gardens Cottage, Clumber Park, Worksop, Notts S80 3AZ. Vehicle parking charges. Dogs admitted. Shop. Cycle hire. Fishing bank. Tricycles, tandems, wheelchairs & special fishing platform for disabled.
Refreshments: Cafeteria open all year daily. Licensed restaurant for lunches daily, evening meals available for pre-booked parties. Telephone: Worksop 484122.

WORKSOP MUSEUM *(Bassetlaw District Council)*
  Memorial Avenue.
Items of local interest. Under development as part of the Bassetlaw Museum (see Retford, Nottinghamshire). Hours of opening as Public Library.

City of Nottingham Museums

Greens Mill Museum

CASTLE MUSEUM: Ceramics, glass, silver, alabasters, archaeology, antiquities, paintings, temporary exhibitions, underground caves and passages, contemporary craft shop.
WOLLATON HALL NATURAL HISTORY MUSEUM: Botany, zoology, geology, British and foreign herbaria.
INDUSTRIAL MUSEUM: Printing, pharmacy, hosiery, lace, beam engine, horse gin, agricultural machinery.
NEWSTEAD ABBEY: Possessions of the poet Byron, pictures and furniture, manuscripts and first editions.
MUSEUM OF COSTUME AND TEXTILES, CASTLE GATE: 17th century costume, map tapestries, period rooms, accessories of all sorts, European and Eastern embroideries. Lace room.
BREWHOUSE YARD MUSEUM: Everyday life in Nottingham from the 17th century to the present day.
CANAL MUSEUM: Canal and river transport through the ages; natural history and archaeology of the Trent Valley.
GEORGE GREEN'S WINDMILL AND SCIENCE CENTRE: Restored working mill. Working scientific exhibits. Life and work of George Green. History of mills and milling.

Oxfordshire

ABINGDON

ABINGDON MUSEUM
(Oxfordshire County Council with Abingdon Town Council)
The County Hall, Market Place. Tel: (0235) 23703.
Displays of the geology, archaeology and history of Abingdon and the surrounding area in the original Sessions Hall of the County Hall, possibly designed by Sir Christopher Wren and begun in 1678, described by Pevsner as the grandest Market Hall in England. Daily 2–5. *Closed* Bank Hols. Adm 10p, Chld 5p.

ALKERTON

BROOK COTTAGE
Telephone: Edge Hill (029 587) 303 or 590
(Mr & Mrs David Hodges)

4 acre landscaped garden, mostly formed since 1964, surrounding 17th century house. Wide variety of trees, shrubs and plants of all kinds; water garden; one-colour borders; collection of shrub roses; many clematis. Interesting throughout season.
Location: 6 m NW of Banbury; ½ m A422 (Banbury/Stratford-upon-Avon). In Alkerton take lane opposite war memorial then right fork.
Opening Times: GARDEN ONLY. Apr 1–Oct 31, Mon–Fri 10–6. Adm £1, Chd free. Evenings and weekends by appointment. *In aid of National Gardens Scheme.*
Refreshments: For parties by prior arrangement.

ASHBURY

ASHDOWN HOUSE, The National Trust

17th century house built by 1st Lord Craven and by him 'consecrated' to Elizabeth, Queen of Bohemia; great staircase rising from hall to attic; portraits of the Winter Queen's family; access to roof, fine views; box parterre and lawns. Avenues and woodland walks.
Location: 2¼ m S of Ashbury; 3½ m N of Lambourn on W side of B4000.
Opening Times: Hall, stairway & roof only (fine views). Apr to end Oct—Weds & Sats 2–6. Guided tours only: at 2.15, 3.15, 4.15 and 5.15, from front door. *Closed* Easter and Bank Holiday Mon. Adm Grounds, hall, stairway & roof £1.20, Chd half-price. **Woodlands** open all year—Sats to Thurs, dawn to dusk, adm free. No reduction for parties (which should pre-book in writing). No dogs allowed in house or grounds. Wheelchair access to garden only.

BANBURY

BANBURY MUSEUM
(Oxfordshire County Council with Cherwell District Council)
8 Horsefair (opposite Banbury Cross). Tel: (0295) 59855.
New permanent exhibition: 'Banburyshire' – Banbury's shops, trades and industries and the town's role as market centre for its rich agricultural hinterland. The Photographer's Gallery houses a reconstructed local photographer's shop, the Parade Studio, of around 1905 and changing temporary exhibitions. Tourist Information Centre, book and gift shop, coffee bar. Apr to Sept: Mon to Sat 10–5. *Closed* Sun. Oct to Mar: Tues to Sat 10–4.30. *Closed* Sun and Mon. Adm free.

BROUGHTON CASTLE
Telephone: Banbury (0295) 62624
(The Lord Saye & Sele)

A moated Tudor mansion with early 14th century nucleus. 16th and 18th century plaster ceilings and 16th century chimney pieces.
Location: 2 m SW of Banbury on the Shipston-on-Stour Road (B4035).
Opening Times: May 18 to Sept 14—Weds & Suns 2–5; also Thurs in July & Aug 2–5; Bank Hol Suns & Bank Hol Mons including Easter 2–5. Adm £2, Chd £1, OAPs/ Students £1.60. Groups on other days throughout the year by appointment (reduced rates).
Refreshments: Buffet teas on open days; by arrangement for groups.

BURFORD

TOLSEY MUSEUM
High Street.
Local history. Daily 2.30–5.30. Apr–Oct.

BUSCOT

BUSCOT OLD PARSONAGE, The National Trust

Built in 1703 of Cotswold stone and stone tiles. On the banks of the Thames. Small garden.
Location: 2 m SE of Lechlade; 4 m NW of Faringdon on A417.
Opening Times: Mar 29 to end Oct—Weds 2–6, by appointment in writing with the tenant. Adm £1. *No parties.* No dogs. No WCs. Unsuitable for wheelchairs.

CHARLBURY

NORTH LEIGH ROMAN VILLA
Telephone: (0993) 881830

This was the home of a 'county' family in the 4th century. Farming was clearly profitable on this good arable land, with Akeman Street nearby to transport the produce to the Roman centres at St Albans and Cirencester. Excavations have revealed an elaborate courtyard villa with over sixty rooms. The site has suffered in the past from souvenir hunters, but it is clear that the villa was equipped with an enviable range of 'comforts' in the form of underfloor heating, painted walls, mosaic tile floors and an elaborate system of hot and cold bath houses.
Location: 4¼ m (6.8 km) south east of Charlbury. OS map ref SP397154.
Opening Times: Good Friday to Sept 30, daily 10–6. Adm 55p, OAPs 40p, Chd 25p.

CHASTLETON

CHASTLETON HOUSE
Telephone: Barton-on-Heath (0608 74) 355
(Mrs Clutton-Brock)

Jacobean Manor House c. 1603. Original Panelling, furniture, tapestries, embroideries. Topiary garden c. 1700.
Location: 4 m from Moreton-in-Marsh off A44 Chipping Norton to Moreton-in-Marsh road; 5 m from Stow-on-the-Wold off A436 Stow to Chipping Norton road.
Opening Times: Good Friday to Sun Oct 1 incl. Fri, Sat, Sun & Bank Hol Mon 2–5. Parties be previous arrangement all year round. Adm £2.50, Chd £1.50. Reductions for parties over 20 in number. Limited free parking. Guided Tours only.

DIDCOT

DIDCOT RAILWAY CENTRE   *(Great Western Society Ltd)*
Tel: (0235) 817200.
Re-creating the Golden Age of the Great Western Railway. Steam trains in the engine shed, reconstructed station, Brunel broadgauge demonstration. Train rides on steaming days. Small exhibits museum. Mar to Dec: Sat, Suns and Bank Hols (*not Christmas*) 11–5, daily Easter to Oct. Steaming Days: first and last Sun each month Mar to Oct, Bank Hols, all Suns and Weds during Aug. Car parking. Meals, snacks and drinks. General Manager: M. Dean.

ENSTONE

DITCHLEY PARK
Telephone: Enstone (060 872) 346
(Ditchley Foundation)

Third in size and date amongst the great 18th century mansions of Oxfordshire. Designed by Gibbs, decoration of Great Hall by Kent.
Location: 1½ m W of A34 at Kiddington; 2 m from Charlbury (B4437).
Station: Charlbury (2 m).
Opening Times: It is unlikely that there will be a set open period in 1989, but private parties will be welcome by special arrangement Mons–Thurs afternoons until early July.

FARINGDON

BUSCOT PARK, The National Trust
Telephone: Faringdon (0367) 20786 (not weekends)

Built 1780. Fine paintings and furniture. Burne-Jones room. Attractive garden walks, lake.
Location: 3 m NW Faringdon on Lechlade/Faringdon road (A417).
Opening Times: Mar 22 to end Sept (incl Good Fri, Easter Sat & Sun)—Weds, Thurs & Fris 2–6; and every 2nd and 4th Sat and each Sun immediately following 2–6. *Last admission to house 5.30.* Adm House & Grounds £2.50, Chd £1.25. Grounds only £1.50, Chd 75p. *No dogs. No indoor photography.* Unsuitable for wheelchairs.

THE GREAT BARN, The National Trust

13th century, stone built, stone tiled roof, exceptionally interesting timber roof construction. Magnificent proportions.
Location: 2 m SW of Faringdon between A420 & B4019.
Opening Times: All year daily at reasonable hours. Adm 50p. Dogs on leads admitted. Wheelchair access.

PUSEY HOUSE GARDENS
Telephone: Buckland 222　　　　　　　&
(Pusey Garden Trust)

Herbaceous borders, walled gardens, water garden, large collection of shrubs and roses. Many fine trees.
Location: 5 m E of Faringdon, ½ m S off A420; 12 m W of Oxford.
Opening Times: Mar 25 to Oct 29 — Tues, Weds, Thurs, Sats & Suns; also Bank Hol Mons: 2–6. Adm £2 (children under 11 free). Parties please book, £1.50 per person. Car park free. Plants for sale.
Refreshments: Teas available.

HENLEY-ON-THAMES

GREYS COURT, The National Trust
Telephone: Rotherfield Greys (04917) 529　　　　&

Beautiful gardens, medieval ruins, a Tudor donkey wheel for raising well water and a 16th century house containing interesting 18th century plasterwork and furniture. The 'Archbishop's' Maze was open for the first time in 1982.
Location: At Rotherfield Greys NW of Henley-on-Thames on the road to Peppard A423.
Opening Times: House: Mar 27 to end Sept — Mons, Weds, Fris 2–6. Garden: Mar 25 to end of Sept — Mons to Sats 2–6. Last admissions half-hour before closing. Adm House & Garden £2.40. Garden only £1.60, Chd half-price. Parties must book in advance. No reduction for parties. *Closed Good Friday.* Dogs in car park only. Wheelchairs provided.
Refreshments: Teas (Mar 27, and May — Weds & Sats; June to end Sept — Mons, Weds, Fris & Sats); also for booked parties at other times by arrangement.

HISTORIC HOUSE & MUSEUM, FAWLEY COURT
(Marian Fathers)

Designed by Sir Christopher Wren, built 1684 as a family residence. The house, decorated by Grinling Gibbons, is situated in a beautiful park designed by "Capability" Brown. The Museum contains documents of the Polish kings and memorabilia of the Polish Army.
Location: 1 m N of Henley-on-Thames via A4155 to Marlow.
Station: Henley-on-Thames (1½ m).
Opening Times: Mar to Nov: Weds, Thurs, Suns 2–5. *Closed Easter and Whitsuntide weeks.* Adm £2, Chd £1, OAPs £1.50. Car park. No dogs. Dec, Feb: open to groups by pre-booked appointment.
Refreshments: Tea, coffee & home-made cakes available July & Aug.

STONOR PARK
Telephone: Turville Heath (049 163) 587
(Lord & Lady Camoys)

Ancient home of the Stonor family and centre of Catholicism. Fine furniture and important sculpture. Magnificent setting.
Location: On B480; 5 m N of Henley-on-Thames, 5 m S of Watlington.
Opening Times: Apr — Suns & Bank Hol Mons only; May to Sept — Weds, Thurs, Suns & Bank Hol Mons, Sats (Aug); 2–5.30 (last adm to house 5); (but *closed Sun June 25.*) Bank Hol Mons 11–5.30. Parties by prior arrangement any Tues, Weds, Thurs (morning or afternoon) and Sun (afternoon only). Adm (1988) £2, OAPs £1.70, Chd (under 14) in family parties free. Party rates on application.

KINGSTON BAGPUIZE

KINGSTON HOUSE
Telephone: (0865) 820259　　　　　　&
(Lady Tweedsmuir)

A superb Charles II manor house surrounded by parkland, a large garden and attractive 17th century stable buildings. The house has a magnificent cantilevered staircase and well-proportioned panelled rooms with fine furniture and pictures. The large and interesting garden contains beautiful trees, lawns, a woodland garden, herbaceous and shrub borders and many lovely bulbs.
Location: 5½ m W of Abingdon at junction of A415 & A420.
Opening Times: May, June, and Sept – Weds and Suns, also May and Aug Bank Hols 2.30–5.30. Adm House and Gardens: £2, OAPs, £1.50, Chd £1. Garden only: 50p. Group rates on request. (Chd under 5 free adm to Gardens, not admitted to House). Groups welcome by appointment. Wheelchairs garden only. No dogs. Gifts, books, plants for sale. Car parking.
Refreshments: Teas.

MILTON

MILTON MANOR HOUSE
Telephone: Abingdon (0235) 831287 or 831871　&
(Mrs Majorie Mockler)

17th century house with Georgian wings. Traditionally designed by Inigo Jones. Walled garden & pleasure grounds.
Location: In Milton village 4 m S of Abingdon; 1 m from Sutton Courtney on B4016; A34, signpost Milton.
Opening Times: Easter Sat to Oct 30 — Sats & Suns and all Bank Hols: 2–5.30. Adm £1.50, Chd 60p. Free car park. *Coach parties welcome by arrangement at reduced rates. Candlelight tours in the evening by arrangement.*
Refreshments: By arrangement.

MINSTER LOVELL

MINSTER LOVELL HALL AND DOVECOTE
Telephone: (0993) 775315
(English Heritage)

Originally a 15th century manor house, the hall was built around a courtyard. The medieval dovecote, complete with nesting boxes, has recently been restored. When the hall was dismantled in the 18th century, a skeleton was found in the cellars. This is thought to have been the Yorkist Lord Lovell who disappeared after the Battle of Bosworth 1485, where he fought on the losing side.
Location: 2½ m (4 km) north west of Witney. OS map ref SP324114.
Opening Times: Good Friday to Sept 30, daily 10–6; Oct 1 to Maundy Thurs, daily 10–4. *Closed* Mons, Dec 24–26, Jan 1. Adm 80p, OAPs 60p, Chd 40p.

NETTLEBED

NUFFIELD PLACE
Telephone: (0491) 641224
(Nuffield College, Friends of Nuffield Place)

The home from 1933–1963 of Lord Nuffield, founder of Morris Motors, Nuffield Place is a rare survival of a complete upper-middle class home of the 1930s. Built in 1914, the house was enlarged in 1933 for Lord Nuffield. Several rooms are still decorated in the '30s style, and all rooms contain furnishings acquired by Lord and Lady Nuffield when they took up residence. Clocks, rugs and some tapestries are of fine quality. Some of the furniture is antique but much was custom made by Cecil A. Halliday of Oxford, and is of skilled craftsmanship. The gardens, with mature trees, stone walls and rockery, were laid out during and just after the First World War. Lady Nuffield's Wolseley car is also on display.
Location: Approximately 7 m from Henley-on-Thames, just off A423 to Oxford.
Opening Times: May to Sept, every 2nd and 4th Sun 2–5. Adm £1.50, Chd 50p. Parties by arrangement. Ground floor and garden suitable for the disabled.
Refreshments: Teas.

OXFORD

THE ASHMOLEAN MUSEUM OF ART AND ARCHAEOLOGY
Beaumont Street. Tel: (0865) 278000.
British, European, Mediterranean, Egyptian and Near Eastern archaeology. Italian, Dutch, Flemish, French and English oil paintings; Old Master and modern drawings, watercolours and prints; miniatures; European ceramics; sculpture and bronzes; English silver; objects of applied art. Coins and medals of all countries and periods. Casts from the antique. Chinese and Japanese porcelain, painting and lacquer. Chinese bronzes, Tibetan art, Indian sculpture and painting, Islamic pottery and metalwork. Tues to Sat 10–4; Sun 2–4. *Closed* Mons and Sept 3, 4 and 5, and a period over Christmas, the New Year and Easter, but open Bank Hol Mons, Easter to late summer 2–5.

BALFOUR BUILDING
(entrance beside no. 60 Banbury Road). Tel: (0865) 274726.
Musical instruments and hunter-gatherers – past and present. Audio-visual facilities. Mon to Sat 1–4.30. May be *closed* Easter and Christmas weeks. Adm free.

BATE COLLECTION OF HISTORICAL INSTRUMENTS
Faculty of Music, St. Aldate's. Tel: (0865) 276139.
Comprehensive collection of Woodwind, Brass, Percussion instruments; Keyboards, Bows; a full Javanese Gamelan. Mon to Fri 2–5. Adm free.

BOTANIC GARDENS
(University of Oxford)

Oldest botanic garden in Britain, founded 1621.
Location: High Street.
Station: Oxford (1 m).
Opening Times: All the year — 9–5, (closes 4.30 winter). Adm free. *Closed Good Fri and Christmas day.*

CHRIST CHURCH LIBRARY
Peckwater Quadrangle. Tel: (0865) 276169.
Statuary, Carrolliana, manuscripts and printed books. Mon to Fri (by special appointment only).

CHRIST CHURCH PICTURE GALLERY
Enter by Canterbury Gate. Tel: (0865) 276172.
Important Old Master paintings and drawings. Mon to Sat 10.30–1, 2–4.30 (5.30 Easter to end Sept); Sun 2–4.30 (5.30 Easter to end Sept). *Closed* for one week at Christmas and Easter. Adm 40p, Chld 20p. Reduced rates for parties by arrangement. Free guided tours of the collections each Thurs 2.15–3.

MUSEUM OF THE HISTORY OF SCIENCE
Broad Street. Tel: (0865) 277280.
Collection of early scientific instruments (astrolabes, armillary spheres, sundials, microscopes, astronomical, electrical, medical and chemical apparatus), photographic apparatus, clocks and watches; also library, manuscripts and photographic records. Mon to Fri 10.30–1, 2.30–4. *Closed* Christmas and Easter weeks and all other Public Hols.

MUSEUM OF MODERN ART
30 Pembroke Street. Tel: (0865) 722733 recorded information: (0865) 728608.
Changing exhibitions of international contemporary art: paintings, drawings,

photographs, ceramics, sculpture, design, architecture. Films, concerts, seminars, workshops. Bookshop. Cafe MoMA. Tues–Sat 10–6; Sun 2–6; *Closed* Mon. Full access for disabled.

MUSEUM OF OXFORD   *(Oxfordshire County Council)*
St. Aldates. Tel: (0865) 815559.
This centrally situated museum guides you through the history of Oxford from the earliest times to the present day. Also temporary exhibitions and a bookshop. Tues to Sat 10–5. *Closed* Sun and Mon. Adm free.

THE OXFORD STORY   *(Heritage Projects Ltd)*
Broad Street OX1 3HA. Tel: (0865) 728822.
The Oxford Story – a brilliantly imaginative presentation of key aspects of the University's story, devised in conjunction with the University itself. The Oxford Story skillfully blends scholarship, technology and audio-visual techniques to bring the University's past to life. You experience eight centuries of the sights, sounds and personalities encountered by Oxford students. Witness great events, Wyclif's translation of the Bible into English, the Martyrdom of Cranmer in Broad Street and the University as a seat of the Royalist cause during the Civil War. Above all you encounter great men and women who shaped both the University and the world. Open daily (except Christmas Day) from 9. Adm £3, Chld £1.50. OAP, Student and family reductions. Individuals and parties may book in advance. Suitable for disabled persons. Gift shop.

OXFORD UNIVERSITY MUSEUM
Parks Road. Tel: (0865) 272950.
Natural history collections in unusual Victorian gothic-style building. Mon to Sat 12–5 (check opening times for Easter and Christmas). Adm free (donations box).

THE PITT RIVERS MUSEUM
South Parks Road (entrance through University Museum).
Tel: (0865) 270927.
Ethnology and prehistoric archaeology of the peoples of the world arranged typologically. Mon to Sat 1–4.30. May be *closed* Easter and Christmas weeks. Adm free.

THE ROTUNDA MUSEUM OF ANTIQUE DOLLS' HOUSES
Grove House, Iffley Turn.
Dolls' Houses 1700–1900 and contents (silver, dinner services, dolls etc.). Sun afternoons from May 1 to Mid-Sept and for parties of 12 or more by written appointment. *Closed* Sept 15 to Apr 31. No children under 16. Adm charge. Ten minutes by bus from central Oxford.

STANTON HARCOURT

STANTON HARCOURT MANOR   &
(Mr Crispin & The Hon Mrs Gascoigne)

Unique medieval buildings in tranquil surroundings—Old Kitchen, Pope's Tower and Domestic Chapel. House contains fine collection of pictures, furniture, silver and porcelain.
Location: 9 m W of Oxford; 5 m SE of Witney; on B4449, between Eynsham & Standlake.
Opening Times: House & Gardens. Mar 26, 27; Apr 6, 9, 27, 30; May 1; (Artists & Craftsmen at work), 11, 14, 25, 28, 29; June 8, 11, 22, 25; July 6, 9, 20, 23; Aug 3, 6, 24, 27, 28; Sept 7, 10, 21, 24: 2–6. **House & Garden** £2, Chd (12 and under) £1. **Garden only** £1, Chd (12 and under) 50p. Large parties and coaches by prior arrangement. Disabled visitors welcome. Home container-grown shrubs & pot plants for sale.
Refreshments: Teas on Suns and Bank Hols in aid of Parish Church.

STEEPLE ASTON

ROUSHAM HOUSE
Telephone: Steeple Aston (0869) 47110
(C Cottrell-Dormer, Esq)

17th century country house with landscape garden by William Kent. Portraits, miniatures.
Location: 12 m N of Oxford off Banbury Road (A423) at Hopcrofts Holt Hotel (1 m).
Station: Heyford (1 m).
Opening Times: Apr to Sept inclusive—Weds, Suns & Bank Hols 2–4.30. Gardens only, everyday 10–4.30. No children under 15. No dogs. *Parties by arrangement on other days.*

THAME

RYCOTE CHAPEL
Telephone: (084 47) 346

It was at the great mansion of Rycote that Sir Henry Norreys entertained that most peripatetic monarch, Elizabeth I. The house has long since disappeared, but the private chapel survives in its entirety. Founded in 1449 by Richard Quatremayne, the chapel still has the original font and some of the early seating. But the superb interior is mainly the work of 17th century craftsmen, and because it has escaped any restoration, it is of outstanding interest.
Location: 3 m (4.8 km) west of Thame. OS map ref SP667046.
Opening Times: Good Friday to Sept 30, daily 10–6; Oct 1 to Maundy Thursday, daily 10–4. *Closed Mons, Christmas and New Year.* Adm 80p, OAPs 60p, Chd 40p.

WALLINGFORD

WALLINGFORD MUSEUM
Flint House, High Street. Tel: (0491) 35065.
Permanent display, regularly updated, illustrating the span of local history; changing exhibitions.

WANTAGE

ARDINGTON HOUSE
Telephone: (0235) 833244
(D. C. N. Baring, Esq.)

Early 18th century of grey brick with red brick facings. Hall with Imperial staircase, panelled dining room with painted ceiling. Magnificent cedar trees.
Location: 12 m S of Oxford; 12 m N of Newbury; 2½ m E of Wantage.
Station: Didcot (8 m).
Opening Times: May to Sept—Mons & all Bank Hols 2.30–4.30. Parties of 10 or more welcomed any day by appointment. Adm House & Grounds £1.50.
Refreshments: Coffee & Teas by arrangement.

KINGSTONE LISLE PARK
Telephone: Uffington (036 782) 223
(Mrs Leopold Lonsdale)

Handsome house with dramatic flying staircase. Fine furnishings and beautiful gardens.
Location: 5 m W of Wantage on B4507.
Opening Times: Easter to Sept 9—Thurs & Bank Hol weekends (Sats, Suns & Mons): 2–5. Parties at other times by arrangement. Adm £2.20, Chd 80p. Parties and OAPs £2.
Refreshments: Teas by arrangement and at Bank Holidays.

VALE AND DOWNLAND MUSEUM CENTRE
(Vale and Downland Museum Trust, Wantage Town Council, Oxon County Council)
Church Street. Tel: (02357) 66838.
Gallery of Vale and Downland Life with the history of Wantage in its setting in the Vale of White Horse. Manned by enthusiastic volunteers; home-made refreshments, snacks, lunches, shop. Open all year: Tues to Sat 10.30–4.30; Sun 2–5, Bank Hol Mons when possible; check in advance. Adm free.

WHEATLEY

WATERPERRY GARDENS
Telephone: Ickford (084 47) 226 and 254

Church of Saxon origin and historical interest in grounds. Famous old glass, brasses and woodwork. Many interesting plants. Shrub, Herbaceous and Alpine Nurseries. Glasshouses and comprehensive Fruit Section.
Location: 8 m E of Oxford. 2 m from Wheatley off old A40. Well signposted locally with Tourist Board 'Rose' symbol.
Opening Times: All the year. Daily—Apr to Sept 10–5.30 (weekdays); 10–6 (weekends); Oct to Mar 10–4.30 *(Teashop closes 30 mins earlier)*. Closed for Christmas and New Year Hols. Open only to visitors to ART IN ACTION July 13–16. Adm to Ornamental Gardens & Nurseries Mar to Oct £1.20, Nov to Feb no charge. Parties and coaches at all times by appointment only. High quality Plant Centre and Garden Shop, telephone: Ickford (084 47) 226. *In aid of National Gardens' Scheme & Gardeners' Sun, June 11 & Aug 13.*
Refreshments: Teashop.

WOODSTOCK

BLENHEIM PALACE
Telephone: Woodstock (0993) 811325 (24 hrs)
(His Grace the Duke of Marlborough)

Masterpiece of Sir John Vanbrugh in the classical style. Fine collection of pictures and tapestries. Gardens and park designed by Vanbrugh and Queen Anne's gardener, Henry Wise. Later construction was carried out by 'Capability' Brown, who also created the famous Blenheim lake. Exhibition of Churchilliana and Sir Winston Churchill's birth room. Churchill paintings on exhibition. Also Blenheim Butterfly House, Garden Centre (open throughout the year), Adventure Playground, Garden Restaurant, Motor Launch and Train. All inclusive ticket.
Location: SW end of Woodstock which lies 8 m N of Oxford (A34).
Opening Times: mid-Mar to Oct 31—Daily 10.30–5.30 (last adm 4.45). Special prices & times apply on Spring Bank Holiday Sunday when the Lord Taverners Charity Cricket Match takes place. *Reduced rates for parties.* Educational service for school parties—Palace, Farm, Forestry, Horticulture & Nature Trail. Adm charges not available at time of going to press.
Refreshments: Licensed Restaurant & self service cafeteria at the Palace. Self Service restaurant at the Garden Centre.

OXFORDSHIRE COUNTY MUSEUM
(Oxfordshire County Council, Department of Leisure and Arts)
Fletcher's House. Tel: (0993) 811456.
The archaeology, crafts, industry and domestic life of the Oxford Region. Temporary exhibition programme. Coffee Bar, bookshop, pleasant gardens; occasional weekend events. May to Sept: Mon to Fri 10–5; Sat 10–6; Sun 2–6. Oct to Apr: Tues to Fri 10–4; Sat 10–5; Sun 2–5.

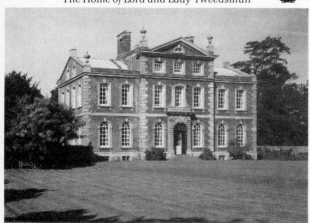

Shropshire

ACTON ROUND

ACTON ROUND HALL
(H L Kennedy, Esq)

Built in 1714 for Sir Whitmore Acton by the Smith Brothers of Warwick and abandoned from 1717–1918, the house remains little altered from its original state.
Location: 6 m W of Bridgnorth; 15 m SE of Shrewsbury.
Opening Times: May, June, July Aug—Thurs 2.30–5.30. Adm £1.50.

ACTON SCOTT

ACTON SCOTT WORKING FARM MUSEUM
(Shropshire County Council)
Wenlock Lodge, near Church Stretton. Tel: Marshbrook (069 46) 306/7.
A working Farm Museum using heavy horses and machinery to demonstrate agriculture as it was at about the turn of the century. Crafts demonstrated regularly, programmes available on application. Apr to Nov: Daily. Adm charge. Car park, picnic area, shops, café. Suitable for disabled visitors.

ALBRIGHTON

AEROSPACE MUSEUM
Royal Air Force, Cosford. Tel: (090 722) 4872/4112.
Britain's largest collection of Military and Civil Transport Aircraft and the history of our civil aviation heritage from DH4A to Concorde in British Airways Exhibition. Huge Missile collection including wartime German experimental weapons, exocet and modern British equipment. Europe's largest collection of Research and Development Aircraft. Open daily 10–4. *Closed* weekends Dec to Feb inclusive. Adm £2.50, Chld/OAPs £1. Special rates for school parties and other groups. Shop, cafe, picnic areas, large car park, all in large parkland setting on an active airfield. On A41, one mile south of Junction 3 on M54. In Royal Oak Country – Shropshire border. Administrator: John Francis.

ASTON MUNSLOW

THE WHITEHOUSE MUSEUM OF BUILDINGS
A Unique Homestead! Where building development has progressed generation by generation from the time Lord Edmund held it in 1043 AD to the present day. Here tutors and students from a wide range of Universities, Colleges, Societies in this and other countries spend days in studying this 6½ acre complex where chemicals have not been used throughout history. Wild flowers are cherished and home supplies of vegetables and herbs are maintained. Further details from Miss C. Purser, the White House, Aston Munslow and from Information Centres. SAE please.

ATCHAM

ATTINGHAM PARK, The National Trust
Telephone: Upton Magna (0743 77) 203

Designed in 1785 by George Steuart for the 1st Lord Berwick. Elegant classical interior decoration. Famous painted boudoir. Nash Picture Gallery. Fine collection of Regency Silver. Park landscape designed by Humphry Repton, 1797. Extensive deer park.
Location: At Atcham; 4 m SE of Shrewsbury, on N side of Telford Road (A5).
Opening Times: Mar 25 to end of Sept—Sats to Weds 2–5.30; Bank Hol Mons 11.30–5.30. Last adm 5. Closed Good Friday. Oct—Sats & Suns 2–5.30. Adm House & Grounds £2.20, Chd £1.10. Deer Park & Grounds only 70p. Family ticket £5.50. Prebooked parties, including evening opening, by arrangement. Dogs in grounds only (not in deer park). Wheelchair provided. Shop. Mother and Baby room.
Refreshments: Home-made teas (parties must pre-book). Lunches Sun only 12.30–2. Light buffet meals by arrangement with The Administrator.

BRIDGNORTH

BRIDGNORTH MUSEUM
(Bridgnorth and District Historical Society)
North Gate, High Street.
Bridgnorth Museum containing many items, mainly local, from Bronze Age tools, Civil War weapons, and Fire marks, to recent past. Apr to Sept: Sats 2–4. Bank Hols, Mid July to Aug: Mon, Tues and Wed 2–4. Adm free – donations welcomed. Parties by previous appointment. Public car parks: Innage, Smithfield and Listley Street. Curator: Mr and Mrs J.S. Ritter.

DUDMASTON, The National Trust
Telephone: Quatt 780866

Late 17th century house; collections of Dutch flower paintings, modern art, botanical paintings and family history. Extensive grounds, woodlands and lakeside garden.
Location: 4 m SE of Bridgnorth on A442.
Opening Times: Easter Sun to end of Sept—Weds & Suns 2.30–6 (last adm 5.30); also Thurs afternoons special opening for pre-booked parties only 2.30–6.

Adm House & Garden £2.20, Family £5.50. Garden only £1. Parties must book in advance. Dogs in garden only, on leads. Shop.
Refreshments: Home-made teas 3–5.30.

MIDLAND MOTOR MUSEUM
Stourbridge Road (A458). Tel: (0746) 761761.
One of the finest collections of sports and sports racing cars and motorcycles in Europe, 1920s to 1980s. Over 100 vehicles. Beautiful grounds, nature trail, picnic and children's play areas. Refreshments. Camping Park. All the year, daily from 10–5. *Closed* Dec 25. Adm charge.

UPTON CRESSETT HALL
Telephone: Morville 307
(William Cash, Esq)

Elizabethan Manor House and magnificent Gatehouse in beautiful countryside by Norman church. Unusually fine medieval timber work and interesting brick and plaster work; 14th century Great Hall.
Location: 4 m W of Bridgnorth; 18 m SE of Shrewsbury off A458.
Opening Times: May to Sept—Thurs 2.30–5. Adm £1, Chd 50p. *Parties at other times throughout the year by appointment.*
Refreshments: Teas & light refreshments by prior arrangement.

BROSELEY

BENTHALL HALL, The National Trust
Telephone: Telford (0952) 882159

16th century stone house with mullioned windows. Interior improved in 17th century. Fine oak staircase and plaster ceilings. Interesting small garden.
Location: 1 m NW of Broseley; 4 m NE of Much Wenlock; 6 m S of Wellington, (B4375).
Opening Times: Easter Sun to end Sept—Tues, Weds, Suns and Bank Hol Mons 2–6 (last adm 5.30). Adm £1.60, Chd 80p. Garden only 80p. *No reduction for parties.* No dogs. Wheelchair access.

THE LAWNS
Telephone: Telford (0952) 882557
(Michael & Molly Berthoud – The Lawns Preservation Trust)

Historic Georgian house where the industrial revolution began. Former home of John Wilkinson, ironmaster, and of John Rose, founder of Coalport. Extensive collections of English pottery and porcelain, 'Cabinet of a Thousand Cups', exhibition of tea and tea wares. Magnificent kitchen. Gardens of 1 acre. Picnic area.
Location: Just off B4373 Bridgnorth/Ironbridge road 6 m N of Bridgnorth.
Station: Telford (5 m).
Opening Times: Apr to Sept – Weds to Suns (& Bank Hols) 2–6. Guided tours on the hour. Last tour 5pm. Adm £2. No reductions. Booked parties for tours, lectures, seminars, MOST WELCOME AT ALL TIMES. Send s.a.e. for full details of 'Learning at Leisure' visits. No dogs, no stilettos. Unsuitable for wheelchairs.
Refreshments: Home made teas 2–5.30. Pre-booked party lunches, teas, suppers by arrangement.

CHURCH STRETTON

CARDING MILL VALLEY & LONG MYND,
The National Trust
Telephone: Church Stretton 722631

Chalet Pavilion in the magnificent scenery of Carding Mill Valley.
Location: 15 m S of Shrewsbury; W of Church Stretton Valley & A49.
Station: Church Stretton (1 m).
Opening Times: Moorland open all year. Chalet Pavilion Information Centre, Shop & Café: Mar 25 to end of Sept and weekends in Oct: Mon–Sat 12.30–5.30 (*closed* Fris Mar 31 to end June, and in Sept); Sun and Bank Holiday Mon 10.30–6. Open for booked parties & special functions. Adm free. Car park charge in Carding Mill Valley. Coaches free. Dogs allowed if kept under control.
Refreshments: Snacks, light lunches, teas, etc at Chalet Pavilion (Dogs not allowed in Pavilion).

CLEOBURY MORTIMER

MAWLEY HALL
(Galliers Trustees)

18th century house attributed to Smith of Warwick. Notable contemporary plasterwork & panelling.
Location: 1 m S of Cleobury Mortimer (A4117); 7 m W of Bewdley.
Opening Times: By written appointment to Administrator. Adm £2.

CLUN

CLUN TOWN TRUST MUSEUM
Tel: (058 84) 247.
Local geology, prehistory earthworks, flints, local history, early photographs etc. Easter to Nov: Tues and Sat 2–5; also Hols: Sat, Mon and Tues 11–1, 2–5; also by appointment. Adm free.

CONDOVER

CONDOVER HALL
(Royal National Institute for the Blind)

"E" shaped building, an excellent example of masons' craft of the late 16th century.
Location: 5 m S of Shrewsbury; 1½ m from A49.
Opening Times: Grounds & exterior of premises (with a limited inspection of the interior) Aug only, by prior appointment.

CRAVEN ARMS

STOKESAY CASTLE
Telephone: Craven Arms (0588) 672544
(Sir Philip & Lady Magnus-Allcroft)

Finest example of a moated and fortified manor house, dating from the 13th century.
Location: 8 m from Ludlow; ¾ m S of Craven Arms on 3rd class Road off A49. *Station: Craven Arms (1 m).*
Opening Times: First Wed in March—Daily (except Tues) 10–5; Apr to Sept—Daily (except Tues) 10–6; Oct—Daily (except Tues) 10–5; Nov—Weekends only 10–dusk. Mons to Fris party bookings only. Last adm half an hour before closing. *Closed Dec, Jan & Feb.* Adm £1, Chd (under 15) 50p. Party bookings in advance. Toilets. Car park. Enquiries to The Custodian, Stokesay Castle, Craven Arms, Shropshire SY7 9AH.
Refreshments: In castle courtyard.

HODNET

HODNET HALL GARDENS
Telephone: (063 084) 202   ♿
(Mr & the Hon Mrs Heber Percy)

The colourful jewel in Shropshire's crown. From the glorious daffodils of Spring to the magnificent roses of Summer, each season brings fresh delights to these award winning gardens. Over 60 acres of magnificent forest trees, sweeping lawns and tranquil pools ensure plentiful wildlife and brilliant natural colour within this beautiful setting.
Location: 12 m NE of Shrewsbury; 5½ m SW of Market Drayton, at junction of A53 to A442; M6 18½ m (junction 15) leading to A53 or M54 (junction 3).
Opening Times: Apr 1 to end of Sept—Weekdays 2–5; Suns & Bank Hols 12–5.30. Adm £1.80, OAPs £1.25, Chd £1. *Reduced rates for organised parties of 25 or over.* Season tickets on application. Free car & coach park. Dogs allowed, but must be kept on leads.
Refreshments: Tearooms open daily 2–5. *Parties to pre-book (menu on request). Gift shop, kitchen garden sales.*

LITTLE NESS

ADCOTE
Telephone: (0939) 260202
(Adcote School Educational Trust Ltd)

"Adcote is the most controlled, coherent and masterly of the big country houses designed by Norman Shaw" (Mark Girouard, 'Country Life' Oct 1970).
Location: 7 m NW of Shrewsbury off A5.
Opening Times: Apr 11 to July 6 (except May 26–29); 2–5. Re-open Sept 1–30, 2–5. Other days throughout the year by appointment. Adm free but the Governors reserve the right to make a charge.

LUDLOW

THE BUTTERCROSS MUSEUM   *(Shropshire County Council)*
Church Street. Tel: (0584) 3857.
The story of the town from the establishment of the Castle to date. Apr to Oct: Daily. Adm charge.

LUDFORD HOUSE
(Mr and Mrs D. F. A. Nicholson)

House dating back to 12th century.
Location: ½ m S of Ludlow, B4361 road.
Opening Times: Grounds and exterior by written permission, with limited inspection of interior. Adm £2. Unsuitable for disabled.
Refreshments: Hotels and Restaurants in Ludlow available.

MUCH WENLOCK

BUILDWAS ABBEY
Telephone: (095 245) 3274

Founded in 1135 as an offshoot of Furness Abbey in Cumbria, the abbey belonged briefly to the Savignac Order, then to the Cistercians. Building continued throughout the 12th century and, once completed, the abbey changed little until the Dissolution. The church is almost complete, except for the roof, and the well-preserved west front typifies the austere style favoured by the Cistercians.

Location: 3¼ m (5.2 km) north east of Much Wenlock. OS map ref SJ642044.
Opening Times: Good Friday to Sept 30, daily 10–6; Oct 1 to Maundy Thursday, daily 10–4. *Closed Mons, Christmas and New Year.* Adm 80p, OAPs 60p, Chd 40p.

MUCH WENLOCK MUSEUM   *(Shropshire County Council)*
High Street. Tel: (0952) 727773.
The geology, natural history and local history of the area of the parish. Apr to Oct: Daily. Adm charge. Suitable for disabled visitors.

WENLOCK PRIORY
Telephone: (0952) 727466
(English Heritage)

The long history of Wenlock stretches back to the 7th century, although nothing visible remains of the religious house founded by St Milburge. After the Norman Conquest, a Cluniac priory was established, which came to be regarded as alien during the Hundred Years' War with France. Decorative arcading from the 12th century chapter house survives and some unusual features in the later, rebuilt church.
Location: In Much Wenlock.
Opening Times: Good Friday to Sept 30, daily 10–6; Oct 1 to Maundy Thurs, daily 10–4. *Closed* Mons, Dec 24–26, Jan 1. Adm 80p, OAPs 60p, Chd 40p.

NEWPORT

LILLESHALL ABBEY
Telephone: (0952) 604431

But for its conversion into a fortified stronghold during the Civil War, more might have survived of this medieval Augustinian abbey. As it is, the sandstone remains of the 12th century church and two well-proportioned doorways, one richly carved and decorated, give tantalising glimpses of past magnificence.
Location: 4½ m (7.2 km) south of Newport. OS map ref SJ738142.
Opening Times: Good Friday to Sept 30, daily 10–6. Adm 80p, OAPs 60p, Chd 40p.

SHIFNAL

BOSCOBEL HOUSE
Telephone: (090 28) 50244

When John Giffard built his tall, gabled, timber-framed hunting lodge in the 17th century, he little knew that it would become a refuge for the future King Charles II after his defeat at Worcester in 1651. In the grounds stands the offspring of the famous oak that sheltered Charles from Cromwell and his search parties. Although still recognisable from contemporary engravings, the house has been much altered over the centuries.
Location: 8 m (12 km) north west of Wolverhampton; 3¾ m (6 km) north of Albrighton. OS map ref SJ837083.
Opening Times: Good Friday to Sept 30, daily 10–6; Oct 1 to Maundy Thursday, daily 10–4. *Closed Mons, Christmas and New Year.* Adm £1.80, OAPs £1.40, Chd 90p.

WESTON PARK
Telephone: Weston-under-Lizard 207
(The Earl of Bradford)

Built 1671 by Lady Wilbraham and contains a superb art collection. Miniature Railway, Adventure Playground, Museum, Aquarium, Nature Trails, Country-side Pottery and Pets Corner.
Location: Entrance from A5 at Weston-under-Lizard, 6 m W of Junction 12, M6 (Gailey); 3 m N of Junction 3, M54 (Tong).
Opening Times: House & Park. Apr 2 to May 31—weekends; Bank Hols, Easter week, Spring Bank Hol week, June 6 to July 24—Daily (except Mons & Fris); July 25–Sept 4—Daily then weekends only until Sept 25. Park 11–7. Last admission 5. Adm Grounds, Aquarium, Museum, Adventure Playground, Pottery, Pets Corner £1.80, Chd & OAPs £1.30. House extra. Special rates for pre-booked parties and school visits. Entry charges may be adjusted on certain days for special events. Free coach and car park. Dogs (on leads) admitted to Park.
Refreshments: In the Old Stables licensed bar and cafeteria. Restaurant service for pre-booked parties.

SHIPTON

SHIPTON HALL
(J N R N Bishop, Esq)

Delightful Elizabethan stone manor and Georgian stable block. Interesting Georgian Roccoco and Gothic plasterwork by T. F. Pritchard. Stone walled garden, medieval dovecote and Parish Church, dating from late Saxon period.
Location: In Shipton; 6 m SW of Much Wenlock junction B4376 & B4368.
Opening Times: May to Sept—Thurs also Suns in July & Aug—Bank Hols (except Christmas and New Year) Suns and Mons: 2.30–5.30. Other times by appointment for parties of 20 or more. Adm £1.20, Chd 60p. Special rate for parties of 20 plus.
Refreshments: Teas/buffets by prior arrangement.

SHREWSBURY

CASTLE GATES LIBRARY
Telephone: Shrewsbury 241487

Former premises of Shrewsbury Grammar School, from 16th and 17th centuries. Now used as a public library. Also houses Shropshire's Local Studies Library. Granted a Civic Trust award for a recent restoration scheme.
Opening Times: Public part of the building Mon–Fri 9.30–6. Thurs 9.30–1. Sats 9.30–5. Private areas by prior appointment only.

CLIVE HOUSE   *(Borough of Shrewsbury and Atcham)*
College Hill. Tel: (0743) 54811.
Fine Georgian House containing outstanding collection of Shropshire ceramics together with art, furniture. Mon 2–5; Tues to Sat 10–5.

COLEHAM PUMPING STATION
(Borough of Shrewsbury and Atcham)
Old Coleham. Tel: (0743) 61196.
Preserved beam engines. Open by appointment only.

HAUGHMOND ABBEY
Telephone: (074 377) 661

William FitzAlan re-established this house for Augustinian canons in 1135. It was rebuilt when FitzAlan became abbot, and further changes and additions were made over the centuries. In 1539 the church was demolished and the abbot's lodging, great hall and kitchens were converted into a private house. Some fine Norman doorways and 14th century statues repay a visit.
Location: 3½ m (5.6 km) north east of Shrewsbury. OS map ref SJ542152.
Opening Times: Good Friday to Sept 30, daily 10–6; Oct 1 to Maundy Thursday, daily 10–4. *Closed Mons, Christmas and New Year.* Adm 80p, OAPs 60p, Chd 40p.

ROWLEY'S HOUSE MUSEUM
(Borough of Shrewsbury and Atcham)
Barker Street. Tel: (0743) 61196.
Recently extended museum set in the 17th century house and mansion of the Rowley family. Containing galleries devoted to archaeology, geology, costume, natural and local history. Shop and publications. Mon to Sat 10–5; Easter to mid Sept: Sun 12–5. Adm charge.

SHROPSHIRE REGIMENTAL MUSEUM
(Borough of Shrewsbury and Atcham and Regimental Trustees)
Shrewsbury Castle. Tel: (0743) 58516.
Newly opened military museum containing fine displays of the military history of the Shropshire regiments. In the superb historic setting of Shrewsbury Castle. Mon to Sat 10–5; Easter to mid Sept: Sun 10–5. Adm charge.

TELFORD

IRONBRIDGE GORGE MUSEUM   *(Ironbridge Gorge Museum Trust)*
A major museum complex based on a unique series of industrial monuments in the Ironbridge Gorge, now a World Heritage Site. Admission to all the museum sites is by "passport" ticket, valid until all sites have been visited once. £4.95; Chld £3.25; Family (2 adults, 5 Chld) £15.

MUSEUM VISITOR CENTRE
Housed in the restored Severn Warehouse the centre outlines the story of the Gorge in the words and pictures of people who visited it over two centuries. Slide-and-tape show in a special auditorium.

BLISTS HILL
A working Victorian industrial community set in 1895. Exhibits incl. fully operational Foundry, Candle Factory, Saw Mill, Printing Shop, Pit Head Winding Engine and the only wrought iron works in the western world. Also shops, cottages and Hay Inclined Plane. 42 acre site.

COALBROOKDALE MUSEUM OF IRON AND FURNACE SITE
Opened in 1979, this museum is beside Abraham Darby's blast furnace and tells the story of iron and steel and the history of Coalbrookdale. The Old Furnace now has a sound and light display.

COALPORT CHINA MUSEUM
Magnificent display of Coalport and Caughley china. Displays on the history of the Works and its people. Housed in the original Coalport factory buildings, and used until 1926. Slide-and-tape show. Mar to Oct: 10–6, Nov to Feb: 10–5.

IRON BRIDGE AND INFORMATION CENTRE
The world's first iron bridge. A small exhibition in the adjacent Toll House tells its history.

JACKFIELD TILE MUSEUM
Housed in the former Craven Dunnill Tileworks, this is the Trust's latest addition. Good display of tiles. Buildings in the process of being restored.

ROSEHILL HOUSE
A restored ironmaster's home, set in the early 19th century, typical of the Darby family houses.

TAR TUNNEL
An 18th century mining tunnel from which natural bitumen was extracted.

For further information and party bookings write to: Ironbridge Gorge Museum Trust, Ironbridge, Telford, Shropshire TF8 7AW. Ironbridge (095 245) 3522.

WENLOCK EDGE

WILDERHOPE MANOR, The National Trust
Telephone: Longville 363   &
Elizabethan manor house with 17th century plaster ceilings. House now run as a Youth Hostel.
Location: 7 m SW of Much Wenlock; ½ m S of B4371.
Opening Times: Mar 25 to end of Sept—Weds & Sats 2–4.30; Oct to Mar—Sats only 2–4.30. Adm £1, Chd 50p. *No reduction for parties. No dogs.*

WESTON RHYN

TYN-Y-RHOS HALL AND SHRINE OF ST. GEORGE
(Greek Orthodox)
Telephone: Chirk (0691) 777898   &
(Brother Demetrius)

Mansion with historic Welsh Royal connections. Featured on HTV Dec 1982. Morning prayers, Sun 11am.
Location: 2½ m from Weston Rhyn, near Bron-y-Garth (off A5).
Station: Chirk (1½ m).
Opening Times: Suns May to end Sept 2.30–5.30. Adm £1, Chd 50p.

WROXETER

WROXETER (VIROCONIUM) ROMAN CITY
Telephone: (074 375) 330

Viroconium was the fourth largest city in Roman Britain and the largest to escape modern development. Deep beneath the exposed walls of the market-hall excavations are revealing a legionary fortress of the first century; while nearby the timber buildings of later settlers are being examined. The most impressive feature is the huge wall dividing the exercise yard from the baths.
Location: 5½ m (8.8 km) south east of Shrewsbury. OS map ref SJ568088.
Opening Times: Good Friday to Sept 30, daily 10–6; Oct 1 to Maundy Thursday, daily 10–4. *Closed Mons, Christmas and New Year.* Adm 80p, OAPs 60p, Chd 40p.

The National Trust

ATTINGHAM PARK

Designed in 1785 – remarkable interior decoration, painted boudoir, Regency silver collection. Landscaped deer park.

BENTHALL HALL

16th century stone house with mullioned windows. Interior improved in 17th century. Fine oak staircase and plaster ceilings. Interesting small garden.

DUDMASTON

Late 17th century house and collections of Dutch flower paintings, modern art, botanical paintings and family history. Extensive grounds, woodlands and lakeside garden.

ADMISSION – SEE EDITORIAL REFERENCE

Shrewsbury's Museums

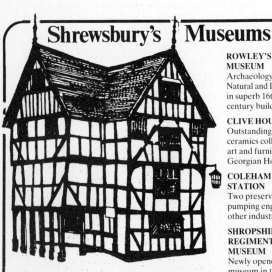

ROWLEY'S HOUSE MUSEUM
Archaeology, Geology, Natural and Local History in superb 16th–17th century buildings.

CLIVE HOUSE
Outstanding Shropshire ceramics collection with art and furniture in a fine Georgian House.

COLEHAM PUMPING STATION
Two preserved steam pumping engines with other industrial exhibits.

SHROPSHIRE REGIMENTAL MUSEUM
Newly opened military museum in the beautiful setting of Shrewsbury Castle.

For further information contact Shrewsbury (0743) 61196

THE IRONBRIDGE GORGE MUSEUM

★ Blists-Hill: A working Victorian Industrial community set in 1895 ★ The Museum's riverside Visitor Centre ★ The World's first Iron Bridge ★ Museum of Iron at Coalbrookdale ★ Coalport China Museum ★ Jackfield Tile Museum Open Daily from 10a.m.–6p.m. (For winter openings please telephone) Free Coach Parking. Good food and drink. Group Discounts. PASSPORT to all sites available. Just 10 minutes from the M54 (junction 4).

Come early to see it all!

**Contact: Visitor Information
Ironbridge Gorge Museum Trust, Ironbridge,
Telford, Shropshire. Tel: Ironbridge (095 245) 3522.**

Somerset

AXBRIDGE

AXBRIDGE MUSEUM: KING JOHN'S HUNTING LODGE
(National Trust administered by Sedgemoor District Council)
The Square. Tel: Axbridge (0934) 732012.
Built c. 1500. Museum of local history, archaeology, geology, ceramics and glass.
Early Tudor merchant's house extensively restored in 1971.
Location: On corner of the Square.
Opening Times: Mar 24 to end Sept—Daily 2–5. Adm free. No dogs, including Guide dogs. Unsuitable for wheelchairs.
Refreshments: In Axbridge.

BARRINGTON

BARRINGTON COURT, The National Trust
Telephone: South Petherton 41480
One of the finest examples of 1920's creativity – thanks to Col. Lyle whose family still live there. A model estate and farm buildings complex, a series of beautiful gardens influenced by Gertrude Jekyll, and a large kitchen garden all designed to support the large Tudor manor house leased by Mr. Lyle to Stuart Interiors, the furniture reproducers. Most recently an estate trail over 200 acres and a farm exhibition centre.
Location: In Barrington village, 5 m NE of Ilminster, off A303, 6 m S of Curry Rivel on A378 between Taunton and Langport. (0460) 40601/52242.
Opening Times: Court and Garden: Mar 25 to Nov 5, Sats to Weds 11–5.30. Adm Gardens £2.50 (parties of 15 or more £2, Chd £1). Coaches by appointment only. Picnic area. Shop (not NT). Children's play area. No dogs. Wheelchair access. Plant sales.
Refreshments: Cream teas, lunches & suppers by arrangement.

BARRINGTON COURT GARDENS
Telephone: (0460) 40601/52242
(Paul Johnson – Estate Manager)
Superb walled gardens – influenced by Gertrude Jekyll. Colonel A.A. Lyle took over the lease of the property in 1920. The gardens are renowned for their lilies and irises and also boast the oldest working Victorian Kitchen Garden in the south-west, comprising of nectarines, peaches, gages, plums, apples and pears as well as asparagus, artichoke, sea kale and celeriac. All produce is available for sale throughout the year. Barrington Court Estate totals some 1000 acres of farmland and woodland situated in a fertile belt of south Somerset and incorporates 7 farms and dairies.
Location: 3 m N of Ilminster off B3168, 25 minutes from M5 (Taunton), 10 minutes from A303.
Opening Times: Open from Good Friday to end Oct: Aug: daily 11–5.30. Apr, May, June, July, Sept and Oct: Sat, Sun, Mon, Tues, Wed 11–5.30. Adm £2.50, Chd £1. Season tickets £10 (for the whole family for as many visits as wished). Parties welcome. Large area of car parking for coaches. Suitable for disabled persons (no wheelchairs available). Garden Centre, Shop, Children's Corner, Nature and Farm Trail, Farm Exhibition.
Refreshments: Licensed restaurant (party bookings for lunches and early evening suppers). Picnic and play area. Strode House offers bed and breakfast.

CASTLE CARY

CASTLE CARY MUSEUM AND PRESERVATION SOCIETY
The Market House.

HADSPEN HOUSE
(N.A. Hobhouse)
8 acre garden on a south-facing slope, containing many unusual plants in an 18th century setting, having a Rare Plant and Old Fashioned Rose Nursery.
Location: 2 m SE of Castle Cary on A371 to Wincanton.
Opening Times: GARDEN ONLY. open all year daily, 9–6 (evenings by request). Adm £1, Chd 50p. *In aid of National Gardens Scheme. Nursery open Apr 1 to Oct 31 closed Mons except Bank Holidays.*
Refreshments: Teas—Sats, Suns & Bank Holidays 2–6, or for groups by request.

CHARD

CHARD AND DISTRICT MUSEUM
High Street.
Displays on the History of Chard, John Stringfellow pioneer of powered flight, early artificial limbs made in Chard, cider making and agriculture, with a complete blacksmith's forge and new costume galleries. May 17 to Oct 1 Mon to Sat 10.30–4.30 (also Sun in July and Aug).

CRICKET ST. THOMAS
Telephone: (0460 30) 755
Estate of Cricket St. Thomas recorded in Domesday Book of 1087. Today it is a wildlife and leisure park of outstanding natural beauty. Animals and birds from all over the world, many leading a free natural life. Visitors can also enjoy the Tropical Aviary, Countrylife Museum, the Heavy Horse Centre, Craft Workshops, lakeside walks, woodland railway and children's Adventure Playground. Film location for BBC TV series 'To The Manor Born'.
Location: 4 m E of Chard on A30. Nearest M5 junction No. 25.
Opening Times: All year round. Daily from 10 am.
Refreshments: Licensed restaurant, tearooms, picnic area.

CHEDDAR

CHEDDAR CAVES MUSEUM AND EXHIBITION
Tel: (0934) 742343.
Upper Paleolithic remains: almost complete skeleton, flints, amber and engraved stones. Now open during winter months.

CHEDDON FITZPAINE

HESTERCOMBE HOUSE AND GARDENS
Telephone: (0823) 87222
(Somerset County Council Fire Brigade Headquarters)
Appearance of present house dates from 1870's with magnificent hallway and wooden staircase, when in ownership of Lord Portman. Main attraction is the historic multi-level garden laid out at the turn of this century by Sir Edwin Lutyens with planting by Miss Gertrude Jekyll. Restoration by County Council over last ten years to portray garden in its original form. Attractive stonework, a long Pergola supported by stone pillars and a magnificent Orangery on the east side of the garden. Best seen in the months of June, July and early Aug. Lovely views across the vale of Taunton Deane.
Location: 4 m NE of Taunton town centre.
Opening Times: All year—Mon to Fri 12–5. Plus last Suns June and July. Donations of £1 requested for garden restoration. Parties welcome – including coach parties. Ample free car parking. Parts of garden suitable for disabled (toilets for disabled).
Refreshments: Only on the Open Suns mentioned above.

CREWKERNE

CLAPTON COURT GARDENS
Telephone: Crewkerne (0460) 73220
(Capt S J Loder)
One of the most beautiful and interesting gardens in the West Country with many rare and unusual trees and shrubs of botanical interest in immaculate formal gardens and fascinating Woodland Garden. The 10 acres includes Terraces, Rose Garden, Rockery and Water Garden. A garden worth visiting at all seasons from springtime bulbs to autumn colours. Plant Centre offering high quality and unusual container shrubs, plants, alpines, etc also specialising in fuchsias and over 220 varieties of pelargoniums. Recently featured on BBC Gardener's World and in Country Life.
Location: 3 m S of Crewkerne on B3165.
Opening Times: GARDENS ONLY. Feb to Nov inclusive—Mons to Fris 10.30–5; Suns 2–5. *Closed Sats (except Easter Sat & all Sats in May 2–5).* Adm £2, OAPs £1.60, Chd 30p. Special rates for pre-booked coach & private parties *(not Suns prior to June).* PLANT CENTRE Feb to Nov inclusive—times as for Gardens above. *No dogs in garden. Free car parking.*
Refreshments: Home-made cream teas and light lunches Apr to Sept, times as garden. Meals by arrangement for parties. Licensed.

DRAYTON

MIDELNEY MANOR
(Mr John Cely Trevilian)
16th to 18th century Manor House. Originally island manor of Abbots of Muchelney and property of Trevilian family since 1500. 17th century Falcons Mews. Gardens; Woodland walks; Heronry.
Location: Signposted from A378 at Bell Hotel; Curry Rivel & from B3168 Hambridge/Curry Rivel Road & in Drayton.
Opening Times: May 1 to Sept 21: Thurs and all Bank Holiday Mons 2.30–5.30 (last tour 4.30). Adm £2, Chd £1. Display of falcon flying Sat Aug 12, 2–5.30. **House not open.** Coach parties and teas by appointment.

DUNSTER

DUNSTER CASTLE, The National Trust
Telephone: Dunster 821314
Castle dating from 13th century, remodelled by Anthony Salvin in 19th century. Fine 17th century staircase and plaster ceilings. Terraced Gardens.
Location: In Dunster, 3 m SE of Minehead on A396.
Station: Dunster (West Somerset Railway) (¾ m).

Opening Times: Mar 26 to end of Sept—Sun to Thurs 11–5. Oct—Sun to Thurs 2–4. Last adm half-hour before closing. Adm £3, Chd £1.50. Parties of 15 or more by written appointment with the Administrator, £2. Garden and grounds open daily Apr to May and Sept—Sun to Thurs 11–5; Oct—Sun to Thurs 2–4; June to Aug —Daily 11–5. Adm £1.50, Chd 50p. Dogs in park only. Shop. Wheelchair access.

Refreshments: Luttrell Arms, Dunster, and village tearooms (not N.T.). National Trust Shop.

ENMORE

BARFORD PARK
Telephone: Spaxton (027 867) 269
(Mr & Mrs Michael Stancomb)

Queen Anne house set in park with fine trees; formal garden, water garden and woodland garden.

Location: 5 m W of Bridgwater.
Opening Times: June 1 to Sept 16—Weds, Thurs and Bank Hol weekends 2–6, or other times by appointment. Please telephone above number. Adm charges not available at the time of going to press.

FARLEIGH HUNGERFORD

FARLEIGH HUNGERFORD CASTLE
Telephone: (02214) 4026

Sir Thomas de Hungerford, Speaker of the House of Commons, fortified the original manor house without permission; he was later pardoned. His mailed effigy, surrounded by the tombs of other Hungerfords, lies in the chapel, a place to stir the imagination.

Location: Farleigh Hungerford 3½ m (5.6 km) west of Trowbridge. OS map ref ST801577.
Opening Times: Good Friday to Sept 30, daily 10–6; Oct 1 to Maundy Thursday, daily 10–4. *Closed Mons, Christmas and New Year.*. Adm 80p, OAPs 60p, Chd 40p.

GLASTONBURY

GLASTONBURY LAKE VILLAGE MUSEUM
The Tribunal, High Street.
Collection of late prehistoric antiquities from Glastonbury Lake village and items of local interest. Adm charge.

GLASTONBURY TRIBUNAL
Telephone: (0458) 32949

Justice was administered here by the Abbot of Glastonbury until the Dissolution. Later a kitchen was added and the building converted to a private house. It is well preserved, with decorative details from three centuries.

Location: High Street. OS map ref ST499390.
Opening Times: Good Friday to Sept 30, daily 10–6; Oct 1 to Maundy Thursday, daily 10–4. *Closed Mons, Christmas and New Year.* Adm 80p, OAPs 60p, Chd 40p.

SOMERSET RURAL LIFE MUSEUM   *(Somerset County Council)*
Abbey Farm, Chilkwell Street. Tel: Glastonbury (0458) 32903.
Museum interpreting Somerset's rural history with award winning permanent exhibitions and a lively programme of events and demonstrations throughout the summer. Temporary exhibitions and magnificent 14th century Abbey Barn. Tea room (summer only) and large car park. Open every weekday 10–5 throughout the year. Sat and Sun 2–6.30 (Easter to Oct) 2.30–5, Nov to Easter. *Closed* Good Friday, Christmas Day and Boxing Day. Adm charge but free adm Fri.

HATCH BEAUCHAMP

HATCH COURT
Telephone: Hatch Beauchamp (0823) 480208
(Commander & Mrs Barry Nation)

A Palladian style Georgian house in Bath stone with superb views of Somerset. A house of great elegance and charm. Small Canadian Military Museum. China room. Deer park.

Location: 6 m SE of Taunton midway between Taunton & Ilminster off A358.
Opening Times: July 6 to Sept 14—Thurs 2.30–5.30, last tour 4.30 *(no coaches)*. Also open Bank Holiday Monday afternoon. Adm £2. Coaches & organised parties by prior appointment only—May to Oct *(except Thurs when House is open)*. Special rates for organised parties. Members of HHA free.
Refreshments: By arrangement. Cups of tea & biscuits available Thurs. Hatch Inn & Farthings Restaurant.

ILCHESTER

LYTES CARY MANOR, The National Trust
Mediaeval manor house with chapel; fine furnishings; formal garden.
Location: On W side of Fosse Way (A37); 2½ m NE of Ilchester signposted on bypass (A303).
Opening Times: Mar 25 to Oct 28—Weds & Sats 2–6 (last adm 5.30). Adm £2, Chd £1. *Dogs in garden only, on leads.* No lavatories. NB. Large coaches cannot pass gate piers.
Refreshments: Refreshments and National Trust Shop at Montacute.

LITTON

PEAR TREE HOUSE
Telephone: Chewton Mendip (076121) 220
(Mr & Mrs John Southwell)

Three acres landscaped into several gardens of distinctive character. Many unusual trees and shrubs; collection of acers; special collection of hollies (about 100 varieties); clematis (over 50 varieties). Ponds with moisture gardens. Pinetum. Featured on 'Gardeners World'. Picnic area. Permanent exhibition of watercolours.

Location: Litton, 8 miles N of Wells on B3114 off A39.
Opening Times: GARDEN ONLY June 17, 18. Oct 7, 8 for National Garden Scheme; also Sat and Mon from June 19 to Sep 11. Other times by appointment. Adm 75p. Open 11–6. Parties by arrangement. Car parking free in adjoining field. Suitable for disabled persons, no wheelchairs available.
Refreshments: Home-made teas on National Garden Scheme days and for parties; at other times tea/coffee available.

MONKSILVER

COMBE SYDENHAM COUNTRY PARK
Telephone: Stogumber (0984) 56284
(Mr and Mrs W. Theed)

Built in 1580 on the site of a monastic settlement and home of Elizabeth Sydenham, wife of Sir Francis Drake. The Cannon Ball associated with their wedding can still be seen in the Great Hall. The Court Room has now been beautifully restored, and onsite work is continuing including the old Corn Mill. Elizabethan-style gardens, Country Park walks and Deer Park. Fly fishing available on valley ponds. Children's play area. Speciality smoked trout/pate. Gift Shop, tea room, free car/coach park.

Location: 5 m N of Wiveliscombe; 3 m S of Watchet on B3188.
Station: Stogumber (2½ m) (West Somerset Railway).
Opening Times: Mar 20 to Nov 3. COUNTRY PARK 11–6. Mar, Apr, May and Oct closing 5 pm. Sun Special admission ticket. Sat morning Gift Shop and Fish sales only. HALL: Last entry to Hall two hours before closing time. House and Garden closed every Sat and Sun throughout the year. School parties welcomed by arrangement throughout the year for activity days. (Winner 1984 Sandford Award for Heritage Education).

MONTACUTE

MONTACUTE HOUSE, The National Trust
Telephone: Martock 823289

Magnificent Elizabethan house of Ham Hill stone begun in the 1590s by Sir Edward Phelips. Fine heraldic glass, tapestries, panelling and furniture. National Portrait Gallery Exhibitions of Elizabethan and Jacobean portraits. Fine formal garden and park.

Location: In Montacute village 4 m W of Yeovil on S side of A3088; 3 m S of A303 nr Ilchester.
Opening Times: House: Mar 25 to Nov 5: Daily (except Tues) 12.30–5.30. Last adm 5 (or sunset if earlier). *Closed Good Fri. Parties by written appointment with the Administrator.* Garden & Park: All the year—Daily 12–5.30 (or sunset if earlier). Adm House, Garden & Park £3, Chd £1.50; Parties of 15 or more £2. Garden & Park only: Oct to May 60p; June to Sept £1, Chd half-price. Dogs in park only. Wheelchairs in garden only.
Refreshments: Light lunches & teas (Apr to end Oct noon–5.30). *Parties catered for by arrangement with the Administrator. National Trust Shop.*

STOKE-SUB-HAMDON PRIORY, The National Trust   &
Complex of buildings begun in 14th century for the priests of the chantry chapel of St Nicholas (destroyed).
Location: Between A303 & A3088; 2 m W of Montacute between Yeovil & Ilminster.
Opening Times: All the year—Daily 10–6 (or sunset if earlier). Adm free. *Great Hall only open to the public.* No dogs.

MUCHELNEY

MUCHELNEY ABBEY
Telephone: (0458) 250664

This was one of the oldest abbeys in Somerset. The church has now vanished but the abbot's house is remarkably intact. Up a stairway of great beauty, the parlour adds flesh to the story that the monks lived well. Two lions smile down from pillars over an ornate fireplace; a wooden settle runs the length of a wall lit by magnificent windows; all are well preserved despite later use as a farmhouse.

Location: 2 m (3.2 km) south of Langport. OS map ref ST428248.
Opening Times: Good Friday to Sept 30, daily 10–6. Adm 80p, OAPs 60p, Chd 40p.

PRIEST'S HOUSE, The National Trust
Telephone: (0458) 250672

Late medieval house, originally the residence of the secular priests who served the parish church. The Tenant shows his own collection of furniture and paintings.
Location: 1 m S of Langport.
Opening Times: All year by appointment with: The Tenant. Priest's House, Muchelney, nr Langport. Adm £1. *No reduction for parties or children.* No dogs. Unsuitable for wheelchairs.

NETHER STOWEY

COLERIDGE COTTAGE, The National Trust
Telephone: Nether Stowey 732662

Home of S T Coleridge from 1797–1800, where he wrote 'The Ancient Mariner'.
Location: At W end of village on S side of A39; 8 m W of Bridgwater.
Opening Times: PARLOUR AND READING ROOM ONLY. Mar 26 to Sept 28— Tues to Thurs & Suns 2–5. *Closed Good Fri.* Adm £1, Chd 50p. *No reduction for parties.* Parties are asked to notify the tenant beforehand. *Adm in winter by written application to the tenant.* No dogs. Unsuitable for wheelchairs & coaches.
Refreshments: In village.

DODINGTON HALL
Telephone: Holford (0278 74) 400
(Lady Gass, occupier P. Birkett)

Small Tudor Manor House on the lower slopes of the Quantock Hills. Great hall with oak roof. Plasterwork. Carved stone fireplace. Display of cowboy and horse equipment. Terraced garden with many varieties of roses.
Location: ½ m from A39. 11 m from Bridgwater; 7 m from Williton.
Opening Times: May, June, July & Aug, Mon 11–5. Adm – donations to Dodington Church. Groups by arrangement. Parking for 15 cars. Unsuitable for disabled.
Refreshments: None at house. Hotels and restaurants in Nether Stowey and Holford.

NORTH NEWTON

MAUNSEL HOUSE
Telephone: (0278) 663413
(Sir Benjamin Slade Bt.)

Home of Sir Benjamin & Lady Slade. Ancestral seat of the Slade family under extensive restoration. Part of the house built before Conquest, most of house built around a Hall erected in 1420. Geoffrey Chaucer was a frequent visitor and guest. He wrote part of the Canterbury Tales whilst staying at the house. Also the ancestral home of Madeline Slade (Mira Behn) devotee to the great Indian leader Mahatma Gandhi. In AD 1086 (Domesday) the Manor was called 'Maunsel' being derived from the French meaning 'sleave of land' and was granted to Count Eustace of Boulogne, Kinsman of William the Conqueror. At the time of Henry II, William de Erleigh granted Maunsel to Philip Arbalistarius as a dowry to his daughter Mabel on payment of two pigs every Whitsuntide at his Court of Durston. His son Philip married the daughter of Sir Hugh D'Auderville and assumed the surname of Maunsel. Philip de Maunsel became progenitor of the family with the surname 'Maunsell' and 'Mansel'. The estate passed to the Bacon family of Norfolk and then to the Slade family.
Location: Bridgwater 4 m, Bristol 20 m, Taunton 7 m, junction 24 M5, turn left North Petherton 1½ m North Newton, ½ m S St. Michael Church.
Opening Times: Apr 1 to Sept 30: Sun & Mon 2.30–5.30. Tues to Sat by appointment only. Adm House and Grounds £2, Chd £1. Coach parties by arrangement. Parties welcome by arrangement – mornings available. Receptions and banqueting by arrangement. Free car parking. Picnic & Barbecue area £1, Chd 50p. Children's adventure play area. *Dogs on leads allowed in grounds only.* Fishing – bring own tackle £1. Boating – bring own boat £1.

PITMINSTER

POUNDISFORD PARK
Telephone: Blagdon Hill (082342) 244   &
(Mr & Mrs R Vivian-Neal)

Delightful 'lived-in' 16th Century house on an intimate scale with 18th Century additions, set in the former Deer Park of Taunton Castle. Particularly fine Elizabethan plaster ceilings, good furniture, china, glass, family pictures, costumes and needle-work. Windowed gallery to hall. Garden contains some interesting plants and a fine brick Gazebo. Rare surviving detached Great Kitchen (now a restaurant).
Location: 3½ m S of Taunton on Trull/Pitminster Road; ½ m W of B3170 Taunton/Honiton Road. Coaches should approach via Staplehay (signposted), from Taunton–Blagdon Hill road only.
Opening Times: HOUSE & GARDEN: July 6 to Sept 14—Thurs & Aug Bank Hol Mons: 11–5. Parties by appointment only, throughout the year. Adm £1.90, Chd (10–16) £1, (under 10 accompanied by adult, free). Parties pre-booked 15 or more £1.60. Disabled to Ground Floor & Garden £1. Guided tours by owners.
Refreshments: For groups – Lunches, Teas & Dinners in the Well House Restaurant (the Tudor Kitchen) by prior appointment only. Tel Blagdon Hill (082342) 566.

SHEPTON MALLET

SHEPTON MALLET MUSEUM   *(Mendip District Council)*
High Street.

SOUTH PETHERTON

EAST LAMBROOK MANOR GARDEN
Telephone: South Petherton (0460) 40328
(Mr & Mrs Andrew Norton)

The garden, created by the late Margery Fish, surrounds the mediaeval house which dates from about 1470. The many books written by Mrs Fish and her extensive lecturing popularised this first of the Cottage style gardens which is now the pattern of many. It is both a traditional English garden and an important collection of unusual and now rare plants. Registered as a grade one garden it is maintained as a living and developing memorial to its creator. The Margery Fish Nursery offers a wide range of plants propagated from the garden.
Location: Off A303 2 m N of South Petherton.
Opening Times: Mon–Sat 9–5 and Bank Hols. *Closed Christmas and New Year.* Adm £1.20 *National Gardens Scheme.* Parties by arrangement only. Car parking limited.

SPARKFORD

HAYNES SPARKFORD MOTOR MUSEUM
Sparkford BA22 7LH. Tel: (0963) 40804.

Fabulous views of the rolling hills and woodland provide a breathtaking backdrop to over 17,000 square feet of pure motoring nostalgia with our unique collection of Classic, Veteran and Vintage cars and Motorcycles. Our rapidly expanding collection includes some of the rarest vehicles in the world with such names as Haynes, Stearns and Doble to name but a few. A 12,000 square foot extension soon to open. The museum also houses the largest exclusively motoring bookshops in the south west of England. Adm £2; OAPs £1.60; Chld, Disabled and UB40s £1.20. Chld under 5 free. Coach parties £1.50 a head. Car parking free. Suitable for disabled. Administrator: Michael Penn.

STREET

THE SHOE MUSEUM
C. & J. Clark, High Street. Tel: (0458) 43131.

Shoes from Roman times to the present, old shoe machines and hand tools, 19th century documents, advertising material and photographs illustrating the early history of C. & J. Clark. Easter Mon to Oct: Mon to Fri 10–4.45; Sat 10–4.30. Adm free. During winter months by appointment only tel: Mrs Brook (0458) 43131.

TAUNTON

SOMERSET COUNTY MUSEUM   *(Somerset County Council)*
Taunton Castle. Tel: Taunton (0823) 255504.

Set in the medieval castle where Judge Jeffreys held the 'Bloody Assize', the museum displays collections relevant to the county of Somerset, including archaeology, geology and palaeontology, natural history, ceramics, costume, dolls and military gallery. Temporary exhibitions Mon to Sat 10–5. Adm charge but free adm on Fri.

TEMPLECOMBE

STOWELL HILL
(Mr & Mrs Robert McCreery)

Spring bulbs; collecton of flowering shrubs, including rhododendrons, azaleas, magnolias, etc Japanese Cherries.
Location: 5 m S of Wincanton, turn at Stowell ½ m from Templecombe on A357.
Opening Times: GARDEN ONLY. Suns May 7, 14, 21, 28. 2–6. Adm 75p, Chd 20p. *In aid of National Gardens Scheme.* No dogs.
Refreshments: Tea available.

TINTINHULL

TINTINHULL HOUSE GARDEN, The National Trust   &

Modern formal garden with borders and ponds surrounding 17th century house (house not open).
Location: 5 m NW of Yeovil; ½ m S of A303 on outskirts Tintinhull village.
Opening Times: Mar 25 to Sept 30—Weds, Thurs & Sats, also Bank Hol Mons 2–6 (last adm 5.30). Adm £2. *No reductions for parties or children.* Coach parties by written arrangement with the tenant. No dogs. Wheelchairs provided —garden only accessible.
Refreshments: Refreshments and National Trust Shop at Montacute.

TOLLAND

GAULDEN MANOR
Telephone: Lydeard St Lawrence (09847) 213
(Mr & Mrs James LeGendre Starkie)

Small historic red sandstone Manor House of great charm. A real lived-in home. Past Somerset seat of the Turberville family, immortalised by Thomas

Hardy. Great Hall has magnificent plaster ceiling and oak screen to room known as the Chapel. Fine antique furniture. Interesting grounds include bog garden with primulas and other moisture loving plants. Herb garden.

Location: 9 m NW of Taunton; 1 m E of Tolland Church. Gaulden Manor signposted from A358 Taunton/Williton Rd just N of Bishops Lydeard and from B3188 Wivelscombe/Watchet Rd (cars only). Nearest village Lydeard St Lawrence (1½ m).

Opening Times: Apr 30 to June 30 — Suns & Thurs; July 1 to Sept 10 — Suns, Weds & Thurs, also Easter Sun and Mon and all Bank Hols: 2–6 (last adm 5.30). House & Garden Adm (1988 rates) £2, Chd (under 14) 80p. Garden only 80p. *Parties on other days by prior arrangement. Mornings, afternoons or evenings & out of season. Shop — books, rare and unusual plants.*

Refreshments: Teas in Garden Tearoom, on Sun, Bank Holidays and Parties.

WASHFORD

CLEEVE ABBEY
Telephone: (0984) 40377

Although little remains of the church, some of the buildings surrounding the cloister of this Cistercian abbey are remarkably complete. A timber roof of outstanding workmanship survives in the 15th century dining hall; also preserved are fragments of pavements, tiles and wall paintings of earlier date.

Location: Washford. OS map ref ST047407.
Opening Times: Good Friday to Sept 30, daily 10–6; Oct 1 to Maundy Thursday, daily 10–4. *Closed Mons, Christmas and New Year.* Adm £1.10, OAPs 80p, Chd 55p.

WELLS

THE BISHOP'S PALACE
Telephone: Wells (0749) 78691
(The Church Commissioners)

The fortified and moated Palace comprises Jocelin's Hall (early 13th century), the Bishop's Chapel and the ruins of the Banqueting Hall (both late 13th century) and the Bishop's Residence (15th century). The grounds which include the wells from which Wells derives its name, provide a beautiful setting for gardens of herbaceous plants, roses, shrubs, mature trees and the Jubilee Arboretum. On the Moat are waterfowl and swans.

Location: City of Wells, at end of Market Place (enter through Bishop's Eye).
Opening Times: Palace, Chapel and Grounds. Easter to end of Oct — Bank Holiday Mons, Thurs & Suns; Aug — Daily: 2–6; May, June, July & Sept also Weds 11–6. Last admission 5.30. Adm £1.75, Chd 30p. Party rates by appointment.
Refreshments: Available in Undercroft.

MILTON LODGE GARDENS
Telephone: (0749) 72168
(Mr & Mrs David Tudway Quilter)

Mature alkaline terraced garden of great charm dating from 1909. Replanned 1962 with mixed shrubs and herbaceous plants, old fashioned roses and ground cover; numerous climbers; old established yew hedges. Fine trees in garden and in separate 7 acre arboretum on opposite side of Old Bristol Road.

Location: ½ m N of Wells. From A39 Bristol–Wells turn N up Old Bristol Road; free car park first gate on left.
Opening Times: GARDEN AND ARBORETUM ONLY: Weds and Suns in May, June and July 2–6. Adm £1, Chd 50p in aid of National Gardens Scheme and the Somerset Red Cross. Parties by appointment throughout the year. No dogs.
Refreshments: Teas available Suns only.

WELLS MUSEUM
Cathedral Green. Tel: (0749) 73477.

Samplers, local bygones, prehistoric cave finds, natural history, Mendip rocks, fossils and minerals. Apr to Oct: Weekdays 10–5.30, Suns 11–5.30. Nov to Mar: Wed to Sun 11–4, (*closed* Dec 21 to Jan 3). Adm 80p, Chld/OAP 30p.

WOOKEY

WOOKEY HOLE CAVES AND MILL
The most spectacular caves in Britain presided over by the famous Witch of Wookey.

YEOVIL

COMPTON HOUSE
Telephone: Yeovil (0935) 74608
(Worldwide Butterflies Ltd)

16th century Manor House with 19th century Tudor style front. Set in tranquil surroundings with lawns and 13th century church, an historic building with a difference: here butterflies are bred and visitors see all stages of their development. Tropical Jungle, Breeding Hall, Palm House. Other display areas include the new Butterfly House, vintage tractors and fire-engine. House still lived in. Visitors also see the Lullingstone Silk Farm which produced the silk for two coronations, the wedding of the Prince and Princess of Wales and other Royal occasions.

Location: On A30 dual carriageway, midway between Sherborne & Yeovil. *Station: Yeovil Pen Mill (2 m), Sherborne (3 m) (Waterloo line).*
Opening Times: Apr 1 to Oct 30 — Daily 10–5. **Visitors should telephone to check the current times and dates in advance of visit.** Adm charges not available at time of going to press. *The gardens of the house are now open to visitors and it is possible to see some of the fine outbuildings which are gradually to be restored.*
Refreshments: Oliver's Coffee House and Restaurant in the house, overlooking the garden.

THE MUSEUM OF SOUTH SOMERSET
(South Somerset District Council)
Hendford Manor Hall. Tel: (0935) 24774.

A museum of local history and archaeology containing the Henry Stiby fire-arm collection and the Bailward costume collection. Mon to Sat 12–5.

YEOVILTON

FLEET AIR ARM MUSEUM AND CONCORDE EXHIBITION
Tel: Ilchester (0935) 840565.

The development of naval aviation is presented in a display of over 50 historic aircraft, many ship and aircraft scale models, photographs, paintings, documents, uniforms and medals all housed under one roof. The interior of Concorde is open to the public. Daily (inc. Bank Hols) 10–5.30 Mar to Oct; 10–4.30 Nov to Feb. *Closed* Dec 24 and 25. Adm charge (party rates, Chld half price, OAPs reduced adm). Free parking, picnic and flying viewing areas. Coaches and caravans welcome. Licensed restaurant. Children's play area. Facilities for disabled. Many special exhibitions including THE FALKLAND ISLANDS CONFLICT, the KAMIKAZE SUICIDE BOMBERS, the WRENS, THE FAIRY SWORDFISH STORY and THE RNAS IN WORLD WAR I.

Staffordshire

ALTON

ALTON TOWERS
Telephone: (0538) 702200

Former estate of the Earls of Shrewsbury set in 500 acres. Gardens developed from 1814. Splendid rock and rose gardens, tree lined valley slopes, pathways bordered by rhododendrons. Woodland walks. Well preserved ruins of Gothic Talbot family mansion. 19th century garden follies including replicas of the To Ho Pagoda of Canton and Choragic Monument of Lysicrates. Fine conservatory.

Location: 12 m Stoke-on-Trent.
Opening Times: Grounds and gardens open all year. Main season with rides and attractions: Mar 18 to Nov 5. Adm – discounts for groups, young people, and senior citizens. Chd under 4 FREE. Afternoon tickets half price after 2.30 pm. Much reduced rates in Winter season: Nov 6 to mid Mar. Disabled facilities. Special Events Calendar all year.
Refreshments: Wide choice of fast food to à la carte. Catering and banqueting facilities.

BARLASTON

WEDGWOOD MUSEUM
(Josiah Wedgwood and Sons Limited, Barlaston)
Josiah Wedgwood and Sons Limited, Barlaston, ST12 9ES.
Tel: (0782) 204218/204141.
A 'Living Museum' displaying the most comprehensive collection of Wedgwood ceramics and art over two centuries, with craft manufacture centre adjacent. Mon to Fri 9–5; Sat 10–4; Sun (Easter to Oct) 10–4. Adm £1.75; Chld, OAPs & Students £1. Special Reductions. Parties. Car Parking. Suitable for disabled persons. Refreshments. Curator: Gaye Blake Roberts.

BREWOOD

CHILLINGTON HALL
Telephone: Brewood 850236
(Mr & Mrs Peter Giffard)

Georgian house. Part 1724 (Francis Smith); part 1785 (Sir John Soane). Fine saloon. Grounds and lake by 'Capability' Brown. Extensive woodland walks.

Location: 4 m SW of A5 at Gailey; 2 m Brewood; 8 m NW of Wolverhampton; 14 m S of Stafford. Best approach is from A449 (Junction 2, M54) through Coven and follow signposts towards Codsall (no entry at Codsall Wood).
Opening Times: May to Sept 14—Thurs (also Suns in Aug) 2.30–5.30. Open Easter Sun & Suns preceding May and late Spring Bank Holidays 2.30–5.30. Adm £1.40; Grounds only 70p. Chd half-price. *Parties other days by arrangement.*

BURSLEM

THE SIR HENRY DOULTON GALLERY
Nile Street, Burslem. Tel: (0782) 575454.
Sir Henry Doulton was recognised by his contemporaries as the greatest potter of his time. This gallery traces the story of Doulton from its foundation in 1815. The gallery also includes the world famous Royal Doulton collection of over 300 rare figures. Weekdays 9–4.15. Factory tours, factory shop.

BURTON UPON TRENT

BASS MUSEUM OF BREWING, HOME OF THE BASS SHIRE HORSES
Horninglow Street (A50). Tel: Burton (0283) 42031 or 45301.
The Museum adjoins the Bass Burton Brewery complex and is housed in buildings formerly occupied by the joiners, wheelwrights and engineers, dating from the mid 19th century. Three floors are devoted to the story of Bass in Burton and the transport of beer. Special displays include a working railway model of Burton in 1921, fine glass and ceramics associated with beer drinking, an Edwardian bar and display of pumping engines. External exhibits include the stables of the prize-winning Bass Shires and their drays, vintage vehicles including a 1920s bottle shaped car. An experimental brewhouse is used for special brews several times a year and a 1905 Robey horizontal cross compound engine is steamed some weekends. A reconstructed railway ale dock is used to exhibit a steam locomotive and items associated with the Bass Private Railway. Open 7 days a week Mon – Fri 10, Sat & Sun 11, last admission 4.30. *Closed* 25, 26 Dec, 1 Jan. Adm charge. Free parking. Bar and refreshments. Brewery tours and/or Education Service by arrangement. The museum completed major extensions in 1988 featuring a new gallery on the process of brewing.

HERITAGE BREWERY MUSEUM
Anglesey Road DE14 3PF. Tel: (0283) 69226.
Traditional working Brewery Museum. Currently undergoing restoration. Organised tours available during initial development phase, by prior arrangement. Various special public Open Days held during the year prior to official opening of the museum. Contact Museum Director Michael Knights for further details.

ECCLESHALL

ECCLESHALL CASTLE
Telephone: Eccleshall (0785) 850250
(Mr & Mrs Mark Carter)

William and Mary Mansion House containing fine collections of porcelain, paintings and furniture. Extensive grounds containing part of the original 14th century castle. Nature Trail, Souvenir shop.

Location: 400 yards N of Eccleshall on A519; 6 m NW of Junct 14 on M6, 9 m SW of Junct 15 on M6.
Opening Times: Easter to Oct 1 from 2–5.30 on Suns, Bank Holidays and Tues following. Also Thurs from June 1 and Tues in Aug. Adm House and Grounds: £2, Chd £1. Family (2 adults & up to 3 Chd) £5.50. Grounds only £1, Chd 50p. Parties (over 20) welcome by appointment at any reasonable time at reduced rates. Reduced rates also available on Tues and Thurs for OAPs and National Trust Members.
Refreshments: Home-made cream teas are available in the Hogarth Restaurant. Full catering service for booked parties.

LEEK

BRINDLEY WATER MILL *(Brindley Mill Preservation Trust)*
Mill Street.
Built in 1752 an operational water-powered corn mill restored in 1974. The James Brindley Museum opened in 1980. Bookstall. Easter to Oct 31: Sat, Sun and Bank Hol Mons (also Mon, Tues and Thurs during July and Aug) 2–5. Minimal adm charges. Parties at any time – please book with Hon. Secretary, 5 Daintry Street, Leek, ST13 5PG.

CHEDDLETON FLINT MILL
(Cheddleton Flint Mill Industrial Heritage Trust)
Between Stoke-on-Trent and Leek on A520.

Twin water-wheels on the River Churnet operate flint grinding pans. The South Mill foundations date back to the 13th century when it ground corn and was a fulling mill. Converted to grinding flint in about 1800 after it was joined by the North Mill which was built specially in the late 18th century to grind flint. The Museum collection includes a Robey 100hp steam engine, model Newcomen engine, rare 1770 haystack boiler, and the narrow boat 'Vienna' moored on the Caldon Canal. The miller's cottage is furnished as it would have looked in the 19th century. Buildings open Sat and Sun afternoons throughout the year. Admission free. Donations welcome. Books, postcards and wallchart on sale; also guides to the Mill in English, French, German and Italian.

LEEK ART GALLERY *(Nicholson Institute)*
Stockwell Street. Tel: (0538) 399181.

Small permanent collection supplemented by mainly local exhibitions. Tues, Wed, Fri 1–5; Sat 10–12.

LICHFIELD

DR. JOHNSON'S BIRTHPLACE
Breadmarket Street. Tel: (0543) 264972.

Relics and pictures of Dr. Johnson and his contemporaries. Apr to Sept: Mon to Sat 10–5; Sun 2–5. Oct to Mar: Mon to Sat 10–4. *Closed* Christmas Day, Boxing Day, New Year's Day, Good Friday and Spring Bank Hol. Adm 50p; Chld and OAPs 25p; Family ticket £1.20. Joint ticket with Heritage Centre 95p.

HANCH HALL
Telephone: Armitage (0543) 490308
(Mr & Mrs Douglas Milton-Haynes)

Original mansion built in reign of Edward I. Seat of the Aston family until end of the 16th century then the Ormes, staunch supporters of Charles I. Home of General William Dyott from 1817, then Sir Charles Forster later in the 19th century. The present house, which is lived in as a family home, exhibits Tudor, Jacobean, Queen Anne and Georgian architecture. Wealth of oak panelling; Observation Tower; interesting collections. Landscaped gardens, trout pool, waterfowl. Tiny Chapel in grounds. Nature trail.
NB. *The owners reserve the right to change days and hours of opening and to close all or parts of the Hall without prior notice.*
Location: 4 m NW of Lichfield on Uttoxeter Road (B5014).
Opening Times: Mar 26 to Oct 1—Suns & Bank Hol Mons & Tues following 2–6; June, July, Aug & Sept—Tues, Weds, Thurs & Sats 2–6 (last tour of House 5). Parties of 20 or more, daily, mornings, afternoons or evenings by arrangement. Adm House & Gardens £2.50, Chd £1.30. Reduction for parties of 20 or more. Free car park. Gift & Bric-a-brac shop. Lengthy tour of the house not really suitable for small children. *Regret no dogs. No stiletto heels in the house.* Candlelight evenings first week in Dec. For further information contact Mrs Milton-Haynes.
Refreshments: Tea & home baking in 17th century Stable Block. Hot or cold meals by arrangement.

LICHFIELD HERITAGE EXHIBITION, TREASURY AND MUNIMENT ROOM
Market Square. Tel: (0543) 256611.

Audio-visual presentation of the Civil War. Civic, Church and Regimental Plate, Maces, State Sword, Ashmole Cup. Superb tapestry of the Bower Procession of 1795. Daily 10–4.30. *Closed* Christmas Day, Boxing Day, New Year's Day and Spring Bank Hol Mon. Adm 70p; Chld, OAPs and Students 30p; Family ticket £1.50. Joint ticket with Dr. Johnson's Birthplace 95p.

MILFORD

SHUGBOROUGH, The National Trust
Telephone: Little Haywood (0889) 881388
(Administered by Staffordshire County Council)

Seat of the Earls of Lichfield. Architecture by James Stuart and Samuel Wyatt. Rococo plasterwork by Vassalli. Extensive parkland with neo-classical monuments. Beautiful formal gardens with Chinese house, Victorian terraces and rose-garden. Guided garden and woodland walks.
Location: 6 m E of Stafford on A513, entrance at Milford. 10 mins drive from M6, junction 13.
Opening Times: House, Museum, Farm, Working Mill & Gardens. Mar 24 to Sept 30—open daily incl. Bank Hol Mons 11–5. Winter opening — Oct 1 to Dec 24—open daily incl. Bank Hol Mons 11–4. Site open all year round to booked parties from 10.30. Adm: House £1.50, (reduced rate £1). Museum £1.50 (reduced rate £1). Farm £1.50 (reduced rate £1). All-in-ticket (House, Museum & Farm) £4 (reduced rate £2). Coach parties: All-in-ticket £2 or £1 per site. (Adm prices subject to change.) Reduced rates available for chd, OAPs and registered unemployed. Chd (under 5) free. NT members free entry to House. Parties can be booked in for guided tours at all sites. School parties can be booked in for guided tours at each site, 60p per head per site, incl. of guide. School All-in-tickets £1.50 per head. When special events are held charges may vary. Guide dogs admitted to House and Museum but not other dogs. Site access for parking, picnic area, parkland, garden and woodland trails £1 per vehicle. Coaches free. National Trust shop and toilets.
Refreshments: Tea-rooms restaurant.

MOSELEY

MOSELEY OLD HALL, The National Trust
Telephone: Wolverhampton (0902) 782808   &

A 17th century formal garden surrounds this mainly Elizabethan house where Charles II hid after the battle of Worcester.
Location: 4 m N of Wolverhampton mid-way between A449 & A460 Roads. Off M6 at Shareshill then via A460. Traffic from S via. M6 and M54 take junction 1 to Wolverhampton and Moseley is signposted after ½ m. Coaches via. A460 to avoid low bridge.
Opening Times: Mar 11–Oct 29. Mar 11–Apr 30 Sat & Sun 2–6; May 1–Jul 12 Wed, Sat & Sun 2–6; Jul 15–Sept 6 Sat–Wed 2–6; Sept 9–27 Wed, Sat & Sun 2–6; Sept 30–Oct 29 Sat & Sun 2–6. Bank Holiday Mon & Tues following (except May 2) 2–6. *Closed Good Friday.* Pre-booked parties at other times including evening tours. Adm £2, Chd half price. Family ticket £5.50. Parties £1.70, evening parties £2. Educational facilities. Wheelchair access ground floor only.
Refreshments: Home-made teas from 2.30. Lunches, dinners, candlelit suppers by arrangement. Licensed.

NEWCASTLE UNDER LYME

BOROUGH MUSEUM AND ART GALLERY
The Brampton. Tel: (0782) 619705.

The museum includes general collections of ceramics, weapons, clocks, textiles, natural history and local history including examples of merchandise produced during the Industrial Revolution. A Victorian street scene, including shops, is open on the first floor. The Art Gallery contains permanent collections of English oil and water-colour painting, 17th to 20th centuries, in addition to which regularly changing exhibitions of contemporary art and sculptures are on show throughout the year. Picture print loan scheme is also available. Museum: Mon to Sat 9.30–1, 2–6; Sun (May to Sept) 2–5.30.

PENKRIDGE

PILLATON OLD HALL
Telephone: Penkridge (078 571) 2200   &
(Mr R. W. & The Hon Mrs Perceval)

15th century gatehouse wing and chapel.
Location: 1 m E of Penkridge on Cannock Road (B5012); turn right at Pillaton Hall Farm.
Opening Times: Open by appointment. Adm 50p.

SHALLOWFORD

ISAAC WALTON COTTAGE
Nr. Eccleshall.

STAFFORD

ANCIENT HIGH HOUSE
Largest timber framed town house in England, dating from 1595. Heritage Exhibition and Tourist Information Centre.
Location: Off junction 13 – A449 to Stafford and junction 14 – A5103 to Stafford off M6.
Opening Times: House and Exhibition Centre: Mon to Fri 9–5; Sat 10–3. Adm £1, Chd/OAPs 50p, reduced rate for parties. Tourist Information Centre: Mon to Fri 9–5; Sat 10–3. No car park.

STAFFORD ART GALLERY AND CRAFT SHOP
(Staffordshire County Council)
Lichfield Road, ST17 4ST. Tel: Stafford (0785) 57303.

Art Gallery showing lively programme of temporary exhibitions of contemporary art, craft and photography with related events. Craft Shop selected for quality by the Crafts Council selling high quality work by outstanding British craftsmen. Tues to Fri 10–5; Sat 10–4.

STOKE ON TRENT

CHATTERLEY WHITFIELD MINING MUSEUM
(Chatterley Whitfield Mining Museum Trust)
Tunstall ST6 8UN. Tel: (0782) 813337.

Collect your helmet and lamp for a fascinating tour of Chatterley Whitfield. Our guides, all ex miners, bring to life the story of coal mining. The guided tour includes the New Pit, steam locomotives, Hesketh steam winding engine, and underground loco rides, shire horse dray rides, pit ponies. 1930's Pit Head canteen, and museum shop. Special events throughout most weekends during the summer. For opening times and admission charges please telephone above number. Free car parking.

CITY MUSEUM AND ART GALLERY
(Stoke-on-Trent District Council)
Bethesda Street, Hanley, ST1 3DE. Tel: (0782) 202173.

Displays one of the largest and most important collections of English pottery and porcelain, primarily Staffordshire; ceramics from Europe, Near and Far East and South America; a collection of archaeological specimens excavated in the area; costumes, samplers, dolls and glassware; social history of the Potteries; local history material, biological and geological; a collection of mainly British 18th–20th century paintings, drawings, prints, water-colours and sculpture and major exhibitions of historical and contemporary interest. Spitfire Gallery. Mon to Sat 10.30–5; Sun 2–5. Adm free. Facilities for disabled people. Shop, cafe and bar.

FORD GREEN HALL *(Stoke-on-Trent District Council)*
Ford Green Road, Smallthorne, ST6 1NG. Tel: (0782) 534771.

16th century timber-framed manor house containing furniture and domestic utensils. Mon, Wed, Thurs and Sat 10–12.30, 2–5; Sun 2–5.

GLADSTONE POTTERY MUSEUM
Uttoxeter Road, Longton. Tel: (0782) 319232.

The Gladstone Pottery Museum is set in a restored Victorian pottery factory complete with cobbled yard, bottle ovens, workshops and steam engine. There are galleries of the rise of the Staffordshire Potteries, tiles, sanitary ware, colour and decoration and social history. Traditional skills are demonstrated by craftsmen in the original workshops. The museum shop sells wares made by Gladstone and other souvenirs. Teashop. Adm £2, OAPs and Students £1.50, Chld £1. Special reductions for booked parties. Car parking for 50 cars. Unsuitable for disabled persons.

MINTON MUSEUM
London Road. Tel: (0782) 744766.

Minton was founded in 1793 and the museum features the many aspects of the company's world famous artistry – parian, majolica, acid gold, pâte-sur-pâte and fine bone china. Weekdays 9–12.30, 1.30–4.30. Factory tours, factory shop.

TAMWORTH

TAMWORTH CASTLE
Telephone: Tamworth 311222, Ext 389.
Weekends only Tamworth 63563
(Tamworth Borough Council)

Norman Keep and tower with Tudor and Jacobean additions. Houses a museum.

Location: In Tamworth; 15 m NE of Birmingham.
Station: Tamworth (¾ m).
Opening Times: All the year—Weekdays (except Fris) 10–5, Suns 2–5. Open Bank Hols. *Closed Fris and Christmas Eve, Christmas Day & Boxing Day.* Adm £1, OAPs and unaccompanied Chd 55p; accompanied Chd 25p.

WALL

WALL (LETOCETUM) ROMAN SITE
Telephone: (0543) 480768

Much of the business of Imperial Rome depended on official couriers who travelled the comprehensive road network. Posting stations were built for them at regular intervals. At Wall, on Watling Street, traces of the hostel and a large part of the bathhouse survive.

Location: 2 m (3.2 km) south west of Lichfield. OS map ref SK099067.
Opening Times: Good Friday to Sept 30, daily 10–6; Oct 1 to Maundy Thursday, daily 10–4. *Closed Mons, Christmas and New Year.* Adm 80p, OAPs 60p, Chd 40p.

WHITMORE

WHITMORE HALL
Telephone: (0782) 680478
(Mr G. Cavenagh-Mainwaring)

Carolinian Manor House, owner's family home for over 800 years. Family portraits dating back to 1624. Outstanding Tudor Stable Block.

Location: Four miles from Newcastle-under-Lyme on the A53 Road to Market Drayton.
Opening Times: Open 2–5.30 every Tues & Weds, May to Aug inclusive (last tour 5). Adm £1.50. *No reduction for parties. Free car parking. Not suitable for disabled. No wheelchairs available.*
Refreshments: Mainwaring Arms Inn, Whitmore & also at Whitmore Art Gallery & Tea rooms, Whitmore.

WILLOUGHBRIDGE

DOROTHY CLIVE GARDEN
(Willoughbridge Garden Trust)

7 acre woodland and rhododendron garden; shrub roses, water garden and a large scree in a fine landscape setting.

Location: 9 m SW Newcastle-under-Lyme. On A51 between junctions with A525 & A53, 1 m E of Woore.
Opening Times: Garden only. Mar 24 to Oct 31—Daily: Suns and Bank Holidays 12–5.30. Sats and weekdays 2–5. Adm £1, Chd 25p. Large car park.

Suffolk

BECCLES

BECCLES AND DISTRICT MUSEUM *(Trustees)*
Newgate (rear of Post Office). Tel: (0502) 712628 (Mr Stock).
Local industry, farming and domestic exhibits; pictures and paintings, items on local government; Printing machine (1842), old Standard Measures (1824); costumes etc.

BUNGAY

BUNGAY MUSEUM *(Waveney District Council)*
Council Office. Tel: (0986) 2176.
Local history museum.

BURY ST. EDMUNDS

THE GERSHOM-PARKINGTON MEMORIAL COLLECTION OF CLOCKS AND WATCHES
(The National Trust and Bury St. Edmunds Borough Council)
8 Angel Hill. Tel: (0284) 60255.
Queen Anne house containing collection of clocks and other instruments for recording time from the 16th century onwards. Mon to Sat 10–5; Sun 2–5. Adm free.

ICKWORTH, The National Trust
Telephone: Horringer 270   &

The house, begun c. 1794, was not completed until 1830. Contents of this architectural curiosity include late Regency and 18th century French furniture, magnificent silver, pictures. Formal gardens, herbaceous borders, orangery. 18th century walks in woodland and around the lake. 35 minute taped guide available.
Location: 3 m SW of Bury St Edmunds on W side of A143.
Opening Times: Rotunda, Corridors & Garden. Mar 25, 26, 27; Apr: Sat & Suns. May 1 to Sept 30: Daily (except Mons & Thurs): 1.30–5.30. Oct: Sat and Sun 1.30–5.30. Open Bank Hol Mons: 1.30–5.30. Adm £3, Chd £1.50. Access to Park, Garden, Restaurant and Shop £1. Parties £2.50. Park open daily. Dogs in park only, on leads. Wheelchair access, one provided; special car park for disabled. Shop.
Refreshments: Lunch & tea in old Servants' Hall. Table licence, restaurant opens 12 noon.

IXWORTH ABBEY
(John Rowe, Esq)

House contains 12th century monastic buildings with 15th to 19th century additions. 13th century Undercroft and 15th century Priors Lodging recently restored.
Location: 6 m NE of Bury St Edmunds; 8 m SE of Thetford; at junction of A143 & A1088.
Opening Times: May 1 to June 6: weekdays only 2–4. Also Spring and Summer Bank Holidays 2–4. Adm £2.20, Chd over 5 £1. Guided visits only.
Refreshments: Meals by prior arrangement only.

MOYSE'S HALL MUSEUM *(Bury St. Edmunds Borough Council)*
Cornhill. Tel: (0284) 69834.
A 12th century dwelling house containing local antiquities.

CAVENDISH

NETHER HALL
(B T Ambrose, Esq)

Listed 15th century Manor House situated in the centre of scenic Stour Valley village, beside its churchyard and famous village green. Surrounded by its own vineyards producing prize-winning Estate white wines.
Location: 12 m S of Bury St Edmunds; beside A1092.
Opening Times: Open daily for tours & wine tasting 11–4. Adm £2, Chd (accompanied) free, OAPs £1.50. Parties by appointment.
Refreshments: Widely available in village.

THE SUE RYDER FOUNDATION MUSEUM
Telephone: Glemsford (0787) 280252
(The Sue Ryder Foundation)

This small Museum is set in beautiful surroundings. It depicts the remarkable story of how the Foundation was established, its work today and its hopes for the future.
Location: On A1092 Long Melford–Cambridge. (Long Melford 4 m: Sudbury 8 m: Bury St Edmund's 16 m: Cambridge 29 m).
Opening Times: Daily—Mon–Sat 10–5.30; Sun 10–11, 12.15–5.30. Parties welcome. For special bookings, please write to:– The Sue Ryder Foundation, Cavendish, Suffolk CO10 8AY.
Refreshments: Coffee shop providing lunches and light meals also gift shop.

COTTON

MECHANICAL MUSIC MUSEUM *(An Independent Museum)*
Blacksmith Road, near Stowmarket. Tel: (0449) 781354.
A large collection of musical items ranging from small polyphons to large fairground organs, all of which are played for visitors. Concerts given on a preserved Wurlitzer Theatre Organ (details from museum). Open every Sun June to Sept 2.30–5.30. Adm £1, Chld 50p. Free car park. Light refreshments.

DUNWICH

DUNWICH MUSEUM
St. James's Street.
History of the lost Medieval town and local wild life. Mar to Oct: Sat and Sun 2–4.30. Also Tues and Thurs, May to Sept and daily in Aug.

EASTON

EASTON FARM PARK
Wickham Market. Tel: (0728) 746475.
Large collection of old farm machinery, country bygones, laundry. Portable steam engine and threshing machine. Easter to end of Sept: Daily 10.30–6. Car parking free. Suitable for disabled persons. Country style tea room. Curator: Stephen Ward.

EUSTON

EUSTON HALL
(The Duke of Grafton)

18th century house. Fine collection of paintings, including Stubbs, Van Dyck, Kneller and Lely. Pleasure grounds by John Evelyn and William Kent. Gardens and 17th century parish church in Wren style.
Location: A1088; 3 m S Thetford.
Opening Times: June 1 to Sept 28—Thurs only 2.30–5.30. Also Sun June 25, 2.30–5.30. Adm £2, Chd 50p, OAPs £1.20. Parties of 12 or more £1 per head.
Refreshments: Teas and shop in Old Kitchen. Picnic area.

EYE

WINGFIELD COLLEGE
Telephone: Stradbroke (037 984) 505
(Ian Chance, Esq)

Founded in 1362 on the 13th century site of the Manor House by Sir John de Wingfield, a close friend of the Black Prince. Magnificent Medieval Great Hall. Surrendered to Henry VIII in 1542 and seized by Cromwell's Parliament in 1549. Mixed period interiors with 18th century neo-classical façade. Walled gardens. Teas. Celebrated Arts and Music Season. Adjacent church with tombs of College founder and Benefactors, The Dukes of Suffolk.
Location: Signposted off B1118; 7 m SE of Diss.
Opening Times: Easter Sat to Sept 25—Sats, Suns & Bank Hols 2–6.
Refreshments: Home-made teas.

FRAMLINGHAM

FRAMLINGHAM CASTLE
Telephone: (0728) 723330
(English Heritage)

The present massive walls and their 13 towers were built by Roger Bigod, second Earl of Norfolk, on a site given to his father by Henry I. The ornamental brick chimneys were added in Tudor times when the arch of the entrance gateway was rebuilt. In 1636 the castle passed to Pembroke College, Cambridge, and in later years the great hall was converted to a poor-house and many of the buildings inside the walls were demolished. It was here, in 1553, that Mary Tudor learned she had become Queen of England.
Location: North side of Framlingham. OS map ref TM287637.
Opening Times: Good Friday to Sept 30, daily 10–6; Oct 1 to Maundy Thurs, daily 10–4. *Closed* Mons, Dec 24–26, Jan 1. Adm £1.10, OAPs 80p, Chd 55p.

SAXTEAD GREEN POST MILL
Telephone: (0728) 82346

In the 13th century Framlingham was a thriving farming community, whose wealth derived from cereals, particularly wheat. This corn-mill, one of the finest in the world, probably dates from 1287 and produced flour until the First World War. The upper part of the mill, containing the machinery, was rotated by a track-mounted fantail. This ensured that the sails always faced square into the wind.
Location: 2 m (3.2 km) west of Framlingham. OS map ref TM253645.
Opening Times: Good Friday to Sept 30, daily 10–6, *closed* Sun. Adm 80p, OAPs 60p, Chd 40p.

IPSWICH

CHRISTCHURCH MANSION
Telephone: Ipswich (0473) 53246
(The Borough of Ipswich)

Extensive Tudor town house in park. Furnished period rooms, 16th to 19th century; outstanding decorative art collections of china, glass etc. Attached art gallery includes work by Gainsborough, Constable and other Suffolk artists up to the present day. Temporary art exhibition programme.
Location: In Christchurch Park, near centre of Ipswich.
Station: Ipswich (1¼ m).
Opening Times: All the year—Mons to Sats 10–5 *(dusk in winter)*; Suns 2.30–4.30 *(dusk in winter)*. Open Bank Hols. *Closed Dec 24, 25 & 26 and Good Fri.* Adm free.

HELMINGHAM HALL GARDENS
(The Lord & Lady Tollemache)

The House was completed in 1510 by the Tollemache family and is surrounded by a wide moat with drawbridges which are raised every night. The large park contains herds of Red and Fallow deer and Highland Cattle and the gardens, which date with the house, are renowned for their herbaceous borders and old fashioned roses. English Heritage Grade I Garden.
Location: 9 m N of Ipswich on B1077.
Opening Times: GARDENS ONLY. Apr 30 to Oct 1—Suns only 2–6. Adm £1.30, Chd 80p, OAPs £1. Safari rides 70p, Chd 50p. Craft shop. *House not open to the public.*
Refreshments: Cream teas. Home-grown plants and produce for sale.

IPSWICH MUSEUM
Telephone: Ipswich (0473) 213761/2
(Ipswich Borough Council)

Geology and natural history of Suffolk; Mankind galleries covering Africa, Asia, America and the Pacific. 'Romans in Suffolk' gallery showing local archaeology. Temporary exhibitions in attached gallery.
Location: High Street, in town centre.
Station: Ipswich.
Opening Times: Mons to Sats 10–5. Temporary exhibition programme. Adm free.

LAVENHAM

GUILDHALL, The National Trust

Early 16th century timber-framed Tudor building; originally hall of Guild of Corpus Christi. Display of local history and industry including a unique exhibition of 700 years of the woollen cloth trade. Delightful small garden.
Location: Market Place Lavenham, Sudbury.
Opening Times: Mar 25 to Nov 4—Daily 11–1, 2–5.30. Closed Good Fri. Adm £1.50, Chd 75p. Parties £1.20, please book with sae to Custodian in charge. School parties 50p by prior arrangement. Shop.
Refreshments: Coffee, light lunches and teas.

LITTLE HALL
(Suffolk Preservation Society)

15th century "hall" house, rooms furnished with Gayer Anderson collection of furniture, pictures, china, books, etc.
Location: E side Lavenham Market Place.
Opening Times: Easter to mid-Oct—Sats, Suns & Bank Hols 2.30–6. *Groups by appointment tel: (0787) 247179.* Adm 80p, Chd 40p.

THE PRIORY
Telephone: Lavenham (0787) 247417
(Mr & Mrs A Casey)

Through the ages the home of Benedictine monks, medieval clothiers, an Elizabethan rector, and now of the Casey family, who rescued the house from a derelict ruin. Beautiful timber-framed building (Grade 1) with stimulating interior design blending old and new, enhanced by paintings, drawings and stained glass by Ervin Bossanyi (1891–1975). Lovely herb garden of unique design. Work still continues on parts of the building. On display is an exhibition of photographs illustrating the restoration.
Location: In Water Street, Lavenham; 10 m S of Bury St Edmunds.
Opening Times: Apr to end Oct—Daily 10.30–5.30. Adm £2, Chd £1. Open by appointment for groups all year, morning, afternoon or evening, please telephone above number. Guided tours can emphasise timber framed buildings and their restoration, history of the house and the area, the Bossanyi collection, interior decor – according to your interests. For winter bookings, there is central heating and log fires!
Refreshments: Coffee, lunches and teas served in the Refectory. Gift shop. Selection of unusual gifts and woven tapestries.

LAXFIELD

JACOBS FARM MUSEUM OF CHILDHOOD
(Mrs Christine Elizabeth Reynolds)
St. Jacobs Hall. Tel: (098 683) 657.
An interesting assortment of antique toys and playthings dating from 1800 to 1960. Dolls, teddys, a working layout of G.I. Edwardian Locos and lots more

besides. Housed in converted period farm buildings, moated grounds with cottage garden surround St. Jacobs Hall which is a Tudor farm house. 12 acres of meadows with rare breeds of farm animals, plus nature trail and picnic area. New craft shop. Easter Sun and Mon, to Oct 31: Tues, Weds, Thurs and all Bank Hols 10–5, Sun all year 12–5. Adm £1, Chld, OAPs and Students 50p. Parties of 12 and over 10% off. Large free car park. Suitable for disabled persons. Situated on the B1117 one mile E from Laxfield.

LEISTON

LONG SHOP MUSEUM
Main Street. Tel: (0728) 832189 or 830550.
Listed building containing Steam Engines and Agricultural etc. Machinery made by Garretts, much other memorabilia. April to Sept 10–4.

LITTLE BLAKENHAM

BLAKENHAM WOODLAND GARDEN
(Lord Blakenham)

5 acre wood with many rare trees and shrubs. Lovely throughout the year, with bluebells, camellias and magnolias followed by azaleas, rhododendrons, roses, hydrangeas and fine autumn colouring.
Location: 4 m NW of Ipswich. The garden is signposted from Little Blakenham which is 1 m off the old A1100 now called B1113.
Opening Times: Apr to Sept—Weds, Thurs, Suns and Bank Hols 1–5. Adm £1. Free car-park. No dogs.

LONG MELFORD

KENTWELL HALL
(J. Patrick Phillips, QC)

Red brick Tudor E-plan mansion surrounded by a broad moat. Exterior little altered. Interior being refurbished. Ancient moats and interconnecting gardens. 15th century Moat House, rare breed farm animals, brick paved Maze and costume display.
Location: Entrance on W of A134, N of Green in Long Melford; 3 m N of Sudbury.
Opening Times: Easter: Good Fri to Thurs following. Easter to June 17—Suns only. July 10 to Sept 30—Weds to Suns 2–6; Bank Hol Sats, Suns & Mons 11–6. Adm £2.40, Chd (5–15) £1.40, OAPs £2.10. Bank Holidays: £3.50, Chd (5–15) £2, OAPs, £3. June 18 to July 19, annual Re-Creation of Tudor Life – weekdays, prebooked school parties only; general public at weekends: 11–5 (special admission charges). Reduction of 20% for prebooked parties over 20 on open days, also groups at other times by arrangement. No dogs.
Refreshments: Teas in the Hall 2–6. Also lunches over Bank Hols.

MELFORD HALL, The National Trust &

Built between 1554 and 1578 by Sir William Cordell, contains fine pictures, furniture and Chinese porcelain. Interesting garden and gazebo. Beatrix Potter display.
Location: In Long Melford on E side of A134; 3 m N of Sudbury.
Opening Times: Principal Rooms & Gardens. Mar: 25, 26, 27; Apr Sat and Sun; May 1 to Sept 30: Wed, Thurs, Sat, Sun, Bank Holidays 2–6. Oct: Sat and Sun 2–6. Adm £2, Chd (with adult) £1. Pre-booked parties of 15 or more £1.60, Weds & Thurs only. No dogs. Wheelchair access, one provided.
Refreshments: In Long Melford.

LOWESTOFT

LOWESTOFT MARITIME MUSEUM
Sparrows Nest Park.
Fishing etc. through the ages.

LOWESTOFT MUSEUM
(Lowestoft Archaeological and Local History Society and Waveney District Council)
Broad House, Nicholas Everitt Park, Oulton Broad.
Lowestoft porcelain, archaeology, local and domestic history, toys. Mar 25–Apr 9, and May 27–Oct 1: Mon–Sat 10.30–1, 2–5; Apr 15–May 21: Sat and Sun 2–5; Oct 7–Oct 29: Sat and Sun 2–4. Adm 40p, Chld/OAPs 20p.

NEWMARKET

THE NATIONAL HORSERACING MUSEUM
Newmarket High Street. Tel: (0638) 667333.
The National Horseracing Museum, which is housed in the Regency Subscription Rooms on the Newmarket High Street, was opened by The Queen on April 30th, 1983. In the Museum's five permanent galleries the great story of the development of Horseracing in this Country is told. Each year, with changing loans and fresh exhibits, the display varies. Another display of fine paintings belonging to the British Sporting Art Trust. A video programme of classic races, wine bar, gift shop, and a walled garden are added attractions to the Museum. Mar 25 to Dec 10: Tues to Sat 10–5, Sun 2–5. *Closed* Mon except for Bank Hols. Aug: Mon to Sat 10–5; Sun 2–5. Adm £1.60, Chld/OAPs 80p. 10% reduction for parties numbering over 20.

ORFORD

ORFORD CASTLE
Telephone: (039 44) 50472

No sooner had Henry II built this castle on the Suffolk coast than rebellion broke out (in 1173). The castle's powerful presence helped to uphold the King's authority and it continued to be an important royal residence for more than 100 years. In 1280 it was granted to the Earl of Norfolk for his lifetime, and from then on it remained in private hands. The design was very advanced for its time, and the keep, much of which remains, is unique in England. The outer wall of the castle, the last section of which collapsed in 1841, was punctuated by rectangular towers, an innovation that provided excellent cover for the defenders.

Location: In Orford. OS map ref TM419499.
Opening Times: Good Friday to Sept 30, daily 10–6; Oct 1 to Maundy Thursday, daily 10–4. *Closed Mons, Christmas and New Year.* Adm 80p, OAPs 60p, Chd 40p.

OTLEY

OTLEY HALL
(Mr and Mrs J G Mosesson)

15th century Moated Hall (Grade 1) and Gardens. Home for 250 years of the Gosnold family. Fine timbers, herring-bone brick, pargetting. Historical associations.

Location: 10 m N of Ipswich, via B1077/B1078; ¼ m NE of Otley village.
Opening Times: Easter Sun & Mon (Mar 26 and 27); Spring Bank Hol Sun & Mon (May 28 and 29); Summer Bank Hol Sun & Mon (Aug 27 and 28): 2–6. Open by appointment to parties, special interest groups, etc. Guided tours. Lectures available on associated history, architectural background, etc. Adm £2.75, Chd (with adult) £1.75.
Refreshments: Tea & light refreshments, buffet meals available by arrangement.

SOMERLEYTON

SOMERLEYTON HALL
(The Lord & Lady Somerleyton)

Early 19th century mansion on which no expense was spared. Beautiful gardens, famous maze, miniature railway (on most days).

Location: 5 m NW Lowestoft off B1074; 7 m Yarmouth (A143).
Station: Somerleyton (1½ m).

Opening Times: House, Maze and Gardens open 1989 – Easter Sun to Jun 1, Thurs, Suns and Bank Holidays. June 1 to Oct 1, Suns, Mons, Tues, Weds & Thurs—2–5.30. Adm £2.50, Chd £1.20, OAPs £2.

SOUTHWOLD

SOUTHWOLD MUSEUM
Bartholomews Green.
Local archaeology, history, natural history and bygones.

STOWMARKET

HAUGHLEY PARK
(Mr & Mrs A J Williams)

Jacobean manor house. Gardens and woods, fine trees and shrubs.
Location: 4 m W of Stowmarket signed on A45 nr Wetherden (not Haughley).
Opening Times: May to Sept—Tues 3–6. Adm £1.50, Chd 50p.

MUSEUM OF EAST ANGLIAN LIFE
Tel: (0449) 612229.

Large open air museum on attractive riverside site in centre of Stowmarket. Reconstructed buildings including Smithy, Watermill and Windpump. New Boby Building houses steam gallery, craft workshops and East Anglian industrial heritage exhibition. Working Suffolk Punch horse, displays on domestic, agricultural and industrial life, steam traction engines. Entrance two minutes walk from Stowmarket market place. Open Apr to Oct: Mon to Sat 11–5; Sun 12–5 (12–6 June to Aug). Adm charge. Reductions for parties. Teas by arrangement.

SUDBURY

GAINSBOROUGH'S HOUSE
Telephone: Sudbury (0787) 72958
(Gainsborough's House Society)

Thomas Gainsborough's birthplace. Pictures and furniture associated with the artist and the 18th century. Exhibitions of historic and contemporary art throughout the year. Contemporary craft gallery. Print workshop; garden.
Location: 46 Gainsborough Street, Sudbury.
Station: Sudbury (¼ m).
Opening Times: Open all the year. Easter to Sept—Tues to Sats 10–5; Sun & Bank Hol Mons 2–5; Oct to Maundy Thursday—Tues to Sats 10–4; Sun and Bank Hol Mons 2–4. *Closed Mons, Good Fri & between Christmas & New Year.* Adm £1, Students/Chd/OAPs 50p.

Surrey

ALBURY

ALBURY PARK
(Country Houses Association Ltd)

Country mansion by Pugin.
Location: 1½ m E of Albury.
Stations: Chilworth (2 m); Gomshall (2 m); Clandon (2 m)
Opening Times: May to Sept—Weds & Thurs 2–5. Adm £1, Chd 50p. Free car park. No dogs admitted.

CAMBERLEY

SURREY HEATH MUSEUM *(Surrey Heath Borough Council)*
Surrey Heath House, Knoll Road GU15 3HD. Tel: (0276) 686252, ext. 528.
A new museum combining permanent displays on local history and environment with a lively programme of temporary displays of local and regional interest. Displays on geology archaeology, natural history, heathland crafts and the military. Open: Tues to Sat 11–5. Adm free. Parties by prior arrangement. Public car park nearby. Suitable for disabled persons.

CATERHAM

EAST SURREY MUSEUM
1 Stafford Road CR3 6JG.
Changing displays of local history, archaeology, natural history, crafts and local artists. Wed and Sat 10–5; Sun 2–5. Adm 20p, Chld and OAPs 10p.

CHERTSEY

CHERTSEY MUSEUM *(Runnymede Borough Council)*
The Cedars, Windsor Street. Tel: (0932) 565764.
The museum contains 18th and 19th century costume, furniture, ceramics, clocks, glass, local history and archaeology. Tues and Thurs 2–5; Wed, Fri and Sat 10–1, 2–5.

CHIDDINGFOLD

RAMSTER
Telephone: (0428) 4422
(Mr & Mrs Paul Gunn)

Mature 20 acre woodland garden of exceptional interest. Laid out by Gauntlett Nurseries of Chiddingfold in early 1900's. Fine rhododendrons, azaleas, camellias, magnolias, trees and shrubs in lovely setting.
Location: On A283 1½ m S of Chiddingfold.
Opening Times: GARDEN ONLY. Apr 22 to June 11—Daily 2–6. Adm £1, Chd 20p. Parties by arrangement. *Share to National Gardens Scheme.*
Refreshments: Teas Sats, Suns & Bank Hol Mons in May only.

CHILWORTH

CHILWORTH MANOR
(Lady Heald)

Garden laid out in 17th century on site of 11th century monastery, 18th century walled garden, spring flowers, flowering shrubs, herbaceous border, 11th century stewponds. House open. Floral arrangements.
Location: 3¾ m SE of Guildford off A248 in Chilworth Village turn at Blacksmith Lane.
Station: Chilworth (¾ m).
Opening Times: GARDEN ONLY: Sats to Weds incl—Apr 8–12; May 13–17; June 17–21; July 15–19; Aug 5–Aug 9. Other times by appointment. Car park open 12.30 for picnics. Adm Garden £1, House (Sats & Suns only) 50p, accompanied Chd free. Cars free. In aid of National Gardens Scheme. Floral decorations.
Refreshments: Tea at the house, Sats & Suns only.

COBHAM

COBHAM BUS MUSEUM *(London Bus Preservation Trust)*
Redhill Road. Tel: (0932) 64078.
A collection of preserved omnibuses dating from the 1920's to recent times. A 'working garage' environment with vehicles in various stages of restoration.

PAINSHILL PARK
Telephone: (0932) 68113
(Painshill Park Trust)

Painshill, contemporary with Stourhead & Stowe, is one of Europe's finest eighteenth century landscape gardens. It was created by The Hon Charles Hamilton, plantsman, painter and brilliantly gifted designer, between 1738 and 1773. He transformed barren heathland into ornamental pleasure grounds and parkland of dramatic beauty and contrasting scenery, dominated by a 14 acre meandering lake fed from the river by an immense waterwheel. Garden buildings and features adorned the Park, including a magnificent Grotto, Temple, ruined Abbey, Chinese Bridge, castellated Tower, and a Mausoleum. Well maintained for 200 years in private ownership, the Park was neglected after 1948 and sank into dereliction. In 1981 the Painshill Park Trust, a registered charity, was formed to restore the gardens to their original splendour, raising the extensive funds needed for such an ambitious project. Already, after nearly 10 years, the Trust has made enormous progress, and this masterpiece is re-emerging from the wilderness.
Location: W of Cobham on A245. 200 yards E of A3/A245. Roundabout.
Opening Times: Apr 15 to Oct 14: Sats 1–6 (last ticket 5). Adm £2, Chd and OAPs £1.50. Pre-booked parties (min. 15) Sun to Fri, excl. Mon. School parties particularly welcome by arrangement with Painshill Park Education Trust. Please ring (0932) 64674 for information and bookings. Much of Park accessible for disabled (no wheelchairs available). Limited facilities and parking. NO DOGS PLEASE.
Refreshments: Light refreshments available.

DORKING

POLESDEN LACEY, The National Trust
Telephone: Bookham 58203 or 52048   &

Originally a Regency villa altered in Edwardian period. Greville collection of pictures, tapestries, furniture. 18th century garden extended 1906, with herbaceous borders, rose garden, clipped hedges, lawns, beeches. Views.
Location: 3 m NW of Dorking, reached via Great Bookham (A246) & then road leading S (1½ m).
Stations: Boxhill or Bookham (both 2½ m).
Opening Times: Mar & Nov—Sats & Suns 1.30–4.30; Apr to end of Oct—Weds to Suns 1.30–5.30. Last adm half hour before closing. Open Good Friday. Open Bank Hol Mons & preceding Suns 11–5.30. Garden open daily all year, 11–sunset. No dogs in formal gardens. Adm Garden only Apr to end Oct £1.20, Nov to end Mar £1. House: Sun & Bank Holiday Mon £1.80 extra. Other open days £1.30 extra. Chd half-price. *Party reductions on Weds, Thurs & Fris only by prior arrangement with the Administrator.* Wheelchairs admitted & provided. Shop open at same times as restaurant.
Refreshments: Licensed Restaurant in the grounds; Mar—Sat & Sun only 11–2.30 & 3–5; Apr to end Oct—Weds to Suns & Bank Hol Mons 11–2.30 & 3–6; Nov to mid-Dec—Weds to Suns 11–2.30 & 3–5. Tel Bookham 56190.

DORMANSLAND

GREATHED MANOR
(Country Houses Association Ltd)

Victorian Manor house.
Location: On the outskirts of the village of Dormansland; 5 m SE of Lingfield.
Stations: Dormans (1½ m); Lingfield (1½ m).
Opening Times: May to Sept—Weds & Thurs 2–5. Adm £1, Chd 50p. Free car park. No dogs admitted.

EAST CLANDON

HATCHLANDS, The National Trust
Telephone: Guildford 222787   &

Built by Admiral Boscawen in 18th century, interior by Robert Adam, with later modifications. Boscawen exhibition. Garden.
Location: E of East Clandon on N side of Leatherhead/Guildford Road (A246).
Station: Clandon (2 m).
Opening Times: Mar 26 to Oct 15—Tues, Weds, Thurs, Suns & Bank Hol Mons only 2–6 (no admission after 5.30). Adm £2, Chd half price. Pre-booked parties £1.50 (Tues, Weds & Thurs only). No dogs. Wheelchair access to ground floor and part of the garden.
Refreshments: Teas.

EGHAM

THE EGHAM MUSEUM *(The Egham Museum Trust)*
Literary Institute, High Street.
Local history and archaeology exhibits from Egham, Englefield Green, Thorpe and Virginia Water, Thurs 2–4.30 and Sats 10.30–12.30, 2.30–4.30. Adm free.

ESHER

CLAREMONT
Telephone: Esher (0372) 67841
(The Claremont Fan Court Foundation Ltd)

Excellent example of Palladian style; built 1772 by "Capability" Brown for Clive of India; Henry Holland and John Soane responsible for the interior decoration. It is now a co-educational school run by Christian Scientists.
Location: ½ m SW from Esher on Esher/Cobham Road A307, turning before entrance to NT Claremont Landscape Garden.
Stations: Claygate (1½ m); Esher (2 m) (not Suns).
Opening Times: Feb to Nov—First complete weekend (Sats & Suns) in each month 2–5. Adm £1, Chd/OAPs 50p. Reduced rates for parties. Souvenirs.
Refreshments: Not available.

CLAREMONT LANDSCAPE GARDEN, The National Trust &

The earliest surviving English landscape garden, recently restored. Begun by Vanbrugh and Bridgemen before 1720, extended and naturalized by Kent. Lake, island with pavilion, grotto and turf amphitheatre, viewpoints and avenues. House not National Trust property.

Location: ½ m SE of Esher on E side of A307. NB: no access from A3 by-pass.
Stations: Esher (2 m) (not Suns); Hersham (2 m); Hinchley Wood (2½ m).
Opening Times: All the year. May to end of Sept–Daily 9–7 (or sunset if earlier). Oct to end of Apr–Daily 9–5 (last adm half hour before closing). *Closed Christmas Day & New Year's Day.* Adm Sun £1.30; Mon to Sat £1 (Chd half price). Guided tours (minimum 15 persons) £1 plus admission price by prior booking, telephone Bookham 53401. Wheelchairs provided. No reduction for parties. Dogs admitted on leads. Shop.
Refreshments: New tea room open Mar: Sat & Sun 11–4; Apr to end Oct: Tues–Sun from 11. Nov to Dec 17: Tues–Sun from 1 pm.

FARNHAM

FARNHAM CASTLE
(The Church Commissioners)

Bishop's Palace built in Norman times with Tudor and Jacobean additions. Fine Great Hall re-modelled at the Restoration.

Location: ½ m N of Town Centre on A287.
Station: Farnham.
Opening Times: Castle–All year Weds 2–4. Parties at other times by arrangement. Adm 70p, Chd and Students 35p. Reductions for parties. All visitors are given guided tours. Centrally heated in winter.

FARNHAM CASTLE KEEP
Telephone: (0252) 713393

Farnham formed part of the estate of the Bishops of Winchester long before the Norman Conquest. And there was still a bishop in residence until 1955–an impressive tenancy. But why should the massive keep be built *around* the mound of earth, and not on top of it? Your guess is as good as the archaeologists'!

Location: Farnham. OS map ref SU839474.
Opening Times: Good Friday to Sept 30, daily 10–6. Adm 80p, OAPs 60p, Chd 40p.

FARNHAM MUSEUM *(Waverley Borough Council)*
Willmer House, 38 West Street. Tel: (0252) 715094.
Early Georgian (1718) front of cut and moulded brick; fine carvings and panelling. Local history and archaeology, William Cobbett, decorative arts. Walled garden. Tues to Sat 11–5; Bank Hol Mons 2–5.

GODALMING

GODALMING MUSEUM
(Godalming Museum Trust/Waverley Borough Council)
109A High Street. Tel: Guildford (0483) 426510.
Medieval Building; Local history and people; Lutyens–Jekyll room; Garden; Shop; Exhibitions. Open Tues–Sat, 10–5.

WINKWORTH ARBORETUM, The National Trust &

99 acres of trees and shrubs planted mainly for Spring and Autumn colour. Two lakes, fine views.

Location: 2 m SE of Godalming on E side of B2130.
Station: Godalming (2 m).
Opening Times: Open all the year during daylight hours. Adm £1, Chd 50p. No reduction for parties. *Coach parties please book to ensure parking space and refreshments.* Bookings Tearoom Concessionaire, The Homestead, Cottage Lane, Thorncombe Street, Bramley, Guildford GU5 0LT. Dogs must be kept under control. Wheelchair access.
Refreshments: Apr to end of Oct–Tues, Weds, Thurs, Fris, Sats, Suns & Bank Hol Mons 2–6 or dusk if earlier. *Closed Tues following Bank Hols.* Also open weekends and some other fine days in Mar.

GUILDFORD

BRITISH RED CROSS HISTORICAL EXHIBITION AND ARCHIVES
(British Red Cross Society)
Barnett Hill, Wonersh. Tel: (0483) 898595.
History of the Red Cross movement from its foundation in 1863, particularly British Red Cross Society from 1870. Includes uniform and other material from First and Second World Wars. Reference library and research facilities available. Adm free. Appointment only. Parties, maximum 12 people. Car parking.

GUILDFORD HOUSE GALLERY
Telephone: (0483) 444741 &
(Guildford Borough Council)

17th century town house now an art gallery. Original fine carved staircase, plaster ceilings and wrought iron window fittings. Temporary exhibitions include historical and modern paintings of local and national importance, photography and craftwork.

Location: 155 High Street, town centre; off A3 (1½ m).
Station: Guildford (½ m).

Opening Times: Mons to Fris 10.30–4.50, Sats 10.30–4.15. *Closed when staging exhibition.* Adm free. Suitable for disabled (ground floor).
Refreshments: Hotels & Restaurants in the town.

GUILDFORD MUSEUM *(Guildford Borough Council)*
Castle Arch. Tel: (0483) 503497.
Archaeological and historical museum for the County, especially West Surrey and Guildford Borough. Needlework collection of general interest. Mon to Sat 11–5.

LOSELEY HOUSE
Telephone: Guildford (0483) 571881 &
(J R More-Molyneux, Esq)

Elizabethan mansion built 1562. Panelling, furniture, paintings, ceilings. Farm tours.

Location: 2½ m SW of Guildford (take B3000 off A3 through Compton); 1½ m N of Godalming (off A3100).
Station: Farncombe (2 m).
Opening Times: May 29 to Sept 30–Weds, Thurs, Fris & Sats 2–5; also Summer Bank Hol Mon 2–5. Adm £2.80, Chd £1.50. Parties of 20 and over £2.20 per person. School parties £1.30 per person. Farm shop. Farm Tours when house is open; at other times, booked parties only.
Refreshments: Home produce, wholefood lunches and teas.

THE WATTS GALLERY
Compton (3 miles from Guildford). Tel: (0483) 810235.
Paintings by G. F. Watts, O.M., R.A. Daily (except Thurs) 2–6 (Oct to Mar, 2–4); also Wed and Sat 11–1. No dogs.

HAMBLEDON

FEATHERCOMBE GARDENS &
(Miss Parker)

Wide views, flowering shrubs, heathers.

Location: S of Godalming 2 m from Milford Station on Hambledon Road, turn to Feathercombe off road between Hydestyle crossroads and Merry Harriers pub.
Opening Times: GARDENS ONLY. Bank Hol Suns & Mons, Apr 30, May 1, 28, 29. 2–6. Adm 60p, Chd 10p. Picnic area. Plants for sale.

VANN
Telephone: Wormley (042 879) 3413
(Mr & Mrs M. B. Caröe)

16th to 20th century house surrounded by 5 acre 'paradise' garden. Water garden by Gertrude Jekyll 1911.

Location: 6 m S of Godalming; A283 to Chiddingfold; turn off at green, signposted Vann Lane at P.O.
Station: Witley (2 m).
Opening Times: GARDENS ONLY: Apr 17–22, May 2–6, 22–27, June 19–24, 10–6. Suns–Apr 16, May 21, June 18, Bank Holiday Mon May 1, 2–7 and by prior appointment Easter–Sept (Tel: Wormley 3413). Plant and vegetable stall. Party bookings and guided tours with morning coffee, lunches or home made teas in house by arrangement. Adm £1, Chd 20p. In aid of National Gardens Scheme and Hambledon Charities.
Refreshments: Home made teas in house, Apr 16, Bank Hol Mon May 1, May 21 and June 18 only.

HASCOMBE

HASCOMBE COURT
Telephone: (048 632) 254
(Mr & Mrs M E Pinto)

Jekyll influences but mainly designed by Percy Cane. Herbaceous border, rhododendron garden, views, Japanese/rock garden with stream, specimen trees.

Location: 2½ m from Godalming off the B2130
Opening Times: Apr 17, May 29, July 30, Aug 28 2–6. Adm £1, Chd 10p (in aid of the National Gardens Scheme). Parties by arrangement. Car park.
Refreshments: White Horse Pub, Hascombe; Winkworth Arboretum.

HASLEMERE

HASLEMERE EDUCATIONAL MUSEUM
High Street. Tel: (0428) 2112.
Fine collection of British birds, geology, zoology, botany, local industries etc.

LIMPSFIELD

DETILLENS
Telephone: Oxted (0883) 713342
(Mr & Mrs D G Neville)

Mid 15th century Wealden House, fine inglenooks, firebacks and panelling. 2½ acres of walled gardens with duck pond.

Location: Centre Limpsfield village opposite Bull Inn off A25.
Station: Oxted (1 m).
Opening Times: May to June–Sats; July to Sept–Weds & Sats: 2–5. *Bank Hols during above periods.* Guided tours at other times by prior arrangement. Adm £2, Chd £1.

PEASLAKE

COVERWOOD LAKES
Telephone: (0306) 731103
(Mr & Mrs C G Metson)

Landscaped water and cottage gardens in lovely setting between Holmbury Hill to the north and Pitch Hill to the south. Rhododendrons, azaleas, primulas, fine trees – both mature and young. Four small lakes and bog garden. Herd of pedigree Poll Hereford cattle and flock of mule sheep in the adjoining farm (Mr Nigel Metson). Garden is included in the Collins Book of British Gardens by George Plumptre and 'Gardens Open Today' – a guide to gardens open to the public through the National Gardens Scheme. It is shortly to be featured in the American publication 'Architectural Digest'.

Location: ½ m from Peaslake village. 8 m from Guildford. 8 m from Dorking (A25). 3 m from A25.
Opening Times: GARDEN ONLY: Suns Apr 30, May 14, 21, 28, 2–6.30. Adm £1, Chd (5 to 16) 50p. GARDEN AND FARM: May, Wed 31, Sun June 4, 11, 2–6.30. Adm £1.50 Chd (5 to 16) 50p. Chd under 5 free. Special reductions for large parties if arrangements made prior to visit. Plenty of free parking space. No dogs please. Suitable for disabled persons (no wheelchairs available). Open for NGS on May 21 & 28, 2–6.30.
Refreshments: Teas and home-made cakes available. Nearest hotel is the Hurtwood, (THF) at Peaslake village (½ m away from garden).

REDHILL

ROYAL EARLSWOOD HOSPITAL MUSEUM
Tel: (0737) 63591.

Divided into eight sections dealing with early history and development, finance, elections, medical and nursing, education, training and occupation, entertainment, building, farm and engineering.

RIPLEY

PYRFORD COURT
Telephone: Woking (048 62) 65880
(Mr & Mrs C. Laikin)

Twenty acres of wild and formal gardens, azaleas, wisteria, rhododendrons, pink marble fountain, venetian bridge.
Location: 2 m E of Woking, B367 junction with Upshott Lane, M25 (exit 10) on to A3 towards Guildford, off to Ripley signposted Pyrford.
Opening Times: Suns May 21, 28, 2–6.30. Sun, Oct 22 12–4. Adults £1, Chd 50p. Open in aid of National Gardens Scheme. For details of operas/concerts and other events in the house please phone above number.
Refreshments: Tea and home made cakes.

TILFORD

OLD KILN AGRICULTURAL MUSEUM
Reeds Road, Tilford. Tel: Frensham (025 125) 2300.

Collection includes wagons, farm implements, hand tools, Dairy, Kitchen, Forge, Wheelwright's shop and Arboretum. Apr to Sept: Wed to Sun and Bank Hols 11–6. Suitable for disabled visitors. Rustic Sunday July 30, 1989.

WEST CLANDON

CLANDON PARK, The National Trust
Telephone: Guildford 222482   &

A Palladian house built 1731–35 by Giacomo Leoni. Fine plasterwork. Collection of furniture, pictures and porcelain. Museum of the Queen's Royal Surrey Regiment. Garden with parterre, grotto and Maori house.

Location: At West Clandon 3 m E Guildford on A247; S of A3 & N of A246. *Station: Clandon (1 m).*
Opening Times: Mar 24 to Oct 15—Daily (except Thurs & Fris) 1.30–5.30 (last adm 5). Open Bank Hol Mons and preceding Suns 11–5.30; open Good Friday. Parties & guided tours by arrangement with the Administrator *(no reduced rate at weekends & Bank Hols).* Adm House & Museum £2.30, Chd £1.10. Shop. Picnic area. Dogs in car park & picnic area only, on leads. Wheelchairs provided.
Refreshments: Restaurant in house 12.30–2 & 3.15–5.30. Prior booking advisable for luncheon, Tel Guildford 222502.

WEYBRIDGE

WEYBRIDGE MUSEUM
Church Street. Tel: (0932) 843573.

Local exhibits of archaeology, social history, natural history and costume. Mon to Fri 2–5; Sat 10–1, 2–5 (Aug: Mon to Sat 10–1, 2–5). Special exhibitions throughout the year. Adm free.

WISLEY

WISLEY GARDEN   &
(The Royal Horticultural Society)

British gardening at its best in all aspects. 250 acres of glorious garden. The wooded slopes with massed rhododendrons and azaleas, the wild daffodils of the alpine meadow, the calm of the pinetum, the gaiety of the herbaceous border, the banked mounds of heathers, the new alpine house, the panorama of the rock garden, the model fruit and vegetable gardens and the range of greenhouse displays are there waiting for you to enjoy them and to learn from them.
Location: In Wisley just off M25 Junction 10, on A3. London 22 m, Guildford 7 m.
Opening Times: All the year—Mons to Sats 10–7 (or sunset if earlier). *Sundays – members & their guests only. Closed Christmas Day.* Adm £2.50, Chd £1. A reduction for parties – tickets for parties must be obtained 14 days in advance of visit. Dogs not admitted other than guide dogs. Information centre, Shop & Plant sales centre.
Refreshments: Licensed restaurant in garden (Jan 7 to mid Dec) & licensed cafeteria.

WOKING

PINEWOOD HOUSE
Telephone: Brookwood (048 67) 3241
(Mr & Mrs J van Zwanenberg)

Four acres of garden. Stream and small lakes – ½ acre of wild garden. Large walled garden – new house built in Roman style, villa also open with oval hall and conservatory.
Location: Woking 4 m, Guildford 5 m. On A322 Guildford to Bagshot road, turning into Heath House Road.
Opening Times: Parties of not more than 25 by appointment Apr, May, June and July. Adm £1. Car parking in drive, courtyard and road. Suitable for disabled persons; ramps for wheelchairs, wide doors to W.C. (no wheelchairs available). Plants for sale. A.R.C.C. stall.
Refreshments: Home made teas by arrangement.

DETILLENS
LIMPSFIELD, SURREY

A medieval Manor House built in 1450 with a vast Crown Post and Tie Beam in the old Hall. The Georgian front was added in 1725. The contents include superb items of furniture, china, militaria and the largest collection of Orders and Decorations of Chivalry in the UK. Another attraction is the Butchers Slaughter House in the grounds which is laid out as a Museum of Country Crafts and Implements especially of local interest.

FARNHAM CASTLE
FARNHAM, SURREY
THE CHURCH COMMISSIONERS

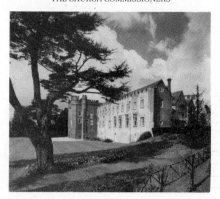

Formerly the seat of the Bishops of Winchester, the Castle was built by Henry of Blois in the 12th century. Its features include the Renaissance brickwork of Waynflete's Tower and the 17th century Chapel.

ADMISSION – SEE EDITORIAL REFERENCE

East Sussex

ALFRISTON

ALFRISTON CLERGY HOUSE, The National Trust
Telephone: Alfriston (0323) 870001

Bought in 1896, the first building acquired by the Trust. Possibly a parish priest's house, c. 1350.
Location: 4 m NE of Seaford just E of B2108; adjoining The Tye & St Andrew's Church.
Station: Berwick (2½ m).
Opening Times: Exhibition Room, Medieval Hall, two other rooms & Garden. Mar 24 to end Oct—Daily 11–6 (or sunset if earlier). Last adm half-hour before closing. Adm 80p, Chd 40p. Pre-booked parties 60p. Shop (open until Christmas). No dogs. Unsuitable for wheelchairs.

BATTLE

BATTLE ABBEY
Telephone: (04246) 3792
(English Heritage)

The Battle of Hastings, 1066—the best-known date in English history. Battle Abbey was built by William the Conqueror as a thanksgiving for his victory, with the high altar on the spot where King Harold died. The church has yet to be fully excavated, but visitors may walk over the battlefield, and see the remains of many of the domestic buildings of the monastery and watch a film on the battle.
Location: Battle. OS map ref TQ749157.
Opening Times: Good Friday to Sept 30, daily 10–6; Oct 1 to Maundy Thurs, daily 10–4. *Closed* Dec 24–26, Jan 1. Adm £1.60, OAPs £1.20, Chd 80p.

BATTLE MUSEUM *(Battle and District Historical Society)*
Langton House.
Facing the Abbey Gateway. Battle of Hastings Diorama and reproduction of the Bayeux Tapestry, Roman–British remains from local sites. Sussex Iron Industry collection of ores and cinders. Easter to early Sept: Mon to Sat 10–1, 2–5; Sun 2.30–5.30. Adm 30p, Chld 10p.

MUSEUM OF SHOPS AND SOCIAL HISTORY
90 High Street, Battle.
A unique collection of packaging and social history items, displayed authentically in 'Victorian Streets' Come shopping with Grandma! Open: Apr–Oct 10–5.30, Nov–Dec 10.30–4.30. *Closed* Thurs. Jan–Mar open weekends & school hols.

BEXHILL

BEXHILL MUSEUM
Egerton Road. Tel: (0424) 211769.
Housed in an Edwardian shelter hall with pleasant views over Egerton Park and lake. Displays interpret the local archaeology, geology and marine biology and the social history of Bexhill. There is also a lively temporary exhibition programme, events and activities for children. Open Tues to Fri 10–5; Sat and Sun 2–5. *Closed* Mon except Bank Hols. Adm 40p; Students and unaccompanied Chld 20p; Family ticket 40p per adult, Chld free. School parties 20p each Chld, Teachers free. Easy roadside parking. Suitable for disabled persons. No wheelchairs available.

BEXHILL MUSEUM OF COSTUME AND SOCIAL HISTORY
Manor House Gardens, Old Town. Tel: (0424) 215361 or 211711.
Open Easter to Sept: Tues to Fri (and Bank Hols) 10.30–1, 2.30–5.30; Sat and Sun 2.30–5.30. Last time of entry 12.30 and 5. Adm 60p, Chld 30p, OAPs 50p. Prices subject to revision.

BODIAM

BODIAM CASTLE, The National Trust
Telephone: Staplecross (058 083) 436

Built 1385–9, one of the best preserved examples of medieval moated military architecture.
Location: 3 m S of Hawkhurst; 1 m E of A229.
Opening Times: Mar 24 to Oct 31 incl. Good Fri. Daily 10–6 (or sunset if earlier). Nov to Mar 23—Mons to Sats only. 10–sunset. Last adm half-hour before closing. *Closed Dec 25 to 28.* Adm £1.30, Chd 70p. *Parties of 15 or more by prior arrangement £1, Chd 50p.* Car park free to members. Museum. Audio visual. Shop. Dogs admitted except in shop & museum. Wheelchair access.
Refreshments: Tea room, Mar 24 to end Oct.

BRIGHTON

THE BOOTH MUSEUM OF NATURAL HISTORY
(Brighton Borough Council)
Dyke Road. Tel: (0273) 552586.
A comprehensive display of British birds, mounted in settings that re-create their natural habitats. Galleries on vertebrate evolution, butterflies of the World and Sussex geology. Frequent temporary exhibitions. Reference collections of insects, osteology, palaeontology, bird and mammal skins, eggs and herbaria. Mon to Sat 10–5; Sun 2–5. *Closed* Thurs, Christmas Day, Boxing Day, Jan 1 and Good Friday. Adm free.

BRIGHTON MUSEUM AND ART GALLERY
(Brighton Borough Council)
Church Street. Tel: (0273) 603005.
The collections include the Willett Collection of English pottery and porcelain; fine and applied art of the Art Nouveau and Art Deco periods; old master paintings, watercolours, furniture, fashion, musical instruments, ethnography, archaeology and Brighton history. Frequent special exhibitions. Tues to Sat 10–5.45; Sun 2–5. *Closed* Mons (except Bank Hols), Christmas Day, Boxing Day, Jan 1 and Good Friday. Adm free. Cafe open Tues to Sat.

THE GRANGE ART GALLERY AND MUSEUM
(Brighton Borough Council)
The Green, Rottingdean. Tel: (0273) 301004.
A Georgian house, adjacent to Kipling's home, displays letters, books and illustrations of the author; History of Rottingdean room and a large display of toys from the Toy Museum. Frequent temporary displays in the Art Gallery. Mon, Thurs and Sat 10–5; Tues and Fri 10–1, 2–5; Sun 2–5. *Closed* Weds, Christmas Day, Boxing Day, Jan 1 and Good Friday. Adm free.

PRESTON MANOR
Telephone: (0273) 603005
(Borough of Brighton)

Georgian house with Edwardian additions. Contains a notable collection of fine furniture, silver, porcelain and pictures. Servants' quarters now open.
Location: On main Brighton to London Road at Preston Park.
Station: Preston Park.

East Sussex – *continued*

Opening Times: All the year—Tues–Sun 10–5. Closed Mons (except Bank Hols) Good Fri, Christmas & Boxing Day. Admission charge. *Reduced rates for parties, families, Chd and OAPs.* Garden free. Parties by arrangement.

THE ROYAL PAVILION *(Brighton Borough Council)*
Tel: (0273) 603005.
The seaside palace of the Prince Regent (King George IV), containing some of the most dazzling and magnificent interiors in the world, now in restoration. Decorations in a fantastic version of 'The Chinese taste', Regency and other contemporary furniture and works of art, including many original pieces returned on loan from H.M. The Queen. Open daily 10–5 (June to Sept, 10–6). Adm fee payable. Reduced for Chld and parties. Guided tours by appointment. *Closed* Christmas Day and Boxing Day. Café opens most days. The Pavilion is currently undergoing extensive structural restoration which may cause the temporary closure of certain rooms and conceal part of the exterior.

Opening times for museums and galleries in the case of Brighton Borough Council are subject to variation. Visitors are advised to telephone to check opening times in advance.

BURWASH

BATEMAN'S, The National Trust
Telephone: Burwash 882302

Built 1634. Rudyard Kipling lived here. Water-mill restored by the National Trust. Attractive garden, yew hedges, lawns, daffodils and wild garden.
Location: ½ m S of Burwash on the Lewes/Etchingham Road (A265).
Opening Times: Mar 24 to end of Oct—Daily (except Thurs & Fris but open Good Fri) 11–6. Last adm 5. Adm House, Mill & Garden £2.50, Chd £1.30, weekends & Bank Hols £2.80, Chd £1.40. Pre-booked parties £2.20., Chd £1.10, weekends and Bank Holidays £2.50, Chd £1.30. No dogs.
Refreshments: Tea room: coffees, light lunches and teas, open as House.

CROWBOROUGH

COBBLERS GARDEN
(Mr & Mrs Martin Furniss)

2 acre garden on sloping site designed and planted by owners since 1968 in informal manner for all-season colour; large range of herbaceous and shrub species; water garden. Featured in RHS Journal, Mar 1978 and two BBC television programmes Aug 1978, 'Country Life' and 'Homes & Gardens' 1981.
Location: At Crowborough Cross (A26) turn on to B2100 (signposted Crowborough station & Rotherfield); at 2nd crossroads turn right into Tollwood Road.
Station: Crowborough (1 m).
Opening Times: GARDEN ONLY—Suns May 21, 28; June 11, 18, 25; July 9, 16, 23; Aug 6, 13. Times 2.30–5.30. Adm £1, Chd 50p. *In aid of National Gardens Scheme and The National Trust.* No dogs please. Plants for sale.
Refreshments: Home made teas.

EASTBOURNE

ROYAL NATIONAL LIFEBOAT INSTITUTION MUSEUM
Grand Parade. Tel: (0323) 30717.
Many types of lifeboats from the earliest date to the present time. Various items used in lifeboat service. Open: mid-Mar to New Year's Day 9.30 to 5.30.

SUSSEX COMBINED SERVICES MUSEUM – REDOUBT FORTRESS
Royal Parade. Tel: (0323) 410300.
Built 1805–10. A circular ten-gun fort with barrack room casemates for a garrison of 350 men. Restored to house the Military Museum for the three services in Sussex. Also contains the Regimental Museum of the Royal Sussex Regiment, and The Queen's Royal Irish Hussars. Collection of cannons on the battlements. Easter to Oct: Daily 10–5.30 (last adm 5). Other times by arrangement.

TOWER NO. 73 (THE WISH TOWER)
King Edwards Parade. Tel: (0323) 410440.
Coastal defence and Invasion Museum. A restored Napoleonic War Martello Tower. The Exhibition illustrates the historical background, the architecture, manning and armament of these small forts. Displays include weapons, uniforms and contemporary documents and models. A coastal defence gun is mounted on the parapet. Easter to Oct: Daily 10–5.30.

TOWNER ART GALLERY AND LOCAL HISTORY MUSEUM
Manor Gardens, High Street, Old Town (A259). Tel: (0323) 411688.
18th century Manor House in public gardens. **Gallery:** Wide ranging programme of temporary exhibitions (see local press for details). Large permanent collection of mainly 19th and 20th century British Art. Concerts and other events. **Local History Museum:** The Eastbourne area from Prehistoric times to the Edwardian era. Photographic archives. Mon to Sat 10–5; Sun 2–5. *Closed Mon Nov–Mar inclusive.* Adm free.

ETCHINGHAM

HAREMERE HALL
Telephone: Etchingham 245
(Jacqueline, Lady Killearn)
Early 17th century Manor House with Minstrel staircase, panelled Great Hall, carved doors and Flemish fireplace. Period furniture. Collections of rugs, ornaments, pottery, plate from Middle and Far East. Terraced gardens.
Location: On A265 between Etchingham & Hurst Green; N of Battle.
Station: Etchingham (5 mins walk).
Opening Times: GARDENS—Daily from Easter to Oct 31. SHIRE HORSE FARM—Daily (not Mons except Bank Hols) from Easter to Oct 31 (demonstrations at 11 & 3). HOUSE open to public Bank Hol weekends 2–5—otherwise to parties of 25 or more by appointment. Hall, Grounds & Gardens £2.50; Gardens only 70p. Party, Chd, OAPs discounts. Registered with English Tourist Board. 5 star accommodation, 4-poster beds, etc, by arrangement with House Manager—brochure and tariff on request.
Refreshments: Luncheon & tea for parties by appointment. Guests for Glyndebourne Opera Festival and Christmas breaks a speciality.

FIRLE

CHARLESTON FARMHOUSE
Telephone: Ripe (032 183) 265
(The Charleston Trust)

17/18th century farmhouse, the home of Vanessa and Clive Bell and Duncan Grant from 1916 until Grant's death in 1978. House and contents decorated by the artists; traditional flint-walled flower garden of the period.
Location: 6 m E of Lewes, on A27, between Firle and Selmeston.
Station: Lewes 6 m; Berwick 3 m.
Opening Times: Mar 25, 26, 27; Apr 1 to Oct 29—Weds, Thurs, Sats (Guided Tours) and Suns and Bank Hol Mons (unguided), 2–6 (last adm 5). Kitchen open Thurs only. Adm £3; car park 50p (no parking charge midweek Apr, May, Oct). Coaches by prior appointment only. Numbers in the House will be limited; no dogs. Student/OAP/ UB40 concessions midweek throughout the season, also weekends Apr, May, Oct. Contact Charleston Office at Farmhouse.

FIRLE PLACE
Telephone: Glynde (079 159) 335
(Viscount Gage)

Important collection of Italian, Dutch and English pictures. Notable Sèvres porcelain, French and English furniture and objects of American interest.
Location: 5 m SE of Lewes on the Lewes/Eastbourne Road (A27).
Station: Glynde (1½ m) or Lewes (5 m, taxis available).
Opening Times: June, July, Aug & Sept—Weds, Thurs & Suns. Also Easter, May, Spring & Summer Bank Hol Suns & Mons: 2 last tickets 5. First Wed in month longer, unguided Connoisseurs' tour of House. Pre-booked group parties of 25 on Open Days (except first Wed in month) at reduced rate. Special exclusive viewings at other times of year for parties over 30 by arrangement. *Party bookings in writing to Showing Secretary, Firle Place, Nr Lewes, East Sussex BN8 6LP (079 159) 335.*
Refreshments: Cold buffet luncheon 12.30–2; Sussex cream teas from 3. Shop and contemporary pictures exhibition. Car park adjacent to house.

FOREST ROW

KIDBROOKE PARK WITH REPTON GROUNDS
(The Council of Michael Hall School)

Sandstone house and stables built in 1730s with later alterations.
Location: 1 m SW of Forest Row, off A22, 4 m S of East Grinstead.
Opening Times: Spring Bank Hol Mon (May 30) then Aug—Daily (inc Bank Hol Mon), 9–6. Application for admission to the Bursar.

HASTINGS

THE FISHERMAN'S MUSEUM
Rock-a-Nore.
The principal exhibit is the Enterprise, the last of the old clinker-built sailing luggers built in Hastings, together with capstan. Included in the exhibits is a large picture of the presentation to Sir Winston Churchill of a golden winkle at the Enterprise on Winkle Island, Sept 1955. End of May to Sept: Daily (except Sat) 10.30–12, 2.30–5; Sun 2.30 to 5.

MUSEUM AND ART GALLERY *(Hastings Borough)*
Cambridge Road. Tel: (0424) 721202.
Paintings, ceramics, Sussex ironwork, local natural history and geology, Oriental, Pacific and American Indian art, The Durbar Hall (Indian Palace). Temporary exhibitions. Mon to Sat 10–1, 2–5; Sun 3–5.

MUSEUM OF LOCAL HISTORY *(Hastings Borough)*
Old Town Hall, High Street.
Displays on maritime history, the Cinque Ports, smuggling, fishing, local personalities such as John Logie Baird. Easter to end Sept: Mon to Sat 10–1, 2–5; Oct to Easter Sun: 3–5. Adm 15p, Chld and OAPs 10p.

SHIPWRECK HERITAGE CENTRE
Rock-a-Nore Road. TN34 3DW. Tel: (0424) 437452.
A new museum whose major exhibits are from three important local wrecks – the warship *Anne* (1690), the Dutch ship *Amsterdam* (1749), and a Danish ship of about 1861. These contain muskets, brandy, wine and a tombstone! A 15th century wreck is displayed in a spectacular sound and light show narrated by film star Christopher Lee. This is the only museum in Britain with working Radar, to monitor shipping in the Channel. Also, weather forecasting can be carried out through our direct link to satellites 500 miles in space which transmit daily pictures of Europe. Open: weekends and public holidays Mar 24–Oct 29; daily: May 27–Sept 17. Will open any other day for groups.

Admission: adults £1, chld 75p. Special family and party reductions. The Centre is adjacent to large car and coach parks. Enquiries to: the Manager.

HEATHFIELD

SUSSEX FARM MUSEUM *(Sussex Farm Museum Trust)*
Horam Manor, TN21 0JB. Tel: (04353) 2597.
Open Easter to Oct, 10–5. Enter from A267.

HOVE

THE BRITISH ENGINEERIUM
Nevill Road. Tel: (0273) 559583.
A unique working steam museum telling the story of Britain's engineering heritage within the building of the fully restored Goldstone Pumping Station. See the huge Eastons & Anderson beam engine of 1876, plus hundreds of models and full size engines depicting the history of steam power on land, sea, road and rail. Conservation and restoration projects of industrial archaeological material for national and private collections worldwide, can be seen under way in the period workshops. Open daily 10–5. Engines in steam Sun and Bank Holidays. Access for disabled. Adm £1.80, Chld/OAPs £1.

HOVE MUSEUM AND ART GALLERY *(Hove Borough Council)*
19 New Church Road BN3 4AB. Tel: (0273) 779410.
Twentieth century paintings and drawings. Eighteenth century pictures, furniture and decorative arts. The notable Pocock collection of British ceramics. Dolls, toys, coins and medals and local history. Special exhibitions of historic and contemporary art and crafts, housed in one of the town's most impressive Victorian villas. Tues to Fri 10–5; Sat 10–4.30. Sun (Mar to Sept only) 2–5. *Closed* Mon, Sun (Oct to Feb) and Bank Hols. Adm free.

LEWES

GLYNDE PLACE
Telephone: Glynde (079 159) 337
(Viscount Hampden)

Beautiful example of 16th century architecture. Pictures, bronzes, historical documents.
Location: 4 m SE of Lewes on Eastbourne/Lewes Road (A27) or A265.
Station: Glynde (½ m).
Opening Times: June 1 to Sept 29—Weds & Thurs and first and last Sun of each month 2.15–5.30 (last adm 5). Open Easter Sun & Mon and Bank Hols. House open for guided tours by prior arrangement (25 or more £1.80 per person). Adm £2.20, Chd £1. Garden only 75p (rebate on entry into house). Free parking.
Refreshments: Home-baked teas in Coach House (parties to book in advance).

LEWES HISTORY CENTRE
(Sussex Archaeological Society and Lewes Town Council)
Barbican House, High Street. Tel: (0273) 474379.
Large scale model of historic Lewes with 25 minute audio-visual programme describing historical evolution, and with substantial static exhibition. Open: Mar to Oct Mon to Sat 10–5; Apr to Oct Sun 11–5. Adm 95p, Chld 50p.

MUSEUM OF LOCAL HISTORY *(Sussex Archaeological Society)*
Anne of Cleves House, Southover High Street. Tel: (0273) 474610.
A picturesque half-timbered building. Collection of household equipment, furniture, Sussex ironwork and pottery and a gallery of Lewes history. Mid-Feb to mid-Nov: Mon to Sat 10–5.30; also Sun (Apr to Oct) 2–5.30. Adm £1, Chld 55p.

MUSEUM OF SUSSEX ARCHAEOLOGY
(Sussex Archaeological Society)
Barbican House, High Street. Tel: (0273) 474379.
Large collection of prehistoric, Romano-British, Saxon and medieval antiquities relating to Sussex. Prints and watercolours of Sussex. Mon to Sat 10–5.30; Sun (Apr to Oct) 11–5.30. Adm £1.25, Chld 65p (includes adm to Lewes Castle).

NEWICK

NEWICK PARK
Telephone: (082 572) 3633
(Viscount Brentford)

Originally an Elizabethan ironmasters house c.1580 this lovely country house is predominantly Georgian (Grade II listed). Home of Viscount Brentford, with some fine furniture and porcelain. The house is open for functions and conferences. Set in 240 acres of farm and parkland. 12 acres of garden (Grade II listed) over Tudor mine workings include specimen ferns, trees and extensive collection of camellias, azaleas and rhododendrons. Beautiful spring flowers, many species over 100 years old. Other interesting features are 19th century ice

house, walled garden with herb nursery. Elizabethan hammer ponds, lakeside walk. National collection of candelabra and sikkimensis primulas.
Location: Lewes 7 m to S, 1 m A272, Haywards Heath 7 m to W, 1 m A275, Uckfield 5 m to E, 3 m A22.
Opening Times: GARDENS: Mar 15–Oct 31, 10.30–6; Adm £1, OAPs 75p, Chd 25p. Reductions for parties 75p per head (4 or more). Car parking for 50 cars, room for up to 6 coaches. Suitable for disabled persons (no wheelchairs).
Refreshments: For garden visitors: teas, lunches (by arrangement). House: available for functions, special parties, day and residential conferences, promotional events.

NORTHIAM

BRICKWALL HOUSE
Telephone: Northiam (07974) 2494 or Curator, Rye 223329
(Frewen Educational Trust)

Home of the Frewen family since 1666. 17th century drawing room with superb 17th century plaster ceilings, and family portraits spanning 400 years of history. Grand staircase. Chess garden and arboretum.
Location: 7 m NW of Rye on B2088.
Opening Times: Apr to end Sept—Sats and Bank Holiday Mons 2–5; Adm £1, OAPs half price. Open at other times by prior arrangement with the curator.

GREAT DIXTER
Telephone: (07974) 3160
(Quentin Lloyd, Esq)

15th century half-timbered manor house in a Lutyens designed garden.
Location: ½ m N of Northiam; 8 m NW of Rye; 12 m N of Hastings. Just off A28.
Opening Times: Good Friday Mar 24 to Sun Oct 15—Daily except Mons (but open all Bank Hol Mons) also weekends Oct 21, 22, 28, 29; open 2 until last adm at 5. Gardens open at 11 on May 27, 28, 29. Suns in July & Aug, also Aug 28. Adm House & Gardens £2.25, Chd 50p. Gardens only £1.50, Chd 25p. Concessions to OAPs and NT members on Fris £1.90 – House and Gardens. Adult guided garden tour for groups £2.75 (minimum charge £19), ask for details. No dogs.
Refreshments: Locally, ask for list.

PEVENSEY

PEVENSEY CASTLE
Telephone: (0323) 762604

The walls that enclose this 10-acre site are from the 4th century Roman fort, Anderida. The inner castle, with its great keep, is medieval. With the fall of France in 1940, Pevensey was put into service again, after centuries of neglect.
Location: Pevensey. OS map ref TQ645048.
Opening Times: Good Friday to Sept 30, daily 10–6; Oct 1 to Maundy Thursday, daily 10–4. *Closed Mons, Christmas and New Year.* Adm £1.10, OAPs 80p, Chd 55p.

RODMELL

MONKS HOUSE, The National Trust
A small village house and garden. The home of Virginia and Leonard Woolf from 1919 until his death in 1969. House administered and largely maintained by tenants.
Location: 3 m SE of Lewes, off C7 in Rodmell village.
Station: Southease (1 m).
Opening Times: Mar 25 to end Apr and Oct—Weds & Sats 2–5; May to end Sept—Weds & Sats 2–6 (last adm ½ hour before closing time). Adm £1.20. No reduction for children or parties. No dogs. Unsuitable for wheelchairs. Maximum of 15 people in house at any one time. Narrow access road.

RYE

LAMB HOUSE, The National Trust
Georgian house with garden. Home of Henry James from 1898 to 1916.
Location: In West Street facing W end of church.
Station: Rye (½ m).
Opening Times: House (Hall & 3 rooms only) & Garden. Apr to end of Oct—Weds & Sats 2–6 (last admission 5.30). Adm £1. No reduction for children or parties. No dogs. Unsuitable for wheelchairs. No lavatories.

RYE MUSEUM
Ypres Tower (administration: 4 Church Square). Tel: (0797) 223254.
Local collections housed in a 13th century tower. Medieval and other pottery from the Rye kilns. Cinque Ports material, shipping, toys and dolls. Easter to mid Oct: Mon to Sat 10.30–1, 2.15–5.30; Sun 11.30–1, 2.15–5.30. Last entry half-hour before closing. Adm charge.

RYE TOWN MODEL

Son et Lumiere, Strand Quay (at the foot of Mermaid Street).
Tel: (0797) 223902.

Rye has a superb new Heritage Centre with Visitor Shop and Local Exhibition. Come and see the fascinating history of the Town of Rye dramatically brought to life in this theatrical combination of a realistic sound and light show and an authentic Town Model. 10 Shows every day from Easter to November; Groups and winter opening by arrangement. Telephone the Town Clerk for rates, parking information and reservations on (0797) 223902.

SEAFORD

SEAFORD MUSEUM OF LOCAL HISTORY

Martello Tower No. 74, Esplanade. Tel: (0323) 893976.

'A trip down Memory Lane'. Period shops, TV, radio, domestic appliances, photographs. Seaford Gallery. Open Summer: Sun, Wed, Sat: 2.30–4.30 and Sun 11–1. Winter: Suns: 11–1, 2.30–4.30. Bank Hols as Sun all year. Parties: appointment only.

SHEFFIELD PARK

BLUEBELL RAILWAY *(Bluebell Railway)*

Sheffield Park Station, nr Uckfield.
Tel: (082 572) 2370 (talking timetable) 3777 (enquiries).

The Bluebell Railway – Living Museum. Operates vintage steam trains between Sheffield Park and Horsted Keynes in Sussex, every Sun, weekends Spring and Autumn, daily June to Sept. Brochure timetable available. Buffet, museum, and shop. Car parking. Suitable for disabled persons.

SHEFFIELD PARK GARDEN, The National Trust

Telephone: Danehill 790655

Large garden with series of lakes linked by cascades; great variety of unusual shrubs.

Location: Midway between East Grinstead & Lewes on E side of A275; 5 m NW of Uckfield.
Opening Times: Mar 25 to Nov 5 — Tues to Sats (closed Good Fri) 11–6 or sunset if earlier; Suns during Oct & Nov: 1–sunset. Last adm one hour before closing. *Closed Tues following Bank Hol Mons.* Liable to overcrowding Suns & Bank Hols. Adm May, Oct & Nov £2.80, Chd £1.40; Mar, Apr & June to Sept £2.20, Chd £1.10. Pre-booked parties £2.10 & £1.60 according to season. *No reduction for parties on Sats, Suns & Bank Hols.* No dogs. Shop. Wheelchairs available.

UCKFIELD

BEECHES FARM

(Mrs Vera Thomas)

16th century tile hung farm house. Lawns, yew trees, borders, sunken garden, roses, fine views.

Location: Off A2102, Buckham Hill 1½ m W Uckfield (on Isfield Road).
Station: Uckfield (1½ m).
Opening Times: All the year — Daily 10–5. Adm Gardens 25p. House (by appointment) 75p. Suns May 7, July 9 & Nov 26. *In aid of National Gardens' Scheme,* and on June 11 *Winged Fellowship.*

UPPER DICKER

MICHELHAM PRIORY

(Sussex Archaeological Society)

Founded in 1229 this Augustinian Priory is surrounded by one of the largest moats in England. Elizabethan wing and 14th century gatehouse. Special exhibitions and events. Tudor barn. Working Watermill restored, grinding wholemeal flour.

Location: ½ m E of Upper Dicker just off London/Eastbourne Road (A22); 10 m N of Eastbourne.
Opening Times: Mar 25 to Oct 31 — Daily 11–5.30. Adm (inc Watermill) £2, OAPs £1.80, Chd (5–16) £1. Reduction for parties booked in advance. *No dogs. 1989:* Sussex Crafts & Small Industries Aug 2–6. Festival of Music & Art and Activities week in Aug & many other events.
Refreshments: At licensed restaurants in Grounds.

WANNOCK

FILCHING MANOR

Telephone: (03212) 7838/7124
(Paul Foulkes-Halbard)

A magnificent example of medieval construction, with central hall open to the roof, the Buttery, (now the drawing room), minstrels' gallery considered to be unique. The oak panelling between the hall and the drawing room represents the earliest type known. An underground passage runs from the cellars to a considerable distance, and is probably an ancient escape hole. The Manor is set in 28 acres of Sussex downland and formal gardens. A special feature of the Manor is the unique and exclusive collection of some of the rarest sports and racing cars in the world, including the 1937 world record breaking Bluebird, pilotted by Sir Malcolm Campbell. Antiquities, arms and armour can also be seen in an historic Manor house which is also very much a family home.

Location: 1¼ m from A22 at Polegate Crossroads. 5 m N of Eastbourne.
Opening Times: Mar to Oct, Thurs to Sun 10.30–4.30, also Bank Holidays. Open at other times by prior appointment. Adm £2, Chd/OAPs £1. Reductions for parties of 10 or more, £1 per person. **Parties must book in advance.** Suitable for disabled, and special toilet facilities for the disabled.
Refreshments: Light refreshments.

WILMINGTON

WILMINGTON PRIORY AND LONG MAN

(Sussex Archaeological Society)
Wilmington Priory. Tel: (0323) 870537.

Remains of 13th century Benedictine Priory with collection of bygone agricultural implements and farmhouse utensils. Mid-Mar to mid-Oct: Mon to Sat (except Tues) 11–5.30; Sun 2–5.30. Adm 80p, Chld 40p.

WINCHELSEA

WINCHELSEA MUSEUM

Court Hall.

Collection illustrating the history of Winchelsea and the Cinque Ports. Handicrafts, archaeological specimens, models, maps, documents. Open May to Sept.

FILCHING MANOR

FILCHING MANOR

A 1904 PEUGEOT FROM THE FOULKES-HALBARD COLLECTION

FOR ADMISSION DETAILS–SEE EDITORIAL REFERENCE

West Sussex

AMBERLEY

AMBERLEY CHALK PITS MUSEUM
(Southern Industrial History Centre Trust)
Houghton Bridge, Amberley, Nr. Arundel. Tel: Bury (0798) 831370

36 acre open air museum of industrial history featuring working craftsmen, operational narrow gauge industrial railway, early motor buses, stationary engines, chalk pits and lime kilns, timber yard with steam crane, metal working shop, forge, pottery, printshop, boat builder's shop, brick display, wireless exhibition, ironmongers shop, domestic display, steam traction engines and rollers, etc. Open from beginning of Apr to end Oct Wed to Sun, plus Bank Hol Mons. Open daily during school summer hols 10–5.

ARDINGLY

WAKEHURST PLACE GARDEN, The National Trust
Telephone: Ardingly (0444) 892701   &
(Administered by Royal Botanic Gardens, Kew)

A wealth of exotic plant species including many fine specimens of trees and shrubs. Picturesque watercourse linking several ponds and lakes. Heath garden and rock walk.

Location: 1½ m NW of Ardingly on B2028.
Opening Times: All the year—Daily Jan, Nov & Dec, 10–4; Feb & Oct, 10–5; Mar, 10–6; Apr to end of Sept, 10–7. Last adm ½ hour before closing. *Closed Christmas Day & New Year's Day.* Adm £1.50, Chd (under 16) 60p. Parties £1. Chd (under 16) 40p.
No dogs. Wheelchairs provided. Exhibition in Mansion. Book shop open all year.
Refreshments: Light refreshments.

ARUNDEL

ARUNDEL CASTLE
Telephone: Arundel 883136   &
(Arundel Castle Trustees Ltd.)

This great castle, situated in magnificent grounds overlooking the River Arun, was built at the end of the 11th century by Roger de Montgomery, Earl of Arundel. It has been the seat of the Dukes of Norfolk and their ancestors for over seven hundred years. Badly damaged in 1643, the castle was restored by the 8th, 11th and 15th Dukes in the 18th and 19th centuries. Fine furniture, tapestries, clocks and portraits by Van Dyck, Gainsborough, Reynolds, Mytens, Lawrence etc. Fitzalan Chapel. Host to Arundel Festival at the end of August each year, which attracts international artists.
Location: In Arundel 9 m W of Worthing: 10 m E of Chichester. Entrance for cars and pedestrians: Lower Lodge Mill Road.
Station: Arundel (¾ m).
Opening Times: Mar 24 to Oct 27—Suns to Fris 1–5 (during June, July & Aug and all Bank Hols 12–5). Last adm any day 4 pm. *The Castle is NOT open on Sats.* Adm charges not available at time of going to press. No dogs. *Special rates for organised parties.*

ARUNDEL TOY AND MILITARY MUSEUM
23 High Street. Tel: (0903) 883101/882908

Intriguing 'Henderson' Private Collection. Toy soldiers galore, militaria, tin toys, teddies, dolls, houses, boats, Goss, Pocillovy, curiosities etc. Open most days Easter to Sept and winter weekends.

MUSEUM AND HERITAGE CENTRE
61 High Street. Tel: (0903) 882726.

Old Arundel on view. Easter to Oct: Open every weekend; also open Tues to Fri and Bank Hols in High Season. Adm 50p, Chld 15p. Parties any time by arrangement.

BRAMBER

ST MARY'S
Telephone: Steyning 816205
(Peter Thorogood Esq)

The foundations of St Mary's go back to the 12 century when land at Bramber was granted to the Knights Templar. The present house (c 1470) was re-fashioned by William Waynflete, Bishop of Winchester, founder of Magdalen College, Oxford, and is classified as "the best late 15th century timber-framing in Sussex". Fine panelled rooms, including unique 'Painted Room' decorated for Elizabeth I's visit. The 'King's Room' has connections with Charles II's escape to France in 1651. Also other Royal and historic associations. Rare 16th century painted wall-leather, splendid carved oak fireplaces, massive 'dragon-beam' in the 'Warden's Room', superb marquetry decoration and strapwork doors. Furniture, pictures, manuscripts. Library contains largest private collection of first editions and illustrated books by celebrated 19th century comic poet and artist, Thomas Hood. Victorian Music room, with elaborate medieval Gothic stone fireplaces, added in 1896 by Hon. Algernon Bourke, son of the Earl of Mayo. Sherlock Holmes connection during ownership (1903–13) of Alfred Musgrave. Ring for details of Summer Festival of Music & Drama, May to October.

Location: 10 m NW of Brighton in village of Bramber on A283.
Station: Shoreham-by-Sea (4 m). Trains from London (Victoria).
Opening Times: Easter Mon to last Sun in Oct—Suns 10–6, Mons & Thurs 2–6, Bank Hol Mons 10–6. Adm £2, OAP £1.80, Chd £1, **Coach party bookings** Mons to Sat by prior arrangement. Reduced rates for parties £1.80 (20 or over). Free coach and car parking in grounds.
Refreshments: Light lunches Suns and Bank Hols. Morning coffee, homemade afternoon tea in the Music Room. Catering for parties including "Palm Court" teas by arrangement.

CHICHESTER

CHICHESTER CATHEDRAL
Telephone: Chichester 782595
(The Dean & Chapter of Chichester)

In the heart of the city, this fine Cathedral has been a centre of Christian worship and community life for 900 years. Site of Shrine of St Richard of Chichester; Romanesque stone carvings; works by Sutherland, Feibusch, Procktor, Chagall, Skelton, Piper, and new Anglo/German tapestry. Treasury. Cloister. Refectory. Shop. Vicars' close and hall.
Location: Centre of city; British Rail; A27, A286.
Opening Times: All year 7.10–7 (6 in winter). Choral Evensong daily (except Weds) during term time; occasionally visiting choirs at other times. Ministry of welcome operates. Guided tours must be booked. No dogs except guide dogs. Wheelchair access (one wheelchair available on application to Vergers). Adm free: suggested donations Adults £1, Chd 20p. Parking in city car parks.
Refreshments: Refectory off Cathedral Cloisters with lavatory facilities (including those for the disabled).

CHICHESTER DISTRICT MUSEUM *(Chichester District Council)*
29 Little London. Tel: (0243) 784683.

Geology, archaeology and local history. Temporary exhibitions programme. Museum shop. Tues to Sat 10–5.30. *Closed* Sun and Mon. Adm free.

GOODWOOD HOUSE
Telephone: Chichester (0243) 774107
(Duke of Richmond)

Bought by the first Duke of Richmond (son of King Charles II and a French female spy!) and home of the Dukes of Richmond ever since, Goodwood House is filled with the treasures collected by all nine Dukes. They include Canalettos, snuff boxes, tapestries, family portraits by Van Dyck, Kneller, Lely, Reynolds, etc; French commodes (!) and Sevres porcelain bought by the Third Duke when (a very bad) British Ambassador at Versailles. There are royal relics. Napoleonic booty and the bits and pieces inevitable after a family has stayed put for 300 years. Chambers, then Wyatt, enlarged the House to hold these Collections. Country Park near the Racecourse on crest of South Downs. Pleasure flights available from the Goodwood Aerodrome together with flying instruction to top standards. Dressage Championships (National & International) and other events in Goodwood Park. Glorious Goodwood Racecourse.
Location: 3½ m NE of Chichester, approach roads A285 & A286, A27. Aerodrome 1 m from House.
Opening Times: Easter Sun & Mon then Apr 30 to Oct 2—Suns & Mons (except June 18, 25, July 9 and event days); also Tues, Weds & Thurs in Aug, 2–5. Large free car park for visitors to House during open hours; House suitable for wheelchairs (no steps); a wheelchair available; Goodwood souvenirs and prints for sale. For all information & group rates contact the House Secretary. Goodwood House, Chichester, West Sussex.
Refreshments: Teas in the State Supper Room for pre-booked parties (min 20); unbooked teas for individuals and families on days when no evening function, or tea and biscuits at The Goodwood Park Hotel Golf and Country Club at the Park Gate (east).

GUILDHALL MUSEUM *(Chichester District Council)*
Priory Park. Tel: (0243) 784683.

Branch of Chichester District Museum, housed in church of 13th century Franciscan Friary and later City Guildhall. Temporary exhibitions. June to Sept. Tues to Sat 1–5. Other times by appointment. *Closed* Sun and Mon. Adm free.

PALLANT HOUSE *(Pallant House Gallery Trust)*
9 North Pallant. Tel: (0243) 774557.

A handsome Queen Anne residence with decorated and furnished period rooms, a collection of modern British art and a temporary exhibitions gallery. Tues to Sat 10–5.30. *Closed* Sun and Mon. Adm charge.

CHITHURST

MALT HOUSE
Telephone: Rogate (073 080)433
(Mr & Mrs Graham Ferguson)

Approximately 4 acres; flowering shrubs including exceptional rhododendrons and azaleas, leading to 60 acres of lovely woodland walks.
Location: 3½ m W of Midhurst via A272, turn N to Chithurst cont 1½ m; or via A3, 2 m S of Liphook turn SE to Milland and Chithurst.
Opening Times: GARDEN ONLY. Suns—Apr 23 to May 28; Bank Hol Mons; May 1 & 29, 2–6. Adm 80p, Chd 40p. *In aid of National Gardens Scheme.* Also open by appointment for parties. Plants for sale.
Refreshments: Tea and biscuits.

CUCKFIELD

CUCKFIELD MUSEUM
Queen's Hall, High Street.
Open Tues, Wed & Sat 10–12.30. (Other times by appointment.)

EAST GRINSTEAD

EAST GRINSTEAD TOWN MUSEUM
A small collection devoted to the town of East Grinstead; occupies part of the East Court Mansion (1769). Wed 2–4 and Sat 2–5 (2–4 in Winter) and Bank Hols. Parties at other times on application to the Curator.

HAMMERWOOD PARK
Telephone: Cowden (0342) 850594 or Woldingham (088 385) 2366
(David Pinnegar, Esq)

Set in 37 acres on the edge of the Ashdown Forest the house was built in 1792 by Latrobe, the architect of The White House and The Capitol, Washington D.C., U.S.A. Although this was his first work it was forgotten for many years. Extensive restoration works have been completed and won numerous awards. Hammerwood Park houses a copy of the Elgin Marbles, various changing exhibitions and the largest private dress collection in the South East. Guided tours, cream teas and musical evenings bring the house to life.
Location: 3½ m E of East Grinstead on A264 to Tunbridge Wells; 1 m W of Holtye.
Opening Times: Easter Mon to end of Sept—Weds, Sats & Bank Hol Mons 2–5.30. Coaches by appointment only. Adm House and Park £2. Additional tours on Weds – 2 pm Garden restoration, £2. 3.30 Dress Collection, £2.

STANDEN, The National Trust
Telephone: East Grinstead (0342) 23029

Built 1894 by Philip Webb. William Morris wallpapers and textiles. Period furniture, paintings. Hillside garden with fine views across Medway Valley.
Location: 1½ m S of East Grinstead signposted from the Turners Hill road (B2110).
Station: East Grinstead (2 m).
Opening Times: Mar 24 to Nov 5—Weds, Thurs, Fris, Sats & Suns 1.30–5.30 (last adm 5). Adm £2.40. Garden only, open from 1, £1.20. Chd half-price. Pre-booked parties £1.80 Weds, Thurs & Fris only; telephone Administrator. *Dogs admitted to car park & woodland walks only.* Wheelchairs provided; disabled drivers may park near house with prior permission from administrator. Shop.
Refreshments: Light lunches and teas served from 1–5.30.

FISHBOURNE

THE ROMAN PALACE *(Sussex Archaeological Society)*
Salthill Road, Fishbourne. Tel: (0243) 785859.
Remains of a first century Palace with many fine mosaic floors including some of the earliest in the country. Finds from the excavations. Re-planted Roman garden. Open daily: Mar, Apr, Oct: 10–5. May–Sept: 10–6. Nov: 10–4. Suns only: Dec, Jan. Feb: 10–4. Adm charge.

FITTLEWORTH

COATES MANOR
(Mrs G. H. Thorp)

One acre garden, mainly shrubs and foliage of special interest.
Location: ½ m S of Fittleworth; SE of Petworth; turn off B2138 signposted 'Coates'.
Opening Times: GARDEN ONLY. Sun, Mon & Tues June 18, 19 & 20, 11–6. Adm 75p, Chd 20p. Also by appointment. *In aid of National Gardens Scheme.*
Refreshments: Tea & cakes.

FONTWELL

DENMANS
Telephone: Eastergate (024 368) 2808 &
(Mrs J. H. Robinson)

Unique 20th century walled garden extravagantly planted for overall, all-year interest in form, colour and texture; areas of glass for tender species. John Brookes School of Garden Design at Clock House, short courses throughout the season.
Location: Between Arundel and Chichester; turn off A27 into Denmans Lane (W of Fontwell racecourse).
Station: Barnham (2 m).
Opening Times: Tues Mar 21 to Sun Oct 29, 10–5—Daily except Mons. Coaches by appointment. Adm £1.60, Chd £1, OAPs £1.40. Groups of 15 or more £1.30. Plant centre. The Country Shop. No dogs. National Gardens Scheme.
Refreshments: Teas shop open 11–5.

HANDCROSS

THE HIGH BEECHES GARDENS
Telephone: Handcross (0444) 400589
(The High Beeches Conservation Trust)

Sixteen acres of enchanting woodland valley gardens, planted with Magnolias, Camellias, Rhododendrons and Azelias, set among sheets of Daffodils and Bluebells in Spring. In Autumn, this is one of the most brilliant gardens for leaf colour, superbly landscaped with Maples, Liquidambers, Amelanchiers and Nyssas. Gentians, Primulas and Iris are naturalised, with Royal Fern and Gunnera in the Water Gardens. There is also three acres of native Wild Flower Meadow, with many species attractive to butterflies.
Location: 1 m E of A23 at Handcross On B2110.
Opening Times: GARDENS ONLY. Easter Mon to Jun 17 and Sept 18 to Oct 29—daily 1–5 *except Weds and Suns.* Special event with plant stall and bazaar on Sun Oct 29, 10–5. Bank Hols also 10–5. Adm £1.50, accompanied Chd free. Guided tour for parties by appointment all year. Landscaped picnic area, toilets and barn shelter. Free car park. No dogs.
Refreshments: Home-made teas and snacks on Spring Bank Hols and Oct 29 only.

NYMANS GARDEN, The National Trust
Telephone: Handcross 400321 or 400002 &

Extensive garden, partly enclosed by walls, with exceptional collection of rare trees, shrubs and plants, herbaceous borders, bulbs. Exhibition on the history of the garden.
Location: At Handcross just off London/Brighton M23/A23.
Opening Times: Garden only. Mar 24 to Nov 5—Daily (except Mons & Fris) 11–7 or sunset if earlier. Open Bank Hol Mons. Last adm 1 hour before closing. Adm £2. Chd half price. Parties of 15 or more by prior arrangement with Head Gardener. No dogs. Wheelchair provided. Shop.
Refreshments: Teas.

HAYWARDS HEATH

BORDE HILL GARDEN
Telephone: Haywards Heath (0444) 450326

Large garden with woods and parkland of exceptional beauty. Rare trees and shrubs, herbaceous borders and fine views. Woodland Walk, water feature, new lake.
Location: 1½ m N of Haywards Heath on Balcombe Road. Brighton 17 m; Gatwick 10 m.
Station: Haywards Heath (1½ m).
Opening Times: Open daily from Good Friday to last weekend in Oct 10–6. Adm £1.50, Chd 50p: parties of 20 or more £1. Parking free. Picnic area. Interesting plants for sale. Dogs allowed on lead.
Refreshments: Licensed—morning coffee, snacks, afternoon tea; full meals by arrangement.

HEASELANDS
(Mrs Ernest Kleinwort)

Over 30 acres of garden with flowering shrubs and trees; water gardens; woodland; small collection of waterfowl.
Location: 1 m SW of Haywards Heath Hospital on A273 to Burgess Hill.
Station: Haywards Heath (1½ m).
Opening Times: GARDEN ONLY. Weds—May 10, 17 & 24; Suns—May 14, 21 & 28, also Sun July 23, 2–6. Parties by arrangement for Autumn colour. Adm £1.20, Chd 30p. Cars free. *In aid of National Gardens Scheme and World Wildlife.* Coaches by appointment. No dogs.
Refreshments: At the house.

HENFIELD

LOCAL HISTORY MUSEUM
Village Hall, High Street.
Open Tues, Thurs, Sat 10–12; Wed 2.30–4.30.

NEW HALL
Telephone: Henfield (0273) 492546
(Mr & Mrs J. N. Carreck)

16th to 18th Century manor house of Henfield, originally owned by the Bishops of Chichester and exhibiting Georgian design and woodwork. A large collection of historic phonographs and gramophones is demonstrated with famous voices of the past from 1888 onward, and other bygones. Also Elizabethan walled garden with bee shelters, Georgian coach house, barn, courtyard and dairy wing. In 3½ acres of gardens with many old trees.
Location: 2 m S of Henfield, off A2037, 4½ m N of Shoreham.
Opening Times: Apr to Oct 11–1, 2.30–5.30. Adm £1.50, Chd 75p. Please telephone beforehand.
Refreshments: In Henfield High Street.

HORSHAM

HORSHAM MUSEUM
9 The Causeway. Tel: (0403) 54959.
16th Century timber-framed house, with walled garden of unusual flowers and herbs. Displays include local history, geology, archaeology, domestic and rural crafts, toys, and early bicycles. Changing temporary exhibitions. Apr to Sept: Tues to Sat 10–5; Oct to Mar: Tues to Fri 1–5, Sat 10–5.

HURSTPIERPOINT

DANNY
(Country Houses Association Ltd)

Elizabethan E-shaped house, dating from 1593.
Location: Between Hassocks and Hurstpierpoint.
Station: Hassocks (1 m).
Opening Times: May to Sept—Weds & Thurs 2–5. Adm £1, Chd 50p. Free car park. No dogs admitted.

LITTLEHAMPTON

LITTLEHAMPTON MUSEUM *(Arun District Council)*
12A River Road. Tel: (0903) 715149.
A fine sea captain's house, magnificent harbour views, maritime paintings, local archaeology and history, temporary exhibitions, summer house, garden and free adm. Tues to Sat 10.30–1, 2–4, and Summer Bank Hol Mons.

LOWER BEEDING

LEONARDSLEE GARDENS
(The Loder Family)
Centenary Year 1889–1989

Extensive spring-flowering shrub garden, listed Grade I, in a valley filled with Rhododendrons, Azaleas and magnificent trees by a series of beautiful lakes. Striking Autumn Tints. Wallabies and Sika Deer. Rock Garden and Wishing Well.
Location: In Lower Beeding, 4½ m SE of Horsham at junction of A279 & A281; 3 m SW of Handcross at bottom of M23.
Opening Times: Spring: Apr 15 to June 18—Daily 10–6. Summer: July, Aug & Sept—Weekends only 12–6. Autumn: Oct—Weekends 10–5. Adm May £2.50 *(50p surcharge on May 14, 21, 28 & 29)*, Apr, June & Oct £2, July, Aug & Sept: £1.50, Chd £1. Coaches welcome by arrangement. Tel: Lower Beeding (040 376) 212. *No dogs please.* Large selection of plants for sale.
Refreshments: New cafeteria; salad bar and teas.

MIDHURST

RICHARD COBDEN COLLECTION *(National Council of Y.M.C.As.)*
Dunford.
Portraits and library of Richard Cobden and family.

PETWORTH

PETWORTH HOUSE, The National Trust
Telephone: Petworth 42207   &

Rebuilt 1688-96 by the 6th Duke of Somerset. Later reconstruction by Salvin, in large and beautiful deer park, landscaped by 'Capability' Brown and painted by Turner. 14th century chapel. Important collection of paintings, sculpture and furniture.
Location: In centre of Petworth 5½ m E of Midhurst.
Opening Times: Mar 24 to Nov 5—Tues, Weds, Thurs, Sats, Suns, Bank Hol Mons and Good Friday 1–5 (last adm 4.30). Adm £2.70, Chd £1.35. Pre-booked parties of 15 or more welcome on Weds, Thurs & Sats only, £2. No dogs in House or Pleasure Grounds. Car park for visitors to House during open hours, 800 yds. Shop. Wheelchairs provided. No prams or pushchairs in showrooms. Deer Park open daily all year—9–sunset, adm free. Car park for Park only on A283, 1½ m N of Petworth. Dogs must be kept under control.
Refreshments: Light lunches and teas in House on open days, 1–5.

PORTFIELD

MECHANICAL MUSIC AND DOLL COLLECTION
Church Road, Portfield. Tel: (0243) 785421.
Music boxes, barrel organs, street pianos, dance organ etc., all fully restored and playing for the visitors. Also fine display of Victorian china dolls. Easter to Sept 30: Daily 10–6. Oct to Easter: Weekends only. Evening bookings by arrangement.

PULBOROUGH

PARHAM HOUSE AND GARDENS
Telephone: Storrington (090 66) 2021

Peaceful Elizabethan House with fine gardens, standing in the heart of a Deer Park at the foot of the South Downs.

Location: A283 Storrington/Pulborough road.
Opening Times: Easter Sun to first Sun in Oct. Suns, Weds, Thurs & Bank Hols 2–6. Gardens 1–6 (last adm 5.30). Adm House & Gardens £2.50, Chd £1.50, OAPs £2. Gardens only £1, Chd 75p (1988 prices), Guided parties for house (£50 min) by prior appointment, Wed & Thurs mornings. Bookings and all enquiries to Administrator. Church. Shop. Picnic enclosure. Dogs on lead in garden only. Arrangements can be made for wheelchair users to see ground floor of house, gardens easily accessible.
Refreshments: In Big Kitchen from 3.

PYECOMBE

NEWTIMBER PLACE
Telephone: Hurstpierpoint (0273) 833104
(His Honour Judge & Mrs John Clay)

Moated house—Etruscan style wall paintings.
Location: 1 m N of Pyecombe 7 m N of Brighton off London Road (A23).
Opening Times: May to Aug—Thurs 2–5. Adm £1.

ROWLANDS CASTLE

STANSTED PARK
Telephone: 0705 412265
(Stansted Park Foundation)

This Neo-Wren house with its ancient chapel and walled gardens and arboretum is surrounded by an enchanting forest through which runs the longest beech avenue in the South of England. John Keats describes the interior of the chapel in his Eve of St. Mark. Organically grown produce will be sold in the garden shop. Cricket matches are played in front of the house on most Sundays throughout the season.
Location: Rowlands Castle, 4 m by road; 2 m walking through forest; Westbourne 3 m; Havant 5 m and Chichester 8 m.
Station: Rowlands Castle (2 m).
Opening Times: Easter Sun and Mon; Apr 30 to Sept 26—Suns, Mons & Tues only 2–6, last entries 5.30. Bus parties by arrangement only. Ample free car parking. Grounds, Chapel, Theatre Museum, Shop and tearoom only suitable for disabled at present. Adm £2, Chd 80p, OAPs £1.40. Party rate (by prior arrangement) £1.40, Chd 60p. Grounds, Chapel and tearoom and shop only £1, Chd 50p, OAPs 80p.
Refreshments: Home made cream teas served in cricket pavilion.

SHARPTHORNE

DUCKYLS
Telephone: (0342) 810352
(Mr & Mrs Michael Taylor)

Twelve acre terraced and woodland garden being gradually restored with collection of azaleas, rhododendrons, camellias; woodland walk, fine views, interesting primroses and auricula.
Location: B2028 S Sharpthorne. 3 m East Grinstead.
Opening Times: Sun Apr 16, Tues Apr 18, 25, May 2, 9, Sun May 14, Tues May 16, 23, 30. Adm £1, Chd 25p. *In aid of National Gardens Scheme.* Parties by arrangement. Car park. Suitable for disabled persons.
Refreshments: Teas etc. at house. White Hart Inn, Ardingly Road, Cat Inn, West Hoathly.

SHOREHAM-BY-SEA

MARLIPINS MUSEUM *(Sussex Archaeological Society)*
High Street. Tel: (07917) 62994.
The building dates from the early 12th century; Maritime and Local History Museum. May to mid-Sept Mon to Sat: 10–1, 2–5; Sun 2–5. Adm free (donations welcome).

SINGLETON

THE WEALD AND DOWNLAND OPEN AIR MUSEUM
Telephone: Singleton (024 363) 348

A collection of historic buildings saved from destruction, including medieval houses, farm buildings, working watermill. 40 acres of park and woodland.
Location: 6 m N of Chichester on A286 just S of Singleton.
Opening Times: Mar 19 to Oct 31—Daily 11–5. Nov 1 to Mar 18—Weds, Suns and Bank Hols only 11–4. Adm £2.50, Chd £1.25, OAPs £1.80. Parties by arrangement. (Group rates available.)
Refreshments: Light refreshments during main season.

WEST DEAN GARDENS
(The Edward James Foundation)

35 acres of informal gardens, fine specimen trees; 300ft pergola; gazebo; borders; wild garden: picnic and play area. Walled garden with Victorian glasshouses containing a collection of lawnmowers and a garden history exhibition.
Location: 6 m N of Chichester on A286, nr Weald & Downland Open Air Museum.
Opening Times: Easter to Sept—Daily 11–6 (last adm 5). Adm £1.40, Chd 65p, OAPs £1.20. Parties by arrangement £1 per person. Garden shop with a wide range of container grown plants for sale. Coach & car parking. No dogs.
Refreshments: Available, outdoor sitting only.

SOUTH HARTING

UPPARK, The National Trust
Telephone: Harting 317 or 458   &

Romantic house (1690) high on the Downs. Interior decoration and furnishings virtually unaltered since 1750. Victorian kitchen with original fittings. Queen Anne dolls' house. Small garden landscaped by Humphrey Repton.

Location: 5 m SE of Petersfield entrance on E side of South Harting/Emsworth road (B2146).
Opening Times: Mar 26 to end of Sept—Weds, Thurs, Suns & Bank Hol Mons 2–6. Last adm 5.30. Adm Sun & Bank Hol Mons £2.50, other open days £2, Chd half price. *Weds & Thurs £1.70 for pre-booked parties of 15 or more by arrangement with Administrator.* Shop. No dogs. Wheelchairs provided.
Refreshments: Teas.

STEYNING

STEYNING MUSEUM
91 High Street.
The Borough Mace and Constable's Staff dating from 1685. Special exhibitions from time to time.

STOPHAM

THE UPPER LODGE
(J. W. Harrington, Esq)

Garden with rhododendrons and azaleas; wide range of shrubs for acid soil.

Location: ½ m N of Stopham Bridge on A283 Pulborough to Petworth.
Station: Pulborough (1 m).
Opening Times: Mar: Fri 24, Sun 26, Mon 27. Apr: Suns 2, 9, 16, 30 (2–5). May: Suns 7, 14, 21, 28, Bank Hol Mons May 1, 29, (2–6). No dogs. Plants for sale. *In aid of the National Gardens Scheme.*

TANGMERE

TANGMERE MILITARY AVIATION MUSEUM
(Tangmere Memorial Museum Co. Ltd.)
Tangmere Airfield, PO Box 50, Chichester. Tel: Chichester (0243) 775223.
Location 3 m E of Chicester off A27. Famous Battle of Britain Airfield now the home of a museum that will interest all ages. A superb collection of exhibits related to 70 years of flying. Personal belongings, relics of wartime air battles, maps, paintings, photos, medals, uniforms, dioramas, static and working models, a Spitfire flight simulator and more besides. New exhibits always being added. Well worth a visit. Tangmere Aeromart – 80 Stalls – normally last Sat in Sept. Open: daily Mar 1 to first weekend in Nov. Adm £1.50, Chld 50p. Special reduction for parties of 12 or more less 10%. Car parking free. Suitable for disabled persons. One wheelchair available. Picnic area. Souvenir shop.

WEST HOATHLY

PRIEST HOUSE *(Sussex Archaeological Society)*
Tel: (0342) 810479.
15th century Clergy House, later converted into a dwelling-house, containing furnished rooms and collection of general bygones, toys, samplers and costume. Apr to mid Oct: Tues to Sat 11–5.30; Sun 2–5.30. Adm 75p, Chld 35p.

WORTHING

WORTHING MUSEUM AND ART GALLERY
(Worthing Borough Council)
Chapel Road. Tel: (0903) 39999, Ext. 121; Sat 204229.
Collections of archaeological material, geology, costume, Sussex bygones and pottery, works of art including early English watercolours, dolls and toys. Apr to Sept: Mon to Sat 10–6. Oct to Mar: Mon to Sat 10–5. *Closed* Sun. Adm free. Parties by arrangement.

YAPTON

BERRI COURT
Telephone: (0243) 551 663
(Mr & Mrs J. C. Turner)

3-acre garden of wide interest, trees, flowering shrubs, heathers, eucalyptus, daffodils, shrub roses, hydrangeas.
Location: Centre of Yapton village.
Station: Barnham (1¾ m).
Opening Times: Suns, Mons, Apr 16, 17, May 14, 15, June 25, 26, Oct 22, 23. 2–4. Adm 70p, Chd 30p. In aid of National Gardens Scheme. Dogs on leads.

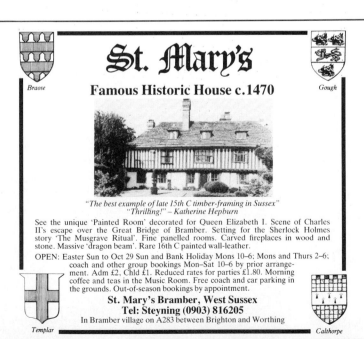

THE HIGH BEECHES

ADMISSION – SEE EDITORIAL REFERENCE

LITTLEHAMPTON MUSEUM
WEST SUSSEX

A Sea Captain's home overlooking the harbour ★ Fine ship paintings ★ Local history & archaeology ★ Temporary exhibitions ★ Garden ★ Free entry.

Tyne & Wear

GATESHEAD

SHIPLEY ART GALLERY
(Tyne and Wear Museums Service)
Prince Consort Road South. Tel: (091) 4771495.

GIBSIDE

GIBSIDE CHAPEL & AVENUE, The National Trust
Telephone: Consett (0207) 542255

Built to James Paine's design soon after 1760. Outstanding example of Georgian architecture approached along a terrace with an oak avenue.
Location: 6 m SW of Gateshead; 20 m NW of Durham between Rowlands Gill and Burnopfield.
Opening Times: Mar 24 to end Oct—Weds, Sats, Suns, Good Fri & Bank Hol Mons 1–5.30. Other times by appointment with the Custodian. Adm to car park, Avenue & Chapel £1, Chd 50p. *Parties please notify Custodian in advance 80p.* Dogs on terrace only, on leads.

JARROW

BEDE MONASTERY MUSEUM
(St. Paul's, Jarrow Development Trust)
Jarrow Hall, Church Bank NE32 3DY. Tel: (091) 4892106.
The museum, on the south bank of the River Tyne, tells the story of the Saxon and Medieval Monasteries of St. Paul's Jarrow – famous as the home of the Venerable Bede. Permanent exhibition of material from archaeological excavations includes Saxon window glass and stone carvings and a scale model of the 7th century monastery. An audio-visual display about the life of the monk. Full educational facilities. Temporary exhibitions. Tea room serving coffee, lunches and teas. Oval Room. Craft shop specialising in Anglo-Saxon related and herbal products. Pleasant gardens, with well established herb garden. Tourist Information Centre. Apr to Oct: Tues to Sat 10–5.30; Sun 2.30–5.30. Nov to Mar: Tues to Sat 11–4.30; Sun 2.30–5.30. *Closed* Mon (except Bank Hols). Adm charge. Curator: Miss S.A. Mills.

NEWCASTLE UPON TYNE

THE CASTLE KEEP MUSEUM
St. Nicholas Street.
The keep of the 'New Castle' built by Henry II in 1170. Interpretation of the history of the Castle site. Apr to Sept: Tues to Sun 9.30–5. Oct to Mar: Tues to Sun 9.30–4. *Closed* Christmas Day, Boxing Day, New Year's Day and Good Friday.

THE GREEK MUSEUM
Percy Building, The Quadrangle. Tel: (091) 2328511, Ext. 3966.
Collection of ancient Greek and Etruscan art ranging from Minoan to Hellenistic times; vases, terracottas, bronzes, gems and armour. Normally open Mon to Fri 10–4.30, and by appointment.

HATTON GALLERY
(situated within the Department of Fine Art)
Tel: (091) 2328511, Ext. 2057.
Organizes a continuous programme of temporary exhibitions of contemporary and historical art. Whenever possible This programme makes use of the Gallery's permanent collection. These exhibitions are of didactic and critical interest. On permanent display are the 'Elterwater Merzbarn' (the last large relief by Kurt Schwitters) and the Fred and Diana Uhlman Collection of African Sculpture. A programme of events and lunchtime discussions is also included in the Gallery's diary. The Gallery is open during exhibition periods Mon to Fri 10–5.30 and Sat 10–4.30.

JOHN GEORGE JOICEY MUSEUM
(Tyne and Wear Museums Service)
City Road, Newcastle Upon Tyne, NE1 2AS. Tel: (091) 2324562
Situated in unique 17th century almshouse (Holy Jesus Hospital) with 19th century addition (the General Soup Kitchen). Displays illustrate aspects of Newcastle's history. Also regimental collections. Exhibition programme. Shop. Coffee area. Tues to Fri 10–5.30; Sat 10–4.30. *Closed* Sun and Mon (except Bank Hols 10–5.30). Adm fee. NCP car park nearby. Not suitable for disabled persons.

LAING ART GALLERY *(Tyne and Wear Museums Service)*
Higham Place, NE1 8AG. Tel: (091) 2327734/2326989.

MUSEUM OF ANTIQUITIES
(jointly with the Society of Antiquaries)
The Quadrangle. Tel: (091) 2328511, Ext. 3844/3849.
Prehistoric, Roman, Anglo-Saxon and Medieval antiquities, chiefly from Northumberland. Scale models of Hadrian's Wall and reconstructions of Roman arms and armour and of a temple of Mithras. Weekdays 10–5. *Closed* Dec 24, 25, 26, New Year's Day and Good Friday.

MUSEUM OF THE DEPARTMENT OF MINING ENGINEERING
Queen Victoria Road. Tel: (091) 2328511, Ext. 3118.
Unique collection of mine safety lamps and water-colours of Northumberland and Durham mines. 1830–40, by T.H. Hair *N.B.* It is advisable for anyone wishing to view the water-colours to do so by previous appointment with the Head of the Department of Mining Engineering. Mon to Fri 9–5.

MUSEUM OF SCIENCE AND ENGINEERING
(Tyne and Wear Museums Service)
Blandford House, Blandford Square. Tel: (091) 2326789.

TRINITY MARITIME CENTRE
(Captain G.W. Clark, MBE, Chairman of Trustees)
29 Broad Chare, Quayside, NE1 3DQ. Tel: (091) 2614691.
The Centre comprises mainly of the history of the Quayside, shipbuilders, and shipping companies associated with the River Tyne. There are ship models, from 18th century to tankers and bulk carriers. Also models of the Quayside

circa 1770 and Walker Naval Yard in the 1950s. The Craft Room contains a ship's lifeboat, diving suit, pumps, and working models of capstans, windlasses and winches. Open Tues to Fri, Summer 10.30–4; Winter 11–3. Adm 50p; Chld 20p, OAP 35p. Reduced prices for parties over 20, schoolteachers with groups free. No car parking. Suitable for disabled. No wheelchairs.

TURBINIA HALL *(Tyne and Wear Museums Service)*
Exhibition Park.

THE UNIVERSITY OF NEWCASTLE UPON TYNE
HANCOCK MUSEUM
(jointly with the Natural History Society of Northumbria)
Barras Bridge. Tel: (091) 2322359.
Comprehensive collections of natural history. Rich Ethnographical section. Major modernisation of displays completed recently, new look for birds, geology, mammals and now "The Rain Forest" and "Abel's Ark". Mon to Sat 10–5; Sun 2–5. Adm 50p, Chld 25p.

SOUTH SHIELDS

ARBEIA ROMAN FORT *(Tyne and Wear Museums Service)*
Baring Street. Tel: (091) 4561369.

MUSEUM AND ART GALLERY *(Tyne and Wear Museums Service)*
Ocean Road. Tel: (091) 4568740.

SPRINGWELL VILLAGE

BOWES RAILWAY
Springwell Village.

SUNDERLAND

GRINDON MUSEUM *(Tyne and Wear Museums Service)*
Grindon Lane. Tel: (091) 5284042.

HYLTON CASTLE
Telephone: (0783) 495048

Heraldic shields and carved figures adorn this splendid castle, shaped like an enormous gatehouse and designed more for comfort than defence. Sir William Hylton built it about 1400 but it was much altered in the 1860s and transformed into a suburban villa. These later additions have now been removed.
Location: 3¾ m (6 km) west of Sunderland. OS map ref NZ358588.
Opening Times: Good Friday to Sept 30, daily 10–6; Oct 1 to Maundy Thursday, daily 10–4. *Closed Mons, Christmas and New Year.* Adm 55p, OAPs 40p, Chld 25p.

MONKWEARMOUTH STATION MUSEUM
(Tyne and Wear Museums Service)
North Bridge Street. Tel: (091) 5677075.

MUSEUM AND ART GALLERY *(Tyne and Wear Museums Service)*
Borough Road. Tel: (091) 5141235.

RYHOPE ENGINES MUSEUM

TYNEMOUTH

TYNEMOUTH CASTLE AND PRIORY
Telephone: 091-257 1090

Two saints were buried within the walls of this Benedictine priory, established in the 11th century on the site of an earlier abandoned monastery. Two walls of the presbytery still tower to their full height and the 15th century chantry chapel has a splendid collection of roof bosses. A fortified gatehouse was added during the Border wars, which persuaded Henry VIII to retain the priory as a royal castle after the Dissolution. The headland remained in use for coastal defence until 1956, one battery is not open to the public.
Location: Tynemouth. OS map ref NZ374695.
Opening Times: Good Friday to Sept 30, daily 10–6; Oct 1 to Maundy Thursday, daily 10–4. *Closed Mons, Christmas and New Year.* Adm 80p, OAPs 60p, Chd 40p.

WALLSEND

WALLSEND HERITAGE CENTRE
(Tyne and Wear Museums Service)
Buddle Street. Tel: (091) 2620012.

WASHINGTON

WASHINGTON OLD HALL, The National Trust
Telephone: Washington (091) 4166879   &
(Leased by Sunderland Borough Council)

Jacobean manor house incorporating portions of 12th century house of the Washington family.
Location: In Washington on E side of Ave; 5 m W of Sunderland (2 m from A1); S of Tyne Tunnel, follow signs for Washington New Town District 4 & then village.
Opening Times: Mar 24 to Sept 30—Daily (except Fri, but open Good Friday) 11–5; Oct—Weds, Sats & Suns 11–5 (last adm 4.30). Adm £1.50; Chd 50p. *Parties of 15 or more £1 each, by prior arrangement only with the Custodian.* Shop. Dogs in garden only, on leads. Wheelchair access.

WASHINGTON 'F' PIT INDUSTRIAL MUSEUM
(Tyne and Wear Museums Service)
Albany Way. Tel: (091) 4167640.

Warwickshire

ALCESTER

COUGHTON COURT, The National Trust
Telephone: Alcester (0789) 762435

Central gatehouse 1509. Two mid-Elizabethan half-timbered wings. Jacobite relics. The home of the Throckmorton family since 1409.

Location: 2 m N of Alcester just E of A435.
Opening Times: Apr—Sats, Suns & Easter Mon to Thurs 2–6; May to Sept—Daily except Mon & Fri, but open Bank Hol Mons 2–6; Oct—Sats & Suns 2–5. Adm £1.80, Chd 90p. Parties by prior arrangement. Shop. Limited access for wheelchairs. Dogs on leads in grounds.
Refreshments: Tea at the House.

RAGLEY HALL
Telephone: Alcester (0789) 762090 or 762455
(The Marquess of Hertford)

Built in 1680. Fine paintings, china, furniture and works of art and mural 'The Temptation'. Gardens, park and lake. Adventure wood, Farm and woodland walks and lakeside picnic places.

Location: 2 m SW of Alcester on Birmingham/Alcester/Evesham Road (A435); 8 m from Stratford-upon-Avon.
Opening Times: HOUSE, GARDEN & PARK: Mar 25 to Oct 1—Daily except Mons and Fris, always open Bank Hol Mons.
GARDEN & PARK, with Adventure Wood and Farm and woodland walk, and lakeside picnic places. Mar, Apr, May & Sept 12–5.30; June, July & Aug 10–6. Licensed Terrace tearooms 12–5. Restaurant for booked parties only.
HOUSE: 12–5.
ADMISSION: HOUSE, GARDEN & PARK, (includes Adventure Wood and Farm and woodland walks) £2.90, Chd £1.90.
GARDEN & PARK ONLY, including Adventure Wood and Farm and woodland walks £1.90, Chd 90p. Coach parties of 30 and over & OAPs £2.40.
Free car park. Dogs welcome on leads in Park and on Country Trail, not in House, Garden or Adventure Wood.
Refreshments: Licensed Terrace tearooms and Restaurant open daily except Mons and Fris, 12 noon–5. Restaurant for booked parties only serving lunches & teas. **Advance Bookings:** (at any time of the year). Coach parties welcome by arrangement. Lunches and teas – parties please write for menus. The Great Hall is available for functions throughout the year. Private dinner parties for any number between 2–150 can be arranged. For further information please contact: The Marquess of Hertford, Ragley Hall, Alcester, Worcestershire. Telephone: Alcester (STD 0789) 762090 or 762455.

CHARLECOTE

CHARLECOTE PARK, The National Trust
Telephone: Stratford-upon-Avon (0789) 840277

Originally built by the Lucy family, 1550s. Refurbished 1830s in Elizabethan Revival style. Deer park.

Location: 5 m E of Stratford-upon-Avon on the N side of B4086.
Opening Times: Mar 25 to Oct—Daily (except Mon & Thurs) 11–6 (open Bank Hol Mons 11–6). Closed Good Fri. Last adm one hour before closing. Evening visits for pre-booked parties second Weds each month. 7.30–9.30. Full price for evening visits (including NT members). School parties by prior arrangement only. Adm £2.60, Chd £1.30. Parties by prior written arrangement only. Family tickets £7.20. No dogs. Wheelchairs provided. Shop.
Refreshments: Refreshments in Orangery.

EDGE HILL

UPTON HOUSE, The National Trust
Telephone: Edge Hill 266

Fine collection paintings, porcelain. Tapestries. Beautiful terraced gardens.

Location: 1 m S of Edge Hill; 7 m NW of Banbury on the Stratford Road (A422).
Opening Times: Mar 25 to end Apr, and Oct: Sat, Sun & Easter Mon 2–6. May to Sept: Sat to Wed 2–6. Last adm to House 5.30. Adm House & Grounds £2.20, Chd £1.10. Parties (except weekends & Bank Hols) by prior arrangement with the Administrator. No indoor photography. Dogs in garden only, on leads. Wheelchairs provided. Wheelchair access ground floor only.

FARNBOROUGH

FARNBOROUGH HALL, The National Trust
(The National Trust)

Mid 18th century house incorporates fine plasterworks and ancient sculpture. ¾ mile terrace walk feature temples and obelisk, but the splendid panoramic views are soon to be marred by M40.

Location: 6 m N of Banbury; ½ m W of A423.
Opening Times: April to end of Sept—Weds, Sats & May Day Bank Hol Sun & Mon 2–6. Adm House, Grounds & Terrace Walk £1.50. Terrace Walk 50p. (Thurs and Fris) 2–6 (But closed Good Friday). Chd half-price. *No reduction for parties.* Parties by prior written arrangement only. Dogs in grounds only, on leads. No indoor photography. NB: The tenants are responsible for the showing arrangements.

KENILWORTH

KENILWORTH CASTLE
Telephone: (0926) 52078
(English Heritage)

One of the grandest ruins in England, this castle was made famous by Sir Walter Scott. Gone now is the great lake that once surrounded it, but still standing is the huge Noman keep with walls nearly 20ft (6m) thick in places. Inside the encircling walls built by King John are the remains of John of Gaunt's chapel and great hall, the Earl of Leicester's stables and gatehouse. The most splendid royal occasion took place in 1575 when Queen Elizabeth I was entertained lavishly by the Earl with music and dancing, fireworks and hunting, for 19 days.

Location: West side of Kenilworth. OS map ref SP278723.
Opening Times: Good Friday to Sept 30, daily 10–6; Oct 1 to Maundy Thurs, daily 10–4. *Closed* Mons, Dec 24–26, Jan 1. Adm £1.10, OAPs 80p, Chd 55p.

STONELEIGH ABBEY
Telephone: 0926 52116
(Lord and Lady Leigh)

The Georgian Mansion, originally a Cistercian Abbey, has now been restored following the disastrous fire in 1960. The North and West Wing State rooms and part of the South wing are now open to visitors. Children's playground, miniature steam railway (Suns and Bank Hols only). Souvenir shop, picnic areas, monks stew ponds, woodland walks. Nature Trail.

Location: 3 m E of Kenilworth; 6 m S of Coventry; 5 m N of Leamington Spa; 6 m NE of Warwick; 1½ m S of Stoneleigh village via B4115 and A444.
Opening Times: Details from: The Administrator, Stoneleigh Abbey, Kenilworth, Warwickshire. Tel: (0926) 52116.
Refreshments: Licensed facilities available.

LAPWORTH

BADDESLEY CLINTON, The National Trust
Telephone: Lapworth (056 43) 3294

A romantically sited medieval moated manor house, with 120 acres, dating back to the 14th century and little changed since 1634.

Location: ¾ m W of A41 Warwick to Birmingham Road, nr Chadwick End; 7½ m NW of Warwick; 13 m SE of Birmingham.
Station: Lapworth (2 m) (not Suns).
Opening Times: Mar 18 to end of Sept—Weds to Suns & Bank Hol Mons 2–6. *Closed Good Fri;* Oct—Weds to Suns 12.30–4.30. Adm £2.30, Chd £1.15, Last admissions 30 mins before closing. Family tickets £6.50 (2 adults and up to 3 chd). Coach parties by prior arrangement only. No prams or pushchairs in the house. No dogs. Wheelchair provided. Shop.
NB: Timed tickets are issued for entry into the house.
Refreshments: Lunches from 12.30 and teas.

PACKWOOD HOUSE, The National Trust
Telephone: Lapworth (056 43) 2024

Elizabethan house with mid-17th century additions. Tapestry, needlework, Carolean formal garden, and yew garden of c. 1650 representing the Sermon on the Mount.

Location: 2 m E of Hockley Heath (which is on A34) 11 m SE of Birmingham.
Stations: Lapworth (1½ m); Dorridge (2 m).
Opening Times: Mar 25 to end of Sept—Weds to Suns & Bank Hol Mons 2–6. *Closed Good Friday.* Oct—Wed to Suns 12.30–4 (last adm ½hr before closing). Adm £1.90, Chd 95p. Family tickets £5.50 (2 adults and up to 3 chd). Parties by prior written arrangement only. No dogs. No prams in House. Wheelchair access to part of garden & ground floor (difficult).

LEAMINGTON SPA

LEAMINGTON SPA ART GALLERY AND MUSEUM
(Warwick District Council)
Avenue Road. Tel: (0926) 26559.

Paintings by Dutch and Flemish masters; 20th century oils and watercolours, mainly English. Sixteenth–nineteenth century pottery and porcelain; 18th century English glass. Mon to Sat 10–1, 2–5 (also Thurs evening 6–8). *Closed* Sun.

NUNEATON

ARBURY HALL
Telephone: Nuneaton (0203) 382804 or Fillongley (0676) 40529
(The Rt Hon the Viscount Daventry)

George Eliot's 'Cheverel Manor 16th century Elizabethan House, gothicized late 18th century, pictures, period furniture etc. Park and landscape gardens.
Location: 2 m SW of Nuneaton off B4102. RAC direction signs.

Opening Times: Suns from Easter Sun to end of Sept. Bank Hol Mons. Tues & Weds in July & Aug. Gardens 2–6, Hall 2–5.30 (last adm 5). Adm Hall and Gardens £2.50 Chd £1.20, Gardens & Park £1.20, Chd 60p. Organised parties any day (25 or over) special terms by prior arrangement with Administrator. School parties also welcome. Free car park.
Refreshments: Available on all open days. Set meals arranged for parties.

NUNEATON MUSEUM AND ART GALLERY
Riversley Park. Tel: (0203) 376473.
Geology, archaeology (local Roman and medieval), ethnography, fine and applied art, George Eliot personalia, continually changing art exhibitions. Mon to Fri 12–7; Sat and Sun 10–7. *Closes* at 5, Oct to Mar. *(Museum opening subject to alteration 1989.)*

RUGBY

RUGBY LIBRARY AND EXHIBITION GALLERY
St. Matthew's Street. Tel: (0788) 542687 or 71813.
Exhibitions by local artists and societies. Mon, Tues, Thurs and Fri 9.30–8; Wed 9.30–5; Sat 9.30–4.

SHIPSTON-ON-STOUR

HONINGTON HALL
Telephone: Shipston-on-Stour (0608) 61434
(Sir John Wiggin, Bart.)

Originally built by the Parker family in 1680. Contains fine 18th century plasterwork.
Location: 10 m S of Stratford-on-Avon; ½ m E of A34.
Opening Times: June, July, Aug—Weds & Bank Hol Mons 2.30–5. Parties at other times by appointment. Adm £1.50, Chd 50p.

STRATFORD-UPON-AVON

THE GRAMMAR SCHOOL
Present-day schoolboys assist your visit to this picturesque half-timbered Guildhall (1417) which includes Shakespeare's schoolroom.
Location: Church Street, Stratford-upon-Avon between the Guild Chapel and almshouses.
Opening Times: Easter and summer school holidays daily 2–6. Times may be changed – details from the Guild School Association. Adm charge.

THE SHAKESPEARE BIRTHPLACE TRUST PROPERTIES
All the properties are open daily except on Good Friday morning, Christmas Eve, Christmas Day, Boxing Day and the morning of Jan 1st. For those needing transport there is a regular guided bus tour service during the summer months connecting the town properties with Anne Hathaway's Cottage and Mary Arden's House.

SHAKESPEARE'S BIRTHPLACE
The half-timbered house where Shakespeare was born, containing many rare Shakespearian exhibits, also BBC Television Shakespeare Costume Exhibition.
Location: Henley Street.
Opening Times: Apr to Oct—Weekdays 9–6 (9–5 Oct); Suns 10–6 (10–5 Oct); Nov to Mar—Weekdays 9–4.30; Suns 1.30–4.30. Adm £1.70, Chd 70p. Adm incl Exhibition £1.90, Chd 80p.

ANNE HATHAWAY'S COTTAGE
The picturesque thatched home of Anne Hathaway before her marriage to Shakespeare.
Location: Shottery (1 m).
Opening Times: Apr to Oct—Weekdays 9–6 (9–5 Oct); Suns 10–6 (10–5 Oct); Nov to Mar—Weekdays 9–4.30; Suns 1.30–4.30. Adm £1.60, Chd 60p.

HALL'S CROFT
A fine Tudor house complete with period furniture and walled garden where Shakespeare's daughter Susanna and Dr John Hall lived.
Location: Old Town.
Opening Times: Apr to Oct—Weekdays 9–6 (9–5 Oct); Suns 10–6 (10–5 Oct); Nov to Mar—Weekdays only 9–4.30. Adm £1.10, Chd 50p.

MARY ARDEN'S HOUSE and THE SHAKESPEARE COUNTRYSIDE MUSEUM
The Tudor farmhouse where Shakespeare's mother lived, with a farming and Shakespeare countryside museum now extended to include the adjoining Glebe Farm. Interesting dovecote. Rural Crafts.
Location: Wilmcote (3 m).
Opening Times: Apr to Oct—Weekdays 9–6 (9–5 Oct); Suns 10–6 (10–5 Oct); Nov to Mar—Weekdays only 9–4.30. Adm £1.60, Chd 70p.

NEW PLACE/NASH'S HOUSE
Foundations of Shakespeare's last home, preserved in an Elizabethan garden setting with Nash's House adjoining which is furnished in period style.
Location: Chapel Street.
Opening Times: Apr to Oct—Weekdays 9–6 (9–5 Oct); Suns 10–6 (10–5 Oct); Nov to Mar—Weekdays only 9–4.30. Adm £1.10, Chd 50p.

Inclusive ticket admitting to all five properties and also the BBC Television Shakespeare costume exhibition £5, Chd £2.
School party permit including the BBC Television Shakespeare costume exhibition £1.50. (One member of staff to each 10 children is admitted free.) Inclusive adm permit for Colleges & University student parties including the BBC Television Shakespeare costume exhibition £2.40. (One member of staff to each 10 students is admitted free.) In both cases, additional adults £5.
Last adm 20 mins before the advertised closing time at all the properties.

STRATFORD-UPON-AVON MOTOR MUSEUM
1 Shakespeare Street. Tel: (0789) 69413.
Only a minute's walk from Shakespeare's Birthplace, this unique presentation features some of the most exotic vintage cars ever made – some specially ordered by the Maharajahs of India – set amidst fashions, music and scenes from that fabulous era – 'The Golden Age of Motoring'. Picnic garden, gallery and speciality shop. Open daily. Adm charge.

THE TEDDY BEAR MUSEUM   *(Gyles Brandreth)*
19 Greenhill Street CV37 6LF. Tel: (0789) 293160.
In an original Elizabethan setting, marvel at hundreds of wonderful teddy bears from around the world – including some of the oldest, most valuable and most unusual on earth. Come to the teddy bears' picnic – browse in the teddy bears' library – see the teddy bears' Victorian dolls' house – meet Winnie the Pooh and Rupert and Paddington in the unique teddy bear hall of fame! Old bears – new bears – giant bears – tiny bears – mechanical bears – musical bears – amazing bears – amusing bears – famous bears and bears of the famous – you'll find them all at the Teddy Bear Museum, home of William Shakesbear, his family and friends. Open daily 9.30–6. Adm £1.50, Chld (under 14) 75p.

WARWICK

DOLL MUSEUM   *(Warwickshire County Council)*
Oken's House, Castle Street. Tel: (0926) 495546.
Displays on the history of dolls and their houses, puzzles and games (18th century to present day). Easter to end Sept: Mon to Sat 10–12.30, 1.30–5; Sun 2–5. Adm 75p; Chld, OAP, unemployed 50p. Concessionary rates for pre-arranged parties of 10 or more. The Joy Robinson collection of antique and period dolls and toys. Daily (inc. Suns) 10.30–5. Adm 70p; Chld 50p.

LORD LEYCESTER HOSPITAL
Telephone: Warwick (0926) 492797
(The Governors of Lord Leycester Hospital)

In 1100 the chapel of St. James was built over the West Gate of Warwick and became the centre for the Guilds established by Royal Charter in 1383. In 1571 Robert Dudley, Earl of Leycester, founded his Hospital for twelve 'poor' persons in the buildings of the Guilds, which had been dispersed in 1546. The Hospital has been run ever since for retired or disabled ex-Servicemen and their wives. The buildings have been recently restored to their original condition including the Great Hall of King James' the Guildhall (museum), the Chaplain's Hall (Queen's Own Hussars Regimental Museum) and the Brethren's Kitchen.
Location: W gate of Warwick (A46).
Station: Warwick (¾ m).
Opening Times: All the year—Mons to Sats 10–5.30 (summer) 10–4 (winter). Gate closes 15 mins earlier. *Closed Suns, Good Fri & Christmas Day.* Adm £1.50, Chd (under 14) 50p, OAPs and students £1. Free car park.
Refreshments: Tea (Easter to Oct). Lunches (for booked parties).

ST. JOHN'S HOUSE   *(Warwickshire County Council)*
Coten End. Tel: (0926) 410410, Ext. 2132.
Warwickshire bygones, period costume and musical instruments. Victorian classroom, kitchen and parlour. Museum of The Royal Warwickshire Regiment is on the first floor. Tues to Sat 10–12.30, 1.30–5.30. *Closed* Mon (except Bank Hols). Sun (May to Sept) 2.30–5. MUSEUM EDUCATION SERVICE, Ext. 2034.

WARWICK CASTLE
Telephone: Warwick (0926) 495421

One of the finest medieval castles, standing on a steep rock cliff beside the River Avon, 8 miles from Stratford. The present castle is a fine example of 14th century fortification with towers and dungeons open to visitors all the year round. The State Rooms contain a magnificent collection of pictures by Rubens, Van Dyck and other Masters. Surrounded by acres of parkland landscaped by 'Capability' Brown, gardens where peacocks roam freely and a river island.
Location: In the centre of Warwick.
Stations: Warwick (½ m); Leamington Spa (2 m).
Opening Times: Open daily (except Christmas Day) all year. Mar 1 to Oct 31—Daily 10–5.30. Nov 1 to Feb 28—Daily 10–4.30. Adm charges not available at time of going to press. Car park.
Refreshments: Licensed restaurant & cafeteria in the Castle. Medieval Banquets.

WARWICKSHIRE MUSEUM *(Warwickshire County Council)*
  Market Place. Tel: (0926) 410410, Ext. 2500; Sat 410619.
Headquarters of the Museum Service. Collection illustrates wild life, geology, archaeology and history of Warwickshire. Frequently changing exhibitions. Displays include the famous Sheldon tapestry map and Warwickshire's giant fossil plesiosaur. Mon to Sat 10–5.30; Sun (May to Sept) 2.30–5.

WARWICKSHIRE MUSEUM OF RURAL LIFE
  (Warwickshire County Council)
  Warwickshire College of Agriculture, Moreton Morrell.
  Tel: Warwick (0926) 410410, Ext. 2021.
The tools and equipment of Warwickshire country life in a rural setting. Open by arrangement only.

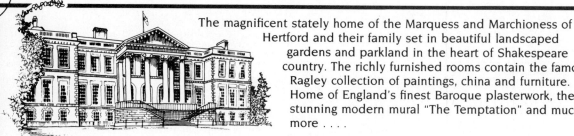

West Midlands

NATIONAL MOTORCYCLE MUSEUM

Coventry Road, Bickenhill. Tel: (06755) 3311.
Hundreds of painstakingly restored British motorcycles dating from 1898 to present day. Restaurant, snack bar, gift and book shop. Conference facilities available. Free car and coach parking. Open daily (except Christmas Day) 10–6. Adm £3, Chld/OAPs £2. Reductions for parties of 20 and over on application.

BIRMINGHAM

ASTON HALL

Telephone: 021-327 0062
(Birmingham Metropolitan District Council)

A fine Jacobean house built 1618–35 with many rooms furnished as period settings. A branch of Birmingham Museums and Art Gallery.
Location: 2½ m from centre of city. Entrance for coaches at Frederick Road; entrance for cars at Witton Lane.
Station: Aston (¾ m).
Opening Times: Mar 18–Oct 29— Daily 2–5. Adm free. School parties can arrange to visit throughout the year.

BIRMINGHAM MUSEUM AND ART GALLERY

Chamberlain Square, B3 3DH. Tel: 021-235 2834.
The Department of Fine Art: Birmingham possesses a representative selection of British and European painting and sculpture from the 14th to the 20th century. Of particular significance are the Italian 17th century paintings and the English Pre-Raphaelite Collection, which is considered to be the finest in the world. There is also an outstanding Collection of English 18th and 19th century drawings and watercolours which may be viewed by prior arrangement.
The Department of Applied Art: The Applied Arts are well represented with collections of ceramics, glass, stained glass, silver, textiles, jewellery, non-precious metalwork, Oriental, Indian and Middle Eastern artefacts and English costume. Much of this material is on display for the first time in the newly refurbished Industrial Gallery. A gallery devoted to items of contemporary craft was established in 1980 with assistance from West Midlands Arts.
The Department of Archaeology and Ethnography: The collections include archaeological objects from the West Midlands and other parts of Britain, the Near East, Egypt, Mediterranean area, India, South and Central America as well as ethnographic material from North America and the Pacific. There are also collections of ancient and Medieval coins with special emphasis on those struck in the West Midlands.
The Department of Local History: The Department of Local History collects, documents and makes available material evidence depicting the origins and growth of Birmingham and its suburbs from the end of the Middle Ages to the present day. Its collections cover social and domestic history, civic life, crafts, trades and industries, local worthies, topographical views and numismatics. The department is also responsible for the Pinto Collection of wooden bygones.
The Department of Natural History: The Department of Natural History has fine collections of British and foreign bird specimens, lepidoptera, minerals, molluscs and plants; also a good series of British fossils and a unique collection of gemstones. The Zoology galleries display several habitat dioramas of European wildlife, the biology of vertebrate animals, including fishes, amphibians, reptiles, birds and mammals, and the Beale gallery of British birds in natural settings. The Fossil gallery has a life-size model of a carnivorous dinosaur as well as the actual skull of another – the plant-eater Triceratops from Montana.
The Department of Conservation: Conservation and restoration work is undertaken on material from the collections, primarily in archaeology, applied art, furniture, paintings, paper and textiles.
Schools Liaison: The Schools Liaison assists teachers wishing to use the museum's collections in their work. It organises courses for serving and student teachers and provides facilities for practical sessions for group visits. It arranges events for all ages including leisure courses, craft demonstrations, talks and exhibitions. During major school holidays a full programme of events is provided for everyone.
Mon to Sat 9.30–5; Sun 2–5. *Closed* Christmas Day, Boxing Day and New Year's Day. Adm free.

BIRMINGHAM NATURE CENTRE

At south-west entrance to Cannon Hill Park, opposite Pebble Mill Road.
Tel: 021472 7775.
The Nature Centre displays living animals of the British Isles and Europe in both outdoor and indoor enclosures, including lynx, fox, badger, polecats, otters and beavers, owls and many others. Conditions have been created to resemble natural habitats and to attract wild birds, butterflies etc. Its grounds of six acres include fishponds, duckponds, stream, rock outcrops, aviaries and beehives. Easter to end Oct: Daily 10–5. Adm free. *Closed* Christmas Day, Boxing Day and New Year's Day.

BLAKESLEY HALL

Telephone: 021-783 2193
(Birmingham Metropolitan District Council)

A timber-framed yeoman's farmhouse c. 1575 carefully furnished to an inventory of 1684. Also contains displays on timber building methods and 17th century pottery from a single excavation. A branch of Birmingham Museums and Art Gallery.
Location: 3 m from city centre; entrance in Blakesley Road.
Stations: Stechford (¾ m); Birmingham New Street. Buses: 16 & 17, 11 on Outer Circle.
Opening Times: Mar 18 to Oct 29—Daily 2–5. Adm free. School parties can arrange to visit throughout the year.

GEOLOGICAL DEPARTMENTAL MUSEUM

The University, Edgbaston. Tel: 021-414 6147.
Collections in palaeontology, stratigraphy, petrology, mineralogy and physical geology, including the Holcroft collection of fossils and the Lapworth collection of graptolites. Daily 9–5 by arrangement.

THE MUSEUM OF SCIENCE AND INDUSTRY

Newhall Street B3 1RZ. Tel: 021-236 1022.
The museum preserves and exhibits a wide range of items of general industrial and scientific interest including steam engines, machine tools, small arms, transport, aircraft and scientific instruments. These are supplemented by temporary exhibitions. Mon to Sat 9.30–5; Sun 2–5. First and third Wed of each month engines on steam. *Closed* Christmas Day, Boxing Day and New Year's Day. Adm free.

THE PATRICK COLLECTION

(J.A. Patrick (Chairman of the Trustees of 'The Patrick Foundation'))
Patrick House, 180 Lifford Lane. Tel: 021-459 9111.
A unique motor museum, which opened in 1985, and has just completed the 2nd stage of an extensive building and refurbishment programme. A changing selection of the Patrick Collection's 230 vehicles are displayed in authentic settings from a 1904 Wolseley, through the rare classic cars of the 1920's the popular cars of the 50s and 60s to such exotic rarities as one of only 25 examples of the incredible Aston Martin Zagato. There is also a Porsche 959. The victorian buildings of the museum are set in lakeside terraced gardens bounded by two canals. Leisure facilities include a children's play area, Le Mans simulators and electric cars. There is a gift shop, refreshment areas and the Lombard Room restaurant and conservatory serving morning coffee, lunch and afternoon tea. Conferences for up to 100 delegates can easily be accommodated together with exhibitions in the grounds. Ample free car parking and coach parties welcome by appointment. Entrance charges and opening times for 1989 are available by telephoning 021 459 9111 on or after Nov 1 1988. Special reductions for parties on application. Suitable for disabled persons. Wheelchairs available. Ample free car parking.

SAREHOLE MILL

Cole Bank Road, Hall Green. Tel: 021-777 6612.
An 18th century water-powered corn mill which ceased production in 1919. The mill was also used for blade grinding and has now been restored to working order. Easter to end Oct: Daily 2–5. Adm free. Educational and group visits by arrangement.

WEOLEY CASTLE

Alwold Road. Tel: 021-427 4270.
The ruins of a fortified manor house dating in its present form from the late 13th century. Excavations have revealed evidence of earlier occupation and the finds are exhibited in a small museum on the site. Easter to end Oct: Tues to Fri 2–5. Adm free. Educational and group visits by arrangement.

BRADMORE

BANTOCK HOUSE *(Wolverhampton Borough Council)*

Bantock Park, Bradmore. Tel: (0902) 313132.
Described as 'one of the finest small scale museums in Europe' (Jeremy Cooper, Sunday Times) Bantock House Museum is famous for its exceptional collections of English painted enamels and West Midlands Japanned ware; the latter has recently benefited from a complete redesign of its display. The panelled rooms also show examples of fine pottery and porcelain, including Worcester, Wedgwood, and the outstanding Balston Collection of Staffordshire portrait figures, on loan from the National Trust. For children, the dolls and toys collection is of special interest; and a newly-opened room now presents displays of local history items. Mon to Fri 10–7; Sat 10–6; Sun 2–5. Adm free. *Closed* New Year's Day, Good Friday to Easter Sunday. Christmas closing subject to annual confirmation. Public holiday opening under review.

BRIERLEY HILL

ROYAL BRIERLEY MUSEUM *(Royal Brierly Crystal)*

North Street. Tel: (0384) 70161.
A fine collection of early glass and crystal, all hand made. One large section includes only fine pieces created over 150 years at Royal Brierley Crystal Ltd (formerly known as Stevens and Williams Limited). Adm free. Parties by arrangement. Plenty of car parking. 20 minutes from junc 2, M5.

COVENTRY

HERBERT ART GALLERY AND MUSEUM
Jordan Well. Tel: (0203) 832387.
Archaeology, natural and local history, visual and decorative arts. Mon to Sat 10–5.30; Sun 2–5. *Closed* Good Friday and part of Christmas period. Adm free.

LUNT ROMAN FORT (RECONSTRUCTION)
Baginton, Nr. Coventry. Tel: (0203) 832381/832433.
Rampart, gateway, gyrus and granary displaying finds from the site and the life of the soldiers in the fort. May–Oct: Tues, Wed, Fri, Sat & Sun 12–6. Adm 50p, Chld/OAPs 25p.

MIDLAND AIR MUSEUM
Coventry Airport, Baginton. Tel: (0203) 301 033.
Over 20 aircraft from diminutive Gnat jet fighter to giant Vulcan bomber and Argosy freighter. Sir Frank Whittle Jet Heritage Centre – exhibition building contains display on work of Coventry born jet pioneer. Apr to Oct: Mon to Sat, 10–4, Sun 11–6. Winter: Sun only. Adm £1, Chld/OAPs 50p (1988 rates). Reductions for parties. Free car parking. Suitable for disabled persons. Souvenir shop, picnic area, refreshments.

MUSEUM OF BRITISH ROAD TRANSPORT
Tel: (0203) 832425.
Over 400 exhibits on display including cars, cycles, motor cycles and commercial vehicles. Apr–Oct: daily 10–5; Nov–Mar: Fri, Sat & Sun 10–5. Adm £1.50, Chld 75p. For further information telephone the above number.

WHITEFRIARS MUSEUM
London Road. Information Tel: (0203) 832387.
The cloister and dormitory of a fourteenth century Carmelite Friary. Built in beautiful pink sandstone, now restored and a regular venue for sculpture exhibitions. Open: Tues to Sat 10–5. Adm free.

DUDLEY

BLACK COUNTRY MUSEUM
Tipton Road. Tel: 021-557 9643.
On a 26 acre site in the heart of the Industrial West Midlands conurbation, buildings and machines from throughout the area are being brought together to create a living tribute to the skills and enterprise of the people of the Black Country. An electric tramcar carries visitors past a colliery and a working replica of the worlds first steam engine. In the village, shops and houses cluster around a chapel and pub next to ironworks and manufactories. Narrowboats rest upon the canal around the village and journey into the Dudley Tunnel and spectacular limestone caverns. Nailmaking and chain-making, glass cutting, bakery, boatbuilding and ironworking all await the visitor. Open Daily 10–5 (reduced hours in winter).

DUDLEY MUSEUM AND ART GALLERY
(Dudley Metropolitan Borough)
St. James's Road. Tel: (0384) 456000.
Fine Geological gallery, especially of local limestone and coal measure fossils. The Brooke Robinson Collection of 17th, 18th and 19th century European paintings, Japanese netsuke and inro, enamels, furniture, Greek, Roman, Chinese and European ceramics. Permanent art collection (in store) and a wide variety of temporary exhibitions throughout the year. Mon to Sat 10–5. *Closed* Sun and Bank Hols.

KINGSWINFORD

BROADFIELD HOUSE GLASS MUSEUM
(Dudley Metropolitan Borough)
Barnett Lane, Kingswinford. Tel: (0384) 273011.
The new permanent home for the Brierley Hill and Stourbridge glass collections. Roman glass to the present day but concentrating on the achievements of the Stourbridge glass makers of the 19th century. Slide and video displays and small museum shop selling modern glass and glass publications. Glass making studios at the rear of the Museum. Tues to Fri 2–5; Sat 10–1, 2–5; Sun 2–5; Bank Holiday Mon 2–5. Adm free.

MOUNT PLEASANT

BILSTON MUSEUM AND ART GALLERY
(Wolverhampton Borough Council)
Mount Pleasant. Tel: (0902) 409143.
The museum contains material relating to Bilston's industrial and social history with special attention drawn to the fine English painted enamels. Most of these date from the 18th century, but the art of producing delicate enamels has survived in Bilston to this day. In the art gallery, exhibitions of contemporary interest are regularly organised, many of them featuring the work of artists from the West Midlands. Mon to Sat 10–5. Adm free. *Closed* New Year's Day, Good Friday, Easter Sunday and May Day. Christmas closing subject to annual confirmation. Public holiday opening under review.

SMETHWICK

AVERY HISTORICAL MUSEUM
Smethwick, B66 2LP. Tel: (021-558) 1112.
A collection of weighing machines, weights, records relating to the history of weighing. During factory hours by appointment.

STOURBRIDGE

HAGLEY HALL
Telephone: Hagley (0562) 882408
(The Viscount & Viscountess Cobham)

The last of the great Palladian Houses, designed by Sanderson Miller and completed in 1760. Superb Italian plasterwork and the fine Lyttelton collection of 18th century paintings and furniture.
Location: Just off A456 Birmingham to Kidderminster; 12 m from Birmingham within easy reach M5 (exit 3 or 4), M6 or M42.
Stations: Hagley (1 m) (not Suns); Stourbridge Junction (2 m).
Opening Times: Jan 2 to Feb 28: daily except Sats. Mar 26, 27, May 28, 29, Aug 27, 28, 2–5. For further details, please telephone Hagley (0562) 882408.
Refreshments: Tea available in the House.

WALSALL

MUSEUM AND ART GALLERY
(Walsall Metropolitan Borough Council)
Lichfield Street. Tel: (0922) 650000, Ext. 3124.
Garman-Ryan collection of paintings, drawings, prints, sculpture and antiquities, including important works by Blake, Degas, Van Gogh and Epstein. Regular loan exhibitions. Local History Museum covering the many facets of the Borough including substantial holdings of both social and industrial exhibits. Mon to Fri 10–6; Sat 10–4.45. Also: LOCAL HISTORY MUSEUM at Willenhall Library. Opening hours as above but *closed* Wed. JEROME K. JEROME BIRTHPLACE MUSEUM at Belsize House, Bradford Street. Tues to Sat 10–5. *Closed* Sun, Mon and Bank Hols.

WALSALL LEATHER CENTRE
(Walsall Metropolitan Borough Council)
56-57 Wisemore, WS2 8EQ. Tel: (0922) 721153.
A fascinating working museum depicting all aspects of the leather industry and its history in Walsall, the leather capital of Britain. Housed in a Victorian factory with displays showing all the various stages of leather production from tanning to finishing, together with fine displays of historic and contemporary products, tools and artefacts. See demonstrations of the leather worker's craft in faithfully reproduced workshops – and have the opportunity to have a go yourself. Open Tues to Sat 10–5; Sun 12–5 (winter 12–4). Adm free. Cafe and gift shop. Facilities for the disabled. Parking facilities opposite.

WEDNESBURY

ART GALLERY AND MUSEUM *(Sandwell Corporation)*
Holyhead Road. Tel: (021-556) 0683.

WEST BROMWICH

OAK HOUSE MUSEUM *(Sandwell Corporation)*
Oak Road. Tel: (021-553) 0759.

WILLENHALL

THE LOCK MUSEUM *(Lock Museum Trust)*
54 New Road. Tel: Willenhall (0902) 634542.
A working museum occupying a Victorian lockmaker's house, with workshops.

WOLVERHAMPTON

CENTRAL ART GALLERY AND MUSEUM
(Wolverhampton Borough Council)
Lichfield Street. Tel: (0902) 312032.
Wolverhampton's major Gallery and Museum has recently been dramatically extended. New visitor amenities include a Gallery Shop and a Tea Room overlooking St. Peter's Gardens. There are two new Museum sections. The Local History Gallery features examples of the town's craftsmanship, manufacturing and transport. The Geology room displays rocks, minerals and the cream of the Fraser Fossil Collection, recently restored and imaginatively displayed. The Oriental Gallery contains a remarkable collection of Chinese and Japanese art and weapons. The Art Gallery features a year-round programme of contemporary art exhibitions. The important collection of 18th and 19th century British paintings includes work by Turner, Landseer, Gainsborough and Zoffany, as well as a popular group of genre paintings by the artists of the 'Cranbrook Colony'. Modern acquisitions include a strong collection of British and American 'Pop Art', including work by Warhol, Lichtenstein, Rosenquist and Hamilton. This collection is acknowledged as being one of the best of its kind outside London. Open: Mon to Sat 10–6. Adm free. *Closed* New Year's Day, Good Friday to following Tues, May Day, Spring Bank Hol Mon & Tues, Summer Bank Hol. Christmas closing subject to confirmation. Public holiday opening times under review.

WIGHTWICK MANOR, The National Trust
Telephone: (0902) 761108

Strongly influenced by William Morris the interiors of this late 19th century house include Morris wallpapers and fabrics, Kempe glass, de Morgan ware and a connoisseurs' collection of pre-Raphaelite paintings. Victorian/Edwardian gardens, terraces & pools.

Location: 3 m W of Wolverhampton, up Wightwick Bank (A454).

Opening Times: All year (except Feb)—Thurs, Sats, Bank Hol Suns & Mons 2.30–5.30. Also open for pre-booked parties only May to end Sept—Weds 2.30–5.30 and Weds & Thurs evenings. Pre-booked school & student tours Weds & Thurs mornings & afternoons. *Closed Dec 25, 26, Jan 1, 2.* Adm £2.50 Sat afternoons £3, (extra rooms shown *but not Bank Hol weekends*). Chd half price. Students £1.50. Gardens only £1. *Parties must book in advance (no reductions).* Photography by permission only. Dogs in garden only, on leads.

Wiltshire

AMESBURY

STONEHENGE

Built between 2800 and 1100 BC, this is Britain's most famous ancient monument and one of the world's most astonishing engineering feats. Many of the stones, some weighing 4 tons each, were brought from the Preseli Mountains in Wales to Salisbury Plain, there to be erected by human muscle power.

Location: 2 m (3.2 km) west of Amesbury. OS map ref SU123422.
Opening Times: Good Friday to Sept 30, daily 10–6; Oct 1 to Maundy Thursday, daily 10–4. *Closed Mons, Christmas and New Year.* Adm £1.60, OAPs £1.20, Chd 80p.

AVEBURY

ALEXANDER KEILLER MUSEUM (English Heritage)
Tel: (067 23) 250.

Pottery and other objects of the Neolithic and Bronze Ages and later date from the excavations at Avebury and Windmill Hill. Mar 15 to Oct 15: Daily 9.30–6.30; Sun 2–6.30 (Apr to Sept: 9.30–6.30). Oct 16 to Mar 14: Daily 9.30–4, Sun 2–4. *Closed* Dec 24, 25, 26 and Jan 1. Adm charge.

AVEBURY MANOR & GARDENS
Telephone: (06723) 203

Avebury Manor a fine Elizabethan manor house, original oak panelled rooms and plasterwork ceilings, fine oak furniture and early paintings fill the house. The attic rooms have been chosen to take you back in time where you will find wax figures of William Sharrington, Sir John Stawell and Sir Richard Holford, late owners of the house. Additional attractions include Sir John Stawell's armoury, supplied by the Royal Armouries, H.M. Tower of London. Replica jewellery and dress of the Elizabethan period. An exhibition of torture instruments and the story of torture and punishment. Within the grounds you will find an Elizabethan market square full of craft shops. See and hear minstrels, jugglers, strolling players, jesters, Lords and Ladies, and become part of Elizabethan life. With all the colour and pageantry of this by-gone age. There are also daily falconry demonstrations, a large adventure playground, nature and adventure trails, topiary, rose and herb gardens, rose centre and gift shop together with 16th century dovecote and wishing well.

Location: 1½ m from A4 London–Bath road; 9 m from Junc. 15, Swindon exit M4. 6 m from Marlborough.
Opening Times: Open daily from Easter to Oct 10–6. All enquiries Estate's Office, Avebury Manor (06723) 203. 1989 Educational group reductions. Groups welcomed – special rates. Car and coach parking within Manor grounds, plus extra parking in Avebury. Suitable for disabled persons (no wheelchairs available).
Refreshments: Restaurant for 60+ and tea rooms for 40+. Banqueting services (banquets, receptions, conferences and corporate hospitality). All enquiries Estate's Office, Avebury Manor.

AVEBURY MUSEUM
Telephone: (0672) 3250

No one knows quite why our ancient ancestors built Silbury Hill or the Sanctuary. But fortunately some of their tools, pottery and weapons have survived and are housed in the museum, which lies at the heart of Britain's earliest beginnings.

Location: In Avebury, 7 m (11.2 km) west of Marlborough. OS map ref SU100700.
Opening Times: Good Friday to Sept 30, daily 10–6; Oct 1 to Maundy Thursday, daily 10–4. *Closed Mons, Christmas and New Year.* Adm 80p, OAPs 60p, Chd 40p.

THE GREAT BARN MUSEUM OF WILTSHIRE FOLK LIFE
Tel: (067 23) 555.

A large aisled and thatched barn of the 17th century, housing displays on the rural and agricultural history of Wiltshire. There are regular craft demonstrations each Sun in season. Apr to Oct: Daily 10–5.30. Open most weekends at other times. Adm charge.

BLUNSDON

SWINDON & CRICKLADE RAILWAY
Blunsdon Station, Nr. Swindon. Tel: (0793) 771615.

Operating steam and diesel locomotives on second Sunday in the month and Bank Holidays April to October. Open every weekend to view restoration work. When completed 4½ miles of M. & S.W.J.R. will be restored. Restaurant, museum, shop and free parking.

BRADFORD-ON-AVON

IFORD MANOR
Telephone: Bradford-on-Avon (02216) 3146 or 2840
(Mrs Cartwright-Hignett)

Iford Manor, a Tudor house with an 18th century façade, stands beside a medieval bridge over the River Frome. Once a busy centre of the woollen trade,

it is now surrounded by a peaceful terraced garden of unique character. Designed in the Italian style, it was the home of Harold Peto, the Edwardian landscape architect. There are pools, statues, a colonnade, antique carvings, cloisters and many plants of botanical interest.

Location: 7 m SE of Bath on A36, signpost Iford 1 m; or from Bradford-on-Avon and Trowbridge via Westwood.
Opening Times: GARDENS ONLY. Weds and Suns in May, June, July & Aug 2–5. Also Summer Bank Hols. Adm £1, Chd & OAPs 70p. At other times by appointment. Coaches by appointment only. Dogs on leads. Free car parking.
Refreshments: On the premises, Sun only.

WESTWOOD MANOR, The National Trust

15th century stone manor house altered in the late 16th century. Fine furnishings. Gardens of clipped yew. Administered for the National Trust by a tenant.

Location: Beside Westwood Church 1½ m SW of Bradford-on-Avon off Frome Road (B3109).
Stations: Avoncliff (1 m); Bradford-on-Avon (1½ m).
Opening Times: Mar 26 to Sept 25—Mons & Suns 2–5. Adm £2. *Other times parties of 15 or more by written application to the tenant. No reduction for parties or children. No photography.* No dogs. Unsuitable for wheelchairs.

CALNE

BOWOOD HOUSE & GARDENS
Telephone: Calne (0249) 812102
(The Earl of Shelburne)

100 acre garden containing many exotic trees, 40 acre lake, waterfall, cave, and Doric Temple, arboretum, pinetum, rose garden and Italian garden. 60 acres of rhododendrons, (flowering season mid-May to June). Interesting rooms in the house include Robert Adam's Library, Dr Joseph Priestley's Laboratory, the Chapel, and a series of Exhibition Rooms featuring classical sculpture, costumes, furniture, Indiana and family jewellery. Important collection of drawings and water colours by English Masters.

Location: 2½ m W of Calne; 5 m SE of Chippenham. Immediately off A4; 8 m of M4.
Opening Times: House, Gardens & Grounds (entrance off A4 at Derry Hill village between Calne & Chippenham). End Mar to mid Oct—Daily incl Bank Hols 11–6. Rhododendron Walks (entrance off A342 at Kennels Lodge) mid-May to mid-June (depending on season) 11–6. Adm rates and information apply Estate Office, Bowood Estate, Calne, Wiltshire. Free car park. No dogs.
Refreshments: Licensed restaurant & Garden Tearoom. Children's Adventure Playground in Pleasure Grounds.

CHIPPENHAM

SHELDON MANOR
Telephone: Chippenham (0249) 653120
(Major Martin Gibbs, DL, JP)

Plantagenet Manor House, lived in as a family home for 700 years. 13th century porch, 15th century detached chapel.

Location: 1½ m W of Chippenham, signposted from A420; eastbound traffic also signposted from A4, E of Corsham (2½ m). M4 exit 17 4 m.
Station: Chippenham (2½ m).
Opening Times: Sun, Mar 26 to Sun, Sept 30—Thurs, Suns & Bank Hols 12.30–6. Gardens open 12.30 for lunches. House open at 2. Other times by arrangement for parties (for whom home-cooked meals can be provided). Majority of property suitable for wheelchairs.
Refreshments: Home-made lunches & cream teas. Coaches welcome by appointment.

YELDE HALL MUSEUM
Market Place.

COATE

COATE AGRICULTURAL MUSEUM
(Thamesdown Borough Council)
Coate.

Temporary displays of the larger items such as waggons, carts, implements etc. Open summer Suns 2–5; at other times on application. Adm free.

RICHARD JEFFERIES MUSEUM (Thamesdown Borough Council)
Coate. Tel: (0793) 26161, Ext. 3130.

Reconstruction of Jefferies' study and cheese room, with personal items, manuscripts, first editions, natural history displays and historical photographs relating to Richard Jefferies and Alfred Williams. Wed, Sat and Sun 2–5. Adm free.

CORSHAM

BATH STONE QUARRY MUSEUM
Bradford Road. Tel: (0249) 716288.

CORSHAM COURT

Telephone: Corsham (0249) 712214   &
(The Lord Methuen)

Elizabethan (1582) and Georgian (1760–70) house, fine 18th century furniture. British, Spanish, Italian and Flemish Old Masters. Park and gardens laid out by "Capability" Brown and Humphrey Repton.

Location: In Corsham 4 m W of Chippenham off the Bath Road (A4).
Opening Times: Staterooms. Jan 1 to Nov 30–Daily except Mons and Fris 2–4.30 (From Good Friday to Sept 30, 2–6 (including Fri and Bank Hols); *Closed* Dec. Last adm 5.30. Other times by appointment. Parties welcome. Adm (incl gardens) £2.50, Chd £1.20; Parties of 20 or more by arrangement. Gardens only £1.20, Chd 60p.
Refreshments: Methuen Arms, Corsham *(parties by prior arrangement)*.

DEVIZES

BROADLEAS GARDENS (Charitable Trust)

Telephone: Devizes 2035
(Lady Anne Cowdray)

A garden with rare and unusual plants and trees. Rhododendrons, magnolias and interesting perennials and ground cover.

Location: 1½ m SW of Devizes on A360
Opening Times: Apr 1 to Oct 31–Suns, Weds & Thurs 2–6. Adm £1, Chd (under 12) half-price. Parties by arrangement. Own plants propagated for sale.
Refreshments: Home-made teas by prior arrangement only.

DEVIZES MUSEUM

(The Wiltshire Archaeological and Natural History Society)
41 Long Street SN10 1NS. Tel: (0380) 77369.
Prehistoric collections of international standing including weapons, exotic ornaments and personal finery. There is a Henge Monument Room and galleries for Roman, Saxon and Medieval periods. Picture gallery and natural history displays. Library offers excellent facilities for study of local history. Open all year Mon to Sat 10–1, 2–5 (closes 4 in winter). Adm 75p, Students and OAPs 50p, Chld 5p. Special arrangements for pre-arranged parties. Shop.

KENNET AND AVON CANAL TRUST

Canal Centre, Couch Lane. Tel: (0380) 71279.
The exhibition tells of the creation of a waterway link which connects the cities of London and Bristol.

DINTON

PHILIPPS HOUSE, The National Trust

Telephone: Teffont 208   &
Classical house completed in 1816 by Sir Jeffry Wyattville for the Wyndham family.
Location: 9 m W of Salisbury; on N side of B3089.
Opening Times: By prior appointment only with the Warden. Adm £1. *No reduction for parties or children.* House leased to YWCA for residential conferences. No dogs.

HOLT

THE COURTS GARDEN, The National Trust

Telephone: North Trowbridge (0225) 782340   &
7 acre garden of mystery–of interest to amateur and botanist. Borders, lily pond and arboretum carpeted with wild flowers.
Location: 2½ m E of Bradford-on-Avon on S side of B3107; 3 m N of Trowbridge.
Station: Bradford-on-Avon (2½ m).
Opening Times: GARDEN ONLY. Mar 24 to Oct 29–Daily (except Sat), 2–5. Adm £1, Chd free (if accompanied). Other times by appointment; please telephone the Head Gardener. House not open. No dogs. Wheelchair access.

LACOCK

FOX TALBOT MUSEUM *(National Trust)*

Tel: (024 973) 459.
Museum of the history of photography with changing exhibitions. Mar to Oct: Daily 11–6. *Closed* Good Friday. Adm £1.20, Chld 60p, parties 80p, subject to price increase.

LACKHAM GARDENS AND MUSEUM

Tel: Chippenham (0249) 656111.
Agricultural implements and tools housed in reconstructed farm buildings. Open Apr–Oct 11–5.

LACOCK ABBEY, The National Trust

Telephone: Lacock 227

13th century abbey converted into a house in 1540, with 18th century "Gothick" alterations for the Talbot family whose home it still is. The medieval cloisters, the brewery and the house are also open to the public. Fine trees.
Location: In the village of Lacock; 3 m N of Melksham; 3 m S of Chippenham just E of A350.

Opening Times: House & Grounds. Mar 25 to Nov 5–Daily (except Tues) 2–6. Last adm 5.30. *Closed Good Fri.* Nov to Mar–Historical and other societies by written arrangement. Grounds only: open Mar to Nov 5–Daily 2–6. Adm House & Grounds £2.50, Chd £1.30. Parties of 15 or more £1.70. Grounds and Cloisters only £1, Chd 50p. *No dogs.* Lavatory for the disabled. Wheelchairs in grounds, village & museum only.

LANDFORD

HAMPTWORTH LODGE

Telephone: Romsey (0794) 390215
(Mr N. Anderson)

Reproduction Jacobean Manor.

Location: 10 m SE of Salisbury on the C44 road between Redlynch and Landford, which is a link road joining the A36 Salisbury–Southampton and the A338 Salisbury–Bournemouth.
Opening Times: House and garden open daily, except Suns, June 1 to July 5 1989, 2.15–5. Conducted parties 2.30 and 3.45. Adm £3, OAPs and Chd 11–18 £2, under 11 free. No special arrangements for parties, but about 15 is the maximum. Car parking. Suitable for disabled ground floor only.
Refreshments: Nearest Hotel is in Salisbury. No refreshments at house.

LUCKINGTON

LUCKINGTON COURT

Telephone: Malmesbury 840 205
(The Hon Mrs Trevor Horn)

Mainly Queen Anne with magnificent group of ancient buildings. Beautiful mainly formal garden with fine collection of ornamental trees and shrubs.
Location: 6 m W of Malmesbury on B4040 Bristol Road.
Opening Times: All the Year–Weds 2–6. Outside only, 50p. Inside view by appointment 3 weeks in advance, £1. Open Sun, May 14, 2.30–6. *Collection box for National Gardens' Scheme.*
Refreshments: Teas in garden or house (in aid of Luckington Parish Church). May 14 only.

LYDIARD TREGOZE

LYDIARD MANSION   &

(Borough of Thamesdown)

Dating from medieval times, reconstructed 1743–49. Outstanding mid-Georgian decoration.
Location: 5 m W of Swindon just N of A420; signpost Lydiard Park.
Opening Times: Weekdays 10–1, 2–5.30; Suns 2–5.30. Adm free, but children under 14 must be accompanied by an adult.

MAIDEN BRADLEY

LONGLEAT HOUSE

Telephone:
Longleat House: Maiden Bradley (098 53) 551
Safari Park: Maiden Bradley (098 53) 328
Caravan Club site: Maiden Bradley (098 53) 663
(The Marquess of Bath)

Longleat House, built by Sir John Thynne in 1580, and still owned and lived in by the same family, was the first truly magnificent Elizabethan House to be built in the Italian Renaissance style. Longleat was also the first Stately Home to be opened to the public in 1949, it is still actively run by the 6th Marquess of Bath and other members of the Thynne family, thus keeping Longleat alive with their presence. Throughout its existence, ancestors have commissioned alterations within the House; ceilings by Italian craftsmen, rooms and corridors by Wyattville, additional libraries to house the vast collection of rare books and of course, the beautiful parkland landscaped by Lancelot 'Capability' Brown. In 1966, Lord Bath, in conjunction with Jimmy Chipperfield established the first drive through wild animals reserve outside Africa and it remains the model for Safari Parks throughout the world. Many other attractions have since been opened, making Longleat a full day's entertainment for all the family. Attractions include, Victorian Kitchens, Lord Bath's Bygones, Dolls Houses, Dr. Who Exhibition, Butterfly Garden, Railway, World's Largest Maze, Pets Corner, Safari Boat Ride, Lord Bath's V.I.P. Vehicle Exhibition. 'Adventure Castle' for children. New for 1989 – 1.25 scale model of Longleat House; in the Safari Park, 'Mayura' the only white tiger in Britain.

Opening Times: Longleat House open all year – Daily (Except Christmas Day) incl. Suns Easter to September 10–6, remainder of year 10–4. Safari Park every day from mid Mar to end Oct, 10–6. (Last cars admitted 5.30 or sunset if earlier.) All other attractions every day from Easter–Oct 30, 11–6 – for Maze, Railway & Adventure Castle last entry 5.30. School Parties welcome at all times of the year – reduced rates for Parties booking in advance. Helicopter landing facilities provided advance notice given.
Refreshments: At the Old Cellar Cafe at the House and in the Restaurant Complex.

MALMESBURY

ATHELSTAN MUSEUM
Tel: (0666) 822143.

Articles concerned with the town and locality – Malmesbury penny (William II) and other coins, Thomas Girtin drawing of Malmesbury Cross, Malmesbury lace making, portraits and photographs, household articles and an 18th century fire engine.

CHARLTON PARK HOUSE
(The Earl of Suffolk and Berkshire)

Jacobean/Georgian mansion, built for the Earls of Suffolk, 1607, altered by Matthew Brettingham the Younger, c. 1770.

Location: 1½ m NE Malmesbury. Entry only by signed entrance on A429, Malmesbury/Cirencester Road. No access from Charlton village.
Opening Times: May to Oct, Mon & Thurs 2–4. Viewing of Great Hall, Staircase and saloon. Adm £1, Chd/OAPs 50p. Car parking limited. Unsuitable for wheelchairs. No dogs. No picnicking.

MELKSHAM

GREAT CHALFIELD MANOR, The National Trust

15th century moated manor house restored in the 20th century. Set across a moat between Parish Church and stables.

Location: 2½ m NE Bradford-on-Avon via B3109, signposted in Holt village.
Opening Times: Apr to Oct—Tues to Thurs 12–1, 2–5 (tours start 12.15, 2.15, 3, 3.45, 4.30). Adm £2. *Historical & other Societies by written arrangement. No reductions for parties or children.* No dogs. Unsuitable for wheelchairs.
Refreshments: Swan Hotel, Bradford-on-Avon; Kings Arms, Melksham.

MERE

MERE CHURCH MUSEUM
The Vicarage, Angel Lane.

MERE MUSEUM
Barton Lane.

POTTERNE

FIRE DEFENCE COLLECTION
Manor House.

PURTON

PURTON MUSEUM
Purton Library, High Street.

REDLYNCH

NEWHOUSE
Telephone: Downton 20055
(Mr & Mrs George Jeffreys)

Brick Jacobean "Trinity" house, c. 1619, with two Georgian wings. Contents include costume collection, Nelson relics and "Hare" picture.

Location: 9 m S of Salisbury; 3 m from Downton, off B3080.
Opening Times: Bank Hol Mons May 1, 29 & Aug 28; Suns in May to Sept inclusive 2–5.30. Adm £1.50, Chd (under 15) 70p.
Refreshments: In stable yard June to Sept inclusive.

SALISBURY

THE KING'S HOUSE
Telephone: Salisbury (0722) 332151   ♿
(Salisbury & South Wiltshire Museum)

The King's House is a Grade 1 listed building dating from the 13th century and is one of the finest houses in the Cathedral Close. It is also the home of the award-winning Salisbury and South Wiltshire Museum with highly-praised galleries on Stonehenge, Early Man, Old Sarum and Salisbury (with its famous Giant and Hob Nob), the Pitt Rivers collection, pictures, ceramics, a pre-N.H.S. surgery and the new Wedgwood room. Temporary exhibitions and lectures throughout the year. Winner – Special Judges' Award, Museum of the Year Award 1985. Winner – Certificate of Distinction, BTA 'Come to Britain' Trophy 1986. **Costume gallery opening 1989.**

Location: In Salisbury Cathedral Close opposite the west door.
Station: Salisbury.
Opening Times: House & Museum. Apr to Sept—Mons to Sats 10–5; Oct to Mar—Mons to Sats 10–4; Suns in July & Aug 2–5. Closed Christmas. Adm £1.50, Chd 50p, OAPs/Students/Unemployed £1. Gift shop.
Refreshments: Apr to Sept. Party bookings all year.

MOMPESSON HOUSE, The National Trust
Fine Queen Anne town house, furnished as the home of a Georgian gentleman; walled garden.

Location: In Cathedral Close on N side of Choristers' Green.
Station: Salisbury (½ m).
Opening Times: Mar 25 to Oct 29—Mons, Tues, Weds, Sats & Suns 12.30–6 (or dusk if earlier). Adm £1.50, Chd 70p. *No reduction for parties.* No dogs.

OLD SARUM
Telephone: (0722) 335398

On the summit of a hill north of Salisbury, huge ramparts and earth mounds are silhouetted against the skyline. Ancient Britons fortified the hill-top which was later inhabited by Romans, Saxons and Normans. Parts of an 11th century castle remain and the foundations of two successive cathedrals are marked on the grass.

Location: 2 m (3.2 km) north of Salisbury. OS map ref SU138327.
Opening Times: Good Friday to Sept 30, daily 10–6; Oct 1 to Maundy Thursday, daily 10–4. *Closed Mons, Christmas and New Year.* Adm 80p, OAPs 60p, Chd 40p.

SALISBURY LIBRARY *(Wiltshire County Council)*
Market Place. Tel: (0722) 24145.

Three art galleries with frequently changing loan exhibitions and exhibitions by local artists. Fine collection of 19th century watercolours (the Edwin Young Collection) and Creasey Collection of Contemporary Art permanently housed in the Library. For further details telephone above No.

SAVERNAKE

TOTTENHAM HOUSE
Telephone: Marlborough 870331
(The Trustees of the Savernake Estate)

Tottenham House, built by the Marquess of Ailesbury, was originally designed by Burlington and built in the early 18th century. About one hundred years later the house was completely rebuilt by Thomas Cundy although some evidence of Burlington's work still remains. The house is let to Hawtreys Preparatory School.

Location: 3 m A4; 6 m Marlborough.
Opening Times: HOUSE ONLY. Open in School holidays—Jan 2–6 1–4 pm; Mar 20–24, and 27–31, Apr 3–7, Aug 28–Sept 1, 4–8: 2–5 pm. Adm £1, Chd (under 14) 50p. No reductions. There are steps to the front door (although there is assistance permanently available), thereafter every room open to the public is on one floor, and the property could not strictly be described as unsuitable for the disabled. Car park.
Refreshments: Savernake Forest Hotel ½ m.

STOURTON

STOURHEAD, The National Trust
Telephone: Bourton (0747) 840348   ♿

The world famous garden was laid out 1741–80; its lakes, temples and rare trees forming a landscape of breath-taking beauty throughout the year. Palladian House designed in 1722 by Colen Campbell. Furniture by Thomas Chippendale the Younger.

Location: 3 m NW of Mere (A303) in the village of Stourton off the Frome/Mere Road (B3092).
Opening Times: HOUSE: Apr & Oct—Sats to Weds 2–6 (or sunset if earlier); May to end Sept—Sat to Thurs 2–6 (or sunset if earlier). *Other times by written arrangement with the Administrator.* Adm £2.50, Chd £1.30. Parties of 15 or more £1.70. GARDENS: All the year—Daily 8–7 (or dusk if earlier). Adm £2, Chd £1. Parties of 15 or more £1.60 (half-price Dec to Feb) May and June £2.50, Chd £1.30, Parties £1.70. Dogs in gardens Oct to end of Feb only. Wheelchairs provided—access to gardens only.
Refreshments: Accommodation, Spread Eagle Inn at Garden entrance, (0747) 840587. National Trust Shop.

SWINDON

GREAT WESTERN RAILWAY MUSEUM
(Thamesdown Borough Council)
Faringdon Road. Tel: (0793) 26161. Ext. 3131.

Historic G.W.R. locomotives, wide range of name-plates, models, illustrations, posters, tickets etc. Mon to Sat 10–5; Sun 2–5. Adm £1, Chld and OAPs 50p (admits also to Railway Village Museum). Party rates.

MOBILE MUSEUM *(Thamesdown Borough Council)*
Bath Road. Tel: (0793) 26161, Ext. 3129.

An ex-Swindon Corporation Transport double-deck bus, purchased and converted through the sponsorship of Burmah Oil and the Area Museum Council for the South-West, to form part of our Schools Service, though it is available for public viewing at Open Days, Fetes, etc. A new exhibition is mounted every term, and adm is free.

MUSEUM AND ART GALLERY *(Thamesdown Borough Council)*

Bath Road. Tel: (0793) 26161, Ext. 3129.

Archaeology, natural history and geology of Wiltshire; local bygones, coins and tokens; the Manners collection of pot lids and ware; the Wiltshire Yeomanry room. Permanent 20th century British art and ceramic collection alternating with travelling exhibitions. Mon to Sat 10–6; Sun 2–5. Adm free.

RAILWAY VILLAGE MUSEUM *(Thamesdown Borough Council)*

34 Faringdon Road. Tel: (0793) 26161, Ext. 3136.

A foreman's house in the original G.W.R. Village, refurnished as it was at the turn of the century. Mon to Sat 10–1, 2–5; Sun 2–5. Adm 40p, Chld and OAPs 20p.

TEFFONT MAGNA

FITZ HOUSE GARDEN

(Major & Mrs Mordaunt-Hare)

Lovely hillside terraced gardens frame a listed group of beautiful ancient stone buildings in one of Wiltshire's prettiest villages. 16th/17th century House (not shown) admired by Nikolaus Pevsner in his Wiltshire Guide. The gardens, bordered by yew and beech hedges and a stream, are a haven of tranquillity, planted with spring bulbs and blossom, azaleas, roses and clematis of all types, honeysuckles, vines and mixed borders. Something of interest throughout the season including much new planting during the last three years. Many scented plants.

Location: On B3089 Barford St Martin (A30) to Mere Road (A303) in the village; 10 m W of Salisbury on direct route Wilton House-Stourhead.
Opening Times: GARDEN ONLY: Easter Sun to end Sept: Suns 2–6; also Sats May 20 and June 17 for the National Gardens Scheme. No dogs. No coaches.

TISBURY

OLD WARDOUR CASTLE

Telephone: (0747) 870487

The ruins stand in a romantic lakeside setting as a result of landscaping and planting in the 18th century. French in style and designed more for living than defence, the castle was built in 1393 by the fifth Lord Lovel, a campaigner in France. It was badly damaged in the Civil War and never repaired. The 18th century Banqueting House contains a small display about the 'Capability' Brown landscape.

Location: 2 m (3.2 km) south of Tisbury. OS map ref ST939263.
Opening Times: Good Friday to Sept 30, daily 10–6; Oct 1 to Maundy Thursday, 10–4 weekends only. *Closed Christmas and New Year.* Adm 80p, OAPs 60p, Chd 40p.

PYTHOUSE

(Country Houses Association Ltd)

Palladian style Georgian mansion.

Location: 2½ m W of Tisbury; 4½ m N of Shaftesbury.
Station: Tisbury (2½ m).
Opening Times: May to Sept—Weds & Thurs 2–5. Adm £1, Chd 50p. Free car park. No dogs admitted.

TROWBRIDGE

TROWBRIDGE MUSEUM *(Trowbridge Town Council)*

Civic Hall.

Interesting articles, pictures, etc. associated with the town's past. Open Tues and Sat mornings.

WESTBURY

CHALCOT HOUSE

(Mr & Mrs Anthony Rudd)

Small 16th century Palladian Manor.

Location: 2 m W of Westbury on A3098 to Frome.
Station: Dilton Marsh (1½ m).
Opening Times: Aug—Daily 2–5. Adm £1.50 including brochure. *Parties at other times by arrangement.*
Refreshments: By arrangement.

WILTON

WILTON HOUSE

(The Earl of Pembroke)

Superb 17th Century state rooms by Inigo Jones (c. 1650) and later James Wyatt (1810). World famous collection of paintings and other treasures. Exhibitions of 7,000 model soldiers set in Diorama scenes, also 'The Pembroke Palace dolls house' and historical tableau of dolls and toys through the ages. Miniature model railway and Adventure Playground. Notable fine cedar trees and Palladian Bridge. Restricted viewing of Double and Single Cube rooms due to restoration. Video of these rooms will be shown. Some exterior restoration work. 14th century Washern Grange, the Holbein Porch and Hunting room may be seen by appointment. Garden Centre.

Location: In town of Wilton, 3 m W of Salisbury on A30. Trains from Waterloo and many other southern and western region stations to Salisbury. Buses from Salisbury Centre every 10 mins.
Station: Salisbury 2½ m. Buses every 10 mins. from Salisbury.
Opening Times: HOUSE and GROUNDS: Mar 24 to Oct 15—Tues to Sats & Bank Hol Mons 11–6; Suns 1–6. Last adm to House & Grounds 5.15. Adm House & Grounds £2.40, OAPs, Students and parties (20 or over) £2, Chd (under 16) £1.80. Adm to HOUSE, GROUNDS and EXHIBITIONS: £3.40, OAPs, Students and parties £2.90, Chd (under 16) £2.50. GROUNDS ONLY: £1.30, Chd 90p. GROUNDS/EXHIBITIONS: £2.30, Chd £1.60. Free car park. No dogs, except guide dogs for the blind.
Refreshments: Licensed Restaurant—self-service.

THE WILTON ROYAL CARPET FACTORY

Wilton (3 miles west of Salisbury on A36) Tel: (0722) 742441, ext. 239.

The oldest carpet factory in the world, occupying the same site since 1655. Exhibition of carpet making crafts, and tour of modern factory. Two museums and photo-gallery. Schools hall, teacher and student facilities. Coffee shop. Reduction for parties over 16, who should book in advance.

WOODFORD

HEALE GARDENS AND PLANT CENTRE

Telephone: Middle Woodford (072 273) 504
(Major David & Lady Anne Rasch)

Winner of Christie's/HHA Garden of the Year 1984 award. Early Carolean manor house where King Charles II hid during his escape. The garden provides an interesting and varied collection of plants, shrub, musk and other roses, growing in the formal setting of clipped hedges and mellow stonework, at their best in June and July. Particularly attractive in Spring and Autumn is the water garden, planted with Magnolia and Acers, surrounding an authentic Japanese Tea House and Nikko Bridge. Many of these plants are for sale in the plant centre.

Location: 4 m N of Salisbury on the Woodford Valley road between A345 and A360.
Opening Times: Garden: Mons to Sats and first Sun of the month and Bank Hols from Easter to Autumn 11–5. **Plant Centre and Shop open throughout the year.** Tours of the house for parties over 20 by arrangement with Lady Anne Rasch.
Refreshments: Lunches & Teas in the House for parties over 20 by arrangement.

WROUGHTON

SCIENCE MUSEUM

Red Barn Gate.

Gala Open Day: Sun, Sept 10, 1989. Also open on selected days in May, June, July and Aug. For further details telephone (0793) 814466 or 01-938 8080.

AVEBURY MANOR

Original oak panelling

Plasterwork ceilings

Topiary

Rose centre

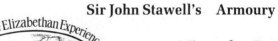

Sir John Stawell's   Armoury

Minstrels   Jugglers

Strolling players

Elizabethan market square

Walled rose and herb gardens   Adventure playground   Falconry demonstrations

16th century Dovecote and much much more

AVEBURY MANOR, WILTSHIRE
All Enquiries Telephone: (06723) 203

"Do please let this one scene fasten upon your memory. Whatever memories of England you carry away, let this be uppermost. For this, to me, is England." *R.C. Hutchinson, novelist.*

FOR ADMISSION DETAILS – SEE EDITORIAL REFERENCE

North Yorkshire

ALDBOROUGH

ALDBOROUGH ROMAN TOWN
Telephone: (090 12) 2768

The little village of Aldborough lies within the bounds of what was once the rich Roman city Isurium Brigantum, Aldborough has even retained part of the Roman street plan—a regular grid with a central open space, once the forum. Part of the Roman town walls survive, and two mosaic pavements may be seen in their original positions. A remarkable collection of Roman objects is on display in the Museum.

Location: ¾ m (1 km) east of Boroughbridge. OS map ref SE405667.
Opening Times: Good Friday to Sept 30, daily 10–6; Oct 1 to Maundy Thursday, daily 10–4. *Closed Mons, Christmas and New Year.* Adm 80p, OAPs 60p, Chd 40p.

AYSGARTH

THE YORKSHIRE MUSEUM OF CARRIAGES & HORSE DRAWN VEHICLES
Yore Mill, By Aysgarth Falls.

CONEYSTHORPE

CASTLE HOWARD
Telephone: Coneysthorpe (065 384) 333
(The Hon. Simon Howard)

Designed by Vanbrugh 1699–1726 for the 3rd Earl of Carlisle assisted by Hawksmoor, who designed the Mausoleum. Fine collection of pictures, statuary and furniture. Beautiful park and grounds. Costume Galleries covering 18th to 20th centuries in the Stable Court. Displays changed every year.

Location: 15 m NE of York; 3 m off A64; 6 m W of Malton; 38 m Leeds; 36 m Harrogate; 22 m Scarborough; 50 m Hull.
Opening Times: Mar 20 to end Oct—Daily. House and Costume Galleries are open 11–4.30. Plant centre, rose gardens, grounds and cafeteria open 10. Adm charges not available at time of going to press. *Special terms for adult booked parties.*
Refreshments: Cafeteria. Licensed restaurant available for advance bookings.

COXWOLD

BYLAND ABBEY
Telephone: (034) 76614

Built in the shadow of the Hambledon Hills, this 12th century Cistercian monastery is still magnificent, both in size and workmanship. The area of the cloister, for example, is larger than either Fountains or Rievaulx Abbeys. Some of the carved stone details are particularly fine, and sections of medieval green and yellow glazed tile floor may be seen.

Location: 1 m (1.6 km) north east of Coxwold. OS map ref SE549789.
Opening Times: Good Friday to Sept 30, daily 10–6; Oct 1 to Maundy Thursday, daily 10–4. *Closed Mons, Christmas and New Year.* Adm 80p, OAPs 60p, Chd 40p.

NEWBURGH PRIORY
Telephone: Coxwold (034 76) 435
(Sir George Wombwell Bt)

Originally 12th century Augustinian Priory with 16th, 17th and 18th century alterations and additions. Rare water garden and collection of rock and alpine plants. Walled garden.

Location: 5 m from Easingwold off A19, 9 m from Thirsk.
Opening Times: May 10 to Aug 30—Weds and Suns, Easter Mon and Aug Bank Hol Mon. House open 2.30–4.45. Grounds 2–6. Adm House & Grounds £1.70, Chd 80p. Grounds only 70p, Chd 30p. *Other days for parties of 25 or more by appointment with the Administrator.*
Refreshments: In the Old Priory Kitchens.

SHANDY HALL
Telephone: Coxwold 465
(The Laurence Sterne Trust)

Exceptional medieval house altered and added to in 17th and 18th centuries but little changed since Laurence Sterne wrote '*A Sentimental Journey*' and most of '*Tristram Shandy*' there. Walled garden with unusual plants.

Location: 20 m from York via A19; 6 m from A19 at Easingwold; 8 m from Thirsk; 13 m from A1 at Dishforth.
Opening Times: June to Sept—Weds 2–4.30. Suns 2.30–4.30. *Any other day or time all year by appointment with Hon Curators.* Adm £1.50, Chd (accompanied) half-price. Book & handicrafts shop. Plants for sale.
Refreshments: Close by in village.

EMBSAY

YORKSHIRE DALES RAILWAY MUSEUM
(Yorkshire Dales Railway Museum Trust)
near Skipton (off A59). Tel: (0756) 4727.

Midland railway station and goods yard. Large collection of ex industrial steam and diesel locomotives. Also wagons and carriages.

HARROGATE

ART GALLERY *(Harrogate District Council)*
Library Buildings, Victoria Avenue. Tel: (0423) 503340.

Permanent collection of oils and watercolours. Many temporary exhibitions. Tel for details.

HARLOW CAR GARDENS
(The Northern Horticultural Society)

60 acres of ornamental gardens and woodlands.
Location: 1½ m from centre of Harrogate, Otley Road B6162.
Station: Harrogate (1½ m).
Opening Times: All the year—Daily 9–7.30 (or dusk if earlier). Adm charge. Free car park. Cafe. Shop and plant sales.

NIDDERDALE MUSEUM
King Street, Pateley Bridge.

ROYAL PUMP ROOM MUSEUM *(Harrogate District Council)*
opposite Valley Gardens. Tel: (0423) 503340.

The museum of spa history now restored to its former splendour.

HAWES

UPPER DALES FOLK MUSEUM *(North Yorkshire County Council)*
Station Yard. Tel: (096 97) 494.

Folk life trades and occupations of the upper Dales. Including sheep and hay farming, peat cutting, hand knitting, Wensleydale cheese making etc. Apr to Sept: Mon to Sat 11–5; Sun 2–5. Oct: Tues, Sat, Sun; Oct half term open every day. Adm charge.

HELMSLEY

DUNCOMBE PARK
(The Rt. Hon. Lord Feversham)

Two 18th century Temples. Landscaped Gardens.
Location: 1 m W of Helmsley.
Opening Times: Gardens only. May to Aug—Weds 10–4. Adm £1. *Apply to Tourist Information Centre, Helmsley Market Place. No access for cars.*

HELMSLEY CASTLE
Telephone: (0439) 70442

Even in its ruined state, Helmsley Castle is spectacular. Begun by Walter Espec shortly after the Norman Conquest, the huge earthworks—now softened to green valleys—are all that remain of this early castle. The oldest stonework is 12th century. Like many English castles, Helmsley rendered indefensible during the Civil War, when it belonged to the notorious George Villiers, Duke of Buckingham. It was abandoned as a great house when its owners built nearby Duncombe Park.

Location: Helmsley. OS map ref SE611836.
Opening Times: Good Friday to Sept 30, daily 10–6; Oct 1 to Maundy Thursday, daily 10–4. *Closed Mons, Christmas and New Year.* Adm £1.10, OAPs 80p, Chd 55p.

NUNNINGTON HALL
Telephone: Nunnington 283
(The National Trust)

Sixteenth century manor house with fine panelled hall and staircase. Carlisle Collection of Miniature Rooms on display.

Location: In Ryedale; 4½ m SE of Helmsley; 1½ m N of B1257.
Opening Times: Easter to end Oct. Closed Good Fri. Open Bank Hol Mons 12–6. Mar 25–30, and Apr weekends only 2–6; May, June, Sept & Oct—Tues, Weds, Thurs, Sats & Suns 2–6; July & Aug—Tues, Weds, Thurs & Sats 2–6; Suns 12–6. Last admission 5.30. School Parties on weekdays by arrangement with administrator. Adm £1.80, Chd 90p, Parties £1.50, Chd 70p. Access to Ground Floor and tearoom only for Wheelchairs. Lavatory for disabled at rear of house. Access to main gardens via ramp. Guide dogs permitted. Dogs in car park only.
Refreshments: Afternoon teas available at all times when house is open 2–5.30 in indoor tearooms or tea garden. Lunches July & Aug. Shop.

RIEVAULX ABBEY
Telephone: (043 96) 228

The fluctuating fortunes of the abbey may be read from the ruins. Within two decades of its foundation in 1131, Rievaulx—the first Cistercian monastery in the north—was vast, with 140 monks and 500 lay brothers. A costly building programme followed, and it is little wonder that by the 13th century the monastery was heavily in debt, and buildings were being reduced in size. By the Dissolution in the 16th century, there were only 22 monks. The church is a beautiful example of early English Gothic. New visitor centre with exhibition and shop.

Location: 3 miles (4.8 km) north west of Helmsley. OS map ref SE577849.
Opening Times: Good Friday to Sept 30, daily 10–6; Oct 1 to Maundy Thursday, daily 10–4. *Closed Mons, Christmas and New Year.* Adm £1.30, OAPs £1, Chd 65p.

RIEVAULX TERRACE, The National Trust
Telephone: Bilsdale 340   &

Beautiful half mile long grass terrace with views of Rievaulx Abbey. Two 18th century Temples and permanent exhibition.

Location: 2½ m NW of Helmsley on Stokesley Road (B1257).
Opening Times: Good Friday to Oct 29 — Daily 10.30–6 (last adm 5.30). Ionic Temple closed 1–2. Adm £1.30, Chd 60p, Parties £1.10, Chd 50p. All dogs on leash. Battery operated 'Runabout' available.
Refreshments: Teas available at Nunnington Hall, 7 m E.

HOVINGHAM

HOVINGHAM HALL
(Sir Marcus & Lady Worsley)

Palladian house designed c. 1760 by Thomas Worsley. Unique Riding School, magnificent yew hedges, dovecot, private cricket ground. Family portraits.

Location: 20 m N of York on Malton/Helmsley Road (B1257).
Opening Times: Open for parties of 15 or more **by written appointment only** — Apr 18 to Sept 28, Tues, Weds & Thurs 11–7. Adm £2, Chd £1.
Refreshments: At the Hall by arrangement. Meals at The Worsley Arms, Hovingham.

HUTTON-LE-HOLE

RYEDALE FOLK MUSEUM *(Crosland Foundation)*
Tel: (075 15) 367.

Open-air museum with interesting collection of rescued buildings rebuilt on an attractive 2½ acre site. Includes a medieval long-house with a witch-post and a 16th century manor house, both cruck-framed and thatched; an 18th/19th century furnished cottage; an Elizabethan glass furnace; workshops with extensive collections of tools of many 19th century crafts. Varied collections illustrating the folk life of Ryedale. Mar 19 to Oct 31: Daily 11–6 (last adm 5.15). Adm charge.

KIRBY WISKE

SION HILL HALL
Telephone: Thirsk (0845) 587206
(The H W Mawer Trust)

Neo-Georgian country house by Walter Brierley, with fine collection of furniture, paintings and porcelain from most periods. R.I.B.A. Architectural Award Winner.

Location: 6 m S of Northallerton, 4 m W of Thirsk, ½ m off A167 signpost Kirby Wiske.
Opening Times: Last Sun in month May–Sept incl. 2–4.30, other times organised groups only by arrangement with the Curator. Adm £2, Chd under 12 free if accompanied. Free parking for cars or coaches.
Refreshments: Teas on open Suns only at Village Hall.

KNARESBOROUGH

ALLERTON PARK
Telephone: (0423) 330927
(The Gerald Arthur Rolph Foundation for Historic Preservation and Education)

The grandest of the surviving Gothic revival stately homes. Its Great Hall and Dining Room are considered amongst the finest carved wood rooms in England. Allerton Park is the ancestral home of Lord Mowbray (c. 1283), Segrave (c. 1283) and Stourton (c. 1448), the premier Baron in England. House designed by George Martin, some interior rooms by Benjamin Baud. Temple of Victory built by Frederick, Duke of York (brother to King George IV) in 18c. The setting for Sherlock Holmes film 'The Sign of Four'. Private collection of mechanical music machines and luxury antique motor cars.

Location: 14½ m W of York; ¼ m E of A1 on York Road (A59); 4½ m W of Knaresborough, 6 m N of Wetherby; 7 m S of Boroughbridge; 14 m N of Leeds.
Opening Times: Easter Sun to end Sept – Suns and Bank Holiday Mons 12–5. Adm House and Grounds £2.50. Students, OAPs and Parties (25 and over) £2. Chd (under 16) with adult £1.50. School Groups £1 each. Free car parking. No dogs, except guide dogs for the blind. Other days by appointment for parties of 25 or more. Enquiries to: Mr. Farr, Administrator, Allerton Park, nr. Knaresborough, N. Yorkshire HG5 0SE. Tel: (0423) 330927.
Refreshments: By request.

KNARESBOROUGH CASTLE AND OLD COURTHOUSE MUSEUM
(Harrrogate District Council)
Castle Grounds. Tel: (0423) 503340.
Local history.

LEYBURN

BOLTON CASTLE
Telephone: (0969) 23981/23674
(The Hon. Harry Orde-Powlett)

One of Britain's best preserved medieval castles now in the first stages of redecoration and refurbishment with period tapestries, arms and suits of armour, a manuscript room and tableaux depicting everyday life in the fifteenth and sixteenth centuries.

Location: Situated within the Yorkshire Dales National Park, 5 m W of Leyburn, 10 m E of Hawes, road signs from the A684.
Opening Times: Daily, Mar to end Oct: 10–5; Nov to Mar – tours by special arrangement. Party visits welcomed: groups of 25 and over, 10 per cent discount and one person free. Car park. Modern toilet facilities.
Refreshments: Tea room with homemade light refreshments. Under cover.

CONSTABLE BURTON HALL
Telephone: Bedale 50428
(M. C. A. Wyvill, Esq.)

Extensive borders, interesting alpines, large informal garden. John Carr house completed in 1768.

Location: On A684, between Leyburn (3 m) & Bedale; A1 (7 m).
Opening Times: Gardens. May 1 to Aug 1 — Daily 9–6. Adm 50p (1987 charge), collecting box.
House: opening dates & adm charges not available at time of going to press. Party rates by arrangement.

LINTON-ON-OUSE

BENINGBROUGH HALL
Telephone: York (0904) 470666   &
(The National Trust)

This handsome Georgian house has been completely restored and in the principal rooms are 100 famous portraits on loan from the National Portrait Gallery. Victorian laundry, potting shed and exhibitions. Garden and Adventure Playground.

Location: 8 m NW of York; 3 m W of Shipton (A19); 2 m SE Linton-on-Ouse; follow signposted route.
Opening Times: Easter to end Oct; Mar 24–30, 12–6. Apr weekends 12–6, School groups & parties on weekdays by prior appointment. May to Oct — Tues, Weds, Thurs, Sats, Suns & Bank Hol Mons 12–6, last adm 5.30. Adm House & Garden £2.50, Chd (accompanied) £1.20. Family ticket (2 adults, 2 Chd) £6.20. Parties £2, Chd £1. Garden & Exhibitions £1.70, Chd (accompanied) 80p. Picnic area. Shop. No dogs. Wheelchairs provided.
Refreshments: The Restaurant serves homemade hot & cold lunches, teas, special suppers. Wheelchair access. Picnic area. Kiosk. Special functions catered for, details from the Administrator.

MALTON

KIRKHAM PRIORY
Telephone: (065 381) 768

The patrons of this monastery, the Lords of Helmsley, are still much in evidence. Their coats of arms adorn the gatehouse, and four family graves have survived amid the ruins of the Church. Built for the monks the Augustinian Order, or Black Canons, Kirkham was founded early in the 12th century by Walter Espec, who also founded Rievaulx Abbey.

Location: 5 m (8 km) south west of Malton. OS map ref SE735657.
Opening Times: Good Friday to Sept 30, daily 10–6; Oct 1 to Maundy Thursday, daily 10–4. *Closed Mons, Christmas and New Year.* Adm 80p, OAPs 60p, Chd 40p.

MALTON MUSEUM
Town Hall, Market Place. Tel: (0653) 695136 or 692610.
Extensive Romano-British collections from the Malton District and the Roman Derventio Fortress, also prehistoric and Medieval material.

MIDDLEHAM

MIDDLEHAM CASTLE
Telephone: (0969) 23899

The great days of Middleham were in the 14th and 15th centuries, when it was the stronghold of the mighty Neville family. After the death of Richard Neville – 'Warwick the Kingmaker' – in 1471, the castle was forfeited to the Crown. The dominant feature of the castle is the great keep, one of the largest in England.

Location: 2 m (3.2 km) south of Leyburn. OS map ref SE128875.
Opening Times: Good Friday to Sept 30, daily 10–6; Oct 1 to Maundy Thursday, daily 10–4. *Closed Mons, Christmas and New Year.* Adm 80p, OAPs 60p, Chd 40p.

NORTHALLERTON

MOUNT GRACE PRIORY
Telephone: (0609) 83249

These 14th century ruins provide a rare opportunity to study the plan of a Carthusian monastery, or 'charterhouse'. The Carthusian monks lived like hermits—in seclusion not only from the world, but from each other. They met together only in chapel, and for religious feasts. Every monk had his own cell—21 in all—a tiny two-storey house with its own garden and workshop. And each cell had running water—a remarkable luxury in the Middle Ages.

Location: 7 miles (11.3 km) north east of Northallerton. OS map ref SE453982.
Opening Times: Good Friday to Sept 30, daily 10–6; Oct 1 to Maundy Thursday, daily 10–4. *Closed Mons, Christmas and New Year.* Adm £1.10, OAPs 80p, Chd 55p.

PICKERING

BECK ISLE MUSEUM OF RURAL LIFE
Regency residence of William Marshall, a noted agriculturist of the late 18th and early 19th centuries. Situated in the centre of an historic town, the many rooms house a considerable collection illustrating the work, social life and customs of the rural community during the past 200 years. Of educational interest to all ages. Apr 1 to end Oct: Daily 10–12.30, 2–5 (Aug 10–6). Adm charge. Parties by arrangement.

PICKERING CASTLE
Telephone: (0751) 74989

Most of the medieval kings visited Pickering Castle. They came to hunt deer and wild boar in the neighbouring forest. It was a sport of which they were inordinately fond, and the royal forests were zealously guarded. Romantics may like to speculate as to why Rosamund's Tower has been linked with 'Fair Rosamund', mistress of Henry II. They should, however, be aware that the tower was built in 1323, a century after the lady died.

Location: Pickering. OS map ref SE800845.
Opening Times: Good Friday to Sept 30, daily 10–6; Oct 1 to Maundy Thursday, daily 10–4. *Closed Mons, Christmas and New Year.* Adm £1.10, OAPs 80p, Chd 55p.

REETH

SWALEDALE FOLK MUSEUM
Reeth, near Richmond. Tel: (0748) 84373.
Depicts how leadmining and sheep farming shaped life in this remote and beautiful Dale.

RICHMOND

EASBY ABBEY
Telephone: (0748) 5224

Founded in 1155 by the wealthy Scrope family, Easby was a monastery of the white-robed Premonstratensian Order. The gatehouse looks much as it did in the 14th century a staircase on the outer wall led to the upper floor where the abbot held his court. Some fine canopied choir stalls taken from Easby when it dissolved may be seen in Richmond parish church, a mile of pleasant riverside walk away.

Location: 1 m (1.6 km) east of Richmond. OS map ref NZ185003.
Opening Times: Good Friday to Sept 30, daily 10–6; Oct 1 to Maundy Thursday, daily 10–4. *Closed Mons, Christmas and New Year.* Adm 80p, OAPs 60p, Chd 40p.

THE GREEN HOWARDS MUSEUM
Trinity Church Square. Tel: (0748) 2133.
Uniform, medals, campaign relics, contemporary MSS, pictures and prints, headdress, buttons, badges and embellishments from 17th century onwards. Apr to Oct: Weekdays 9.30–4.30; Sun 2–4.30. Nov, Feb and Mar: Weekdays 10–4.30. *Closed Sun Nov, Feb and Mar and throughout Dec and Jan.*

RICHMOND CASTLE
Telephone: (0748) 2493

Surrounded on three sides by high moorland, Richmond Castle is in a strongly defensible position. However, the castle has seen little active service, which accounts for the remarkable amount of early Norman stonework that has survived. Built by Alan the Red, shortly after 1066, the castle went with the title 'Duke of Richmond' and has had many royal and powerful owners.

Location: Richmond. OS map ref NZ174006.
Opening Times: Good Friday to Sept 30, daily 10–6; Oct 1 to Maundy Thursday, daily 10–4. *Closed Mons, Christmas and New Year.* Adm £1.30 OAPs £1, Chd 65p.

THE RICHMONDSHIRE MUSEUM
(The Richmondshire Museum Trust)
Ryders Wynd. Tel: (0748) 5611.
The history of Richmond. Cruck House, lead and copper mining; farming; needlecrafts. Model of Richmond railway complex; local crafts; displays of Victorian and Edwardian costumes and children's toys; Herriot Surgery Set from TV series. Mar 24 to Oct 29: 11–5. Parties by appointment. Adm 40p, Chld/OAPs 20p. Hon Curator: Mr L.P. Wenham.

RIPLEY

RIPLEY CASTLE
Telephone: Harrogate (0423) 770152
(Sir Thomas Ingilby Bt)

Has been the home of the Ingilby family since early 14th century. Main gateway dates from reign of Edward IV. Extensive gardens.

Location: In Ripley 3½ m N Harrogate; 7½ m from Ripon.
Opening Times: Castle: Apr, May and Oct—Sats & Suns, 11.30–4.30; June to Oct (incl)—Daily except Mons and Fri 11.30–4.30. Good Friday and all Bank Holidays in season 11–4.30. Booked parties: Groups can visit the castle on any day during the year, by prior appointment. Gardens only: Daily Apr 1 to Oct.
Refreshments: Licensed restaurant (The Butlers Pantry) in village: Tearoom in castle courtyard, serving home-made teas.

RIPON

FOUNTAINS ABBEY & STUDLEY ROYAL, The National Trust
Ruins of Cistercian monastery. Ornamental gardens laid out by John Aislabie, 1720. Exhibition and video film in Fountains Hall. Awarded World Heritage status.

Location: 2m W of Ripon; 9 m W of Harrogate; NW of A61.
Opening Times: DEER PARK. Open all year during daylight hours, adm free. ABBEY & GARDENS. Jan, Feb, Mar, Nov & Dec—Daily except Christmas Eve, Christmas Day and Fri in Jan, Nov & Dec 10–5 or dusk if earlier. Apr, May, June & Sept 10–7; July & Aug 10–8; Oct 10–6 or dusk if earlier. FOUNTAINS HALL. Apr to Sept, 11–6; Oct to Mar, 1–4. Adm £1.90, Chd 90p. Family ticket £4.70 (2 Adults/2 Chd). Parties (up to 40) £1.50, Chd 70p. Parties of 40 and more (Mon to Fri) £1.30, Chd 60p. Car parking: Cars 70p, Motorcycles 30p. Coaches (Mon to Fri) no charge, Sat & Sun £3. *Closed Christmas Eve & Christmas Day.*
Refreshments: Light lunches, sandwiches, cakes, soup, tea, coffee, cold drinks available Studley Cafe, Studley Park. Open Jan to end March, 11–5; Apr to Oct, 10–5.30; Oct to Jan, 11–5. Fountains Cafe open Apr to Oct 10–5.30. Nov and Dec: weekends only 11–5. Wheelchair access. Picnics can be taken anywhere on Estate. Dogs on leashes only. Studley Royal Shop—Tel: (0765) 4246. Open all year Jan to end Mar, 11–5. Apr to Oct, 10–6 and Oct to Dec, 11–5. Abbey Stores – open Apr – Oct 10–5.

MARKENFIELD HALL
(The Lord Grantley, MC)

Fine example of English manor house 14th, 15th & 16th century buildings surrounded by moat.

Location: 3 m S of Ripon off the Ripon/Harrogate Road (A61). Access is up a road marked 'Public Bridleway Hell Wath Lane'.
Opening Times: Apr to Oct—Mons 10–12.30, 2.15–5. Adm 50p, Chd (accompanied by adult) free. Exterior only outside courtyard and moat all other days in May—times as above. Adm free.

NEWBY HALL & GARDENS
Telephone: (0423) 322583
(R. E. J. Compton, Esq.)

One of the most famous Adam houses beautifully redecorated, contains superb Gobelins tapestries, fine collection of antique sculpture and furniture. 25 acres of glorious Gardens. Miniature Railway through the Gardens and Adventure Gardens for children. Woodland discovery walk. Steam boat on Suns. Gift shop. Plant stall. Picnic area.

Location: 4 m SE of Ripon on Boroughbridge Road (B6265). 3 m W of A1; 14 m Harrogate; 20 m York; 35 m Leeds; 32 m Skipton.
Opening Times: Mar 24 to Oct 29—Daily except Mons (but open Bank Hol Mons). House open until Oct 1 from 12–5. Garden open until Oct 29, 11–5.30 last adm 5 pm. Adm charges not available at time of going to press. Enquiries to: Opening Administrator, The Estate Office, Newby Hall, Ripon HG4 5AE.
Refreshments: Licensed Restaurant for lunches & teas in the Garden Restaurant.

NORTON CONYERS
Telephone: Melmerby (076 584) 333
(Sir James Graham, Bt)

This late medieval house with Jacobean and Georgian additions has belonged to the Grahams since 1624. James I, Charles I and James II stayed here. Family pictures, furniture and wedding dresses. Relics of Charlotte Brontë who paid a visit in 1839, the house is one of the originals of Thornfield Hall in 'Jane Eyre', and a family legend was reputedly the inspiration for the mad Mrs Rochester.

Location: 3½ m NW of Ripon nr Wath; 1½ m from A1.
Opening Times: Suns from June 4 to Sept 17, also all Bank Holiday Suns & Mons, and daily from July 29 to Aug 5, 2–5.30. Any time for booked parties; inquiries to Beatrice, Lady Graham at above address. Adm £1.50, Chd (4–14) 70p, OAPs £1, parties of 15 or more £1. Small gift shop, free parking. Dogs (excluding guide dogs) in grounds only. Visitors are requested not to wear stiletto heels.
Interesting **Small Garden Centre** in the 18th century walled garden, specialising in unusual hardy plants. Open all year Mons to Fris 9–5; Sats & Suns Apr 1 to Oct 1, 2–5.30.
Refreshments: Bank holiday and charity openings. Also for booked parties by request.

RIPON PRISON AND POLICE MUSEUM
St. Marygate. Tel: (0765) 3706.

A former Victorian prison with cells converted to museum use. The displays deal with crime, punishment, imprisonment and law enforcement over recent centuries. May to Sept: Daily 1.30–5; (July/Aug: Mon–Sat 11–5). Groups welcome by appointment, at other times. Free car park opposite.

SCARBOROUGH

EBBERSTON HALL
(W. de Wend Fenton, Esq.)

Palladian Villa of 1718 designed by the architect Colin Campbell. Water gardens attributed to William Benson and Switzer. Elaborate woodwork and cornices comparable to Castle Howard and Beningbrough.

Location: 11 m W of Scarborough on A170 Scarborough/Pickering Road.
Opening Times: Easter to Oct 1 – Daily 10–6. Adm £1.50.

ROTUNDA MUSEUM *(Scarborough Borough Council)*
Vernon Road. Tel: (0723) 374839.

Archaeological collections of all periods represented in N.E. Yorkshire. Local history and bygones.

SCARBOROUGH ART GALLERY
(Scarborough Borough Council)
The Crescent. Tel: (0723) 374753.

Local artists. Laughton Collection (English School). Frequent loan exhibitions.

SCARBOROUGH CASTLE
Telephone: (072 3) 72451

Standing on the massive headland between the North and South Bays, the castle commands magnificent views. There was a prehistoric settlement here, and a Roman signal station, but the first mention of the castle is in the 12th century, when it was seized by Henry II. During the Civil War the castle was besieged and changed hands several times. A hundred years later it was still in use to detain political prisoners – notably George Fox, founder of the Society of Friends (Quakers).

Location: East of town centre. OS map ref TA050893.
Opening Times: Good Friday to Sept 30, daily 10–6; Oct 1 to Maundy Thursday, daily 10–4. *Closed Mons, Christmas and New Year.* Adm £1.10, OAPs 80p, Chd 55p.

WOOD END MUSEUM *(Scarborough Borough Council)*
The Crescent. Tel: (0723) 367326.

Former home of Sitwell family; two rooms devoted to paintings and first editions of this literary family. Exhibitions of local natural history and geology. Conservatory and aquarium. Tues to Sat 10–1, 2–5; Sun (Spring Bank Hol to end Sept) 2–5. *Closed* Mon.

SETTLE

MUSEUM OF NORTH CRAVEN LIFE *(North Craven Heritage Trust)*
6 Chapel Street. Tel: (072 92) 2854.

The museum is situated in a 17th century building close to the centre of Settle. Includes a comprehensive permanent display illustrating the landscape, settlement, farming and other aspects of life in North Craven. Special exhibitions are mounted on special features and personalities connected with the locality. May to June: Sat, Sun 2–5. July to Sept: Daily (not Mon) 2–5. Oct to Apr: Sat 2–5. Small adm charge. (Please telephone for party bookings.) Suitable for disabled persons on ground floor only. Free public car park nearby.

SHERIFF HUTTON

SHERIFF HUTTON PARK
Telephone: Sheriff Hutton (034 77) 442
(The East 15 Acting School Limited)

Grade I historic house, originally King James I's Royal Hunting Lodge. Open to public are 3 rooms of significant importance and main staircase; they include 2 magnificent Jacobean plaster ceilings and a beautiful screens passage. Extensive grounds with routed walkways, picnic areas, lily pond, lake, statues. Croquet introduced here mid 19th Century by Leonard Thompson whose rules were published by Cordeaux & Ernest 1864.

Location: Park entrance clearly signposted ¼ m S of Sheriff Hutton village centre, at junction York and Flaxton/Lilling roads.
Opening Times: Apr 1 to Oct 31, daily except Mon 10–6. Winter weekends by appointment only. Adm £1, Chd/OAPs 50p, under 5 free. Group adm 12 – £10, 16 – £13, 50 – £40. Family ticket £2. Adequate free car parking. Section of grounds traversible in wheelchair by request, lift to ground floor rooms in Hall (no wheelchairs available). Sheriff Hutton Park is the venue of the Galtres Theatre Company and productions are frequently presented here and open to tourists. In 1989 numerous performances will be staged in the Company's new Greek-style amphitheatre by the lakeside.
Refreshments: Picnic venues and tearoom provided; hotel next door.

SKIPTON

CRAVEN MUSEUM
Town Hall, High Street. Tel: (0756) 4079.

Craven antiquities, social history, natural history, geology specimens. Apr to Sept: Mon, Wed, Thurs and Fri 11–5; Sat 10–12, 1–5; Sun 2–5. Oct to Mar: Mon, Wed, Thurs and Fri 2–5; Sat 10–12, 1.30–4.30.

SKIPTON CASTLE
Telephone: Skipton (0756) 2442

First-time visitors are delighted to discover that this most popular Yorkshire castle is still complete and fully roofed. Skipton Castle's massive mediaeval towers and beautiful Conduit Court featured on TV in 'Treasure Hunt'.

Location: Head of High Street.
Railway Station: (½ m).
Bus Station: (town centre).
Opening Times: Every day, except Christmas Day. Adm £1.60; under-18's half price; under-5's free! Everyone under 18 gets a Skipton Castle Explorer's badge. Guides are available for pre-booked parties; otherwise, illustrated Tour Sheets in English, French, German or Japanese are provided. Party visits are welcomed: School parties 80p each including accompanying adults; 10% discount for other parties of 15 or more. Large coach and car park nearby, off High Street.

SNAPE

THORP PERROW ARBORETUM
(Sir John & Lady Ropner)

60 acres of landscaped grounds containing an arboretum of over 2,000 species of trees and shrubs, including some of the largest and rarest in England.

Location: N of Ripon on the Well/Bedale Road.
Opening Times: End of Mar to end of Oct. Adm £1, Chd under 12 & OAPs 50p. Free car park. Picnic area.

SUTTON-ON-THE-FOREST

SUTTON PARK
Telephone: 0347 810249
(Mrs Sheffield)

Most welcoming early Georgian house, the home of Mrs Nancy Sheffield, built in 1730. Historical contents include Chippendale, Sheraton and French furniture, decorative plasterwork by Cortese, fine paintings and porcelain, with fresh flower arrangements in every room. Very beautiful landscaped gardens and parkland created by Capability Brown. Georgian Ice House, Woodland/Daffodil Walks, Nature Trail and Gift Shop.

Location: 8 m N of York; on the B1363 York/Helmsley road. Also signposted from the A19 York/Thirsk road in the Easingwold area.
Opening Times: GARDENS: open daily from Easter to Oct 1 (*except Sat*) from 11–5.30. HOUSE AND GARDENS: open all Easter weekend, Apr: Suns only from 1.30; May to Sept 12: Sun, Tues and Bank Holiday Mons from 1.30. Adm charges not available at time of going to press. Booked parties of 20 or more welcome every day. Contact: The Secretary, Sutton Park, Sutton-on-the-Forest, York, YO6 1DP. Tel: (0347) 810249.
Refreshments: Tea room/restaurant.

THIRSK

THIRSK MUSEUM
16 Kirkgate Y07 1PQ. Tel: (0845) 22755.

Local history and antiquities. Birthplace of Thomas Lord, founder of Lord's Cricket Ground. Open daily. Easter to end of Oct. Adm charge. Free car parking nearby.

WHITBY

PANNETT ART GALLERY *(Whitby Town Council)*
Pannett Park.

Collections of early and contemporary English watercolours and oil paintings; also works by Turner, Bonington, David Cox, Peter de Wint and the Weatherills. Special exhibitions in summer.

WHITBY ABBEY
Telephone: (0947) 603568

Founded in 655 and presided over by an abbess, Whitby was a double monastery for both men and women – a feature of the Anglo-Saxon church. This early history has been chronicled by the Venerable Bede, who tells us that here the poet Caedmon lived and worked. Destroyed by invading Danes in 857, the monastery was refounded after the Norman Conquest, but its exposed clifftop site continued to invite attack by sea pirates. The building remains are from the later Benedictine monastery.

Location: Whitby. OS map ref NZ904115.
Opening Times: Good Friday to Sept 30, daily 10–6; Oct 1 to Maundy Thursday, daily 10–4. *Closed Mons, Christmas and New Year.* Adm 80p, OAPs 60p, Chd 40p.

WHITBY MUSEUM OF WHITBY LITERARY AND PHILOSOPHICAL SOCIETY
Pannett Park. Tel: (0947) 602908.

Fine collection of fossils. Relics of prehistoric man and of Roman occupation. Local history and bygones. Shipping gallery. Captain Cook relics. Natural history. May to Sept: Weekdays 9.30–5.30; Sun 2–5. Oct to Apr: Weekdays 10.30–1 (Wed to Sat 2–4); Sun 2–4. Adm charge.

YORK

THE BAR CONVENT MUSEUM
Blossom Street YO2 2AH. Tel: (0904) 643238.
The Bar Convent Museum tells the fascinating story of Christianity in Britain. The Museum is housed in a beautiful eighteenth century building with a magnificent neo-classical chapel, built secretly in defiance of anti-Catholic laws. A permanent display outlines the progress of Christianity from Roman times through the turbulent Reformation to the founding and development of the Bar Convent. The story is brought up to date with the work of the Sisters today in an ecumenical world. Temporary exhibitions focus on aspects of Christian life and art and there is a varied lecture programme. On the upper floors of the building is a Youth Centre where visiting groups of children can stay for £12.50 including all meals. Open Mon–Sat 10–5; Sun 2–5. *Closed* New Years Day, Good Friday, Christmas Eve, Christmas Day, Boxing Day. Adm £1.75, Concessions £1.50, 5–16 year olds £1, Chld under 5 free. Family rate £3.50. 10% discount for pre-booked parties. Café and gift shop. The Museum is available for private viewings and receptions (by appointment). Coach parking by prior arrangement.

THE CHOCOLATE EXPERIENCE *(Rowntree plc)*
Rowntree plc Y01 1XY. Tel: (0904) 612261.
Sited on the banks of the River Foss in York 'The Chocolate Experience', believed to be the first visitors centre of its kind in the UK, is planned to open by the end of 1989. The centre will provide an opportunity to experience a chocolate factory environment from the turn of the century and include demonstrations of present day manufacturing processes. There will also be numerous exhibits and hands-on opportunities, fascinating activities using the latest high-tech forms of presentation and a chance to learn about Joseph Rowntree, the man who pioneered social welfare in the industry. 'The Chocolate Experience' is being designed to entertain, educate, and give enjoyment to the whole family. Admission charge.

CLIFFORD'S TOWER, YORK
Telephone: (0904) 646940.
York Castle, like the city itself, has had a long and turbulent history. Clifford's Tower was built on an earlier motte (or mound) in the 13th century. The tower is named after a Lancastrian leader from the Wars of the Roses, Sir Robert Clifford, who was defeated in 1322, and his body hung in chains from the tower.
Location: Near Castle Museum. OS map ref SE605515.
Opening Times: Good Friday to Sept 30, daily 10–6; Oct 1 to Maundy Thursday, daily 10–4. *Closed Christmas and New Year.* Adm 80p, OAPs 60p, Chd 40p.

FAIRFAX HOUSE *(York Civic Trust)*
Castlegate YO1 1RN. Tel: (0904) 655543.
An 18th century house designed by John Carr of York and described as a classic architectural masterpiece of its age. Certainly one of the finest townhouses in England and saved from near collapse by the York Civic Trust who restored it to its former glory during 1982/84. In addition to the superbly decorated plasterwork, wood and wrought iron, the house is now home for an outstanding collection of 18th century Furniture and Clocks, formed by the late Noel Terry. Described by Christie's as one of the finest private collections of this century, it enhances and complements the house and helps to create a very special 'lived in' feeling. The gift of the entire collection by Noel Terry's Trustees to the Civic Trust has enabled it to fill the house with appropriate pieces of the period and has provided the basis for what can now be considered a fully furnished Georgian Townhouse. Permanent exhibition on 'Life in Georgian York'. Open Mar 1 to Dec 31: Mon to Thurs and Sat 11–5; Sun 1.30–5 (last adm 4.30). *Closed* Fri. Adm £2, Chld 75p, OAP £1.75. Parties, Adult (prebooked 15 or more) £1.25, Chld 50p. Public car park within 50 yards. Suitable for disabled persons only with assistance (by telephoning beforehand staff can be available to help). A small gift shop offers selected antiques, publications and gifts. Opening times are the same as the house.

IMPRESSIONS GALLERY OF PHOTOGRAPHY
(Paul Wombell – Director)
17 Colliergate. Tel: (0904) 654724.
Impressions was the first photographic gallery to open outside London, in 1972. There are three gallery areas showing a wide range of photographic exhibitions, both contemporary and historical, also darkroom with courses and workshops. The gallery has an exciting photographic bookshop selling a variety of posters and postcards. Mon to Sat 10.30–5.30. *Closed* Bank Hols and the week between Christmas and New Year. Adm free. Unsuitable for disabled persons.

JORVIK VIKING CENTRE *(York Archaeological Trust)*
Coppergate. Tel: (0904) 643211.
Uncovered by archaeologists Jorvik is the Viking city untouched since the Vikings lived in York a thousand years ago. Cooking-ware, shoes, fragments of clothing. A market, busy wharf, houses re-created in accurate detail. The Viking Dig, reconstructed where it took place, with the preserved 10th century buildings replaced where they were found. Apr to Oct: Daily 9–7. Adm £2.75, Chld £1.35. Special rates (Nov to March incl), OAP's £2.

MERCHANT ADVENTURERS' HALL
Telephone: (0904) 654818
(The Governor and Company of Merchant Adventurers)
One of the finest surviving medieval gild halls in Europe.
Location: Next to Clifford's Tower, the Castle Museum and Fairfax House.
Station: York (½ m).
Opening Times: Mid-Mar to early Nov—Daily 8.30–5; early Nov to mid-Mar—Daily (except Sun) 8.30–3.30. Adm £1, OAPs 80p, Chd 50p. Suitable for the disabled, including lavatory for disabled. No car parking, except in city of York.

NATIONAL RAILWAY MUSEUM *(Science Museum)*
Leeman Road. Tel: (0904) 621261.
An internationally important collection of imposing locomotives and historic railway carriages, all beautifully restored to their former glory. Highlights are the steam-speed record holder "Mallard" and Queen Victoria's magnificent Saloon. An enormous range of memorabilia is displayed: Children's toys, tickets, ornate silverware, uniform buttons and intricately crafted models all help to tell the story of the railways in Britain. Telephone for details of locomotive working days and other activities. Open Mon to Sat 10–6; Sun 11–6, except Christmas Eve, Christmas Day, Boxing Day, New Year's Day. Restaurant, Gift Shop, Car Park. Facilities for disabled visitors. Adm £1.50; Chld, Student, Senior Citizen, disabled UB40 holder 75p; Parties £1.25/concessions 50p; Family Rate (2 adults and up to 3 children) £4.

TREASURER'S HOUSE, The National Trust
Telephone: York (0904) 624247
Large 17th century house of great interest. Fine furniture and paintings. Exhibition.
Location: Behind York Minster.
Station: York (½ m).
Opening Times: Good Friday to Oct 29—Daily 10.30–5. Last adm 4.30. Guided tours by arrangement. Adm £1.50, Chd 70p, Parties £1.30, Chd 60p. Wheelchair access—part of ground floor only. No car parking facilities. Dogs not allowed, except for guide dogs. Shop.
Refreshments: Available in licensed tea rooms serving morning coffee, light lunches, teas. Open for pre-booked parties during and outside normal opening hours and for private functions. Tel: York 646757.

YORK CASTLE MUSEUM *(York City Council)*
Eye of York YO1 1RY. Tel: (0904) 653611.
An outstanding social history museum based on the Kirk collection of bygones and including period rooms, a cobbled street, domestic and agricultural equipment, costumes, toys, arms and armour, an Edwardian street and park and a water-driven corn mill. Apr to Oct: Mon to Sat 9.30–last admission 5.30; Sun 10–last admission 5.30; Nov to Mar: Mon to Sat 9.30–last admission 4; Sun 10–last admission 4. Last admission one hour before closing. Adm £2.50, Chld, OAPs and Students £1.25. Party rate (Nov to Mar) £1.95, Chld and OAPs £1 (prices apply to Mar 31 1989).

YORK CITY ART GALLERY *(York City Council)*
Exhibition Square. Tel: (0904) 623839.
Outstanding collections of European and British paintings from c. 1350 to the present, including the Lycett Green collection of Old Masters and works by York artists, notably William Etty; water-colours, drawings and prints mostly devoted to the topography of York; modern stoneware pottery. Lively and varied programme of changing exhibitions. Mon to Sat 10–5, Sun 2.30–5 (last adm 4.30). *Closed* Dec 25, 26, Jan 1 and Good Friday. Shop open during all Gallery hours, last sales at 4.45 daily. Facilities for the disabled. Adm free to the collections and most exhibitions.

THE YORKSHIRE MUSEUM *(North Yorkshire County Council)*
Museum Gardens. Tel: (0904) 629745.
Contains extensive Roman, Anglo-Saxon and Viking collections, Yorkshire pottery and important medieval architectural sculptures. Many major temporary exhibitions throughout the year. The botanical gardens contain the Roman Multangular Tower, the Medieval ruins of St. Mary's Abbey, the Hospitium and Astronomical Observatory. Mon to Sat 10–5; Sun 1–5. Adm charge.

YORKSHIRE MUSEUM OF FARMING
(Yorkshire Museum of Farming Ltd)
Murton. Tel: (0904) 489966.
Set in 8 acres of country park, just 3 miles from York.

YORK STORY *(York City Council)*
The Heritage Centre, Castlegate. Tel: (0904) 28632.
Britain's finest Heritage Centre, set up in 1975 to interpret the social and architectural history of the City of York. The exhibitions, which include many notable pieces by modern artists and craftsmen, is equipped with a new audio-visual presentation which shows the history of York, highlighting the surviving buildings and objects. Models and dioramas. A Heritage 'Walk Around York' is available, guiding visitors to the major buildings in the city. Mon to Sat 10–5; Sun 1–5. Adm 80p, Chld, OAPs and Students 40p (prices apply to Mar 31 1989).

South Yorkshire

BARNSLEY

COOPER GALLERY *(Barnsley Metropolitan Borough Council)*
Church Street, S70 2AH. Tel: (0226) 242905.

17th century Dutch, 18th and 19th century French and Italian paintings and a fine collection of English drawings and watercolours, including the Sir Michael Sadler collection. Focusing on contemporary art and craft and including thematic exhibitions from the permanent collection. Continuous programme of temporary exhibitions and related activities. Tues 1–5.30; Wed to Sun 10–5.30; *closed* Mon.

MONK BRETTON PRIORY
Telephone: (0226) 20489

The monastery was founded about 1154, initially for monks of the Cluniac Order. The priory was involved in violent arguments with another Cluniac monastery at Pontefract, and more than once an armed force was sent to occupy Monk Bretton. Their differences were only resolved by Monk Bretton leaving the Order to become a Benedictine house. The remains show the layout of the monastery. One of the best-preserved buildings is the 14th century prior's lodging, which stands three storeys high.

Location: 2 m (3.2 km) north east of Barnsley. OS map ref SE373065.
Opening Times: Good Friday to Sept 30, daily 10–6; Oct 1 to Maundy Thursday, daily 10–4. *Closed Mons, Christmas and New Year.* Adm 55p, OAPs 40p, Chd 25p.

WORSBROUGH MILL MUSEUM
(Barnsley Metropolitan Borough Council)
Worsbrough Bridge, S70 5LJ. Tel: (0226) 203961.

17th and 19th century corn mills restored to working condition. Daily demonstrations of water-powered machinery. Programme of milling days and craft weekends. Different types of flour produced for sale. Set in 200 acre country park. Wed to Sun 10–5.30. *Closed* Mon and Tues.

CAWTHORNE

CANNON HALL
Telephone: Barnsley 790270
(Barnsley Metropolitan Borough Council)

18th century house by Carr of York. Collections of fine furniture, paintings, glassware, pewter and pottery. Also the Regimental Museum of the 13th/18th Royal Hussars. 70 acres of parkland.
Location: 5 m W of Barnsley on A635; 1 m NW of Cawthorne.
Opening Times: All the year—Weekdays 10.30–5; Suns 2.30–5. Adm free. *Closed Christmas Day, Boxing Day, December 27, New Year's Day & Good Friday.*

VICTORIA JUBILEE MUSEUM
Cawthorne. Tel: (0226) 791273.
Natural history, geology and objects of local interest.

CONISBROUGH

CONISBROUGH CASTLE
Telephone: (070 986) 3329

Sir Walter Scott's novel 'Ivanhoe' made Conisbrough Castle famous. The magnificent keep—still largely intact—is one of the finest examples of 12th century building in England. Sited by the River Don, the castle we see today was probably the work of Hamelin Plantagenet, illegitimate half-brother of Henry II.

Location: 4½ m (7.2 km) south west of Doncaster. OS map ref SK515989.
Opening Times: Good Friday to Sept 30, daily 10–6; Oct 1 to Maundy Thursday, daily 10–4. *Closed Mons, Christmas and New Year.* Adm £1.10, OAPs 80p, Chd 55p.

DONCASTER

DONCASTER MUSEUM AND ART GALLERY
(Doncaster Metropolitan Borough Council)
Chequer Road, DN1 2AE. Tel: (0302) 734287.
Natural history, prehistoric, Roman and medieval archaeology and local history, militaria, costume, paintings, sculpture, silver, ceramics and glass. The Regimental Collection of the King's Own Yorkshire Light Infantry. Mon to Sat 10–5; Sun 2–5. *Closed* Fri.

MUSEUM OF SOUTH YORKSHIRE LIFE
(Doncaster Metropolitan Borough Council)
Cusworth Park, DN5 7TU. Tel: (0302) 782342.
Social history collections, agriculture, industry, costume and toys. Mon to Sat 11–5; Sun 1–5. *Closed* Fri. (*Closes* at 4 in Winter).

HICKLETON

THE SUE RYDER HOME, HICKLETON HALL
(The Sue Ryder Foundation)
This Home cares for 50 physically handicapped and others who are homeless and unable to cope on their own.
Location: 6 m NW of Doncaster; on A635 Doncaster/Barnsley Road (behind Hickleton Church).
Opening Times: Individuals wishing to visit the Home may do so, Mons to Fris 2–4 without prior appointment. Please report your arrival to the Office in the main entrance.
Refreshments: Hotels & Restaurants in Doncaster.

MALTBY

ROCHE ABBEY
Telephone: (0709) 812739

Most medieval monasteries are near running water, since the monks were more fastidious about sanitation than their contemporaries. The two founders of Roche gave land on either side of a stream, and parts of the building bridge the water. Founded in 1147 for monks of the Cistercian Order, the name 'Roche' derives from its rocky site. Sadly, the only part of the abbey's history of which we know any detail, is the Dissolution. When the monks left, the monastery was plundered and the carved wood from the church burnt in order to melt the lead taken from the roof.

Location: 1½ m (2.4 km) south of Maltby. OS map ref SK544898.
Opening Times: Good Friday to Sept 30, daily 10–6; Oct 1 to Maundy Thursday, 10–4 weekends only. *Closed Christmas and New Year.* Adm 80p, OAPs 60p, Chd 40p.

MEERSBROOK

BISHOPS' HOUSE *(Sheffield Metropolitan District Council)*
Meersbrook Park. Tel: (0742) 557701.
Tudor timber-framed house, with exhibitions of local and social history. Wed to Sun 10–5 (Sun from 11). Adm 40p, Chld 20p.

ROTHERHAM

ART GALLERY *(Rotherham Metropolitan Borough Council)*
Brian O'Malley Library and Arts Centre, Walker Place.
Tel: (0709) 382121, Ext. 3624 or 3635.
Continuous programme of temporary exhibitions in-cluding, at times, 19th and 20th century paintings from the museum collections. Tues to Sat 10–5. *Closed* Sun, Mon and Bank Hols.

CLIFTON PARK MUSEUM
(Rotherham Metropolitan Borough Council)
Clifton Park. Tel: (0709) 382121, Ext. 3628 or 3635.
Late 18th century mansion, reputedly by John Carr of York. Contains 18th century furnished rooms, family portraits, period kitchen. Displays of Victoriana, local history, local Roman antiquities, numis-matics, glass and glassmaking, Church silver, 19th and 20th century paintings, British ceramics including Rockingham, local geology and natural history. Temporary exhibitions. Activities for Schools and other Educational Groups; Junior Museum Club; holiday activities. Apr to Sept: Weekdays (excluding Fri) 10–5; Sun 2.30–5. Oct to Mar: Weekdays (excluding Fri) 10–5; Sun 2.30–4.30.

THE YORK AND LANCASTER REGIMENTAL MUSEUM
Brian O'Malley Library and Arts Centre, Walker Place.
Tel: (0709) 382121, Ext. 3625.
Uniforms, medals (including seven V.C.'s), campaign relics and insignia covering the history of the Regi-ment and its forebears, the 65th. and 84th. Foot, from 1758 to 1968. For times of opening see Art Gallery entry. Adm free.

SHEFFIELD

ABBEYDALE INDUSTRIAL HAMLET
(Sheffield Metropolitan District Council)
Abbeydale Road South. Tel: (0742) 367731.
An 18th century scytheworks comprising a Huntsman crucible steel furnace, water-powered tilt-hammers, grinding hull, hand-forges and workman's cottage and manager's house. Mon to Sat 10–5; Sun 11–5 *(please check in advance for Mon and Tues opening).* Adm £1, Chld 50p. Premium adm for special events. Special events – Working Days, Children's Working Days and Craft Fair: for Information regarding dates and to confirm opening times please telephone the above number.

GRAVES ART GALLERY *(Sheffield Metropolitan District Council)*
Surrey Street. Tel: (0742) 734781.
Presents an introduction to British art of the 20th century and important examples of European painting. Among the artists represented are Murillo, Ribera, Cézanne, Corot and Matisse in addition to a large collection of English water-colours. Changing displays focus on different aspects of the permanent collection. Also important collections of Chinese, Indian, Islamic and African art. Frequent loan exhibitions. Cafe. Mon to Sat 10–6; *Closed* Sun . Adm free.

KELHAM ISLAND INDUSTRIAL MUSEUM
(Sheffield Metropolitan District Council)
Alma Street, S3 8RY. Tel: (0742) 722106.
Major new museum of Sheffield industry past and present includes 12,000h.p. steam engine (regularly demonstrated), traditional "little mesters" at work, reconstructed workshops (cutlery, die-sinking). Educational facilities, shop, cafe, publications. Wed to Sat 10–5; Sun 11–5. Open Bank Hol Mons. Adm £1, Chld/OAPs and party rate 50p.

MAPPIN ART GALLERY *(Sheffield Metropolitan District Council)*
Weston Park. Tel: (0742) 26281 or 754091.
Paintings and sculpture mainly representative of the British School of the 18th, 19th and 20th centuries including pictures by Turner, Constable, Morland, Millais, Burne-Jones and sculpture by Chantrey, Watts and Stevens. Living artists represented include Moore, Hoyland, Greaves and Jones; changing displays focus on different aspects of the permanent collection. Frequent loan exhibitions of contemporary painting, sculpture and graphic art are held. Tues to Sat 10–5; Sun 2–5. *Closed* Mon. Cafe. Adm free.

RUSKIN GALLERY *(Sheffield Metropolitan District Council)*
101 Norfolk Street, S1 2JE. Tel: (0742) 734781.
This recently opened gallery houses the collection founded by the Victorian artist and writer John Ruskin in 1875 for the artisans of Sheffield. The collection comprises pictures, prints, minerals, illustrated manuscripts, plaster-casts of architectural details and a library. Temporary exhibitions from aspects of the collection are displayed on the mezzanine floor. Recipient of a Museum of the Year Award 1986. Mon to Fri 10–6; Sat 10–5. *Closed* Sun. Adm free.

SHEFFIELD BOTANIC GARDENS
(Sheffield City Council)
Begun as a private venture in 1833, transferred to the Town Trust in 1898, and to Sheffield Corporation 1951. Demonstration gardens, conservation area and garden, and garden and chalet for the disabled, together with the Paxton Pavilion complex, which includes aviary, aquarium and half hardy house.
Location: 1 m from centre of Sheffield.
Opening Times: Daily all year. Admission free.

SHEFFIELD CITY MUSEUM
(Sheffield Metropolitan District Council)
Weston Park. Tel: (0742) 768588.
Collections of natural history, geology, ceramics and coins; specialised collections of cutlery, Old Sheffield Plate and local archaeology. Temporary

SHEPHERD WHEEL *(Sheffield Metropolitan District Council)*
Whiteley Wood, Hangingwater Road. Tel: (0742) 367731.
A water-powered grinding establishment. Wed to Sun 10–12.30, 1.30–5 (Sun from 11). *Closes* at 4 in winter. Party bookings telephone the above number.

DONCASTER METROPOLITAN BOROUGH
MUSEUMS AND ARTS SERVICE

MUSEUM AND ART GALLERY
CHEQUER ROAD

Established 1908, moved to the present building in 1964. Regional collections of Archaeology, Natural History, Geology and Art. Frequent temporary Exhibitions. Admission Free.

MUSEUM OF SOUTH YORKSHIRE LIFE
CUSWORTH HALL

The 18th Century mansion of the Wrightson family used to depict everyday life of local people during the past two centuries. Programme of temporary exhibitions and family activities. Admission Free.

THE KING'S OWN YORKSHIRE LIGHT INFANTRY

The Regimental Collection of the King's Own Yorkshire Light Infantry displayed in the newly constructed gallery. The origins of this famous Yorkshire Regiment go back to the raising of the 51st of foot in 1755. Uniforms, badges, equipment, weapons and medals. The life of a soldier over two hundred years.

West Yorkshire

ABERFORD

LOTHERTON HALL
(Leeds Metro District Council)

Edwardian house with attractive gardens. Gascoigne collection of pictures and furniture.

Location: 1 m E of A1 at Aberford on the Towton Road (B1217).
Opening Times: All the year—Tues to Sun 10.30–6.15 (or dusk if earlier); Thurs from May to September 10.30–8.30. *Closed Mons except Bank Hol Mons.* Adm 75p, Chd & OAPs 30p. Students free. Season ticket £3.15 (includes Temple Newsam, see below).

BAILDON

BRACKEN HALL COUNTRYSIDE CENTRE
(Bradford Metropolitan Council)
Glenn Road, Baildon. Tel: (0274) 584140.

Situated at the local beauty spot of Shipley Glen, housing displays and exhibits relating to the natural history, geology and local history of the area. Please 'phone for details and opening times.

BATLEY

ART GALLERY *(Kirklees Metropolitan Council)*
Market Place. Tel: (0924) 473141.

Collections of fine art and temporary exhibitions. Mon to Fri 10–6; Sat 10–4. *Closed Sun.*

BAGSHAW MUSEUM *(Kirklees Metropolitan Council)*
Wilton Park. Tel: (0924) 472514.

Exotic Victorian building housing local collections, natural history, ethnography and Oriental arts. Mon to Sat 10–5; Sun 1–5.

YORKSHIRE FIRE MUSEUM
Bradford Road.

BIRSTALL

OAKWELL HALL and COUNTRY PARK
Telephone: Batley 474926
(Kirklees Metro Council)

Elizabethan moated manor house (1583) with Civil War and Brontë connections. It was 'Fieldhead' of Charlotte Brontë's novel 'Shirley'. The Hall was completely refurbished in 1988 and is now displayed as a seventeenth century gentleman's house. The Hall is surrounded by period gardens and 87 acres of country park. Features include a wildlife garden, arboretum, countryside information centre, equestrian arena and adventure playground. New facilities include a visitor complex with interpretive centre, craft workshops, converted barn for indoor events and shop. SANDFORD AWARD 1989.

Location: Birstall, Batley.
Opening Times: Open all year – Mons to Sats 10–5; Suns 1–5. Adm free.
Refreshments: Tea room.

BOSTON SPA

BRAMHAM PARK
Telephone: Boston Spa (0937) 844265
(Mr & Mrs George Lane Fox)

The house was created during the first half of the 18th century and affords a rare opportunity to enjoy a beautiful Queen Anne mansion containing fine furniture, pictures and porcelain—set in magnificent grounds with ornamental ponds, cascades, tall beech hedges and loggias of various shapes—unique in the British Isles for its grand vistas design stretching out into woodlands of cedar, copper beech, lime and Spanish chestnut interspersed with wild rhododendron thickets.

Location: 5 m S of Wetherby on the Great North Road (A1).
Opening Times: GROUNDS ONLY. Easter weekend, May Day, Spring Bank Hol weekend. HOUSE & GROUNDS. June 11 to Aug 31—Suns, Tues, Weds & Thurs also Bank Hol Mon (Aug 28) 1.15–5.30. Last adm 5 pm. For adm charges concessionary rates contact The Estate Office, Bramham Park, Wetherby, W. Yorks LS23 6ND.
BRAMHAM HORSE TRIALS—June 1–4, 1989.

BRADFORD

BOLLING HALL *(Bradford Metropolitan Council)*
Bolling Hall Road. BD4 7LP. Tel: (0274) 723057.

A fine example of West Yorkshire domestic architecture, ranging in date from the Pele Tower (c. 1450) to the Carr Wing (1779–80). There are very good ceilings in the Ghost Room (early 17th century) and the Carr drawing room. Fine 17th and 18th century furniture. The rooms are furnished appropriately for their period. Tues to Sun 10–6 (Oct to Mar, 10–5). *Closed* Mon (except Bank Hols) and Christmas Day, Boxing Day and Good Friday.

CARTWRIGHT HALL ART GALLERY
(Bradford Metropolitan Council)
Lister Park, BD4 9NS. Tel: (0274) 493313.

The permanent collection of important late Victorian and Edwardian art include Rossetti, Ford Madox Brown, Clausen, Wadsworth, Eurich, Hockney and 20th century British art. The British International Print Biennale is held here, reflected in the collection of contemporary prints. There is a lively programme of touring and cultural art, craft and photography exhibitions. Tues to Sun 10–6 (Oct to Mar, 10–5). *Closed* Mon (Open Bank Hols), Good Friday, Christmas Day and Boxing Day.

COLOUR MUSEUM *(The Society of Dyers and Colourists)*
82 Grattan Road, off Westgate. Tel: (0274) 390955.

Step into the world of colour. A fascinating museum with many interactive exhibits which allow you to explore what colour is, how we react to it and how we use it. Displays look at how we see in colour, light and colour and colour in everyday life. Visitors can also step behind the high street shop windows to find out how our clothes and the fabrics in our homes are dyed and printed. Tues to Fri 2–5, Sat 10–4; school and other parties also on mornings of Tues to Fri by prior booking.

COMMUNITY ARTS *(Bradford Metropolitan Council)*
17-21 Chapel Street, Little Germany, BD1 5DT. Tel: (0274) 721372.

Community Arts Centre open July 1988. Good physical access, ramp and lift to all floors, loop systems and braille signs. The centre offers skills, equipment, workshops, exhibitions and meeting space. Please 'phone for details of opening times and events.

INDUSTRIAL MUSEUM *(Bradford Metropolitan Council)*
Moorside Road BD2 3HP. Tel: (0274) 631756.

Sited in a former spinning mill the collections reflect the woollen and worsted industries, engineering and transport, with the Mill Owner's house furnished in turn of century styles. Tues to Sun 10–5. *Closed* Mon (Open Bank Hols) and Good Friday, Christmas Day, Boxing Day.

NATIONAL MUSEUM OF PHOTOGRAPHY, FILM AND TELEVISION
(A joint venture between the Science Museum and Bradford Metropolitan Council)
Prince's View. Tel: (0274) 727488.

Britain's "most dramatic and accessible new museum" (Sunday Times) explores and examines photography in all its aspects: from camera obscuras to full-scale 1930's portrait studio; from processing and developing films to photography in medicine, space and science; from photojournalism and pictures in news context to a chance meeting with "Lord Lichfield". ALSO houses Britain's only IMAX cinema – with the biggest screen in Europe – 52ft high × 63ft wide: shows daily. The Kodak Museum telling the story of photography and cinematography is now at the Museum and will open in 1989. New galleries cover: the story of British Television with interactive displays where visitors can read the news, and try vision mixing, editing etc. Two floors of the Museum house special temporary exhibitions looking at the work of one particular photographer or themes and issues current in photography. Change approx every 3 months. Tues to Sun 11–7.30 (*N.B. Some galleries close at 6), closed* Mons, but open all Bank Hols except May Day. Adm to museum is free. Cinema (and IMAX) adm £2.50, Chld £1.30, Students/OAPs/UB40s £2. Parties catered for during ordinary opening hours, group rates for cinema, or can be especially accommodated – telephone for details. Ample parking. Suitable for disabled persons; wheelchairs accommodated. Wine and coffee bar, the Prince's View, open daily 11–7.30. Museum shop stocks extensive ranges of books and postcards etc. Mail order. **Winner of the Museum of the Year Award, 1988.** Keeper: Colin Ford.

BRIGHOUSE

SMITH ART GALLERY *(Calderdale Borough Council)*
Halifax Road, Brighouse. Tel: (0484) 719222.

Permanent collection of about 450 pictures, oils and water-colours – and a changing programme of temporary exhibitions. Mon to Sat 10–5; Sun 2.30–5. *Closed* Sun, Oct to Mar.

CASTLEFORD

CASTLEFORD MUSEUM *(Wakefield Metropolitan District Council)*
(Room in Castleford Library), Carlton Street. Tel: (0977) 559552.

Castleford Museum Room has changing displays of Roman finds, local pottery etc. Mon to Fri 2–5. *Closed* weekends and local government and public holidays.

LEDSTON HALL
(G. H. H. Wheler, Esq.)

17th century mansion with some earlier work.

Location: 2 m N of Castleford off A656.
Station: Castleford (2¾ m).
Opening Times: Exterior only. May, June, July and Aug—Mon to Fri 9–4. Other days by appointment.
Refreshments: Chequers Inn, Ledsham (1 m).

CLECKHEATON

RED HOUSE *(Kirklees Metropolitan Council)*
Oxford Road, Gomersal. Tel: (0924) 474926.
1660 house with strong associations with the Brontës. *Closed* for structural repairs 1988–89.

DEWSBURY

DEWSBURY EXHIBITION GALLERY
(Kirklees Metropolitan Council)
Wellington Street. Tel: (0924) 465151.
Exhibition gallery devoted to local history of area and frequent exhibitions of a varied nature. Mon to Fri 10–5; Sat 10–4. *Closed* Sun.

DEWSBURY MUSEUM *(Kirklees Metropolitan Council)*
Crow Nest Park, Heckmondwike Road. Tel: Dewsbury (0924) 468171.
Devoted to the theme of 'Childhood'. Temporary exhibitions throughout the year. Open Mon to Sat 10–5; Sun 1–5.

HALIFAX

BANKFIELD MUSEUM AND ART GALLERY
(Calderdale Borough Council)
Akroyd Park, Halifax. Tel: (0422) 54823/52334.
Textiles and costume, art and local history. Natural history collections. The Duke of Wellington's Regimental Museum is also at Bankfield. Lively programme of temporary exhibitions. Mon to Sat 10–5; Sun 2.30–5.

CALDERDALE INDUSTRIAL MUSEUM
(Calderdale Borough Council)
Entrances Piece Hall and Winding Road, Halifax. Tel: (0422) 59031.
150 years of Calderdale's Industrial history with working machinery. Tues to Sat 10–5; Sun 2–5. *Closed* Mons except for Bank Hols. Adm 50p, Chld/OAPs and unwaged 25p. Group visits can be arranged at 25p each.

THE PIECE HALL *(Calderdale Borough Council)*
Halifax. Tel: (0422) 59031.
A handsome Italian Piazza style building with a preindustrial Museum and Art Gallery. Cloth production from the fleece to the 'piece' before the Industrial Revolution, plus a varied programme of exhibitions. Mon to Sat 10–5 (Apr to Sept, 10–6), Sun 10–5.

SHIBDEN HALL & FOLK MUSEUM
Telephone: Halifax (0422) 52246
(Calderdale Metropolitan Borough Council)

15th century timber-framed house.
Location: ¼ m SE of Halifax on the Halifax/Hipperholme Road (A58).
Opening Times: Apr to Sept—Mons to Sats 10–6, Suns 2–5. Oct, Nov & Mar—Mons to Sats 10–5, Suns 2–5. Feb—Suns only 2–5. *Closed December to January.* Adm Summer 60p, Chd 30p; Low season 50p, Chd 25p. *Conducted tours after normal hours (Fee payable).*
Refreshments: At the Hall.

WEST YORKSHIRE FOLK MUSEUM *(Calderdale Borough Council)*
Shibden Hall, Shibden Park, Halifax. Tel: (0422) 52246.
1420 half-timbered hall with 17th century furniture; a 17th century barn; early agricultural implements; coaches and harness; craft workshops. Café. Apr to Sept: Mon to Sat 10–6; Sun 2–5. Oct, Nov and Mar: Mon to Sat 10–5; Sun 2–5. Feb: Sun 2–5. *Closed* Dec and Jan. Conducted tours other times by arrangement. Adm 50p, Chld/OAP 25p (May to Sept 60p and 30p).

HAWORTH

BRONTË PARSONAGE
Telephone: Haworth 42323
(The Brontë Society)

Georgian Parsonage, containing many relics of the Brontë family, including furniture, clothes, manuscripts and drawings. Small formal garden.
Location: 4 m SW of Keighley on A6033 at Haworth.
Opening Times: All the year—Daily Apr to Sept, 11–5.30; Oct to Mar, 11–4.30. Adm Good Fri–Aug 31 inclusive, £1, OAPs & Students 50p, Chd 25p; all other times, 60p, OAPs & Students 30p, Chd 25p. *Closed Dec 24, 25 and 26 and Feb 1 to 21 incl.*

HEBDEN BRIDGE

AUTOMOBILIA *(Brian Collins)*
Billy Lane, Old Town, Wadsworth. Tel: (0422) 844775.
Telex: 517395 COLFIB G.
A restored stone built 19th century cloth warehouse, 3 storeys, with attractive pitchpine beam features.

HEPTONSTALL

HEPTONSTALL OLD GRAMMAR SCHOOL MUSEUM
(Calderdale Borough Council)
Hebden Bridge.
17th century stone school building with local history display and old grammar school furniture. Easter week 11–12.30, 1.15–4. Apr to Sept: Sat and Sun 2–6. May to Aug: Mon, Wed, Thurs and Fri 11–12.30, 1.15–4; Sat and Sun 12–5. Oct to Mar: Sat and Sun 1–5. Adm 15p, Chld/OAPs 5p.

HOLMFIRTH

HOLMFIRTH POSTCARD MUSEUM
(Kirklees Metropolitan Council)
Huddersfield Road. Tel: (0484) 682231.
Britain's first Postcard Museum, based on the local firm of Bamforth & Co. Ltd., famous for its production of saucy postcards. Mon to Sat 10–5; Sun 1–5.

HUDDERSFIELD

ART GALLERY *(Kirklees Metropolitan Council)*
Princess Alexandra Walk. Tel: (0484) 513808.
Permanent collection of fine art from mid-19th century. Temporary exhibition throughout the year. Mon to Fri 10–6; Sat 10–4. *Closed* Sun.

TOLSON MEMORIAL MUSEUM *(Kirklees Metropolitan Council)*
Ravensknowle Park. Tel: (0484) 530591.
Natural science, archaeological transport and farming collections tell the story of life in Northern England. Mon–Sat 10–5; Sun 1–5.

ILKLEY

MANOR HOUSE
Telephone: Ilkley 600066
(Bradford Metro Council)

Small 16th/17th century Manor built on part of the site of a Roman fort. Lively exhibition programme.
Location: Castle Yard, Ilkley.
Station: Ilkley.
Opening Times: All year—Daily (except Mons but open Bank Hol Mons) Oct to Mar 10–5. Apr to Sept 10–6. *Closed Christmas Day, Boxing Day & Good Friday.* Adm free (Public Museum).

WHITE WELLS *(Bradford Metropolitan Council)*
Ilkley Moor.
Restored 18th century plunge baths. Easter to mid-Oct: Sat, Sun and Bank Hols 2–5.

KEIGHLEY

CLIFFE CASTLE MUSEUM AND ART GALLERY
(Bradford Metropolitan Council)
Spring Gardens Lane BD20 6LH. Tel: (0274) 758230.
A former Victorian mansion housing a wide range of natural history and folk life material. Victorian reception rooms, the Airedale gallery. Molecule to Minerals and temporary exhibitions areas. Tues to Sun 10–6 (Oct to Mar, 10–5). *Closed* Mon (except Bank Hols) and Christmas Day, Boxing Day and Good Friday.

EAST RIDDLESDEN HALL, The National Trust &

17th century manor house. Magnificent tithe barn. Small formal garden.
Location: 1 m NE of Keighley on S side of A650, on N bank of Aire.
Station: Keighley (1½ m).
Opening Times: Easter to end Oct: Mar 24–31: 2–5.30. Apr—Weekends only 2–5.30. School groups and parties on weekdays by prior arrangement. May, June, Sept & Oct, Wed–Sun and Bank Holiday Mons 2–5.30; July & Aug, Weds to Suns & Bank Hol Mons 12–5.30 (last adm 5). Tearoom open 2–5. Adm £1.50, Chd 70p, Parties £1.30, Chd 60p. Dogs, with the exception of guide dogs, allowed in grounds only and must be on leash. Only ground floor and garden accessible for disabled visitors. Shop and Information Centre. Large camera bags are not allowed in house – photography by permission only.
Refreshments: Afternoon teas and refreshments in Bothy Tearoom adjacent to house (on first floor), special arrangements for disabled visitors contact Administrator.

KEIGHLEY & WORTH VALLEY RAILWAY
Haworth Station.

LEEDS

HAREWOOD HOUSE AND BIRD GARDEN
Telephone: (0532) 886225
(The Earl of Harewood)

18th century house designed by John Carr and Robert Adam and still the home of the Lascelles family. As well as superb ceilings, plasterwork and Chippendale furniture it contains fine English and Italian paintings and Sevres and Chinese porcelain. In the grounds, landscaped by 'Capability' Brown, are lakeside and woodland walks, displays of roses and rhododendrons and a herbaceous border running the length of the Terrace.

Location: 7 m S of Harrogate; 8 m N of Leeds on Leeds/Harrogate road; Junction A61/659 at Harewood village; 5 m from A1 at Wetherby 22m from York.
Opening Times: HOUSE, GROUNDS, BIRD GARDEN AND ALL FACILITIES — Easter to Oct 31 daily. Gates open 10 House open 11. Limited opening Nov, Feb and Mar — Suns. Concession rates for Coach parties, school parties welcome at all times. Adm charges and details of Summer and Weekend Events — including Car Rallies and Leeds Championship Dog Show available from Gerald Long, Visitors Information, Estate Office, Harewood, Leeds LS17 9LQ. State Dining Room (max 48) available.
Refreshments: Cafeteria; Restaurant; also Courtyard Functions Suite for Conference/ Product launches throughout the year.

LEEDS CITY MUSEUM *(City of Leeds)*
Municipal Buildings LS1 3AA.
Collections illustrating nearly every aspect of natural history, ethnography and archaeology. Although their scope is worldwide, they particularly concern the Yorkshire region. Tues to Fri 9.30–5.30; Sat 10–4. *Closed* Sun and Mon.

MUSEUM OF LEEDS *(City of Leeds)*
Tel: (0532) 637861 (Armley Mills).
Industrial Museum of the year 1983. This extensive open-air museum includes the following:
The Museum of Leeds Trail: This canalside footpath trail follows six miles of the Aire Valley from the centre of Leeds to the village of Rodley, linking the following museums with over 40 historic sites. Daily 9–dusk. Guidebook available from local museums and bookshops.
Armley Mills: (Canal Road, Armley). Once the world's largest woollen mills, this museum is housed in a unique fireproof building of 1806 on an impressive island site in the River Aire. The exhibits illustrate the industrial history of Leeds and include a working water wheel, locomotives, engines, textile, clothing and printing machinery. Apr to Sept: Tues to Sat 10–6; Sun 2–6. Oct to Mar: Tues to Sat 10–5; Sun 2–5 (last admission 30 mins. before closing). *Closed* Mon.
Kirkstall Abbey: (Kirkstall). Britain's finest early monastic ruin, founded by Cistercian monks in 1152. Daily 9–dusk.
Abbey House: (Kirkstall). The 12th century abbey gatehouse now houses a folk museum showing the life of Leeds people and includes three full-size streets of local shops and cottages. There are also displays detailing the history of Kirkstall Abbey. Apr to Sept: Mon to Sat 10–6; Sun 2–6. Oct to Mar: Mon to Sat 10–5; Sun 2–5.

TEMPLE NEWSAM
(Leeds Metro District Council)
Tudor-Jacobean house, birthplace of Lord Darnley, with collection of pictures and furniture.
Location: 5 m E of Leeds; 1 m S of A63 (nr junction with A642).
Station: Cross Gates (1¾ m).
Opening Times: All the year — Tues to Sun 10.30–6.15 (or dusk if earlier); Weds from May to Sept 10.30–8.30. *Closed Mons except Bank Hol Mons.* Adm 75p, Chd & OAPs 30p. Students free. Season tickets £3.15 (includes Lotherton Hall, see above).

OTLEY

OTLEY MUSEUM
Civic Centre, Cross Green.

OVERTON

YORKSHIRE MINING MUSEUM
Caphouse Colliery, New Road, Overton, WF4 4RH
Tel: Wakefield (0924) 848806.
Opens from June 6, 1988, 10–5 daily. Major new Museum of the Yorkshire coalfields. Includes guided tour 450 feet underground to original workings where methods and conditions of mining from 1820 to the present day have been reconstructed. Extensive outdoor and indoor displays, 'paddy' train rides, parking, picnic area, shop and refreshments. Party bookings welcome.

PONTEFRACT

ACKWORTH SCHOOL
Telephone: Hemsworth (0977) 611401
(Co-educational Boarding School Society of Friends)
Georgian building (1750) — only remaining building of London Foundling Hospital.
Location: 3½ m S of Pontefract on A628.
Opening Times: During School vacations — Monday to Fri 10–4 (by appointment). Adm: voluntary donation.

PONTEFRACT MUSEUM *(Wakefield Metropolitan District Council)*
Salter Row. Tel: (0977) 797289.
Displays on the history of Pontefract including fine early 17th century painting of Pontefract Castle. Temporary exhibition programme. Mon to Sat 10.30–5, Sun 2.30–5. Open all Spring and Summer Bank Holidays.

RIPPONDEN

RYBURN FARM MUSEUM *(Calderdale Borough Council)*
Ripponden, Sowerby Bridge.
A small farmhouse with adjoining barn – a typical 19th century Penine hill farm. Open Mar to Oct: Sat, Sun and public holidays 2–5. Adm 10p, Chld/OAPs 5p.

SALTAIRE

MUSEUM OF VICTORIAN REED ORGANIS & HARMONIUMS
(Phil & Pam Fluke)
Victoria Hall, Victoria Road. Tel: (0274) 585601 After 5 pm.
A private collection of over 44 reed organs, which organists are invited to play.

SHIPLEY

THE WORLD AND SOOTY EXHIBITION
Windhill Manor, Leeds Rd BD18 1BP. Tel: (0274) 531122.
Brand new museum based on the life of Sooty since 1948. Photos and film take you back to your childhood, while the youngsters can enjoy the Sooty of today in the charming animated displays and novelties. Open daily 10–5.30. *Closed* Christmas Day, Boxing Day and New Years Day.

WAKEFIELD

ELIZABETHAN GALLERY
(Wakefield Metropolitan District Council)
Brook Street. Tel: (0924) 370211, Ext. 540 (after 5 and weekends 370087).
Temporary exhibitions of paintings, sculptures, photography, crafts etc. Mon to Sat 10.30–5, Sun 2.30–5, and Spring and Summer Bank Holidays during exhibitions only.

NOSTELL PRIORY, The National Trust
Telephone: Wakefield 863892
Built for Sir Rowland Winn by Paine; a wing added in 1766 by Robert Adam. State rooms contain pictures and famous Chippendale furniture made especially for the house.
Location: 6 m SE of Wakefield, on N side of A638.
Station: Fitzwilliam (1½ m).
Opening Times: Mar 25–28, Apr, May, June, Sept & Oct — Sats 12–5, Suns 11–5; July & Aug — Daily (except Fris) 12–5, Sun 11–5. Bank Hol Openings: Easter Bank Hol — Mon & Tues; May Bank Hol — Mon; Spring Bank Hol — Mon & Tues; Aug Bank Hol — Mon: Mons 11–5, Tues 12–5. Adm House & Grounds £2.40, Chd £1.20; Party rate (30 or more) £2, Chd £1. Grounds only £1.30, Chd 60p; Parking free. Pre-booked parties welcome outside normal published opening times. However, on these occasions, a charge will be made to National Trust members. *Dogs in grounds on leashes, not in house (except guide dogs). Lift available for disabled.*
Refreshments: Lunches and afternoon teas available in stable tea rooms (not NT).

WAKEFIELD ART GALLERY
(Wakefield Metropolitan District Council)
Wentworth Terrace. Tel: (0924) 375402.
Wakefield Art Gallery is the administrative headquarters of Wakefield Art Galleries and Museums. It is nationally and internationally well known for its fine collection of 20th century art, including important work by Barbara Hepworth and Henry Moore, and work by the Camden Town and Bloomsbury Group artists. There is a small collection of older work, with some particularly fine 18th and 19th century paintings of Wakefield. Artists' Print Loom Scheme, and a full temporary exhibition programme. Mon to Sat 10.30–5, Sun 2.30–5. Open all Spring and Summer Bank Holidays.

WAKEFIELD MUSEUM *(Wakefield Metropolitan District Council)*
Wood Street. Tel: (0924) 370211, Ext. 7190; (after 5 and weekends 361767).
Archaeology, local and social history displays. Extensive new displays of Charles Waterton's famous collection of exotic birds and animals. Temporary exhibition programme. Mon to Sat 10.30–5, Sun 2.30–5. Open all Spring and Summer Bank Holidays.

WETHERBY

STOCKELD PARK
Telephone: Wetherby (0937) 66101
(Mr & Mrs P. G. F. Grant)
Small country mansion, one of the finest examples of the work of James Paine, built in the Palladian style 1758–63. Main feature is the central hall and staircase. Attractive grounds and gardens.
Location: 3 m N of Wetherby; 7 m SE of Harrogate on A661.
Opening Times: July 1 to 30 1989, daily (*except Mons*) 2.30–5.30. Other times by appointment. Adm charges not available at time of going to press.
Refreshments: Teas at weekends only.

Cartwright Hall

BRADFORD
ART GALLERIES & MUSEUMS

BOLLING HALL
CARTWRIGHT HALL
INDUSTRIAL MUSEUM
CLIFFE CASTLE, Keighley
THE MANOR HOUSE
WHITE WELLS, Ilkley

BRONTË PARSONAGE MUSEUM
HAWORTH, KEIGHLEY, WEST YORKSHIRE

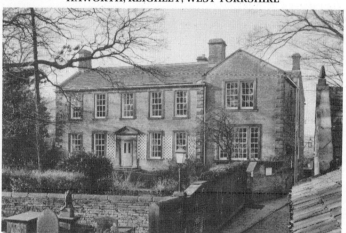

Once the home of the famous Brontë family this Georgian Parsonage has rooms furnished as in the Brontës' day with displays of their personal treasures. See where the writers of Jane Eyre and Wuthering Heights lived.
Become a member of the Brontë Society and enjoy the many privileges this offers. Write for details.

SHIBDEN HALL
HALIFAX
WEST YORKSHIRE FOLK MUSEUM

An early 15th century half-timbered house with later additions, furnished with 17th and 18th century material. The 17th century barn and outbuildings are equipped with early agricultural implements and craft workshops, the museum is set in a large park and surrounded by terrace gardens. Snack bar facilities. Admission: Summer—Adults 60p. Children 30p. Low Season—Adults 50p. Children 25p.

ADMISSION – SEE EDITORIAL REFERENCE

Experience a trip through time with Sooty having fun - from his beginning in 1948 to the present day.

The ever-lovable mischievious character is shown here in many guises. See original photos, animated sets, film, sound and sight, plus much more.

Browse through the shop or relax in the cafe. Bring the complete family for a very different experience. Four miles from Bradford airport, six miles from the M606, two and a half miles from the Bradford rail and bus interchange and only five minutes walk from Shipley rail or bus station.

Open: 10am - 5.30pm 7 days a week, (closed Xmas day, Boxing day, New Year day).

The World and Sooty, Windhill Manor, Leeds Road, Shipley, West Yorkshire, BD18 1BP. Tel: 0274 – 531122.

LOTHERTON HALL
ABERFORD, near LEEDS, West Yorkshire

Lotherton Hall was built round an earlier house dating from the mid-eighteenth century. The extensions to the east were completed in 1896 and those to the west in 1903. The Hall, with its art collection, park and gardens, was given to the City of Leeds by Sir Alvary and Lady Gascoigne in 1968 and opened as a country house museum in 1969. The Gascoigne collection, which contains pictures, furniture, silver and porcelain of the 17th and 18th centuries, as well as works of a later period, includes a magnificent portrait by Pompeo Batoni and an impressive group of silver race cups ranging in date from 1776 to 1842. The first floor and costume galleries were opened in 1970 and the oriental gallery in 1975. There is also a Museum shop and audio visual room.

WALES

Clwyd

BERSHAM

BERSHAM INDUSTRIAL HERITAGE CENTRE
(Clwyd County Council)
  Bersham, Nr. Wrexham LL14 4HT. Tel: Wrexham (0978) 261529.
Displays on the 18th century Wilkinson Ironworks, Davies Bros. Gatesmiths, lead-mining and blacksmithing. Regular programme of temporary exhibitions and craft residences. Free guided tours of the Bersham & Clywedog Industrial Trail in the Summer. Parking and adm free. Access for disabled. Sales point. For opening times and trail booking please telephone the Curator.

BODELWYDDAN

BODELWYDDAN CASTLE
Telephone: (0745) 583539
(Clwyd County Council)

Bodelwyddan Castle has been authentically restored as a Victorian Country House and contains a major collection of portraits and photography on permanent loan from the National Portrait Gallery. The collection includes works by many eminent Victorian Portraitists such as G. F. Watts, William Holman Hunt, John Singer Sargeant, Sir Edwin Landseer and Sir Thomas Lawrence. The portraits are complemented by furniture from the Victoria & Albert Museum and sculptures from the Royal Academy. The Castle is situated in beautiful countryside and is a member of the National Garden Scheme. The extensive formal gardens have been restored and many original features have been retained. For children, there is an adventure woodland and a funland play area.
Location: Just off the A55 near St. Asaph (opposite the Marble Church).
Opening Times: To Mar 19, 1989: Thurs to Sun 11–3. Mar 21 to Oct 1 1989: Open daily except Mons (but open Bank Holiday Mons) 11–5; from Oct 5, details on application. Adm £2, Chd £1, Family group £5.60 (2 Adults 3 Chd), OAPs/ Unemployed £1.50, Students £1. Discount rates available for groups of 20 or more. Ample car parking. Suitable for disabled persons (no wheelchairs available). Gift Shop, Picnic area, Woodland walk.
Refreshments: Victorian Tea Room, Pavilion Restaurant, Cafeteria.

CHIRK

CHIRK CASTLE, The National Trust
Telephone: Chirk 777701

Built 1310; a unique, unaltered example of a border castle of Edward I's time, inhabited continuously for 660 years. Interesting portraits, tapestries etc. Gardens.
Location: ½ m from Chirk (on A5 trunk road) then 1½ m private driveway; 20 m NW of Shrewsbury 7 m SE of Llangollen.
Station: Chirk (2 m).
Opening Times: Mar 24 to Sept 29—Daily except Mons & Sats 12–5, Gardens open 12–6. (Open Bank Holiday Mons 12–5). Sept 30 to Oct 29—Sats and Suns only 12–5, Gardens open 12–6. (Last adm to Castle 4.30, Gardens 5.30.) Adm £2.30, Chd £1.15, Family £5.75. Pre-booked parties of 20 or more £1.85. Shop. No dogs. Very limited access for wheelchairs.
Refreshments: Tea rooms (light lunches & teas).

HAWARDEN

EWLOE CASTLE
(Cadw: Welsh Historic Monuments)

Native Welsh castle with typical round and aspidal towers.
Location: 1 m NW of Hawarden.

HOLWAY

GRANGE CAVERN MILITARY MUSEUM *(A. Pearce)*
  Grange Lane. Tel: (0352) 713455.
The world's largest underground military museum of 2½ acres. Quarried in the early 19th century, and situated in an area of outstanding natural beauty with panoramic views over the Dee estuary. Ex World War II Bomb Store, which housed the Dambuster Bouncing Bombs, over 70 vehicles of all ages, heavy guns, motorbikes, collection of militaria, Falklands display, and much much more. Refreshments, licensed bar, free film show, souvenir shop. Ample free parking, picnic area. Easter to end Oct: daily 9.30 to 6 (last adm 5); Feb and Mar: weekends only 10–5 (last adm 4). *Closed* Nov, Dec, Jan. Party visits by appointment, 10% reduction over 20. £1.95, OAPs £1.65, Chld £1.45. Suitable for disabled. On A55 between Holywell and St. Asaph.

LLANASA

GYRN CASTLE
Telephone: (074 56) 3500
(Sir Geoffrey Bates, BT, MC)

Dating, in part, from 1700; castellated 1820. Large picture gallery, panelled entrance hall. Pleasant woodland walks.
Location: 26 m W of Chester (off A55); 4 m SE of Prestatyn.
Opening Times: All the year—by appointment. Adm £1.50, parties welcome.
Refreshments: By arrangement.

LLANGOLLEN

PLAS NEWYDD MUSEUM *(Glyndwr District Council)*
  Hill Street. Tel: (082 42) 2201.
Black-and-white house, home from 1780–1831 of the 'Ladies of Llangollen' eccentric 'blue-stockings'. May to Sept: Mon to Sat 10–7; Sun 11–4. Oct to Apr: by arrangement. Adm (1988 rates) 70p, Chld 35p.

VALLE CRUCIS ABBEY
(Cadw: Welsh Historic Monuments)

Impressive 13th century Abbey, still with its own fishpond.
Location: On Horseshoe Pass, 1 m N of Llangollen.

MOLD

ORIEL THEATR CLWYD *(Clwyd County Council)*
  County Civic Centre. Tel: Mold (0352) 56331.
Regular programme of local and touring exhibitions. Free parking and admission with access for disabled. Cafeteria and sales point. Open all year including weekends and bank holidays.

PONTBLYDDYN

PLAS TEG
Telephone: (0352) 771335
(Mrs C Bayley)

Built in 1610, one of the finest buildings of its kind, at each corner there are projecting towers with corbelled eaves, and a ogee-shaped roof supporting wooden copulas and finials, this is of architectural interest. As you enter this fine Jacobean mansion (recently restored to its former glory) notice the remarkable carved oak staircase, with massive newels, moulded finials and pendants. Enjoy a relaxed atmosphere as you discover rooms with influences from Europe, India and the Orient, four poster beds dating back to 1627, wall hangings, rare baths especially an 1815 coal fired bath with shower, plus a delight of rare carpets, wall brackets, fine furniture and china. Plas Teg can also cater for banquets, conferences, concerts and weddings. The long gallery is available for temporary exhibitions. We now have a collection of Parrots and Macaws on view, not forgetting Martin the Toucan.
Location: 1¾ m N of Caergwrle on the Wrexham-Mold Road (A541).
Opening Times: Daily including Bank Holidays, closed Tues 11–6, Sun 12–6. Adm £2, Chd £1. Parties of over 20 pre-booked 10% off. Car park. Unsuitable for wheelchairs except ground floor. No dogs in the house.
Refreshments: Teas, coffee, cake etc.

RHUDDLAN

BODRHYDDAN HALL
(Col the Lord Langford)

17th century manor house of historic interest. Famous portraits, armour, furniture. Extensive garden, Arboretum and picnic area.
Location: 4 m SE of Rhyl, midway between Rhuddlan & Dyserth.
Opening Times: June to Sept—Tues & Thurs 2–5.30. Adm £1, Chd 50p. *Special terms for parties.*
Refreshments: At the hall. Picnic areas.

RHUDDLAN CASTLE
(Cadw: Welsh Historic Monuments)

Begun by Edward I in 1277; concentric castle of simple design.
Location: In Rhuddlan.

RHYL

RHYL LIBRARY, MUSEUM & ARTS CENTRE
(Clwyd County Council)
  Church Street. Tel: Rhyl (0745) 53814/53833.
Displays and early films on video set in an exciting recreated pier scene. Regular programme of local and touring exhibitions throughout the year. *Closed* on Suns. Free admission and parking with access for disabled. Cafeteria and sales point.

RUTHIN

RUTHIN CRAFT CENTRE
Park Road LL15 1BB. Tel: (08242) 4774/5675/3992.

The Gallery, housed within a purpose-built Craft Centre in the beautiful Vale of Clwyd, specialises in work by top British artists and designer-makers, but also reflects the wealth of talent within the principality. With an exciting programme of selling exhibitions which change monthly and a stock of work in glass, leather, wood, ceramics, jewellery, textiles and paper, it produces a constant variety of excellence. There are also thirteen studios where craftsmen work on a daily basis, situated around a landscaped courtyard. Licensed restaurant. Opening hours 10–5 seven days a week. Adm free. Parking. Advanced notice for parties. Suitable for disabled persons – all areas have access ramps for wheelchairs. For information, telephone (08242) 4774/3992/5675.

WREXHAM

ERDDIG, The National Trust
Telephone: Wrexham (0978) 355314   &

Late 17th century house with 18th century additions and containing much of the original furniture, set in a garden restored to 18th century formal design and containing varieties of fruit known to have been grown there during that period. Range of domestic outbuildings include laundry, bakehouse, sawmill and smithy, all in working order; the extensive restoration work on house and garden is now complete. Visitor Centre containing early farm implements.

Location: 2 m S of Wrexham off A525.
Stations: Wrexham Central (1¾ m); Wrexham General (2½ m), includes 1 m driveway to House.
Opening Times: Mar 24 to June 30: Daily except Thurs & Fri (open Good Friday) 11–6; House open 12–5; (last adm House 4, Gardens 5.30). July 1 to Sept 1: Daily except Fri 11–6. House open 12–5; (last adm House 4, Gardens 5.30). Sept 2 to Oct 22: Daily except Thurs and Fri 11–6; House open 12–5; (last adm House 4, Gardens 5.30). School and Youth Groups by arrangement. Adm £3, Chd £1.50, Family £7.50. Prebooked groups of 20+ £2.40.
NB: Certain rooms have no electric light; visitors wishing to make a close study of pictures & textiles should avoid dull days early & late in season. Due to extreme fragility the Tapestry & Chinese Rooms will be open only on Weds & Sats.
Refreshments: Light lunches & teas.

WREXHAM LIBRARY ARTS CENTRE *(Clwyd County Council)*
Rhosddu Road. Tel: (0978) 261932.

Local and touring exhibitions, drama and musical events. Contact Exhibitions Officer for details of programmes and opening times. Admission free, parking adjacent and access for disabled. Cafeteria and sales point.

Dyfed

ABERGWILI

THE CARMARTHEN MUSEUM *(Dyfed County Council)*
Abergwili. Tel: (0267) 231691.

Situated in the former Palace of the Bishop of St. David's, the museum is surrounded by seven acres of beautiful parkland. Displays cover the history and natural history of the region and include archaeology, costume and folk life material. Mon to Sat 10–4.30. Adm 50p, Chld 25p. Reductions for parties, OAPs, Students and the unemployed.

ABERYSTWYTH

ABERYSTWYTH ARTS CENTRE EXHIBITIONS
Tel: (0970) 623232 *(Theatre Box Office)*; (0972) 624278 *(Exhibitions)*.

Continuous programme of exhibitions throughout the year covering painting, prints, sculpture, craft plus monthly changing exhibitions of photography and ceramics. Also major collection of studio pottery (housed in our new Ceramics Gallery). Craft shop, bookshop and cafe. Mon to Sat 9.30–5.

THE CATHERINE LEWIS GALLERY AND PRINT ROOM
(The Hugh Owen Library, The University College of Wales)
Tel: (0970) 62339/623591.

Permanent collection of graphic art from 15th–20th century particularly 1860's illustration, 1920's/30's and contemporary prints, 20th century Italian and British photography. Changing exhibitions from the collection and special exhibitions of graphic art (see posters or telephone). Reference available by appointment. Open Mon to Fri 9.30–5; Sat (College Term only) 9.30–12.30 (except for Christmas, Easter and Bank Hols). Adm free. Parties by arrangement. Car parking. Suitable for disabled persons.

CEREDIGION MUSEUM
Coliseum, Terrace Road.

Mainly folk collection including agriculture, reconstructed cottage interior of 1850 and various local crafts. Also archaeology, weights and measures, 'Development of Aberystwyth', seafaring, leadmining, Welsh furniture and other domestic objects, small costumed figures, clocks, transport, education, dentistry and slate enamelling. The museum is housed in a restored Edwardian theatre. Mon to Sat 10–5.

THE NATIONAL LIBRARY OF WALES
Aberystwyth SY23 3BU. Tel: (0970) 623816. Telex: 35165.
Fax: (0970) 615709.

Collection of books, manuscripts and records relating to Wales and the Celtic countries; topographical prints, maps, drawings etc. of historical interest. One of six Copyright Libraries in Britain. Exhibitions. Mon to Fri 9.30–6; Sat 9.30–5. *Closed Bank Hols, Easter, Tues and first full week of Oct.*

AMROTH

COLBY LODGE GARDEN, The National Trust
Telephone: Llandeilo 822800

Formal and woodland gardens; walks through a secluded valley along open and wooded pathways with rhododendrons and azaleas. Mr and Mrs A. Scourfield Lewis kindly allow access to the Walled Garden during normal visiting hours.
Location: NE of Tenby off A477; E of junction A477/A478.
Station: Kilgetty (2½ m).
Opening Times: Daily all year during daylight hours. Adm free.

CILGERRAN

CILGERRAN CASTLE
(Cadw: Welsh Historic Monuments)

A 13th century castle which has been a favourite subject for painters since the 18th century.
Location: 3 m from Cilgerran itself along River Tefi.

DRE-FACH FELINDRE

MUSEUM OF THE WOOLLEN INDUSTRY
(a branch museum of the National Museum of Wales)
Dre-Fach Felindre, near Newcastle Emlyn. Tel: (0559) 370929.

Situated in the most important woollen manufacturing centre of Wales, it contains an extensive section of textile machinery and tools dating back to the 18th century along with an exhibition of photographs tracing the development of Wales' most important rural industry from the middle ages to the present day. The evolutionary stages in the development of the woollen industry may be seen at the museum.
Four miles East of Newcastle Emlyn on the A484 Carmarthen to Cardigan road. Open Apr 1 to Sept 30. Mon to Sat 9–5. Oct 1 to Mar 31. Mon to Fri 9–5. *Closed* Christmas Eve, Christmas Day, Boxing Day, New Year's Day, Good Friday, May Day.

HAVERFORDWEST

THE CASTLE MUSEUM AND ART GALLERY
Haverfordwest. Tel: (0437) 3708.

Town and Military museum incorporating Art Gallery and Cultural Exhibition Centre showing local fine Art Collection and temporary exhibitions. Displays include the history of the former Town and County of Haverfordwest and the Collection of the Pembroke Yeomanry Historical Trust. Tues to Sat 10–5.30 (winter 10–4). *Closed* Mon (but open Mons in tourist season) and Good Friday, Christmas Day, Boxing Day and New Year's Day. Car park. Museum shop. Small adm charge. For all enquiries and party visits contact the Curator (see below).

GRAHAM SUTHERLAND GALLERY
The Rhos.

A unique collection of works by Graham Sutherland; drawings, paintings, graphics. Apr to Sept: Daily *(except Mon but open Bank Hol Mons)* 10.30–5.

PICTON CASTLE
(The Picton Castle Trust)

A scheduled ancient monument, but also a beautiful home, occupied continuously since the 15th century by the Philipps family who are still in residence.
Location: 4 m SE of Haverfordwest S of A40 via the Rhos.
Opening Times: CASTLE: Easter Sun & Mon, and following Bank Hols. Also every Sun & Thurs from mid-July to mid-Sept: 2–5. GROUNDS: Easter Sat to Sept 30—Daily 10.30–5, except Mon. GRAHAM SUTHERLAND GALLERY: dates and times of opening under review. Craft Shop. Free car park. Charges not available at time of going to press.
Refreshments: Tea shop. *Closed* Mon.

KIDWELLY

KIDWELLY CASTLE
(Cadw: Welsh Historic Monuments)

A very substantial castle possessing a notable chapel built out over the river bank.
Location: In Kidwelly.

KIDWELLY INDUSTRIAL MUSEUM
(Kidwelly Heritage Centre and Tinplate Museum Trust/Llanelli Borough Council)
Kidwelly. Tel: (0554) 891078.
Located in remains of tinplate works. Also features locomotives, colliery winding engine and headgear, interpretive exhibitions. Industrial machinery and tools. Special exhibitions on heritage of the area, and on coal industry of the area. Easter to Sept: 10–5 weekdays; 2–5 weekends. Open Bank Hols. Adm (1988 prices) 75p, Chld/OAPs/students/unemployed 30p. Family ticket £1.80. 20% reduction parties of 15 or more, school parties free. Car parking available. Suitable for disabled persons. Basic refreshments.

LAMPHEY

LAMPHEY PALACE
(Cadw: Welsh Historic Monuments)
Substantial remains of the medieval Bishops of St David's country residence.
Location: 2½ m E of Pembroke on A4139.

LLANELLI

PARC HOWARD AND ART GALLERY *(Llanelli Borough Council)*
Tel: (0554) 773538.
Collection of Llanelli pottery. Exhibits of Welsh artists. Items of local interest. Travelling exhibitions.

PUBLIC LIBRARY GALLERY *(Llanelli Borough Council)*
Tel: (0554) 773538.
Collection of local artists; travelling and other exhibitions. Mon to Sat 10–6.

LLANYCEFN

PENRHOS COTTAGE
Llanycefn, near Maenclochog (map reference SM102258).
Traditional Welsh Cottage, furnished. Branch Museum and Information Centre, near Preseli Hills, not far from the Gors Fawr Stone Circle. May to Sept: Daily (except Sun morning and Mon) 10–12.30, 2.30–6. Small adm charge. All enquiries to the Curator (see below).

LLAWHADEN

LLAWHADEN CASTLE
(Cadw: Welsh Historic Monuments)
Built to protect the Church's estates in West Wales.
Location: Llawhaden, off A40(T).

PEMBROKE

NATIONAL MUSEUM OF GYPSY CARAVANS, ROMANY CRAFTS AND LORE
Commons Road. Tel: (0646) 681308.
An outstanding collection of Gypsy caravans and representation of Gypsy life.

PONTERWYD

LLYWERNOG SILVER-LEAD MINE MUSEUM
Ponterwyd. Tel: Ponterwyd (097085) 620 for details.
An award winning restoration of a Victorian water-powered metal-mine which captures the spirit and atmosphere of the 'boom-days'.

ST. DAVIDS

ST DAVIDS BISHOPS PALACE
(Cadw: Welsh Historic Monuments)
A most impressive mediaeval Bishop's Palace within the Cathedral Close.
Location: In the centre of St Davids.

SPITTAL

SCOLTON MANOR MUSEUM
Spittal, near Haverfordwest (on B4329). Tel: (0437) 82328.
New regional museum, study centre etc. in course of development. Grounds (40 acres) include Nature Trail, 'Tree Trail', picnic sites. The Manor House, Stables and Exhibition Hall contain human, social, domestic and industrial history, rural crafts, costume and railway collections (including 100 year old steam locomotive). Open tourist season only 10.30–6. *Closed* Mon. Museum shops, large car park, refreshments (high season only). Small adm charge. For parties out of season visits and other enquiries, contact the Curator or tel: (0437) 82 328.

STRATA FLORIDA

STRATA FLORIDA ABBEY
(Cadw: Welsh Historic Monuments)
A remote, 13th century Cistercian site in a lovely setting.
Location: Up minor road, 2 m from Pontrhydfendigaid.

TALLEY

TALLEY ABBEY
(Cadw: Welsh Historic Monuments)
A small 12th century monastic site founded for the Premonstratensian Order.
Location: ¼ m from Talley Village.

TENBY

TENBY MUSEUM AND PICTURE GALLERY
Castle Hill. Tel: (0834) 2809.
An outstanding display of the geology, archaeology and natural history of Pembrokeshire. The maritime gallery commemorates Tenby's seafaring past and its achievements as a lifeboat station; there are special exhibitions of local history. Pictures of local interest and by artists with local connections, including Augustus and Gwen John and Nina Hamnett are on view in the gallery. Open Daily Easter to Oct: 10–6. Winter times from Nov 1. Adm charge. School parties, by appointment, free.

TUDOR MERCHANT'S HOUSE, The National Trust
An example of a merchant's house of the 15th century.
Location: Quay Hill, Tenby.
Station: Tenby (8 mins walk) (not Suns, except June-Aug).
Opening Times: Easter Sun to end Sept, Mon–Fri 10–1 & 2.30–6. *Closed Sat.* Open Sun 2–6. Last adm 5.45. Adult £1, Chld 50p. No dogs. Unsuitable for wheelchairs.

TRAPP

CARREG CENNEN CASTLE
(Cadw: Welsh Historic Monuments)
A 13th century castle dramatically perched on a limestone crag.
Location: Signposted from Trapp Village near Llandeilo.

TRE'R DDOL

YR HEN GAPEL
(a branch Museum of the National Museum of Wales, administered by the Welsh Folk Museum)
Tre'r Ddôl, near Aberystwyth. Tel: (0970) 86407.
10 miles North of Aberystwyth on the A487 Aberystwyth to Machynlleth road. This museum of 19th century religious life in Wales reflects those activities which had such far reaching effects on the social life of both rural and industrial Wales. The collection consists of a permanent exhibition and also temporary displays of related interest. The museum is housed in a former Wesleyan Methodist chapel which was linked with the momentous 1859 religious revival. Open Apr 1 to Sept 30 Mon – Sat 10–5. *Closed* Sun.

Mid Glamorgan

COITY

COITY CASTLE
(Cadw: Welsh Historic Monuments)
A typical Norman stronghold guarding a fertile area of the Vale of Glamorgan.
Location: Coity Village, nr Bridgend (on M4).

MERTHYR TYDFIL

CYFARTHFA CASTLE MUSEUM
Tel: (0685) 723112.
Situated in an ironmasters gothic mansion the collections cover paintings, ceramics, silver furniture and decorative art. There are displays on local history, industrial history, enthnography, archaeology and Egyptology. New gallery with programme of temporary exhibitions throughout the year. Weekdays 10–1, 2–6 (Fri close 5). Sun 2–5. During winter Oct 1 to Apr 1 close one hour earlier. *Closed* Christmas and Good Friday. Adm 20p, Chld 10p. Educational Groups free. Schoolroom available.

JOSEPH PARRY'S BIRTHPLACE *(Merthyr Tydfil Heritage Trust)*
4 Chapel Row, Georgetown CF48 7BN. Tel: 73117 & 83704.
The cottage contains exhibitions on the history of Merthyr Tydfil, and on the life and works of Dr Joseph Parry the musician and composer. He was born here in 1841 into a family who were employed at nearby Cyfarthfa Ironworks. At the time of his death in 1903 he was well established as the Head of the Music department at University College Cardiff and had composed well over 400 works including 'Myfanwy'. Easter to Sept 30: Open Mon–Sat 11–1, 2–5; Bank Hols & Sun 2–5. Winter: Open Mon–Fri 11–1, 2–5. *Closed* Dec 24–Jan 2. Adm free. Parties – please book in advance. Car parking adjacent to cottage. Guided walks around Merthyr Tydfil are available covering many different aspects of its industrial/social/urban history.

South Glamorgan

CAERPHILLY

CAERPHILLY CASTLE
(Cadw: Welsh Historic Monuments)
Second largest castle area in Europe.
Location: In Caerphilly; 6 m N of Cardiff.

CARDIFF

BURGES DRAWINGS COLLECTION
The Burges Rooms, Cardiff Castle.

CARDIFF CASTLE
(Cardiff City Council)
Begun 1090 on remains of Roman Fort. Rich interior decorations. Location for Cardiff Searchlight Tattoo.
Location: In centre of Cardiff city.
Station: Cardiff Centre (½ m).

THE NATIONAL MUSEUM OF WALES
Main Building, Cathays Park. (Amgueddfa Genedlaethol Cymru)
Tel: (0222) 397951.
The story of Wales from earliest times is told in the main building of the National Museum of Wales. Welsh plants and animals and the geological forces that have given the country its present shape are illustrated in the departments of Botany, Zoology and Geology while the work and art of man are displayed in the departments of Archaeology, Art and Industry. A remarkable collection of modern European paintings and sculpture has helped the museum earn its International status.

WELSH INDUSTRIAL AND MARITIME MUSEUM
(a branch museum of the National Museum of Wales)
Tel: (0222) 481919.
Working exhibits tell the story of motive power and the roles played by a variety of machines over two centuries of industrial production and progress in South Wales. Many large out-door exhibits are also on show including a pilot cutter, a canal boat, cranes, an industrial locomotive and a working replica of Richard Trevithick's famous Penydarren locomotive.

PENARTH

TURNER HOUSE
(A branch art gallery of the National Museum of Wales)
Tel: (0222) 708870.
A small gallery holding temporary exhibitions of pictures and objets d'art from the National Museum of Wales and other sources.

ST. FAGANS

WELSH FOLK MUSEUM
(A branch museum of the National Museum of Wales)
Nr. Cardiff. Tel: (0222) 569441.
An open air museum of about 100 acres representing the life and culture of Wales.

TONGWYNLAIS

CASTELL COCH
(Cadw: Welsh Historic Monuments)
13th century castle, restored on original lines for the Marquess of Bute in 19th century and made habitable. Unique Neo Gothic decorations.
Location: 6 m N of Cardiff off Pontypridd Road by village of Tongwynlais.

West Glamorgan

NEATH

CEFN COED COLLIERY MUSEUM
(West Glamorgan County Council)
Blaenant Colliery, Crynant, SA10 8SN. Tel: Crynant (0639) 750556.
The museum vividly portrays the story of men and machines involved in the mining of coal at the former Cefn Coed Colliery. A massive steam winding engine, now electrically driven, realistic simulated underground mining gallery. Apr to Oct: Daily 10.30–6. Adm (1988 opening times and charges) 70p, Chld/OAPs 45p, Chld under five and registered disabled free. 10 or more persons pre-booked 45p, Chld/OAPs 35p. West Glamorgan schools free. Free car parking. Suitable for disabled persons. Refreshments. Curator: R. Merrill.

NEATH ABBEY
(Cadw: Welsh Historic Monuments)
In the 16th century the 'fairest building in Wales'.
Location: In Neath.

SWANSEA

MARITIME AND INDUSTRIAL MUSEUM *(Swansea City Council)*
Museum Square, Maritime Quarter. Tel: (0792) 470371/50351.
See the working woollen mill; transport, maritime and industrial displays. Step aboard the boats floating alongside museum. Activities for all. Open daily 10.30–5.30. Adm free.

SWANSEA MUSEUMS SERVICE, GLYNN VIVIAN ART GALLERY AND MUSEUM
(Swansea City Council)
Alexandra Road. Tel: (0792) 55006/51738.
Pictures, sculpture, glass and Swansea China. Top quality visiting exhibitions programme. Free films and many other activities. Open daily 10.30–5.30. Adm free.

UNIVERSITY COLLEGE OF SWANSEA AND ROYAL INSTITUTION OF SOUTH WALES MUSEUM
(Swansea Museum)
Victoria Road. Tel: (0792) 53763.
Collections of antiquarian interest; archaeology, ceramics. Welsh folk culture, 19th century Welsh Kitchen, reclamation of the Lower Swansea Valley, natural history, numismatics, art. Tues to Sat 10–4.30. Adm 30p, Chld and OAPs 15p (accompanied Chld 10p).

WEOBLEY

WEOBLEY CASTLE
(Cadw: Welsh Historic Monuments)
A fortified mediaeval manor house.
Location: Minor road from Llanrhidian, Gower Peninsula.

Gwent

ABERGAVENNY

ABERGAVENNY AND DISTRICT MUSEUM
(Monmouth District Council)
The Castle, Castle Street. Tel: (0873) 4282.
Local history of the town and surrounding area. Castle grounds open to visitors.

BLAENAVON

BIG PIT MINING MUSEUM
Tel: (0495) 790311.
Mining museum with temporary and permanent exhibitions; underground tour of the coal mine, and historical exhibitions relating to the history of the area, with particular emphasis on mining and local industries. Adm Surface and underground: £3.45, OAP £3, Chld £2.45; surface only: £1.25, OAP £1, Chld 75p. Open daily Mar – Dec, other times by arrangement. Reductions for parties over 30. Refreshments. Facilities for disabled by arrangement. Ample car parking.

CAERLEON

CAERLEON ROMAN FORTRESS BATHS AND AMPHITHEATRE
(Cadw: Welsh Historic Monuments)
The only excavated Legionary baths in Europe; in a town still boasting many other Roman remains.
Location: Caerleon 2 m N of Newport, off M4 junction 25.

ROMAN LEGIONARY MUSEUM
(a branch archaeological gallery of the National Museum of Wales)
Tel: Newport (0633) 423134.
The refurbished Roman Legionary Museum was officially opened in June 1987. On display are three life-size Roman soldiers – a centurion, a standard bearer and a legionary – sculpture, inscriptions, tombstones, a labyrinth mosaic, military equipment, pottery, glass and jewellery – including a remarkable collection of engraved gemstones from the Fortress Baths.

CALDICOT

CALDICOT CASTLE MUSEUM
(Monmouth District Council)
The Castle. Tel: Caldicot (0291) 420241.
Local history, furniture, costume and temporary exhibitions in the restored remains of a frontier castle.

CHEPSTOW

CHEPSTOW CASTLE
(Cadw: Welsh Historic Monuments)
Great Tower dates from late 11th century.
Location: On W bank of the Wye, near Chepstow Bridge.

CHEPSTOW MUSEUM *(Monmouth District Council)*
Bridge Street. Tel: (029 12) 5981.
Local history of the town and surrounding area featuring Chepstow at work, Wye Valley, river trade and fishing, castle and temporary exhibitions.

CWMBRAN

LLANYRAFON FARM *(Torfaen Museum Trust)*
Tel: (063 33) 61810.
A 17th century manor house furnished to show the lives of the Griffiths family who lived in it; also exhibitions on the agricultural history of the South Wales Valleys. OPENING SPRING 1989: telephone for further details.

LLANTILIO CROSSENNY

WHITE CASTLE
(Cadw: Welsh Historic Monuments)
One of the border castles of the Norman Marcher Lords.
Location: Minor roads, signposted from B4521 & B4233.

MONMOUTH

MONMOUTH MUSEUM *(Monmouth District Council)*
Priory Street.

NELSON COLLECTION AND LOCAL HISTORY CENTRE
Tel: (0600) 3519.
One of the finest collections of Nelson relics and memorabilia. Displays on the development of the town, C.S. Rolls (of Rolls-Royce), temporary exhibitions.

NEWPORT

MUSEUM AND ART GALLERY
(Newport Borough Council)
John Frost Square. Tel: (0633) 840064.
Natural science displays including geology; fine and applied art, specialising in early English watercolours, teapots and contemporary crafts; Prehistoric and Romano-British remains from Caerwent; local history including the Chartist movement. Regular travelling exhibitions and lectures. Mon to Thurs 9.30–5; Fri 9.30–4.30; Sat 9.30–4.

TREDEGAR HOUSE
Telephone: Newport (0633) 815880
(Newport Borough Council)
One wing of the 16th century house survives, but Tredegar House owes its character to lavish 17th century rebuilding in brick. The Country Park includes gardens, lake (boating and coarse fishing), adventure play farm, carriage rides and craft workshops.
Location: SW of Newport; signposted from M4 junction 28, A48.
Station: Newport (2¾ m).
Opening Times: COUNTRY PARK. Daily 6.15–Sunset. HOUSE & ATTRACTIONS. Good Fri to last Sun in Sept. Weds to Suns & Public Hols. House Tours every ½ hour from 12.30–4.30. House open at other times by appointment. Adm (1988 rates) £1.80, Chd/OAPs £1. Family £4. Carriage Rides £1, Chd 50p. Boats £1.50 per ½ hour. Fishing £1, Chd 50p during season. Touring Caravans £2–£4, Tents £1.20–£4. Coach & school parties welcome if booked in advance.
Refreshments: Lunch & teas at the Old Brewhouse Bar & Tea Room.

PENHOW

PENHOW CASTLE
Telephone: Penhow (0633) 400800 and bookings/enquiries (0633) 400555
(Stephen Weeks Esq.)
Location: On A48, midway between Chepstow and Newport. M4 junctions 22 or 24.
Opening Times: Good Fri to end of Sept – Weds to Suns inclusive and Bank Holidays, 10–6 (last adm 5). Winter opening: Wed only, 10–5. Adm £2.25, Chd and concessions £1.15. Family tickets (2 2): £5.50. *Price includes Soundalive Walkman Tour.* 'Candlelit Tours' by appointment and on summer Weds at 7. Inn, craft centre, gift shop, accommodation, events, restaurant. Please call the Administrator for full information on educational and out-of-hours visits. The Penhow Castle Visitor Centre is open all year round.

PONTYPOOL

JUNCTION COTTAGE PONTYMOEL *(Torfaen Museum Trust)*
Tel: (049 55) 52036.
A canal toll-keeper's cottage with exhibitions on the canals of South-East Wales. Apr to Sept: Daily 2–5.

THE VALLEY INHERITANCE *(Torfaen Museum Trust)*
Tel: (049 55) 52036.
Audiovisual presentation and exhibitions on social and industrial development of a South Wales valley and its people. Temporary exhibitions. Weekdays 10–5; Sun 2–5. *Closed* Christmas Day. Adm charge.

RAGLAN

RAGLAN CASTLE
(Cadw: Welsh Historic Monuments)
A most impressive 15th century castle: possibly the last truly mediaeval castle.
Location: N of Raglan, signposted from A40 Raglan by-pass.

TINTERN

TINTERN ABBEY
(Cadw: Welsh Historic Monuments)
One of Britain's most complete Cistercian Abbeys, the Abbey Church is inspiringly beautiful.
Location: In Tintern.

USK

GWENT RURAL LIFE MUSEUM
The Malt Barn, New Market Street. Tel: (029 13) 3777 or (063 349) 315.
Agricultural and craft tools, wagons, vintage machinery, farmhouse kitchen, laundry, dairy. Winner of Prince of Wales Award. Apr–Sept: Mon to Fri 10–5; weekends 2–5. Oct–Mar: please telephone museum. Parties by arrangement. Adm charge. *An Independent Museum.*

Gwynedd

BANGOR

PENRHYN CASTLE, The National Trust
Telephone: (0243) 353084
The 19th century Castle is a unique and outstanding example of neo-Norman architecture. The garden and grounds have exotic and rare trees and shrubs. There is an Industrial Railway Museum and exhibition of dolls. Victorian formal garden. Superb views of mountains and Menai Strait.
Location: 3 m E of Bangor, on A5122.
Station: Bangor (3 m).
Opening Times: Mar 24 to Nov 5 – Daily except Tues 11–6. Please note: Castle and Museums 12–5, July & Aug 11–5 (except Tues), last adm 30 mins prior to closing. Adm £2.50, Chd £1.25, Family £6.25, Groups £2.
Refreshments: Light lunches & teas at Castle.

BEAUMARIS

BEAUMARIS CASTLE
(Cadw: Welsh Historic Monuments)
Last of great castles of the Edwardian conquest.
Location: In Beaumaris.

BEAUMARIS GAOL
(Gwynedd Archives and Museums Service)
Beaumaris.
Built in 1829 Beaumaris Gaol is a grim reminder of the harshness of justice in Victorian Britain. Visitors can see the prison cells, the punishment cell, the unique tread-wheel, the condemned cell and the condemned man's final walk to the scaffold. There is an exhibition of documents illustrating prison life in the nineteenth century. Also on display is the Scott Police exhibition. May to Sept: Daily 11–6. Also Beaumaris's Victorian Courthouse. May to Sept: 11.30–5.30.

BEDDGELERT

SYGUN COPPER MINE
Tel: (0766 86) 595.
A British Tourist Authority Award winning family attraction in the heart of the stunning Snowdonia National Park. Guided audio/visual tours take the visitor into the underground world of the 19th century copper miner. Magnificent stalactite and stalagmite formations. Adm £2.20, OAPs £1.75, Chld £1.35. Special group rates. Free parking. Unsuitable for disabled.

BLAENAU FFESTINIOG

LLECHWEDD SLATE CAVERNS
Tel: (0766) 830306.
Preserved section of a slate mine offering mine tours to visitors. Slate mine and associated buildings and equipment. Easter or Apr 1 (whichever is earlier) to end Oct: 10am (last tour 5.15pm, Oct 4.15). Adm free to surface. 1988 underground tours £2.55, Chld £1.60, OAPs £2. Reductions for parties of 20+. Free car parking. Only partly suitable for disabled persons. Cafe, pub, soup kitchen, licensed restaurant.

CAERNARFON

CAERNARFON CASTLE
(Cadw: Welsh Historic Monuments)
The most important of Edward I's castles.
Location: In Caernarfon.

THE ROYAL WELCH FUSILIERS
Queen's Tower, Caernarfon Castle.
Hat ribbon worn by King William of Orange 1690, Keys of Corunna, Officer's Mitre Cap 1750, nine V.C.s, Gold Peninsular War medals; large collection of Campaign medals, full size Tableau and Royal and other portraits by Dennis Fields, Oswald Birley and Gerald Kelly. Mid-Mar to mid-Oct: Daily 9.30–6.30. Mid-Oct to mid-Mar: Weekdays 9.30–4; Sun 2–4. Adm to Castle £2, Regimental Museum free.

SEGONTIUM ROMAN FORT MUSEUM
(a branch museum of the National Museum of Wales)
Tel: (0286) 5625.
The Museum stands on the site of one of Britain's most famous forts and maintained by the Welsh Office, contains mostly material excavated there. May to Sept: Mon to Sat 9.30–6; Sun 2–6. Mar, Apr and Oct: Mon to Sat 9.30–5.30; Sun 2–5. Nov to Feb: Mon to Sat 9.30–4; Sun 2–4. *Closed* Dec 24, 25, 26, New Year's Day, Good Friday and May Day.

SEIONT II MARITIME MUSEUM
Victoria Dock.
Step back in time when you board the Museum's operational centrepiece, the steam dredger *Seiont II* and in the Museum itself absorb the development, hardships and drama of the area's maritime history. Open: Easter, May to Sept: Daily 1–5 (often open 10 to dusk during the summer holidays).

CONWY

ABERCONWY HOUSE, The National Trust
Telephone: Conwy (049259) 2246

Town house that dates from 14th century, now housing the Conwy Exhibition, depicting the life of the borough from Roman times to the present day.
Location: In the town at junction of Castle Street & High Street.
Station: Llandudno Junction (¾ m).
Opening Times: Mar 24 to Nov 5 – Daily (except Tues) 11–5.30 (last admission 5.15); Adm 80p, Chd 40p, Family £2. Pre-booked parties 60p. Shop.

CONWY CASTLE
(Cadw: Welsh Historic Monuments)
Built by Edward I to command Conwy ferry.
Location: In Conwy.

PLAS MAWR
(Royal Cambrian Academy of Art)
Built by Robert Wynne 1577–80.
Location: High Street Conwy.
Station: Conwy (200 yards).
Opening Times: Nov, Feb & Mar – Weds to Suns 10–4; Apr to Sept – All week 10–6; Oct – All week 10–4. *Closed Dec & Jan.* Adm 75p, Chd 25p, OAPs/Students 50p.

CRICCIETH

CRICCIETH CASTLE
(Cadw: Welsh Historic Monuments)
Native Welsh castle dating mainly first half 13th century.
Location: In Criccieth.

LLOYD GEORGE MEMORIAL MUSEUM
Llanystumdwy.
In the 'Lloyd George Village' where he was raised, by whose river he is buried, are displayed caskets, deeds of freedom, photographs, mementoes and cartoons of the great statesman. Highgate, the boyhood home, is also open to the public. A/V presentation, 'Talking Head'. Easter, mid May to Sept: Daily 10–5 and at other times by appointment.

CYMER

CYMER ABBEY
(Cadw: Welsh Historic Monuments)
A small Cistercian foundation on the banks of the Mawddach.
Location: 2 m NW of Dolgellau on A494.

HARLECH

HARLECH CASTLE
(Cadw: Welsh Historic Monuments)
Built 1283–9 by Edward I. Concentric plan.
Location: In Harlech.

HOLYHEAD

HOLYHEAD MARITIME MUSEUM
Rhos-y-Gaer Avenue (close to Railway Station).
May to Sept: Daily 1–5, but *closed* Mon (except Bank Hols).

LLANBERIS

ORIEL ERYRI *(a branch of the National Museum of Wales)*
Tel: (0286) 870636.
This new environmental centre interprets the rich and varied natural and human history of Snowdonia. May to Sept: Mon to Sat 10–5; Sun 2.30–5. *Closed* May Day.

WELSH SLATE MUSEUM
(administered by the National Museum of Wales in conjunction with CADW, Welsh Historic Monuments)
Tel: (0286) 870630.
When the extensive Dinorwic Quarry was closed in 1969 the workshops and most of the machinery and plant were preserved and a branch museum of the National Museum of Wales was established. Much of the original atmosphere remains in the fitting and erecting shops, repair shops, smithy, dressing and sawing sheds, foundry office, mess room and yard. Open Easter to Sept 30 9.30–6.30. Sun 2–6.30. *Closed* Oct to Good Friday, May Day.

LLANDUDNO

LLANDUDNO MUSEUM
17-19 Gloddaeth Street. Tel: (0492) 76517.

MOSTYN ART GALLERY/ORIEL MOSTYN
12 Vaughan Street.
This major public gallery organises temporary exhibitions covering a wide range of the contemporary arts from Britain and abroad, work by artists working in Wales and historical exhibitions of the fine and applied arts which are of particular regional interest. Open during exhibitions, Tues to Sat: all year 11–5; Suns 2–6 (Apr–Sept). Adm free. Easy access for disabled. Bookshop, postcards, crafts, prints.

LLANFAIRPWLL

PLAS NEWYDD, The National Trust
Telephone: Llanfairpwll (0248) 714795   ♿

18th century house by James Wyatt in unspoilt position adjacent to Menai Strait. Magnificent views to Snowdonia. Fine spring garden. Rex Whistler exhibition and mural painting. Military museum.
Location: 1 m SW of Llanfairpwll on A4080 to Brynsiencyn; turn off A5 to Llanfairpwll at W end of Britannia Bridge.
Station: Llanfairpwll (1¾ m).
Opening Times: Mar 24 to Oct 1 – Daily except Sats 12–5. Shop, tearoom and gardens only 11–5. (July & Aug 11–5 except Sat). Shop, tearoom and gardens only 11–5. Last adm 4.30. Oct 6 to Nov 5, Fri and Sun only 12–5 (last adm 4.30). Adm £2.20, Chd £1.10, Family £5.50, Group £1.80.
Refreshments: Tea rooms (light lunches & teas).

LLANRUG

BRYN BRAS CASTLE
Telephone: Llanberis 870 210
(Mr & Mrs N E Gray-Parry)

The Castle, Grade II* listed, was built in c.1830 in the Romanesque style on an earlier structure built before 1750. There are fine examples of stained glass, panelling, interesting ceilings and richly carved furniture in this romantic castle, which was built by a Welshman, and is still a Welsh family home. The extensive and tranquil Victorian gardens of natural beauty, with much wild life, gradually merge into the foothills of Snowdon. They include peaceful lawns, walled Knot Garden, stream and pools, woodland walks and a ¼ mile mountain walk with magnificent panoramic views of Snowdon, Anglesey and the sea.
Location: 4½ m E of Caernarfon; 3½ m NW of Llanberis; ½ m off A4086.
Opening Times: Spring Bank Hol to mid-July & Sept—Daily (except Sats) 1–5. Mid-July to end Aug—Daily (except Sats) 10.30–5. Adm £1.50, Chd 75p. *25% reduction for parties.* Free car park. Picnic area. No dogs.
Refreshments: Home made Welsh teas (including Bara Brith) in charming tea room & the tea garden. Castle Apartments for holidays available all year.

LLANRWST

GWYDIR UCHAF CHAPEL
(Cadw: Welsh Historic Monuments)

A 17th century private chapel with elaborately painted ceilings and walls.
Location: On Forestry Commission land S of Llanrwst.

MENAI BRIDGE

MUSEUM OF CHILDHOOD
Water Street, Menai Bridge.

NEFYN

LLEYN HISTORICAL AND MARITIME MUSEUM
Old St. Mary's Church, Church Street.
This museum recreates the atmosphere of the area's maritime traditions by recording mainly through visual displays, the life and activities of the local community from the early 19th century to the present day. Open July 1 to early Sept: Mon to Fri 10.30–12.30; 2.30–4.30.

PENMACHNO

TY MAWR WYBRNANT, The National Trust
Telephone: Penmachno (069 03) 213

The birthplace of Bishop William Morgan. (c. 1541–1604), the first translator of the Bible into Welsh.
Location: At the head of the little valley of Wybrnant, 3½ m SW of Betws-y-Coed; 2 m W of Penmachno.
Opening Times: Mar 24 to Oct 1 daily excluding Mon and Sat (open Bank Holiday Mons) 12–5. Last adm 15 mins before closing. Oct 6 to Nov 5: Fri and Sun only 12–4. Adm £1, Chd 50p, Family £2.50.

PORTHMADOG

FESTINIOG RAILWAY MUSEUM *(Festiniog Railway Co.)*
Harbour Station.
Museum in former Goods Shed illustrating the Railway's history from the 1830s to the present day. Open daily during train service hours.

PORTHMADOG MARITIME MUSEUM
Situated on one of the old wharves of Porthmadog harbour, the last remaining slate shed houses a display on the maritime history of Porthmadog. Easter week, end of May to end of Sept: Daily 10–6.

TALYBONT

COCHWILLAN OLD HALL
Telephone: Bangor 364608
(R. C. H. Douglas Pennant, Esq)

Fine example of medieval architecture (restored 1971).
Location: 3½ m Bangor; 1 m Talybont village off A55.
Opening Times: Open by appointment.

TAL-Y-CAFN

BODNANT GARDEN, The National Trust
Telephone: Tyn-y-Groes (0492) 650460   &

Begun in 1875 by Henry Pochin. Amongst the finest gardens in the country. Magnificent collections of rhododendrons, camellias, magnolias and conifers.

Location: 8 m S of Llandudno & Colwyn Bay on A470; Entrance along Eglwysbach Road.
Station: Tal-y-Cafn (1½ m).
Opening Times: Mar 18 to Oct 31—Daily 10–5 (last adm 4.30). Adm £2, Chd £1. Pre-booked parties of 20 or more £1.80. Free car park. *No dogs (except guide dogs for the blind).* Wheelchairs provided but garden is steep & difficult. Braille guide.
Refreshments: Tea at car park Kiosk.

TYWYN

NARROW GAUGE RAILWAY MUSEUM
(The Narrow Gauge Railway Museum Trust)
Wharf Station, Tywyn. Tel: (0654) 710472.
A fine collection of steam locomotives, wagons, signals and other equipment from narrow gauge railways of the British Isles. Easter to end of Oct: Daily.

Powys

BRECON

BRECKNOCK MUSEUM *(Powys County Council)*
Collections illustrating the local and natural history of Brecknock. Archaeological, agricultural and domestic material, pottery, porcelain and lovespoons. Assize Court reconstruction, library and archives collection. Mon to Sat 10–5. *Closed* Good Friday, Christmas Day, Boxing Day and New Year's Day.

BWLCH

TREBINSHWN HOUSE
(Robin Watson, Esq)

A medium sized 16th century manor house which underwent extensive restoration in 1800. Fine courtyard and walled garden.
Location: 7 m SE of Brecon; 1½ m from Bwlch & A40; 4 m from Llangorse (B4560).
Opening Times: May 1 to Aug 31—Mons & Tues 10–5. Adm charge not available at time of going to press.
Refreshments: Red Lion Hotel, Llangorse (4 m).

CRICKHOWELL

TRETOWER COURT & CASTLE
(Cadw: Welsh Historic Monuments)

One of the finest medieval houses in Wales.
Location: 3½ m NW Crickhowell between A40 & A479 Roads.

LLANDRINDOD WELLS

LLANDRINDOD MUSEUM *(Powys County Council)*
Temple Street. Tel: (0597) 4513.
Archaeological material, mainly from Castell Collen excavations (Roman). Paterson Doll Collection. Mon to Sat 10–12.30, 2–5. *Closed* Sat afternoons from Oct to Apr and Bank Hols.

LLANIDLOES

MUSEUM OF LOCAL HISTORY AND INDUSTRY
(Powys County Council)
Market Hall.
Articles of local interest and industry. Easter week and Spring Bank Hol to Sept: Mon to Sat 11–1, 2–5.

NEWTOWN

ROBERT OWEN MEMORIAL MUSEUM (INDEPENDENT)
The Cross, Broad Street. Tel: (0686) 26345.
Illustrates the remarkable life of Robert Owen, (1771–1858), model employer, social reformer, inspirer of the Co-operative movement. Mon to Fri 9.45–11.45, 2–3.30. Sat 10–11.30. Adm free.

W.H. SMITH MUSEUM *(W.H. Smith Ltd.)*

24 High Street, Newtown. Tel: (0686) 626280.

The museum is on the first floor of the Newtown branch of W.H. Smith. The shop has been completely restored to its 1927 appearance, when the branch first opened. It has the original oak shop front, tiling and mirrors, plaster relief decoration and other details. The displays, which include models, photographs and a variety of historical mementoes, illustrate the history of W.H. Smith from its beginning in 1792 until the present day. Mon, Thurs, Sat 9–5; Tues, Wed, Fri 9–5.30. *Closed* Sun and Bank Hols. Adm free. Some street parking and public car park approx ¼ mile away. Not suitable for disabled persons.

WELSHPOOL

POWIS CASTLE, The National Trust

Telephone: Welshpool (0938) 4336   ♿

The medieval stronghold of the Welsh princes of Upper Powys, the home of the Herbert family since 1587. Clive of India Museum. Fine plaster work, murals, furniture, paintings and tapestry. Historic terraced garden; herbaceous borders, rare trees and shrubs.

Location: 1 m S of Welshpool on A483; Pedestrian access from High Street (A490); Cars enter road to Newtown (A483); 1 m.

Stations: Welshpool (1¼ m); Welshpool Raven Square (1¼ m); BR service Aug only.

Opening Times: Mar 24 to June 30: Wed to Sun 12–5 (open Bank Holiday Mon). NB *closed Apr 20 & 21*. July 1 to Aug 31: daily except Mon 11–6 (open Bank Holiday Mon). Sept 1 to Nov 5: Wed to Sun 12–5, last adm 30 mins prior to closing. Nov 6 to Apr 8 1990, Sun only 2–4.30. Gardens, Clive Museum and tearoom open.

Refreshments: Tea rooms (light lunches & teas).

POWYSLAND MUSEUM *(Powys County Council)*

Tel: (0938) 4759.

Material of folk life, archaeological and historical interest relating to the area. Mon to Fri 11–1, 2–5; Sat 2–4.30. *Closed* Wed in winter.

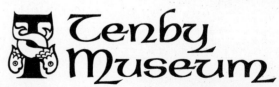

IRELAND (REPUBLIC OF)

ASHFORD

MOUNT USHER GARDENS
Telephone: (0404) 40205
(Mrs Madelaine Jay)

The Gardens extend along the Vartry river in beautiful County Wicklow. They are laid out in the informal 'Robinsonian' style comprising rare plants, shrubs and trees, collected from many parts of the world.

Location: Ashford, 1 m from Wicklow on Dublin-Bray-Wexford Road.
Opening Times: Mar 17 to Oct 31, open daily including Suns and Bank Holidays 10.30–6. Adm IR £2, OAPs, Chd, Students IR £1.50. Groups (20) IR £1.50, OAPs, Chd, Students IR £1.20. Car parking. Suitable for the disabled. No wheelchairs provided. Shopping courtyard.
Refreshments: Tea room at entrance, snacks, light lunches. Hunters Hotel 1 m.

BAGENALSTOWN

DUNLECKNEY MANOR
Telephone: (0503) 21932

Built c.' 1835 by Daniel Robertson incorporating original Manor of 1610. Dunleckney is perhaps the finest example of early 19th century Tudor Gothic architecture in Ireland. Magnificent stairwell and fine oak and walnut panelling throughout the house.

Location: ½ m N Bagenalstown. 60 m S Dublin. 8 m S Carlow.
Opening Times: June to Sept 2–6. Otherwise by appointment. Adm £1.50, Chd 50p.

BANTRY

BANTRY HOUSE
Telephone: (027) 50047
(Mr & Mrs Egerton Shelswell-White)

Partly-Georgian mansion standing at edge of Bantry Bay, with beautiful views. Seat of family of White, formerly Earls of Bantry. Unique collection of tapestries, furniture etc. Terraces and Statuary in the Italian style in grounds.

Location: In outskirts of Bantry (½ m); 56 m SW of Cork.
Opening Times: Open all year–Daily 9–6 *(open until 8 on most summer evenings)*. Adm House & Grounds £2, Chd (up to 14) accompanied by parents, free, OAPs/Students £1. Parties of 20 or more £1.50. Craft shop.
Refreshments: Tea room. Bed and Breakfast. Lunch/dinner in main dining room for groups of 10–30. (Advance Booking.)

BEAUFORT

DUNLOE CASTLE HOTEL GARDENS
Telephone: (064) 44111

The gardens at Dunloe Castle contain an extensive and interesting collection of plants, several of which are rarely, if at all, found elsewhere in Ireland. Each season brings its own specialities, camelias and rhododendron in spring, magnolias and sun roses in summer, Irish heaths and richly tinted leaves in autumn, are just a few of the many attractions. This combination of wild grandeur and garden exotica is situated in a setting of incomparable views of mountains and lakes.

Location: Situated adjacent to the Deluxe 140 bedroomed Hotel Dunloe Castle, off the main Killarney/Killorglin road, on the route to the Gap of Dunloe, approximately 8 km from Killarney.
Opening Times: May 1 to end Sept. Adm free. Catalogue of plants and trees available at hotel reception.
Refreshments: Available at Hotel Dunloe Castle.

BIRR

BIRR CASTLE DEMESNE
Telephone: (353509) 20056

Over 100 acres of gardens, rivers with waterfalls, lake and lake walks, terraces and parkland, scenically laid out and planted with most important collection of plants, many introduced directly from the wild. The Park contains the nineteenth century's largest telescope. Facilities include exhibition gallery, educationally explained tree trail, picnic and play area, coffee shop and tourist office.

Opening Times: Jan to Apr and Oct to Dec: Adm £2, Chd £1. Exhibition season (May to Sept): Adm £2.40, Chd £1.20; Group rates £2, Chd £1. (Admission free to all subscribing Friends of the Demesne.) Open daily throughout the year: 9–1 and 2–6 (or dusk in winter).
Refreshments: Morning coffee, lunch, afternoon teas.

BLARNEY

BLARNEY CASTLE AND BLARNEY HOUSE   &
(Sir Richard Colthurst, Bart)

Blarney Castle and Rock Close. Situated 5 miles from Cork City, the Castle is famous for its Stone which has the traditional power of conferring eloquence on all who kiss it. The word "Blarney" has found its way into the English language and has been described as conferring upon anyone who kisses it "a cajoling tongue and the art of flattery, or of telling lies with unblushing effrontery". The battlements crowning the fine intact keep are typically Irish in form and set in the walls below the battlements is the Stone. To kiss it one has to lean backwards out from the parapet walk. Adjacent to the Castle is the Rock Close, said to have Druidic connections and containing the gardens laid out by the Jefferies family in 1759 and now containing many old specimens and much new planting of shrubs, trees and beds, amongst the fine old limestone rocks scattered in 25 acres. **Blarney House & Gardens:** 200 yards from the Castle is Blarney House and Gardens, a fine Scottish Baronial type house, with distinguished corner turrets and bartizans with conical roofs and now restored inside with fine rooms and stairwell. Outside, the formal gardens and fine view of Blarney Lake together with the walk down to it and between the House and the Castle a large area of new planting, with shrubs, trees, beds and walks.

Location: 7 m from Cork City. 9 m from Cork Airport; 9 m from Ringaskiddy Port.
Opening Times: Blarney Castle & Rock Close: Mon to Sat, May, 9–7. June/July, 9–8.30. Aug, Sept, 9–7.30. Oct–Apr, 9–sundown. Sun, Summer 9.30–5.30. Winter 9.30–sundown. **Blarney House & Gardens:** June–mid Sept Mons to Sat only 12–6. (Last adm 30 mins before stated closing times.) Adm **Blarney Castle and Rock:** IR £2.30, Chd IR £1, OAPs and Students IR £1.50. **Blarney House & Gardens:** IR £2, Chd IR £1, OAPs and Students IR £1.50. Car and Coach Parking.
Refreshments: Sweet and soft drink kiosk; three hotels, three public houses; tea houses.

BLESSINGTON

RUSSBOROUGH
Blessington, Co. Wicklow   *map (iii)Z*
Telephone: (045) 65239
(Alfred Beit Foundation)

Palladian house in romantic setting in the Wicklow mountains, built 1740–50 and housing the Beit Art Collection.

Location: 20 m SW of Dublin; 2 m SW of Blessington on N81.
Opening Times: Easter to Oct 31: Easter to May 31, and Sept to Oct 31: Suns and Bank Holidays only 2–5.30. June 1 to Aug 31: daily 2–5.30. Adm £2.50, Chd (accompanied) 50p. Chd (over 12 accompanied) £1, Student/OAP £1.50. Upstairs – £1, Chd (accompanied) free. Shop. Children's playground. Extensive wooded parkland. Adjacent lakeside amenity and picnic area.
Refreshments: Tea room.

BRAY

KILLRUDDERY HOUSE & GARDENS
Telephone: (01) 863405

Home of the Earl and Countess of Meath. The Garden and Park is the only surviving 17th century layout in Ireland. The House is fully furnished with an interesting period collection.

Location: 23 km S of Dublin. The main entrance 2 km beyond Bray on the Greystones road.
Opening Times: May, June and Sept daily 1–5. Open at other times and dates for groups by prior arrangement. Adm House: £2.50, Chd £1.50, Gardens only: £1, Chd 50p.

BUNRATTY

BUNRATTY CASTLE & FOLK PARK
Telephone: (061) 361511
(Shannon Free Airport Development Company)

Bunratty Castle, built in 1469, is the most complete and authentic example of a Mediaeval Castle in Ireland. Its furniture, tapestries and works of art are displayed to give the visitor an idea of the furnishings and arrangement of a Castle of the late 16th or early 17th century. The Folk Park, in the grounds of the Castle, contains typical rural dwellings recreated and furnished to reflect life in Ireland at the turn of the century. The Park also features the complete reconstruction of a 19th century Irish village street, including craft shops, post office and general stores. **Bunratty House** (1805) has also been restored and furnished.

Location: 7 m from Shannon International Airport—N18 on Map.
Opening Times: Daily–9–5.30 (last adm 4.30). Adm: Bunratty Castle and Folk Park £3.10, Chd £1.60. Special group rates and family tickets. Car Parking. Suitable for disabled persons in Folk Park only.
Refreshments: Tea room in grounds of Folk Park, providing tea, coffee, scones, etc. Mediaeval Banquets and Entertainment nightly in Bunratty.

CASTLEREA

CLONALIS HOUSE
Telephone: (0907) 20014

Clonalis is the ancestral home of the O'Conor's of Connaught, descendants of the last High Kings of Ireland and traditional kings of Connaught. The Gaelic history of the family is recorded through the collection of archives, documentation and portraits in the house.
Location: Situated to the W of Castlerea town.
Opening Times: June 18 to Sept 7 – Daily 11–5.30. May to June 18 – Sats and Suns only 2–5.30. Other times by arrangement. Craft shop.
Refreshments: Tea room.

CASTLETOWNROCHE

ANNES GROVE GARDENS
Telephone: 022-26145
(Mr & Mrs Patrick Grove Annesley)

Extensive Robinsonian woodland and riverside gardens with notable collection of rhododendrons and other exotica. Edwardian flower garden.
Location: 1 m N of Castletownroche, signposted from N72 Fermoy/Killarney road.
Opening Times: Apr 1 to Sept 30—Mons to Fris 10–5; Suns 1–6; Sats by appointment only. Guided tours for pre-booked groups. Adm £1.80, Chd/OAPs £1, disabled free. Free car park, adjacent picnic site.
Refreshments: Lunches and teas for pre-booked groups by arrangement.

CELBRIDGE

CASTLETOWN HOUSE
(Castletown Foundation)

Built in 1722, the finest Georgian country house in Ireland.
Location: 12 m W of Dublin.
Opening Times: Open daily all year. Mon to Fri 10–5; Suns and Bank Hols 2–6. Adm £2.50, Chd 90p. Group rates available.
Refreshments: At the House at weekends.

CRAGGAUNOWEN

THE CRAGGAUNOWEN PROJECT
Telephone: 061-61511
(Shannon Free Airport Development Company)

The Craggaunowen project is pleasantly situated in the wooded farmland of County Clare. The site consists of a mediaeval Tower House containing a display of furniture and art objects, including some rare Irish pieces. There are two iron-age dwellings – a lake dwelling and a ring fort – and the leather boat 'Brendan' sailed by Tim Severin from Ireland to Newfoundland. In the summer months experiments and displays are conducted on the techniques associated with milling, pottery making and weaving in the iron age.
Location: 6 km E of Quin, 4 km N of Sixmilebridge. 24 km NW of Limerick.
Opening Times: May to Sept 10–6. Adm £2.30, Chd £1.35, Adult Groups £2, Student Groups £1. Car parking. Access to all exhibits for disabled.
Refreshments: Teas, home made scones.

CRATLOE

CRATLOE WOODS HOUSE
Telephone: Ireland (061) 87306
(Mr & Mrs J.G. Brickenden)

Cratloe Woods House is one of the few roofed examples of a Longhouse to survive. The Longhouse is a singularly Irish type of building. Exhibition of works of art and curios. Craft shop. Display of horse drawn farm machinery.
Location: 5 m from Limerick and 10 m from Shannon Airport on the Limerick-Shannon and Ennis dual carriageway.
Opening Times: June 1–Mid Sept – daily 2–6 except Suns. Adm £1.50, Chd 80p. Parties and special reductions by arrangement. Car park. Suitable for disabled persons.
Refreshments: Afternoon Teas.

DONABATE

NEWBRIDGE HOUSE
Telephone: Dublin 436534/5
(Ann Chambers, Administrator)

Newbridge House is an 18th century mansion in its own magnificent parkland of 300 acres. The Great Drawing room, in its original state, is one of the finest Georgian interiors in Ireland. Kitchen and laundry capture the 'below stairs' atmosphere of the big house, and the courtyard, with its coach house and various workshops, connect the past with the present.
Location: 12 m from the centre of Dublin.
Opening Times: Apr to Oct – Mon–Fri 10–12.45 & 2–5. Suns & Bank Holidays 2–6. Nov to Mar – Suns & Bank Holidays 2–5. Adm £2, OAPS & Students £1.50, Chd £1.10, Family ticket £5.95. Parties £1.75, OAPs & Students £1.25, Chd 90p. Bus & public car parks. Unsuitable for the disabled.
Refreshments: Coffee Shop serving teas, coffees, cakes, sandwiches.

DUBLIN

CHESTER BEATTY LIBRARY AND GALLERY OF ORIENTAL ART
20 Shrewsbury Road.

DOUGLAS HYDE GALLERY OF CONTEMPORARY ART
Trinity College, Nassau St.

DUBLIN CIVIC MUSEUM
City Assembly House, South William St.

GUINNESS MUSEUM
(Arthur Guinness, Son & Co. (Dublin) Ltd.)
The Old Hop Store, Rainsford Street.

THE HUGH LANE MUNICIPAL GALLERY OF MODERN ART
(Dublin Corporation)
Charlemont House, Parnell Square, Dublin 1. Tel: (0001) 01 741903.
European painting and sculpture c. 1880–1987. The Lane Room includes 'Lavacourt' by Monet, 'Jour d'Ete' by Berthe Morisot. Regular temporary exhibitions. Tues to Sat 9.30–6; Sun 11–5. *Closed* Mon.

IRISH LIFE VIKING ADVENTURE
Telephone: Dublin 797104

An authentic reconstruction of a street in Dublin in the year 988 brought to life by characters. They play the part of the typical merchant or house builder or other inhabitants that one would have met a thousand years ago. Visit these people in their houses, see how they live and experience the sounds and smells of Viking Dublin.
Location: Dublin City.
Opening Times: Daily 9–4 (last admission). Adm £2.75, Chd (under 14) £2 (under 5 free), Students/OAPs £2.25. Group rates for 20+.

NATIONAL GALLERY OF IRELAND
Merrion Square (West). Tel: (01) 615133.
Paintings, drawings and sculptures of all European countries and the United States of America from 1300–1900. Bookshop and restaurant. Mon, Tues, Wed, Fri and Sat 10–6; Thurs 10–9; Sun 2–5.

NATIONAL MUSEUM OF IRELAND *(a National Museum)*
Tel: (0001) 765521.
Contains the National collections of archaeology, the fine arts, history, folk life, zoology and geology. Outstanding exhibition of Prehistoric gold and Early Christian metalwork. Exhibitions of silver, ceramics and textiles, including Irish lace. Special display of Japanese decorative art. Archaeological, historical and fine arts collections located at Kildare Street, Zoological collections in the Natural History Museum at Merrion Street. Temporary exhibitions at the Exhibition Centre, 7–9 Merrion Row. Open Tues to Sat 10–5; Sun 2–5. Adm free.

POWERSCOURT TOWNHOUSE CENTRE
Telephone: Dublin 687477

Built in 1771 for Richard Wingfield – Third Viscount Lord Powerscourt. Designed by Robert Mack and contains fine plasterwork by James McCullagh and Michael Staplcton.
Location: 59 South William Street, Dublin 2.
Opening Times: Open daily 9.30–5.30. *Closed* Bank Holidays. Adm free. Wheelchair access to three floors.

ENNISKERRY

POWERSCOURT GARDENS & WATERFALL
Telephone: Dublin 867676/7/8   &

Powerscourt is owned by the Slazenger family and has been welcoming visitors for more than 50 years. Powerscourt is a magnificent example of an artistocratic garden laid out with taste and imagination. The breathtaking location nestling under the Great Sugar Loaf, the beauty of its Italian and Japanese Gardens, the splendid statuary and the incomparable iron work make it a fairytale demesne. The Waterfall is 398 feet high, which makes it one of the most spectacular in Ireland. Restaurant, souvenir gift and craft shop and children's play areas, garden centre and house-plant shop.
Location: ¼ mile Enniskerry, 12 miles S of Dublin.
Opening Times: Gardens: Mar 1 to Oct 31—Daily 9–5.30. Garden Centre open all year. Waterfall open all year 10.30–7. Closes dusk wintertime. Guided tours for specialist groups on request. Adm charges Gardens: £1.90, Chd 95p; Waterfall: £1, Chd 50p. Group reductions, season tickets. Property suitable for disabled persons. Wheelchair available.
Refreshments: Gardens: small restaurant (50 people) serving lunches, teas etc. Waterfall: Teas, light lunches available in high season.

FOTA

FOTA
Telephone: Cork (021) 812555   &
(Richard Wood)

Regency mansion with fine neo-classical and French Revival rooms, contains an important collection of Irish period landscapes. Furnished with Irish 18th and 19th century pieces. Also world famous arboretum and 70 acre wildlife park. **European Museum of the Year Award Winner.**

Location: 10 m E of Cork City, on Cobh Road, off main Waterford Road.
Station: Fota.
Opening Times: Mar 17 to end Oct—Mons to Sats 11–6, Suns 2–6. Remainder of year, Suns & Bank Hols 2–6. Parties any time by prior arrangement with the Administrator. Adm £2, Chd 50p, OAPs, Students & Unemployed £1. Disabled free (ground floor only suitable).
Refreshments: Light teas available. Lunches and dinners organised for groups by prior arrangement. Coffee shop in Wildlife Park. Restaurants and Hotels in Cobh (4 m).

GLANMIRE

DUNKATHEL
(Mrs Geoffrey Russell)

Classic Ducart style Georgian House with fine furniture and a superb Bath Stone Staircase. The Beatrice Gubbins water colour collection is on view and an Orchestrion dating from 1880 may be heard by visitors.
Location: 3½ m from Cork on the Waterford Road.
Opening Times: May 1 to Oct 31—Weds–Suns 2–6. Adm IR £1.50, Chd IR 50p. Parties at other times by arrangement.
Refreshments: Afternoon teas available.

RIVERSTOWN HOUSE

The House was originally built in 1602. It became the seat of Doctor Jemmett Brown, Bishop of Cork, who rebuilt it in 1745 with fine plasterwork by the Francini brothers.
Location: 6 km from Cork City on the Cork/Dublin road.
Opening Times: May to Aug, Thurs to Sat. At other times by appointment. Adm £1.50.

GLASNEVIN

NATIONAL BOTANIC GARDENS
(Department of Agriculture)

Founded 1795. 47 acres in extent containing 25,000 different living plant species and varieties. Flowering shrubs. Dwarf conifers. Orchids. Herbarium, 500,000 specimens.
Location: 2 m from city centre.
Opening Times: All the year—Daily (except Christmas Day); Weekdays 9–6 (summer); 10–4.30 (winter). Sundays 11–6 (summer); 11–4.30 (winter). Conservatories. Mons to Fris 9–12.45, 2.15–5 (summer); 10–12.45, 2.15–4.15 (winter). Sats 9–12.15, 2.15–5.45 (summer); 10–12.15, 2.15–4.15 (winter). Suns 2–5.45 (summer); 2–4.15 (winter). Adm free.

GLENEALY

ROBERT SHEANE'S AGRICULTURAL MUSEUM
  Tel: (0404) 5608 or 5626.
Old farm machinery and accessories etc. Open business hours Mon–Fri or by appointment. Adm £1 (incl booklet). Car parking (20 cars). Suitable for disabled persons.

GLIN

GLIN CASTLE
Telephone: Ireland (068) 34173/34112
(The Knight of Glin and Madam Fitz-Gerald)

A Georgian Gothic castle with a series of battlemented folly lodges on lands held by the Knights of Glin for over 700 years. The interiors possess elaborate neo-classical plaster ceilings, a flying grand staircase and a notable collection of 18th century Irish mahogany furniture, family portraits and Irish landscapes. Formal gardens.
Location: On N69 32 m W of Limerick and 3 m E of Tarbert.
Opening Times: May 1 to May 31, 10–12, 2–4, and at other times groups by arrangement. Adm IR £2, Chd IR £1, groups IR £1.50. Car Parking. Suitable for disabled persons.
Refreshments: At the Glin Castle Gate Shop in one of the Gothic lodges on main road. Proprietress Joan Stack Tel. (068) 34188. Open Apr–Oct inclusive.

GORT

THOOR BALLYLEE
Telephone: (091) 31436
(Senator Michael Yeats)

16th Century Norman Tower with thatched cottage attached. Summer home of W.B. Yeats for 12 years 1917–1929. Location of inspiration of the 'Tower' and 'Winding Stair' poems.
Location: 4 m from Gort Town. 1 m from N18 Galway/Gort road. 1 m from N66 Gort/Loughrea road.
Opening Times: Open daily June–Sept 10–6. Large car park suitable for buses. Unsuitable for the disabled. Bus groups and large parties given lecture.
Refreshments: Tea room in grounds of Tower supplying tea, coffee, minerals, pastries, biscuits etc.

KILKENNY

ROTHE HOUSE
Telephone: (056) 22893

Rothe House is a 16th century merchant house built by the Rothe family. It is being restored by Kilkenny Archaeological Society and contains the Society's Museum with costumes, pictures, and artifacts of Kilkenny interest. The house is a charming Tudor style composition built around two courtyards.
Location: Centre of Kilkenny city, 75 m from Dublin.
Opening Times: Apr to Oct 10.30–12.30, 2–5. Mon to Sat and Sun 3–5. Nov to Mar 3–5, Sat and Sun. Adm £1, Chd 30p, OAPs/Students 50p, group rate adults 60p.
Refreshments: Coffee shop serving teas, coffee and snacks during summer period.

KILLARNEY

MUCKROSS HOUSE AND GARDENS
Telephone: (064) 31440

Muckross House is a 19th century manor house, beautifully situated close to Muckross Lake, second largest of Killarney's three lakes. The house has many items of historic interest including locally carved period furniture, prints, maps and items which illustrate a traditional way of life of the people of Kerry. Skilled craftworkers at Muckross House carry on some of the traditional crafts of Kerry as their predecessors did in bygone days. The gardens, informal in design, are noted for their fine collection of rhododendrons and azaleas, extensive water gardens and an outstanding rock garden on natural limestone.
Location: 6 km (3.5 m) from Killarney on the Kenmare road.
Opening Times: Open all year. Mar 17 to June 30 daily 9–6. July 1 to Aug 31 daily 9–7. Sept 1 to Oct 31 daily 9–6; Rest of year daily, except Mons when the house is closed 11–5. Free car park, suitable for buses. Adm IR £2, Chd IR £1, group rates for 20+ IR £1.50. Free adm to the gardens.
Refreshments: Tea Room located in the old coach-house, serving teas, coffees, soup, sandwiches, pastries, minerals, etc.

KILMAINHAM

THE ROYAL HOSPITAL
Telephone: (01) 718666

Founded in 1680 by the Duke of Ormond as a hospice for pensioner soldiers, the Royal Hospital Kilmainham is the earliest surviving public building in the country. Recently restored, it is now the National Centre for Culture and the Arts.
Location: Situated 2 m W of Dublin city; 300 metres from Heuston Station.
Opening Times: For information please tel: (031) 718666. Adm: Tues free; Wed to Fri £1, Chd 50p, Family ticket (2 adults plus children) £3; Sat, Sun £2, Chd 50p, Family ticket £4. OAPs free.
Refreshments: Sunday Brunch: adults £6, Chd £3 each.

KINSALE

KINSALE REGIONAL MUSEUM
  Tel: (021) 772044.
17th century Market House, Charters and general collection depicting life in town and port through the centuries. Daily at reasonable times. Adm 40p, Chld 10p.

KINVARA

DUNGUAIRE CASTLE
Telephone: (091) 37108

Dunguaire was the stronghold of Guaire, King of Connaught in the 7th century. The 15th century Dunguaire Castle, now beautifully restored overlooks Galway Bay and gives an insight into the lifestyles of those that lived there. Dunguaire features mediaeval banquets nightly, May to September.
Location: The Castle is on the Ennis/Galway road.
Opening Times: Open daily Apr (from Easter) to Sept 30, 10–5. Adm £1.60, Chd 90p. Special Group rates. Souvenir Shop.
Refreshments: Tea room. Snacks.

KYLEMORE

KYLEMORE ABBEY
Telephone: (095) 41146, or shops (095) 41113.

The only home of the Benedictine Nuns in Ireland. The Castle was acquired by the Nuns in 1920, and a precious heirloom was preserved, both for and on behalf of the people of Ireland, and visitors from all over the world. Built by Mr Mitchell Henry, MP for County Galway, and a native of Manchester. The Abbey is set amidst the lakes and mountains of Connemara in an area of outstanding beauty.
Location: 50 m from Galway city, between Galway and Clifden, near Letterfrack.
Opening Times: The grounds and part of the Abbey are open daily, Mar to Nov 10–6. Adm free. Pottery, gift and craft shop.
Refreshments: Light lunches, teas and snacks.

LISMORE

LISMORE CASTLE
Telephone: Dungarvan (058) 54424
(Trustees of the Lismore Estates)

Beautifully situated walled and woodland gardens, containing a fine collection of camellias, magnolias and other shrubs. There is a remarkable yew walk.
Location: In town of Lismore; 45 m W of Waterford; 35 m NE of Cork.
Opening Times: GARDENS ONLY. May 8 to Sept 8—Daily (except Sats) 1.45–4.45. Adm £1, Chd (under 16) 50p. Reduced rates for parties.

LONGFORD

CARRIGGLAS MANOR
Telephone: Ireland (043) 45165
(Mr & Mrs Lefroy)

Tudor Gothic Revival House with beautifully furnished interiors. Fine Georgian stableyard by James Gandon with costume museum. Tea room & shop. Woodland Garden.
Location: 3 m from Longford on T15/R194 Ballinalee/Granard Road. 2 m N of main N4 Route on signed turn-off avoiding Longford Town congestion.
Opening Times: House, Stableyard, Costume Museum, Tea Room & Shop. June 2 to Sept 10, daily except Wed & Thurs 12.30–4.30 (Aug 5.30). Pre-booked parties at other times by arrangement. Hourly House Tours – Last Tour 3.30 (Aug 4.30). Adm £2, Chd £1, Adult Group rate £1.50, Chd Group rate 75p.
Refreshments: Tea room, light lunches & afternoon teas. Hotels, pubs etc. in Longford (3m). Dinner, Bed & Breakfast available IR£75 per person. Pre-booking absolutely essential.

LOUGH GUR

LOUGH GUR VISITOR CENTRE
Telephone: (061) 85186

Lough Gur Visitor Centre is modelled on Neolithic circular and rectangular houses and illustrates the story of man and his landscape through audio-visuals, artifacts and replicas of materials found in this historic place.
Location: Lough Gur – 16 m SE of Limerick City on the road to Kilmallock.
Opening Times: May 1 to Sept 30 – daily 10–6. Adm IR £1.50 (includes free cup of tea), Chd/Students 75p. Group rates available. Car parking free. Unsuitable for the disabled.

LOUGHREA

LOUGHREA MUSEUM
St. Brendan's. Tel: (091) 41212.
Ecclesiastical Museum, vestments, chalices, statues. 13th century.

MALAHIDE

MALAHIDE CASTLE
Telephone: 452655/452371
(Ann Chambers, Administrator)

One of Ireland's oldest and most historic castles containing a unique collection of Irish period furniture and Irish historical portraits, most of which are on permanent loan from the National Gallery of Ireland. In the adjacent gardens there are in excess of 5000 species and varieties of shrubs.
Location: 8 m from centre of Dublin.
Opening Times: Open all year Mon–Fri 10–12.45 & 2–5; Apr to Oct Sats 11–6; Suns and Bank Holidays 2–6; Nov–Mar Sats, Suns, Bank Holidays 2–5. Adm £2.15, OAPs & Students £1.50, Chd £1.15, Family £6. Parties £1.85, OAPs & Students £1.30, Chd £1. Bus & public car park. Unsuitable for the disabled.
Refreshments: Restaurant open in Castle during opening hours. Private evening banquets on request for groups; Local Hotel, Grand Hotel, Malahide, Co. Dublin.

MONAGHAN

MONAGHAN COUNTY MUSEUM
(Monaghan County Council)
Hill Street. Tel: 047 82928.
Heritage and contemporary art at present on show. Exhibitions planned on archaeology, local history, folklife, crafts and lace. Awarded Council of Europe Museum Prize. Tues to Sat 11–1, 2–5. *Closed* public hols.

NEW ROSS

THE JOHN F. KENNEDY ARBORETUM
Telephone: (051) 88171
(The State/Forest Service)

A comprehensive, scientifically laid-out arboretum with plant collections arranged in botanical circuits. Incorporated are forest plots and areas devoted to plant research. Reception building with display panel, Lecture Hall with A/V. Special collections of conifers, rhododendrons etc. A road gives access to a view point (890 ft) from which six counties may be seen.
Location: 12 km (7½ m) S of New Ross on R733.
Opening Times: Daily all year, except Christmas Day and Good Friday. May to Aug 10–8; Apr & Sept 10–6.30; Oct to Mar 10–5. Charge for car parking – Car £1.80 (IR £2), Season ticket £7.20 (IR £8), Coach £7.20 (IR £8), Minibus £3.60 (IR £4). Suitable for the disabled.
Refreshments: Cafe/Shop (May to Sept and weekends Apr). Tea, coffee, soup, sandwiches, salads etc. Five counties Hotel, New Ross 11km (7 m), Horse & Hound, lounge bar, Ballynabola 10km (6 m).

PORTLAOISE

EMO COURT
Telephone: Ireland (0502) 26110
(C.D. Cholmeley-Harrison)

Outstanding neo-classical house by James Gandon completed in 1796. Extensive gardens containing a wealth of specimen trees & flowering shrubs, spectacular in spring and autumn.
Location: Portlaoise 6 m on N7.
Opening Times: Apr to end Oct. GARDENS – daily 2.30–5.30 (last entry), Adm £1.50, Students & OAPs £1. HOUSE – Mon 2–6, Adm £2.50 *(no reductions and no children)*. Free car park. Suitable for disabled persons.
Refreshments: Montague Hotel 1½ m – on N7.

QUIN

KNAPPOGUE CASTLE
Telephone: (061) 71103
(Mr and Mrs M E Andrews)

Knappogue Castle is one of the forty-two Castles built by the great McNamara Tribe which ruled over the territory of Clancullen from the 5th to the mid-15th centuries. The Castle has undergone extensive restoration work with its furnishings giving an authentic 15th century atmosphere. Craftshop.
Location: Quin – R469 on Map.
Opening Times: Easter to Sept 30 9.30–5.30. Adm £1.90, Chd £1.15, Special Group rates. Car Parking. Mediaeval Banquets and Entertainment twice nightly at 5.45 and 8.45 from May 1 to Oct 31. Souvenir shop in beautifully restored courtyard.

RATHKEALE

CASTLE MATRIX
Telephone: (069) 64284

This Norman tower was built upon a Celtic Santuary from which the original name *Matres* was derived: later Anglicized to *Matrix*. Constructed in 1440 by the 7th Earl of Desmond who along with his father are the earliest recorded Norman poets in the Irish language. Here in 1580, Raleigh and Spenser first met and began their lifelong friendship.
Location: 18 m SW of Limerick City on the main Killarney road; the castle is at the SW edge of Rathkeale village.
Opening Times: May 15 to Sept 15, Sats to Tues 1–5. Open at other times by prior arrangement. Adm £2, Chd £1. Spit-roasted mediaeval banquets available to groups by arrangement.
Refreshments: Teas and luncheons available to groups by arrangement.

ROSCREA

DAMER HOUSE – ROSCREA HERITAGE CENTRE
Telephone: (0505) 21850
(William Hayes, Administrator)

An important early 18th century house situated in the courtyard of the 13th century Roscrea Castle, a polygonal fortification with gate-tower, corner turrets and curtain wall. The centrepiece of the house is the richly carved stairway. The house and attached 19th century Georgian annexe contain exhibitions relating mainly to the history of the Midlands. Computerised ancestral research service is available.
Location: Castle Street, centre of town, on main Dublin–Limerick road, close to Round Tower and 12th century Romanesque church gable.
Opening Times: May to Sept, Mon to Fri 10–5, Sat 11–5, Sun 2–5. Oct to Apr, Mon to Fri 10–5. Adm including guided tour of castle and house £1.75, OAPs and Students £1, Parties £1.50, Family £3.75.
Refreshments: Coffee Shop serving teas, coffees, sandwiches, scones, etc.

SANDYCOVE

THE JAMES JOYCE TOWER
Telephone: Ireland (01) 809265/808571
(Dublin and East Tourism)

Martello Tower built in 1804 as part of defence system against threatened Napoleonic invasion. Lived in briefly by James Joyce in 1904, and made the setting for the opening of his famous novel *Ulysses*. Opened as the James Joyce Museum in 1962. First and rare editions, personal possessions and other Joyce memorabilia, various military fittings preserved. Commanding view of Dublin Bay. Books of Joycean and Irish interest, posters, cards etc. on sale. Occasional evening lectures, slide shows etc.

Location: 1¼ m SE of Dun Laoghaire. Turn L from Sandycove Road along Sandycove Avenue to Sandycove Harbour and footpath to the Tower.
Opening Times: Apr 1 to Oct 31 (including Bank Holidays), Mon–Sat 10–1, 2–5, Suns 2.30–6. Rest of the year by appointment. Tel. Ireland (01) 808571. Adm £1.20, Students and OAPs 90p, Chd 60p. Parties (20+) 80p, School parties negotiable. Guided tours for parties by arrangement in advance. Suitable for disabled persons on ground floor only.
Refreshments: Fitzgerald's Pub, Sandycove: Wishbone Restaurant, Glasthule: Carney Arms Hotel, Dun Laoghaire: Royal Marine Hotel, Dun Laoghaire.

SLANE

SLANE CASTLE
Telephone: Drogheda (041) 24207
(The Earl of Mount Charles)

Dramatic 18th century Castle on river Boyne, featuring work of James Wyatt, Francis Johnston, James Gandon and Capability Brown, with fine pictures and furniture.
Location: 29 m from Dublin. 8 m from Navan. 9 m from Drogheda. Slane village on N2. Castle entrance on N51 (to Navan).
Opening Times: Mar 17 to Oct 30 – Suns and Bank Holiday Mons 2–6. Adm £1.65, Students & OAPs 50p, Family Rate £3.50, Parties (20) £1.25. Car park for 100. Suitable for the disabled, no wheelchairs available.
Refreshments: Steak bar/restaurant fully licensed. Open Wed–Sun 12–10.30 pm.

SLIGO

LISSADELL
(Josslyn Gore-Booth, Esq)

The finest Greek-revival country house in Ireland. Splendid views of the surrounding countryside. The home of Countess Markiewicz.
Location: 8 m NW of Sligo overlooking Sligo Bay.
Opening Times: Easter week then May 1 to Sept 30 — Weekdays 2–5.15. Last tour 4.30. *Closed Suns.* Adm £1.50.

TIMOLEAGUE

TIMOLEAGUE CASTLE GARDENS
Telephone: (023) 46116 or (021) 831512
(Mr N.R.E. Travers)

Seven acres of old fashioned gardens in a beautiful and historic setting. Palm trees and other frost-tender shrubs flourish in the mild climate of this beautiful part of West Cork.

Location: Adjoining Timoleague village, Bandon 8 m.
Opening Times: GARDEN ONLY Easter Weekend, then daily mid May to mid Sept 12–6. Adm £1.08 (IR £1.20), Chd 56p (IR 60p). Parties by arrangement. Car park. Suitable for the disabled.
Refreshments: At local hotels.

TULLY

JAPANESE GARDENS
Telephone: (045) 21617
(Irish National Stud)

Created between 1906–1910, the Japanese Gardens symbolise the Life of Man from the Cave of Birth to the Gateway to Eternity. Special features include the Tea House, Red Bridge and some very old bonsai trees.
Location: Co. Kildare 1 m from Kildare Town and 5 m from Newbridge.
Opening Times: Easter to Oct 31 – Mon to Fri 10–5, Suns 2–5.30, Sat and Bank Holidays 10–5.30. Adm £1.50, Students and OAPs £1, Chd 80p. Family (2 adults and 2 children) £4. Groups (25) £1.40. Unsuitable for the disabled. Entrance to The Irish National Stud is at the same gate.
Refreshments: Tea, coffee, soup, salads, sandwiches etc. Groups can be catered for with some notice.

WEXFORD

IRISH AGRICULTURAL MUSEUM
(The Irish Agricultural Museum (J.C.) Ltd)
Johnstown Castle. Tel: 053-42888.
National museum of agriculture and Irish rural life. Housed in estate farmyard set in the 50 acre gardens of Johnstown Castle. Specialist sections on rural transport, country furniture and rural crafts. New exhibits being added annually. Open High Season: (June–Aug) Mon to Fri 9–5; Sat & Sun 2–5. Mid Season: (May & Sept–2 Nov) Mon to Fri 9–12.30, 1.30–5; Sat & Sun 2–5. Low Season: (3 Nov–30 Apr) Mon to Fri 9–12.30, 1.30–5. Adm £1.25, Chld/Students 50p. 20% reduction for groups paid in advance. Free car parking. Suitable for disabled persons (no wheelchairs available). Coffee shop open in high season. Invalid toilets. Specialist bookshop.

JOHNSTOWN CASTLE   ♿
(An Foras Taluntais (Land-use & Grassland Research Centre))

Grounds and gardens only. Many acres of well laid out grounds, with artificial lakes and fine collection of ornamental trees and shrubs. Agricultural museum.
Location: 5 m SW of Wexford.
Opening Times: All the year — Daily 9–5. Guidebook available at Castle. Adm to be decided.
Refreshments: Coffee shop during July & Aug.

BLARNEY HOUSE
Co. CORK

JOHNSTOWN CASTLE

**Land-use & Grassland Research Centre,
Wexford, Ireland
An Foras Taluntais**

ADMISSION – SEE EDITORIAL REFERENCE

KYLEMORE ABBEY

ADMISSION—SEE EDITORIAL REFERENCE

IRELAND (NORTHERN)

ANNAGHMORE

ARDRESS HOUSE, The National Trust
Telephone: Annaghmore 851236

17th century country house with fine plasterwork. Small garden, agricultural display in farmyard. Woodland play area.
Location: 7 m W of Portadown on Portadown/Moy Road (B28); 2 m from Loughgall intersection on M1.
Opening Times: Easter: Mar 24 to Apr 2: daily 12–6. Apr and May: Sat, Sun & Bank Holidays 12–6. June, July and Aug: daily except Tues 12–6. Sept: Sat and Sun 12–6. Booked parties by arrangement throughout the season. Adm House: £1, Parties 75p (outside normal hours £1.20). Farmyard: 50p, Parties 40p. Parking 50p. Wheelchairs admitted. Picnic areas.
Refreshments: Picnic teas available on summer Suns.

ARMAGH

ARMAGH COUNTY MUSEUM *(County of Armagh)*
The Mall East.
Local antiquities, Prehistoric weapons, implements. Period costumes, uniforms. Natural history and bygones. Mon to Sat 10–1, 2–5. *Closed* certain Public Hols.

BANGOR

BANGOR VISITORS AND HERITAGE CENTRE
(North Down Borough Council)
Town Hall, Bangor Castle. Tel: (0247) 270371.
Local history and works of art reflecting aspects of North Down's historical and cultural past. Audio-visual shows; varying temporary exhibitions. Tues to Sat 11–4.30; Sun 2–4.30. July and Aug 10.30–5.30; Sun 2–5.30. Adm free. Parties by prior arrangement. Suitable for disabled persons. Curator I.A. Wilson B.A., Dip.Ed.

BELFAST

ULSTER MUSEUM
Botanic Gardens, BT9 5AB. Tel: (0232) 668251.
Collections of Irish antiquities, ethnography, local history, industrial archaeology including a splendid collection of linen textile machinery, numismatics, geology including the Dinosaur Show, featuring a complete anatosauras skeleton and the natural history of Ireland with a unique feature on the 'Living Sea'.

COLERAINE

DOWNHILL CASTLE, The National Trust
Built by the Earl of Bristol, Bishop of Derry, in 1783 with Mussenden Temple, the Bishop's Gate, the Black Glen and the Bishop's Fish Pond.
Location: 5 m W of Coleraine on Coleraine/Downhill Road (A2).
Station: Castlerock.
Opening Times: Temple: Apr to end Sept: daily 12–6. Glen and grounds always open. Grounds free at all times. Glen open free at all times. Dogs admitted. Limited wheelchair access.

HEZLETT HOUSE, The National Trust
Telephone: Castlerock 848567

Thatched cottage of particular importance because of the unusual cruck/truss construction of the roof.
Location: 4 m W of Coleraine on Coleraine/Downhill Coast Road (A2).
Opening Times: Easter: Mar 24 to Apr 2: daily 12–6. Apr to June: Sat, Sun and Bank Holidays 12–6. July and Aug: daily except Tues 12–6. Sept: Sat and Sun 12–6. Adm 50p, Chd 25p, Parties outside normal hours 60p. No dogs. Unsuitable for wheelchairs.

COOKSTOWN

WELLBROOK BEETLING MILL, The National Trust
A water-powered mill built in 18th century with 19th century modifications.
Location: 3 m from Cookstown on Cookstown/Omagh Road.
Opening Times: Easter: Mar 24 to Apr 2: daily 12–6. Apr and May: Sat, Sun and Bank Holidays 12–6. June to end Aug: daily except Tues 12–6. Sept: Sat and Sun 12–6. Adm 50p, Chd 25p. Parties 50p (outside normal opening hours 60p). No dogs. Unsuitable for wheelchairs.

DOWNPATRICK

DOWN MUSEUM *(Down District Council)*
The Mall. Tel: (0396) 615218.
Local archaeology, history and natural history. Housed in 18th century county gaol which is undergoing phased restoration. Tues–Fri 11–5, Sat 2–5. *Closed* Sun and Mon. Extended opening and Sunday opening in July and August. Adm free. Car parking. Partly suitable for disabled persons.

ENNISKILLEN

CASTLE COOLE, The National Trust
Telephone: Enniskillen 22690

Magnificent 18th century mansion by James Wyatt with plasterwork by Joseph Rose.

Location: 1½ m SE of Enniskillen on Belfast/Clogher/Enniskillen Road (A4).
Opening Times: The estate is open from dawn to dusk free of charge from Apr 1 to Sept 30. Picnickers welcome. House open Easter: Mar 24 to Apr 2: daily 12–6. Apr and May: Sat, Sun and Bank Holidays 12–6. June, July and Aug: daily except Tues 12–6. Sept: Sat and Sun 12–6. Adm House: £1.50, parties £1.25 (outside normal hours £2). Parking 50p.

FERMANAGH COUNTY MUSEUM *(Fermanagh District Council)*
Castle Barracks.
15th century castle. Regional pre-history and history using large-scale models. Audio-visual programme on Medieval and Plantation life, and special exhibitions. Open all year Mon–Fri 10–1, 2–5. Sat (May–Sept) 2–5; Sun (July and Aug) 2–5.

FLORENCE COURT

FLORENCE COURT, The National Trust
Telephone: Florence Court 249   &

Important 18th century house built by John Cole. Excellent rococo plasterwork. Pleasure Gardens.

Location: 8 m SW of Enniskillen via A4 and A32; 1 m W of Florence Court village.
Opening Times: Easter: Mar 24 to Apr 2: daily 12–6. Apr to end Sept: daily except Tues 12–6. Last adm 5.15. Grounds open all year round, 10am to one hour before dusk. Adm £1.50, Chd 75p. Parties £1.25 (outside normal opening hours £2). Parking 50p. Dogs in pleasure gardens only, on leads. Wheelchair access—ground floor only.
Refreshments: Tearoom open as house.

MONEYMORE

SPRINGHILL, The National Trust
Telephone: Moneymore 48210   &

House dating from 17th century. Magnificent oak staircase and interesting furniture & paintings. Costume museum. Cottar's kitchen.
Location: On Moneymore/Coagh Road (1 m from Moneymore).
Opening Times: Easter: Mar 24 to Apr 2: daily 12–6. Apr and May: Sat, Sun and Bank Holidays 12–6. June to end Aug: daily except Tues 12–6. Sept: Sat and Sun 12–6. Adm £1.25. Parties £1 (outside normal opening hours £1.50). Dogs in grounds only, on leads. Wheelchair access to ground floor & museum.
Refreshments: Light refreshments and shop in Servants Hall. Lunches, high teas & dinners at Manor House, Main Street, Moneymore. Tel Moneymore 48206.

MOY

THE ARGORY, The National Trust
Telephone: Moy 84753   &

295 acre estate with neo-classical house, built c. 1820.
Location: 4 m from Moy on Derrycaw Road; 3 m from Coalisland intersection.
Opening Times: Easter: Mar 24 to Apr 2: daily 12–6. Apr and May: Sat, Sun and Bank Holidays 12–6. June, July and Aug: daily except Tues 12–6. Sept: Sat and Sun 12–6. Adm £1.25, Chd 65p, Parties £1, Chd 35p, (parties outside normal hours £1.50). Parking 50p. Dogs in grounds only on leads. Wheelchairs provided – access to ground floor only.
Refreshments: Tea room Apr, May and Sept: Sat, Sun and Bank Holidays 2–6; open all Easter week. June to Aug: daily except Tues 2–6.

NEWTOWNARDS

MOUNT STEWART HOUSE, GARDEN AND TEMPLE, The National Trust
Telephone: Greyabbey 387   &

Interesting house with important associations with Lord Castlereagh. Gardens designed by Lady Edith, Marchioness of Londonderry. Fine topiary work, flowering shrubs and rhododendrons. Temple of the Winds, modelled on that at Athens, built 1783.

Location: On E shore of Strangford Lough; 5 m SE of Newtownards; 15 m E of Belfast (A20).
Opening Times: House & Temple: Easter: Mar 24 to Apr 2: daily 12–6. Apr: Sat and Sun 12–6. May: Wed to Sun 12–6. June to end Aug: daily except Tues 12–6. Sept: Sat and Sun 12–6. **Garden:** Mar 17, then Mar 24 to Apr 2: 12–6. Apr: Sat and Sun 12–6. May: Wed to Sun 12–6. June to end Aug: daily except Tues 12–6. Sept and Oct: daily except Tues 12–6. Adm House, Garden and Temple £2. Parties £1.50 (outside normal hours £1.75). Garden and Temple £1.50. Parties £1 (outside normal hours £1.50). Dogs in garden only, on leads. Wheelchairs provided. Booked parties by arrangement throughout the season. Open Bank Hols falling on a Monday.
Refreshments: Tea room open as house.

OMAGH

ULSTER–AMERICAN FOLK PARK
Camphill, Co. Tyrone.
The Ulster–American Folk Park tells the story of migrations of Ulster people to the New World and of the contribution they made to the U.S.A. throughout the period of its birth and growth. Restored and recreated buildings, log dwellings, craft demonstrations, modern exhibition building. Education service. Easter to Early Sept: Mon to Sat 11–6.30; Sun and Public Hols 11.30–7. Mid Sept to Easter: Mon to Fri 10.30–5 (except Public Hols). Adm £1.50, Chld 75p. Reduction for disabled and parties of 20 or more.

SAINTFIELD

ROWALLANE GARDEN, The National Trust
Telephone: Saintfield 510131   &

Beautiful gardens containing large collection of plants, chiefly trees and shrubs. Of particular interest in spring and autumn.
Location: 11 m SE of Belfast; 1 m S of Saintfield on the W of the Downpatrick Road (A7).
Opening Times: Easter (inc. Good Friday) and Apr: daily 12–6. May and June: daily 12–9. July to end Sept: daily 12–6. Oct to end Mar: Mon to Fri 12–4.30. *Closed* Dec 25 and 26, Jan 1. Open all Bank Holidays. Adm Apr to end Oct £1. Parties 80p. Nov to end Mar 50p. Parties 35p. Outside normal opening hours £1.20. Dogs admitted on leads, to indicated areas. Wheelchair access (1 provided).
Refreshments: Tea room, Apr to Sept: daily 2–6.

STRABANE

GRAY'S PRINTING PRESS, The National Trust

The shop was in existence in 18th century. It has close links with Scots-Irish tradition in America.
Location: In Main Street, Strabane.
Opening Times: Press: Mar 24 to end of Sept—Daily (except Thurs & Suns) 12–6. Shop (not N.T.): Every day except Thurs, Suns & public hols, 9–1 and 2–5.30. Adm 50p, Chd 25p.

STRANGFORD

CASTLE WARD, The National Trust
Telephone: Strangford 204   &

Built by the first Lord Bangor in 1765 in a beautiful setting. Laundry museum. Wildfowl collection on lake. Strangford Lough Information Centre in converted barn on edge of shore.
Location: 7 m NE of Downpatrick; 1½ m W of Strangford village (A25).
Opening Times: Easter: Mar 24 to Apr 2: daily 12–6. Apr: Sat and Sun 12–6. May: Wed to Sun and Bank Holiday Mons 12–6. June, July and Aug: daily except Tues 12–6. Sept and Oct: Sat and Sun 12–6. Estate and grounds open all year dawn to one hour after dusk. (Charge for car park only.) Adm House: £1.25, parties £1 (outside normal opening hours £1.50). Parking £2.50 (£1 when house and other facilities are closed). Wheelchairs access (3 provided).
Refreshments: Refreshments available. Open as house.

TEMPLEPATRICK

TEMPLETOWN MAUSOLEUM, The National Trust

Built 1783 by Robert Adam.
Location: Castle Upton Graveyard, Templepatrick (A6).
Opening Times: All year during daylight hours. Adm free. Dogs admitted. Access difficult for wheelchairs.

🌿 The National Trust
Northern Ireland Properties

For further information about properties in the care of the National Trust in Northern Ireland apply to
The National Trust, Rowallane, Saintfield, Co. Down. Telephone: Saintfield 510721.

SPRINGHILL
MONEYMORE, CO. LONDONDERRY

CASTLE WARD
STRANG FORD, CO. DOWN

MOUNT STEWART
HOUSE & GARDEN
GREYABBEY, CO. DOWN

CASTLE COOLE
ENNISKILLEN, CO. FERMANAGH

ARDRESS
CO. ARMAGH

ROWALLANE GARDEN
SAINTFIELD, CO. DOWN

ADMISSION DETAILS — SEE EDITORIAL REFERENCE

SCOTLAND

Borders Region

COLDSTREAM

THE HIRSEL GROUNDS & DUNDOCK WOOD
Telephone: Coldstream (0890) 2834

Snowdrops, aconites and daffodils in Spring in grounds. Fantastic rhododendrons and azaleas May/June Dundock wood and grounds. Marvellous Autumn colouring. Picnic areas. Parking. Homestead museum, Craft Centre and workshops.
Opening Times: All reasonable daylight hours throughout the year. Adm by donation.
Refreshments: In main season.

DRYBURGH

DRYBURGH ABBEY
(Secretary of State for Scotland)

Sir Walter Scott and Field Marshal Earl Haig are buried in this 12th century Abbey.
Location: 5 m SE of Melrose, nr St Boswells.
Opening Times: Apr 1 to Sept 30—Weekdays 9.30–7; Suns 2–7; Oct 1 to Mar 31—Weekdays 9.30–4; Suns 2–4. *Closed Dec 25, 26 & Jan 1 & 2).* Adm £1, Chd & OAPs 50p.

DUNS

MANDERSTON
Telephone: Duns (0361) 83450
(Mr and Mrs Adrian Palmer)

The finest Edwardian house in the classical style in Britain. Remarkable picturesque group of farm and dairy buildings; gardens.
Location: 2 m E of Duns on A6105; 14 m W of Berwick upon Tweed.
Opening Times: May 11 to Sept 24—Thurs & Suns also Bank Hol Mons May 29 & Aug 28, 2–5.30. Adm charges not available at time of going to press. Parties at any time. Gift shop.
Refreshments: Cream Teas.

EYEMOUTH

AYTON CASTLE
Telephone: (089 07) 81212

Victorian castle in red sandstone.
Location: 7 m N of Berwick-upon-Tweed on A1.
Opening Times: May to Sept—Suns 2–5 or by appointment. Adm £1, Chd (under 15) free.

EYEMOUTH MUSEUM
Auld Kirk, Market Place. Tel: (08907) 50678.
Opened in 1981, the museum houses a 15' tapestry made to commemorate the centenary of the Eyemouth Fishing Disaster of 1881. Other features include a reconstruction of a 19th century fisherman's kitchen, the wheelhouse and a prow of a modern fishing boat, rural and natural history collections. Exhibition gallery. Opening times as shown at Tourist Information Centre in foyer. Adm charge.

GALASHIELS

OLD GALA HOUSE *(Ettrick and Lauderdale District Council)*
Scott Crescent. Tel: (0896) 4751 ext. 132 or (0750) 20096.
This historic house, dating from 1583, once the home of the Lairds of Gala, was re-opened as an interpretive centre in 1988. Displays tell the story of the Lairds of Gala and their involvement in the development of the town. Particularly memorable are the painted ceiling (1635) and painted wall (1988). Open Easter to end of Oct, Mon–Sat 10–4 *(Closed* Tues); Sun 2–4. Adm by donation.

GORDON

MELLERSTAIN
Telephone: Gordon (057 381) 225
(The Earl of Haddington)

Scotland's famous Adam mansion. Beautifully decorated and furnished interiors. Terraced gardens and lake. Gift shop.
Location: 9 m NE of Melrose; 7 m NW of Kelso; 37 m SE of Edinburgh.
Opening Times: Easter weekend (Mar 24–27) then May 1 to Sept 30—Daily (except Sats) 12.30–5. Last adm to House 4.30. Adm charges not available at time of going to press. Free parking. *Special terms for organised parties by appointment, apply Curator.*
Refreshments: Tea rooms.

HAWICK

MUSEUM AND THE SCOTT ART GALLERY
(Roxburgh District Council)
Wilton Lodge Park. Tel: (0450) 73457.
Social history, local industries (particularly knitwear), natural history and fine local collections. Scottish paintings and temporary exhibitions in the Scott Gallery. Apr to Sept: Mon to Sat 10–12, 1–5; Sun 2–5. Oct to Mar: Mon to Fri 1–4; Sun 2–4. *Closed* Sat. Adm 50p, Chld/OAPs/students and the unemployed 25p. Roxburgh district residents and Borders Regional schools free.

INNERLEITHEN

ROBERT SMAIL'S PRINTING WORKS
(The National Trust for Scotland)

The buildings contain vintage working machinery, including a 100-year-old press which was originally driven by water wheels. The Victorian office is on display complete with its acid-etched plate-glass windows and examples of historic items printed in the works.
Location: In Innerleithen High Street, 30 m S of Edinburgh.
Opening Times: Mar 24 to Dec 24, Mon–Sat (except Tues) 10–5. Adm free.

TRAQUAIR
Telephone: Innerleithen (0896) 830323
(P. Maxwell Stuart of Traquair)

A house full of beauty, romance and mystery. Rich in associations with Mary Queen of Scots, the Jacobites and Catholic persecution. Priest's room with secret stairs. The Bear gates have remained closed since 1745. The present Laird brews his world famous Traquair House Ale in the 18th century Brew House. Extensive grounds and newly planted maze.
Location: 1 m from Innerleithen; 6 m from Peebles; 29 m from Edinburgh at junction of B709 & B7062 (40 minutes by road from Edinburgh Turnhouse Airport, 1½ hours from Glasgow).
Opening Times: Easter Sat, Sun & Mon. Suns and Mons in May, then daily from May 27 to Sept 30, 1.30–5.30; (July and Aug only 10.30–5.30). Last adm 5. Grounds: May to Sept: 10.30–5.30. Gift Shop, Antique Shop.
Refreshments: Home cooking at the 1745 Cottage Tea Room from 12.30.

JEDBURGH

CASTLE JAIL *(Roxburgh District Council)*
Castlegate. Tel: (0835) 63254.
A Howard reform jail, built 1823, on the site of the former Jedburgh Castle and gallows. Contains articles associated with prison life and the history of the Royal Burgh. Apr to Sept: Mon to Sat 10–12, 1–5; Sun 2–5. Adm 50p, Chld/OAPs/students and the unemployed 25p. Reductions for pre-booked parties over 20. Roxburgh district residents and Borders Regional schools free.

JEDBURGH ABBEY
(Secretary of State for Scotland)

Founded by David I this Augustinian Abbey is remarkably complete. Recent excavations are now open to the public. New Visitor Centre.
Location: In Jedburgh.
Opening Times: Apr to Sept—Weekdays 9.30–7; Suns 2–7; Oct to Mar—Weekdays 9.30–4; Suns 2–4. Adm £1, Chd & OAPs 50p.

MARY, QUEEN OF SCOTS' HOUSE *(Roxburgh District Council)*
Queen Street. Tel: (0835) 63331.
Recently refurbished to an exceptional standard, the house tells the story of the life of the tragic queen, who herself visited Jedburgh in 1566. The displays offer a new and thought-provoking interpretation of the theme which has become one of Scotland's top visitor attractions. Apr to Oct: Daily 10–5 Adm 75p, Chld/OAPs/students and the unemployed 50p. 5% discount for parties over 20. Roxburgh district residents and Borders Regional schools free.

KELSO

FLOORS CASTLE
Telephone: Kelso (0573) 23333
(The Duke of Roxburghe)

Built in 1721 by William Adam and later added to by Playfair. Magnificent tapestries, fine French and English furniture, paintings, porcelain.
Location: N of Kelso.
Opening Times: Easter Sun & Mon Mar 26, 27 and from Apr 30 to Sept 28—Suns to Thurs (incl Bank Hol Mons); July and Aug: also open Fris. Grounds, Gardens and Castle—10.30–5.30 (last adm to Castle 4.45). Oct: Sun and Wed, 10.30–4. The Castle will open on Fris during Apr, May, June & Sept to coach parties by appointment only. Closed Sats. Adm £2.20, Chd (aged 8 and over) £1.50, OAPs £2; Family ticket £6. Party rates on request from The Factor, Roxburghe Estate Office, Kelso, Roxburghshire. Garden Centre and coffee shop open seven days.
Refreshments: Licensed restaurant, gift shop and coffee shop.

KELSO MUSEUM *(Roxburgh District Council)*
Turret House, Abbey Court. Tel: (0573) 25470.
A new award winning museum in a charming 18th century building owned by the National Trust for Scotland. Once used as a skinner's workshop, the house has displays reconstructing a skinner's business as well as areas reflecting Kelso's growth as a market town and about Kelso Abbey. The Museum shares the building with the Tourist Information Centre. Open Apr–Oct, times as Tourist Information Centre. Adm 50p, Chld, OAP's, students, unemployed 35p. Parties of over 20, 5% discount. Good car park nearby (200 yds). Only ground floor display suitable for disabled. Roxburgh district residents and Borders Regional schools free.

LAUDER

THIRLESTANE CASTLE
Telephone: Lauder (05782) 430

Described as one of the oldest and finest Castles in Scotland, Thirlestane has its roots in an original 13th century fort overlooking the Leader Valley. The main keep was built in 1590 by the Maitland family who have lived in the Castle for over 400 years; it was extended in 1670 and again in 1840. The Restoration Period plasterwork ceilings are considered to be the finest in existence. The family nurseries now house a collection of over 7,000 historic toys and children are encouraged to dress up. Visitors see the old kitchens, pantries and laundries as well as the Country Life Exhibitions portraying day to day life in the Borders through the centuries. Grounds, picnic garden, woodland walk, free car park, gift shop.
Location: 28 m S of Edinburgh off A68 – follow signs on all main approach roads.
Opening Times: Easter Sun and Mon, May, June and Sept – Wed, Thur and Sun only. July and Aug – daily except Sat. Castle 2–5. Grounds 12–6. Adm £2, Chd/OAPs and party rate £1.50, family ticket (parents and children only) £5. Booked party tours any time by arrangement.
Refreshments: Tea room.

LIDDLESDALE

HERMITAGE CASTLE
(Secretary of State for Scotland)

Here in 1566. Queen Mary visited her wounded lover Bothwell.
Location: In Liddlesdale; 5½ m NE of Newcastleton.
Opening Times: Apr 1 to Sept 30—Weekdays 9.30–7, Suns 2–7; Oct 1 to Mar 31—Weekends only. *Closed Dec 25, 26; Jan 1, 2.* Adm 60p, Chd & OAPs 30p.

MELROSE

ABBOTSFORD HOUSE   &
(Mrs P Maxwell-Scott)

The home of Sir Walter Scott. containing many historical relics collected by him.
Location: 3 m W of Melrose just S of A72; 5 m E of Selkirk.
Opening Times: 3rd Mon of Mar to Oct 31—Daily 10–5; Suns 2–5. *Cars with wheelchairs or disabled visitors enter by private entrance.* Gift shop.
Refreshments: Teashop.

MELROSE ABBEY
(Secretary of State for Scotland)

Beautiful Cistercian Abbey founded by David I.
Location: In Melrose.
Opening Times: Apr 1 to Sept 30—Weekdays 9.30–7, Suns 2–7; Oct 1 to Mar 31—Weekdays 9.30–4, Suns 2–4. *Closed Dec 25, 26; Jan 1, 2.* Adm £1.00, Chd & OAPs 50p.

PRIORWOOD GARDEN
Telephone: Melrose (089 682) 2555
(The National Trust for Scotland)

Garden featuring flowers suitable for drying. Shop and Trust visitor centre.
Location: In Melrose.
Opening Times: Mar 24 to Apr 27, Nov 1 to Dec 24: Mon–Sat 10–1, 2–5.30. Apr 28 to June 30, Oct 1 to 31: Mon–Sat 10–5.30, Sun 1.30–5.30. July 1 to Sept 30: Mon–Sat 10–6, Sun 1.30–5.30. Adm by donation.

PEEBLES

DAWYCK BOTANIC GARDEN
(Royal Botanic Garden, Edinburgh)

Impressive woodland garden.
Location: 8 m SW of Peebles; 28 m S of Edinburgh.
Opening Times: Apr to Oct—Daily 10–6. Adm 30p. No animals.

KAILZIE GARDENS   &
(Mrs A M Richard)

Beautifully situated private gardens re-created in the last 20 years. Magnificent spring show of snowdrops and daffodils; mature timber. Herbaceous borders, shrub and floral beds in old walled garden. Formal rose garden. Greenhouse. Wild Garden and Burnside walk with Primulas, Meconopsis and Rhododendrons. A garden for all seasons.
Location: 2½ m SE from Peebles on B7062.
Opening Times: Fri Mar 24 to Sun Oct 8—Daily 11–5.30. Adm £1, Chd 45p. Car park. Picnic area. Shop. Art Gallery. Owls. Waterfowl pond. Plants for sale when available.
Refreshments: Licensed tea room; lunches & teas.

NEIDPATH CASTLE
Telephone: Aberlady (087 57) 201
(Lady Elizabeth Benson)

Medieval castle updated in the 17th century, situated on a bluff above the River Tweed. Pit prison, well hewn out of solid rock and fine views.
Location: 1 m W of Peebles on A72.
Opening Times: Mar 23 to Apr 2; Apr 29 to Oct 8—Mons to Sats 10–1, 2–5; Suns 1–5 Adm £1, Chd 50p, OAPs 50p. Parties at reduced rates—enquiries to The Factor, Estates Office, Longniddry, East Lothian EH32 0PY.
Refreshments: Hotels in Peebles.

TWEEDDALE MUSEUM *(Tweeddale District Council)*
Chambers Institute, High Street. Tel: (0721) 20123.
Local museum which has displays relating mainly to Tweeddale District, its history, environment and culture. Open all year Mon to Fri 10–5; Apr–Oct: Sat 12–4 and public holidays.

ST. BOSWELLS

MERTOUN GARDENS
Telephone: St Boswells 23236
(His Grace the Duke of Sutherland)

20 acres of beautiful grounds with delightful walks and river views. Fine trees, herbaceous plants and flowering shrubs. Walled garden and well-preserved circular dovecot.
Location: 2 m NE of St Boswells on the B6404.
Opening Times: Garden only. Sats and Suns, Mons on Bank Holidays only—Apr to Sept 2–6 (last entry 5.30). Parties by arrangement. Adm 80p, Chd 30p, OAPs 30p. No dogs. Car parking.
Refreshments: Dryburgh Abbey Hotel, Buccleuch Arms Hotel, St Boswells.

SELKIRK

BOWHILL
Telephone: Selkirk (0750) 20732   &
(His Grace the Duke of Buccleuch & Queensberry KT)

Border home of the Scotts of Buccleuch. Famous paintings include 8 Guardis, Canaletto's Whitehall, Claudes, Gainsboroughs, Reynolds and Raeburns. Superb French furniture and porcelain. Monmouth, Sir Walter Scott and Queen Victoria relics. For details of our specialist courses, run in conjunction with Sotheby's please tel: Buccleuch Heritage Trust Selkirk (0750) 20732. Restored Victorian kitchen. Audio-Visual programme. Lecture Theatre. Exciting Adventure Woodland Play Area. Walks to historic Newark Castle and by lochs and rivers along nature trails.
Location: 3 m W of Selkirk on A708 Moffat-St. Mary's Loch road. Edinburgh, Carlisle, Newcastle approx 1½ hours by road.
Opening Times: House open July 1 to July 31—Daily 1–4.30 (Suns 2–6). Grounds (includes Adventure Woodland Play Area, Nature Trails)—July 1 to July 31—Daily 12–5 (Suns 2–6). Last entry 45 mins before closing time. Riding Centre and Pony Trekking (0750) 20192 open all day all year. Adm House & Grounds £2.50. Parties over 20 £1.75. Grounds only £1. Wheelchair users and Chd (under 5) free. Free car & coach parking. Open by appointment at additional times for museums and specialist or educational groups.
Refreshments: Gift shop and licensed tea room open daily during 'House open' period.

HALLIWELL'S HOUSE MUSEUM
(Ettrick and Lauderdale District Council)
Halliwell's Close, Market Place. Tel: (0750) 20096.
The town's oldest surviving dwelling house after extensive renovation, which was commended in the Civic Trust 1984 Awards, now creates for the present day visitor its past role as a dwelling house and ironmonger's shop. First floor galleries tell the tale of the development of this historic Royal Burgh of Selkirk. The stories are told by objects, text, drawings, videos and a talking post and the Museum was a winner in the British Tourist Authority's 'Come to Britain' Awards for 1984. A temporary Exhibition Gallery (displays changing monthly) and Tourist Information Centre included. Free parking. Apr to Oct: Daily 10–12.30, 1.30–5; Sun 2–4. Adm 50p, Chld/OAP/unemployed 25p. Nov to Dec: Mon to Fri 2–4.30; Sat 10–12; Sun 2–4. Adm free.

SMAILHOLM

SMAILHOLM TOWER
(Historic Buildings and Monuments)

Simple tower house displaying a collection of costume figures and tapestries relating to Sir Walter Scotts' 'Minstrelsy of the Scottish Borders'.

Location: nr Smailholm Village 6 m NW of Kelso.
Opening Times: Apr 1 to Sept 30—Weekdays 9.30–7, Suns 2–7. Oct 1 to Mar 31, *closed.* Adm 60p, Chd & OAPs 30p.

WALKERBURN

SCOTTISH MUSEUM OF WOOLLEN TEXTILES
(Clan Royal of Scotland)
Tweedvale Mill, EH43 6AH. Tel: (089 687) 281/3.
A history of the woollen industry. Easter to Oct Daily. Arrangements can be made for school parties all year. Adm charge.

Central Region

BO'NESS

BIRKHILL CLAY MINE *(Bo'ness Heritage Trust)*
Birkhill. Tel: (0506) 825855.
The Birkhill Clay Mine is an ambitious project to tell the story of fireclay – how and why it was mined and what life was like for the miners. The first phase of the project was opened in 1988 with escorted tours of the mine workings and vivid audio and visual displays. The mine itself is located at the foot of the beautiful steeply-wooded Avon Gorge, 3 miles from Bo'ness. Operation is in conjunction with the Bo'ness & Kinneil Steam Railway (see separate entry) which brings visitors on a 40 minute vintage train journey from the centre of Bo'ness to the Mine area. Adm £1.50, Chld 80p. Advance notice for groups essential. No access for disabled.

BO'NESS & KINNEIL RAILWAY
(Scottish Railway Preservation Society)
Bo'ness Station, Union Street. Tel: (0506) 822298.
Victorian railway centre with a Scottish emphasis has steam hauled trains on a branch line offering a 7 mile round trip. Bo'ness station has buffet facilities, a souvenir shop, a visitors' trail and a picnic area. There is ample free car parking and foreshore walks with fine views over the Forth. Follow the M9 to Linlithgow for A706 or to Grangemouth for A904. Nearest BR stations are Falkirk, Grahamston and Linlithgow. Bus services from these towns plus Glasgow & Edinburgh. Steam trains run Sats, Suns and Bank Holiday Mons, Easter to end of Sept. Five day steam train operation 3rd week July to 2nd week in Aug. First three Suns in Oct. Also Santa steam trains at weekends in Dec. Charges to be fixed for 1989. Special rates for parties. Car parking free. Suitable for disabled persons (no wheelchairs available). Steam railway system run by volunteers.

KINNEIL HOUSE
(Secretary of State for Scotland)
Stately home of the Dukes of Hamilton.
Location: To the west of Bo'ness.
Opening Times: Apr 1 to Sept 30—Daily 9.30–7, Suns 2–7; Oct 1 to Mar 31—Daily 9.30–4, Suns 2–4. *Closed every Tues pm & Fris in winter. Dec 25, 26; Jan 1, 2.* Adm 60p, Chd & OAPs 30p.

KINNEIL MUSEUM AND ROMAN FORTLET
Kinneil Estate, Bo'ness.
Local history, interpretive exhibition for Kinneil Estate. May to Oct: Mon to Sat 10–5; Nov to Apr: Sat only 10–5.

DOLLAR

CASTLE CAMPBELL
(Secretary of State for Scotland)
15th century oblong tower with later additions, set in a steep sided glen. Sometimes known as "Castle Gloom".
Location: 1 m N of Dollar; on N slope of Ochil Hills at head of Dollar Glen.
Opening Times: Apr 1 to Sept 30—Weekdays 9.30–7, Suns 2–7; Oct 1 to Mar 31—Weekdays 9.30–4, Suns 2–4. *(Closed Thurs pm & Fris in winter, also Dec 25, 26; Jan 1, 2).* Adm 60p, Chd & OAPs 30p.

DOUNE

DOUNE MOTOR MUSEUM
Carse of Cambus (on the A84). Tel: (0786) 841203.
A unique collection of vintage and post vintage thoroughbred cars. The display includes examples of Hispano Suiza, Bentley, Jaguar, Aston Martin, Lagonda and many others, including the second oldest Rolls-Royce in the world. Apr to Oct. Daily. Gift shop, cafeteria. Adm charge. Free car parking.

DUNBLANE

DUNBLANE CATHEDRAL MUSEUM
(Society of Friends of Dunblane Cathedral)
The Cross. Tel: Dunblane (0786) 822217.
Large collection of pictures of Cathedral before restoration. Large collection of Communion tokens. Collection of reproductions of Bishops' seals. Leightoniana,

medieval carving, library, archives room, local history. Late May to early Oct 10.30–12.30, 2.30–4.30. Other times on request.

STIRLING

SMITH ART GALLERY AND MUSEUM
Dumbarton Road FK8 2RQ. Tel: (0786) 71917.
Stirling's lively award winning museum and art gallery features exhibitions, art events, shop and theatre. Collection of art, archaeology, natural history, local and social history. Admission free, assisted disabled access. Open Tues to Sun. Phone for details of opening hours and current exhibitions.

STIRLING CASTLE
(Secretary of State for Scotland)
Royal Castle on a great basalt rock dominating the surrounding countryside.
Location: In Stirling.
Station: Stirling (¾ m).
Opening Times: Apr 1 to Sept 30—Weekdays 9.30–6.00. Suns 10.30–5.30. Oct 1 to Mar 31—Weekdays 9.30–5.05. Suns 12.30–4.20. *Closed Dec 25, 26; Jan 1, 2 and 3.* Adm £1.50, Chd & OAPs 75p, Family £4. Last ticket sold 45 mins before closing time.

Dumfries & Galloway

CASTLE DOUGLAS

CASTLE DOUGLAS ART GALLERY
Permanent collection of paintings by Ethel S.G. Bristowe. Open for special exhibitions only.

THREAVE GARDEN
Telephone: Castle Douglas (0556) 2575
(The National Trust for Scotland)
The Trust's School of Gardening. Gardens now among the major tourist attractions of SW Scotland. Visitor centre.
Location: 1 m W of Castle Douglas off A75.
Opening Times: GARDENS. All the year—Daily 9-sunset. WALLED GARDEN & GLASSHOUSES—Daily 9–5. Visitor Centre. Shop Mar 24 to Oct 31—daily 9–6, tearoom Mar 24 weekend to Oct 31 daily 10–5. Adm £2, Chd £1. Adult parties £1.60, Schools 80p, Chd under 5 years free. OAPs & Students (on production of their cards) adm at half the standard adult rate.

DUMFRIES

BURNS HOUSE *(Nithsdale District Council)*
Burns Sreet. Tel: (0387) 55297.
House in which Robert Burns lived for the three years prior to his death. 50p, concessions 25p. Opening times as Dumfries Museum.

CAERLAVEROCK CASTLE
(Secretary of State for Scotland)
One of the finest examples of early classical Renaissance building in Scotland and chief seat of the Maxwell family.
Location: 8 m SSE of Dumfries on the Glencaple Road (B725).
Opening Times: Apr 1 to Sept 30—Weekdays 9.30–7, Suns 2–7; Oct 1 to Mar 31—Weekdays 9.30–4, Suns 2–4. Adm 60p, Chd & OAPs 30p.

DUMFRIES MUSEUM *(Nithsdale District Council)*
The Observatory. Tel: (0387) 53374.
Natural history, archaeological and folk collections. Weekdays 10–1, 2–5; Sun 2–5. *Closed* Sun and Mon, Oct to Mar. Adm free. Camera obscura 50p, concessions 25p. Obscura *closed* Oct to Mar.

GRACEFIELD – ARTS CENTRE
28 Edinburgh Road. Tel: Dumfries 62084.
Gracefields Arts Centre houses a permanent collection of over 400 Scottish paintings. Temporary exhibitions change every four weeks and in addition to the Gallery Spaces there are also four studios, dark room, cafe/bar and pottery. Open all week 10–5 during Summer; 12–5 Winter. Adm free. Phone for details on above number.

OLD BRIDGE HOUSE MUSEUM *(Nithsdale District Council)*
Tel: (0387) 56904.
Seventeenth century house with six period and historical rooms. Adm free. Opening times as Dumfries Museum, *closed* Oct to Mar.

ROBERT BURNS CENTRE *(Nithsdale District Council)*
Old Town Mill, Mill Road. Tel: (0387) 64808.
Exhibition on Burns and his life in Dumfries. AV theatre, shop, café. Adm free, except to AV theatre, 50p, concessions 25p. *Combined ticket for Camera Obscura, Burns House and Burns Centre AV theatre £1 only.* New – Quality feature films 5 evenings a week. Apr to Sept: Mon to Sat 10–8; Sun 2–5. Oct to Mar: Tues to Sat 10–1, 2–5.

SANQUHAR MUSEUM *(Nithsdale District Council)*
1735 Adam-designed town house; covers local history, geology etc. Adm on request to Mr. Johnston, Hon. Curator at 42 High Street, Sanquhar or Miss Millar, Local Government Offices, High Street, Sanquhar.

SAVINGS BANK MUSEUM
Ruthwell.

SHAMBELLIE HOUSE MUSEUM OF COSTUME
(National Museums of Scotland) (Outstation)
New Abbey, Dumfries. Tel: 038-785 375.
Collection of 200 years of fashionable dress. Open May to Sept: Thurs to Mon 10–5.30; Sun 12–5.30. Closed Tues and Wed.

ECCLEFECHAN

CARLYLE'S BIRTHPLACE
Telephone: Ecclefechan (057 63) 666
(The National Trust for Scotland)

Thomas Carlyle was born here in 1795. Mementoes and MSS.
Location: 5 m SE of Lockerbie on the Lockerbie/Carlisle Road (A74).
Opening Times: Mar 24 to Oct 31—daily 12–5. Adm 90p, Chd 45p (under 5 free). OAPs & Students (on production of their cards) adm at half the standard rate. Adult parties 70p, school parties 35p.
Refreshments: Ecclefechan Hotel.

KIRKBEAN

ARBIGLAND GARDENS
(Captain J B Blackett)

Woodland, formal and water gardens arranged round a secluded bay. The garden where Admiral Paul Jones worked as a boy.
Location: 15 m SW of Dumfries on A710.
Opening Times: Gardens: May to Sept incl—Tues, Thurs & Suns 2–6. House and Gardens: May 20–28, 1989: 2–6; Aug 19–27, 1989: 2–6. Adm £1, Chd 50p. Toddlers free. Car park free. Picnic area by sandy beach. Dogs on leads please. Produce Shop.
Refreshments: Tea room. Hotels in Dumfries or Southerness (2 m).

KIRKCUDBRIGHT

BROUGHTON HOUSE
Telephone: (0557) 30437
(The Hornel Trust)

Home of the artist E. A. Hornel 1864–1933. Mainly 18th century. Fine furniture, Scottish paintings. George III–Victorian samplers. Special exhibitions: The Artist in his Studio: House Laundry 1920's. Superb town garden and Japanese garden.
Location: 12 High Street, Kirkcudbright DG6 4JX.
Opening Times: Easter to Oct 14: weekdays 11–1, 2–5, Sun 2–5. *Closed* Tues. Adm 60p, OAPs/Chd half price. Conducted tours for parties available. Car parking nearby in town park. Suitable for disabled persons (no wheelchairs available).
Refreshments: Many in Kirkcudbright.

THE STEWARTRY MUSEUM
Independent Museum depicting the history and culture of Galloway. Easter to Oct: Mon to Sat 11–4, (July and Aug 11–5). Adm 50p, Chld 25p.

NEW ABBEY

SWEETHEART ABBEY
(Secretary of State for Scotland)

Cistercian monastery famous for the touching and romantic circumstances of its foundation by Lady Dervorgilla.
Location: 7 m S of Dumfries on coast road (A710).
Opening Times: Apr 1 to Sept 30—Weekdays 9.30–7, Suns 2–7; Oct 1 to Mar 31—Weekdays 9.30–4, Suns 2–4. Adm 60p, Chd & OAPs 30p.

PORT LOGAN

LOGAN BOTANIC GARDEN
(Royal Botanic Garden, Edinburgh)

A wide collection of plants from the warm temperate regions of the world.
Location: 10 m S of Stranraer.
Opening Times: Apr to Oct—Daily 10–6. Adm 60p, Chd/OAPs 30p. No animals.
Refreshments: Teas available.

STRANRAER

CASTLE KENNEDY GARDENS
Telephone: Stranraer (0776) 2024
(The Earl and Countess of Stair)

Beautiful gardens laid out on a peninsula between two lochs, Rhododendrons, azaleas, magnolias, embothriums and many other plants from overseas.
Location: 3 m E of Stranraer on A75; Stranraer/Dumfries Road (entrance by Castle Kennedy Lodge only).
Opening Times: Apr to Sept—Daily 10–5. Adm £1.50, Chd (under 16) 50p, OAPs £1. Party rates on application. Free parking. Plant Centre.
Refreshments: Light refreshments only. Hotels Eynhallow, Castle Kennedy & Stranraer.

WIGTOWN DISTRICT MUSEUM
55 George Street. Tel: (0776) 5088.
Changing exhibitions on local and national topics.

THORNHILL

DRUMLANRIG CASTLE AND COUNTRY PARK
Telephone: Thornhill (0848) 30248
(Home of the Duke of Buccleuch & Queensberry KT)

Magnificent pink sandstone castle with outstanding art treasures – Leonardo, Rembrandt, Hobein – beautiful silverware, superb furniture and porcelain, Bonnie Prince Charlie's relics. Extensive grounds and woodland includes gardens, exciting adventure woodland play area, nature trails and picnic sites. Tearoom and giftshop. Working craft centre, lecture room and cycle hire.
Location: 18 m N of Dumfries; 3 m N of Thornhill off A76; 16 m from A74 at Elvanfoot; approx 1½ hrs by road from Edinburgh, Glasgow & Carlisle.
Opening Times: Castle and Grounds – Sat, Apr 29 to Sun Aug 20. Daily (*except Thurs*) 11–5. Sun 2–6. Grounds and Adventure Woodland only – open daily through season and until Sept 30. Adm Castle and Grounds £2.50. Grounds only £1. Chd under 16, Castle and Grounds £1 (under 5 free). Discounts for groups of 20 or over, OAPs and students.
Refreshments: Lunches, Afternoon Teas and snacks at above times.

Fife Region

ABERDOUR

ABERDOUR CASTLE
(Secretary of State for Scotland)

A 14th century tower with the remains of a terraced garden and bowling green. There is also a splendid dovecot and panoramic views across the Firth of Forth.
Location: At Aberdour.
Opening Times: Apr 1 to Sept 30—Daily 9.30–7 (Suns 2–7); Oct 1 to Mar 31—Daily 9.30–4 (Suns 2–4). *Closed Thurs pm and Fri in winter, also Dec 25, 26; Jan 1, 2.* Adm 60p, Chd & OAPs 30p.

ANSTRUTHER

THE SCOTTISH FISHERIES MUSEUM
(Scottish Fisheries Museum Trust Ltd.)
St. Ayles, Harbourhead. Tel: (0333) 310628.
16th to 19th century buildings housing marine aquarium, fishing and ships' gear, model and actual fishing boats, period fisher-home interiors, reference library. Apr to Oct: Weekdays 10–5.30. Nov to Mar: weekdays 10–5, Sun all year 2–5. Adm £1; Chld/OAPs/Unemployed 50p. *Reduced rates for pre-booked parties.* Tearoom. Shop.

CULROSS

CULROSS PALACE
(Secretary of State for Scotland)

Built between 1597 and 1611. Contains very fine series of paintings on wooden walls and ceilings.
Location: In the village of Culross on the Firth of Forth between Kincardine and Dunfermline (A985).
Opening Times: Apr 1 to Sept 30—Weekdays 9.30–7 (Suns 2–7); Oct 1 to Mar 31—Weekdays 9.30–4 (Suns 2–4). *Closed Dec 25 & 26; Jan 1 & 2.* Adm £1, Chd & OAPs 50p.
Refreshments: Dundonald Arms, Culross.

DUNIMARLE MUSEUM
Tel: Newmills (0383) 229.
Napoleonic furniture, oil paintings, library, ceramics, glass, silver and objets d'art. Adm charge.

THE TOWN HOUSE & THE STUDY
Telephone: Newmills (0383) 880359
(The National Trust for Scotland)

Outstanding survival of Scottish 17th century burgh architecture carefully restored to 20th century living standards.

Location: 12 m W of Forth Road Bridge, off A985.
Opening Times: Town House (with visual presentation) open Mar 24 to Mar 27, and Apr 28 to Oct 1 daily 11–1, 2–5. Adm 60p, Chd 30p. The Study open Apr 1 to 23, Jun 1 to Aug 31 and Oct 7 to 29, Sat and Sun 2–4. Other times by appointment only. Adm 40p, Chd 20p. Joint ticket—adults £1, Chd 50p. Students (on production of their cards) adm at half the standard adult rate.

CUPAR

FIFE FOLK MUSEUM
Ceres.
A varied local collection displayed in a unique setting.

HILL OF TARVIT
Telephone: Cupar (0334) 53127
(The National Trust for Scotland)

Mansion house remodelled 1906. Collection of furniture, tapestries, porcelain and paintings. Gardens.

Location: 2½ m SW of Cupar A916.
Station: Cupar (2½ m).
Opening Times: House: Mar 24 to Mar 27 daily 2–6. Apr 28 to Sept 30; also weekends Apr 1 to Apr 23, Oct 1 to Oct 29 (last tour 5.30). Gardens & grounds all year. 10–sunset. Adm House & Gardens £2, Chd £1. Adult parties (20 or more) £1.60. Schools 80p. Gardens only £1, Chd 50p. Chd under 5 free, OAPs & Students (on production of their cards) adm at half the standard adult rate.

DUNFERMLINE

ANDREW CARNEGIE BIRTHPLACE MUSEUM
Junction of Moodie Street and Priory Lane. Tel: (0383) 724302.
'The man who dies rich dies disgraced.' Born in a humble weaver's cottage, Andrew Carnegie became the greatest steelmaster in 19th century America – and gave away $350 million. Exciting displays in his Birthplace Cottage and the adjoining Memorial Hall tell his fascinating story and illustrate the work of the major Trusts and Foundations he established in Britain, Europe and America. Audio-visual programme. Guided tours available during summer weekends. Provision for disabled. Shop. Apr to Oct: Mon to Sat 11–5; Sun 2–5. Nov to Mar: Daily 2–4. Adm free.

DUNFERMLINE DISTRICT MUSEUM AND THE SMALL GALLERY
(Dunfermline District Council)
Viewfield. Tel: (0383) 721814.
Local history and natural history of the district. Small gallery: monthly art and craft exhibitions. Mon to Sat 11–5. *Closed* Sun and public holidays.

PITTENCRIEFF HOUSE MUSEUM *(Dunfermline District Council)*
Pittencrieff Park. Tel: (0383) 722935/721814.
Local history and costume displays; temporary painting and photographic exhibitions. May 8 to Sept 2: Daily (except Tues) 11–5.

DYSART

MCDOUALL STUART MUSEUM *(Kirkcaldy District Museums)*
Rectory Lane, Dysart. Tel: (0592) 260732.
This small museum occupies one of Dysart's many National Trust for Scotland restored 'little houses' which form the 18th century burgh, with its historic harbour. The house is the birthplace of John McDouall Stuart, first explorer to cross Australia 1861–2 and displays describe his harrowing journeys, the Australian wilderness, and the Aborigines who made a life there. Sales area and starting point for self-guided tours around this attractive burgh. June 1 to Aug 31: Daily (incl. Sun) 2–5.

FALKLAND

FALKLAND PALACE & GARDEN
Telephone: Falkland (033 757) 397
(Her Majesty the Queen. Hereditary Constable, Capt & Keeper: Ninian Crichton Stuart. Deputy Keeper: The National Trust for Scotland)

Attractive 16th century royal palace, favourite retreat of Stuart kings and queens. Gardens now laid out to the original Royal plans. Town Hall, Visitor Centre, Exhibition and Shop.

Location: In Falkland, 11 m N of Kirkcaldy on A912.
Opening Times: Mar 24 to Sept 30—Mons to Sats 10–6; Suns 2–6. Oct 1 to 29—Sats 10–6; Suns 2–6. Last tour of Palace 5. Adm Palace & Gardens £2.10, Chd £1.05. Adult parties £1.70. Schools 85p. Gardens only £1.30, Chd 65p (under 5 free). OAPs & Students (on production of their cards) adm at half the standard adult rate. Visitor centre and Trust shop.
Refreshments: Bruce Arms, Falkland.

INVERKEITHING

INVERKEITHING MUSEUM *(Dunfermline District Council)*
Queen Street. Tel: (0383) 413344.
Small local history museum with a collection of material relating to Admiral Sir Samuel Greig (native of Inverkeithing) who became "Father of the Russian Navy" in the mid-17th century. Museum is situated in a 14th century Friary. There is little of the Friary still in existence except the Hospice which among other things houses the museum. Wed to Sun 11–5. *Closed* Mon and Tues, 25 and 26 Dec, 1 and 2 Jan. Adm free. Car parking outside museum. Unsuitable for disabled persons.

KIRKCALDY

KIRKCALDY MUSEUM AND ART GALLERY
(Kirkcaldy District Museums)
By Kirkcaldy Railway Station. Tel: (0592) 260732.
Come and discover the heritage of Kirkcaldy District through a unique collection of Scottish paintings, fascinating new historical displays and a full programme of changing art, craft and historical exhibitions. Gallery shop for crafts, cards and local publications. Special enquiry and schools services available. Open Mon to Sat 11–5; Sun 2–5. Adm free.

MARKINCH

BALGONIE CASTLE
Telephone: (0592) 750119
(The Laird and Lady of Balgonie and Eddergoll)

One of the finest late 14th century Ashlar built towers in Scotland. Once more a family home after being abandoned for 160 years. Consisting of five floors with the two lower ones being vaulted. Around the large courtyard are buildings from 1496 to 1702. The gatehouse also contains a prison. 17th century home of Sir Alexander Leslie, the Lord General of the Covenanting Army of Scotland. He was later created the 1st Earl of Leven. During the Jacobite rising of 1715, the castle was garrisoned by Rob Roy McGregor. The present owners have a long-term project for total restoration for public and educational usage. They are also professional leather carvers and tapestry weavers. A wild-life garden has been established between the castle and the River Leven.

Location: B921 2 m E of Glenrothes; 4 m N of Kirkcaldy.
Opening Times: Tours through the tower 2–5 all year round. Otherwise by appointment. Studios and courtyard open daily all year round. Adm £1, Chd/ OAPs special reductions. Parties by prior booking. Car parking. Property suitable for disabled persons in courtyard and ground floors only.
Refreshments: Picnic area only.

PITTENWEEM

KELLIE CASTLE AND GARDEN
Telephone: Arncroach (033 38) 271
(The National Trust for Scotland)

Fine example of 16th-17th century domestic architecture of lowland countries of Scotland.

Location: 3 m NNW of Pittenweem on B9171.
Opening Times: CASTLE and GARDEN: Mar 24 to Mar 27—Daily, Apr 28 to Sept 30—Daily 2–6. Last tour 5.30, also weekends Oct 1 to Oct 29, and Apr 1 to Apr 27. GARDENS: All the year—Daily 10–sunset. Adm £2, Chd £1. Adult parties (20 or more) £1.60. Schools 80p. Gardens only 80p, Chd (accompanied by adult) 40p (under 5 free). OAPs & Students (on production of their cards) adm at half the standard adult rate. *Gardens only suitable for disabled.*

ST. ANDREWS

CRAWFORD CENTRE FOR THE ARTS
93 North St. Tel: (0334) 74610.
Monthly programme of temporary exhibitions including contemporary and historical Scottish and international art, photography, architecture, crafts, etc. Also drama and music performances and workshops. Open all year: Mon to Sat 10–5, Sun 2–5. *Closed* Christmas and New Year. Adm free. Suitable for disabled persons.

Grampian Region

ABERDEEN

ABERDEEN ART GALLERY *(Aberdeen District Council)*
Schoolhill. Tel: (0224) 646333.
Permanent collection of 18th, 19th and 20th century art with emphasis on contemporary art – oil paintings, watercolours, prints, drawings, sculpture, decorative arts. Full programme of special exhibitions. Music. Dance. Poetry. Events. Film. Coffee shop; Gallery shop. Mon to Sat 10–5 (Thurs 10–8); Sun 2–5. Adm free. Parking (275m.) 250 places.

ABERDEEN MARITIME MUSEUM *(Aberdeen District Council)*
Provost Ross's House, Shiprow. Tel: (0224) 585788.
Display themes on local shipbuilding, fishing, North Sea oil, ship models and paintings within the restored 16th century building. Special Exhibitions. Museum shop. Mon to Sat 10–5. Adm free. Parking (45m.) 400 places.

ABERDEEN UNIVERSITY ANTHROPOLOGICAL MUSEUM
Tel: (0224) 273131 Ext. 3132.
General archaeological and ethnographical museum with Classical, Oriental, Egyptian, American and Pacific collections and local antiquities. Mon to Fri 10–5; Sun 2–5. *Closed* Sat.

ABERDEEN UNIVERSITY NATURAL HISTORY MUSEUM
Zoology Department, Tillydrone Avenue. Tel: (0224) 40241.
Teaching and study collections of natural history. By appointment.

JAMES DUN'S HOUSE *(Aberdeen District Council)*
61 Schoolhill. Tel: (0224) 646333.
18th century town house renovated for use as a museum with permanent displays and special exhibitions. Museum shop. Mon to Sat 10–5. Adm free. Parking (360m.) 250 places.

PROVOST ROSS'S HOUSE *(National Trust for Scotland)*
Shiprow, off Castle Street. Tel: (0224) 572215.
Houses the Aberdeen Maritime Museum, operated by the City of Aberdeen District Council, in one of the oldest surviving houses in Aberdeen, built 1593. Open all year (except Christmas and New Year Hols) Mon to Sat 10–5. *Closed* Suns. Adm free.

PROVOST SKENE'S HOUSE *(Aberdeen District Council)*
Guestrow (off Broad Street). Tel: (0224) 641086.
17th century furnished house with period rooms and displays of local history and domestic life. Video programme showing daily. Provost Skene's Kitchen has been restored and serves coffee, tea and light meals. Mon to Sat 10–5. Adm free. Parking (25m.) 35 places.

ALFORD

GRAMPIAN TRANSPORT MUSEUM
(Grampian Transport Museum Association)
Alford AB3 8AD. Tel: (0336) 2292.
Purpose-built buildings house an extensive collection of road transport vehicles and items. Most of the vehicle exhibits have strong local associations. All types of vehicle are represented including steam and horse-drawn. Regional road transport history is reflected by photographs and displays. A separate railway exhibition is housed in the reconstructed GNSR village station. Alford Cavalcade 23 July 1989, 24 July 1988. A monumental gathering of the regions preserved transport. The railway station also incorporates a Tourist Information Centre and acts as a terminus of the Alford Valley Railway, a two foot gauge passenger carrying railway. Daily 1 Apr to 30 Sept 10.30–5. Adm charge. Special reductions for parties. Car parking free. Suitable for disabled persons.

BALLATER

BALMORAL CASTLE
(Her Majesty the Queen)

Grounds and Exhition open.
Location: 8 m W of Ballater on A93.
Opening Times: Gardens and Exhibition open during May, June & July—Daily (except Suns) 10–5. Adm (1987 rates) £1.20, OAPs £1, Chd free. Donation to charities. Pony trekking.
Refreshments: Refreshment room at Balmoral.

BANCHORY

BANCHORY MUSEUM *(North East of Scotland Museum Service)*
The Square. Tel: Peterhead (0779) 77778.
Local history and bygones. June to Sept.

CRATHES CASTLE & GARDEN
Telephone: Crathes (033 044) 525   &
(The National Trust for Scotland)

Fine 16th century baronial castle. Remarkable early painted ceilings. Beautiful gardens.
Location: 3 m E of Banchory on A93; 15 m W of Aberdeen.
Opening Times: CASTLE & VISITOR CENTRE: Mar 24 to Mar 27, weekends: Apr **only** (Apr 1 to 23). Apr 28 to Oct 31—Daily 11–6; (last tour 5.15). Adm Castle & Grounds £2.20, Chd £1.10. Garden & Grounds £2, Chd £1. Combined ticket (Castle, Garden & Grounds) £2.80, Chd £1.40, Adult parties £2.20, Schools £1.10. Booked parties also accepted on weekdays in Apr and Oct. GARDENS & GROUNDS. All the year—Daily 9.30–sunset. Chd under 5 years free. OAPs & Students (on production of their cards) adm at half the standard adult rate. Visitor Centre.
Refreshments: Shop and Restaurant.

BANFF

BANFF MUSEUM *(North East of Scotland Museum Service)*
High Street. Tel: Peterhead (0779) 77778.
Local history, natural history, James Ferguson relics. June to Sept.

DUFF HOUSE
(Secretary of State for Scotland)

18th century mansion designed by William Adam.
Location: ½ m S of Banff.
Opening Times: Apr 1 to Sept 30—Weekdays 9.30–7, Suns 2–7. Oct 1 to Mar 31—apply keykeeper. Adm 60p, Chd & OAPs 30p.

BRAEMAR

BRAEMAR CASTLE
Telephone: Braemar (033 83) 219 – *out of season* 224
(Captain A A C Farquharson of Invercauld)

Romantic 17th century castle, originally of the Earls of Mar of architectural and historical interest. A fully furnished private residence of surprising charm.
Location: ½ m NE of Braemar on A93.
Opening Times: May to early Oct—Daily 10–6. Adm £1.30, Chd 65p. Special rates for groups and OAPs. Free car and bus park.

BUCKIE

BUCKIE MARITIME MUSEUM *(Moray District Council)*
Cluny Place. Tel: Forres (0309) 73701.
Fishing, lifeboats, coopering, local history. Peter Anson paintings. Mon to Fri 10–8; Sat 10–12.

BURGHEAD

BURGHEAD MUSEUM *(Moray District Council)*
Tel: Forres (0309) 73701.
Local archaeology, history and natural history. Tues 1.30–5; Thurs 5–8.30; Sat 10–12.

DONSIDE

KILDRUMMY CASTLE GARDEN
Telephone: Kildrummy (09755) 71264 or 71277   &
(Kildrummy Castle Garden Trust)

Approximately 10 acres of garden with shrubs, heaths, gentians, rhododen-drons, lilies etc. Alpine and water garden dominated by ruins of 13th century castle. Walks, play area and video room.
Location: On A97 off A944 10 m W of Alford; 15 m S of Huntly; 35 m W of Aberdeen.
Opening Times: GARDENS ONLY. Apr to Oct—Daily 10–5. Adm £1 (1988 rates). Car park inside hotel main entrance free. Coach park inside hotel trade entrance free. Plants for sale. Wheelchairs.
Refreshments: At Kildrummy Castle Hotel in the grounds (please make reservations) Kildrummy (09755) 71288. The Kildrummy Inn, Kildrummy (09755) 71227.

DRUMOAK

DRUM CASTLE
Telephone: Drumoak (033 08) 204
(The National Trust for Scotland)

The oldest part of the historic Castle, the great square tower—one of the three oldest tower houses in Scotland—dates from the late 13th century. Charming mansion added in 1619.
Location: 10 m W of Aberdeen, off A93.
Opening Times: Apr 28 to Oct 1—Daily 2–6 (last tour 5.15). Adm Castle £2.10, Chd £1.05. Adult parties £1.70, Schools 85p. Chd under 5 years free. OAPs & Students (on production of their cards) adm at half the standard adult rate. Grounds open all year 9.30–sunset. Adm by donation.

DUFFTOWN

BALVENIE CASTLE
(Secretary of State for Scotland)

A 13th century castle visited by Mary Queen of Scots in 1562.
Location: At Dufftown.
Opening Times: Apr 1 to Sept 30—Daily 9.30–7 (Suns 2–7). *Closed Oct to Mar.* Adm 60p, Chd & OAPs 30p.

DUFFTOWN MUSEUM *(Moray District Council)*
The Tower. Tel: Forres (0309) 73701.
Local history, Mortlach Kirk. Temporary exhibitions. Mid May to Sept: Daily 10–6.

THE GLENFIDDICH DISTILLERY *(The Grant Family)*
Dufftown. Tel: (0340) 20373.
The Glenfiddich distillery is a living museum, still using the same skills as employed in Victorian times and exhibiting whisky and Grant family memorabilia from throughout that period. Also links with Culloden, Balvenie Castle, Mortlach Church etc. Special exhibitions include Coopers tools, bagpipes, Gordon Highlanders, distilling memorabilia and appropriate references to Scottish history. Open all year: Weekdays 9.30–4.30. May 14 to Oct 16: Sats 9.30–4.30; Sun 12–4.30. *Closed* Christmas and New Year. Adm free. Parties numbering more than 12 accepted (preferably if booked in advance). Car parking. Suitable for disabled persons. Complimentary dram or soft drink. Curator Mr. Mike Don.

ELGIN

ELGIN CATHEDRAL
(Secretary of State for Scotland)
Probably Scotland's most beautiful cathedral with certainly the finest chapter house.
Location: In Elgin.
Opening Times: Apr 1 to Sept 30—Daily 9.30–7, Suns 2–7; Oct 1 to Mar 31—Daily 9.30–4. Suns 2–4. *Closed Dec 25, 26; Jan 1, 2.* Adm 60p, Chd & OAPs 30p.

FETTERCAIRN

FASQUE
Telephone: Fettercairn (056 14) 201
(The Gladstone Family)
1809 Home of the Gladstone family with a full complement of furnishings and domestic articles little changed for 160 years.
Location: 1 m N of Fettercairn on the B974 Cairn O Mount pass road; 34 m Aberdeen and Dundee; 17 m Stonehaven; 12 m Montrose; 18 m Banchory.
Opening Times: House open May 1 to end of Sept every day except Fris 1.30–5.30 with last entry at 5 pm. Adults £2, Chd 90p. Parties £1.75 over 25 pre-booked. Evening opening for parties by arrangement.

FOCHABERS

FOCHABERS FOLK MUSEUM
Largest collection of horse drawn vehicles in North Scotland. Downstairs there is a virtual Alladin's Cave, mostly concerned with bygone days in Fochabers and the surrounding area. Collected by the Christie family with the help of friends, the museum gives a unique picture of Fochabers. There is a complete village shop in authentic style of the turn of the century – well before the era of plastic wrappings and prepacked provisions. There are clocks, model engines, wedding dresses, pictures of events and personalities. Winter: Daily 9.30–1, 2–5; Summer: Daily 9.30–1, 2–6. Adm 40p; Chld and OAPs 20p.

FORRES

FALCONER MUSEUM *(Moray District Council)*
Tel: Forres (0309) 73701.
Local history 'The Story of Forres'; Natural history; Exhibits on Hugh Falconer and other prominent local people. Temporary exhibitions. Mid May to Sept: Daily 9.30–5.30. Other periods Mon to Fri 10–12.30, 1.30–4.

FYVIE

FYVIE CASTLE
Telephone: Fyvie (065 16) 266
(The National Trust of Scotland)
The oldest part of the castle dates from the 13th century and its five great towers are the monuments to the five families who owned the castle. The building contains the finest wheel stair in Scotland and a magnificent collection of paintings.
Location: Off A947, 8 m SE of Turriff.
Opening Times: Apr 28 to May 25—Daily 2–6; May 26 to Oct 1—Daily 11–6 (last tour 5.15). Adm Castle: £2.10, Chd £1.05, Adult parties £1.70, Schools 85p. Parkland free. Chd (under 5) free. OAPs & Students (on production of their cards) adm at half the standard adult rate. Permanent exhibition – Castles of Mar.

HUNTLY

BRANDER MUSEUM *(North East of Scotland Museum Service)*
Public Library Building. Tel: Peterhead (0779) 77778.
Small display of local bygones and travelling exhibitions. Open all year.

HUNTLY CASTLE
(Secretary of State for Scotland)
A magnificent ruin of an architectural and heraldic house built in the 16th and 17th centuries.
Location: In Huntly.
Opening Times: Apr 1 to Sept 30—Daily 9.30–7, Suns 2–7; Oct 1 to Mar 31—Daily 9.30–4, Suns 2–4. *Closed Dec 25, 26; Jan 1, 2.* Adm 60p, Chd & OAPs 30p.

INVERURIE

INVERURIE MUSEUM *(North East of Scotland Museum Service)*
Public Library Building, The Square. Tel: Peterhead (0779) 77778.
Collection of Prehistoric material from locality. Small geological and natural history collections. Special exhibitions. Open all year.

KEITH

KEITH ART GALLERY *(Moray District Council)*
Church Road. Tel: Forres (0309) 73701.
Local history. Temporary exhibitions. June to Sept: Daily 9.30–6.

KENNETHMONT

LEITH HALL AND GARDEN
Telephone: Kennethmont (046 43) 216   ♿
(The National Trust for Scotland)
Home of the Leith family from 1650. Jacobite relics, and major exhibition of family's military collection. Charming garden.
Location: 1 m W of Kennethmont on B9002; 34 m NW of Aberdeen.
Opening Times: Apr 28 to Oct 1—Daily 2–6 (last tour 5.15). Gardens and Grounds all the year—Daily 9.30–sunset. Adm House and garden £2.10, Chd £1.05 (under 5 free). Adult parties £1.70, Schools 85p. OAPs & Students (on production of their cards) adm at half the standard adult rate. Admission to gardens & grounds by donation. Picnic area.

LUMPHANAN

CRAIGIEVAR CASTLE
Telephone: Lumphanan (033 98) 83635
(The National Trust for Scotland)
Exceptional tower house. Structurally unchanged since its completion in 1626.
Location: 6 m S of Alford on A980; 26 m W of Aberdeen.
Opening Times: Apr 28 to June 30, Sept 1 to Oct 1—Daily 2–6. July 1 to Aug 31, daily 11–6 (last tour 5.15). Parties of 12 or more at other times by arrangement. Adm £2.10, Chd £1.05. Adult parties £1.70, Schools 85p. Chd under 5 years free. OAPs & Students (on production of their cards) adm at half the standard adult rate. Grounds open all year 9.30–sunset. Adm by donation. *It is recommended that all coach parties should book in advance.*

METHLICK

HADDO HOUSE
Telephone: Tarves (065 15) 440   ♿
(The National Trust for Scotland)
Georgian house designed in 1731 by William Adam. Home of the Gordons of Haddo for over 500 years. Terraced gardens.
Location: 4 m N of Pitmedden; 19 m N of Aberdeen (A981 & B999).
Opening Times: Mar 24 to Mar 27; Apr 28 to Oct 31 daily 2–6. Apr 2 to Apr 23, Suns only 2–6 (last tour 5.15). Adm £2.10, Chd £1.05 (under 5 free). Adult parties £1.70, Schools 85p. OAPs & Students (on production of their cards) adm at half the standard adult rate. Gardens & grounds open all year 9.30–sunset, adm by donation. Wheelchair access. Permanent exhibition, shop and Restaurant open Mar 24 to 27, and Apr 28 to Oct 31 daily 11–6.
Refreshments: Restaurant.

MINTLAW

NORTH EAST OF SCOTLAND AGRICULTURAL HERITAGE CENTRE
(Leisure and Recreation Dept., Banff and Buchan District Council)
Aden Country Park, by Peterhead AB4 8LD. Tel: (0771) 22807/22857.
Set amid Aden Country Park's beautiful surroundings, the Centre portrays everyday life on the former Aden estate during the 1920s within the finely restored home farm by use of displays, audio visual programme and costume guides. A wide ranging exhibition tells the exciting story of North East farming innovation over the past two centuries, with dioramas, soundtrack, and video cartoon. Regularly changing temporary exhibitions. Nature walks by prior appointment with Ranger Service. Nature trail, Craftworkers, Restaurant, Shop. Aden Farm and Field Day 11th June 1989 – farming in action, vintage machinery, heavy horse and demonstrations. Open May to Sept daily 11–5; Apr and Oct weekends only 12–5. No charge for Centre or Country Park. Parties welcome by arrangement. Free car parking. Access for disabled. One wheelchair available at Reception. Visitors are welcome to picnic in the Country Park.

Nr. NAIRN

BRODIE CASTLE
Telephone: Brodie (030 94) 371
(The National Trust for Scotland)

Ancient seat of the Brodies, burned in 1645 and largely rebuilt, with 17th/19th century additions. Fine furniture, porcelain and paintings.
Location: Off A96 between Nairn & Forres.
Opening Times: Mar 24 to Sept 30: Mons to Sats 11–6; Suns 2–6 (last tour 5.15). Also open weekends only Oct 1 to Oct 22, Sat 11–6, Sun 2–6. Grounds open all year 9.30–sunset. Adm £2.10, Chd £1.05 (under 5 free). Adult parties £1.70, Schools 85p. OAPs & Students (on production of their cards) adm at half the standard adult rate. Grounds by donation.

PETERHEAD

ARBUTHNOT MUSEUM *(North East of Scotland Museum Service)*
St. Peter Street. Tel: (0779) 77778.
Collection illustrating local history; whaling and Arctic section; coins. Open all year.

PITMEDDEN

MUSEUM OF FARMING LIFE *(National Trust for Scotland)*
Gordon, on A920, 1m W of Pitmedden village and 14m N of Aberdeen. Tel: (06513) 2352.
Collection of agricultural and domestic artifacts. May 1 to Sept 30: 10–6 (last admission 5.15). Adm Museum and Garden £1.80, Chld 90p. Adult parties £1.40, schools 70p.

PITMEDDEN
Telephone: Udny (065 13) 2445
(The National Trust for Scotland)

Reconstructed 17th century garden with floral designs, fountains and sundials. Display on the evolution of the formal garden. Museum of Farming Life.
Location: 14 m N of Aberdeen on A920.
Opening Times: Garden & grounds open all year—Daily 9.30–sunset. Museum, Visitor Centre & other facilities—Apr 28 to Oct 1—Daily 11–6 (last adm 5.15). Adm Garden & Museum (May to Sept) £1.70, Chd 85p (under 5 free). Adult parties £1.40, Schools 70p. Adm Garden only £1, Chd 50p. OAPs & Students (on production of their cards) adm at half the standard adult rate. No dogs in garden please. *House not open.*

SAUCHEN

CASTLE FRASER
Telephone: Sauchen (033 03) 463
(The National Trust for Scotland)

One of the most spectacular of the Castles of Mar. Z-plan castle begun in 1575 and completed in 1636.
Location: 3 m S of Kemnay off B993; 16 m W of Aberdeen.
Opening Times: Apr 28 to Oct 1—Daily 2–6 (last tour 5.15). Adm £2.10, Chd £1.05. Adult parties £1.70, Schools 85p. Chd under 5 years free. OAPs & Students (on production of their cards) adm at half the standard adult rate. Garden & grounds open all year, 9.30–sunset, adm by donation. Picnic area.

SPEY BAY

TUGNET ICE HOUSE *(Moray District Council)*
Tel: Forres (0309) 73701.
Exhibition on salmon fishing and the River Spey. June to Aug all reasonable hours.

STONEHAVEN

MUCHALLS CASTLE
(Mr & Mrs Maurice A Simpson)

Early 17th century elaborate plaster work ceilings and fireplaces. Built by Burnetts of Leys, 1619.
Location: 5 m N Stonehaven; 9 m S Aberdeen; ¾ m off Aberdeen/Stonehaven Road (A92).
Opening Times: July and Aug. Sun and Tues 2.30–4.30. Other times by written application only. Adm 60p, Chd/OAPs 20p.

TOLBOOTH MUSEUM *(North East of Scotland Museum Service)*
The Harbour. Tel: Peterhead (0779) 77778.
Local history and fishing displays. June to Sept.

TOMINTOUL

TOMINTOUL VISITOR CENTRE *(Moray District Council)*
The Square. Tel: Forres (0309) 73701.
Wildlife, landscape, geology, climate, local history, reconstructed farm kitchen and village smithy. Easter to Oct: Daily 9.30–6.

Highlands Region

ARDERSIER

FORT GEORGE
(Secretary of State for Scotland)

One of the most outstanding military fortifications virtually unaltered from the 18th century. Re-creations of 18th & 19th century barrack rooms. Seafield collection of arms.
Location: At Ardersier. 11 m NE of Inverness.
Opening Times: Apr 1 to Sept 30—Daily 9.30–7, Suns 2–7; Oct 1 to Mar 31—Daily 9.30–4, Suns 2–4. *Closed Dec 25, 26; Jan 1, 2.* Adm £1.50, Chd & OAPs 75p. Family £4.

ARMADALE

THE MUSEUM OF THE ISLES
Clan Donald Centre, Armadale. Tel: (047 14) 227/305.
The Exhibition traces the origins of Gaeldom, the rise and fall of the Lords of the Isles and the cultural influence of Clan Donald. The Audio-Visual Theatre features an 18 minute presentation 'The Sea Kingdom'. The award winning Clan Donald Centre has a Restaurant, craft/bookshop, woodland gardens, nature trails and Ranger service. Open daily Easter to mid Oct, 10–5.30. Adm £1.20, groups, Chld and OAPs 80p. Entire facility designed with our disabled visitors in mind. Free parking. **Runner-up in Scotland's Museum of the Year Awards 1986.**

CROMARTY

HUGH MILLER'S COTTAGE
Telephone: Cromarty (038 17) 245
(The National Trust for Scotland)

Birthplace (10 Oct 1802) of Hugh Miller, stonemason, eminent geologist, editor and writer. Furnished thatched cottage built c 1711 for his grandfather contains an interesting exhibition on his life and work. Captioned video programme.
Location: In Cromarty 22m from Inverness A832.
Opening Times: Mar 24 to Mar 27 and Apr 28 to Oct 1—Mons to Sats 10–12, 1–5; Suns 2–5. Adm 90p, Chd 45p (under 5 free). OAPs & Students (on production of their cards) adm at half the standard adult rate.

DORNIE

EILEAN DONAN CASTLE
Telephone: Dornie (059 985) 202
(J D H MacRae, Esq)

13th century Castle. Jacobite relics—mostly with Clan connections.
Location: In Dornie, Kyle of Lochalsh; 8 m E of Kyle on A87.
Opening Times: Apr to Sept 30—Daily (inc Suns) 10–12.30, 2–6. Adm £1.

DRUMNADROCHIT

URQUHART CASTLE
(Secretary of State of Scotland)

Remains of one of the largest Castles in Scotland
Location: On W shore of Loch Ness 1½ m SE of Drumnadrochit.
Opening Times: Apr 1 to Sept 30—Weekdays 9.30–7, Suns 2–7; Oct 1 to Mar 31—Weekdays 9.30–4, Suns 2–4. *Closed Dec 25, 26; Jan 1, 2.* Adm £1, Chd & OAPs 50p.

DUNVEGAN

BORRERAIG PIPING CENTRE *(Ian Stirling)*
Borreraig, Dunvegan. Tel: (047 081) 213.
The Centre is located on ancestral holdings of the MacCrimmons, hereditary pipers to MacLeod chiefs (1500-1800), and the first composers, players and teachers of Pibroch. Exhibits depict various aspects of the remarkable story of the Highland bagpipe and its music.

DUNVEGAN CASTLE
(John MacLeod of MacLeod)

Dating from the 13th century and continuously inhabited by the Chiefs of MacLeod. Fairy flag.
Location: Dunvegan village (1 m); 23 m W of Portree on the Isle of Skye.
Opening Times: Mar 24 to Sept 30: 10–5; Oct 2 to Oct 28: 11–4.30; Nov to Mar: by appointment; Suns: garden, grounds, craft shop and restaurant open, castle closed. Adm £2.80, Chd £1.50. Parties – special rates on application.

FORT WILLIAM

THE WEST HIGHLAND MUSEUM
Cameron Square. Tel: (0397) 2169.

Historical, natural history and folk exhibits. Prince Charles Edward Stuart and the '45 Rising. Items of local interest from pre-history to modern industry. Tartans. Mon to Sat: June and Sept 9.30–5.30; July and Aug 9.30–9; remainder of year 10–1, 2–5. *Closed* Sun. Small adm charge.

GAIRLOCH

GAIRLOCH HERITAGE MUSEUM
Tel: (044 583) 243.

Local history museum illustrating all aspects of past life in a West Highland Parish.

GLENCOE

GLENCOE AND NORTH LORN FOLK MUSEUM
Thatched restored 'Cruck' cottage in Glencoe village. Exhibits include domestic bygones, costume, weapons, Jacobite relics, agricultural implements and natural history. Late May to end of Sept: Mon to Sat 10–5.30.

GOLSPIE

DUNROBIN CASTLE
(The Countess of Sutherland)

One of Scotland's oldest inhabited houses. Historic home of the Sutherland family. Furniture, paintings and plate. Exhibits of local and general interest. Victorian Museum in grounds.

Location: ½ m NE of Golspie on A9.
Station: Golspie (2 m).
Opening Times: June 1 to Sept 15—Mons to Sats 10.30–5.30; Suns 1–5.30. Last adm half hour before closing. Coaches welcome all year by appointment. Adm £2.20, Chd £1.10. Parties (12 or more) £2, Chd £1. OAPs £1.40. Family ticket £5.50 (incl Guide Book).
Refreshments: Tearoom.

INVERNESS

CAWDOR CASTLE
Telephone: Cawdor (066 77)615   Telex 75225
(The Earl of Cawdor, FRICS)

The 14th century Keep, fortified in the 15th century and impressive additions, mainly 17th century, form a massive fortress. Gardens, nature trails and splendid grounds. Shakespearian memories of Macbeth. The most romantic castle in the Highlands.

Location: S of Nairn on B9090 between Inverness and Nairn.
Opening Times: May 1 to Oct 1—Daily 10–5.30 (last adm 5). Adm £2.60, Chd (aged 5–15) £1.40, OAPs and disabled £2.10. Parties of 20 or more adults £2.40; 20 or more children £1.15. Family ticket (2 adults and up to 5 children) £7.50. Gardens & grounds only £1.30. Free coach & car park. Gift shop. Picnic area. Pitch & Putt course. Putting Green, Nature Trails. No dogs allowed in Castle or Grounds.
Refreshments: Licensed restaurant (self-service); Snack bar.

INVERNESS MUSEUM AND ART GALLERY
(Inverness District Council)
Castle Wynd. Tel: (0463) 237114.

The social and natural history, archaeology and culture of the Highlands. Important collection of Highland silver; displays on 'The Life of the Clans' and Highland wildlife including a reconstruction of the last taxidermist's workshop in the Highlands. Active programme of temporary exhibitions and events. Books, crafts, replicas on sale. New exhibition galleries, coffee shop and other facilities. Mon to Sat 9–5. *Closed* Sun. Adm free.

KINGUSSIE

THE HIGHLAND FOLK MUSEUM
Tel: (054 02) 307.

A comprehensive collection of old Highland artefacts including examples of craft-work and tools, household plenishings, tartans etc. In the grounds there is a furnished cottage with a mill and an extensive farming museum. Apr to Oct: Weekdays 10–6; Sun 2–6. Nov to Mar: Weekdays 10–3.

LOCHALINE

ARDTORNISH
(Mrs John Raven)

Garden of interesting mature conifers, rhododendrons and deciduous trees and shrubs set amidst magnificent scenery. ½ m from Kinlochaline Castle (open by donation) 14th century tower house on the river Aline.

Location: Off A82; 41 m SW of Fort William via A82, Corran Ferry & A884.
Opening Times: Apr 1 to Oct 31—Daily 10–6. Adm (by collecting box for garden upkeep) £1, Chd (under 16) free. Also Sun May 28 *in aid of the Scottish Gardens Scheme & Morvern Parish Church* when teas are provided.
Refreshments: Sun May 28—teas in main house, otherwise self catering accommodation available by the week.

POOLEWE

INVEREWE
Telephone: Poolewe 229 (Information Centre)   &
(The National Trust for Scotland)

Remarkable garden created by the late Osgood Mackenzie. Rare and sub-tropical plants.

Location: 7 m from Gairloch; 85 m W of Inverness, A832.
Opening Times: Garden open all the year—Daily 9.30–sunset. Visitor Centre: Mar 24 to May 4 & Sept 4 to Oct 22—Mons to Sats 10–5; Suns 12–5. May 5 to Sept 3—Mons to Sats 9.30–6.30; Suns 12–6. Adm £2, Chd £1. Cruise and adult parties £1.60, Chd 80p. Chd under 5 years free. OAPs & Students (on production of their cards) adm at half the standard adult rate. Ranger Naturalist Service.
Refreshments: (Licensed) restaurant in garden (Apr 1 to May 4 and Sept 5 to Oct 15—Mons to Sats 10.30–4.30, Suns 12–4.30. May 5 to Sept 4—Mons to Sats 10–5, Suns 12–5). Poolewe (044 586) 200.

STORNOWAY

MUSEUM NAN EILEAN
Town Hall.

STRATHPEFFER

THE DOLL MUSEUM
Spa Cottage, The Square. Tel: (0997) 21549.

Dolls, toys, Victoriana, lace, cradles etc. Easter to Oct: Mon to Fri 10–12, 1–3, and in June, July and Aug: Mon, Tues, Thurs 8–9.30. Other days, times, all year, those interested admitted if owner is in. Adm charge.

THURSO

THURSO MUSEUM
The Library. Tel: (0847) 3237.

Zoological, geological and botanical collections. The Dick collection of plants and mosses. Weekdays 10–1, 2–5.

WICK

CARNEGIE LIBRARY
Tel: (0955) 2864.

Wick Society Museum, mainly concerned with the fishing industry.

Lothian Region

ABERLADY

GOSFORD HOUSE
Telephone: Aberlady (08757) 201
(Lord Wemyss Trust)

Robert Adam Mansion, central block surviving; striking maritime situation. Original wings replaced 1890; South wing contains celebrated Marble Hall, fine collection of paintings etc. Part of Adam block burnt 1940, re-roofed 1987. Policies laid out with ornamental water. Grey Lag Geese and other wildfowl breeding.

Location: On A198 between Aberlady & Longniddry; NW of Haddington.
Station: Longniddry (2 m).
Opening Times: June and July— Weds, Sats & Suns 2–5. Adm £1, Chd 50p, OAPs 75p. Wemyss & March Estates, Longniddry, East Lothian EH32 0PY.
Refreshments: Hotels in Aberlady.

HARELAW FARMHOUSE
Telephone: Aberlady (08757) 201
(Lord Wemyss' Trust)

Harelaw Farmhouse. An early 19th Century 2-storey farmhouse built in the old fashioned way, as an integral part of the steading, which is also distinguished by a dovecote over the entrance arch surmounted by a windvane.
Location: Between Longniddry and Drem on the B1377.
Opening Times: Exteriors only. By appointment, Wemyss and March Estates, Estate Office, Longniddry, East Lothian EH32 0PY.

MYRETON MOTOR MUSEUM
East Lothian. Tel: 087-57 288.

BALERNO

MALLENY GARDEN   ♿
(The National Trust for Scotland)

A delightfully personal garden with a particularly good collection of shrub roses. National Bonsai Collection for Scotland.
Location: In Balerno, off A70.
Opening Times: GARDEN ONLY. All the year—Daily 10—sunset. Adm £1, Chd 50p (under 5 free). OAPs/Students (on production of their cards) adm at half the standard adult rate. No dogs in garden please.

DIRLETON

DIRLETON CASTLE & GARDEN
(Secretary of State for Scotland)

Well preserved 13th century castle, attractive gardens.
Location: In the village of Dirleton on Edinburgh/North Berwick Road (A198). *Station: North Berwick (2 m).*
Opening Times: Apr 1 to Sept 30—Weekdays 9.30–7, Suns 2–7; Oct 1 to Mar 31—Weekdays 9.30–4, Suns 2–4. *Closed Dec 25 & 26; Jan 1 & 2.* Adm £1, Chd & OAPs 50p.

EAST LINTON

PRESTON MILL
Telephone: East Linton (0620) 860426
(The National Trust for Scotland)

The oldest (16th century) of its kind still working and only survivor of many on the banks of the Tyne. Popular with artists. Renovated machinery.
Location: 5½ m W of Dunbar, off A1.
Opening Times: Preston Mill and Phantassie Doo'cot: Mar 24 to Sept 30—Mons to Sats 10–1, 2–5; Oct 1–31—Mons to Sats 10–1, 2–4.30, Suns 2–4.30; Nov 1 to Nov 30—Sats 10–12.30 and 2–4.30, Sun 2–4.30. Adm £1.10, Chd 55p (under 5 free). OAPs/Students (on production of their cards) adm at half the standard adult rate. Adult parties 90p, school parties 45p.

EDINBURGH

BRAIDWOOD AND RUSHBROOK MUSEUM
Lauriston Place.

BRASS RUBBING CENTRE *(City of Edinburgh)*
Trinity Apse, Chalmers Close, High Street *(opposite Museum of Childhood)*. Tel: 031-556 4634.
Display of replica brasses and Scottish carved stones. Facilities for making rubbings. Opening arrangements under review.

CANONGATE TOLBOOTH *(City of Edinburgh)*
163 Canongate. Tel: 031-225 2424, Ext 6638.
Was burgh courthouse and prison for more than 300 years. Due to reopen in early 1989 as 'The People's Story', dealing with the life and work of Edinburgh's people.

NO. 7 CHARLOTTE SQUARE *(National Trust for Scotland)*
Tel: 031-225 2160.
The lower floors of this Georgian House are furnished as it might have been by its first owners, showing the domestic surroundings and reflecting the social conditions of that age. Easter to Oct 31: Daily 10–5; Sun 2–5. Last adm ½hr before closing times. Adm (including audio-visual presentation) £1.80, Chld 90p. Adult parties £1.40, schools 70p.

CITY ART CENTRE *(City of Edinburgh)*
2 Market Street. Tel: 031-225 2424, Ext 6650.
Art collections of works by late 19th and 20th century artists, mostly Scottish. Frequent temporary exhibitions. Mon to Sat 10–5 (June to Sept 10–6). During Festival period open Sun 2–5. Adm free.

DALKEITH PARK
Telephone: Edinburgh (031-663) 5684
(The Buccleuch Estates)

Woodland and riverside walks in extensive grounds of Dalkeith Palace. Tunnel walk, and beautiful Adam Bridge, Nature trails and Exciting Adventure Woodland Play Area. Attractive Barbeque Area.
Location: 7 m S of Edinburgh City Centre from E end of Dalkeith High Street, off A68.
Opening Times: Mar 25 to Oct 30—Daily 11–6; Nov—Sats & Suns only. Adm £1 (Chd in parties of over 20, 70p). Educational facilities. Free car park & coach parking.

EDINBURGH CASTLE
(Historic Buildings and Monuments)

Ancient fortress of great importance. St Margaret's Chapel has Norman features.
Location: Castlehill, Edinburgh.
Opening Times: Apr 1 to Sept 30—Weekdays 9.30–5.50, Suns 11–5.50; Oct 1 to Mar 31—Weekdays 9.30–5.05, Suns 12.30–4.20. Last tickets sold 45 mins before closing. *Castle closed Dec 25, 26; Jan 1, 2 & 3.* Adm £2.20, Chd & OAPs £1.10, Family £5.

EDINBURGH WAX MUSEUM
142 High Street. Tel: 031-226 4445.
Scottish history throughout the ages depicted in wax. Fantasy land for children.

THE FRUITMARKET GALLERY
29 Market Street, EH1 1DF. Tel: 031-225 2383.
Changing programme of exhibitions of contemporary artists. Tues to Sat 10–5.30; Sun 1.30–5.30. *Closed Mon.*

THE GEORGIAN HOUSE
Telephone: 031-225 2160
(The National Trust for Scotland)

The north side of Charlotte Square is classed as Robert Adam's masterpiece of urban architecture. The main floors of No. 7 are open as a typical Georgian House. Audio-visual shows.
Location: In Edinburgh city centre.
Opening Times: Mar 24 to Oct 31—Mons to Sats 10 5, Suns 2–5. *Last admission ½ hour before closing time.* Adm incl Audio-Visual, £1.70, Chd 85p (under 5 free). Adult parties £1.40, schools 70p. OAPs/Students (on production of their cards) adm at half the standard adult rate.

GLADSTONE'S LAND
Telephone: 031-226 5856
(The National Trust for Scotland)

Built 1620 and shortly afterwards occupied by Thomas Gledstanes. Remarkable painted wooden ceilings; furnished as typical 'Old Town' house of the period.
Location: 483 Lawnmarket, Edinburgh.
Opening Times: Mar 24 to Oct 31—Mons to Sats 10–5, Suns 2–5. *Last admission ½ hour before closing time.* Adm £1.60, Chd 80p (under 5 free). Adult parties £1.30, schools 65p. OAPs/Students (on production of their cards) adm at half the standard adult rate.

HUNTLY HOUSE *(City of Edinburgh)*
142 Canongate. Tel: 031-225 2424, Ext 6689.
Local history and topography; important collections of Edinburgh silver, glass and Scottish pottery. Reconstruction of an old Scots kitchen. Original copy of the 'National Covenant' of 1638. Also personal collection of Field Marshal Earl Haig. Mon to Sat 10–5 (June to Sept 10–6). During Festival period open Sun 2–5. Adm free.

JOHN KNOX HOUSE MUSEUM
Royal Mile. Tel: 031-556 6961.
A picturesque house said to be the only 15th century house now in Scotland. By tradition it has connections with John Knox, the famous Scottish Reformer. Adm £1, Chld and OAPs 70p. Special rates for parties.

LADY STAIR'S HOUSE *(City of Edinburgh)*
Lady Stair's Close, Lawnmarket. Tel: 031-225 2424, Ext 6593.
A reconstructed town house dating from 1622. Relics connected with Robert Burns, Sir Walter Scott and R.L. Stevenson. Mon to Sat 10–5 (June to Sept 10–6). During Festival period open Sun 2–5. Adm free.

LAURISTON CASTLE
(City of Edinburgh District Council)

A beautifully furnished Edwardian home, associated with John Law (1671–1729) founder of first bank in France.
Location: Cramond Road South, Davidsons Mains, 4½ m from GPO, Edinburgh.
Opening Times: Castle. All the year. Apr to Oct—Daily (except Fris) 11–1, 2–5; Nov to Mar—Sats & Suns only 2–4. Adm £1, Chd 50p. Guided tours only (last tour 40 mins before closing time). Grounds—Daily 9–dusk.

MUSEUM OF CHILDHOOD *(City of Edinburgh)*
42 High Street (opposite John Knox's house). Tel: 031-225 2424 Ext. 6645.
Re-opened 1986 following complete re-display and extension. Still the noisiest museum in the world! Mon to Sat 10–5; Jun to Sept 10–6; during festival period open Sun 2–5. Adm free.

MUSEUM OF COMMUNICATION *(C.H.C. Matthews)*
University of Edinburgh, Mayfield Road. Tel: (0506) 824507.
A collection of telephones, spark transmitters, crystal sets, early valve sets, communication receivers, transmitters, Fultophone, teleprinters, hearing aids, wire and tape recorders, television, radar, valves from midgets to giants.

MUSEUM OF THE ROYAL COLLEGE OF SURGEONS OF EDINBURGH
Nicolson Street. Tel: 031-556 6206.
Exhibits of surgical, dental, pathological and historical interest. By appointment.

NATIONAL GALLERY OF SCOTLAND
The Mound, EH2 2EL.
An outstanding collection of paintings, drawings and prints by the greatest artists from the Renaissance to Post Impressionism, including Velasquez, El Greco, Rembrandt, Vermeer, Gainsborough, Turner, Constable, Degas, Monet and Van Gogh; shown alongside the national collection of Scottish art – Ramsay, Raeburn, Wilkie and McTaggart.

NATIONAL MONUMENTS RECORD OF SCOTLAND
(Royal Commission on the Ancient and Historical Monuments of Scotland)
6–7 Coates Place, EH3 7AA. Tel: (031 225) 5994.
Collection of about 450,000 drawings, 600,000 photographs, 12,000 maps and 12,000 printed books relating to Scottish archaeology and historic architecture. Mon to Thur 10.30–4.30, Fri 10.30–4 or by appointment.

PALACE OF HOLYROODHOUSE
Telephone: 031-556 7371
(Royal Palace)

The Official Residence of H.M. The Queen in Scotland. The ridge, known as the Royal Mile, that slopes downwards from Edinburgh Castle, comes to a majestic conclusion at Holyroodhouse, where Palace and Abbey stand against the spectacular backdrop of Salisbury Crag. Throughout history, Holyrood has been the scene of turbulent and extraordinary events, yet the Palace retains a modern appeal to a Royal residence still in regular use.
Location: Central Edinburgh.
Opening Times: Summer season: Mar 27 to May 9, June 1 to June 12, July 7 to Oct 23: fully open – adm £1.60, Chd/Students/OAPs 80p. May 10 to July 5, 6: partly open – adm £1, Chd/Students/OAPs 50p. *Closed May 16 to May 31, and June 13 to July 4.* Winter season: Jan 5 to Mar 26, and Oct 23 to Dec 31: fully open – adm £1.60, Chd/Students/OAPs 80p. *Closed Dec 26 and 27.* All visitors are conducted by Palace Wardens in groups leaving at about 10 minute intervals. From Nov to Mar pre-paid groups of 15 or more receive a 20% discount, and accompanied school parties are admitted free Mon to Fri; in both cases, prior application must be made. Special interest tours can sometimes be arranged, particularly during off-season. *The Palace and Abbey may sometimes be closed at short notice.*
Refreshments: Tea room outside Main Gate.

QUEENSFERRY MUSEUM *(City of Edinburgh)*
Tel: 031-331 1590.
Situated between the two Forth bridges in the Council Chambers of the former Royal Burgh of Queensferry. Local history collection. May to Aug: opening arrangements under review. Adm free.

ROYAL BOTANIC GARDEN
Edinburgh   *map F14*
(Royal Botanic Garden, Edinburgh)

Founded 17th century. Beautiful rock garden. Exhibition Plant Houses.
Location: Inverleith Row, Edinburgh.
Opening Times: All the year. Mar to Oct (during BST)—Weekdays 9–one hour before sunset, Suns 1–one hour before sunset. Remainder of year—Weekdays 9–sunset, Suns 11–sunset. *Closed Christmas Day & New Year's Day.* Plant-houses and Exhibition Hall—Weekdays 10–5, Suns 11–5. Adm free.
Refreshments: Tea in the garden *(Apr to Sept).*

ROYAL MUSEUM OF SCOTLAND
(National Museums of Scotland)
Chambers Street, EH1 1JF. Tel: 031-225 7534.
Houses the national collections of decorative arts of the world, ethnography, natural history, geology, technology and science. Displays range from primitive art to space material, from ceramics to fossils, from birds to working models in the hall of power. Items of importance in all fields. Additional major displays in course of preparation. Main Hall of architectural interest. Temporary exhibitions. Lectures, gallery talks, films at advertised times: Mon to Sat 10–5; Sun 2–5. Adm free. Tea room 10–4 (except Sun). Shop.

ROYAL MUSEUM OF SCOTLAND
(National Museums of Scotland)
Queen Street, EH2 1JD. Tel: 031-255 7534.
Collections cover the whole of Scotland from the Stone Age to recent times; prehistoric and Roman objects, sculptured stones, relics of the Celtic church, Scottish coins and medals, Stuart relics, Highland weapons, domestic life, costumes and textiles; also reference library. Mon to Sat 10–5; Sun 2–5. Adm free.

RUSSELL COLLECTION OF HARPSICHORDS AND CLAVICHORDS
(University of Edinburgh)
St. Cecilia's Hall, Niddry Street, Cowgate. Tel: 031-667 1011, Ext. 4415.
Forty-seven keyboard instruments, including harpsichords, clavichords, forte-pianos, regals, spinets, virginals and chamber organs. Pictures (Pannini etc.). Tapestries and textiles. Sat and Wed 2–5 throughout year. Daily during Edinburgh Festival (mornings). Adm 25p.

SCOTCH WHISKY HERITAGE CENTRE
358 Castlehill, Royal Mile EH1 2NE. Tel: 031-220 0441.
The Scotch Whisky Heritage Centre provides an entertaining explanation of the making of Scotch Whisky from the barley to the bottle. Travel through 300 years of Scotch Whisky history in a Barrel Car, with commentary in English or six other languages. Open daily from 9–7 (summer), 9–5 (winter). Adm fee.

SCOTTISH NATIONAL GALLERY OF MODERN ART
Belford Road, EH4 3DR.
Scotland's choice collection of the painting, sculpture and graphic art of this century. The work of the established masters – Picasso, Matisse, Ernst, Kirchner, Dix, Moore; major Scottish artists; and the leading figures of the contemporary international scene.

SCOTTISH NATIONAL PORTRAIT GALLERY
Queen Street, EH2 1JD.
Portraits in all media of people who have played a significant role in Scottish history from the 16th century to the present, recorded by the most famous artists of the day; also the national collection of photography.

Study Rooms
The **Department of Prints and Drawings** at the National Gallery, and the **Print Room and Reference Section** at the Portrait Gallery are open to visitors by arrangement at the front desk of the Galleries: Mon to Fri 10–12.30, 2–4.30. The **Prints and Drawings Study Room** at the Gallery of Modern Art is open by prior appointment only: Mon to Fri 10–1.
Further information about the Galleries, the collections and activities is available from the Information Department. Tel: 031-556 8921.

SCOTTISH UNITED SERVICES MUSEUM
(National Museums of Scotland)
Edinburgh Castle. Tel: 031-225 7534.
Illustrates by its display of uniforms, head-dress, arms and equipment, medals, portraits and models, the history of the armed forces of Scotland. Extensive library and comprehensive collection of prints of uniforms. New gallery – Musket, Fife and Drum: 300 years of British Military Music. Opening times as for Edinburgh Castle.

HADDINGTON

AMISFIELD MAINS
Telephone: Aberlady (08757) 201
(Lord Wemyss Trust)

Georgian farmhouse with "Gothick" Barn and Cottage.
Location: Between Haddington & East Linton on A1 Edinburgh/Dunbar Road.
Opening Times: Exteriors only. By appointment, Wemyss & March Estates, Estate Office, Longniddry, East Lothian EH32 0PY.

BEANSTON

Telephone: Aberlady (08757) 201
(Lord Wemyss Trust)

Georgian farmhouse with Georgian Orangery.

Location: Between Haddington & East Linton on A1 Edinburgh/Dunbar Road.
Opening Times: Exteriors only. By appointment, Wemyss & March Estates, Estate Office, Longniddry, East Lothian EH32 0PY.

LENNOXLOVE

Telephone: Haddington (062 082) 3720
(His Grace the Duke of Hamilton)

Formerly Lethington Tower, ancient home of the Maitlands. The Lime Avenue, known as Politician's Walk, was laid out by William Maitland, Secretary to Mary Queen of Scots.

Location: 1½ m S of Haddington on B6369; 18 m E of Edinburgh off A1.
Opening Times: Easter weekend, then May to Sept—Weds, Sats & Suns 2–5. At other times by appointment (minimum of 10 people); apply to Estate Office, Lennoxlove, Haddington. Adm £2, Chd £1. Pre-booked parties of 10 or more £1.50, Chd 50p. Price includes guided tour of House, entry to gardens and parking.

STEVENSON HOUSE

Telephone: Haddington (062 082) 3376 Mrs. J. C. H. Dunlop
(Trustees of the Brown Dunlop Country Houses Trust)

A family home for four centuries, of charm and interest and dating from the 13th century when it belonged to the Cistercian Nunnery at Haddington, but partially destroyed on several occasions, and finally made uninhabitable in 1544. Restored about 1560 and the present house dates mainly from this period, with later additions in the 18th century.

Location: 20 m approx from Edinburgh; 1½ m approx from A1; 2 m approx from Haddington. (See Historic House direction signs on A1 in Haddington.)
Opening Times: July to mid-Aug—Thurs, Sats & Suns 2–5. Guided tours 2.30–4. Other times by arrangement. Adm £1.50, OAP 75p, Chd (under 14) 75p. Special arrangement parties welcome. Car parking. Suitable for wheelchairs in garden only.
Refreshments: Appointment parties morning coffee etc at Stevenson. Nearest hotels and restaurants are in Haddington, i.e. 2 m from Stevenson.

INVERESK

INVERESK LODGE AND GARDEN
(The National Trust for Scotland)

New garden, with large selection of plants.

Location: In Inveresk village; 6 m E of Edinburgh off A1.
Opening Times: GARDEN ONLY. All year—Mons to Fris 10–4.30; Suns 2–5. Adm 50p, Chd (with adult) 25p, under 5 free, OAPs/Students (on production of their cards) adm at half the standard adult rate. Honesty Box.

LEITH

LAMB'S HOUSE

Telephone: 031-554 3131
(The National Trust for Scotland)

Residence and warehouse of prosperous merchant of late 16th or early 17th century. Renovated 18th century. Now old people's day centre.

Location: In Leith.
Opening Times: Mons to Fris—Daily 9–5. *(Except Christmas/New Year.)*

LINLITHGOW

THE HOUSE OF THE BINNS

Telephone: Philipstoun (050 683) 4255
(The National Trust for Scotland)

Historic home of the Dalyells. Fine plaster ceilings. Interesting pictures. Panoramic viewpoint.

Location: 3½ m E of Linlithgow on Queensferry Road (A904).
Opening Times: Mar 25 to Mar 27 daily 2–5; Apr 29 to Oct 1—Daily (except Fris) 2–5 (last adm 4.30). Parkland open 10–7. Adm £2, Chd £1 (under 5 free). Adult parties £1.60, Schools 80p, OAPS/Students (on production of their cards) adm at half the standard adult rate. *Members of the Royal Scots Dragoon Guards (in uniform) admitted free.*

LINLITHGOW PALACE
(Secretary of State for Scotland)

Birthplace of Mary Queen of Scots.

Location: In Linlithgow.
Station: Linlithgow (½ m).
Opening Times: Apr 1 to Sept 30—Daily 9.30–7 (Suns 2–7). Oct 1 to Mar 31—Daily 9.30–4 (Suns 2–4). *Closed Dec 25, 26, Jan 1 & 2.* Adm £1, Chd & OAPs 50p.

LIVINGSTON

LIVINGSTON MILL FARM
(Livingston Mill Farm Community Project)
Millfield Livingston Village. Tel: (0506) 414957.
Restored 18th century farm steading and watermill. Milling and threshing machinery. Farm implements and tools. Farm carts. Apr to Oct: daily 10–5. Nov, Feb, Mar weekends only 1–4; *closed* Dec and Jan. Adm charges. Special reductions by arrangement. Parties by arrangement. Parking for 40 cars. Suitable for disabled persons. Refreshments.

NEWBRIDGE

SCOTTISH AGRICULTURAL MUSEUM
(National Museums of Scotland) (Outstation)
Ingliston, Newbridge (in Royal Highland Showground). Tel: 031-225 7534. Ploughing and harvesting farm life, room settings, crafts, animal husbandry etc May to Sept: Mon to Fri 10–5. *Closed* Sat and Sun.

NEWTON GRANGE

SCOTTISH MINING MUSEUM
Lady Victoria Colliery EH22 4QN. Tel: (031) 663-7519.
A recently renovated Victorian colliery. The Grant Ritchie steam winding engine is just one of the attractions. The visitor centre displays a tableaux, employing the latest technology to recreate a day in the life of a Victorian pit village. The museum has a period licensed tearoom and shop. Open all year *(closed* Mon) Tues–Fri 10–4.30, Sat and Sun 12–5. Adm £1, Chld 60p. Ample parking. Part access for the disabled.

NORTH BERWICK

MUSEUM OF FLIGHT
(National Museums of Scotland) (Outstation)
East Fortune Airfield, nr. North Berwick. Tel: 062-088 308 or 031-225 7534. Over 30 aircraft and aero engines including a Comet 4C and Vulcan. Open daily in July and Aug and at other advertised times. Mon to Sun 10–5.

TANTALLON CASTLE
(Secretary of State for Scotland)

Famous 14th century stronghold of the Douglases occupies a magnificent situation on the rocky coast of the Firth of Forth.

Location: On the coast approx 3 m E of North Berwick.
Opening Times: Apr 1 to Sept 30—Weekdays 9.30–7, Suns 2–7; Oct 1 to Mar 31—Weekdays 9.30–4, Suns 2–4. *Closed Weds & Thurs am in winter, and Dec 25, 26; Jan 1, 2.* Adm £1, Chd & OAPs 50p.

PENCAITLAND

WINTON HOUSE

Telephone: Pencaitland (0875) 340 222
(Sir David & Lady Ogilvy)

Built 1620. Famous twisted stone chimneys and beautiful plaster ceilings in honour of Charles I's visit. Enlarged 1800. Fine pictures and furniture. Terraced gardens.

Location: Drive entrances with wrought-iron gates and lodges in Pencaitland (A6093) and towards New Winton village on B6355. Tranent (A1) 3 m, by B6355; Haddington (A1) by A6093 6 m; Pathhead (A68) 6 m by A6093.
Opening Times: Restricted to groups of ten or more (and others very specially interested) at any time by prior arrangement with the owner. Adm (Party rate) House *(personally conducted tour)* grounds and car park £1.50.
Refreshments: Tea and biscuits can be arranged in the house, or Old Smiddy Inn, Pencaitland (1 m).

PRESTONPANS

HAMILTON HOUSE

Telephone: 031-336 2157
(The National Trust for Scotland)

Built in 1628 by John Hamilton, a prosperous Edinburgh burgess.
Location: 8½ m E of Edinburgh on A198.
Station: Prestonpans.
Opening Times: By prior arrangement.

SCOTTISH MINING MUSEUM
Nr. Prestonpans.
The site has a history of over 800 years of coal mining, the museum contains a Cornish Beam Pumping engine, an exhibition hall and visitor centre. Colliery engines are steamed every first Sun of the month from Apr to Sept. Open all year *(closed* Mon) Tues to Fri 10–4, Sat and Sun 12–5. Adm free. Ample parking. Part access for the disabled. (See Lady Victoria Colliery.)

SOUTH QUEENSFERRY

DALMENY HOUSE
Telephone: (031 331) 1888   &
(The Earl of Rosebery)

Rosebery Collection of paintings; Napoleonic and other historical items. Mentmore collection of superb French furniture, Goya tapestries and porcelain.
Location: 3 m E of South Queensferry; 7 m W of Edinburgh; on B924 (off A90).
Station: Dalmeny (2 m).
Public Transport: From St. Andrew Sq. Bus Station to Chapel Gate (1 m from house).
Opening Times: May 1 to Sept 28 — Suns to Thurs 2–5.30. Conducted tours. Adm £1.90, Chd & Students £1.30, OAPs £1.50. Special party rate £1.60 (minimum 20). Special parties at other times throughout the year by arrangement with the Administrator.
Refreshments: Tea.

HOPETOUN HOUSE
Telephone: 031 331 2451
(Hopetoun House Preservation Trust)

Home of the Marquess of Linlithgow. Fine example of 18th century Adam architecture. Magnificent reception rooms, pictures, antiques.
Location: 2 m from Forth Road Bridge nr South Queensferry off A904.
Opening Times: Easter, then Sat Apr 29 to Sun Oct 1. Daily 11–5.30. Adm House and Grounds: £2.50. Special concessions for students, children and OAPs, also for groups of 20 or more, and family group. Free parking. Gift shop. Deerpark. Picnic areas. Free Ranger service. Magnificent views of the Forth and the Bridges. The house is also available for special private evening functions. Enquiries to Administrator's Office 031-331 2451.
Refreshments: Licensed restaurant and snack bar.

WINCHBURGH

NIDDRY CASTLE
Telephone: Winchburgh 890 753
(Peter and Janet Wright)

Late 15th century Scottish Castle, built by the Seton family. Following her escape from Loch Leven, Mary Queen of Scots was given brief shelter at Niddry by the 5th Lord Seton in 1568. Early in the 18th century Niddry Castle was abandoned and lay in ruins for over 250 years. It is now being restored over a seven year period (1984–91) by Peter and Janet Wright. Niddry is a scheduled ancient monument and the subject of a conservation agreement with the National Trust for Scotland.
Location: By Winchburgh. Turn off A89 1 m West Newbridge – 1 m, or turn off B9080 in Winchburgh – 1 m.
Opening Times: Open Wed and Sun only, May to Sept incl 10–4.30. Adm by donation. Parties by arrangement. Car parking is available, adjacent to the Castle. Not suitable for disabled. Outdoor footwear and clothing advisable. For safety reasons children must be adequately supervised.

Orkney Isles

HARRAY

THE ORKNEY FARM AND FOLK MUSEUM
(Orkney Islands Council)
Two restored farmsteads illustrating tradition and change in island life, at **Kirbuster** and **Corrigall**. Apr – Sept: Mon to Sat 10.30–1, 2–5; Sun 2–7. Adm charge.

KIRKWALL

TANKERNESS HOUSE MUSEUM *(Orkney Islands Council)*
Orkney archaeology and local history. Special exhibitions. Mon to Sat 10.30–12.30, 1.30–5; Sun (May to Sept) 2–5. Adm charge (Apr to Sept).

ST. MARGARET'S HOPE

ORKNEY WIRELESS MUSEUM
Church Road.
Featuring wartime radio and defences at Scapa Flow.

STROMNESS

THE PIER ARTS CENTRE *(The Pier Arts Centre Trust)*
Permanent collection of 20th century British art; also a programme of changing exhibitions. Adm free.

STROMNESS MUSEUM *(Orkney Natural History Society)*
Orkney Maritime and natural history displays; Scapa Flow and the German Fleet. Mon to Sat 10.30–12.30, 1.30–5. (Thurs 11–1, additionally 3–5 during July and Aug). *Closed* Sun and Public Hols. Adm charge.

Shetland Islands

LERWICK

BÖD OF GREMISTA
Gremista. Tel: (0595) 4386.
Birthplace of Arthur Anderson, co-founder and main developer of P&O Company. Open May to Sept: every afternoon except Thurs 2–5. Tel: (0595) 4386 (when open); other times (0595) 4632.

LOWER HILL HEAD

SHETLAND CROFT HOUSE MUSEUM *(Shetland Islands Council)*
c/o Shetland Museum, Lerwick ZE1 0EL. Tel: (0595) 5057.
A restored (c.1870s) Croft house, Steading and Water mill, at Voe, Dunrossness. May 1 to Sept 30: Daily (except Mons) 10–1, 2–5. Adm 50p, Chld 20p.

SHETLAND MUSEUM *(Shetland Islands Council)*
Lerwick ZE1 0EL. Tel: (0595) 5057.
The theme of the museum is 'Life in Shetland through the Ages'. Our disciplines comprehend local archaeology, folk life, history, a large maritime section with many fine ship and boat models and a growing natural history collection. We also hold an extensive photographic collection, c.30,000 negatives and a growing archive. Open all year: Mon, Wed and Fri 10–7; Tues, Thurs and Sat 10–5. Adm free. Town centre site with adjacent car parking.

Strathclyde Region

ALEXANDRIA

TOBIAS SMOLLETT
Cameron Farm. Tel: Alexandria 56226.
Unique collection of 1st and other editions of the works of Tobias Smollett and items connected with his life.

ALLOWAY

BURNS COTTAGE
(Trustees of Burns Monument)

Thatched cottage in which Robert Burns was born, 1759. Museum with Burns' relics.
Location: 1½ m SW of Ayr.
Station: Ayr (1½ m).
Opening Times: Open all year round — June to Aug 9–7, Suns 10–7; Apr to May, Sept to Oct 10–5, Suns 2–5. During winter 10–4 (*closed Suns*). Adm Cottage & Monument £1.20, Chd & OAPs 60p, includes entry to Burns Monument.
Refreshments: Tea at cottage in Summer.

APPIN

APPIN WILDLIFE MUSEUM
Appin Home Farm.

AYR

AYR CARNEGIE LIRBARY *(Kyle and Carrick District Council)*
12 Main Street. Tel: (0292) 269141, Ext. 5227.
Occasional Exhibitions. Mon to Fri 9–7.

MACLAURIN GALLERY AND ROZELLE HOUSE
(Kyle and Carrick District Council)
Rozelle. Tel: (0292) 45447.
Variety of exhibitions 3 to 5 weeks' duration. Fine art, craft, photography, contemporary art. Local history and military exhibits in house. Mon to Sat 11–5; Sun 2–5 (Apr to Oct only).

TAM O'SHANTER MUSEUM
High Street.

BALLOCH

BALLOCH CASTLE COUNTRY PARK
Telephone: Alexandria (0389) 58216
(Dumbarton District Council)

200 acres. Situated beside Loch Lomond contains many conifers, rhododendrons and other shrubs. Walled garden. Fairy Glen. Castle Visitor Centre, site of old castle and moat. Nature trail and countryside ranger service. Guided walks in summer.
Location: Balloch, Dumbartonshire.
Station: Balloch (¾ m).
Opening Times: All the year—Daily 10 to dusk. Adm free. Car parks.

BIGGAR

ALBION ARCHIVE
17 North Back Road.
Records of Scotland's most successful commercial motor. Details of over 165,000 vehicles. Photographs, memorabilia. H.Q. of Albion Owners Club and Blackwood Murray Vintage Rally (Aug). Open by appointment, details from Moat Park (below).

GLADSTONE COURT
North Back Road. Tel: (0899) 21050.
Small indoor street of shops, workshops, a bank, telephone exchange and village library. Easter to Oct: Mon to Sat 10–12.30, 2–5; Sun 2–5. Adm charge (under 8 free). Reduced charges for joint ticket with Greenhill (below).

GREENHILL COVENANTER'S HOUSE
Burn Braes. Tel: (0899) 21050.
Two-storey farmhouse, rescued in ruinous condition in upper Clyde valley and re-erected at Biggar. Relics of local Covenanters. Donald Cargill's bed (1681), 17th century furnishings, costume figures. Rare breeds of stock and poultry. May to mid-Oct: Daily 2–5. Adm charge (under 8 free).

JOHN BUCHAN CENTRE
Broughton (6 miles).
Life and times of the author of 'The 39 Steps', lawyer, politician, soldier, historian, biographer, poet and Governor General of Canada. Easter to mid-Oct: Daily 2–5. Adm charge. Details from Moat Park below.

MOAT PARK HERITAGE CENTRE
Burn Braes. Tel: (0899) 21050.
Flagship of a growing number of local museums, Moat Park was opened by HRH The Princess Royal in 1988. Geological history of the area from five hundred million years ago. Microsm of life in the Upper Clyde and Tweed valleys from seven thousand years ago to the present day illustrated by models. Fine display of patchwork and samplers, including a unique Tailor's Quilt. Open Mar to Oct: Daily 10–5; Sun 2–5. Other times admission during normal office hours (side entrance). Adm charge. (Reduced charges for joint ticket with other museums.)

BISHOPBRIGGS

THOMAS MUIR MUSEUM *(Strathkelvin District Council)*
Bishopbriggs Library. Tel: (041 775) 1185.
Display illustrating the life of Thomas Muir. Open Mon–Fri 9.45–8. Sat 10–1.

BLANTYRE

THE DAVID LIVINGSTONE CENTRE
Tel: (0698) 823140.
Includes 'THE LIVINGSTONE MEMORIAL'. The birthplace of David Livingstone (1813) containing personal relics, tableaux and working models. The AFRICA PAVILION, with exhibition describing life in modern Africa, and SHUTTLE ROW (Social History) MUSEUM. Cafeteria, picnic area and gardens. Open all year Mon to Sat 10–6; Sun 2–6. Adm £1, Chld 50p, OAPs 70p. Cafeteria open Apr to Sept only. Free parking.

BOTHWELL

BOTHWELL CASTLE
(Secretary of State for Scotland)

The largest and finest 13th century Stone Castle in Scotland.
Location: At Bothwell but approached from Uddingston.
Opening Times: Apr 1 to Sept 30—Weekdays 9.30–7, Suns 2–7; Oct 1 to Mar 31—Weekdays 9.30–4. *(Closed Thurs pm and Fris in winter)*, Suns 2–4. *Closed Dec 25, 26; Jan 1, 2.* Adm 60p, Chd & OAPs 30p.

BRODICK

BRODICK CASTLE, GARDEN AND COUNTRY PARK
Telephone: Brodick (0770) 2202   &
(The National Trust for Scotland)

Historic home of the Dukes of Hamilton. The castle dates in part from the 13th century. Paintings, furniture, objets d'art. Formal and woodland gardens, noted for rhododendrons. Country park.

Location: 1½ m N of Brodick pierhead on the Isle of Arran.
Station: Ardrossan Harbour and Claonaig in Kintyre (& hence by Caledonian MacBrayne ferry).
Ferry enquiries to Caledonian MacBrayne. Tel. Gourock (0475) 33755.
Opening Times: CASTLE. Mar 24–27: 1–5; Mar 28 to Apr 27 Mon, Wed, Sat 1–5; Apr 28 to Oct 1: daily 1–5; Oct 2 to Oct 14: Mon, Wed, Sat 1–5. *(Last tour 4.30).* Tea room.
COUNTRY PARK & GARDEN. All the year—Daily 9.30–sunset. Adm Castle & Gardens £2.10, Chd £1.05; Parties £1.70, Chd 85p. Gardens only £1.30, Chd 65p, Chd under 5 free, OAPs/Students (on production of their cards) adm at half the standard adult rate. Car park free. Shop.
Refreshments: Tea at the Castle.

ISLE OF ARRAN HERITAGE MUSEUM
Rosaburn, Brodick.
A collection of traditional buildings: Smithy, cottage furnished in late 19th and early 20th century styles, stable block with displays of local social history, archaeology and geology. Car park, picnic area. Tearoom. May to end Sept: Mon to Fri. Weekends as advertised. Adm charge.

CAMPBELTOWN

CAMPBELTOWN MUSEUM *(Argyll and Bute District Council)*
Archaeological, geological and natural history of Kintyre. Mon, Tues, Thurs and Fri 10–1, 2–5, 6–8; Wed and Sat 10–1, 2–5.

CLYDEBANK

CLYDEBANK DISTRICT MUSEUM
Old Town Hall, Dumbarton Road. Tel: 041-941 1331 ext. 402.
Find us beside the shipyards where the world-famous "Queens" were built. The Museum tells the story of the shipyards and the "Risingest Burgh" which grew up around them. There are displays on trade unions and on the 1941 Blitz, when the town was destroyed. On show are sewing machines dating from 1851 to 1980. Singer's in Clydebank was the largest sewing machine factory in Europe. Mon and Wed 2–5; Sat 10–5 or at other times by prior arrangement.

COATBRIDGE

SUMMERLEE HERITAGE TRUST
West Canal Street, Coatbridge, ML5 1QD. Tel: (0236) 31261.
Open air museum of social and industrial history, with working electric tramway, extensive operating belt driven machinery, coal mine. Social history exhibitions, Tea Room. Adm charge. Open end Feb to Dec 22. Accessible to wheelchairs, parties by appointment, guided tours available. Free car parking, convenient access from BR Sunnyside and Coatbridge Central Stations.

CRAIGNURE

TOROSAY CASTLE AND GARDENS
Telephone: Craignure (068 02) 421
(Mr Christopher James)

Early Victorian house by David Bryce with 11 acres of unexpected terraced gardens laid out by Sir Robert Lorimer with 18th century Italian statues by Antonio Bonazza.
Location: 1½ m SE of Craignure by A849, by Forest Walk or by Steam Railway.
Opening Times: Castle. May 1 to Sept 30—Daily 10.30–5.30 (last adm 5). Late Apr and early Oct according to Easter and weather. Gardens. All the year during daylight hours. *Parties to Castle at other times by appointment only.* Adm Castle not available at time of going to press. Gardens only £1.50, Chd (between 5–16), OAPs/Students 75p (by Honesty box when Castle closed). Car park free. Dogs on leads in Garden only. Gardens and tearooms only suitable for wheelchairs. Local craft shop.
Refreshments: Home baked teas in Castle.

CRARAE

CRARAE GLEN GARDEN
Telephone: (0546) 86607/86614
(Crarae Garden Charitable Trust)

50 acres of trees, shrubs and plants in natural surroundings with waterfalls and magnificent panoramic views over Loch Fyne.
Location: 10 m SW of Inverary on A83 to Lochgilphead (14 m).
Opening Times: Daily throughout the year – summer 9–6, winter during daylight hours. Adm fixed charge, Chd up to age 5 free. Car parking free. Visitor centre, crafts, tea/coffee. Plants for sale Apr–Oct 10–4.30.

CUMBERNAULD

CUMBERNAULD & KILSYTH DISTRICT MUSEUM
Ardenlea House, The Wynd.

CUMNOCK

BAIRD INSTITUTE MUSEUM
Lugar Street. Tel: (0290) 22024.
A local history museum featuring local pottery and wooden ware, in conjunction with a programme of temporary exhibitions. Fri 9.30–1, 1.30–4; Sat 11–1. Adm free.

DALMELLINGTON

SCOTTISH INDUSTRIAL RAILWAY CENTRE
(Ayrshire Railway Preservation Group)
Minnivey Colliery, Burnton, Dalmellington, 12 miles South East of Ayr, just off the A713.
Steam and diesel locomotives, rolling stock and cranes.

DUMBARTON

THE DENNY TANK
Castle Street G82 1QS. Tel: (0389) 63444.
The Denny Tank occupies a unique place in maritime history. Established in 1883 by Wm. Denny III, it was the first commercial ship model testing Tank in the world. Through the years, it has been the origin of many outstanding innovations in ship design; eg: the Denny/Brown Ship Stabilizing System, Hydrofoils, and Side-wall Hovercraft. Also in the Tank, ships as diverse as P&O liner 'Canberra', and Sir Thomas Lipton's 'Shamrock III' have been tested. Presently, the Tank is a working artifact, owned by Scottish Maritime Museum, and visitors can see in the Tank, a memorial to the Clyde's originality in shipbuilding science. Open Mon–Fri 10–4. For advanced bookings and further information contact: Education Officer, Denny Ship Model Experiment Tank, Castle Street, Dumbarton G82 1QS or telephone (0389) 63444.

DUMBARTON CASTLE
(Secretary of State for Scotland)
Sited on a volcanic rock overlooking the Firth of Clyde.
Location: At Dumbarton.
Opening Times: Apr 1 to Sept 30—Daily 9.30–7, Suns 2–7; Oct 1 to Mar 31—Daily 9.30–4, Suns 2–4. *Closed Dec 25, 26; Jan 1, 2.* Adm 60p, Chd & OAPs 30p.

DUNOON

BENMORE YOUNGER BOTANIC GARDEN
(Royal Botanic Garden, Edinburgh)
A woodland garden on a grand scale.
Location: 7 m NW of Dunoon (off A815).
Opening Times: Daily—Apr to Oct 10–6. Adm 60p, Chd/OAPs 30p.
Refreshments: Tea at main entrance.

EASDALE ISLAND

EASDALE ISLAND FOLK MUSEUM *(Jean Adams, Curator)*
By Oban, Argyll. Tel: Balvicar (08523) 370 (evenings).
A pictorial history of the Slate Islands in the 1800s, showing the industrial and domestic life of the people. Apr to Oct: weekdays 10.30–5.30; Sun 10.30–4.30. Adm 70p, Chld 20p.

GIRVAN

PENKILL CASTLE
Telephone: Old Dailly (046 587) 261
(Elton A Eckstrand, JD.)

15th century Castle, impressive later additions. Fine furniture, tapestries and paintings. Favourite haunt of the Pre-Raphaelites, an inspiration to Dante Gabriel Rossetti and his sister Christina and other well known visitors.
Location: 2½ m E of Girvan on B734 Barr Road (off A77 Stranraer/Ayr Road).
Station: Girvan (2½ m).
Opening Times: By appointment. Guided tour with coffee and cakes in Banqueting Hall £5.50 incl. For details of other programmes contact Administrator.

GLASGOW

ART GALLERY AND MUSEUM
Kelvingrove G3 8AG. Tel: 041-357 3929.
Fine Art: Collection includes works from all major European schools, notably the Dutch 17th century and French Barbizon, Impressionist and Post-Impressionist periods. Also British painting 17th to 20th centuries with emphasis on Scottish art, especially Glasgow Boys and Scottish Colourists. Decorative Art: Collections include important specimens of Western European ceramics, glass, silver, and furniture. Recently opened gallery displays Glasgow decorative arts 1880–1920. Armour: The Scott Collection of arms and armour including the Milanese Armour c.1450, the Whitelaw Collection of Scottish arms. Archaeology and History: Neolithic, Bronze and Iron Age material; items from the Egyptian, Greek and Cypriot collections. Ethnography: Implements, clothing, weapons, religious and ceremonial objects relating to non-European societies. Natural History: Collection contains important botanical, geological and zoological material, being particularly strong in Scottish fossils, world-wide non-flowering plants (Stirton Collection), birds, fish and molluscs, for example. There are many historically interesting specimens, including type specimens. Weekdays 10–5; Sun 2–5. Self-service restaurant and coffee bar.

BELLAHOUSTON PARK
(City of Glasgow District Council)

171 acres. Sunk, wall and rock gardens. Dry ski-slope. Athletic and indoor sports centre.
Location: Paisley Road West.
Station: Cardonald (1¼ m).
Opening Times: All the year—Daily 8 to dusk. Adm free.

BOTANIC GARDENS
(City of Glasgow District Council)

Covering 40 acres. Extensive botanical collections, tropical plants, herb and systematic gardens.
Location: Great Western Road.
Opening Times: All the year—Daily (incl Suns) 7–dusk. Kibble Palace 10–4.45 (winter 10–4.15). Main range of glasshouses 1–4.45 (winter 1–4.15). Suns all year 12–4.45, (winter 12–4.15). Adm free.

THE BURRELL COLLECTION
Pollok Country Park G43 1AT. Tel: 041-649 7151.
Housed in new building opened in 1983. World famous collection of textiles, furniture, ceramics, stained glass, silver, art objects and pictures (especially 19th century French), gifted to Glasgow in 1944 by Sir William and Lady Burrell. Weekdays 10–5; Sun 2–5. Self-service restaurant.

CHARLES RENNIE MACKINTOSH SOCIETY – QUEEN'S CROSS
Queen's Cross, 870 Garscube Road, G20 7EL. Tel: 041-946 6600.
The CRM Society was formed in 1973 and in 1977 undertook the care of Queen's Cross Church, Maryhill, Glasgow, designed by Mackintosh (1897–99). Now the international headquarters of the Society, an information centre with exhibition area, reference library and shop for the enthusiast. Open: Tues, Thurs, Fri 12–5.30; Sun 2.30–5.

COLLINS GALLERY *(University of Strathclyde)*
University of Strathclyde, Richmond Street.
Tel: 041-552 4400, Extns. 2682/4145.
The Collins Gallery is part of the University of Strathclyde and is situated 5 minutes walk from the city centre. Throughout the year it presents a varied programme of temporary exhibitions and other related events. Subjects include Fine and Applied art, architecture, local history, photography, both historical and contemporary. Collections – fine art, coins, scientific equipment. Special exhibitions 11/12 per annum. Mon to Fri 10–5; Sat 12–4. *Closed* Christmas, New Year's Day and Easter. Adm free. Parties welcome, free. Car parking nearby. Suitable for disabled persons.

GREENBANK GARDEN
Telephone: 041-639 3281
(The National Trust for Scotland)

Walled garden, woodland walk and policies. Wide range of plants, flowers and shrubs. Garden for disabled. Regular garden walks and events. Best seen Apr–Oct. Attractive series of gardens, extending to 2½ acres, surrounding Georgian house (not open to the public).
Location: Flenders Road, near Clarkston Toll.
Station: Clarkston (1¼ m).
Opening Times: Garden. All the year—Daily 9.30–sunset. Adm £1.10, Chd (accompanied by adult) 55p; Chd party 45p. Adult parties 90p. Chd under 5 free, OAPs/ Students (on production of their cards) adm at half the standard adult rate. *House closed.*

HAGGS CASTLE
100 St. Andrews Drive G41 4RB. Tel: 041-427 2725.
A museum of history for children with work space for children's activities. Weekdays 10–5; Sun 2–5.

HUNTERIAN ART GALLERY
Hillhead Street, Glasgow University. Tel: 041-330 5431.
Unrivalled collections of C. R. Mackintosh, including reconstructed interiors of the architect's house, and of J. A. M. Whistler. Works by Rembrandt, Chardin, Stubbs, Reynolds, Pissarro, Sisley, Rodin plus Scottish painting from the 18th century to the present. Large collection of Old Master and modern prints. Sculpture Courtyard. Varied programme of temporary exhibitions. Mon to Fri 9.30–5; Sat 9.30–1. Mackintosh House *closed* Mon to Fri 12.30–1.30. Adm 50p to Mackintosh House on weekday afternoons and Sats.

HUNTERIAN MUSEUM
Glasgow University G12 8QQ. Tel: 041-330 4221.
Scotland's oldest public museum, opened in 1807. Situated in Sir George Gilbert Scott's magnificent Victorian Gothic building. Collections include geological, archaeological, historical, ethnographic and numismatic material. Temporary exhibitions. Book shop. Small 18th century coffee shop. Mon to Fri 9.30–5; Sat 9.30–1.

Strathclyde Region – *continued*

HUTCHESONS' HALL
Telephone: 041-552 8391
(The National Trust for Scotland)

Described as one of the most elegant buildings in Glasgow's city centre, the Hall was built in 1802–5 to a design by David Hamilton.
Location: 158 Ingram Street, nr SE corner of George Square.
Opening Times: Visitor Centre: open all year, Mons–Fris 9–5. Shop: Mons–Sats 10–4. Entry free.

LINN PARK
(City of Glasgow District Council)

212 acres pine and deciduous woodlands with enchanting riverside walks. Nature centre, Nature trail and Children's Zoo.
Location: Clarkston Road; Netherlee Road; Simshill Road, Linnview Avenue.
Station: Minrend (¾ m).
Opening Times: All the year—Daily 8 to dusk. Adm free. Car park at golf course & Netherlee Road.

MUSEUM OF TRANSPORT
Kelvin Hall, 1 Bunhouse Road, G3 8DP. Tel: 041-357 3929.
Opened Spring 1988. A new and considerably enlarged museum of the history of transport, including a reproduction of a typical 1938 Glasgow street. Other new features are a larger display of the ship models and a walk-in Motor Car Showroom with cars from the 1930s up to modern times. Other displays include Glasgow trams and buses, Scottish built cars, fire engines, horse-drawn vehicles, commercial vehicles, cycles and motorcycles, railway locomotives and a Glasgow Subway station. Restaurant, fast food and bar facilities are shared with the adjacent indoor Sports Centre. Weekdays 10–5; Sun 2–5.

PEOPLE'S PALACE
Glasgow Green G40 1AT. Tel: 041-554 0223.
Museum of Glasgow history from 1175 to the present day. Collections cover early Glasgow, the rise of the tobacco trade in the 18th century and domestic, social and political life in the 19th and 20th centuries. Snack bar. Weekdays 10–5; Sun 2–5.

POLLOK HOUSE & PARK
Telephone: 041-632 0274
(City of Glasgow District Council)

Built 1747–52, additions by Sir Rowand Anderson 1890–1908. Contains Stirling Maxwell collection of Spanish and other European paintings; displays of furniture, ceramics, glass and silver. Nearby in Pollok Park is the Burrell Collection, winner of 1985 Museum of the Year Award and numerous other awards. Opening times as Pollok House.
Location: 3½ m from City Centre.
Station: Pollokshaws West (1 m).
Opening Times: All the year—Weekdays 10–5, Suns 2–5. Adm free. *Closed Christmas Day & New Year's Day.*
Refreshments: Tea room (reservations Tel 041-649 7547).

PROVAND'S LORDSHIP
Castle Street G4 0RB. Tel: 041-552 8819.
Facing the Cathedral, the only other surviving medieval building in Glasgow built 1471. Period displays ranging in date from 1500 to 1918. Weekdays 10–5; Sun 2–5.

PROVANHALL HOUSE
Auchinlea Park, Auchinlea Road, G34. Tel: 041-771 1538.
House dating from 17th century with some period displays, maintained in conjunction with Department of Parks and Recreation. Weekdays 10–5; Sun 2–5.

ROSS HALL PARK
(City of Glasgow District Council)

33 acres. Majestic trees by River Cart. Extensive heather and rock gardens, with water features, nature trails.
Location: Crookston Road SW.
Opening Times: All the year—Daily 8–dusk. Adm free.

RUTHERGLEN MUSEUM
King Street G73 1D4. Tel: 041-647 0837.
A museum of the history of the former Royal Burgh of Rutherglen with regularly changing displays and temporary exhibitions. Weekdays 10–5; Sun 2–5.

SPRINGBURN MUSEUM & EXHIBITION CENTRE
(Springburn Museum Trust)
Ayr Street G21 4BW. Tel: 041-557 1405.
Local history of an area which was once the greatest centre of steam locomotive manufacture in Europe. Open Mon–Fri 10.30–5, Sat 10–1, Sun and Bank Hols 2–5. Adm free. Car parking in streets nearby. Suitable for disabled persons though no wheelchairs available.

THE TENEMENT HOUSE
Telephone: (041) 333 0183
(The National Trust of Scotland)

A restored first floor flat in a Victorian tenement building, built 1892, presents a picture of social significance.

Location: No 145 Buccleuch Street, Garnethill (N of Charing Cross).
Opening Times: Jan 7 to Mar 19 – Sat and Suns 2–4; Mar 24 to Oct 31 – Daily 2–5; Nov 4 to Dec 17 – Sat and Suns 2–4. Weekday morning visits by educational & other groups (no more than 15) to be arranged by advance booking only. Adm £1.10, Chd 55p; Adult parties 90p, school parties 45p.

VICTORIA PARK
(City of Glasgow District Council)

Fossilised tree stumps, 300 million years old, in Fossil Grove Building. 58 acres. Extensive carpet bedding depicting centennial events.
Location: Victoria Park Drive North.
Opening Times: Park: All the year—Daily 8–dusk. Fossil Grove Building: Mon–Fri 8–4, Sat & Sun pm only. Adm free.

GREENOCK

THE MCLEAN MUSEUM *(Inverclyde District Council)*
9 Union Street, West End. Tel: (0475) 23741.
Picture gallery and ethnography, natural history, and shipping exhibits. Relics of James Watt. Mon to Sat 10–12, 1–5. (Part closed 1988/89 for renovation work.)

HAMILTON

HAMILTON DISTRICT MUSEUM *(Hamilton District Council)*
129 Muir Street, ML3 6BJ. Tel: (0698) 283981.
17th century coaching inn now housing a local history collection. Includes 18th century Assembly Room, Fives Court and stable. Contains displays of costume, art, historical photographs, agriculture, handloom weaving, lace-making, coalmining etc. Also extensive transport gallery and reconstructed Victorian kitchen. Mon to Sat 10–12, 1–5.

HELENSBURGH

THE HILL HOUSE
Telephone: (0436) 3900
(The National Trust for Scotland)

Overlooking the estuary of the River Clyde the house is considered to be the finest example of the domestic architecture of Charles Rennie Mackintosh. Commissioned in 1902 and completed in 1904 for the Glasgow publisher Walter W Blackie. Audio-visual programme on life of Charles Rennie Mackintosh.
Location: In Upper Colquhoun Street, Helensburgh; NW of Glasgow via A814.
Opening Times: Open all year (except Christmas and New Year Hols)—Daily 1–5 (last adm 4.30). Adm £1.70, Chd 85p. Adult parties £1.40, schools 70p.

INVERARAY

AUCHINDRAIN OPEN AIR MUSEUM OF COUNTRY LIFE
(Auchindrain Museum Trustees)
5 miles SW of Inveraray on A83.
Complete old Highland township on original site giving fascinating glimpse into the past. Many cottages and outbuildings, restored and under restoration, which are furnished and equipped to various periods.

INVERARAY CASTLE
Telephone: Inveraray (0499) 2203.
(The Trustees of the 10th Duke of Argyll)

Since 15th century the headquarters of the Clan Campbell. Present castle built 18th century by Roger Morris and Robert Mylne.
Location: ¾ m NE of Inveraray on Loch Fyne 58 m NW of Glasgow.
Opening Times: First Sat in Apr to second Sun in Oct. Apr, May, June, Sept & Oct: daily (except Fri) 10–1, 2–6. Sun 1–6. (During June, the Castle will remain open at lunch time.) July & Aug: daily 10–6, Sun 1–6. Last admission 12.30 & 5.30. **Note: The Castle will be closed Aug 9–15 1989 inclusive.** Gardens open by appointment, woodland walk open all year. Craft shop. *Enquiries:* The Factor, Dept HH, Cherry Park, Inveraray, Argyll. Telephone: (0499) 2203.
Refreshments: Tearoom.

IRVINE

GLASGOW VENNEL CONSERVATION AREA
Tel: (0294) 75059.
A street steeped in history: lodging room and workplace of Scotland's national Bard, Robert Burns. Adm free. Adjacent car parks.

SCOTTISH MARITIME MUSEUM
(Scottish Maritime Museum Heritage Trust)
Laird Forge, Gottries Road, Irvine, KA12 8QE. Tel: (0294) 78283.
The Scottish Maritime Museum contains, on four sites, full size ships, an exhibition of small boats and shipping pictures and a restored Tenement Flat, with Museum Shop and Education Centre. There is also a Workshop and Research Unit and the site of the reconstruction of the 1872 Linthouse Engine Shop which will provide an increase in Museum Display Area over the next decade. Come and discover the world of Scotland and the sea, board the Puffer, Tug and Lifeboat in the Harbour and learn about boatbuilding ashore. Open Apr 1 to Oct 31: Daily 10–5. Other times by appointment. Adm £1.50; Chld and OAPs 75p; Family £3; School Party Organiser and Unemployed 75p. Car parking nearby. Suitable for disabled. No wheelchairs available.

ISLE OF GIGHA

ACHAMORE GARDENS
Telephone: Gigha Hotel 05835 254
(D W N Landale, Esq)

50 acre woodland garden of great botanical interest, with world famous Gigha collection of rhododendrons, azaleas, and camellias.
Location: Isle of Gigha. Ferry from Tayinloan on A82, 17 miles south of Tarbert.
Opening Times: Garden only, all year round—9 to sunset. Adm £2 (1988 rate). Dogs on leads allowed. Plants sold.
Refreshments: Gigha Hotel. Boathouse Bar.

KILBARCHAN

WEAVER'S COTTAGE
(The National Trust for Scotland)

Typical cottage of 18th century handloom weaver: looms, weaving equipment, domestic utensils.
Location: In Kilbarchan village; 8 m SW of Glasgow off A737.
Station: Johnstone (2½ m).
Opening Times: Mar 25 to May 25 and Sept 2 to Oct 31 – Tues, Thurs, Sats & Suns 2–5; May 26 to Aug 31 – daily 2–5 (last tour 4.30). Adm 90p, Chd 45p (under 5 free); Adult parties 70p; Chd party 35p, OAPs/Students (on production of their cards) adm at half the standard adult rate. Video programme.

KILMARNOCK

DEAN CASTLE *(Kilmarnock and Loudoun District Council)*
Dean Road, off Glasgow Road. Tel: (0563) 26401 ext. 36 or (0563) 34580.
Medieval arms and armour, musical instruments, tapestries. Daily 12–5 (*closed* Dec 25, 26 and Jan 1, 2). Adm £1, Chld free. Organised parties must book. All enquiries to Dick Institute, see below.

DICK INSTITUTE MUSEUM AND ART GALLERY
(Kilmarnock and Loudoun District Council)
Elmbank Avenue. Tel: (0563) 26401.
Paintings, geology, archeology, natural history, industry. Frequent temporary exhibitions.

KIRKINTILLOCH

THE AULD KIRK MUSEUM *(Strathkelvin District Council)*
Cowgate. Tel: 041-775 1185.
Temporary exhibitions only, including art, photography, local history, archaeology and social and industrial history. Opening hours as for Barony Chambers.

THE BARONY CHAMBERS MUSEUM
(Strathkelvin District Council)
The Cross. Tel: 041-775 1185.
Local social and industrial history, weaving, coalmining, transport, shipbuilding, ironfounding, domestic collections on display. Apr to Oct: Tues, Thurs and Fri 2–5; Sat 10–1, 2–5. Nov to Mar: Tues, Thurs 2–5; Sat 10–1, 2–5.

KIRKOSWALD

SOUTER JOHNNIE'S COTTAGE
Telephone: Kirkoswald (065 56) 603
(The National Trust for Scotland)

Thatched home of the original Souter in Burns' "Tam o' Shanter", Burns' relics. Life-sized stone figures of the Souter, Tam, the Innkeeper and his wife, in garden.
Location: In Kirkoswald village 4 m W of Maybole on A77.
Opening Times: Mar 24 to Oct 31—Daily 12–5 (or by appointment) Adm 90p, Chd 45p. Adult parties 70p, Schools 35p, (under 5 free) OAPs/Students (on production of their cards) adm at half the standard adult rate.

LANARK

NEW LANARK CONSERVATION VILLAGE
(New Lanark Conservation Trust)
New Lanark Mills, Lanark ML11 9DB. Tel: (0555) 61345.
Award-winning 200 year old Cotton Mill Village, site of Robert Owen's social and educational experiments. Nominated as a World Heritage site, the village is undergoing major restoration. Set in the Clyde Gorge, surrounded by beautiful woodlands and the Falls of Clyde, New Lanark is Europe's premier Industrial Heritage Site. Visitor Centre, Exhibitions, coffee bar, gifts, craft shops, picnic areas, children's playground. Special Exhibitions: Mar 26/27 (Easter Sun/Mon) – Egg Decorating workshops and Magic Shows. Apr 29/30 and May 1 – 3 day Steam Fair. Sept 3 – Victorian Fair. Open: Daily from 11–5. *Closed* Christmas Day and New Years Day. Adm 50p; Chld, OAPs and Unemployed 25p. Pre-booking advisable – special rates for schools. Car parking in visitor car park. Suitable for disabled persons. No wheelchairs available. Access to village free at all times. Limited disabled parking in village square.

LANGBANK

FINLAYSTONE HOUSE AND GARDENS
Telephone: Langbank 285
(Mrs G MacMillan)

Formerly home of fifteen Earls of Glencairn; now the home of the chief of Clan MacMillan. Exhibitions of international dolls, flower books and prints, and Celtic art. Woodlands, with picnic/play areas. Ranger service.
Location: On A8 between Langbank & Port Glasgow; 20 minutes W of Glasgow on S bank of the Clyde.
Station: Longbank (1¼ m).
Opening Times: Beautiful gardens and woods open ALL THE YEAR. Adm 90p, Chd 60p. House: Apr to Aug—Suns 2.30–4.30, **and** by appointment any time. Pre-booked groups welcome.
Refreshments: Home-baked afternoon teas Sats & Suns in summer in Old Laundry.

LARGS

KELBURN COUNTRY CENTRE AND KELBURN CASTLE
Telephone: Fairlie (0475) 568685
(The Home and Park of the Earls of Glasgow on the Firth of Clyde.)

Waterfalls, gardens, famous trees, spectacular walks and views. Adventure course, Commando Assauli course, pet's corner, children's stockade, pony trekking. Shop, exhibitions.
Location: On the A78 between Largs and Fairlie in Ayrshire.
Station: Largs (2 m).
Opening Times: Kelburn Country Centre: Open with all facilities daily 10–6 from Good Friday to mid-Oct. Adm £1.80, Chd/OAPs £1.20. Reductions for booked parties. Dogs admitted on leads. **Winter opening:** Grounds only mid-Oct to Apr 12. Adm £1 and 60p. **Kelburn Castle:** Open to visitors from Sat Apr 22 to Sun May 29 only. Closed at all other times, except to special parties by prior arrangement. Adm £1.50 per person excluding admission to Kelburn Country Centre.
Refreshments: Licensed cafe, lunches, snacks, home baking, ice cream parlour, picnic areas. Open from Good Friday to mid-Oct.

MAYBOLE

CULZEAN CASTLE, GARDEN AND COUNTRY PARK
Telephone: Kirkoswald (065 56) 269
(The National Trust for Scotland)

One of the finest Adam houses in Scotland. Spacious policies and gardens. Adventure playground.
Location: 12 m SW of Ayr just off A719.
Opening Times: CASTLE. Mar 24 to Mar 31: 10–6; Apr 1 to Apr 27: 10–5; Apr 28 to Aug 31: 10–6; Sept 1 to Oct 31: 10–5. Last adm ½ hour before closing. Adm £2.10, Chd £1.05 (under 5 free). Adult parties £1.70, Schools 85p. OAPs/Students (on production of their cards) adm at half the standard adult rate. House not suitable for wheelchairs.
CULZEAN COUNTRY PARK *(Charges under review). (NTS and Kyle & Carrick; Cunninghame; Cummock & Doon Valley District Councils & Strathclyde Region)*— open all year. Adm free to members. Cars £3.50, mini buses & caravans £5, Coaches £15, charges Apr 1 to Oct only, vehicles (except school coaches) free at other times. Open all year, daily 9–sunset. Visitor Centre, Shop and Tourist Information Centre. Visitor Centre, Shop and Tourist Information Centre Mar 24–31, Apr, Sept and Oct: 10–5; May to Aug: 10–6. Ranger-Naturalist service.
Refreshments: Restaurant, Apr 1 to Apr 30 and Sept 1 to Oct 31, daily 10.30–5; May 1 to Aug 31, daily 10.30–6.

MILLPORT

ROBERTSON MUSEUM AND AQUARIUM
Marine Station. Tel: (0475) 530581/2.
The museum and aquarium exhibit marine life found in the Clyde sea area. Mon to Sat 9.30–12.30, 2–5. *Closed* Sat during winter. Adm 40p, Chld 25p.

MILNGAVIE

LILLIE ART GALLERY
(Bearsden and Milngavie District Council)
Station Road. Tel: 041-956 2351.
Collection of 20th century Scottish paintings; temporary and loan exhibitions of art and crafts (*see diary of exhibitions*). Tues to Fri 11–5, 7–9; Sat and Sun 2–5. *Closed* Mon.

OBAN

MCGAIG MUSEUM
Corran Halls.

PAISLEY

PAISLEY MUSEUM AND ART GALLERIES
(Renfrew District Council)
High Street. Tel: (041-889) 3151.
Paisley shawls; Renfrewshire history, geology and natural history; Arbuthnot manuscripts; general collections. Gallery of Scottish painters; large collection of ceramics. Mon to Sat 10–5. *Closed* Sun.

ROTHESAY

BUTESHIRE NATURAL HISTORY SOCIETY MUSEUM
Stuart Street.
Collections of the natural history, archaeology, geology and history of the island of Bute.

SALTCOATS

NORTH AYRSHIRE MUSEUM *(Cunninghame District Council)*
Kirkgate. Tel: (0294) 64174.
History, industry and life in North Ayrshire. Adm free. Free car park adjacent.

STRAITON

BLAIRQUHAN CASTLE AND GARDENS
Ayrshire   *map D12*
Telephone: Straiton (065 57) 239
(James Hunter Blair)

Magnificent Regency castellated mansion approached by a 3 m private drive beside the river Girvan. Walled gardens and pinetum. Plants and trees for sale. Picture gallery.
Location: 14 m S of Ayr; off A77. Entrance Lodge is on B7045 ½ m S of Kirkmichael.
Opening Times: Aug 1 to Aug 31 *(not Mons)*. Adm £2.50, Chd £1.50, OAPs £2. Parties by arrangement at any time of year. Car parking. Wheelchairs—around gardens and principal floor of the castle.
Refreshments: Tea in castle.

STRATHAVON

JOHN HASTIE MUSEUM
A local history collection. Mon to Fri 2–5 (Thurs 2–4.30); Sat 11–1, 2–5. (May to Sept.)

TARBOLTON

BACHELORS' CLUB
Telephone: Tarbolton (0292) 541 or 940
(The National Trust for Scotland)

17th century thatched house where Burns and his friends formed their club in 1780. Period furnishings.
Location: In Tarbolton village 7½ m NE of Ayr (off A758).
Opening Times: Mar 24 to Oct 31—Daily 12–5. Adm 90p, Chd 45p (under 5 free), OAPs/Students (on production of their cards) adm at half the standard adult rate. Adult parties 70p, school parties 35p. *Other times by appointment.*

Tayside Region

ARBROATH

ARBROATH ART GALLERY *(Angus District Council)*
Public Library, Hill Terrace.
Collection of paintings by local artists and local views, in particular the works of J.W. Herald, watercolourist. Also two oil paintings by Peter Breughell II. Mon to Fri 9.30–6; Sat 9.30–5.

ARBROATH MUSEUM *(Angus District Council)*
Signal Tower, Ladyloan.
Local collections cover the history of Arbroath from Prehistoric Times to the Industrial Revolution. Special features include the Bellrock Lighthouse, Fishing and the Wildlife of Arbroath Cliffs. Apr to Oct: Mon to Sat 10.30–1; 2–5. July and Aug: Sun 2–5. Nov to Mar: Mon to Fri 2–5; Sat 10.30–1; 2–5.

BLAIR ATHOLL

ATHOLL COUNTRY COLLECTION
(Mr and Mrs John and Janet Cameron)
The Old School. Tel: (079 681) 232.
Tells the interesting story of life for the villagers and glen folk in years gone by. Designed with children in mind. Easter, then end of May to early Oct.

BLAIR CASTLE
Telephone: (079 681) 207
(His Grace the Duke of Atholl)

13th century home of The Duke of Atholl, Blair Castle is Scotland's most visited Historic House and has 32 rooms of infinite variety displaying beautiful furniture, fine collection of paintings, Arms and Armour, china, lace and embroidery, children's games and Jacobite relics. The Duke of Atholl has Europe's only official private army – The Atholl Highlanders.
Location: 8 m NW of Pitlochry off A9.
Station: Blair Atholl (1½ m).
Opening Times: Open Mar 23 to Oct 29 Mon to Sat 2–6, Sun (June to Sept) 12–6, Suns (Apr, May & Oct) 2–6. Last adm 5. Adm £2.50, Chd £1.50, reductions for pre-booked groups, Family tickets available. Picnic areas, Deer Park, Nature trails, pony trekking, free car and coach parking. Gift shop. Children's Guide Book. Up to 2,000 visitors a day can be accommodated.
Refreshments: Self Service Restaurant. Catering for pre-booked groups of up to 200 in separate rooms with waitress service can be provided. Further details available from The Administrator, Tel: 079 681 207. Fax: 079 681 487.

BRECHIN

BRECHIN MUSEUM *(Angus District Council)*
Public Library, St. Ninian's Square.
Local collections tell the story of the development of Brechin from the Celtic church of the 10th century to the last days of the Burgh in 1975. There is a small display of some of the works of D. Waterson, etcher and watercolourist. Mon to Fri 9.30–6 (Wed 9.30–7); Sat 9.30–5.

COMRIE

SCOTTISH TARTANS MUSEUM
Comrie, PH6 2DW (on the A85). Tel: (0764) 70779.
The Scottish Tartans Society studies tartan and Highland dress and maintains the Scottish Tartans Museum in Comrie, Perthshire. The museum incorporates a working weaver's cottage and dye garden. Easter to Oct: Mon to Sat 10–5; Sun 2–4. Tel for winter opening times. Adm 95p, Chld, OAPs 60p. Family ticket (not exceeding 2 adults and 3 Chld) £2.20. Members Scottish Tartans Society free. Groups of more than 20, 60p each. Car parking in village. Suitable for disabled persons.

DUNDEE

BARRACK STREET MUSEUM *(City of Dundee District Council)*
Barrack Street.
Museum of Natural History, currently in process of redevelopment. Displays of Scottish wildlife, including highland, lowland, coastal, urban habitats. Displays of geology, exotic wildlife. Special exhibits include skeleton of Great Tay Whale, celebrated in verse by poet William McGonagall. Observation beehive. Occasional touring exhibitions. Public enquiry and identification service. Mon to Sat 10–5. *Closed* Sun.

BROUGHTY CASTLE MUSEUM *(City of Dundee District Council)*
Broughty Ferry.
Former estuary fort overlooking River Tay, adjacent to large recreation area and sandy beach. Displays on: History of Broughty Ferry, fishing, ferries, lifeboat, railway, Victorian holiday resort; Whaling – Scotland's finest collection of whaling memorabilia; Seashore-creatures of rocky and sandy shores; Military History, arms and armour. Viewing room on top floor offers fine views over Tay Estuary. Mon to Thurs and Sat 10–1, 2–5; Sun (July to Sept) 2–5. *Closed* Fri all year.

MCMANUS GALLERIES *(City of Dundee District Council)*
Albert Square.
Principal local history museum and art galleries, housed in one of Scotland's finest Victorian buildings by architect Gilbert Scott, recently subject of major redevelopment. New local history displays: Trade and Industry – Shipping, Flax and Jute, Printing and Publishing, Railways, Tay Bridge Disaster, Trades Unions; Social History – Reconstructed bar, shop, school room and tenement kitchen, old town model, crime and punishment; Mary Slessor memorial; Archaeology – Stone Age burial, giant dug-out canoe, bronze age house reconstruction, Romans, Pictish stones, Egyptian mummy. Major Scottish art gallery with fine collections, notably Victorian Scottish paintings and Scottish Colourist paintings. Furniture, silver, glass, ceramics. Regular programme of temporary and touring exhibitions. Public enquiry and identification service. Facilities for disabled visitors. Mon to Sat 10–5. *Closed* Sun.

MILLS OBSERVATORY *(City of Dundee District Council)*
Balgay Hill. Tel: Dundee (0382) 67138.
Britain's only full-time public observatory. Historic 10-inch refracting telescope gives fine views of moon and planets. Displays on astronomy, space exploration. Small planetarium. Regular slide shows. Balcony gives fine views over River Tay to Fife. Viewing of sky weather permitting. Public enquiry and information service. Apr to Sept Mon–Fri 10–5, Sat 2–5; Oct to Mar, Mon to Fri 3–10, Sat 2–5. *Closed* Sun.

ROYAL RESEARCH SHIP DISCOVERY *(Dundee Heritage Trust)*
Victoria Dock, Dundee. Tel: (0382) 25282 or 201175.
Captain Scott's famous Antartic Exploration Ship built in Dundee in 1901. Now open to the public while undergoing final restoration. The first of the Dundee Heritage Trust's projects. Apr to May: daily 2–5, weekends and Bank Hols 11–5. Jun to Sept daily: 10–5. Guided tours. Adm: Adults 1.75, concessions £1, Dundee Heritage Club members free.

ST. MARY'S TOWER *(City of Dundee District Council)*
  Nethergate.
Dundee's oldest building. Fifteenth century steeple tower, restored in nineteenth century. Viewpoint. *Closed* for repairs. Enquiries to the McManus Galleries.

Enquiries for all City of Dundee Museums should be made at the McManus Galleries, Albert Square, Dundee, DD1 1DA. Tel: Dundee (0382) 23141.

EDZELL

EDZELL CASTLE & GARDENS
(Secretary of State for Scotland)

16th century castle. Unique renaissance garden. New Visitor Centre.

Location: 1 m W of Edzell; 6 m N of Brechin off B996.
Opening Times: Apr 1 to Sept 30—Weekdays 9.30–7, Suns 2–7; Oct 1 to Mar 31—Weekdays (*except Tues and Thurs morning*) 9.30–4, Suns 2–4. *Closed Dec 25 & 26; Jan 1 & 2.* Adm 60p, Chd & OAPs 30p.

FORFAR

FORFAR MUSEUM *(Angus District Council)*
  Public Library, Meffan Institute, High Street.
Closed until further notice. All enquiries to N.K. Atkinson, Dip Ed., AMA, MBOU, FSA (Scot), District Curator, Museums and Art Galleries, Panmure Place, Montrose, Angus DD10 8HE. Tel: (0674) 73231.

GLAMIS

ANGUS FOLK MUSEUM
(The National Trust for Scotland)

Row of 19th century cottages with stone-slabbed roofs, restored by the Trust. Adapted to display the Angus Folk Collection, one of the finest in the country.

Location: In Glamis village; 12 m N of Dundee A94.
Opening Times: Mar 24 to Mar 27, Apr 28 to May 25 and Sept 1 to Oct 1—Daily 12–5; May 26 to Aug 31—Daily 11.30–5.30 (last adm ½ hour before closing). Adm £1.20, Chd 60p (under 5 free). Adult parties £1, Schools 50p. OAPs/Students (on production of their cards) adm at half the standard adult rate.

GLAMIS CASTLE
(Mary, Countess of Strathmore and Kinghorne)

Family home of the Earls of Strathmore and Kinghorne and a royal residence since 1372. Childhood home of H.M. Queen Elizabeth The Queen Mother and birthplace of H.R.H. The Princess Margaret. Legendary setting of Shakespeare's play 'Macbeth'. Five-storey L shaped tower block dating from 13th century, remodelled 1606, containing magnificent rooms with wide range of historic pictures, furniture, porcelain etc.

Location: Glamis.
Opening Times: Good Friday to Easter Monday, then Apr 29 to Oct 16—daily 12–5.30 (last tour 4.45). Adm £2.50, reductions for Chd, OAPs and groups. Ample bus and car parking. Picnic area, Shops, Garden and Nature Trail.
Refreshments: Licensed Restaurant at the Castle.

KIRRIEMUIR

BARRIE'S BIRTHPLACE
Telephone: Kirriemuir (0575) 72646
(The National Trust for Scotland).

Contains mementoes of Sir James Barrie. Peter Pan display and A/V programme.

Location: No 9 Brechin Road, in Kirriemuir.
Opening Times: Mar 24 to Mar 27, Apr 28 to Oct 1—Mons to Sats 11–5.30, Suns 2–5.30 (last tour 5). Adm 90p, Chd 45p (under 5 free). OAPs/Students (on production of their cards) adm at half the standard adult rate. Adult parties 70p, schools 35p.
Refreshments: Airlie Arms Hotel.

MONTROSE

HOUSE OF DUN
Telephone: (067481) 264
(The National Trust for Scotland)

Modest size Palladian house overlooking the Montrose Basin, built in 1730 for David Erskine, Lord Dun, to designs by William Adam. Exuberant plasterwork in the saloon.

Location: 3 m W of Montrose.
Opening Times: Apr 28 to Oct 29 (last tour of House ½ hr before closing). House, courtyard and tea room 11–5.30. Grounds open all year. Adm £2.10, Chd £1.05, Adult parties £1.70, schools 85p.

MONTROSE MUSEUM *(Angus District Council)*
  Panmure Place. Tel: (0674) 73232.
Extensive local collections cover the history of Montrose from prehistoric times to local government reorganisation, the maritime history of the port, the Natural History of Angus and local art. Pictish stones, Montrose silver and pottery; whaling artefacts; Napoleonic items (including a cast of his death mask). Paintings by local artists and local views, sculpture by W. Lamb. Apr to Oct: Mon to Sat 10.30–1, 2–5. July and Aug: Sun 2–5. Nov to Mar: Mon to Fri 2–5; Sat 10.30–1, 2–5.

SUNNYSIDE MUSEUM *(Tayside Health Board)*
  Sunnyside Royal Hospital, Hillside. Tel: (067 483) 361.
This museum outlines the history of psychiatry in Scotland. Exhibits include slides, audio/visual shows.

WILLIAM LAMB MEMORIAL STUDIO *(Angus District Council)*
  24 Market Street.
The working studio of the famous Montrose sculptor includes displays of his sculptures, etchings, paintings and drawings. Also featured are his workroom and tools and his living room with self-styled furniture. July and Aug: Sun 2–5 or by arrangement.

MUTHILL

DRUMMOND CASTLE GARDENS
(The Grimsthorpe & Drummond Castle Trust Ltd)

Gardens only are open.

Location: 3 m S of Crieff, W off Crieff/Muthill Road (A822)—East Lodge.
Opening Times: May to Aug—Daily 2–6 (last admission 5); Sept—Weds & Suns 2–6. Adm £1.20, Chd/OAPs 60p. Free car park. *Gardens only are open to the public, according to the Rules in force.*

PERTH

BRANKLYN GARDEN
Telephone: Perth (0738) 25535
(The National Trust for Scotland)

One of the finest gardens of its size in Britain (2 acres).

Location: 1½ m E of Perth on Dundee Road (A85).
Opening Times: Mar 1 to Oct 31—Daily 9.30–sunset. Adm £1.10, Chd 55p (under 5 free) OAPs/Students (on production of their cards) adm at half the standard adult rate. Adult parties 90p, schools 45p.

HUNTINGTOWER CASTLE
(Secretary of State for Scotland)

Two fine and complete towers in which are excellent painted ceilings.

Location: 2 m W of Perth.
Opening Times: Apr 1 to Sept 30—Daily 9.30–7, Suns 2–7; Oct 1 to Mar 31—Daily 9.30–4, Suns 2–4. *Closed Dec 25, 26; Jan 1, 2.* Adm 60p, Chd & OAPs 30p.

PERTH MUSEUM AND ART GALLERY
  (Perth and Kinross District Council)
  Tel: (0738) 32488.
Permanent collections of fine art, ceramics, glass, silver, local history, archaeology, ethnography, costume and communion tokens. Major new displays of local natural history. Changing programme of exhibitions. Mon to Sat 10–1, 2–5. *Closed* Sun. Branch Museums at Alyth and Kinross, open May–Sept: Thurs to Sat, 1–5.

SCONE PALACE
Telephone: Perth (0738) 52300
(Rt Hon the Earl of Mansfield)

This medieval palace was Gothicised for the third Earl of Mansfield in the early 19th century. Superb collections of French furniture, china, ivories, clocks, Vernis Martin vases and objets d'art.

Location: 2 m NE of Perth on the Braemer Road (A93).
Station: Perth (2½ m).
Opening Times: Mar 24 to Oct 16—Mons to Sats 9.30–5, Suns 1.30–5 (July and Aug 10–5). Adm £2.70. Special rates for booked parties. Free car park. Shops. Picnic park. Playground. Winter tours by special arrangment.
Refreshments: Coffee shop. Old Kitchen Restaurant (licensed). Home baking. State Room dinners.

WEEM

CASTLE MENZIES
(Menzies Clan Society)

Magnificant example of a 16th century fortified house, seat of the Chiefs of Clan Menzies, situated in the beautiful valley of the Tay. It was involved in the turbulent history of the Central Highlands and here "Bonnie Prince Charlie" rested on his way to Culloden in 1746.

Location: 1½ m from Aberfeldy on B846.
Opening Times: Apr to Sept—Weekdays 10.30–5, Suns 2–5. Adm £1.50, Chd 50p, OAPs 75p. Reductions for parties by prior arrangement.

HIGHLAND HOSPITALITY
BLAIR CASTLE

From the moment you set foot in the ancient stronghold of the Dukes of Atholl, Blair Castle welcomes you to a feast of historic memories and traditional hospitality.

Set in 32 exquisite rooms, the unique treasures and priceless antiques are glorious reminders of seven hundred years of Scottish and European culture.

Scotland's most visited House is set just off the new scenic A9 route through the central Highlands and welcomes you every day from 23rd March to 27th October. It is open from 10am to 6pm (2pm to 6pm Sundays). Last admissions 5pm. Parking is free.

For further information, leaflets and Party Booking forms, telephone 079 681 207.

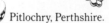

Pitlochry, Perthshire.

BRAEMAR CASTLE
ABERDEENSHIRE

"The Standard on the Braes o' Mar, is up and streaming rarely"

Built in 1628 by the Earl of Mar. Attacked and burned by the celebrated Black Colonel (John Farquharson of Inverey) in 1689. Repaired by the government and garrisoned with English troops after the rising of 1745. Later transformed by the Farquharsons of Invercauld, who had purchased it in 1732, into a fully furnished private residence of unusual charm. L-plan castle of fairy tale proportions, with round central tower and spiral stair. Barrel-vaulted ceilings, massive iron 'Yett', and underground pit (prison). Remarkable star-shaped defensive curtain wall. Much valuable furniture, paintings and items of Scottish historical interest. Exhibition of International Costumes.

OPEN 10 am to 6 pm Daily. MAY to early OCTOBER. Admission £1.30. Children 65p. Group and O.A.P. rates. Guided Tours. Souvenirs. Gifts Selection.

Welcome !

Castles and Great Houses Museums and Little Houses

Historic Places Mountains and Wild Places

Gardens and Parklands Restaurants and Gift Shops

Over 100 beautiful places for you to visit

Free brochures and helpful service from the Marketing Department (MG), The National Trust for Scotland, 5 Charlotte Square, Edinburgh EH2 4DU Tel. 031-226 5922 Telex 72379 MTS G Offices in Inverurie, Aberdeenshire, Glasgow, Inverness, Perth, London

 National Trust for Scotland

BOWHILL NEAR SELKIRK

Edinburgh 42 miles,
Berwick 43,
Carlisle 56,
Glasgow 75.

Opening dates 1989.
House and Grounds
1 July – 13 August daily.

Grounds only: 29 April –
28 August daily except
Fridays.

See line entry for times
and admission charges.

Free car and coach
parking.

For details of our specialist one, three or five day Arts Courses run in conjunction with
Sotheby's. please telephone Buccleuch Heritage Trust (0750) 20732.

DALKEITH PARK
Nr EDINBURGH

Dalkeith House from the Nature Trail

Nature Trails and Exciting Adventure Woodland Play
Area. Attractive Barbecue Area. Woodland and riverside
walks in the beautiful grounds of Dalkeith Palace. Tunnel
Walk. Adam Bridge. Educational packs and special
facilities for School parties with Ranger Service.
Information Centre. Light Refreshments.

Open daily—March 25 to October 30; Saturdays &
Sundays only in November, 11 am to 6 pm. Access from
East end Dalkeith High Street, 3 miles from Edinburgh
City Boundary off A68.

CASTLE MENZIES
PERTHSHIRE

Magnificent example of a 16th century fortified house, seat of the Chiefs of
Clan Menzies. Situated in the beautiful valley of Tay. It was involved in the
turbulent history of the Central Highlands, and here 'Bonnie Prince Charlie'
rested on his way to Culloden in 1746.

HAMILTON DISTRICT MUSEUM

Step into the past at Hamilton District Museum, the
oldest building in the town. It was originally the
Hamilton Arms Inn, built in 1696, and London
coaches stopped here daily. Re-live that era in our
restored stable and fascinating transport gallery with
four-in-hand coach and other early vehicles. Stroll
through the elegant 18th century Assembly Room
with its original plasterwork and musicians' gallery,
and then savour the atmosphere of our reconstructed
Victorian kitchen. We also have a wide range of local
history displays, including costume, archaeology,
lacemaking, handloom weaving, coalmining and
much more.

129 MUIR STREET, HAMILTON
Telephone 283981

18th century Assembly Room

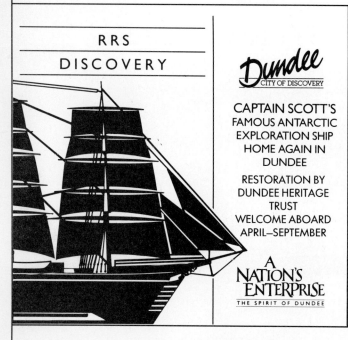

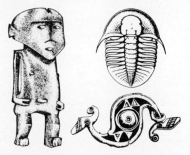

Alphabetical Index to properties

Key to Map Sections

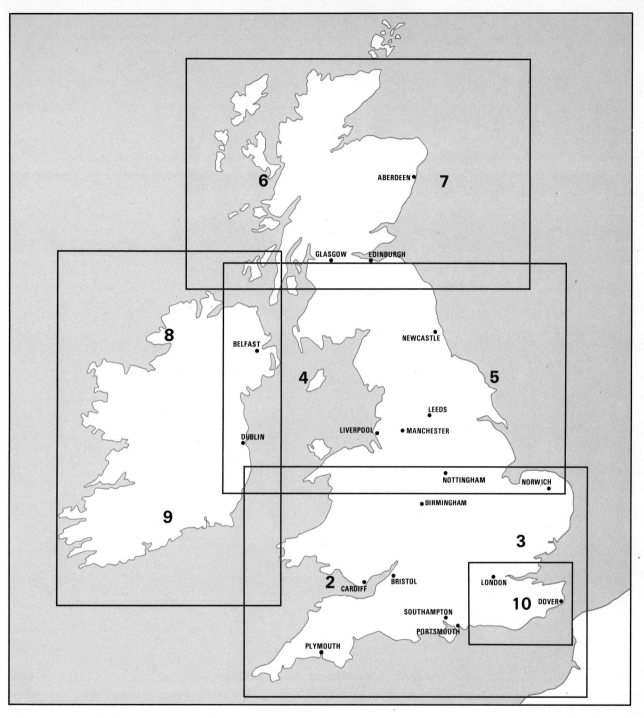

ABERDEEN

6 7

GLASGOW EDINBURGH

NEWCASTLE

BELFAST

8

4 5

LEEDS

LIVERPOOL MANCHESTER

DUBLIN

NOTTINGHAM NORWICH

BIRMINGHAM

9

3

LONDON

2 CARDIFF BRISTOL

10 DOVER

SOUTHAMPTON

PORTSMOUTH

PLYMOUTH

LEGEND

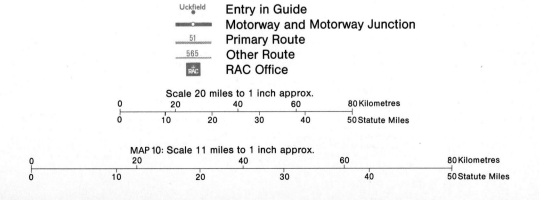

Scale 20 miles to 1 inch approx.

| 0 | 20 | 40 | 60 | 80 Kilometres |
| 0 | 10 | 20 | 30 | 40 | 50 Statute Miles |

MAP 10: Scale 11 miles to 1 inch approx.

| 0 | 20 | 40 | 60 | 80 Kilometres |
| 0 | 10 | 20 | 30 | 40 | 50 Statute Miles |

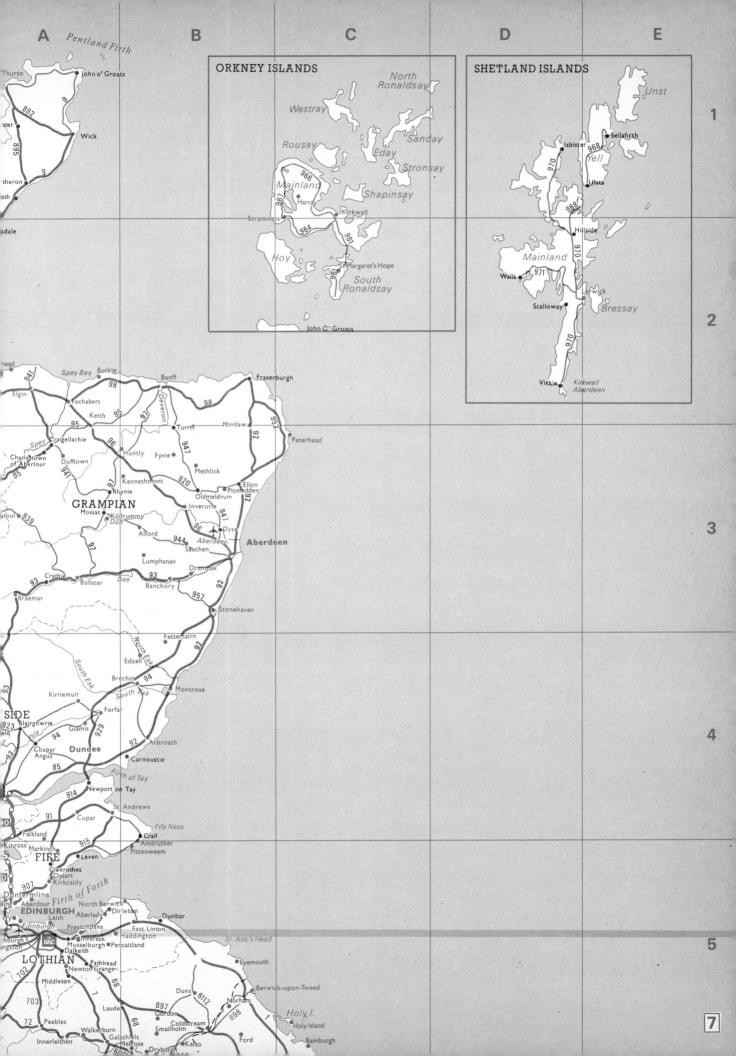

献身

親愛なる友人レイモンドへ、人生という広大なタペストリーの中で、旅の途中に消えない痕跡を残す人間関係はほとんどありません。私は幸運なことに、あなたを稀有で大切な魂の一人に数えることができ、その揺るぎないサポートが私の道を最も深く照らしてくれました。心からの感謝とあふれる感情を込めて、このささやかな作品をあなたに捧げます。栄枯盛衰を経て、あなたは揺るぎない力の柱であり続け、私の能力に対する信念は決して揺らぎませんでした。言葉と想像力の領域において、あなたは私の導きの光であり、疑いが私の決意を曇らせたときは私を前に押し出し、夢がとらえどころのないように思えたときは星に手を伸ばすよう私を鼓舞してくれました。あなたの存在は友情の枠を超えて共鳴します。なぜなら、あなたは親友でありミューズでもあり、私の中に創造性の残り火を点火してくれるからです。あなたの鋭い知性、揺るぎないアドバイス、そして比類のない共感力が私の言葉に命を吹き込み、この本のページ全体で踊る物語に実体と真実性を与えてくれました。心の奥底からインクが流れ出るように、深い感謝の気持ちを込めてこの言葉を書きます。それはあなたの揺るぎない優しさ、私に対する揺るぎない信頼、そして揺るぎない友情の証です。あなたがそばにいて、逆境の時には慰めを与え、勝利の時には祝福を与えてくれるのは、私にとって何と幸せなことでしょう。この献身を込めて、私はあなたの揺るぎないサポートと真の友情の体現者であることに永遠に感謝しつつ、冒頭のページにあなたの名前を刻みます。最大限の賞賛の意を表します、ロック・ジェーン

昔々、絆の強い小さな町に、トミーという名の少年がいました。わずか５歳の彼は、ほとんどの大人には理解できない困難にすでに直面していました。トミーはトランスジェンダーの少年で、女性の体で生まれましたが、自分を少年として認識し、生きていました。彼は明るく想像力豊かな子供で、自分の架空の世界に慰めを見つけることがよくありました。しかし、この日を境に、彼の現実は過酷な戦場となった。

トミーの子供時代の陽気な日々は長くは続かず、彼の人生は悲しみと痛みに彩られていました。トミーが物心ついた頃から、彼の愛する母親サラは癌と闘っていました。彼女は勇敢に戦った強くて回復力のある女性でしたが、病気が大きな被害をもたらしました。無数の化学療法と利用可能な最先端の治療にもかかわらず、サラの病気は治癒が不可能と思われる段階まで進行していました

トミーは幼い肩に重い荷を負っていましたが、できる限りの方法で母親を喜ばせたいという決意を持ち続けました。彼は彼女の話を聞くのが大好きで、彼女の声は彼の心を慰めてくれました。トミーの想像力豊かな心にアイデアが閃いたのは、そうしたストーリーテリング セッションの1つでした。

「お母さん、私たちの町には魔法の生き物が隠れていると思う？」彼は目を好奇心に輝かせながら尋ねた。サラは弱いながらも常に協力的で、微笑んで優しくうなずいた